3-

THE CHAMPAGNE GUIDE

For Jody Rolfe

Published in 2017 by Hardie Grant Books, an imprint of Hardie Grant Publishing

Hardie Grant Books (Melbourne)
Building 1, 658 Church Street
Richmond, Victoria 3121

Hardie Grant Books (London)
5th & 6th Floors
52–54 Southwark Street
London SE1 1UN

hardiegrantbooks.com

A Cataloguing-in-Publication entry is available from the catalogue of the
National Library of Australia at www.nla.gov.au
The Champagne Guide 2018–2019
ISBN 978 1 74379 318 3

Publishing Director: Jane Willson
Managing Editor: Marg Bowman
Project Editor: Loran McDougall
Editor: Katri Hilden
Design Manager: Mark Campbell
Designer: Susanne Geppert
Cover Designer: Andy Warren
Photographers: Tyson Stelzer and Jody Rolfe
Production Manager: Todd Rechner
Production Coordinator: Rebecca Bryson

Colour reproduction by Splitting Image Colour Studio
Printed in China by 1010 Printing International Limited

2018–2019

THE CHAMPAGNE GUIDE

THE DEFINITIVE GUIDE TO CHAMPAGNE

TYSON STELZER

hardie grant books

CONTENTS

OPPOSITE, CLOCKWISE FROM TOP LEFT: *Midsummer on the premier cru slopes of Grauves in the Côte des Blancs; late winter snow on the hillsides of Aÿ; riddling racks at Armand de Brignac; the cathedral of Notre-Dame in Reims; the maison of William Deutz in Aÿ; ripe pinot noir in Rilly-la-Montagne.*

UNDER THE SURFACE

ehind an inconspicuous doorway hidden amidst the lush trees of a secret walled garden in the middle of the city of Reims, in the shadows of the fairytale turrets of Pommery, lies a timeless passageway of 106 spiral stairs descending into a mythical, ancient world hiding the very deepest secrets of Champagne. With each step deeper, deeper into the underworld of Charles Heidsieck, the temperature plummets and the chill of expectation rises. The final step falls into a vast subterranean 'crayère', a chalk mine of cathedral proportions. Walls of stark, white chalk tower to the surface 38 metres above in a perfect pyramid, looming and dramatic in its cavernous expanse, like a gigantic sculpture of buried ice art frozen in time.

Time itself stands still in the silence of this place. Immortalised for 1700 years, the vast chamber reverberates with 3rd century Roman picks, scoring the chalk, carving blocks to build the cities of the ancient world above. Tunnels disappear into oppressive darkness in every direction, whispering with the hushed voices of Middle Age smugglers, squirrelling away their shady chattels in secret drives. Hundreds of interconnected crayères resonate with the century-old cries of children taking refuge as booming echoes of World War I German shells raze Reims to the ground, shaking the stone to the core of the earth.

Soft, damp, salty chalk walls are alive with the rich memories of the aeons, inscribed with a record of a dramatic history in centuries of graffiti, bearing names, dates, pictures, manifestos and love notes, as if they were carved yesterday. The air that has breathed through these caverns for millennia is oblivious to the passage of time, too, devoid of any dank, musty, old-cellar heaviness, enlivened with a bewildering freshness, as if somehow rejuvenated by the ancient chalk itself.

This chalk is the key to the ageing of champagne and the invisible secret that blesses its vines with vitality and energy. Given birth 90 million years ago under an ocean stretching across the Parisian basin, Champagne's chalk plunges to depths of hundreds of metres below the surface. It is this chalk that blesses

The 3rd century crayères of Charles Heidsieck are among the last remnants of the ancient city of Reims.

its finest vineyards with hydration, freshness and the crystalline mineral texture that infuses grand longevity in its wines.

And it is from this chalk that a city is carved under the city. An astonishing maze of more than 250 kilometres of passages under Reims alone became home to entire communities seeking years of refuge from the ravages of the world wars, transforming drives into schools, churches, hospitals, shops, municipal offices and homes.

To the Champenois today, these caverns are more than just an idyllic haven. They are a silent and constant spirit, the sure and strong foundation of a volatile region, the bedrock that firms and sustains all that transpires in the wild and ravaged world above. A symbol of immovable resilience, of enduring continuity, of rock-solid consistency.

The ancient chalk has defined generations of Champenois. A people of quiet and resilient strength, of confident assurance in spite of impossible odds, with natural, political and economic climates stacked against them, and of grand ambition to battle the elements and transform austere and acidic grapes into the most celebrated beverage on earth.

'In Champagne we have the poorest soils in the world,' reveals Louis Roederer chef de cave Jean-Baptiste Lécaillon. 'It is hard to grow anything here. And we were destroyed by every war. So we have to be resilient. We are survivors. It is not a beautiful place. And yet in spite of all this, we make the wines of celebration, of life and of resilience. All of this suffering has made this possible.'

It is impossible to visit this place, to delve deep under the surface of Champagne, and not be deeply moved by the spirit that flows through these ancient chalk caverns. The earth deep under Reims is infused with a calm, assuring silence. An all-consuming peace. An agelessness that transcends the very passage of time itself.

The only rhythm here is the slow drip of water, seeping through the sodden chalk, counting each moment in tiny droplets whose echoes awaken the silence of endless tunnels. Lit only by the distant glow of dim light through tiny grates high above, there is no passage of the pale northern sun or waning of the shining moon to mark the passing of the seasons here. Nothing changes. It is a cool 10°C and a damp 90% humidity. Always. This place is oblivious to the march of the world above – the tranquil, eerie silence of winter snowfall, the stony, grey austerity of springtime rain, the ravages of fierce summer storms, the pastel glow of autumn harvest, and the destruction of Champagne's tumultuous extremes.

On Wednesday 22 April 2016, the Côte des Bar froze to death. Not an isolated chill, but a blanket of devastating, all-consuming ice like the region had never seen before. Its timing could not have been more disastrous, just two weeks after tender young buds were awakened by the arrival of spring. The result was instantaneous and catastrophic, and in that icy moment on that chilling spring morning, two-thirds of the region's harvest was erased. One devastated grower with a projected harvest of more than 100 tonnes would, five months of toil later, harvest just 1.5.

The volatile world of Champagne has been buffeted by fast-changing economic times, too. Global sales

Taittinger's breathtaking 4 km of crayères and galleries cradle 3 million bottles of Comtes de Champagne at a constant 10°C.

were conservative in 2016 as Brexit wounded sales to Champagne's biggest export market. Meanwhile, domestic sales were depressed in the wake of terrorism attacks. Champagne's recovery after its record sales of 2007 has been slow, hampered by global and European crises, though value has grown slowly, achieving a new record of €4.7 billion in 2015 and again in 2016. Champagne is poised for growth, and its two biggest players and most ambitious exporters, Moët et Chandon and Veuve Clicquot, are currently scurrying to construct vast new facilities to substantially increase production. Champagne's long-aged style calls for long lead times, and the region currently boasts more than 1.4 billion bottles stockpiled in warehouses and buried in the silence of the earth.

The peace and calm of its chalk caverns define not only its people but infuse the character of its wines, for it is time that makes champagne. For centuries, the cold, humid stability far below the surface has been the secret to maturing champagne, for the cooler and slower the second ferment and ageing, the finer the bubbles and the more elegant the champagne. The work of the yeast continues long beyond its short days of life creating bubbles in the bottle. Even in its afterlife as dead 'lees', the slow passage of time coaxes out enticing complexity and silky texture, softening the raw acidity of austere young champagne.

There is no compromise for time. Countless winemakers the world over have devised all manner of shortcuts in sparkling wine production, but none comes close to the age-old *méthode traditionnelle*. No bottle rests in the depths of Champagne for less than 15 months, and most lie dormant for much, much longer. Charles Heidsieck Blanc des Millénaires 1995 has slumbered in these caverns more than 20 years, the oldest current-release champagne of all.

Some champagnes remain in the depths far longer, sometimes by design and sometimes by glorious accident. In 2010, Bollinger assigned a trainee oenologist the task of cleaning out a little drive 15 metres under its headquarters in Aÿ, stacked from floor to ceiling and back wall to entry with row after row of empty bottles. He was astounded by what he discovered hidden behind: a trove of 600 undisgorged bottles. Even the oldest workers in the cellar had no knowledge of this treasure, which must have been lost for almost a century. The only clue to the identity of the bottles lay in a code on a small wooden panel that identified each batch. The house worked through its archives with two historians over six months to decipher the codes, revealing the true extent of the discovery. The youngest bottles were identified to be

Champagne's climate is one of the most extreme and volatile in the wine world, gripped by icy extremes and buffeted by violent storms.

magnums of 1921. There were hand-blown magnums of 1886, the second vintage ever to be bottled in magnums. And, most remarkable of all, 54 bottles of 1830, just one year after the founding of the house.

The arduous task of restoring these ancient bottles ensued, and it took a team of three a month to complete. To determine whether disgorgement was required, an innovative tool known as a 'laser aphrometer' was used to measure the pressure inside the bottles without opening them. It was ultimately decided to open them all and, on tasting, more than half were discarded as mushroomy or corky. Of the 54 bottles of 1830, only 13 were found to be in good condition.

At 186 years of age, no bubbles remained in this hedonistic, copper-gold nectar, nuanced with flavours of madeira, cedar, wood spice, nutmeg and bees wax, more reminiscent of sherry or *vin jaune* than champagne as we know it, yet with an integrity and intrigue truly astonishing.

Such remarkable discoveries are not uncommon in Champagne. Drives were walled up to hide stock from the plundering hands of raiders during the wars. To hide the evidence, these new walls were painted with yoghurt to accelerate the growth of mould. So successful was this disappearing trick that some remain undiscovered to this day. Bollinger has two walled-up drives it's keen to investigate. Who knows what secrets may yet be unearthed from Champagne's depths?

Such rare curios will fascinate and intrigue, but it is the maturation of its commercial releases that truly sets Champagne apart. A decade of suppressed sales and the ever-present, though as yet unrealised, promise of record demand has blessed the region with the privilege of holding back its releases for longer. Factoring in the age of reserve stocks, champagne now boasts an incredible average age on release of more than 4.5 years. It has been said that to produce great champagne, age is the second most important priority after the quality of the grapes. On this basis, Champagne has never been in a stronger position.

There is optimism in ascending from the depths of Champagne's mythical world. To climb those 106 stairs to the surface is to return to the present from 1700 years of dramatic history. Our world today yearns for the peace and calm of this ancient place as fervently as it has at any time in its war-ravaged past.

Following the tragic terrorist attack on its Paris offices in 2015, French satirical magazine *Charlie Hebdo* published the headline cover, *Ils ont les armes. On les emmerde, on a le champagne!* – 'They have guns. F*** them, we have champagne!' If one beverage has won the right to represent peace in our torn world, to stand as the universal symbol of celebration, of unity, of hope, transcending cultures and creeds, surely it is the one from the region destroyed by every war, fashioned by resilient survivors and raised in the very crayères that provided refuge through countless wars.

You will recall that Jean-Baptiste Lécaillon called champagne the wine of celebration, life and resilience. And it is infused with the rock-solid, ageless spirit of ancient chalk crayères.

BIENVENUE!

Welcome to the fifth edition of The Champagne Guide

*T*here's a dazzling world of champagne to be discovered. Never has a greater variety of styles, wider diversity of brands or more exquisite quality emerged from the source of the finest fizz on earth. Champagne offers more options than ever to add sparkle to your occasion, your cuisine, your mood and your taste. It's a thrilling chase to find just the right bottle, but it can be a daunting task, too. This book dares to present the most up-to-date picture of Champagne, to get under the surface of this vast and complex place to uncover the character of every cuvée and take the guesswork out of your next bottle of bubbles.

The intricate personality of a bottle of champagne is shaped by a grand plethora of ingredients: its house style, vintage, grape varieties, reserve wines, winemaking techniques, chef de cave preferences, maturation time, dosage, time since disgorgement and, of course, the terroir of the vineyards themselves.

In the following pages, you'll discover not just what these things mean but, most importantly, how they smell, taste and feel in 625 champagnes from 113 of the best and most important houses, all of which have been tasted recently, providing an up-to-date snapshot of champagnes just as you'll find them this year.

UP-TO-THE-MOMENT GUIDE

Champagne is fast on the move, and an up-to-the-minute guide to the champagnes to drink this year is just as critical as it is for any other wine. This is why this book is very different to every other champagne guide. Time is everything in the development of champagne, and the landscape of the wines on the shelves is changing rapidly.

Since my last edition, new vintages have landed and non-vintages have rolled on to new blends. On occasions when last year's vintage is still current, I've retasted the wine and written an all-new review. I'm amazed how quickly some have blossomed, and others have wilted.

Champagne is the most intricately complex of all wines to craft, and hence to assess. Every bottle is different, according to how long it has relied upon the sustaining presence of lees prior to disgorgement, how long it has evolved post-disgorgement, the composition

of the blend and the dosage for that disgorgement, not to mention how it has travelled. Even non-vintage blends change every vintage as an ever more temperamental mother nature foils even the most skilful blenders. This presents a dilemma in communicating meaningful guidance on each cuvée, and I have again earnestly sought to retaste as many wines outside Champagne as possible, in some cases in as many as five different places.

This has all led me to a bold step which I believe to be unprecedented in champagne publishing – inclusion not only of disgorgement date, base vintage and location of tasting, but also of different scores for the same cuvée when these details change. A complex undertaking, but I'm convinced there's no other way to fairly interpret champagne for its markets across the globe.

To guarantee that you're up to date with the very latest in Champagne, I've added a new chapter with my top ten tips for buying champagne this year to get you right up to speed on all the latest trends and developments (see pages 18–19), added a chapter on champagne and food matching (pages 29–30), updated all 95 champagne producers, dropped a few lesser estates and added 40 new players. There simply aren't enough pages to include everything, so 19 houses and scores for 52 cuvées that didn't make the cut are featured in the index.

A new era in champagne has arrived, and there has never been a better time to raise a glass to discover the intricate personality of the most celebrated beverage on earth. Get ready to sparkle.

The Champagne Guide

USING THIS GUIDE

*C*hasing the best fizz that money can buy? Bienvenue! Your glass is about to froth over. You'll be astounded at what champagne has to offer if you know what to look for this year, and the following pages will guarantee you don't miss a thing.

WHAT DO MY SCORES MEAN?

Points are a quick way to highlight the best champagnes in each category. There has been much controversy surrounding wine scores in recent years. It is of course a travesty to reduce the grand complexities of champagne to a single number, but I persist in doing so because many readers find this useful in honing in on the best cuvées of the year. As always, my descriptions are infinitely more informative than scores, and more detailed than ever this year.

I persevere with the international 100 point system, not because I endorse it, but simply because it is universally understood. Broadly, anything less than 85 is faulty, less than 90 is sound but unexciting, and 91 is where all the real fun begins. A 94 point champagne has impeccable purity and immaculate balance – a gold medal in a wine show. Beyond, it's not greater concentration of flavour, more obvious fruit or more clever winemaking tricks that set it apart. True greatness is declared by something more profound: the inimitable stamp of place – 'terroir' to the French, articulated most eloquently in length of finish and palate texture. Persistence of aftertaste and depth of mineral character distinguish the very finest champagnes.

100 The pinnacle of character, balance and persistence. This year, just 0.6% of champagnes tasted scored 100 points. Only one is currently available. Sadly, it's ear-splittingly expensive.

99 Almost perfection (20 on the 20 point scale). Less than 2% of champagnes tasted. Look out for one $$$ cuvée in the stratosphere this year.

98 An exceedingly rare calibre of world-class distinction. Around 3% of champagnes tasted. The prestige cuvées of the top houses tend to rule this territory.

97 More than exceptional. Just 3% of champagnes tasted. Look out for two $$$ blanc de blancs.

96 Exceptional. Top gold or trophy standard in a wine show (19/20); just 8% of champagnes tasted. There's something for everyone here this year, including five $$ cuvées.

95 Offering an edge that pushes beyond excellent; less than 11% of champagnes tasted. Look out for 13 $$ cuvées.

94 Excellent champagne that I love. Gold medal in a wine show (18.5/20). Less than 12% of champagnes tasted. Look out for two $ cuvées.

93 Almost excellent; 13% of champagnes tasted.

92 A very good wine that characterises its place and variety; 14% of champagnes tasted.

91 Better than good, offering an edge of distinction. Silver medal (17/20); 7% of champagnes tasted. With more than 450 champagnes at 91 or above this year, why drink anything less?

90 A good wine that I like; 7% of champagnes tasted. Only buy if it's cheap.

89 Better than sound and almost good; 7% of champagnes tasted.

88 Sound. Worth buying if it's cheap. Bronze medal standard (15.5/20); 5% of champagnes tasted.

87 Almost sound; 3% of champagnes tasted.

86 Simple and ordinary; 2% of champagnes tasted.

85 Ordinary and boring, though without notable faults (14/20); 2% of champagnes tasted.

84 Borderline faulty. Less than 1% of champagnes tasted.

83 Faulty. Caution!

82 Distinctly faulty (12/20).

81 Exceedingly faulty. Stand well clear.

80 Horrid. You've been warned.

See page 357 for a full list of wines by score.

PRICE

Whether you're on the hunt for a bargain or a decadent splurge, this guide will help you find the right bottle in no time. Each cuvée is price-coded to indicate what you can expect to pay in an average retail store. Champagne is one of the most readily discounted wines on the shelves, so shop around and you're sure to find the big brands on special. Back-vintage champagnes not currently available are listed without indication of price, featured throughout the guide to provide an insight into the potential of the most age-worthy cuvées.

	Euros (France)	Great British Pounds	US Dollars	Australian Dollars	Hong Kong Dollars	Singapore Dollars
$	<€25	<£30	<$50	<$60	<$400	<$80
$$	€25–50	£30–50	$50–80	$60–100	$400–550	$80–140
$$$	€51–65	£51–65	$81–100	$101–150	$551–650	$141–160
$$$$	€66–140	£66–130	$101–200	$151–300	$651–1100	$161–250
$$$$$	>€140	>£130	>$200	>$300	>$1100	>$250

ON THE HOUSE

The Best Champagnes of the Year lists on the following pages highlight the most important wines in this book. These are the finest fizzes that money can buy this year, the most reliable bargains, the most pristine big blends, the most sought-after growers, the most sublime rosés, the most brilliant blanc de blancs, the most balanced low-dosage champagnes, and the upper reaches of the stratosphere of prestige.

The Champagne Guide 2018–2019 Hall of Honour acknowledges the finest houses of the year. A house is only as worthy as its current cuvées, so its rating is based exclusively on the quality of its wines in the market this year, not on past performance or museum wines. History and reputation count for nothing if the wines you can buy don't live up to expectation.

I have made a small exception to this, in compensating for the difficult 2011 and 2010 base vintages where these have let down non-vintage cuvées. Under-performing houses do not deserve your attention nor mine, so unless a house scores at least 5 out of 10, it does not score at all.

Roughly, to rate 10 out of 10, the entry non-vintage cuvée of the house would typically score 95/100, vintage cuvées around 96, and prestige cuvées 97. To attain 5 out of 10, these drop to 91, 93 and 94 respectively.

There is a prudent saying in Champagne that if you make a good brut NV, you are a good house. The entry-level cuvées that comprise the majority of the house's production bear a strong weighting in its rating.

These ratings are by their nature highly controversial. As Champagne house styles increasingly diversify, it is ever more challenging to reduce their grand complexities to a single number. I encourage you to use these only as a guide to quickly home in on the very best houses.

HALL OF HONOUR

The Champagne Guide

• 2018—2019 •

The Best Champagnes of the Year

BÉRÊCHE & FILS VALLÉE DE LA
MARNE RIVE GAUCHE MEUNIER 2012
$$$ • 95 POINTS • PAGE 55

BERNARD BRÉMONT AMBONNAY
GRAND CRU BRUT MILLÉSIME 2008
$$$ • 95 POINTS • PAGE 58

BILLECART-SALMON CUVÉE SOUS
BOIS BRUT NV
$$$ • 95 POINTS • PAGE 66

BRUNO PAILLARD ASSEMBLAGE 2008
$$$ • 95 POINTS • PAGE 81

CHARLES HEIDSIECK MILLÉSIME
VINTAGE BRUT 2005
$$$ • 95 POINTS • PAGE 92

DEVAUX D DE DEVAUX MILLÉSIME
2008
$$$ • 95 POINTS • PAGE 123

LANSON EXTRA AGE BRUT NV
$$$ • 95 POINTS • PAGE 228

VEUVE CLICQUOT VINTAGE 2008
$$$ • 94 POINTS • PAGE 345

Under $$$$

BILLECART-SALMON CUVÉE NICOLAS
FRANÇOIS BILLECART 2002
$$$$ • 99 POINTS • PAGE 68

DEUTZ AMOUR DE DEUTZ ROSÉ
MILLÉSIME BRUT 2008
$$$$ • 99 POINTS • PAGE 119

PIERRE PÉTERS CUVÉE SPÉCIALE
BLANC DE BLANCS LES CHÉTILLONS
2008
$$$$ • 99 POINTS • PAGE 302

DEUTZ AMOUR DE DEUTZ BRUT
MILLÉSIME 2008
$$$$ • 98 POINTS • PAGE 118

DEUTZ CUVÉE WILLIAM DEUTZ
BRUT MILLÉSIME 2008
$$$$ • 98 POINTS • PAGE 117

EGLY-OURIET GRAND CRU
EXTRA BRUT VP VIEILLISSEMENT
PROLONGÉ NV
$$$$ • 98 POINTS • PAGE 141

JACQUESSON DIZY TERRES ROUGES
2012
$$$$ • 98 POINTS • PAGE 199

KRUG GRANDE CUVÉE 158ÈME
EDITION NV
$$$$ • 98 POINTS • PAGE 211

PIERRE PÉTERS CUVÉE SPÉCIALE
BLANC DE BLANCS
LES CHÉTILLONS 2002
$$$$ • 98 POINTS

BILLECART-SALMON BLANC DE
BLANCS BRUT 2004
$$$$ • 97 POINTS • PAGE 67

BOLLINGER LA GRANDE ANNÉE
2007
$$$$ • 97 POINTS • PAGE 76

DEUTZ AMOUR DE DEUTZ BRUT
MILLÉSIME 2007
$$$$ • 97 POINTS • PAGE 118

DEUTZ AMOUR DE DEUTZ BRUT
MILLÉSIME 2006
$$$$ • 97 POINTS • PAGE 118

DEUTZ AMOUR DE DEUTZ ROSÉ
MILLÉSIME BRUT 2006
$$$$ • 97 POINTS • PAGE 119

EGLY-OURIET GRAND CRU
MILLÉSIME 2006
$$$$ • 97 POINTS • PAGE 140

GOSSET CELEBRIS 2002
$$$$ • 97 POINTS

KRUG GRANDE CUVÉE 163ÈME
EDITION NV
$$$$ • 97 POINTS • PAGE 211

ROBERT MONCUIT LES CHÉTILLONS
BLANC DE BLANCS GRAND CRU 2008
$$$$ • 97 POINTS • PAGE 315

ALFRED GRATIEN CUVÉE PARADIS
BRUT 2008
$$$$ • 96 POINTS • PAGE 38

BÉRÊCHE & FILS LE CRAN LUDES
PREMIER CRU 2008
$$$$ • 96 POINTS • PAGE 55

BRUNO PAILLARD N.P.U. NEC PLUS
ULTRA 1999
$$$$ • 96 POINTS • PAGE 81

CHARLES HEIDSIECK MILLÉSIME
ROSÉ 2006
$$$$ • 96 POINTS • PAGE 92

DEUTZ AMOUR DE DEUTZ ROSÉ
MILLÉSIME BRUT 2007
$$$$ • 96 POINTS • PAGE 119

DEUTZ CUVÉE WILLIAM DEUTZ
BRUT MILLÉSIME 2006
$$$$ • 96 POINTS • PAGE 117

DUVAL-LEROY FEMME DE
CHAMPAGNE BRUT GRAND CRU NV
$$$$ • 96 POINTS • PAGE 137

EGLY-OURIET GRAND CRU
AMBONNAY ROUGE 2012
$$$$ • 96 POINTS • PAGE 141

EGLY-OURIET GRAND CRU BRUT
ROSÉ NV
$$$$ • 96 POINTS • PAGE 140

GOSSET CELEBRIS ROSÉ EXTRA BRUT
2007
$$$$ • 96 POINTS • PAGE 161

JACQUESSON DIZY TERRES ROUGES
ROSÉ EXTRA BRUT 2009
$$$$ • 96 POINTS • PAGE 200

KRUG GRANDE CUVÉE 159ÈME
EDITION NV
$$$$ • 96 POINTS • PAGE 211

PAUL DÉTHUNE CUVÉE A
L'ANCIENNE BRUT 2008
$$$$ • 96 POINTS • PAGE 277

PIERRE PÉTERS CUVÉE SPÉCIALE
BLANC DE BLANCS LES CHÉTILLONS
2007
$$$$ • 96 POINTS • PAGE 302

PIERRE PÉTERS CUVÉE SPÉCIALE
BLANC DE BLANCS LES CHÉTILLONS
1996
$$$$ • 96 POINTS

PIERRE PÉTERS CUVÉE SPÉCIALE
BLANC DE BLANCS LES CHÉTILLONS
OENOTHÈQUE 2000
$$$$ • 96 POINTS

POL ROGER BRUT ROSÉ 2008
$$$$ • 95 POINTS • PAGE 310

Under $$$$$

KRUG CLOS DU MESNIL BLANC DE
BLANCS BRUT 2002
$$$$$ • 100 POINTS • PAGE 212

DUVAL-LEROY FEMME DE
CHAMPAGNE 1996
$$$$$ • 99 POINTS • PAGE 137

KRUG VINTAGE 2002
$$$$$ • 99 POINTS • PAGE 210

TAITTINGER COMTES DE
CHAMPAGNE BLANC DE BLANCS
2008
$$$$$ • 99 POINTS • PAGE 327

BILLECART-SALMON GRANDE CUVÉE
1998
$$$$$ • 98 POINTS • PAGE 69

BOLLINGER R.D. EXTRA BRUT 2002
$$$$$ • 98 POINTS • PAGE 78

BOLLINGER VIEILLES VIGNES
FRANÇAISES 2006
$$$$$ • 98 POINTS • PAGE 78

CHARLES HEIDSIECK BLANC DES
MILLÉNAIRES 1995
$$$$$ • 98 POINTS • PAGE 93

DOM PÉRIGNON P2 1998
$$$$$ • 98 POINTS • PAGE 128

EGLY-OURIET GRAND CRU BLANC
DE NOIRS VIEILLE VIGNE NV
$$$$$ • 98 POINTS • PAGE 141

GOSSET 15 ANS DE CAVE A MINIMA
BRUT NV
$$$$$ • 98 POINTS • PAGE 159

KRUG ROSÉ BRUT NV
$$$$$ • 98 POINTS • PAGE 209

LOUIS ROEDERER CRISTAL ROSÉ
2009
$$$$$ • 98 POINTS • PAGE 249

LOUIS ROEDERER CRISTAL ROSÉ
2007
$$$$$ • 98 POINTS • PAGE 249

TAITTINGER COMTES DE
CHAMPAGNE BLANC DE BLANCS
2007
$$$$$ • 98 POINTS • PAGE 328

BOLLINGER LA GRANDE ANNÉE
ROSÉ 2007
$$$$$ • 97 POINTS • PAGE 77

KRUG CLOS D'AMBONNAY 2000
$$$$$ • 97 POINTS • PAGE 213

PIPER-HEIDSIECK RARE MILLESIME
2002
$$$$$ • 97 POINTS • PAGE 306

POL ROGER CUVÉE SIR WINSTON
CHURCHILL 2006
$$$$$ • 97 POINTS • PAGE 310

TAITTINGER COMTES DE
CHAMPAGNE BLANC DE BLANCS
2006
$$$$$ • 97 POINTS • PAGE 328

LOUIS ROEDERER CRISTAL BRUT
2007
$$$$$ • 96 POINTS • PAGE 248

The Best Blanc de Blancs
Champagnes of the Year $$-$$$

J.L. VERGNON RÉSONANCE
MILLÉSIME GRAND CRU BLANC DE
BLANCS EXTRA BRUT 2008
$$$ • 97 POINTS • PAGE 185

PIERRE GIMONNET & FILS SPECIAL
CLUB GRANDS TERROIRS DE
CHARDONNAY 2008
$$$ • 97 POINTS • PAGE 295

PIERRE GIMONNET & FILS CUVÉE
FLEURON 1ER CRU BLANC DE BLANCS
2008
$$ • 96 POINTS • PAGE 294

PIERRE GIMONNET & FILS SPECIAL
CLUB GRANDS TERROIRS DE
CHARDONNAY 2012
$$$ • 96 POINTS • PAGE 295

PIERRE GIMONNET & FILS SPECIAL
CLUB GRANDS TERROIRS DE
CHARDONNAY 2010
$$$ • 96 POINTS • PAGE 295

AYALA BLANC DE BLANCS BRUT
2008
$$$ • 95 POINTS • PAGE 50

AR LENOBLE GRAND CRU BLANC DE
BLANCS CHOUILLY BRUT 2008
$$ • 95 POINTS • PAGE 44

BRUNO PAILLARD BLANC DE BLANCS
BRUT 2004
$$$ • 95 POINTS • PAGE 81

CLAUDE CAZALS MILLÉSIME GRAND
CRU BLANC DE BLANCS BRUT 2008
$$ • 95 POINTS • PAGE 98

DE SOUSA CUVÉE DES CAUDALIES
BLANC DE BLANCS GRAND CRU
EXTRA BRUT NV
$$$ • 95 POINTS • PAGE 108

DELAMOTTE BLANC DE BLANCS 2007
$$$ • 95 POINTS • PAGE 112

J. LASSALLE BLANC DE BLANCS
MILLÉSIME PREMIER CRU BRUT
2007
$$$ • 95 POINTS • PAGE 182

LE BRUN-SERVENAY CUVÉE
CHARDONNAY VIEILLES VIGNES
EXTRA BRUT 2006
$$ • 95 POINTS • PAGE 240

LE BRUN-SERVENAY CUVÉE
EXHILARANTE VIEILLES VIGNES
MILLÉSIME 2008
$$$ • 95 POINTS • PAGE 241

PIERRE GIMONNET & FILS EXTRA
BRUT CUVÉE OENOPHILE 1ER CRU
BLANC DE BLANCS NON DOSÉ 2008
$$ • 95 POINTS • PAGE 294

PIERRE GIMONNET & FILS SPECIAL
CLUB OGER GRAND CRU BLANC DE
BLANCS 2012
$$$ • 95 POINTS • PAGE 296

PIERRE PÉTERS CUVÉE MILLÉSIME
L'ESPRIT BLANC DE BLANCS 2012
$$$ • 95 POINTS • PAGE 300

POL ROGER BLANC DE BLANCS BRUT
VINTAGE 2009
$$$ • 95 POINTS • PAGE 309

DELAMOTTE BLANC DE BLANCS NV
$$ • 94 POINTS • PAGE 111

LALLIER BLANC DE BLANCS GRAND
CRU BRUT NV
$$ • 94 POINTS • PAGE 223

LE BRUN-SERVENAY BRUT
SELECTION BLANC DE BLANCS
GRAND CRU NV
$$ • 94 POINTS • PAGE 240

PIERRE GIMONNET & FILS CUVÉE
GASTRONOME 1ER CRU BLANC DE
BLANCS BRUT 2012
$$ • 94 POINTS • PAGE 293

VEUVE FOURNY & FILS BLANC DE
BLANCS VERTUS PREMIER CRU BRUT
NATURE NV
$$ • 94 POINTS • PAGE 351

PHILIPPONNAT GRAND
BLANC BRUT 2007
$$ • 92 POINTS • PAGE 287

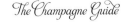
The Champagne Guide

The Best Rosé Champagnes of the Year $$-$$$

BOLLINGER ROSÉ BRUT NV
$$$ • 96 POINTS • PAGE 76

BRUNO PAILLARD PREMIÈRE CUVÉE ROSÉ EXTRA BRUT NV
$$$ • 96 POINTS • PAGE 80

CHARLES HEIDSIECK ROSÉ RÉSERVE NV
$$$ • 96 POINTS • PAGE 91

DEUTZ BRUT ROSÉ MILLÉSIMÉ 2012
$$$ • 96 POINTS • PAGE 116

ROBERT MONCUIT LES ROMARINES GRAND CRU ROSÉ BRUT NV
$$ • 96 POINTS • PAGE 315

ALFRED GRATIEN BRUT ROSÉ NV
$$$ • 95 POINTS • PAGE 37

BILLECART-SALMON BRUT ROSÉ NV
$$$ • 95 POINTS • PAGE 65

DE SOUSA ROSÉ DE SAIGNÉE GRAND CRU BRUT NV
$$ • 95 POINTS • PAGE 106

DEUTZ BRUT ROSÉ NV
$$ • 95 POINTS • PAGE 115

GATINOIS AŸ GRAND CRU BRUT ROSÉ NV
$$ • 95 POINTS • PAGE 153

HENRIOT ROSÉ MILLÉSIME 2008
$$$ • 95 POINTS • PAGE 174

LARMANDIER-BERNIER ROSÉ DE SAIGNÉE PREMIER CRU EXTRA BRUT NV
$$$ • 95 POINTS • PAGE 233

LOUIS ROEDERER VINTAGE ROSÉ 2010
$$$ • 95 POINTS • PAGE 247

PIERRE PÉTERS ROSÉ FOR ALBANE NV
$$ • 95 POINTS • PAGE 301

VEUVE FOURNY & FILS ROSÉ LES ROUGESMONTS EXTRA BRUT NV
$$$ • 95 POINTS • PAGE 352

ANDRÉ CLOUET ROSÉ No 3 BRUT NV
$$ • 94 POINTS • PAGE 41

GEOFFROY ROSÉ DE SAIGNÉE BRUT PREMIER CRU NV
$$ • 94 POINTS • PAGE 157

J. LASSALLE PREMIER CRU BRUT ROSÉ NV
$$ • 94 POINTS • PAGE 181

J.L. VERGNON ROSÉMOTION GRAND CRU EXTRA BRUT NV
$$ • 94 POINTS • PAGE 184

L. BÉNARD-PITOIS BRUT ROSÉ PREMIER CRU NV
$$ • 94 POINTS • PAGE 216

MARC HÉBRART BRUT ROSÉ PREMIER CRU NV
$$ • 94 POINTS • PAGE 254

PIERRE GIMONNET & FILS ROSÉ DE BLANCS 1ER CRU BRUT NV
$$ • 94 POINTS • PAGE 293

Rosé is going gangbusters, now representing more than 10% of champagne exports and a huge 23% of my best buys this year.

TOP TIPS FOR BUYING CHAMPAGNE

*C*hampagne is a fast-moving target, recording record global turnover in recent years not always in step with the region's best buys. For all of its record-smashing, cork-popping success, there is still much to embrace in the diversity of styles, producers and prices that Champagne has to offer. Here are my top ten tips for making the most of the region's finest this year.

BUY VINTAGE

It's a travesty that the smallest-selling champagne category remains the best value. Excluding prestige and rosé, vintage champagne represents a minuscule 1.6% of champagne bottles exported. And yet this same category represents an enormous 62% of my best of lists this year! (See page 14.)

BUY 2008

2008 is the most refined and long-lived vintage in many decades, and it's on the shelves right now.

BUY NVs BASED ON 2012

2012 is the predominant non-vintage base in the market this year, and it's the best since 2008. Where possible, I've explained throughout this guide how to decode bottling codes to ascertain base vintages.

BUY ROSÉ

Champagne rosé continues its flamboyant growth curve, up 8.6% in 2016, now representing more than 10% of champagne exports. And yet its performance in the glass far outranks its sales success, representing a huge 23% of my best of lists this year. See page 17 for my top rosé recommendations.

BUY PRESTIGE

This year I discovered an unusually small number of high-scoring cuvées in $, $$ and $$$ price brackets, making an investment in prestige cuvées all the more rewarding. I have lined up 56 astonishing champagnes at $$$$ and $$$$$ prices in my 'Best of' list (see page 15).

Prestige champagne remains a tiny category, and although exports grew by 4.6% in 2016, they still coincidentally represent just 4.6% of all champagnes sold.

SPEND UP

Champagne remains the bargain of the luxury wine world, with prestige champagne ranking as the most affordable and most accessible of all flagship global benchmark wine styles. When was the last time you found a mature First Growth Bordeaux or Grand Cru Burgundy for the same price as Krug Grand Cuvée?

In 1904, Moët & Chandon Carte Bleue sold for the same price as Château Latour, Château Margaux and Château Haut-Brion. A 30-year-old Château Lafite was just double the price of a bottle of Louis Roederer, Mumm Cordon Rouge or Veuve Clicquot. Today, these Bordeaux wines are 20 times the price! Champagne does not rank even once among the top 20 most expensive wines in the world.

And yet Champagne pays its growers the highest grape price in the world of €6.20 per kilogram, more than 60% up on the price 15 years ago. It takes 1.2 kilograms of grapes to make a bottle of wine, not to mention a production process more complex and more labour-intensive than any other in the wine world. Besides fortified, champagne is the only wine style matured to its prime prior to release. Champagne currently has 1.43 billion bottles stockpiled in waiting, more than 4.5 years of supply.

When I recently hosted an intimate group of champagne lovers for a special week of visits in the region, they arrived sceptical about the high price of champagne and left astounded by its value, exclaiming that they now knew just what went into its production.

Champagne is the envy of the wine world, the universal and inimitable symbol of celebration. It accounts for 20% of French wine sales, from just 4% of the country's vineyards.

Can champagne maintain its bargain prices? It can, and it will, until demand hits a record high in the coming years. Since a record of 338.8 million bottles in 2007, champagne achieved a post-GFC sales record of 312.5 million in 2015, softening to 306 million in 2016. Average ex-cellar bottle prices have risen by just 14% over the past nine years, making €4.7 billion in sales in both 2015 and 2016 all-time records for global champagne turnover.

GO MONTAGNE & CÔTE DES BLANCS

Pinot noir ranks as Champagne's most planted varietal (38%), followed by meunier (32%) and chardonnay (30%). The blanc de blancs cuvées of the greatest villages of the Côte des Blancs and the pinot-driven blends of the Montagne de Reims uphold their reputations as the greatest sparkling wines on earth.

DON'T MISS CHAMPAGNE GROWERS

A tremendous 4461 of Champagne's 15,800 growers produce their own champagnes, compared with just 306 houses and 39 coopératives. However, growers have declined to less than 20% of champagne sales.

Since 2007, the volume of sales from champagne houses has ebbed and flowed with European and global economic instability, but stabilised at 219.4 million bottles in 2016, unchanged from 2010 levels. Coopérative sales likewise remained stable since 2010 at 27.1 million bottles. By comparison, grower champagne sales suffered a steady and consistent decline since 2008, dropping 24% from 78.5 million to just 59.5 million in 2016.

This year, the growers most worthy of your attention are Egly-Ouriet, André Clouet, De Sousa, Gatinois and Pierre Gimonnet & Fils. I include De Sousa here even though, like Bérêche et Fils, this estate recently relinquished its Récoltant-Manipulant status for the flexibility to purchase grapes. Both will always remain growers in my mind. The sharp distinction drawn around the world between Champagne growers and négociant houses is simply a contrived fallacy.

BEWARE OF FAULTY BOTTLES

Of more than 800 cuvées I tasted for this guide, I'm delighted to report that I encountered less than 1% cork taint and less than 1% random oxidation, by far the lowest results I have ever seen for bottle variation.

Imparted randomly by natural corks, cork taint gives a mouldy, 'wet cardboard' or 'wet dog' character to champagne. It suppresses fruit and shortens the length of finish. In its most subtle form, it may simply have a slight dulling effect on the bouquet and palate.

Champagne is the most fragile of all wine styles, and particularly susceptible to degradation in contact with oxygen. Oxidation shows itself in champagne as premature development, flattening fruit expression,

contributing characters of burnt orange or vinegar, and drying out the finish.

Positive trends in both cork taint and oxidation are thanks in part to more than 60 million bottles (a little more than 20%) of champagne now sealed with Mytik DIAM, a micro-agglomerate closure moulded from granulated fragments of cork which have been treated to extract cork taint and some 150 other molecules that might produce 'off' characters. I have never seen cork taint in any DIAM-sealed wine.

'Lightstruck' is the menacing effect of degradation of wine exposed to ultraviolet light from fluorescent lamps and, worse, sunlight. There is no wine more susceptible to lightstruck than champagne in clear glass bottles, diminishing citrus aromas and producing reductive characters such as sulphur, corn, gherkin, bacon, gun smoke or burnt rubber.

As always, request a replacement of any faulty bottle.

GET OFF THE LOW SUGAR DIET

For the first time this year, I have made the bold move of dropping the 'Low Dosage Champagnes of the Year' as a dedicated category in my 'Best of' lists. There simply aren't enough worthy cuvées this year.

Over the centuries, dosage levels have gradually lowered, and in recent years the catch cry seems to have become 'how low can you go?' Until recently, to qualify as 'brut', champagne required less than 15g/L of sweetness – a little less than a teaspoon of sugar in a cup of coffee. This has now been lowered to a maximum of 12g/L. 'Extra brut' requires less than 6g/L, and 'brut nature' or 'brut zero' less than 3g/L. Most champagnes now boast a refreshingly low dosage of 5–10g/L.

Champagne's sweet dreams may be a thing of the past, but has it gone too far? 'Zero dosage' is all the rage, and the intent of the 'Coke Zero' movement of the wine world is certainly noble, but too many champagne brands have joined the parade simply because it's the thing to do. Dogmatically slashing dosage to zero purely for the sake of branding is self-defeating.

A carefully tweaked low dosage is not designed to make a wine taste sweet. The effect of just 5g/L (a spoonful of sugar in an entire bottle) can be astounding. Floral aromas are lifted, the palate is softened and more harmonious, the fruit is more expressive and, in the most delightful way, it doesn't taste sweet. Sugar also builds longevity, reacting with amino acids to give roasted, honeyed characters.

Champagne's most progressive makers carefully tweak the dosage of every cuvée, every year, to create a precise balance. Beware of zero-dosage cuvées built on the same base as the brut cuvée of the house.

CHAMPAGNE VINTAGES

The vast complexity and diversity of Champagne and the varied micro-climates of its 320 villages have long driven me to resist writing generic vintage reports. But the more I taste champagne, the more I see distinctive moods of each season underscoring the voice of each terroir and house style. 'The magic of champagne belongs to the climate, not the soil,' says Louis Roederer chef de cave Jean-Baptiste Lécaillon. 'The climate is stronger, and the wines tell the story of the rain and the sun.'

This is particularly pronounced in the wines released this year. The last edition of this guide caught many new vintage releases from the tricky 2005 and ordinary 2006 harvests, and a great deal of non-vintage wines marked by the harrowing 2011 and tricky 2010 seasons. This year, the news is much more optimistic, as most vintage releases have shifted to the reasonable 2007 and 2009 seasons, and most importantly the spectacular 2008, while the great 2012 vintage is the predominant non-vintage base in the market.

The tumultuous climate of Champagne makes the stamp of the season more dramatic than in any other wine region, so an insight into the personality of every harvest is pertinent again this year.

There's a disconcerting trend in Champagne to release vintage wines more often. While some chef de caves argue that a progressive warming of the climate has rendered more seasons capable of standing alone, I am increasingly unconvinced of the merits of warm seasons like 2001, 2003 and 2005. Many houses and growers were ambitious in releasing vintage wines from 2003 and 2005. Now we are seeing 2010 and 2011 vintage wines beginning to emerge. Buyer beware! We have entered an era in which greater consumer discernment is necessary in selecting vintages. There are notable exceptions highlighted throughout this guide, but the general rule for the first decade of the new millennium is to stick with the even years.

I've introduced a little twist to traditional historic vintage reports. Each of the following assessments is written according to how this vintage is looking today, and the cuvées I've singled out have all been tasted recently. In cool, stable, dark conditions, the enduring vintages of 1996, 2002, 2004, 2008 and 2012 are capable of maturing magnificently for decades, and I hope you might be enticed to lay down a bottle or two.

2016

A season of catastrophic climactic events that decimated yields, though there is surprised optimism for the grapes that survived. This was the vintage that Pierre Larmandier (Larmandier-Bernier) dubbed 'the year of living dangerously!' April and May frosts, hail and torrential rain obliterated an estimated 22% of the Champagne harvest, with the majority of the crop in the Côte des Bar completely wiped out, said to be the most widespread devastation in the area's history. April through July delivered double the average rainfall, bringing on particularly aggressive mildew and oïdium, leaving Bollinger wondering in June if they would pick any grapes at all. Late August delivered a four-day heatwave, and with canopies opened up to facilitate ventilation, an estimated 3–5% of the crop was burnt by the sun. The result was an average yield of just 9000kg/hectare, the lowest since 2003. The region will maintain supply thanks to high levels of reserves from the four strong preceding vintages. An otherwise idyllic August and September saved the harvest, with sunny days and cool nights producing good ripeness while upholding bright acidity. Jean-Baptiste Lécaillon (Louis Roederer) found the vintage to require no chaptalisation or malolactic fermentation, and compared the ripeness and acidity with the great seasons of 2012, 2002, 1964 and 1949. 'At the vintage celebration at the end of harvest, I told my team that if you wanted proof that god is Champenois, this harvest was it!' he said.

2015

A season of generous, ripe maturity, producing wines of concentration, body and structure, yet in the right hands, upholding excellent acid profile, freshness and definition. Outstanding pinot noir and exceptional meunier, though chardonnay experienced over- and under-ripeness in places. Vineyards largely fared well through the driest and sunniest summer in Champagne since records began after World War II, thanks to near-record soil moisture furnished by strong early spring rainfall. Chardonnay fared worst in the heat, though cool nights upheld acid levels not far below normal. Some rain in August and early September provided some relief without disease pressure, but hampered flavour, acid and sugar ripeness, making the decision of when to harvest more difficult than ever before. The result was high ripeness, frequently over 11 degrees natural potential and a record of 12.5 degrees in Bollinger's La Côte aux Enfants. Perrier-Jouët harvested Cramant at 11.9 degrees, prompting a small addition of tartaric acid for the first time in Hervé Deschamps' 20 years. Others attempted to uphold freshness by partially or fully blocking malolactic fermentation, with minimal impact due to particularly low levels of malic this year. Even the seniors of the region found it difficult to identify another vintage like it, though some drew comparisons with 1947, 1959, 1964, 1976 and 2002: 'We were expecting 1947 but we got 1976 or 1990, which was not so bad!' said Anselme Selosse (Jacques Selosse); 'we have not had such a good vintage since 2002!' declared Antoine Roland-Billecart (Billecart-Salmon); 'I definitely think 2015 is better than 2002!' enthused Jean-Baptiste Lécaillon (Louis Roederer). I tasted the vins clairs extensively during blending in early 2016 and was impressed by the levels of acidity supporting this generous harvest. Some vineyards display tropical ripeness, and I tend to agree with Pol Roger's Laurent d'Harcourt's caution that 'maybe we got a bit too much sun to keep the acidity at a level that will allow the wines to age long'.

2014

An exceptional season on the Montagne de Reims and Côte des Bar, excellent in the Côte des Blancs, though the Vallée de la Marne suffered from rot and lacked maturity. The vivacity of a cold summer contrasts the rounded fleshiness of a warm harvest. The wettest August on record and the coldest summer in 20 years were followed by an idyllic September. Those who spent the harvest in Champagne recall a compacted vintage saved by the warm autumn sun. There was no rescuing meunier after twice the usual summer rainfall in the Vallée de la Marne, though diligent viticulture helped in the Côte des Blancs, producing chardonnay charged with excellent acidity and ripeness, leading Veuve

Fourny chef de cave Emmanuel Fourny to dub this *l'année du vigneron*, the year of the vine grower. The Montagne de Reims received only 10% more summer rainfall than usual, and Louis Roederer chef de cave Jean-Baptiste Lécaillon reported 'some of the best fruit we have produced'. When I visited Eric Rodez in Ambonnay just after he'd emptied his last press load, he was excited like a boy at Christmas, declaring, 'This may be the harvest of my career!' Houses sourcing predominantly from the northern Montagne de Reims and Côte des Blancs declared vintage cuvées.

2013

A late, cool, elongated harvest of high acidity. The early-ripening villages of the Côte des Blancs, southern Montagne de Reims and eastern Vallée de la Marne suffered poor flowering, which proved to be a blessing, tempering yields in an otherwise higher-yielding vintage, advancing ripeness, with good results. Rodolphe Péters (Pierre Péters) now ranks it alongside 2008 as his favoured vintage of recent decades, and suggests the highlights of the season will trump the best of 2012, although 2012 will be better on average. For Moët & Chandon chef de cave Benoît Gouez, 'On paper, 2013 was as good as 2012 for chardonnay and pinot noir in the grand and premier crus.' Later-ripening villages were delayed by high yields, afflicted by rain in September and a cold, windy October. It was not until well into that month that ripeness was achieved, with stringent selection required to avoid rot. This proved a particularly challenging year in the western Marne and Côte des Bar. Such were the acidities that Louis Roederer put a record number of parcels through malolactic fermentation. Severe July hailstorms battered some 3000 hectares, with more than 300 hectares completely destroyed, particularly around Épernay and the Côte des Blancs, where 10–20% of the grand cru crop was lost.

2012 • 8/10

A stark reminder that blanket generalisations are grossly inadequate in Champagne's grand diversity. I visited and tasted the vins clairs in early 2013 and was amazed at their scintillating acidity, expressive concentration, entrancing purity and classic refinement, yet surprised by the polarising reports about the vintage.

Superlatives rolled: 'The vintage of my career' (Dumangin), 'amazing' (Veuve Clicquot), 'very, very good' (Jacquesson), 'perfect balance' (Mumm), 'spectacular, one of the three classic vintages so far this century' (Louis Roederer), 'very similar to 2002' (Taittinger), 'better than 2002 or 2008' (Pierre Gimonnet), 'better than 1996' (Vilmart), 'challenging yet beautiful' (Devaux), 'just fantastic, wow!' (Billecart-Salmon).

Then this: 'One of the toughest seasons I can recall in 25 years' (Larmandier-Bernier), 'challenging' (Dom Pérignon), 'very difficult' (Piper Heidsieck), 'tough' (Pierre Péters). 'For a good vintage in Champagne, we do not want a good summer,' clarifies Didier Gimonnet. 'The grapes must suffer!'

Record rainfall between March and July made diligence in controlling rot paramount, a nightmare for some organic and biodynamic growers. While a few of the most fanatical growers reported bumper yields, most lost one-third of their crop. A cool summer upheld dizzying acidity, while perfect conditions from mid-August produced generous sugar ripeness, so much so that some growers saw no need to chaptalise.

Those who waited and picked ripe were rewarded, and there will be many spectacularly concentrated, acid-driven, long-lived vintage cuvées made this season, though there are notable exceptions: Ruinart did not see the stamina in chardonnay to produce a Dom Ruinart in 2012, and Krug will not release a vintage cuvée, instead keeping its small crop in reserve. The greatest 2012 vintage champagnes released to date are Deutz Rosé Brut, Egly-Ouriet Grand Cru Ambonnay Rouge and Pierre Gimonnet & Fils Special Club Grands Terroirs de Chardonnay, with many more still to come.

2011 · 2/10

A dismal vintage marked by underripeness, dilution and widespread rot. I visited at the height of summer in mid-July, and for two weeks there was not one day of sunshine to ripen the harvest. Misty mornings made way for sullen, grey days, frequently sodden with downpours. Summer was otherwise hot, furnishing a short growing cycle and grapes devoid of complexity and character. In spite of a lack of ripeness, the threat of rot during a rain-interrupted harvest prompted the CIVC to announce some of the earliest harvest dates in history. For all the inconsistencies of 2011, Veuve Clicquot chef de cave Dominique Demarville upholds the season as evidence Champagne is still capable of producing strong acidity. Very few vintage wines were produced. This year, 2011 still hovers on the shelves as the base of some non-vintage champagnes, marked by dusty, dry, mushroomy rot. Its impact is exacerbated by the weakness of 2010, hampering any hopes of resurrecting non-vintage cuvées with generous reserves. Disappointingly, I am yet to taste a 2011 vintage champagne rating above 91 points.

2010 · 3/10

A challenging season, with ripe fruit marred by dilution, low acidity and rampant rot. A hot, dry summer ended abruptly in a mid-August deluge, prompting a devastating outburst of botrytis across the Marne. 'There was such a fog of dry rot in the air I couldn't see the guys throwing the grapes into the press!' one Montagne de Reims grower revealed. Sorting was paramount, and some houses elected to keep less than their appellation allowance. This proved to put a timely damper on production after the global financial crisis significantly dented champagne sales in 2009. The greatest 2010 vintage champagne released to date is Pierre Gimonnet & Fils Special Club Grands Terroirs de Chardonnay.

2009 · 6/10

Dry, hot continental weather produced a sunny, ripe vintage of rounded exuberance, clean and appealing right away, without the acidity to age, making 2009 the antithesis of the tense, enduring 2008. While this vintage will forever lurk in the shadow of its predecessor, it is a season with some surprises. 'An excellent vintage!' found Jacquesson's Jean-Hervé Chiquet, and for Didier Gimonnet of Pierre Gimonnet, one of the best of the decade after 2002. The greatest 2009 vintage champagnes today are Deutz Brut Rosé, Louis Roederer Cristal Rosé, Jacquesson Dizy Terres Rouges Rosé Extra Brut and Pierre Péters Cuvée Spéciale Blanc de Blancs Les Chétillons, though very few vintage wines were made, as much in response to the global financial crisis as the pedigree of the season.

2008 · 10/10

A vintage of classic finesse, crystalline purity, tightly clenched acidity and monumental longevity, 2008 is the essence of champagne. It will be decades before the full distinction of this transcendental season becomes truly apparent, but I have ever-rising confidence that it will eclipse even 1996 and every season since. There is no more exquisite recipe for champagne than a wet spring, a cool, not particularly sunny, yet dry, summer, followed by idyllic, bright days and cool nights, lingering gloriously for the entire duration of harvest. The result was textbook ripeness of 9.6–9.8 degrees potential, and heightened acidities of 8.5–8.6g/L. To Vazart-Coquart chef de cave Jean-Pierre Vazart, 2008 is 1996 with balance. Even many lesser growers and houses produced admirable results in this near-perfect vintage, while the flagship cuvées of the top houses will endure for half a century. The greatest 2008 vintage champagnes today are Deutz Amour de Deutz Brut, Deutz Amour de Deutz Rosé Brut, Deutz William Deutz Brut, J.L. Vergnon Résonance Millésime Grand Cru Blanc de Blancs Extra Brut, Pierre Gimonnet & Fils Special Club Millésime de Collection Blanc de Blancs, Pierre Péters Cuvée Spéciale Blanc de Blancs Les Chétillons, Robert Moncuit Les Chétillons Blanc de Blancs Grand Cru and Taittinger Comtes de Champagne, with many, many more stunners yet to be released.

2007 · 7/10

A vintage of delicacy and finesse, with endurance, if not concentration, terroir expression or distinctive character. A warm winter made for an early season, retarded by a wet, cold and rot-inducing summer. Harvest was saved by a north wind and sunny days from mid-August, furnishing adequate maturity while upholding good acid levels. This proved to be a highly variable vintage from one village to the next, largely dependent upon picking date, vineyard care and sorting regime. Following the warm, sunny style of 2006, the elegance of 2007 is sometimes compared to that of 1997 following 1996. To Dom Pérignon chef de cave Richard Geoffroy, '2007 was slight – it never happened!' Those who harvested later were rewarded with better expression and character. The greatest 2007 vintage champagnes today are Bollinger La Grande Année, Bollinger La Grande Année Rosé, Deutz Amour de Deutz Brut, Gosset Cuvée Celebris Rosé Extra Brut, Louis Roederer Cristal, Louis Roederer Cristal Rosé, Pierre Péters Cuvée Spéciale Blanc de Blancs Les Chétillons and Taittinger Comtes de Champagne.

2006 · 6/10

A soft, fruity, approachable vintage, without particularly distinct structure, already at its peak at less than a decade of age. A warm June, record hot July, cold, rainy August and sunny September produced ripe, clean fruit of 10.2% average degrees potential and low acidity of just 7g/L. Moët & Chandon chef de cave Benoît Gouez says 2006 is about 'amplitude, volume and expansive mouthfeel', likening it to 1999. To Didier Gimonnet, it has the structure and 'clumsy richness' of 2005 and the minerality of 2004. The greatest 2006s today are Bollinger Vieilles Vignes Françaises, Deutz Amour de Deutz Brut, Deutz Amour de Deutz Rosé Brut, Egly-Ouriet Grand Cru Millésime, Emmanuel Brochet Extra Brut Premier Cru Millésime, Louis Roederer Cristal,

Paul Bara Special Club Rosé, Pierre Péters Cuvée Spéciale Blanc de Blancs Les Chétillons, Pol Roger Sir Winston Churchill and Taittinger Comtes de Champagne Blanc de Blancs, with more yet to be released.

2005 · 5/10

A hot, tricky season of overripe character and dry phenolic grip, lacking freshness and elegance, with most cuvées already at their peak. Extremes of heat spikes alternating with heavy rainfall triggered mildew attacks in July, though a cool August and mild September prompted an elongated harvest. Ultimately, a mature vintage of 9.8% degrees potential, with some pinot noir and meunier afflicted by botrytis. The greatest 2005 vintage champagnes today are Bollinger La Grande Année Rosé, Jacquesson Avize Champ Caïn Récolte Extra Brut, Jacquesson Aÿ Vauzelle Terme Récolte Extra Brut, Jacquesson Dizy Corne Bautray Récolte Extra Brut, Pierre Gimonnet & Fils Millésime de Collection Blanc de Blancs, Pierre Gimonnet & Fils Special Club Blanc de Blancs, Pierre Péters Cuvée Spéciale Blanc de Blancs Les Chétillons, Taittinger Comtes de Champagne Rosé, and more yet to be released.

2004 · 8/10

A magnificent vintage of fine aromatic profile, lightness, finesse, energy, mineral definition and terroir expression. Record high yields took everyone by surprise in producing champagnes of beauty and stamina. With energy in the vines in reserve after the tiny 2003 season, the enormous 2004 harvest was evidence that you can make great champagne from high yields, provided the vines are in balance. A warm, sunny July was followed by a cool, wet August, but the crucial first three weeks of September were idyllically sunny and dry, producing properly ripe fruit of well-structured acidity. 'One would expect that high yields would mean less minerality, but in 2004 we had both, testimony to the extraordinary terroir of Champagne!' exclaims Didier Gimonnet. The greatest 2004s today are Billecart-Salmon Blanc de Blancs Brut, De Sousa Cuvée des Caudalies Grand Cru Millésime Brut, Dom Pérignon, Louis Roederer Cristal Rosé, Mailly Grand Cru Exception Blanche Blanc de Blancs Brut, Perrier-Joüet Belle Epoque Blanc de Blancs, Pierre Péters Cuvée Spéciale Blanc de Blancs Les Chétillons, Pol Roger Cuvée Sir Winston Churchill, Ruinart Dom Ruinart, Salon Cuvée S Blanc de Blancs, Taittinger Comtes de Champagne Blanc de Blancs, Veuve Clicquot La Grande Dame Brut, Veuve Clicquot La Grande Dame Rosé.

2003 · 2/10

A calamitous vintage of pronounced concentration, overripe flavour profile, low acidity and hard phenolic bitterness that leaves most cuvées finishing astringent, coarse, dry and short. The most devastating April frosts in 70 years decimated 43% of the crop, hitting Côte des Blancs chardonnay hardest, wiping out 90% of Avize and Le Mesnil-sur-Oger; in early June, violent hailstorms battered the Montagne de Reims and Vallée de la Marne. Summer was the hottest to ever hit Champagne, with a sweltering August averaging 10°C above the norm, shrivelling grapes like raisins, prompting the earliest start to harvest since 1822. Of what little fruit remained in the Marne, opulent, overripe pinot noir and meunier boasted high sugar levels and low acidity. 'The perfect description of a nightmare,' in the words of Charles Heidsieck chef de cave Cyril Brun. Dom Pérignon registered the lowest acidity it has ever recorded. Says Richard Geoffroy, '2003 is border territory for Champagne, as border as it can be'. This is not a vintage for the cellar, and most are now well past their prime. Krug is the grand exception that proves the rule, testimony to stringent selection and tiny production. The greatest 2003 vintage champagnes today are Gosset Cuvée Celebris Rosé Extra Brut, Krug Clos du Mesnil, Krug Vintage and Le Brun-Servenay Cuvée Chardonnay Brut Millésime Vielles Vignes.

2002 · 9/10

A benchmark harvest that balances finesse, power and structure like no other in Champagne's recent history. The best wines possess decades of potential. A well-mannered season of continental climatic influence, with perfect harvest conditions from 10 September of dry, sunny days fostering ripe fruit intensity, and cool nights maintaining acidities a fraction below average. 'The 2002 was revenge for the challenging 2001, with nature giving everything that it withheld!' exclaims Piper-Heidsieck chef de cave Régis Camus. Didier Gimonnet considers it the greatest vintage since 1990, 'exemplifying the ultimate balance between elegance, concentration and freshness, nearly the best wine we could obtain'. It's impossible to list all the greatest 2002 vintage champagnes, but the very best today are Billecart-Salmon Cuvée Elisabeth Salmon Brut Rosé, Billecart-Salmon Cuvée Nicolas François Billecart, Bollinger R.D. Extra Brut, Dom Pérignon, Gosset Celebris, Jacquesson Aÿ Vauzelle Terme Recolte Brut, Krug Clos du Mesnil, Krug Vintage, Pierre Péters Cuvée Spéciale Blanc de Blancs Les Chétillons, Piper-

Heidsieck Rare Millésime, Pol Roger Cuvée Sir Winston Churchill, Taittinger Comtes de Champagne Blanc de Blancs, with more yet to come.

2001 · 1/10

Olivier Krug rates 2001 as Champagne's worst vintage in two decades. A dire season of incessant rain from early in the season all the way through to harvest, with particularly violent rain and hail from the latter part of July destroying 800 hectares across 55 communes. A cold September was accompanied by torrential rain and less sun than Champagne had seen in 45 years, cementing the fate of the season, diluting the wines and producing low ripeness of just 8.5% degrees potential. Virtually no vintage wines were produced.

2000 · 7/10

A warm, voluptuously ripe year of deep colour and rich fruit well suited to early drinking, with many cuvées now a deep yellow hue and quickly reaching the end of their peak. Dubbed *gourmandise orageuse* ('stormy indulgence') by Krug, 2000 was a tumultuous season delivering some of the most destructive hailstorms ever to lash Champagne, with 2900 hectares completely devastated across 114 communes. Warm, dry conditions arrived in August, after a hot June and cold July, and held out throughout harvest, producing abundant, large grapes, blessed with above-average levels of sugar (9.8% degrees potential), slightly lower than average acidities, and very little disease. The greatest 2000 vintage champagnes today are Billecart-Salmon Cuvée Nicolas François Billecart, Billecart-Salmon Cuvée Elisabeth Salmon Brut Rosé, Bollinger La Grande Année, Dom Pérignon Rosé, Duval-Leroy Femme de Champagne, Krug Clos d'Ambonnay, Krug Clos du Mesnil, Krug Vintage, Pierre Péters Cuvée Spéciale Blanc de Blancs Les Chétillons, Pol Roger Cuvée Sir Winston Churchill, and Taittinger Comtes de Champagne Blanc de Blancs.

1999 · 6/10

A fruity, soft season lacking acid drive, with most cuvées now past their prime; a warm vintage of continental climatic influence, recording Champagne's hottest summer since 1959 (though 2003 trumped it), and higher than usual rainfall. Harvest started optimistically, but hopes were diluted by heavy, persistent rain. The result was a vintage of high maturity and low malic acidity (just 6.5g/L total acidity), likened to 1989 by Jean-Baptiste Lécaillon. The greatest 1999s today are Billecart-Salmon

Blanc de Blancs Brut, Billecart-Salmon Le Clos Sainte-Hilaire, Bollinger La Grande Année Rosé, Larmandier-Bernier Special Club, Pol Roger Cuvée Sir Winston Churchill, Salon Cuvée S Blanc de Blancs, and Taittinger Comtes de Champagne Blanc de Blancs.

1998 • 7/10

The most enduring cuvées of 1998 retain elegant freshness amidst the expressive presence of the season, though lesser cuvées are now tired and heavy. Evidence that it is ultimately the weather at harvest that bears the strongest influence on the calibre of the vintage, 1998 followed a dismal progression of a wet, rot-inducing July, debilitating August heatwave, and rain storms in early September. It was not until mid-September that the weather finally delivered warm, dry conditions for harvest. Balanced ripeness of 9.8% degrees potential and strong acid levels of 9.8g/L came as the first surprise; the unwavering stamina of the best cuvées of the season the second. The greatest 1998 vintage champagnes today are Billecart-Salmon Cuvée Nicolas François Billecart, Billecart-Salmon Grande Cuvée, Billecart-Salmon Le Clos Saint-Hilaire, Dom Pérignon P2, Gosset Cuvée Celebris Extra Brut Vintage, Gosset Cuvée Celebris Rosé Brut, Krug Clos du Mesnil, Krug Clos d'Ambonnay, Krug Vintage, Piper-Heidsieck Rare Millesime, Pol Roger Cuvée Sir Winston Churchill, Taittinger Comtes de Champagne Blanc de Blancs, and Veuve Clicquot La Grande Dame Brut.

1997 • 4/10

The least vintage of the latter years of that century, 1997 was a ripe, rounded, accessible season, forever lost between the memory of 1996 and 1998. A tough lead-up to harvest saw 1997 plagued by frost, hail, uneven set and rot, producing the lowest yields since 1985. A hot July and very warm August were finally rescued by a bone-dry harvest, producing a high 10.2% degrees potential, and surprisingly good acidities for such ripeness. Salon registered acidity on equal par with 1996, infusing freshness and brightness. Few vintage wines were released; most are now well past their peak. The most notable exceptions are Jacquesson Avize Dégorgement Tardif Extra Brut, Salon Cuvée S Blanc de Blancs, and Pierre Péters Cuvée Spéciale Blanc de Blancs Les Chétillons.

1996 • 10/10

One of Champagne's most enduring, spectacular and lauded vintages, with both acidity and ripeness in extreme proportions, rendering its wines unbalanced in their youth. They are only beginning to find their poise after two decades, and the best will effortlessly endure for a lifetime. This vintage has gone down in history as the perfect 10/10 season of 10 degrees potential alcohol and 10g/L acidity – to this day the highest acidity ever recorded for Dom Pérignon. A less than ideal summer alternating between rain and intense heat was followed by rain until 20 September, then clear, sunny days, cool nights, and a strong north wind. This wind proved the key to the vintage, not only evaporating the threat of rot but, crucially, dehydrating the grapes and concentrating sugar and acidity to levels not seen since 1928. Quickly hailed among the greatest vintages of all time, some have since raised reservations, as some cuvées matured in flavour before their intense acidities softened. No such fear for the finest cuvées, the best of which are only now coming into their own, with glorious years of potential stretching ahead. The greatest 1996 vintage champagnes today are Billecart-Salmon Cuvée Nicolas François Billecart, Billecart-Salmon Grande Cuvée, Bollinger R.D. Extra Brut, Dom Pérignon Oenothèque, Duval-Leroy Femme de Champagne, René Geoffroy Cuvée Autrefois, Henriot La Cuvée des Enchanteleurs, Krug Vintage, Larmandier-Bernier Special Club, Louis Roederer Brut Rosé, Pierre Péters Cuvée Spéciale Blanc de Blancs Les Chétillons, Pol Roger Cuvée Sir Winston Churchill, Salon Cuvée S Blanc de Blancs, and Taittinger Comtes de Champagne Rosé.

1995 • 8/10

A vintage of elegant opulence, refined power and classic endurance, marvellously evidenced in a set of cuvées that have attained a lofty magnificence at 20 years of age, with a bright future stretching before them. Long forgotten in the shadow of 1996, 1995 is more classic and arguably more consistent, if less showy. This was Champagne's finest season since 1990, with a hot, dry summer accelerating maturity, and a sunny, late harvest furnishing good ripeness of 9.2% degrees potential and normal acidity. In 2014 Didier Gimonnet hosted a tasting with the French press to ascertain the best vintage of the 1990s. After 1990 was deemed too rich and 1996 too acidic, the winner was 1995. The greatest 1995 vintage champagnes today are Billecart-Salmon Cuvée Nicolas François Billecart, Charles Heidsieck Blanc des Millénaires, Dom Pérignon P2 Rosé, Jacquesson Dégorgement Tardif Extra Brut Millésime, Louis Roederer Cristal, and Salon Cuvée S Blanc de Blancs.

DOWN TO EARTH

On a small range of hills rising less than impressively from a chalk plain 145 kilometres north-east of Paris lies the patchwork of 33,762 hectares of vineyards that is Champagne. Too exposed to wind and rain and not sufficiently blessed by the sun, there is no chance of ripening grapes on the flatter land here. And yet this land sends a shiver down my spine every time I come close. By some miracle, its drab hillsides produce fruits that thousands of winegrowers around the globe strive desperately to emulate, yet none have equalled.

Austere and impoverished soft white chalk is Champagne's secret, a remnant of a 90 million-year-old seabed. Its true blessing is espoused not only in cool, damp 17-century-old cellars, but especially in the vineyards, bestowing its fruits with crystalline minerality, reflecting and storing heat and retaining moisture – a perfectly regulated vine humidifier.

Champagne comprises five departments: the Marne (most importantly the Montagne de Reims, Côte des Blancs and Vallée de la Marne), the Côte des Bar, the Aisne, the Haute-Marne and the Seine-et-Marne.

THE MONTAGNE DE REIMS

The Montagne de Reims is no mountain – more a wooded hillock, rising to an unimpressive 180 metres above the surrounding plains and just 275 metres above sea level. Yet even this elevation is sufficient to orientate some of Champagne's mightiest vineyards. The vines of the Montagne de Reims follow the slope of a hillside topped with dense forest, in a backward 'C' formation from Villers-Allerand on the northern slopes, reaching a crescendo in the thundering grand crus of Bouzy and Ambonnay in the south. These stand alongside Verzenay as the Montagne de Reims' finest villages. Pinot noir is king of these chalky sites, and nowhere in Champagne produces its equal. There are also substantial plantings of meunier, and chardonnay is on the rise.

The 'Petite Montagne' is a north-western extension of the Montagne de Reims, extending north of Reims itself, nurturing Champagne's most northerly vineyards on soils of sand and clay, well suited to meunier.

CÔTE DES BLANCS

Chardonnay is left largely to the Côte des Blancs, 96% of which is planted to the variety, the remainder largely pinot noir in the commune of Vertus in the south.

With dramatic slopes, warmer days and thinner topsoils making chalk more accessible than anywhere in the region, the Côte des Blancs produces Champagne's most regular fruit, and most reliable, exhilarating and mineral-infused wines. This is why many are sold unblended as blanc de blancs. These are among Champagne's most searingly structured and long-lived wines. There is perhaps no village in Champagne that stands alone as confidently as Le Mesnil-sur-Oger, though Cramant, Avize, Oger and the premier cru of Vertus command great respect.

VALLÉE DE LA MARNE

More than half of the Vallée de la Marne is planted to meunier, although pinot noir plantings are on the increase. The south-facing sites of Aÿ and Mareuil-sur-Aÿ towards its eastern end rival the great grand crus of the Montagne de Reims. Its cooler western reaches of clay soils are exclusively the territory of meunier, easier to grow and ripen than pinot noir and chardonnay.

CÔTE DE SÉZANNE

The Côte de Sézanne is a little way south of the Côte des Blancs in the Marne and shares the same southeast orientation and dominance of chardonnay. Its soils are heavier and its wines more rustic.

CÔTE DES BAR

More than 100 kilometres south-east of the Côte des Blancs, the outpost of the Aube (Côte des Bar) is closer to Burgundy than to Reims. Pinot noir is the principal grape here, comprising four-fifths of the region's plantings, producing vigorous and more rustic wines. Planted largely during the late 1980s, vine maturity is now in step with the rest of the region, and the Aube has enjoyed significant increases in quality in recent years. Its finest villages are Celles-sur-Ource, Les Riceys and Urville.

The Champagne Guide

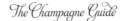

THE CHEF IN THE CELLAR
How champagne is made

*C*hampagne must be the most successfully processed creation in all of agricultural history, through a convoluted, painstaking method designed expressly to transform an insipidly austere and undrinkably acidic juice into the most celebrated beverage in the world. Every element of the champagne process is geared towards making its searing acidity less challenging – bubbles, yeast, chaptalisation, dosage, blending and ageing. The genius of champagne production calls on more tricks than any other wine style to create flavour, complexity, texture and balance. The traditional method by which this is achieved is known as Méthode Traditionnelle.

PRESSING

How can white wine be made from the dark-skinned grapes of pinot noir and meunier? The secret is careful, selective harvesting and immediate, gentle pressing, to avoid staining the clear juice. All grapes in Champagne are handpicked and gently pressed nearby as whole bunches in four-tonne lots. By law, only the first 2550 litres of juice from every four tonnes of grapes may be used. On current yields, this equates to an average production of 10,000 bottles per hectare.

The *coeur de la cuvée*, the 'heart of the cuvée', is the middle of the pressing, yielding the purest juice.

The tailles – coarser, inferior juice that flows last from the press – is used in varying levels according to the house style, and rarely at all in the finest cuvées.

SETTLING

Débourbage is the settling of solids and impurities from the must (pressed grape juice), allowing clear juice to be drawn off from the top.

This process is taken to another level by the houses of Billecart-Salmon and Pol Roger, who perform a second settling of the must at cold temperature, producing particularly exquisite and fresh champagnes.

FIRST FERMENTATION

The 'alcoholic' fermentation of champagne takes place in stainless steel tanks. Traditional oak barrels are coming back into vogue for fermentation and/or maturation, to increase suppleness, texture, power and complexity. The 'degrees potential' ripeness at which grapes are picked roughly equates to the potential alcohol of the finished wine. Most champagne producers 'chaptalise' prior to fermentation by adding sugar or concentrated grape juice to increase the alcoholic strength. Some makers 'inoculate' the ferment with cultured yeasts, while others rely on wild yeasts.

MALOLACTIC FERMENTATION

Malolactic fermentation converts tart 'malic' (green apple) acid into softer 'lactic' (dairy) acid. This process is practised by most houses to soften their wines. Notable exceptions include Gosset, Lanson and Salon.

With the advent of warmer vintages, an increasing number of houses are experimenting with blocking malolactic fermentation.

ASSEMBLAGE

Skilful blending is Champagne's answer to its erratic seasons. Challenging vintages are handled by blending wines from different vineyards, different vintages (reserve wines) and different grapes.

Champagne is usually a blend of chardonnay (for structure, elegance and finesse), pinot noir (for perfume, body and richness) and meunier (for plump fruitiness). Blanc de blancs ('white wine from white grapes') is usually chardonnay, and blanc de noirs ('white wine from red grapes') usually pinot noir/meunier.

The key distinguishing factor between champagne houses lies in the cuvée – the blend created in assembling different wines. There is no skill in the winemaking world that I envy more than that of the chef de cave in blending a fine champagne, uniting different ingredients according to each harvest in a blend today that must be consistent with the house style when it emerges from the cellar in years to come.

RESERVE WINES (FOR NV BLENDS)
Non-vintage wines are deepened by a portion of older vintage 'reserve' wines stored in tank, barrel or bottle. These are crucial for maintaining consistency in Champagne's wildly fluctuating seasons.

TIRAGE
Prior to bottling, a *liqueur de tirage* of sugar and wine is added (see 'Second fermentation', further down).

BOTTLING
Wines are bottled and sealed under crown seal, or occasionally cork. They may be filtered and cold stabilised at this time to remove any solids.

SECOND FERMENTATION
The sugar added to champagne prior to bottling induces a secondary fermentation in the bottle known as the *prise de mousse*. Under the pressure of a sealed bottle, the carbon dioxide produced dissolves in the wine, creating sparkling wine. The finer the still wine and the cooler the cellar in which this fermentation occurs, the smaller the bubbles. Larger bottles ferment more slowly – one reason why magnums are superior and half bottles are inferior to standard bottles. A finer bead is an indicator of quality.

MATURATION
Acidity is the key to champagne, but its astringency makes these wines unapproachable in their youth. The mellowing, softening effect of age is crucial to the champagne style. Dead yeast cells ('lees') from the second fermentation remain in the bottle and contribute subtly to champagne's complexity. The longer this process of 'autolysis' persists the better, improving mouthfeel and longevity, and adding biscuity, bready nuances to the flavour profile.

The mandatory minimum in champagne is 15 months for non-vintage and three years for vintage wines, but reputable producers always far exceed these minima, typically ageing non-vintage cuvées 3–4 years, vintage cuvées 7–8 years, and prestige cuvées sometimes 10 years or more.

RIDDLING (*REMUAGE*)
In the early 19th century, Antoine Müller, cellar master of the widow Clicquot (Veuve Clicquot), invented a method of cleaning the wine of the sediment created when it ferments in bottle, without losing its bubbles. A wooden desk (*pupitre*) pierced with holes holds the mature bottles sideways. Each bottle is given a quarter-rotation every day, and slowly tilted from horizontal to upside down. The lees sediment collects in the neck of the bottle. This process of 'remuage' is performed by a 'riddler', who can turn 50,000–60,000 bottles every day!

In modern times, the riddling process has been taken over by gyropalettes in most champagne houses. These giant robotic arms slowly rotate large cages of bottles. The effect is the same, perhaps even more consistent, albeit without the romance.

A gyro can riddle a cage of bottles in as little as three days, but many estates use a longer cycle of a week or more.

DISGORGEMENT (*DÉGORGEMENT*)
After riddling, the sediment is settled on the inside of the cork or crown cap. The neck of the bottle is then frozen, the cap released, and the plug of sediment shot out (*dégorgement*), leaving perfectly clear wine behind.

DOSAGE (THE FINAL ADDITION)
To replace the volume lost through disgorgement, the bottle is topped up with sweetened wine (*liqueur d'expédition*) and a new cork is inserted.

'Zero dosage' champagnes are topped up with dry wine. See page 19 for dosage trends.

MAKING ROSÉ CHAMPAGNE
About 10% of champagne production is rosé, growing every year in response to global demand. It is made in the same manner as white champagne, with a subtle difference. Colour is achieved in one of three ways.

Most commonly, a 'blending method' (*rosé d'assemblage*) is used, in which a tiny quantity of pinot noir or meunier (made as a table wine) is added – often only 5–10%, but sometimes as much as 20%. A rapid increase in demand for rosé has recently put pressure on supplies of quality red wine for blending in Champagne.

The *saignée* method adds free-run juice from just-crushed red grapes, producing the finest, palest wines. A 'limited maceration' method produces darker, heavier wines through a quick soak on red grape skins.

Rosé production is tricky, not only in marrying champagne's acidity with red wine tannin, but in determining the desired depth of colour long before it is set. Yeast is a highly effective fining agent, leaching colour during both primary and secondary fermentations.

THE CHAMPAGNE INGREDIENT
The art of matching champagne and food

atching champagne with the right dish can be one of the most thrilling culinary experiences of all. But getting it wrong can diminish both the wine and the dish. A talented chef friend insists it's the hardest of all wine styles to match with food. That's probably why he does it better than anyone I know.

I have the privilege of hosting regular champagne tastings and dinners, under great chefs around the world, hosting intimate tour groups in Champagne's finest restaurants and the private dining rooms of its greatest houses, or winging it myself in my own kitchen. Here are some insights I've discovered to help you in your pursuit of the ultimate champagne match.

Champagne is one of the most elegant and subtle of all beverages. In aligning food to complement, I've come to realise the most important rule is that less is more. Less intense flavour, less cooking, less sugar and fewer ingredients that might confuse the experience.

Champagne is primarily an apéritif, and the Champenois don't pretend that this is a wine that will comfortably handle any cuisine. They will quickly switch to Bordeaux or Burgundy with main-course red meats, and Sauternes or Port with dessert.

Refreshing, tangy acid is the ultimate palate kick-starter, inducing an appetite and energising the taste-buds for what is to come. No other wine is blessed with more acid than champagne, and this is what makes it the ultimate apéritif!

BLANC DE BLANCS AND YOUNG NVs

The vast diversity of champagne styles calls for careful consideration of the right cuvée to sit alongside a dish. Lighter dishes, such as many vegetarian dishes, and crustacea like crabs, scallops and prawns will partner neatly with the elegance of younger, non-vintage or blanc de blancs cuvées. Champagne loves all seafood, and lobster or crayfish make for a particularly decadent combination – one for the bucket list. Start saving!

VINTAGE, OAKED AND PINOT-LED

Fuller flavours – oily fish, pork, ham, prosciutto, chicken, turkey, rabbit, pigeon, quail, pheasant and other game birds – deserve a mature vintage, barrel-fermented or pinot-led cuvée from Champagne's stronger grand crus, such as Bouzy, Ambonnay or Aÿ. The more the meat is cooked (particularly if it's fried, roasted or grilled), the more you can push out into more hedonistic champagne territory.

ROSÉ

Rosé in a light and airy style calls for the most subtle flavours of all, but a fleshy and structured rosé can confidently handle anything up to pork or turkey proportions. Salmon is rosé's best friend, a captivating match of colour and flavour!

OYSTERS

Oysters are widely touted as a classic champagne match, but in truth they're much easier to partner with a stronger and saltier wine like manzanilla-style sherry. For a champagne, try a salty, mineral Côte des Blancs grand cru or a tightly strung zero dosage.

VEGETABLES

Most vegetables are subtle in flavour and won't generally trouble champagne. Avoid chargrilling as it tends to dominate. Sweetcorn, fennel, mushrooms, potatoes and pumpkin are some of my favourite champagne matches. Chips are great with any champagne (seriously!).

EGGS

Eggs are particularly versatile and most egg-based dishes like quiches, omelettes and – my personal favourites – soufflés and gougères, make a beautiful marriage with champagne. Opt for a fuller-bodied style with fried or baked dishes, and a more elegant style with poached or steamed dishes.

BREADS ETC
Grain-based foods such as bread (don't spare the butter!), pasta, rice, risotto and gnocchi are friendly with most wines and will happily sidle up alongside any champagne. I love nuts with champagne, especially if they're roasted (go for unflavoured versions, but salt is great!).

CHEESE
Cheese matching with champagne can be complicated, but a few simple rules provide a reliable starting point. Hard cheeses are ideal, particularly aged, salty styles like parmesan, parmigiano reggiano, pecorino, romano, and the number one favourite of the Champenois, comté! Soft, creamy cheeses tend to play havoc with champagne, and the intensity of washed rind and blue cheeses makes these the worst offenders. Muscatelles and quince paste are a great addition to the cheese board with sweet dessert wines, but leave them off with champagne.

DELICACIES
There are a few decadent specialties I always love with champagne: foie gras, truffles, caviar, snails! If you're shelling out for these delicacies, you can afford prestige champagne to match. And an elegant bottle of affordable NV is always my ally at our local sushi train (get on board!).

RED MEATS
Red meat dishes are a tough match for any elegant white wine and particularly so with champagne. There will always be exceptions, but it's almost always much smarter to pull out a red wine instead – as the Champenois do.

CHAMPAGNE ASSASSINS!
Other likely champagne assassins to be wary of are vinegar, pickled anything, capers, olives, soy sauce, overt spice heat (chilli, curry, wasabi or mustard), coffee and chocolate (désolé!).

DESSERTS
The age-old rule for dessert is that the wine should be sweeter than the dish. Unless you have a particularly sweet champagne on hand, opt for an ever so slightly sweet dessert. Fresh berries or cherries are the simplest option. Sweet dishes are tricky with champagne, and only oh so rarely do I encounter a great combination. I prefer to serve champagne with a hard cheese course and instead reach for a dessert wine with dessert.

WATER
The final ingredient to truly set off a great champagne is mineral water. Select a very pure and subtle style of low minerality, to highlight the minerality of the champagne. 'Antipodes' is my favourite. Always avoid chlorinated tap water as this will destroy champagne.

Think of champagne like an ingredient in your culinary journey, and enjoy experimenting with matching it with subtle flavours. You'll be enthralled by just how brilliantly the right dish can make a great champagne shine.

Cuisine in the maison of William Deutz relies upon subtle flavours to complement the elegant champagnes of the house.

AWASH WITH BUBBLES
How to serve champagne

CHAMPAGNE GLASSES

Using decent glassware is essential for fully appreciating wine, and all the more for champagne.

How important? 'We worked with wine glass company Riedel for more than a year to develop a glass which was ideal for Krug Grande Cuvée,' Olivier Krug told me. 'They proposed 26 glasses and I would take them home to try with my wife until very late at night!'

The more I visit and taste with the Champenois, the more I appreciate the way a large glass draws a champagne out of itself. Champagne holds its bead longest in an elongated glass, but don't select one so narrow that you can't get your nose in to appreciate the bouquet. 'It's not just about the bubbles. Champagne is a wine, not just scenery!' says Duval-Leroy Sales Manager Michel Brismontier, who serves champagne in normal wine glasses rather than flutes.

The Champenois prefer slightly wider glasses than typical champagne flutes, to allow their finest cuvées sufficient space to open out. Think halfway between a flute and a fine white wine glass. All good glasses curve in slightly at the top. The finer the glass, the better they look at the table, and the less the champagne will warm up when you pour it. Cut, engraved or coloured glasses make it harder to appreciate the wine's appearance.

The glass I use most often is the Riedel Vinum XL Champagne. This is the largest glass I've found, with a bowl of white wine glass proportions that draws down into the stem sufficiently to produce a focused stream of bubbles. Moët & Chandon use these as their tasting glass and tell me they were designed in the 1960s. They'll set you back as much as a bottle of non-vintage champagne (each!), making for an expensive but worthwhile investment in champagne enjoyment.

My second-favourite glass is one-fifth of the price. The Luigi Bormioli Magnifico Flute is very nearly as large as the Riedel and just a little heavier. If you can't find these, grab a medium-sized white wine glass over a champagne flute for any serious bottle of fizz.

Champagne houses have done away with narrow flutes in favour of larger glasses to highlight the full magnificence of their cuvées.

The traditional flat champagne 'coupe' glasses are now practically unheard of in Champagne, except in historical ceremony. They are inferior because their large surface area evaporates both bead and aroma rapidly. The wide, flanged rim also spills the wine to the sides of the tongue, where sensitivity to acidity is heightened.

It's paramount that there is not the slightest residue of detergent in the glass, as this will instantly destroy the mousse (bubbles) and the taste. Riedel recommends washing under warm water without detergent, and polishing with microfibre towels. Never dry a glass by holding the base and twisting the bowl, as this may snap the stem.

SERVING TEMPERATURE

'The temperature of service is very important,' emphasises Oliver Krug, who admits to being obsessed with the quality of service. 'We may work for 10 or 20 years to create Grande Cuvée, ship it in the best refrigerated container, and then you might be served the first Krug of your life in a stupid flute as cold as ice, and you miss 99% of the pleasure and the message!'

Antoine Roland-Billecart of Billecart-Salmon says wine is like a human being in the cold. 'Put yourself out in the snow and you won't show anything either, you'll be all covered up!' he says. 'Three degrees breaks everything in champagne. It should be served at cellar temperature, and never below 8°C.' Cellar temperature for the Champenois means 10°C.

Champagne is often served much too cold. Poured at fridge temperature, it will taste flavourless and acidic. The only exceptions are particularly sweet styles, which are best toned down with a stern chill. In general, the finer the wine, the warmer I tend to serve it. The Champenois suggest 8–10°C for non-vintage and rosé styles, and 10–12°C for vintage and prestige wines.

If you're pulling a bottle out of a climate-controlled cellar, it will need to be cooled a little further, so pop it in the fridge for half an hour. If it's at room temperature to start with, 3–4 hours in the fridge or 15 minutes in an ice bucket might be in order. On a warm day, serve champagne a touch cooler, as it will soon warm up.

Always hold a champagne glass by its base or stem, to avoid warming the wine in your hand. This will also reduce the likelihood of any aromas on your hands interfering with its delicate bouquet.

AGE AND CELLARING

Twenty-year-old champagne is one of my favourite indulgences, and a top vintage wine or prestige cuvée will comfortably go the distance. Generally, aim to drink vintage champagnes between eight and 15 years after vintage, and non-vintage wines within five years. Most entry-level NVs have little to gain from bottle ageing, but exceptions are noted throughout this guide. Late-disgorged vintages are held on lees in the cellar and can improve over many decades.

Late-disgorged champagne is generally best consumed within a few years of disgorgement, as it doesn't tend to cellar confidently post-disgorgement. 'Disgorgement is a shock for a wine, like a human going into surgery,' explains Antoine Roland-Billecart. 'When you're young, you recover much better. When an old champagne is disgorged, it may oxidise.' This is why Billecart disgorges its museum stock at the same time as its standard releases. Different houses have different philosophies, and there are always exceptions. I've tasted very old late-disgorged bottles that have held up magnificently five years after disgorgement.

Champagne spends the first years of its life in a dark, humid, chalk cellar under Champagne at a constant temperature of 8–10°C, so it will get a rude shock if it's thrust into a warmer environment. Champagne is highly fussy when it comes to proper cellaring conditions and, unless you live somewhere particularly cold, if you don't have a climate-controlled cellar, err on the side of caution and drink it within a few years.

Champagne in clear glass bottles is remarkably light sensitive, so keep it in the dark at all times. If it comes in a box, bag or cellophane wrap, keep it covered until you serve it.

HOW TO OPEN A BOTTLE OF FIZZ

Opening a champagne bottle is pretty easy, but some people make such a fuss about it that they end up stuffing it up altogether. There are a few basic points to grasp before spraying your friends with fizz.

First, ensure that nobody has shaken the bottle before you get hold of it (not funny!). Always have a target glass nearby to pour the first gush into, but not too close (I once inadvertently shot the bowl clean off one of those expensive Riedels with a stray cork!). Check the firing range for chandeliers and unsuspecting passers-by and re-aim if necessary.

Remove the capsule using the pull-tab, if it has one. Hold the bottle at 45 degrees and remove the cage with six half-turns of the wire, keeping your thumb firmly over the end of the cork, in case it attempts to fire out of the bottle. I prefer to loosen the cage and leave it on the cork, which can assist with grip.

Twist the bottle (not the cork) slowly and ease the cork out gently. If you encounter a stubborn, young cork, use a clean tea towel to improve your grip. When the cork is almost out, tilt it sideways to release the gas slowly. It should make a gentle hiss, not an ostentatious pop. This is important, as it maintains the maximum bead (bubbles) in the wine and reduces the risk of a dramatic gush.

HOW TO POUR CHAMPAGNE

Check that the wine tastes right, then pour half a glass for each drinker, topping them up after the 'mousse' has subsided. You can choose to tilt the glass to minimise frothing – I do. Sparkling wine is the only style where you can break the rule of never more than half-filling a glass, but do leave sufficient room for your nose so you can appreciate the bouquet!

The Champenois sometimes recommend decanting champagne. This does offer some advantages in encouraging older or more robust champagnes to open up, but I have never been successful without losing most of the bubbles.

A light veil of snow catches the first light of dawn on the south-facing grand cru slopes of Aÿ.

AGRAPART & FILS

(A-gra-pah e Feess)

7/10

57 AVENUE JEAN JAURÈS 51190 AVIZE
www.champagne-agrapart.com

CHAMPAGNE
AGRAPART & Fils

AVIZE - GRAND CRU

'If we have good grapes we have good wines,' is Pascal Agrapart's refreshing philosophy. While many others rigidly pursue regimes in the vineyard and winery because that's the way it's always been done, or is the latest fad, the ethos and practice of Agrapart are quite the antithesis. This fanatical Avize grower upholds practices not far from organics or biodynamics, yet has never sought certification under either, preferring to maintain the freedom to listen sensitively to the rhythm of the seasons and respond to the benefit of his vines. His restless pursuit of a detailed expression of place is articulated in the purity and crystalline mineral expression of his wines.

In Champagne it is a rare claim to be the fourth generation to produce champagne from one's own vineyards. Yet Pascal and brother Fabrice Agrapart do so not with a staid reliance on the ways of their forebears, but with a progressive and at times courageous sense of spontaneity.

Inspired by Burgundy to make wines of character true to their place, Agrapart upholds terroir as being more important than variety. Chardonnay comprises 95% of almost 10 hectares of enviable estate plantings, mainly in the grand crus of Avize, Oger, Cramant and Oiry, divided across 62 plots of vines of an impressive average age of 40 years – some more than 65 years.

Every effort is focused on encouraging the roots of these old vines into the mother rock to draw out the mineral character of each site. Vineyard management is painstakingly eco-friendly, with no chemical pesticides or herbicides used. Vineyards are ploughed to break up surface roots, aerate the soil and maintain microbial life, while organic fertilisers, compost and manure are adapted according to soil analyses.

Pascal Agrapart upholds that '25% of the wine is made by the soil and 25% by the weather', and points out that the micro-climates are very different in each of his parcels. This poses a greater challenge to an organic regime than would a single site.

'I don't want to have certification because I want to be able to plough the soil when I can, and use chemicals when I need to,' he says. The disease threat of the wet 2012 vintage necessitated chemical treatments.

Agrapart works his 1959 vines in his 'La Fosse' vineyard in Avize only by hand and horse, and he's more down-to-earth about this than anyone else I've met in Champagne. 'There is no compacting of the soil, and perhaps there is more oxygen and microbial life, and perhaps the roots go deeper, and perhaps there is more minerality in the wine. Perhaps, perhaps! Perhaps it is better – and perhaps it's just sentimental!'

Each winemaking element is designed to preserve the detail of the vineyard. Sensitive, intelligent use of large, old oak for vinification and ageing of finer parcels

The Champagne Guide

for vintage wines and non-vintage reserves are not for woody flavour, but oxidation – for Agrapart, 'oxidation is not the enemy of wine'. He buys five-year-old barrels from Burgundy and the Loire and maintains them until they're very old. Larger 600-litre puncheons are favoured, for a higher ratio of wine to wood.

Wild yeasts from the vineyards further draw out the character of each site. Full malolactic fermentation is encouraged, for stability, balance and evolution of the wine, which he suggests removes the need for sterile filtration and high levels of sulphur dioxide preservative. The results are usually clean and precise.

The energy of Agrapart's grand cru chardonnay vineyards and the endurance infused through barrel fermentation make these very long-lived cuvées that appreciate extended lees ageing prior to release. Ageing a minimum of three years for non-vintage and seven for vintage cuvées necessitates a stock of 360,000 bottles

to sustain an annual production of 90,000. This is a significant production for hand-riddling, but the hands-on approach of the estate is maintained.

Most of Agrapart's seven cuvées are blanc de blancs, with a little pinot in his entry wine, and a single-field blend of six grape varieties. Low dosages are used throughout, which he suggests reduces the importance of ageing the wine between disgorgement and release. While disgorgement dates aren't printed on back labels, they're easy to decode from the cork. The number is the year of disgorgement, and the letter is the month (A for January, B for February, and so on).

Agrapart's wines are characterful, deeply mineral expressions of the great, enduring terroirs of the Côte des Blancs, given articulate voice through diligent attention to detail.

These are long-enduring cuvées of an exceptional custodian of remarkable terroirs.

AGRAPART & FILS TERROIRS BLANC DE BLANCS GRAND CRU EXTRA BRUT NV $$$

89 points • 2012 BASE VINTAGE • TASTED IN AUSTRALIA

A classification of better parcels than 7 Crus; 20–40-year-old vines in Avize, Oger, Cramant and Oiry; 50% reserves; full malolactic fermentation; aged 4 years on lees; low dosage of 5g/L

A toasty and nutty cuvée of hazelnut bitterness that contrasts the tang and tension of grapefruit and bruised apple fruit. It finishes dry and grainy, with some coarseness to its structure. Excellent acid line and well-integrated, low dosage define a long finish.

AGRAPART & FILS COMPLANTÉE GRAND CRU EXTRA BRUT NV $$$$

93 points • TASTED IN AUSTRALIA

A blend of 80% 2013 and 20% 2012 of co-planted pinot noir, meunier, pinot blanc, chardonnay, arbane and petit meslier from young vines planted in 2002 in the single vineyard La Fosse in Avize; co-fermented in oak barrels; full malolactic fermentation; aged on lees under cork; unfiltered; low dosage of 5g/L

Complantée is on the rise as these vines gain maturity. The result is as complex as the recipe anticipates, layered with apple, pear, grapefruit and lemon, with subtle hints of tropical fruits on the sides. For all of its fruit salad of complexity, it commands a tightly honed and focused finish of excellent acid drive and all the texture of prominent, salt-infused Avize chalk minerality. It lingers with excellent persistence and surprising tension, harmony and focus for such a mix, with acidity showing prominently. A refreshing surprise.

ALFRED GRATIEN

(Al-fre Gra-shah)

7/10

30 RUE MAURICE CERVEAUX 51201 EPERNAY

www.alfredgratien.com

Alfred Gratien is a small house, producing 300,000 bottles annually, with a long history of making wines of complexity. Its champagnes are made in a rigorously classical way, with the first fermentation and at least six months of ageing taking place exclusively in 900 small 228-litre neutral barriques, of 12-years average age, previously used at least four times in Chablis. Reserve wines are stored in large oak barrels. Malolactic fermentation is systematically avoided, to ensure that cuvées retain their original character, maintaining freshness as they age and preserving the aroma of the grapes and the land from which they came. Barrel fermentation without malolactic is no trivial balancing act, though Alfred Gratien pulls it off with more than a little accomplishment, and never as seamlessly or triumphantly as in the current set of cuvées.

Alfred Gratien was acquired by the Henkell & Co group in 2004, retaining its own small holdings of just four hectares of vineyards and 65 growers from which grapes are sourced. The house considers its barrels a key to its relationship with its growers, allowing it to keep every plot separate. Each of 900 barrels is labelled with the name of the village and the grower, and each grower is invited to come to taste their own wines every second year.

Henkell & Co invested considerably in the house, building a new cuverie for blending of the young wines. At just 9°C, its cellars are some of the coldest in

Champagne. This is too cold for the second fermentation to kick off, so bottles are first held in the barrel hall for two weeks. It then takes 70–80 days to complete the second fermentation in the cellar below. The house maintains a considerable stock of 1.5 million bottles, since long ageing is important for softening malic acidity.

Since 2007, the new owners have wisely left the house in the hands of young Nicolas Jaeger, the fourth generation of the Jaeger family to serve as chef de cave of the house. If the cuvées since his tenure began are anything to go by, the house is in more than capable hands. All the more laudable because production has doubled in the past 14 years, with a target to reach the capacity of the facility of 400,000–450,000 bottles by 2020.

Chardonnay is the theme of the house, blessed by great sources in the finest crus of the Côte des Blancs. In concert with malic acidity, this chardonnay focus brings a zingy freshness to the deeply complex Gratien style, softened gently by barrel fermentation and long bottle ageing. Current non-vintage releases have enjoyed five years on lees in bottle, and vintage cuvées more than eight. Vintage wines are aged under natural cork, which Jaeger claims assists in preventing oxidation and enhancing tertiary aromas, complexity and firmness. He tastes every bottle as it is disgorged and rejects 1% to cork taint and 2% to leakage or other variation. With full barrel vinification and no malolactic fermentation, these are captivating and long-ageing champagnes of fine, creamy bead, lively acid line and well-managed, barrel-matured complexity.

ALFRED GRATIEN BRUT NV $$

94 points • 2011 BASE VINTAGE • DISGORGED MARCH 2016 • TASTED IN AUSTRALIA

46% chardonnay from Le Mesnil-sur-Oger, Avize, Chouilly, Vertus and Cramant; 30% meunier from Leuvrigny, Damery and Reuil-sur-Marne; 24% pinot from Ludes and Bouzy; reserves from 2010 and 2009; fermented and aged 6 months in oak barrels; aged 5 years on lees; no malolactic fermentation; 9g/L dosage

There is quite some skill entwined into this cuvée, evenly and compellingly harmonising the fleshy stone fruits and red apples of ripe fruit with a flash of bright lemon juice and citrus zest, the taut twang of malic acidity and all the spicy, toasty complexity of full barrel fermentation and maturation. To achieve this seamless accord with such confidence in the challenging 2011 base vintage is especially laudable. The creamy texture of barrel fermentation supports fine chalk mineral focus on a finish that evenly and beautifully unites body, cut and drive.

ALFRED GRATIEN BRUT ROSÉ NV $$$

95 points • 2011 BASE VINTAGE • DISGORGED MARCH 2016 • TASTED IN AUSTRALIA

56% chardonnay from Le Mesnil-sur-Oger, Avize, Chouilly, Vertus and Cramant; 23% pinot from Ludes and Bouzy; 21% meunier from Leuvrigny, Damery and Reuil-sur-Marne; reserves from 2010 and 2009; fermented and aged 6 months in oak barrels; aged 5 years on lees; no malolactic fermentation; 8g/L dosage

The Gratien house style is particularly flattering to rosé, and this medium salmon-tinted style is alive and full with layers of precise red cherry, raspberry, strawberry and watermelon fruit, accented with pink pepper. The textural synergy that defines the house is no easy balancing act, calmly uniting the creamy, silky texture of barrel fermentation, the fine mouthfeel of carefully managed tannins, the fine chalk mineral definition of great terroirs and the enlivening cut of malic acidity. Barrel and bottle age contribute subtle savoury allure of toast and dried nectarines, eloquently supporting and never competing with bright red fruits focus. Like the Brut NV, a captivating cuvée, and a triumph for the 2011 base vintage.

ALFRED GRATIEN GRAND CRU BLANC DE BLANCS BRUT 2007 $$$

93 points • DISGORGED FEBRUARY 2016 • TASTED IN AUSTRALIA

Avize and Cramant; fermented and aged 6 months in oak barrels; aged 8 years on lees; no malolactic fermentation; 8g/L dosage

Two more years on lees and a touch more dosage since its inaugural release have flattered this blend of the great northern Côte des Blancs grand crus of Cramant and Avize. It upholds its full-straw hue and notes of fresh lemon zest, barrel and bottle-derived characters of brioche and hint of fennel. The clash of malic acidity with wood lends a hint of sappiness, yet concludes with a flourish of bright malic acid drive, harmony and fine chalk mineral texture.

ALFRED GRATIEN CUVÉE PARADIS BRUT 2008 $$$$

96 points • DISGORGED FEBRUARY 2016 • TASTED IN AUSTRALIA

65% chardonnay fro Le Mesnil-sur-Oger, Avize, Chouilly, Vertus and Cramant; 35% pinot noir from Ludes and Bouzy; a blend of the best barrels from the cellar; fermented and aged 6 months in oak barrels; aged 7 years on lees; no malolactic fermentation; 8g/L dosage

Gratien is a master of harmonising the sabre of malic acid, the impact of ripe fruit and a universe of barrel-fermented complexity, and nowhere is this more dramatically exemplified than in the heightened tension of the great 2008 season. Fleshy stone fruits meet crunchy lemon zest, tussling with layers of mixed spice, fig and wild honey. Structurally it's at once intriguing and irresistible, simultaneously creamy, silky and dramatically tense, with the softening touch of barrel fermentation calming its lightning bolt of malic shock. It concludes very long and complete, engaging now, and it's only going to get better. Marvellous.

A radiant afternoon at the end of harvest 2014 on the slopes overlooking Épernay.

The Champagne Guide

ANDRÉ CLOUET

(On-dray Cloo-ay)

8/10

8 RUE GAMBETTA 51150 BOUZY

Bouzy and Ambonnay are the epicentre of pinot noir in Champagne, and the Clouet family is the privileged custodian of eight hectares of estate vines in the best middle slopes of both villages. These are rich and concentrated expressions of pinot noir, wines of deep complexity, multifaceted interest and engaging character, yet with remarkable restraint and sense of control. Tasting after tasting confirm my impression that this small and relatively unknown grower ranks high among Champagne's finest practitioners of pinot noir — and represents one of the best value of all.

When I first met extroverted young chef de cave Jean-François Clouet, he didn't show me through his winery or cellars, didn't walk me through rows of vines, or even pour his champagnes. He took me to the top of the vineyards, on the edge of the forest overlooking Bouzy, and recounted the remarkable sweep of history that had played out in view of this place over two millennia: Attila the Hun, the Battle of the Catalaunian Fields, the birth of the monarchy, the crusades, the Templars, Marie Antoinette. On another visit he showed me original documents of his village in his family archives, and took me to another part of town to recount another branch of history. 'To understand Champagne you need to understand its political history,' he said.

For Clouet's family, that history began here in 1492, and his family still resides in the house his ancestors built in Bouzy in 1741. 'My family was making wine in Champagne at the same time Dom Pérignon was starring!' he exclaims. This history lives on, not only in the spectacular labels designed by Jean-François' great-grandfather in 1911 (harking back to the family's printer heritage, making books for the king since 1491), but in a traditional approach in the vineyards. 'I like the idea of the work of human hands in pruning, performing the same actions as my grandfather and even the Romans, who planted vines here 2000 years ago.'

The flamboyant Jean-François is one of the upcoming rock stars of Champagne. He is inherently talented as a winemaker, keenly insightful, at once deeply rooted in his family's history and yet daringly creative, with a distinctly modern twist to his approach. It is his goal that some day none of his champagnes will have any dosage at all, an ideal that he rightly describes as revolutionary.

'Not to be snobby or arrogant, but I have a real sense that a zero-dosage wine from a single village can really showcase the pedigree of the village,' he suggests. 'You have to be an extremely good winemaker to make zero-dosage champagne.' And if anyone can do it anywhere,

Jean-François can in Bouzy and Ambonnay. To this end, for some years he has experimented with using Sauternes barriques from Château Doisy Daëne for alcoholic fermentation. 'It gives the illusion of the wine being sweet, when it is not sweet at all!' he claims. The result, to my astonishment, is quite magnificent.

When Clouet began working on the estate over a decade ago, he took note of those embarking on organic and biodynamic regimes. 'Biodynamics and organics look good on paper,' he says, 'but my idea is that it is simply important to take care of the ground by hand without the use of herbicides.' Stringent sorting during harvest maintains freshness and purity in his cuvées.

Clouet's focus remains resolutely on pinot noir, which comprises 100% of every cuvée except his Millésime, a 50/50 blend of pinot noir and chardonnay. 'I am frustrated with the idea of blending from everywhere!' he exclaims. 'I love pure pinot noir! No make-up and no compromise!'

Clouet is fascinated by the geological history of his soils, and makes it his goal to express the minerality of pure chalk in his wines. 'Fantastic minerality and low dosage are important for good pinot noir,' he claims. His cuvées receive low dosages of 6g/L.

In 2011 Clouet created 'Clouet world', a substantial logistics facility for disgorgement, remuage and bottling on land he inherited just outside the village.

As seriously as he takes his responsibilities, Clouet doesn't take himself too seriously. 'Champagne is always for flirting!' he grins. And he likens his wines to independent films. 'I love Hollywood movies, but sometimes I want to watch something independent. Winemaking in Champagne is the same,' he says. 'One is not better than the other. Dom Pérignon and Pol Roger are fantastic, with all the action of James Bond in *Skyfall*, but sometimes I have a taste for something else.'

His champagnes offer that something else, without the Hollywood budget, yet with pyrotechnics all of their own.

ANDRÉ CLOUET GRANDE RÉSERVE BLANC DE NOIRS BRUT NV $$

92 points • 2013 BASE VINTAGE • TASTED IN AUSTRALIA

100% Bouzy and Ambonnay pinot noir; 2013 base vintage with reserves from 2011, 2010, 2008, 2005 and 2002; 8g/L dosage

Clouet captures the full, exuberant stature of Bouzy pinot noir in this luscious, succulent and generous style. Ripe, sweet red cherry, wild strawberry and plum fruits of fleshy, expansive mouthfeel are backed by a fanfare of bottle-derived complexity of mixed spice, gingernut biscuits and toffee. It lingers very long, enlivened softly by the expressive chalk mineral definition of Bouzy.

ANDRÉ CLOUET SILVER BRUT NATURE NV $$

92 points • 2012 BASE VINTAGE • TASTED IN AUSTRALIA

Grande Réserve with zero dosage; 100% Bouzy and Ambonnay pinot noir; reserves from 2009, 2008, 2005 and 2002; 2.5 years on lees; 30% fermented in Sauternes barriques from Doisy Daëne; zero dosage

Jean-François Clouet's zero-dosage ideal is manifested with superb clarity, showcasing pinot noir of such depth and richness that it has absolutely no need for dosage. The great 2012 season brings tension and precision, still upholding a taut acid line and primary freshness of lemon and white cherry fruit. Barrel fermentation unites with bottle age to lay out a magnificently complex landscape of gingernut biscuits, hazelnuts, fruit mince spice, coffee and praline. Pronounced chalk mineral acidity provides sea salt definition, with a creamy, frothy texture which contrasts notes of fine but firm dry extract heightened in barrels. A zero dosage of persistence, tension and confidence.

The Champagne Guide

André Clouet Rosé No 3 Brut NV $$

94 points • 2012 BASE VINTAGE • TASTED IN AUSTRALIA

100% Bouzy and Ambonnay pinot noir; 15% 2012, 35% 2011 and 50% reserves from a solera of 10 vintages; 15% red wine from the four best lieux-dits of the estate in Bouzy, macerated on skins for 2 weeks; 8g/L dosage

Jean-François' 'Clouet No 3' was inspired by Coco Chanel, the number introduced to denote the style, recognising that the colour is different each year, with the number 3 representing a light, elegant apéritif style. Elegance and freshness are his goals for rosé, avoiding what he describes as the 'full, rustic and heavy' styles of the past.

Clouet's rosé epitomises elegance and focus, while flamboyantly celebrating the generous wild strawberry, raspberry, red cherry and watermelon fruit of Bouzy. It encapsulates that wonderful talent of pinot noir to build and rise on the finish, with more body and presence than ever this year. This is quite an achievement based on the 2011 vintage, though Jean-François deploys a cunningly strategic recipe of just 35% 2011, freshened with 2012 and deepened with 50% reserves from a deep solera. Structure is fine and confident, driven both by the chalk minerality of the village and a finely executed tannin presence. It finishes with great length and poise of exquisite red berry fruits. An engaging and enticingly priced rosé of primary integrity.

André Clouet Le Clos 2008 $$$$$

96 points • TASTED IN CHAMPAGNE

Single vineyard; only released in magnums; zero dosage

The Clouet Clos between the house and the cuverie on the lower edge of Bouzy is not the family's finest terroir, without the characteristic chalk mineral definition of their hillside sites, and it takes an exceptional season to infuse it with the confidence to stand alone. However, 2008 delivered that season, with a captivating tension and introverted reticence containing grand complexity waiting to burst out. And burst out it has, two years after release. Deep and luscious plums, black cherries and violets declare the depth and impact of Bouzy, rising to the rhythm of an exceptional season, abounding with a cornucopia of gingernut biscuits, anise, glacé orange, fig, mixed spice, baked white peach, golden fruit cake and roast almonds. The tension and focus of 2008 acidity draws out the finish long and true, coaxing out a pronounced chalk mineral texture of glittering, crystalline definition. Give it at least another five years yet.

The ebullient Jean-François Clouet was described as 'a combination of winemaker and circus ringmaster' by my group of visiting guests.

AR LENOBLE

(A.R. Ler-nob-ler)

7/10

35–37 RUE PAUL DOUCE 51480 DAMERY
www.champagne-arlenoble.com

'*The two important things for making great champagne are the quality of your grapes and the size of your stock,' declares Antoine Malassagne, who is richly blessed with both. With his sister Anne, he is the fourth generation to manage the family cellars and vineyards of the Graser-Malassagne family. The 18 hectares of the small house of Lenoble transcend its position in the centre of the village of Damery, in the middle of the Vallée de la Marne, thanks to a majority of holdings in the core of the Côte des Blancs grand cru of Chouilly. The chardonnay from these vines defines Lenoble's finest cuvées, supplemented with chardonnay and pinot noir from estate vineyards in Bisseuil and Damery. The remainder of its needs, including all meunier, is sourced from Damery growers. For an annual production of 400,000 bottles, Lenoble's cellar stock of 1.5 million is sizeable, furnishing long ageing of 3–4 years for non-vintage cuvées, and six or more for vintage wines. True to its name, a noble approach in the vines and the cellar produces well-composed and tantalisingly affordable cuvées that exemplify Malassagne's philosophy of 'full body with elegance', showcasing the strength, structure, definition and opulence of Chouilly.*

Lenoble was established in 18th century cellars in Damery almost a century ago. When Antoine Malassagne returned to the family company in 1996, he was unimpressed with traditional techniques and set about improving practices in the vineyards and winery in 1998. 'I am starting to see the results of our efforts in the past three or four vintages,' he told me.

A natural approach in the vineyards has seen the elimination of herbicides and pesticides, ploughing to control weeds and aerate the soil, use of organic manure, and cultivation of grasses in the mid-rows of some vineyards to moderate yields and increase ripeness. 'I am nearly organic but not quite, as I am concerned

about using copper sulphate to combat mildew,' says Malassagne, a qualified chemical engineer. For these initiatives, Lenoble was the second in Champagne after Bollinger to receive High Environmental Value certification.

Malassagne's philosophy of making champagne is to vinify it like still wine. The winery was rebuilt in 2008 and maintains three wooden presses between 30 and 45 years of age. All parcels are vinified separately, with the best parcels from the finest seasons fermented in small Burgundy barrels for oxidative character. 'Champagne is a very delicate wine, and the barrel needs to support the wine rather than dominating,' he emphasises. For the most part, his cuvées reflect sensitive use of oak, generally with no more than one-third of any blend vinified in barrels, though a foray into 100% small-barrel fermentation is disconcerting.

'I like buying new barrels, as you know what you're getting.' To reduce new oak character, the first year's fermentation is sold for distillation – a costly and time-consuming process. Four brand new 5000-litre foudres have been recently acquired for ageing reserves for 4–5 months post-fermentation. 'I buy more and more big barrels, because they impart less oaky flavour than small barrels and produce clear, clean wines of finesse and complexity.'

Lenoble adapts vinification to suit the harvest, with malolactic fermentation used selectively, according to the season and the parcel, and not at all in reserve wines. 'It's difficult to find a balance between finesse and intensity,' Malassagne admits. Dosage is very low, no more than 5g/L.

Back labels are particularly informative, detailing base vintage, reserves and vinification.

Driven by a scientific mind, Malassagne is constantly experimenting to refine the details and improve his wines, rather than following trends. He has trialled wild yeasts, bâtonnage and Hungarian oak, though is not convinced of any. He doesn't produce the same non-vintage wines each vintage. 'I try to improve and make the best wines I can every year,' he explains. 'Generation after generation, we try to improve vinification and practices in the vines.'

AR Lenoble Cuvée Intense Brut NV $

93 points • 2012 base vintage • Tasted in Australia

Chouilly, Bisseuil, Damery and other villages of the Vallée de la Marne; 35% reserves without malolactic; 20% vinified in barrels; 6g/L dosage

An impeccably crafted wine from noble fruit sources, offering value for money. Crunchy apple and grapefruit define a well-focused fruit profile, backed by the biscuity complexity of bottle age and a touch of oak, culminating in a finish of well-focused malic acid line and neatly integrated low dosage. A touch of phenolic texture does not interrupt its flow or mineral mouthfeel. A cuvée of integrity and poise.

AR Lenoble Brut Nature Dosage Zero NV $$

92 points • 2011 Base Vintage • Tasted in Australia

Chouilly, Bisseuil, Damery and other villages of the Vallée de la Marne; 35% reserves without malolactic; 18% vinified in barrels; 0g/L dosage

A zero-dosage cuvée based on the harrowing 2011 season is not a recipe that instils confidence, yet the Lenoble team have done a laudable job of creating a wine of poise and appeal. Depth of apple and pear fruit is layered with the toasty, roast hazelnut character of bottle age and a touch of barrel vinification. The dry dustiness of the season is present, though there is sufficient fine chalk mineral texture, ripe fruit presence and even malic acid flow to create a finish of appeal and harmony without any need for dosage. A monumental feat!

AR Lenoble Grand Cru Blanc de Blancs Chouilly Brut NV $$

92 points • 2012 BASE VINTAGE • TASTED IN AUSTRALIA

At least 35% reserves; 20% vinified in barrels; less than 5g/L dosage

Classic Chouilly, and this year a more profound showcase than ever for the ripe opulence of the village, a full and unabashed explosion of glowing locut, yellow mirabelle plum, grilled pineapple, golden delicious apple, even mango. Strategic retention of some malic acidity provides much needed control through a well-defined acid line, which draws out the finish amidst soft, rounded chalk minerality and the creamy texture and toasty, nutty character of barrel vinification. In all, there's nothing subtle about this rendition, though it upholds admirable balance and appeal.

AR Lenoble Grand Cru Blanc de Blancs Chouilly Brut 2008 $$

95 points • TASTED IN AUSTRALIA

10% vinified in oak; 4g/L dosage

The tension and definition of the energetic 2008 vintage is endearing in the opulent village of Chouilly, and Malassagne has sensitively matched the elegance of the vintage with a subtle 10% oak vinification and a very light dosage. Good gracious, such is the stamina of the season that this cuvée has not evolved one iota since its release two years ago, upholding youthful lemon, pear and apple fruit of impressive poise and proportion amidst notes of lemon meringue. It's propelled by a wonderful line of glistening 2008 acidity and pronounced, frothing salt mineral texture, elongating a finish of magnificent line and persistence. Oak lends an appealing, almost invisible note of vanilla and almond. A masterful and age-worthy contrast between the rounded intensity of Chouilly and the vivacious drive of a terrific season.

AR Lenoble Rosé Terroirs Chouilly-Bisseuil NV $$

93 points • 2012 BASE VINTAGE • TASTED IN CHAMPAGNE AND AUSTRALIA

92% Chouilly chardonnay, 8% Bisseuil pinot noir red wine; 28% reserves; 20% vinified in barrels; less than 5g/L dosage

Lenoble's pinot noir and meunier is too rich to stand alone as a rosé, so the house tactically calls upon the structure and fresh acid drive of its Chouilly chardonnay. A philosophy of elegance is upheld by just 8% pinot noir red wine and the result is an altogether more toned demeanour in medium salmon copper, tannin structure and spicy oak presence. It's a precocious thing, with a momentary fanfare of tangelo, candied strawberry, red cherry and musk, proclaiming Bisseuil pinot noir more dramatically than its small inclusion would suggest, then immediately vanishing. The citrus fruits of Chouilly are articulated through the discreetly handled texture of a glimpse of oak. It concludes elegant and fine, thanks to the tension and chalk mineral structure of Chouilly.

The Champagne Guide

AR Lenoble Cuvée Gentilhomme Grand Cru Blanc de Blancs Millésime Brut 2009 $$$

92 points • Tasted in Champagne and Australia

100% Chouilly chardonnay; 100% fermented in small barrels for the first time; partial malolactic fermentation; 3g/L dosage

A glowing, bright medium-straw hue introduces a cuvée that contrasts the exuberance of ripe white fruits of 2009 with a sour acid core and the pronounced charcuterie character of full barrel vinification, disrupting Lenoble's hitherto impeccable record of sensitive use of oak. It consequently lacks something of the dignified refinement that this cuvée has exuded in the past, a powerful wine that collides ripe lemon and grapefruit with firm acidity and prominent oak character. It achieves the accord with poise and harmony, thanks to the tension of malic acidity and the prominent, fine chalk minerality of Chouilly, drawing out a long and accurate finish.

AR Lenoble Les Aventures Grand Cru Chouilly Blanc de Blancs Brut NV $$$

93 points • 2006 base vintage • Tasted in Australia

100% Chouilly chardonnay from a single half-hectare plot; 40% reserves from 2002; 22% vinified in oak; aged on cork; 3g/L dosage; just 2000 bottles released each year

Blended only from seasons released as vintages in their own right, the philosophy of 'The Adventures of Lenoble' is to showcase what a small terroir in Chouilly can produce in top years. Quite a quest it is, engineered and structured with a scaffold of Chouilly tension, amplified by barrel fermentation. Never has it looked finer, and this blend has softened and toned magnificently over quite some years since its release, exemplified by long age on tirage under cork; its tense, coiled acidity still well defined, though now calm and integrated, and the classic yellow fruits of Chouilly now further progressed on their journey towards toast, roast nuts, green olives and coffee beans. Wood work remains pronounced, in notes of savoury, spicy charcuterie complexity and a creamy texture of gentle phenolic grip, yet it preserves the salty chalk mineral texture of Chouilly and upholds its poise, enduring persistence and characterful definition. This is a powerful and formidable experience for the adventurous, yet never heavy nor broad, promising a journey that will linger for some years yet. It's main-course ready, and deserves to be served a little warmer, in large glasses.

AR Lenoble Collection Rare Grand Cru Blanc de Blancs Millésime 1988

89 points • Tasted in Champagne

100% Chouilly chardonnay; full malolactic; disgorged on the spot

A grand old vintage that has sadly grown tired. A medium-golden hue and flavours of gingernut biscuits, mixed spice, honey on toast and some burnt-orange notes on the finish reflect some maderisation.

ARMAND DE BRIGNAC

(Ah-mon de Brin-yak)

———

6 RUE DOM PÉRIGNON 51500 CHIGNY-LES-ROSES

www.armanddebrignac.com

*W*hen the house of Cattier set out to make the most expensive champagne in the world in 2000, they could not have dreamed of the exposure it would receive. In what Cattier describes as 'a great miracle', US hip-hop sensation Shawn Carter (Jay Z) discovered the wine in New York shortly after its release in 2006. To Cattier's 'great surprise' and delight, Jay Z immediately featured the champagne in his new video clip. On the day of the clip's release, Armand de Brignac's US distributor received more than 700 requests for the champagne. A decade later, more than 100,000 bottles are sold in 110 countries annually and Jay Z is the proud owner of the brand.

The striking gold, silver, pink and emerald-clad livery and glam pewter Ace of Spades branding are among Champagne's most lux designs of recent times. But is the wine inside worth the hype and not inconsiderable price?

The focus of Armand de Brignac is said to be pinot noir and meunier, though the current blend comprises 40% of each pinot noir and chardonnay. There are now five cuvées, with Brut Gold representing nearly 80% of production, Rosé 15%, Blanc de Blancs 5%, Blanc de Noirs 2.5% and Demi Sec 2.3%.

Each cuvée is a young, fruity, non-vintage blend of three harvests, to contrast with Cattier's older Clos du Moulin, the inspiration for the three-vintage recipe. *Liqueur de dosage* is aged for a full year, mostly in new Argonne oak barrels to add a touch of wood to the blends.

Armand de Brignac is made by Cattier alongside its own cuvées in its home of Chigny-les-Roses, 150-year-old cellars in neighbouring village Rilly-la-Montagne and a 3600m² warehouse in Reims (largely to facilitate the space required for a big production of large-format bottles, according to Jean-Jacques Cattier). The house

created what is believed to be Champagne's biggest bottle. Dubbed the 'Titan', its 45 kilogram, 37.5-litre bulk holds 50 standard bottles. The first is yet to be opened (assuming it can be lifted!).

Underneath its Rilly facility, Armand de Brignac's gloriously glam and spectacularly lit display of shiny bottles resides in some of Champagne's deepest cellars, no less than 136 steps below the street. The premises were bought by the Cattier family 17 years ago and progressively rebuilt, though in contrast to the showpiece cellars, the production facilities are still quite rustic. Work is underway, and when I visited in 2016, old epoxy resin-lined concrete tanks were being replaced with temperature-controlled stainless steel, important for temperature stability, particularly for malolactic fermentation.

The decision to allocate a wine to Armand de Brignac or to Cattier is made not in the vineyards but based on the fermented wines in tank prior to blending. 'The best for Armand de Brignac, of course,' explains Jean-Jacques. When I questioned the impact of this on the quality of Cattier, he reasoned it away on the

The Champagne Guide

basis that Cattier produces eight times the volume of Armand de Brignac.

Fruit is sourced from Cattier's estate vineyards in the premier cru villages of the northern slopes of the Montagne de Reims, particularly Rilly-la-Montagne, Chigny-les-Roses and Ludes, supplemented with growers from across the Marne, including the villages of Avize, Verzenay and Bouzy, with a desire to increase supplies from the Côte des Blancs and Aÿ. Unclassified villages comprise about 10% of the mix.

Dosages are higher than they need to be, which Jean-Jacques justifies on the basis that the target audience is a young demographic seeking young and fresh champagnes, and this style demands sweetness to soften it.

The philosophy and recipe are sound, though on paper there's nothing to distinguish them from the entry NV blends of many houses. Like them, the current release is based on the 2012 vintage. But does that glam bottle justify ten times the price?

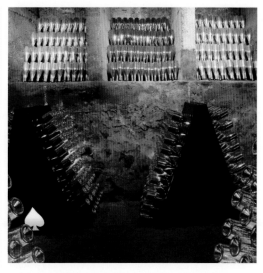

Armand's grand display of shiny bottles deep under Rilly.

ARMAND DE BRIGNAC BRUT GOLD NV $$$$$

91 points • 2012 BASE VINTAGE • TASTED IN CHAMPAGNE

40% chardonnay, 40% pinot, 20% meunier; 2010 and 2009 reserves; around 3 years on lees; *liqueur de dosage* aged in oak; 9.5g/L dosage

The citrus of chardonnay meets the strawberry and red apple of pinot noir and meunier in a fresh and bright style of medium-straw hue and primary, crunchy fruit definition, supported by the honeyed sweetness of dosage. Three years on lees has built subtle praline and nougat notes, but the focus remains primarily on the fruit. Fine chalk minerality is gentle and subtle. A simple, fresh and lively champagne of reasonable persistence in a clean, non-vintage style, finishing a little sweet and honeyed, with more dosage than it calls for. It's otherwise evenly balanced and well made, albeit very young and straightforward for its price.

ARMAND DE BRIGNAC ROSÉ NV $$$$$

92 points • 2012 BASE VINTAGE • TASTED IN CHAMPAGNE

50% pinot, 40% meunier, 10% chardonnay; 2010 and 2009 reserves; 17% pinot noir red wine made partly by the house and partly purchased from Verzenay (mostly), Mailly-Champagne and Bouzy; 9.5g/L dosage

Showcasing the presence and structure of pinot noir, this is a rosé of medium crimson-copper hue and deep cherry and strawberry fruits, becoming cherry liqueur in time, with savoury tamarillo notes. A fleshy, pinot-driven mid-palate is offset by phenolic grip of considerable tannin structure, which counters honeyed dosage on the finish. Three years on lees has built subtle nutty complexity, but the focus remains primarily on its fruit, which is nonetheless impressive, though let down a little by the clash of tannins and dosage. A rosé for pink-meat main courses to tone its tannins.

ARMAND DE BRIGNAC BLANC DE BLANCS NV $$$$$

93 points • 2009 BASE VINTAGE • TASTED IN CHAMPAGNE

2008 and 2006 reserves; ~5.5 years on lees; usually half estate vineyards on northern Montagne premier crus and half Côte des Blancs, mainly Cramant and Avize; 10g/L dosage; ~5000 bottles

With a medium yellow straw–hue, Armand de Brignac's Blanc de Blancs is surprisingly considerably deeper in hue than its Gold, reflecting a few years of additional age. This maturity has delivered wonderfully silky, creamy structure and all of the joy of nougat and brioche, even coffee bean and caramel in time, bringing depth, complexity and integration to succulent white peach fruit. The fine chalk minerality of the northern Côte des Blancs is toned to an elegant background level. The result is creamy, immediate and poised, with alluring balance and style. Honeyed dosage of 10g/L is a little more prominent on the finish than it needs to be, though it has the acidity and chalk minerality to handle it.

ARMAND DE BRIGNAC BLANC DE NOIRS NV $$$$$

92 points • 2009 BASE VINTAGE • TASTED IN CHAMPAGNE

100% pinot noir from Chigny-les-Roses, Mailly-Champagne, Verzy, Verzenay and Bouzy; 2008 and 2006 reserves; ~5.5 years on lees; 8g/L dosage; 2500 bottles

Capturing the restraint of northern Montagne de Reims pinot noir, this is a pale straw coloured, crunchy red apple and pear blanc de noirs. Its pale hue is said to reflect the first-press cut of the juice, though some phonolic presence gives an apple skin-like grip to the finish, evenly balanced by 8g/L dosage. It concludes with good length and fresh poise.

ARMAND DE BRIGNAC DEMI SEC NV $$$$$

89 points • 2008 BASE VINTAGE • TASTED IN CHAMPAGNE

40% chardonnay, 40% pinot, 20% meunier; 2007 and 2006 reserves; an older blend of Gold with 33g/L dosage; 2300 bottles

Said to be the only prestige cuvée demi-sec, this is a toasty and buttery style of medium yellow straw–hue and flavours of French pâtisserie, tropical fruits and honey. Sweet, candied dosage feels disjointed and clashes with phenolic grip, which cuts the finish off firm and abrupt.

The Champagne Guide

AYALA

(Eye-yah-lah)

6/10

2 BOULEVARD DU NORD 51160 AŸ

www.champagne-ayala.fr

Big changes are at hand at Ayala, and its wines are beginning to shine. A youthful enthusiasm is breathing through its grand, historic premises of Château d'Aÿ. The house that had been left sleeping until it was purchased by Bollinger in 2005 is now wide awake, and its elegant, chardonnay-charged cuvées have been refreshed.

In 2011, Ayala assistant chef de cave and former Bollinger quality manager Caroline Latrive was appointed chef de cave at the age of 36. A year later, former Bollinger chief administrative officer, Hadrien Mouflard, was appointed managing director of Ayala at the age of 32. In the same year, the production facilities of the house were modernised with the purchase of new, small 25–100hL temperature-controlled vats.

'For me, it is a big change,' Mouflard explained when I visited. 'We need to capitalise on 150 years of great heritage and history of the house and to translate this into a contemporary style and feel, with the energy and the freedom to innovate.' This means reinventing the house with new packaging and a wine style to differentiate it from Bollinger and other houses.

Labels have recently been changed to stately black, the style of the house a century ago, but the big changes at Ayala go much deeper, boring to the core of the house style. In an attempt to emphasise freshness, elegance and balance, average dosage levels have been lowered from 11g/L of sweetness to just 7g/L. To distinguish it from the pinot-dominant style of

Bollinger, the percentage of chardonnay in the key wine of the house, Ayala Brut Majeur, has been raised from 25–30% to more than 40%. And, again in contrast to its stablemate, every cuvée is vinified in stainless steel tanks, in a quest for minerality, purity and freshness.

Ayala sources from some 50 growers and 75 hectares, laying claim to less than five hectares of its own vineyards, but this is somewhat misleading, as it continues to access fruit from the original 40 hectares retained by its previous owners. It is also in the fortunate position of sharing vineyard sources with Bollinger – an easy share, thanks to Ayala's strong reliance on chardonnay.

Ayala is a medium-sized house with an annual production of 700,000 bottles, up from 400,000 a decade ago, with a medium-term aspiration to increase to 1 million, equal to its production a century ago. There are currently 3 million bottles in its 2.5 kilometres of cellars, 25 metres under Aÿ, where non-vintage wines spend 30 months on lees, vintage wines six years, and prestige wines up to ten. Perle d'Ayala wines are aged under natural cork, said to produce a wine more resilient to the effects of oxygen during ageing. As with Bollinger, this necessitates hand disgorgement, and every bottle must be checked for taint. All wines undergo full malolactic fermentation.

Ayala's long history with dry wines began in 1870, just a decade after the house was founded, with the release of a champagne of 22g/L residual (in a market of typically 100–150g/L). The house claims to have produced the first zero-dosage champagne (in contention with Perrier-Jouët). However, Ayala's success with this style is uncontested, with its Brut Nature Zero Dosage finding tremendous popularity by the glass in London.

Ayala's noble practice of printing the disgorgement date on the back of each bottle gives consumers a chance to identify a fresh disgorgement – an opportunity precious few champagne houses deliver. Its new website boasts particularly informative data sheets on each cuvée.

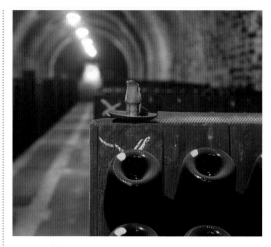

A house on the rise, Ayala's cuvées spend a minimum of 30 months in its 2.5 kilometres of cellars deep under the house in Aÿ.

Ayala Brut Majeur NV $$

90 points • Disgorged August 2016 • Tasted in Australia

40% chardonnay, 40% pinot noir, 20% meunier; sourced from 25 villages; aged 3 years on lees; 7g/L dosage; 80% of production of the house

The vivacity of chardonnay proclaims its presence in this white-fruited style of lemon juice, grapefruit zest, pear and apple, with subtle almond meal and nougat nuances from lees age. Integrated acidity and soft phenolic presence unite in an even and gentle finish of lingering persistence. An appealing and well-balanced Brut Majeur.

Ayala Blanc de Blancs Brut 2008 $$$

95 points • Disgorged March 2016 • Tasted in Australia

60% Chouilly and 40% Le Mesnil-sur-Oger; aged on lees more than 6 years; 6g/L dosage; 30,000–40,000 bottles

Managing director Hadrien Mouflard considers this the flagship of the new Ayala, and never has he been more on the money than in the scintillating 2008 vintage. This is the pinnacle of the chardonnay personality of Ayala, in all its lively, vibrant, energetic and crystalline mineral pizzazz. It is at once deep and light, full and ethereal, built on a core of grand cru depth of white peach, apple and lemon, even hints of fig, graced with subtle complexity of brioche and nougat. The fine, bright, dancing acidity of 2008 energises fine, salt chalk minerality in a stunning display that holds with profound energy and line. A brilliant display of grand terroirs in a sublime season and a thrilling showpiece of the new Ayala.

The Champagne Guide

BARRAT-MASSON

(Bah-raht Mah-soh)

---

20 RUE JAILLARD 10370 VILLENAUXE-LA-GRANDE

https://champagne-barrat-masson.com

CHAMPAGNE

BARRAT • MASSON

Aurélie and Loïc Barrat-Masson established their tiny estate in Villenauxe-la-Grande in the Côte de Sézanne in 2010, having taken over the family farm in 2005, converting seven hectares of vineyards to organic farming and transforming the old buildings into a cuverie and cellars. Planted to 90% chardonnay and 10% pinot noir, these are characterful and precise cuvées of no chaptalisation and low dosage, possessing the complexity of fermentation roughly half in stainless steel tanks and half in oak barrels and demi-muids. Back labels are informative.

BARRAT-MASSON GRAIN D'ARGILE EXTRA BRUT NV $$

90 points • 90% 2013 BASE VINTAGE • DISGORGED APRIL 2016 • TASTED IN AUSTRALIA

63% chardonnay, 37% pinot; 10% 2012 reserve wine; 1.5 years on lees; partial malolactic; aged on lees in barrel and tank for 9 months; 2g/L dosage; 333 cases

A young, precise, zesty, fresh, chardonnay-led cuvée that celebrates Sézanne fruit in primary lemon zest, nashi pear and grapefruit. It's clean, clear, bright and pure, though its youth and low dosage conspire to create a hard acid finish. It would benefit from longer on lees, deeper reserves and a touch more dosage.

BARRAT-MASSON FLEUR DE CRAIE 2012 $$

91 points • DISGORGED FEBRUARY 2016 • TASTED IN AUSTRALIA

100% chardonnay; 2 years on lees; fermented and aged 9 months in 50% barrel and 50% tank; 0g/L dosage; 550 cases

A characterful and precise Sézanne blanc de blancs, taking well-handled barrel fermentation in its stride to uphold the purity and focus of lemon, bitter grapefruit, fennel and nashi pear. A spicy dimension adds interest without hindering focus. Fine-tuned acidity flows comfortably on a bone-dry finish of subtle salt mineral texture.

BÉRÊCHE & FILS

(Bair-aysh e Feess)

(7/10)

LE CRAON DE LUDES 51500 LUDES

www.champagne-bereche-et-fils.com

GRAND VIN DE CHAMPAGNE

PROPRIÉTAIRES DE VIGNES

Young brothers Raphaël and Vincent Bérêche exemplify an enthusiastic and talented new generation that is transforming some of Champagne's smaller, longstanding estates. Working alongside their father, Jean-Pierre, the brothers represent the fifth generation of the family to grow and make champagnes with a very real sense of purity and craftsmanship. They are rightly celebrated among the leading minds of Champagne's young generation, and their extensive range of current cuvées is proof of their talent. Theirs are intelligent and perceptive minds, not afraid to change and adapt, reflected resoundingly in an ever more refined house style.

While many would uphold organic or biodynamic certification as the holy grail of viticulture, Champagne's tumultuous climate makes such ideals in many sites infeasible at best. After many visits to Bérêche's cellars on the edge of the forest above Craon de Ludes, I have been left with the overwhelming impression that any philosophy in force in the vines and wines of Bérêche is one of intuitive sensitivity, agile adaptability and good sense.

'We take a bit of this and a bit of that,' Raphaël declares unassumingly. 'We work in an organic way, but if there is too much rain in July and disease breaks out, we use a systemic chemical and then continue with our organic approach.' He's the first to admit Champagne is a difficult place to attempt to control everything, particularly in an estate as far-flung as this.

Since 1950, Bérêche's holdings have grown from just 2.5 hectares in Ludes to a total of 9.5 hectares, centred around Ludes and neighbouring Chigny-les-Roses, and extending as far as Trépail in the eastern Montagne de Reims, Ormes west of Reims, and Mareuil-le-Port and Festigny in the Vallée de la Marne.

Raphaël emphasises the importance of managing all the vines themselves, to control yields. A modest production of 85,000 bottles from 9.5 hectares of mature vines averaging 38 years of age reflects particularly low yields. 'One problem of Champagne is that the yields are sometimes too high,' he admits. His brother Vincent has managed the vineyards since 2008, achieving balanced vines and fully mature fruit by maintaining yields of just 60–65hL/hectare – less than two-thirds the regional average. 'If we have higher yields, we need to put more products on the vines and there is a greater risk of disease,' Raphaël explains. 'It's like me: if I ate at [nearby restaurant] Le Grand Cerf every day I would die in two weeks!'

Bérêche encourages balance in his vines through spontaneous grass grown in the mid-rows. Herbicide use

The Champagne Guide

has been eliminated since Raphaël began in 2004. He believes this is the most important treatment to avoid, for the sake of the pH and acidity of the finished wines.

Biodynamics has been trialled since 2007 on a three-hectare plot in front of the house, as a test for the whole estate, but Raphaël admits that it's easier to manage nearby than 40 kilometres away in Festigny. 'We are just nine people and 9.5 hectares, so it's very important that we don't lose our crop!' he says.

Bérêche's simple and natural approach in the vineyard carries into the cellar, where labour-intensive, traditional techniques are favoured, from pressing and first fermentation to disgorgement. The brothers visit the vineyards three or four times to choose the right moment to harvest, and pickers are paid by the hour, not by the kilogram, to encourage stringent selection. Everything is pressed at the estate in Craon de Ludes. When I visited one Sunday morning two-thirds of the way through vintage 2014, I found Raphaël had been working until 2am and was at the press again by 7.30. He is hard-working, reflective and intuitive in responding to the seasons. While long, slow, natural primary fermentations are the goal, if the ferments run too long, they are energised with commercial yeasts. He likes the idea of yeasts from the domaine and the grape, but admits they're really derived from the cellar and barrels.

Fermentation is equally divided between oak barrels and small stainless steel tanks, which have recently replaced old enamel-lined concrete tanks. Slightly larger and older 300-litre Burgundy barrels are preferred to Champagne's traditional 205-litre barrels, as their more subtle influence on the wine maintains fruit precision. Vinification in barrels has recently increased to 80%.

Wines are matured for extended periods in both barrels and tanks prior to bottling. Ageing on lees with a little bâtonnage allows the wines to become slightly reductive, providing protection from oxidation, even with only very small additions of sulphur dioxide. A low-sulphur regime is a priority, with small additions to maintain freshness only on the press and after fermentation, and none at bottling or disgorgement. Bérêche prizes low pH, dissolved carbon dioxide gas and sugar in the dosage ahead of sulphur dioxide for preserving freshness. This seems to work most of the time, although I have occasionally noted funky barrel notes in some cuvées. To his credit, Raphaël has recognised when sulphur levels are too low and corrected in subsequent releases.

Even with such low sulphur levels, Bérêche has no trouble fully blocking malolactic fermentation, thanks to very cold (8°C) cellars at the top of Craon de Ludes. 'Historically, Champagne did not have malolactic fermentation,' Raphaël points out. 'This was only introduced in the 1980s, to make it easier to drink, and to reduce the time in the cellar.'

Bérêche is working to increase the time each cuvée is aged, with a new cellar under the house to increase capacity for reserve wines. With the exception of the entry Brut NV and Extra Brut NV, all cuvées are aged on cork instead of crown seal, to increase oxygen interaction and produce a creamier bead and a more open, characterful and complex wine, with a more logical coherence of nose and palate.

Cork ageing necessitates hand disgorgement, and it takes two people to taste and disgorge 1200 bottles a day. A traditional *liqueur d'expédition* is used in place of grape concentrate, at very low levels of dosage, so as to faithfully preserve tension and minerality in the wines. Raphaël highlights that even 2–3g/L of dosage is important for ageing, and does not regard his Extra Brut NV as a style to age for more than five years. Back labels of all cuvées are impressively informative, disclosing dosage, disgorgement date and base vintage. A very classy website discloses more detail again. The number of bottles produced has recently been added to the front label of each cuvée.

Bérêche recently relinquished its Récoltant-Manipulant status in favour of Négociant-Manipulant, so as to have the flexibility to purchase more vineyards and buy from growers. 'We wanted to buy a 0.3 hectare plot in Mailly-Champagne, but the authorities only permitted us to buy half because they said we were too big,' Raphaël explains. Their NM status has opened up the opportunity to selectively purchase single-vineyard fruit for new cuvées (not to adapt existing blends) as well as tiny quantities of mature champagnes *sur latte* from top terroirs to sell under their Raphaël et Vincent Bérêche label. This year they assessed 30 different champagnes in this way and selected three, for which they managed disgorgement and dosage.

In an age when champagne markets religiously celebrate Récoltant-Manipulant status, such relinquishment, like that of De Sousa in Avize recently, is testimony to the higher esteem in which this is upheld outside of Champagne than it is within. Like their approach in the vineyard and the cellar, Raphaël and Vincent are driven to change and adapt for the betterment of their cuvées, rather than subscribing to dogmatic regimes.

The wines of Bérêche are vinous champagnes of dry complexity. Even as young vins clairs, they are generously expressive of both ripe fruit intensity and the mineral signature of their sites. Raphaël and Vincent have succeeded in progressively toning the assertive temperament of malic acidity, barrel fermentation and low dosage, making for champagnes that will keep fanatics enthralled.

Bérêche & Fils Brut Réserve NV $$

95 points • 70% 2013 base vintage • Disgorged September 2015 • Tasted in Champagne

30% chardonnay, 35% pinot, 35% meunier; 30% 2012 and perpetual reserve; 2 years on lees; no malolactic; 60% vinified in barrels; 10-15% tailles aged 2 years in little barrels for more oxygen to soften the finish; 6.5g/L dosage; 70,000 bottles

Bérêche admits that this is his most difficult wine to make, with an aspiration of richness, finesse, chalk minerality, creamy texture and a clean, bright finish. He has pulled this off as brilliantly as I have ever seen it with the 2013 base. To achieve such impeccable expression of red berry fruits, stone fruits and citrus even with a majority of barrel fermentation is a feat few in Champagne can achieve. Bérêche melds all this seamlessly with nuances of toast and almonds from lees age, contrasting with bright malic acidity and softly mineral chalk texture, finishing with wonderful, lingering, bright red cherry fruit and the energy to age confidently for the short term.

Bérêche & Fils Les Monts Fournois Ludes 2012 $$$$

93 points • Disgorged December 2015 • Tasted in Champagne

100% chardonnay; Les Monts Fournois single plot planted 1961 at the bottom of Ludes bordering Rilly; extra brut; no malolactic fermentation; 100% vinified in large oak barrels; 3g/L dosage; 1709 bottles

From a plot accessed by Bérêche for five years, on which the grower has never used fertilisers, encouraging the roots very deep into the chalk. The result is frothy, salty minerality, amplified by high-tensile malic acidity that screams out for age to soften. Picked at 12 degrees potential and fermented to 13%, this is a ripe style of intense apple, pear and lemon fruit and even gentle notes of red cherries surprising for chardonnay. Crunchy grapefruit bite contrasts the elegant spiciness of barrel fermentation.

Bérêche & Fils Les Beaux Regards Chardonnay 2012 $$$

94 points • Disgorged February 2016 • Tasted in Champagne

Single-plot Ludes; vinified in 1-4-year-old barrels; no malolactic fermentation; tasted a week after disgorgement; 3g/L dosage; 3821 bottles

A jousting contest between the focused lemon, grapefruit and apple of ripe chardonnay and the fruit cake and fruit mince spice of barrel fermentation, impaled by the structure of firm, high-tensile malic acidity and pronounced, fine chalk mineral structure. Mineral personality leaps from the glass with sea salt aromas and flavours. Again this year a cuvée of great drive, texture, confidence and energy, demanding a decade in the cellar.

Raphaël & Vincent Bérêche Cru Sélectionné Vallée Brut Premier Cru Extra Brut NV $$$

92 points • Disgorged January 2016 • Tasted in Champagne

50% chardonnay and 50% pinot from Aÿ, Dizy and Hautvillers; 5 years on lees; vintage 2010 but not declared on the bottle; 100% vinified in tank; full malolactic fermentation; 6g/L dosage; 2371 bottles

Intentionally more accessible and fruity, this cuvée presents a compelling contrast in terroirs and production (tank fermented with full malolactic) to the Bérêche & Fils style. The result is appealing and ready to drink, an engaging presentation of spice and praline with strawberry and raspberry fruits, culminating in a rounded, red apple finish.

BÉRÊCHE & FILS LE CRAN LUDES PREMIER CRU 2008 $$$$

96 points • DISGORGED NOVEMBER 2015 • TASTED IN CHAMPAGNE

50% chardonnay, 50% pinot; chardonnay planted 1969 and pinot planted 1973 on pure chalk in Craon de Ludes; 84 months on lees; vinified in barrels of 1-3 years of age; no malolactic fermentation; 3g/L dosage; 2500 bottles

Bérêche has been refining the ripeness, oak and sulphur of this cuvée for five vintages, and the scintillating 2008 season has delivered his finest work yet. It's a beautifully evocative and complex cuvée that captures the golden fruit cake and spice of barrel fermentation while projecting a wonderful fruit core of impeccable white peach, apple and lemon, even the ripeness of pineapple. All these theatrics are pulled into line by piercing 2008 malic acidity, awash with fine chalk mineral texture that froths long into the finish. It's still very tense and young at eight years of age and screams out for at least another decade – if not three.

BÉRÊCHE & FILS REFLET D'ANTAN BRUT NV $$$

93 points • 2010 BASE VINTAGE • DISGORGED MAY 2015 • TASTED IN CHAMPAGNE

The reserve wine for Brut Reserve NV from perpetual solera reserve; 35% pinot noir from Ludes, 35% meunier from Mareuil-le-Port and 30% chardonnay from both villages; vinified in barrels and demi-muids; no malolactic fermentation; 41 months on lees; 6g/L dosage; 4500 bottles

Each year the brothers take just two-thirds of each 600L demi-muid of reserves, allocating the best to this cuvée and the rest to the Brut Reserve. Raphaël describes the result as an old-fashioned style. It's found a harmony between the definition of red apple and dried fruits, and the spice, creamy texture, toast, nuts and complex savoury charcuterie notes of barrel fermentation. With a full-straw hue and copper tint, it's powerful, yet never heavy or imposing, with well-toned malic acidity holding a long and full finish. A champagne of expression and character before comfortable appeal.

BÉRÊCHE & FILS VALLÉE DE LA MARNE RIVE GAUCHE MEUNIER 2012 $$$

95 points • DISGORGED NOVEMBER 2015 • TASTED IN CHAMPAGNE

Single plot from the family's best parcel of old meunier planted on clay soils in 1969 on the left bank of Mareuil-le-Port in the Vallée de la Marne; 32 months on lees; vinified in 2-5-year-old barrels; no malolactic fermentation; 3g/L dosage; 3776 bottles

This vineyard was blessed by the great 2012 season and the result is a benchmark meunier of wonderfully evocative presence. A full straw with a blush tint heralds exact red cherry and strawberry fruits and lifted rose petal perfume, propelled effortlessly by all the spice of barrel fermentation. Bright yet well integrated malic acidity declares a lively and refreshing finish which lingers long with red fruits and spice. Wow.

Raphaël & Vincent Bérêche Cru Sélectionné Côte Grand Cru 2007 $$$

93 points • Disgorged January 2016 • Tasted in Champagne
100% Cramant chardonnay; 4g/L dosage; 4000 bottles

The persistence and power of Cramant are on display in this dry style of grapefruit, apple, pear and spice. The signature salty, chalky minerality of the village is on prominent display. A compelling take on a great terroir.

Raphaël & Vincent Bérêche Cru Sélectionné Montagne 2004 $$$

95 points • Disgorged January 2016 • Tasted in Champagne
75% pinot, 25% chardonnay; Verzenay; 5g/L dosage; 1200 bottles

Verzenay is just on the other side of Mailly-Champagne from Ludes. The Bérêche brothers love the village and what they describe as its 'stony northern aromas', though admit that it demands a long time in the cellar. Hence their enthusiasm to find this mature cuvée from 'a typical old champagne grower who kept some bottles to sell to fund his retirement'. It's signature Verzenay of medium-straw hue, upholding red cherry and strawberry fruit, while basking in the blessing of 12 years of age in notes of brioche, fruit mince spice and gingernut biscuits. It projects the elegant mood of the village with confidence and poise, finishing softly textured and long, supported by gently integrated acidity.

Bérêche & Fils Les Monts Fournois Coteaux Champenois Ludes Blanc 2013 $$$

91 points • Disgorged November 2015 • Tasted in Champagne
Ludes chardonnay planted in 1961; matured for 18 months in barrels; 3g/L dosage; 294 bottles

A rare still white champagne made in miniscule volumes just for the estate and three Michelin-starred Reims restauant L'Assiette Champenois. This is the first vineyard that the brothers harvest, achieving a full 12 degrees natural potential and a tense 2.83pH, an unusual contrast of acid and sugar. The result is a young Coteaux Champenois of prominent, classy vanillin/toasty oak and a core of impressively ripe fruit presence of white peach, grapefruit and lemon. It showcases its considerable fruit ripeness, backed by a tense acid line that draws out a long finish, promising impressive potential in the cellar.

Bérêche & Fils Coteaux Champenois Rouge Les Montées 2013 $$$

92 points • Disgorged November 2015 • Tasted in Champagne
75% pinot, 25% meunier; single plot of just 0.38 hectare planted in 1965 in Ormes close to Vrigny; 75% whole-bunch fermentation; vinified and matured in barrels on lees for 18 months; 880 bottles

In spite of low yields of just 35hL/ hectare from this tiny 0.38 hectare plot, the Bérêche brothers can't get this fruit any riper than 11.5 degrees potential. The result is just five barrels, four for this cuvée and one for their Campania Remensis rosé. This is an enticingly spicy still red champagne of fruit mince spice, pepper, and a savoury beetroot core, fleshed out with strawberry and red cherry fruits. Fine tannins of impressively textured poise and good acid line define a long and balanced finish that will endure long in the cellar.

The Champagne Guide

BERNARD BRÉMONT

(Behr-nah Breh-moh)

6/10

<small>1 RUE DE REIMS 51150 AMBONNAY</small>

www.champagne-bremont.fr

Bernard Brémont

ernard and Michèle Brémont established their estate in Ambonnay in 1965, when Bernard and his father hand carved their underground cellars for maturing their champagnes. This hands-on approach prevails, and all operations from viticulture through to disgorgement are now capably handled by their son Thibault and daughter Anne. The family is privileged to have 12 hectares of pinot noir and three hectares of chardonnay of vines (of average age 30 years) located almost entirely in the magnificent grand cru of Ambonnay, and just 0.3 hectare in neighbouring Bouzy. Their finest cuvées accurately capture all the fanfare and chalk mineral definition of Ambonnay, within a style of precision and poise.

BERNARD BRÉMONT AMBONNAY GRAND CRU BRUT NV $$

92 points • 2012 BASE VINTAGE • DISGORGED JANUARY 2016 • TASTED IN AUSTRALIA

68% pinot, 32% chardonnay from Ambonnay; 38% reserve wines; aged 3 years on lees; 8g/L dosage; DIAM closure

Bernard Brémont captures the poise and power of Ambonnay in a style that contrasts pear and apple fruit with the roast hazelnut complexity of bottle age. Acidity and dosage meld in a harmonious finish, energised by the fine chalk minerality of the village, with just a touch of phenolic grip closing off.

BERNARD BRÉMONT AMBONNAY GRAND CRU BRUT ROSÉ NV $$

91 points • 2013 BASE VINTAGE • DISGORGED APRIL 2016 • TASTED IN AUSTRALIA

60% chardonnay, 25% pinot noir white wine from Ambonnay; 15% pinot noir red wine from Bouzy; 38% reserve wines; aged a little under 3 years on lees; 8g/L dosage; DIAM closure

A bright, medium crimson hue heralds a characterful rosé alive with musk, wild strawberries and freshly picked raspberries. It's fruity and precocious, structured with fine tannin grip and culminating in a finish defined more by fruit sweetness than dosage. The effect is simple and short, though nonetheless balanced and appealing.

BERNARD BRÉMONT GRAND CRU DE 50 ANS PASSION NV $$

94 points • 2009 BASE VINTAGE • DISGORGED MAY 2016 • TASTED IN AUSTRALIA

80% pinot noir, 20% chardonnay from Ambonnay; aged a little under 7 years on lees; 8g/L dosage; DIAM closure

A commemorative release to celebrate the 50th anniversary of the house, this is a cuvée that captures all the fanfare of Ambonnay in a powerful and ripe base vintage, brimming with mirabelle plums, figs, succulent peach and baked apple, bolstered with grand complexity of reserves and bottle maturity in deep golden fruit cake, wild honey, mixed spice and toast. It culminates in a finish of great presence and persistence, toned by fine chalk mineral mouthfeel. An exuberant and jubilant Ambonnay.

BERNARD BRÉMONT AMBONNAY GRAND CRU BRUT MILLÉSIME 2008 $$$

95 points • DISGORGED MAY 2016 • TASTED IN AUSTRALIA

55% pinot noir, 45% chardonnay from Ambonnay; aged a little under 7 years on lees; 8g/L dosage; DIAM closure

Gorgeous aromas and flavours of pure red cherries, plums and mixed spice evoke all the glory of one of Champagne's greatest grand crus. The purity and poise of the scintillating 2008 season are presented with pinpoint accuracy within the generosity of the village. Eight years of age has built an undercurrent of toasty, spicy complexity, but the focus remains on the impeccable, tense acid definition of 2008, framed immaculately in the pronounced, fine chalk mineral texture of Ambonnay. This is a 2008 ready to drink now.

BESSERAT DE BELLEFON

(Bess-rah der Bell-foh)

22 RUE MAURICE CERVEAUX 51200 ÉPERNAY

www.besseratdebellefon.com

A medium-sized house in Épernay under the banner of the Lanson-BCC group, Besserat de Bellefon produces 1.3 million bottles annually from 25 hectares of estate vineyards situated mainly in the Vallée de la Marne, substantially supplemented with supply from some 100 growers. The house style is distinctive in a lower pressure of 4.5 atmospheres (compared with 6 in most champagnes), but more importantly in a complete absence of malolactic fermentation in all cuvées. The softening effect of age is consequently important, with non-vintage cuvées aged for a minimum of three years and vintage cuvées a minimum of five years, though even this is insufficient to tame the hard malic acidity that marks the house style. This makes non-vintage blends challenging, but confidently balances warm seasons like 2006. Cédric Thiébault has been with the house since 1999 and immediately introduced DIAM across the range when he became cellar master in 2006. Disgorgement dates are printed on back labels.

BESSERAT DE BELLEFON CUVÉE DES MOINES MILLÉSIME BRUT 2006 $$

93 points • DISGORGED SEPTEMBER 2014 • TASTED IN AUSTRALIA

57% chardonnay, 33% pinot, 10% meunier; 8g/L dosage; DIAM closure

This is Besserat's first vintage release since 2002, admirably sidestepping the challenging 2003 and 2005 vintages, though surprisingly not releasing the 2004. A confident chardonnay lead in the absence of malolactic is well poised to counter the exuberance of the ripe 2006 season, while a decade of age has blessed it with prominent layers of spice of all kinds, gingernut biscuits, butter cake, dried nectarines, even caramel and golden fruit cake. The bright, signature Besserat malic acidity keeps the finish lively and well-defined, and it holds its line and length admirably. The result is a substantial step up from Besserat's non-vintage releases, making this the cuvée of the range most worthy of your attention this year.

Besserat de Bellefon Cuvée des Moines Brut NV $$

90 points • Disgorged September 2015 • Tasted in Australia

35% chardonnay, 20% pinot, 45% meunier; 9g/L dosage; DIAM closure

Besserat's non-vintage entry point is a cuvée of power and tension, presenting the depth of meunier in black cherry fruit and considerable bottle-age secondary complexity of roast hazelnuts and toast. This contrasts with a taut finish of firm malic acidity, engulfing dosage and concluding bright and tense. This is quite a juxtaposition and is pulled off confidently.

Besserat de Bellefon Cuvée des Moines B de B Brut NV $$

91 points • Disgorged April 2014 • Tasted in Australia

45% chardonnay, 45% pinot, 10% meunier; 9g/L dosage; 7000 bottles; DIAM closure

The B de B Cuvée was launched in 2013 to commemorate the 170th anniversary of the house. It carries an exuberant and exotic feel, with ripe nectarine and even mango suggestions underlined by layers of spice and all the biscuity fanfare of lees age. Creamy bead declares depth of maturity. It culminates in a long finish of tense malic acid line, marked by some phenolic bitterness.

Besserat de Bellefon Cuvée des Moines Extra Brut NV $$

89 points • Disgorged November 2015 • Tasted in Australia

25% chardonnay, 75% pinot; 5g/L dosage; DIAM closure

Besserat de Bellefon Cuvée des Moines Grand Cru Blanc de Blancs Brut NV $$

88 points • Disgorged September 2015 • Tasted in Australia

9g/L dosage; DIAM closure

Besserat de Bellefon Cuvée des Moines Grand Cru Blanc de Noirs Brut NV $$

89 points • Disgorged October 2015 • Tasted in Australia

100% pinot; 8g/L dosage; DIAM closure

Besserat de Bellefon Cuvée des Moines Rosé Brut NV $$

86 points • Disgorged September 2014 • Tasted in Australia

25% chardonnay, 25% pinot, 50% meunier; 9g/L dosage; DIAM closure

BILLECART-SALMON

(Bill-khah Sal-moh)

9/10

40 RUE CARNOT 51160 MAREUIL-SUR-AŸ

www.champagne-billecart.fr

CHAMPAGNE
BILLECART-SALMON
Maison Fondée en 1818

The art of crafting elegant, graceful champagne requires the most exacting skill. Sweetness, richness and breadth cover all manner of sins in champagne, but a wine in its unadorned, raw nakedness reveals even the slightest blemish for all to see. The mark of Billecart is made not by the heavy footfall of concentration, power and presence, but rather by the fairy touch of delicacy and crystal-clear fidelity. Every one of its dozen cuvées articulately speaks the house philosophy of 'respecting the integrity of the fruit, freshness and acidity'.

On the surface, there appears little to distinguish the fruit sources of this medium-sized house in Mareuil-sur-Aÿ. Vineyard holdings are small, servicing a 2.4 million bottle annual production with just 20 hectares of estate vines and more than 300 hectares of purchased fruit managed by 185 growers. How does Billecart maintain such transcendental standards in each of its cuvées?

Antoine Roland-Billecart, who manages the house with his brother François, answers this question with a refreshingly frank honesty. 'We are not very focused on marketing,' he begins in impeccable English. 'Vinification is the key for us, and all the rest is bullshit.'

Its elegant delicacy places Billecart dizzyingly high among Champagne's finest houses, but also infuses its cuvées with an inherent fragility, rendering them particularly vulnerable to imperfections in closure, transportation or storage. Without disgorgement dates indicated on bottles, it's difficult to ascertain the age of non-vintage cuvées, but be sure to ask for fresh stock that hasn't lingered on retail shelves.

Billecart's vintage wines can be coiled up tight in their youth and appreciate plenty of time to open up in a large glass.

Over many hours of visits and intensive tastings with Antoine and cellar master François Domi, an enlightening picture emerges, illuminating some 11 spheres that account for the astounding performance of Billecart-Salmon.

LONGSTANDING FAMILY MANAGEMENT

Although not exclusively owned by the family, Billecart has been under family management since it was founded in 1818. The family still lives on site, and there is a long-visioned continuity at play. The eighth generation of the family, Nicolas Roland-Billecart, came on board alongside his father François, uncle Antoine and grandfather Jean in 2010.

'We are very lucky that my father still joins us for every tasting,' Antoine reflects. 'He began working in

Antoine Roland-Billecart takes a sample from a fermentation tank. The family maintains active involvement in every stage of production.

wine when he was 16 and has over 70 harvests in his memory. His experience of terroir is so great that he can comment on the effect of every parcel in a blend and challenge us to consider what a wine will be like in 20 years. 'This sample won't last, and in 15 years you're going to cry!' he tells us. He has such experience that he can feel a vintage by smelling and tasting the musts, building the blend in his mind before we even taste it.'

HANDS-ON VINEYARD MANAGEMENT

'It's easy to work for a company that is searching for quality as the goal across the whole process,' François Domi says. Starting with the fruit. 'The best grapes on the best terroirs are expensive, but this is our priority.'

Billecart's production has trebled in the past 20 years, and since that time they have set about acquiring vineyards centred around Mareuil-sur-Aÿ. In 2004, the family sold a 45% share in the firm, and in so doing secured access to an additional 80 hectares of grand cru fruit.

Today, the company also manages 100 hectares (and rising) under lease arrangement, taking full control, from pruning to harvest. 'This is very important,' explains Antoine, 'because it enables us to conduct the vineyard the way we want, yielding 70hL/hectare rather than 85–90, ensuring consistent ripeness and balanced concentration and acidity.' A team of 40 local pickers is paid by the hour to be particularly selective in the most sensitive vineyards.

In vineyards under company control, there has been a return to a more natural way of growing vines and promoting soil health through an absence of pesticides and herbicides. Clos Saint-Hilaire has been worked biodynamically for 12 years, and other estate vineyards

are working towards the same regime. All growers are encouraged to grow grasses in the mid-rows to limit yields. A generational approach to farming, rather than a full biodynamic regime, is the aspiration.

PARCEL SELECTION

Even at a modest 70hL/hectare, Billecart's output is tiny for an estate sourcing from 320 hectares. Antoine considers the flexibility of sourcing grapes from 185 growers to be strategic, permitting vinification of 140% of production every year, with lesser parcels sold as still wines, or declassified to Billecart's second label, Charles Le Bel.

'It's great to own your own vineyards, but the opportunity to be selective is something fantastic!' Antoine exclaims. The decision was made recently to cap production at the current level of 2 million bottles.

METICULOUS PRODUCTION REGIME

The precision of Billecart is proclaimed in a squeaky-clean winery, even during my visit at the height of vintage 2014. Each element of its meticulous production is geared towards capturing every nuance in the fruit. Billecart presses half the fruit it purchases and uses a pneumatic press for larger parcels, because it's more gentle than the traditional press. One hundred 40hL tanks and some 450 barrels maintain individual control over every one of 280 parcels.

'We have to be very precise, increasing quality by being overly selective, keeping what we want and getting rid of what we don't want to keep,' explains Antoine. A massive new blending tank was commissioned in 2009 to lower the risk of oxidation and increase the consistency of the blends.

COLD SETTLING AND COOL FERMENTS

Perhaps Billecart's most revolutionary technique is its practice of double débourbage. After the standard clarification process to settle out solids, the juice is settled a second time at 4°C for at least 48 hours without use of enzymes. The house pioneered this technique in 1952, inspired by the brothers' maternal grandfather's experience in brewing beer. At this temperature, the coarser lees are removed without risk of oxidation, delivering pristine juice for fermentation. The process is expensive and time-consuming. 'Most of our colleagues thought we were crazy!' admits Antoine.

The juice is then brought up to just 13°C – never more than 14°C – for the primary fermentation. Antoine has growers and houses tell him it's impossible for yeast to work at this temperature. At 13°C, cultured yeasts from the natural yeasts of nearby villages take 3–4 weeks to complete fermentation. Such cool, long ferments are crucial for retaining greater freshness and delicacy than a standard champagne ferment of one week at 20°C, particularly in a warm vintage like 2015. Parcels then stay on lees in tank for six months, crucial for development of personality, structure and aroma.

All parcels for non-vintage blends pass through malolactic fermentation, but for vintage wines this is dependent upon the season. For Antoine, 'respecting the style of the vintage is more important than anything else', and winemaking is adapted each year to suit.

INCREASING USE OF OAK
When Antoine comes to work every day he asks himself what can be done to improve vinification within the house style. As a devotee of Krug Clos du Mesnil – he openly volunteers the inaugural vintage as his favourite blanc de blancs of all time – it's no surprise Billecart has increased the use of oak barrels for fermentation since 1996. Fifty barrels in that year became 80 in 1997. A new barrel room now houses 500 barrels and two new large oak foudres, ranking Billecart fourth for barrels in Champagne, after Krug, Bollinger and Alfred Gratien. The plan is to replicate this room to add thirty 80hL oak foudres this year.

Old barrels, having seen six or seven vintages in Burgundy, are used for the fermentation of all grand cru fruit, and bâtonnage is conducted weekly, according to taste. Barrels currently range from five to 15 years of age. The goal at Billecart, as always, is to encourage subtle complexity rather than overt character. 'Just to add some spice,' as Antoine puts it.

Pinot noir harvest in Billecart's home of Mareuil-sur-Aÿ, where the house will celebrate its 200th birthday in 2018.

LOW DOSAGE
Antoine considers a decrease in dosage over the past decade as crucial in allowing the fruit to show its full character. 'It is like make-up,' he proposes. 'You don't need it if there is no problem, and you want to show the real character of the wines.' Dosage levels are low: typically 8g/L in non-vintage wines, and around just 4g/L in vintage wines ('Extra Brut'). Any more sweetness might play havoc with such delicate styles.

DIFFERENT LIQUEUR FOR EACH DOSAGE
The final nuance comes at disgorgement: every cuvée has a different liqueur at Billecart. François Domi conducts many tastings with different dosages, from wines aged in barrel and those in tank, to determine which best suits each wine. A different liqueur is used for every disgorgement, so completely different liqueurs can be chosen for the start, the middle and the end of a cuvée.

LONG AGEING
Billecart's non-vintage wines are aged for 3–4 years, and its millésime collection a minimum 8–10 years (the 2002 Cuvée Nicolas François Billecart was released in 2013). Brut Réserve NV is released after 28 months in the cellar, rather than the 24 months of recent years, with a goal to exceed 30 months. Billecart holds a deep collection of reserves, with at least one-third of every harvest kept in reserve. The precision and freshness of the Billecart house style is all the more compelling in the context of such deep reserves and long ageing.

SUPERIOR CLOSURE
Finally, and crucially, all non-vintage wines except blanc de blancs have been sealed with DIAM cork since 2006. DIAM is not perfect, but it is demonstrably superior to natural cork. Billecart's Australian agent reported an immediate drop in returned bottles as soon as DIAM was introduced. Billecart is currently nine years into a 10-year trial of ageing of vintage wines under DIAM. I look forward to the day when Billecart's top wines are entrusted to a reliable closure.

THE GENIUS OF FRANÇOIS DOMI
Alongside the enthusiastic energy of Antoine Roland-Billecart, François Domi is the quietly spoken and reflective genius. He started in the lab at Billecart as an oenologist 30 years ago and describes himself today as part of the furniture. His unassuming manner means his name is never listed among Champagne's rockstars, but his greatest hits of the past two decades surely place him at the top of the charts.

BILLECART-SALMON BLANC DE BLANCS GRAND CRU BRUT NV $$$

92 points • 2011 BASE VINTAGE • DISGORGED MARCH 2016 • TASTED IN AUSTRALIA

A blend of Avize for structure, Cramant for florals, Chouilly for depth and Le Mesnil-sur-Oger for definition; 50% reserves from 2010, 2009 and 2008; partial malolactic fermentation; 6g/L dosage; DIAM closure

'In your dreams,' responded Jean Roland-Billecart when his son Antoine proposed a non-vintage blanc de blancs. 'We don't have sufficient quantity of chardonnay, but if you find the grapes to produce it, go ahead.' And find them he did. Not just anywhere, but in the five grand crus of the Côte des Blancs, and in 1997 Billecart made its first non-vintage blanc de blancs.

This is a compelling result for the 2011 base year, bolstered in no small part by 50% reserves (twice the usual level), which build layers of pâtisserie, butter and nougat, though don't quite go all the way to countering the dry, earthy finish that marks 2011. Nonetheless, it upholds the creamy, soft and textural signature of the style, energised by nicely poised acidity and a softly rumbling undercurrent of grand cru minerality.

BILLECART-SALMON EXTRA BRUT NV $$

93 points • 2012 BASE VINTAGE • DISGORGED DECEMBER 2015 • TASTED IN CHAMPAGNE AND AUSTRALIA

40% meunier from Vallée de la Marne; 30% pinot from Aÿ, Mareuil-sur-Aÿ, Ambonnay, Rilly-la-Montagne, Verzenay and Verzy; 30% chardonnay from Vitry, Sézannais and Côte des Blancs; 50% reserves from 2010, 2009 and 2008, and chardonnay from 2011; full malolactic fermentation; zero dosage; DIAM closure

The precision of Billecart lends itself well to this style, making for one of the most refined zero-dosage champagnes, built on the same base as Brut Réserve – but crucially, not simply a zero-dosage version of the same. It's older, with an extra year on lees – 'not so it has more fat', explains Antoine, 'but so it is more rounded, with less angles'. The liqueur in the dosage is different, too, with 5mL of reserve wines contributing volume, structure and persistence. Age has built considerable depth of complexity in almond meal, toast, nougat and brioche, preserved in a brittle shell of bone-shaking purity and citrus minerality, with excellent focus and drive of vibrant lemon, apple, grapefruit and crunchy pear. Zero dosage makes for a firm finish which would benefit from even the slightest touch of sweetness.

Long ageing is one of the many keys to the Billecart style. Its cuvées rest for a minimum of 28 months deep under Mareuil-sur-Aÿ.

The Champagne Guide

BILLECART-SALMON BRUT RÉSERVE NV $$

94 points • 2013 BASE VINTAGE • DISGORGED NOVEMBER 2015 AND JUNE 2016
• TASTED IN CHAMPAGNE AND AUSTRALIA

40% meunier from Vallée de la Marne; 30% pinot from Aÿ, Mareuil-sur-Aÿ, Ambonnay, Rilly-la-Montagne, Verzenay and Verzy; 30% chardonnay from Vitry, Sézannais and Côte des Blancs; 45% reserves from 2012, 2010 and 2009; full malolactic fermentation; aged 28 months on lees; 8g/L dosage; DIAM closure; around 1.2 million bottles annually

Billecart's enchanting Brut Réserve upholds its aspiration of impressive freshness and elegance, even in the presence of impressive levels of reserve wines, a generous 45% of the blend. This cuvée is a captivating contradiction, dressing one of Champagne's higher representations of meunier in one of the most delicate and graceful of attires. It glides onto the stage and sings with the pristine signature of the house, energised by the red apple and red berry fruits of meunier, with a breathtakingly refined melody of pure lemon zest, in a dazzling display of elegant, soft, crystalline chalk minerality and understated, fragrant elegance. Lees age furnishes subtle brioche and almond notes, while meunier lends supple approachability, without for a moment dipping its gaze from purity and definition, concluding with fresh, bright acidity, well-integrated dosage, gentle phenolic presence, good persistence and fine chalk mineral drive. Classic Billecart.

BILLECART-SALMON BRUT ROSÉ NV $$$

95 points • 2012 BASE VINTAGE • DISGORGED OCTOBER 2015 AND AUGUST 2016
• TASTED IN CHAMPAGNE AND AUSTRALIA

40% chardonnay from Vitry and Côte des Blancs; 30% pinot from Aÿ, Mareuil-sur-Aÿ, Ambonnay, Rilly-la-Montagne, Verzenay and Verzy; 30% meunier from Vallée de la Marne; 40% reserves from 2010, 2009 and 2008; just 7% pinot noir red wine from Mareuil-sur-Aÿ, more for aromatic effect than colour; full malolactic fermentation; 9g/L dosage; DIAM closure

Some 20% of Billecart's production is rosé (400,000 bottles), claimed to be the biggest proportion of rosé among Champagne's larger houses (though Moët may have just caught up). The utter restraint of the house places delicate rosés very close to its heart, dubbed internally 'champagne rosé' rather than 'rosé champagne'. Antoine recounts a tasting in which he poured the wine into black glasses for sommeliers. Not one identified it as a rosé. 'When my grandfather began producing rosés in the early 1960s, most thought it a fanciful, artificial wine that lacked purity,' he recalls. 'He persevered, convinced it would have its place. Those sceptics are now making their own!'

As precise and pretty as ever, this is classically restrained Billecart of epic refinement, pale-salmon hue and gorgeously restrained rose petal, red cherry and strawberry hull fruit. This cuvée has attained that wonderful place where lees age contributes great texture and mouthfeel, without diminishing purity or freshness. Delightfully understated, eminently fresh and elegantly persistent, it carries with grace and poise amidst fine chalk mineral texture, taut acid focus, impeccably pure persistence and a fine, creamy bead. Enjoy it in its ravishing youth.

BILLECART-SALMON EXTRA BRUT VINTAGE 2006 $$$

92 points • Disgorged June 2014 and August 2015 • Tasted in Champagne
and Australia

75% pinot noir from Aÿ; Mareuil-sur-Aÿ, Ambonnay, Rilly-la-Montagne, Verzenay, Verzy; 25%
chardonnay from Côte des Blancs; a little less than 20% pinot barrel-fermented; partial malolactic
fermentation; aged 6 years on lees; 3g/L dosage

Billecart is striving for more personality in its wines, and this release reveals the character and
dry structure of a ripe season, showcasing the diversity of the house in bridging its elegant cuvées
and its richer *sous bois* style. This cuvée has evolved into a more savoury and secondary style, with
a full straw yellow–hue, contrasting the roast nuts, brioche, spice and honey of lees age with the
grilled toast and gunpowder of reduction. In the current arc in its evolution it lacks generosity,
the ripe white peach and grilled pineapple of the season having faded, and its firm, dry phenolic
structure and grapefruit pith grip remaining, accented by partial barrel fermentation. This is
purposely a food champagne and is true to a lesser vintage, though it finishes with good length
of expansive pinot noir presence and well-integrated dosage.

BILLECART-SALMON CUVÉE SOUS BOIS BRUT NV $$$

95 points • 2007 base vintage • Disgorged November 2015 • Tasted in
Champagne and Australia

One-third of each champagne variety; meunier from Vallée de la Marne, pinot from Vallée de la
Marne and Montagne de Reims, chardonnay from Côte des Blancs; one-third reserve wines from
2006, 2005 and 2004, which Antoine describes as 'the fourth third so it doesn't fit in the bottle!';
partially oak-fermented; aged on lees in barrel with bâtonnage for 6 months; less than 10%
malolactic fermentation; 7g/L dosage; DIAM closure

Sous Bois is as distinctive for Billecart as its bold, modern label. 'With the diversity of
Champagne's regions and the rise of growers, it's increasingly important for us to produce
more interesting, small-production wines,' points out Antoine. *Sous bois* is literally 'under wood',
inspired by oak-fermented parcels destined for Billecart's top cuvées. Its aspiration is to uphold
the mandate of Billecart in freshness, tightness and elegance. With an average age of more than
a decade, this is a particularly mature non-vintage. It was released after the 2008 base due to
the level of malic acidity sustained in the ripe, powerful and rounded 2007 season. Retention
of 90–100% of malic acidity charges it with lively drive and toned lemon juice freshness,
contrasting an epic, swirling undercurrent of impressive magnitude and richness, with deep
strokes of caramel, honey, crème brûlée and roast nuts. It sings with classic Billecart precision,
while basking in the richness of barrel fermentation, beautifully integrated thanks to a decade of
lees age. It's silky, creamy, buttery and alluring, and as bold and commanding as its controversial
label. Don't serve it too cold, and be sure to present it in large glasses.

BILLECART-SALMON DEMI-SEC NV $$

89 points • 2013 BASE VINTAGE • DISGORGED APRIL 2015 • TASTED IN AUSTRALIA

40% meunier from Vallée de la Marne; 30% pinot from Aÿ, Mareuil-sur-Aÿ, Ambonnay, Rilly-la-Montagne, Verzenay and Verzy; 30% chardonnay from Vitry, Sézannais and Côte des Blancs; 45% reserves from 2012, 2010 and 2009; full malolactic fermentation; 45g/L dosage; DIAM closure

Again one of the better-crafted sweet champagnes on the shelves this year; the same base as the Brut Réserve charges it with the acidity and poise to handle its honeyed sweetness, up from 40g/L to 45g/L this year. This transforms the clean fruit precision that defines Billecart into candied citrus, lemon drops and glacé figs, with a creamy, sweet finish, well toned by balanced acidity, though marked by an earthiness on the finish I've not seen in this cuvée before. Well executed, but nothing on the clean purity of Brut Réserve.

BILLECART-SALMON BLANC DE BLANCS BRUT 2004 $$$$

97 points • DISGORGED FEBRUARY 2016 • TASTED IN AUSTRALIA

A blend of Le Mesnil-sur-Oger, Cramant, Avize and Chouilly; one-third fermented in 228-litre Burgundy barrels of around 10 years of age; 6g/L dosage

BdB 2004 makes a monumental declaration: from Billecart's proud position in the heart of pinot territory, this shows its command of the fabled chalk terroirs of the Côte des Blancs' A-list. From its introverted and stately magnificent stance two years ago it has intensified into a brilliantly luminous beacon that will continue to dazzle for decades. A wine of graceful allure, euphoric freshness and profound poise, it's breathtakingly elegant yet innately intense. Crystalline poise of fine-ground, salty chalk minerality, faintly flinty nuances and pronounced acid line announce expansive presence that has blossomed after 13 years. Four years on from its release, white citrus, apple and white stone fruits have gently begun to dim to reveal the magnificent hallmarks of maturity in brioche, butter and subtle spice. It culminates in profound persistence and an enticing interplay between chalk structure and long-aged complexity.

BILLECART-SALMON CUVÉE ELISABETH SALMON BRUT ROSÉ 2006 $$$$$

96 points • DISGORGED DECEMBER 2015 • TASTED IN CHAMPAGNE AND AUSTRALIA

50% pinot from Aÿ, Mareuil-sur-Aÿ, Ambonnay, Verzenay, Verzy; 50% chardonnay from Côte des Blancs; 8% pinot red wine from 40+ year-old vines yielding 25–30hL/hectare on a full south-facing slope in Valofroy on Mont du Gruguet in Mareuil-sur-Aÿ; 6g/L dosage; DIAM closure

The tightrope balance of long-aged rosé is one of Champagne's most challenging arts, and the restrained style of Billecart is flattering in the generous presence of the 2006 season. Strawberry and red cherry fruits have evolved to a toasty place of dark chocolate and coffee, though upholding the poise and definition of the house, thanks to a fine, long-lingering, beautifully focused acid line and the ever-present texture of fine, strong, mouth-filling chalk minerality. Côte des Blancs chardonnay confidently tones the presence of pinot noir. It holds with persistence and confidence, albeit developing faster, without the vibrancy and delicacy of the mesmerising 2002 before it. (No 2004 was made, since the red wine was not deemed to be of sufficient standard.)

Billecart-Salmon Cuvée Nicolas François Billecart 2002 $$$$

99 points • Disgorged October 2012 and April 2014 • Tasted in Australia and Champagne

60% pinot noir from Aÿ, Mareuil-sur-Aÿ, Ambonnay, Verzenay and Verzy; 40% Côte des Blancs chardonnay; 18% barrel-fermented in old oak casks; partial malolactic fermentation; 4g/L dosage; 50,000 bottles

Some champagnes volunteer their life story within seconds of first introduction, like overworked movie trailers that leave you fully convinced you've seen the film. Others churn in your consciousness for days, slowly unravelling their story long after the credits have rolled. NFB 2002 has played out a captivating script since my first dramatic encounter in mid-2013. Four years on, it's opening magnificently to display remarkable complexity, yet at every moment clinging to impeccable elegance, coiled focus of malic acid tension and exhilarating chalk mineral texture. Even at 15 years of age, it has barely moved, upholding brilliant primary definition of icy lemon citrus and fennel, with only subtle, graceful evolution of nougat, butter, honey, roast almonds and toast, promising decades of potential yet. As always, the greatness of Billecart is proclaimed not by impact or power, but by slowly rising complexity, astonishing chalk mineral presence of mouth-enveloping texture and a revelation of stunning persistence. Minerality cascades in ultra-fine detail, to the point of silkiness, yet simultaneously poised and confident. Delightful grace and intricate craftsmanship proclaim one of the great Billecarts of the modern era, a champagne with many characters and subplots to reveal, to be enjoyed slowly in the presence of the most intimate company – and ideally not for at least another decade.

Billecart-Salmon Cuvée Nicolas François Billecart 1996

99 points • Tasted in Champagne

Testimony to the sheer endurance of NFB in the greatest seasons, this is a magnificent bottle in impeccable condition, backward and fresh for 20 years of age. It preserves an excellent core of intensity of white peach fruit, fig and preserved lemon, holding with outstanding persistence and line. Tertiary hints of green olives and sweet pipe-smoke complexity are the only suggestions of its maturity, all the while sustaining excellent freshness and definition of lemon zest purity. It's still on the upward incline, with decades before it. Goodness.

Billecart-Salmon Cuvée Nicolas François Billecart 1995

98 points • Tasted in Champagne

Having attained its glorious peak at a grand 21 years of age, the outstanding and underrated 1995 season will hold its integrity for a decade yet. An excellent core of ripe lemon, white peach and fig is finished with gentle minerality and excellent persistence. Time has blessed it with wonderful allure of green olives, saffron, hints of smoke, even suggestions of chocolate and dried fruits. Wow.

The Champagne Guide

BILLECART-SALMON GRANDE CUVÉE 1998 $$$$$

98 points • DISGORGED OCTOBER 2009 • TASTED IN AUSTRALIA

60% pinot from Aÿ, Mareuil-sur-Aÿ, Ambonnay, Verzenay, Verzy; 40% chardonnay from Côte des Blancs; partial malolactic fermentation; 4.5g/L dosage

Grande Cuvée is no more, but one of the great champagnes of recent times has not gone quietly into the night. Its final vintage holds its own, returning for yet another rousing encore this year. At a full 19 years of age, Grande Cuvée has grown into an iridescent gleam of yellow straw. Its core of white fruits of all kinds has evolved through thick orchestral scoring of toasty, spicy complexity and reductive, flinty gunpowder. Tightly wound and enchantingly focused, it has now morphed into all the fanfare of tertiary complexity of pipe smoke, green olives, burnt butter and mixed spice, all the while tightly hugging rails of crystalline-pure acidity. It holds long on the finish with outstretched magnificence, an epiphany of relentless persistence underlined by consummately fine-spun, deep-set textural presence that froths and foams with sea salt minerality. Grand Cuvée has finally achieved its peak. Billecart's resolve to redirect its top fruit to Nicolas François Billecart is certainly noble, but Grande Cuvée will forever be missed. Farewell, old friend.

BILLECART-SALMON LE CLOS SAINT-HILAIRE 1999 $$$$$

95 points • DISGORGED JULY 2014 • TASTED IN AUSTRALIA

1 hectare clos in Mareuil-sur-Aÿ on silty-clayish-limestone 7 metres above chalk; planted exclusively to pinot noir since 1964 and managed biodynamically since 2003; yielding a minuscule 40-45hL/ hectare, less than one bottle per vine; harvested in two passes at full ripeness; two cuvées vinified in situ; fully fermented in 15-year-old oak barrels; no malolactic fermentation; zero dosage; 6750 bottles, only in top vintages

Le Clos Saint-Hilaire has no right to its profound echelon. It is but a premier cru, although this is more a reflection on the inadequacies of an oversimplified cru system. More significantly, in soil (deeper and less chalky than, for instance, the Clos des Goisses at the other end of the village) and in aspect (due east, far from the sought-after south-facing orientation), it has no claims to greatness. It is but a flat expanse beside the press house in the village. The genius of François Domi and the painstaking attention to detail of Billecart play a dramatic role. I could not name another wine at this level, anywhere in the world, of which the same could be said.

Alongside Krug Clos d'Ambonnay, Billecart Le Clos Saint-Hilaire is the king of blanc de noirs. It was conceived as Antoine and François Roland-Billecart stood on the wall of the clos late one night during harvest in 1995. With plenty of red wine in stock for rosé, they decided they could afford to put this pinot noir in the cellar for a decade to see how it looked on its own.

Le Clos Saint-Hilaire's fourth release is not the towering masterpiece of its predecessor, with its impeccable freshness and profound mineral clarity. François Domi describes it as opposite in personality to the 1998. I was the first outside the house to taste it, and on pouring he exclaimed, 'Le rosé de Saint-Hilaire!' It's deep in colour, a full yellow-gold hue, true to its power and depth in encapsulating a warm season at 18 years of age. Le Clos Saint-Hilaire has attained monumental proportions in the generous 1999 season. Its ripe generosity is flung to the extremes of pineapple, golden delicious apple and fig. Eighteen years of maturity have piled on mixed spice, golden fruit cake and roast hazelnuts, even the beginning of nuances of green olives and pipe smoke. It finishes dry and firm, with chalk minerality and bitter phenolic grip conspiring, its dryness accentuated by zero dosage and full retention of malic acidity. A Clos Saint-Hilaire to drink now.

BOIZEL

(Bwah-zel)

5/10

46 AVENUE DE CHAMPAGNE 51200 ÉPERNAY

www.boizel.com

ÉPERNAY   FRANCE

CHAMPAGNE

BOIZEL

MAISON FONDÉE EN 1834

Evelyne Roques-Boizel is the fifth generation to head Boizel. Seven hectares of estate vineyards are complemented with long-term contracts with growers in about 50 villages, boosted in 1994 after an injection of funds from the Lanson-BCC group. Boizel's clean, fruity style is achieved through fermentation in stainless steel vats at 18°C, full malolactic fermentation, and long ageing of non-vintage cuvées of at least three years. Vintage wines are aged five to seven years, after a small proportion of vinification in barrel. Back labels declare the blend and disgorgement date.

BOIZEL BRUT RÉSERVE NV $$

91 points • 2012 BASE VINTAGE • DISGORGED JULY 2015 • TASTED IN AUSTRALIA

55% pinot from Mailly-Champagne, Venteuil and Pierry; 30% chardonnay from Vertus, Chouilly, Cuis and Nogent-l'Ábbesse; 15% meunier from Mont-Saint-Pére, Vandières and Châtillon-sur-Marne; 30% reserve wines; 3 years on lees; 8g/L dosage

Boizel's entry wine is a citrusy and fruity style that contrasts lemon zest crunch and strawberry hull notes with the subtle nougat and brioche characters of three years on lees. Low dosage keeps the acid tension in focus through a finish of line and length. There's character and fruit integrity here, albeit in a somewhat coarse and simplistic style.

Boizel Brut Rosé NV $$$

91 points • 2012 BASE VINTAGE • DISGORGED JULY 2015 • TASTED IN AUSTRALIA

50% pinot from Cumières and Les Riceys; 30% meunier; 20% chardonnay from Vertus, Chouilly and Nogent-l'Ábbesse; 20% reserve wines; 3 years on lees; 8% pinot noir red wine; 8g/L dosage

A delicate rosé that proclaims pinot noir in gentle tones of pomegranate, watermelon, strawberry hull and red cherries, framed in a creamy mouthfeel and subtle almond meal notes derived from three years on lees. Tannin grip is firm yet fine and well-poised for its restrained mood.

Boizel Grand Vintage 2004 $$$

94 points • TASTED IN AUSTRALIA

50% chardonnay from Le Mesnil-sur-Oger, Chouilly and Vertus; 40% pinot from Mailly and Bisseuil; 10% meunier from Cumières; 7-10 years on lees; 6g/L dosage

An impressively bright medium-straw hue at 12 years of age heralds a complex take on the enduring 2004 season, charged with primary grapefruit, lemon zest, fennel and apple, and layered with an enticing complexity of struck flint. Its bottle-developed secondary complexity is building slowly, with understated nuances of almond meal and brioche, but declared more dramatically in the finely structured mouthfeel of long lees age. Impressive.

Boizel Joyau de France Brut Millésimé 2000 $$$$

92 points • DISGORGED MARCH 2014 • TASTED IN AUSTRALIA

65% pinot noir from Mailly-Champagne, Pierry, Vertus and Cumières; 35% chardonnay from Le Mesnil-sur-Oger, Avize, Oger and Vertus; 13 years on lees; 10% oak; 7g/L dosage

Two years ago I wrote that this cuvée had attained the end of its life with confidence and grace. The same disgorgement today has begun to teeter over the brink. It upholds the glowing full straw-yellow hue of the 2000 harvest at 16 years of maturity, presenting tertiary complexity of coffee bean, cocoa, gingernut biscuits and now nuances of pipe smoke and smouldering hearth. The finish is beginning to contract and dry out, though acidity, dosage and texture remain confidently entwined.

A winter wonderland in Trépail, one of the highest villages on the Montagne de Reims, where the snow lingers long.

BOLLINGER

(Boh-lahn-zhay)

10/10

20 BOULEVARD DU MARÉCHAL DE LATTRE DE TASSIGNY 51160 AŸ

www.champagne-bollinger.com

CHAMPAGNE
BOLLINGER
MAISON FONDÉE EN 1829

It's another world at Bollinger. Take everything you know about large champagne houses, the way champagne tastes, the way it's fermented, the way it's aged, even the ownership of the vineyards and the companies, and brace yourself for a very different story at Bollinger. I've met with the good Bollinger folk numerous times in recent years in Australia and in their illustrious maison in Aÿ, and on every occasion I have been astounded by the pace of change. If Bollinger wasn't your style ten years ago, come hither! There's never been a better time to bask in the glory of this legendary house. These are ravishing champagnes that now rank high among the very best of the region. James Bond, you've finally got it right.

The Bollinger house style has long been a love-it-or-hate-it champagne, oft maligned for the aldehydes that can develop as a result of oxidation during barrel ageing. Oxidation during fermentation is positive, but prior to fermentation it suppresses fruit, and post-fermentation it dulls the wine. The priority now is to suppress oxidation, creating fresher and less aldehydic wines, an imperative that the house balances delicately with its mandate of using as little sulphur dioxide preservative as possible. Exacting attention to the finer details has transformed Bollinger over the past decade, lifting its wines to the cleanest, most precise, least aldehydic it has ever made.

In early 2013 Mathieu Kauffmann announced his surprise resignation as chef de cave of Bollinger. The house appointed Gilles Descôtes as his replacement. After almost a decade of experience on Bollinger's tasting panel, overseeing the estate vineyards, managing grower relations and taking charge of production in 2012, he was a natural choice. While some questioned his appointment, the house was rightfully proud to introduce a chef de cave with a background in viticulture rather than oenology.

There are eleven facets that set Bollinger apart among champagne houses, beginning in the vineyards.

ESTATE VINEYARDS

Bollinger is a champagne of cathedral proportions: massive, impacting and magnificent. Its weight derives foremost from estate-grown pinot noir. 'We have pinot noir in our blood,' says Descôtes. 'We are nicknamed "The Burgundy house"!' Every cuvée has a minimum of 60% pinot noir, and an impressive 60% of the grapes come from estate vineyards. (The only other house boasting such proportions is Louis Roederer.) Centred around Aÿ, Champagne's pinot noir epicentre, Bollinger's mighty 164 hectares comprise 85% grand cru and premier cru vineyards. 'We liken ourselves more with champagne growers than houses, since our vineyards are such an important part of our house,'

Ageing reserve wines on cork necessitates the tedious and expensive process of riddling by hand at Bollinger.

Descôtes declares. Bollinger allocates 500 man hours per hectare each year to manage its vineyards, compared with 380 on average in Champagne.

The house has grown production from 2.5 to 3 million bottles in recent years, though always upholding at least 60% of supply from estate vineyards. In 2015, Bollinger purchased one hectare of grand cru vineyard at a cost ot €1.5 million. 'We aspire to grow a bit in volume and a bit in price,' explains president Jérôme Philipon. 'Our long-term plan in 10 to 15 years is to be able to supply 3.5 million bottles.'

The policy of the house is to only buy grapes that it can assess visually. It thus only sources from the Marne, and favours Aÿ and the nearby villages of Louvois, Mareuil-sur-Aÿ, Verzy and Verzenay, though the great Côte des Blancs crus of Le Mesnil-sur-Oger, Cramant, Oger and especially Avize and Cuis are also important. Aÿ is at the core of every Bollinger blend and Verzenay ranks second, with elegance to foil the opulence of Aÿ. Bouzy holds a special place, too. The house is also privileged to strong holdings in Avenay-Val-d'Or and Tauxières-Mutry.

Grape maturity is pushed a little further at Bollinger through careful choice of harvest date, a blessing the house attributes to vineyard ownership. When I visited on the second-last day of harvest 2014, Bollinger's red wines for rosé had only just started fermenting, while most at Veuve Clicquot had already finished. Bollinger's balance of fruit is sourced from winegrowers who have worked with the house for many generations (every one of 120 parcels is vinified separately at Bollinger; there is no purchase of *vins sur lattes*). This accounts for the consistency, depth and complexity in Bollinger's wines.

The house is experimenting with organics in a few of its plots, though doesn't aspire to seeking certification.

NEW PRESS HOUSE

To reduce pre-ferment oxidation, a new press centre was constructed in neighbouring Mareuil-sur-Aÿ, within line of sight of the maison in Aÿ, in time for the 2003 vintage. Almost all the grapes of estate vineyards are transported by truck or tractor to Mareuil, where eight-tonne pneumatic presses are worked 24/7 to press 200 tonnes daily. Every grape variety, every cru and sometimes even individual growers are kept separate. To facilitate long ageing, no tailles is used in Bollinger's cuvées.

In 2013, Bollinger doubled its red wine processing capacity in response to increasing demand for rosé. Since 2005, the house has produced all of its own red wine from tiny yields of just 30hL/hectare. When I visited during harvest 2014, I was impressed by a stringent team of eight, fanatically working the sorting table as tiny grapes for red wines arrived at the press centre.

BARREL FERMENTATION

Bollinger uses only the cuvée (the first and best pressing) and ferments under temperature control in both stainless steel tanks and oak barrels. Use of barrels for fermentation and ageing is a key element in reinforcing Bollinger's house style, and Descôtes goes to great lengths to retain freshness and fruit purity through diligent barrel cleaning and cellar hygiene. Every barrel is tasted post-fermentation and again before blending.

The magnitude of this task becomes apparent after witnessing more than 3300 champagne barrels of 225-litre capacity stacked long and high, row after row, plus 208 barrels of 400-litre capacity, made by Bollinger in 1903, and some recently acquired new 350–400L 'pipes'. The house has grown its barrel stocks from 2500 in 2005 to 3500 today. To increase consistency, old barrels of at least three years of age are purchased annually from Bollinger-owned Burgundy négociant Chanson and maintained until they are 20–30 years old, by what Bollinger claims to be the last in-house cooper in Champagne. Bollinger's vintage wines are 100% barrel fermented, as are all of its reserve wines, and any other parcels with sufficient acidity to handle 6–7 months in barrel.

Comparing vins clairs (fermented still base wines) fermented in stainless steel and oak is enlightening, the barrel-fermented samples in no way woody (thanks to the age of Bollinger's barrels), but better integrated, more textured, more complex and better balanced. Bollinger considers barrels an insurance policy for the wine, providing controlled oxidation, and drawing out the longevity of Grande Année to 20 years and beyond.

FAMILY OWNERSHIP

Bollinger is the largest independent champagne house after Louis Roederer, owned and run completely by members of the Bollinger family. This provides the freedom to uphold practices, such as longer ageing under cork, that might be considered infeasible under a large owner.

LONGER AGEING

Bollinger keeps its cuvées on lees for long periods: a minimum of three years and an average of three and a half years for non-vintages (until recently two and a half years), and eight years or longer for Grande Année (previously six). This is considered crucial for producing small bubbles and very fine, velvety textures.

More than 12 million bottles are held in storage in Bollinger's 5.5 kilometres of cellars over four levels under Aÿ, plus an additional 750,000 reserve magnums (and growing) of grand and premier cru pinot noir and chardonnay, fermented in barrels, bottled with natural corks and kept for between five and 15 years, or longer. There is a desire to increase production, but only at the very slow rate of 5000 bottles per year, so as to uphold quality. To sell one more bottle in five years' time, the house needs to put five more bottles in the cellar now.

Infused with the resilience of barrel maturation, Bollinger's white cuvées are rock-solid, and I rarely encounter bottle variation whenever and wherever in the world I taste them. They also possess propensity for great longevity (but its rosés are best drunk as youthful as possible). Her Majesty the Queen of England cellars her Special Cuvée for 10 years, and reportedly did not pop the 2001 disgorgement until 2010!

DEEP RESERVES

Bollinger's non-vintage cuvées are blessed with astonishing depth of reserves, unrivalled by any other house besides Krug itself. As this book is going to print, the house is blending its 2016 base Special Cuvée, comprising just 43% 2016 and an enormous 57% of reserve wines – the majority from 2015, along with 2014, 2013, 2012, 2011 and reserve magnums of 2005, 2006 and 2007. The small percentage of older reserves are considered crucial for maintaining consistency in this blend of a massive total of 400 wines in all.

AGEING UNDER CORK

Bollinger upholds that ageing its reserve wines in magnum on natural cork rather than crown seal affords more complexity, a practice followed by a small number of growers and small houses, but no other sizeable house. Six grams of sugar is added for a *prise de mousse*

(carbonic fermentation) to produce a light sparkle of two atmospheres to retain fresh flavour and aroma in these reserve magnums, dubbed 'aromatic bombs' by the house.

It's not hard to see why very few houses age reserve wines under cork: it necessitates riddling and disgorgement by hand, not to mention wastage to cork taint. It takes a team of 10 people three weeks to open 75,000 reserve magnums by hand for Special Cuvée and Rosé. It's a tedious and expensive process to check every bottle for cork taint by nose. Workers are instructed not to wear perfume on disgorgement days, and not to front up at all if they have a cold. The house reports a rejection rate to cork taint of less than half of 1%, but admits that even this is too much. The benefits of DIAM corks in eliminating cork taint are acknowledged, but they are considered aesthetically inferior by the house, and the preference is for contact with natural, unglued cork.

It's not only Special Cuvée that's produced using a labour-intensive process at Bollinger. Vintage wines are hand disgorged, with every bottle tasted at disgorgement, and non-vintage rosé is hand riddled.

Asked about the practice of ageing under cork, Christian Pol Roger allegedly replied: 'It's a great idea, but we are not as crazy as you are at Bollinger!'

MALOLACTIC FERMENTATION

In the past, malolactic fermentation occurred haphazardly, only in those barrels and tanks that happened to progress naturally. In pursuit of greater consistency, malolactic bacteria are now introduced to ensure systematic completion of malolactic fermentation.

ONE BLEND

All 2 million bottles of Bollinger's Special Cuvée are tiraged at once in a single blend in February, to maintain the consistency of each blend. To further promote freshness, Bollinger disgorges three times a year, with each disgorgement from the same original blend, yet subtly different due to a different length of time on lees. Bottles are aged on lees at least three years, and on average three and a half years.

Disappointingly, disgorgement dates are not stamped on non-vintage bottles, although they are on the vintage wines, and regrettably the house now declines to volunteer disgorgement dates and base and reserve vintages when asked. This is a pity, especially for a cuvée blessed with such incredible depth of reserves. Labelling occurs shortly after disgorgement, so the labelling date provides a good indication. The first two digits of the labelling code on the neck of Special Cuvée and Rosé are the year, and the next three digits are the number of the day of that year, so L1626010 means the 260th day of 2016.

The letter on the cork is the month of disgorgement and the number is the year, so 6I is September 2016.

MODERN FACILITIES

To further reduce post-ferment oxidation, in 2012 Bollinger installed one of Champagne's most modern disgorgement lines. A computerised system checks for defects in the seal of cork-sealed bottles, and rejects 3–4%. (If only it could detect cork taint, too!) When I visited, a cart was stacked 10 high with rejects destined to be used as liqueur for dosage.

Since 2013, Bollinger has introduced a system of 'jetting' at disgorgement. A tiny droplet of water is sprayed to foam the wine and push out oxygen. Internal trials have revealed this process to greatly diminish oxidation during disgorgement. Bottling facilities were updated in 2005, 2008 and again in 2012, this time in preparation for a new bottle design.

NEW BOTTLE

In 2012, Bollinger launched its gloriously refined '1846' bottle with a wider base, narrower neck and elegant curves, based on an original champagne bottle found in the Bollinger cellars dated 1846. The benefits are more than just aesthetic. With a neck three millimetres narrower, the new bottle has a neck cross-sectional area 20% smaller than the last, which slows the oxygen exchange, better for ageing. This neck is also said to take up 40–50% less oxygen during disgorgement.

This year I have been disconcerted to encounter random oxidation in bottles of Bollinger La Grande Année 2007, 2005 and R.D. 2002. Subsequent bottles were on form. As always, request a replacement if you encounter a bottle out of condition.

For a champagne of breadth, depth and grandeur, and one that is readily available and affordable, Bollinger is in a world of its own. It's no surprise the house broke all its sales records in value and volume in 2015 and cannot keep up with demand, imposing allocations in every market.

BOLLINGER SPECIAL CUVÉE BRUT NV $$

95 points • 2012 BASE VINTAGE • DISGORGED APRIL 2016 • TASTED IN AUSTRALIA
95 points • 2011 BASE VINTAGE • DISGORGED MARCH 2015 • TASTED IN CHAMPAGNE

The complexity and richness of Special Cuvée is unparalleled among the entry-level non-vintage blends of every champagne house, short of ascending to the mesosphere of Krug. Its grand recipe explains why. A blend of 60% pinot noir, 25% chardonnay and 15% meunier, it's built on incredible depth of 50–60% reserves (see 'Deep Reserves', opposite). Further intensity is derived from 30–40% of the blend in oak barrels, and a very high proportion of grand cru and premier cru fruit sources (more than 85%). Post-blending, the wine matures for between three and four years on lees in the cellar before it is disgorged and a light dosage of 8g/L is added. This cuvée represents 90% of the production of the house – more than 2.5 million bottles annually.

Benchmark Bollinger, fresh and vivacious, yet wonderfully resonant with all the depth and triumphant complexity that set Special Cuvée apart. A universe of complexity spans light years of black cherries, plums, fresh lemon zest, red apple, even the richness of ripe peach and fig. Deep reserves allow primary fruit to speak articulately, reverberating softly with Bollinger's signature notes of ginger, dried nectarine, mixed spice, toast, brioche, honey and roast nuts. For all this, it upholds achingly pristine citrus zest freshness throughout, riding on a vibrant acid line, culminating in a masterful crescendo of fine, frothing, salt and iodine-infused minerality. Black cherry fruit lingers long and profound. Special Cuvée remains one of the finest entry NVs on the planet.

Bollinger Rosé Brut NV $$$

96 points • Disgorged September 2016 • Tasted in Australia
96 points • Disgorged October 2015 • Tasted in Champagne

Bollinger Rosé NV has doubled in volume since its much-celebrated introduction in 2008, though it still represents just 250,000 bottles, merely one-tenth of Special Cuvée. The blend is now slightly different to Special Cuvée, here 62% pinot noir, 24% chardonnay and 14% meunier. Pinot noir red wine from the grand cru villages of Verzenay (predominantly) and Aÿ is given long pre-ferment maceration and matured in barrel for 12 months. The house prides itself on its red wine, and such is its strength, concentration, depth of colour and robust tannin structure that a tiny 5–6% is all that is required. Like Special Cuvée, it is matured 3–4 years on lees. The blend is more than 85% grand crus and premier crus, with a light dosage of 8g/L.

This is breathtaking rosé, full-bodied in every way, with magnificent body, spellbinding purity and impeccable poise. Greater elegance is the mandate, and it meets the brief with effortless grace, a medium-salmon hue and vibrant liveliness in the midst of profound depth. Characterful poise of red cherry, pink grapefruit, wild strawberry and fig expresses greater freshness than ever, meeting the subtle spice, coffee bean and dark chocolate nuances of secondary development. It's all intricately laced together with fine-tuned acidity, a creamy bead and subtle tannin texture that reinforces soft chalk mineral texture, lingering long on a refined finish.

Bollinger La Grande Année 2007 $$$$

97 points • Disgorged September 2016 • Tasted in Australia

70% pinot, mainly from Aÿ and Verzenay; 30% chardonnay, mainly from Avize, Cramant and Oger; a blend of 14 crus, 91% grand cru and 9% premier cru; entirely fermented and matured in oak barrels; aged under natural cork 8 years on lees; 7g/L dosage

Radiating through a bright, full straw-yellow hue, this is a succulent and enticing LGA that contrasts the tension of 2007 with the reverberating depth of Aÿ pinot noir and all the structure and fanfare of small-barrel fermentation. Layers of spice are packed around a magnificent core of pronounced black cherry fruit, before exploding into a universe of Bollinger complexity of mixed spice, ginger and roast nuts. The depth and character of pinot noir build incrementally on the palate to profound proportions. The creamy and silky effect of barrel fermentation caresses fine chalk minerality, flowing seamlessly into a very long, full and captivating finish of dark chocolate. One bottle was oxidised.

Bollinger 007 Millésime 2009 $$$$

95 points • Tasted in Australia

68% pinot noir, 39% from Aÿ and 29% from Verzenay; 32% chardonnay, 16% from Le Mesnil-sur-Oger, 8% from Avize and 8% from Cramant, entirely fermented and matured in oak barrels; aged under natural cork 6 years on lees; 7g/L dosage

All the fast-paced action of Bolly is on show in wide-screen high definition in this warm vintage grand cru blend of more than two-thirds pinot noir. As ever for Bollinger, fermentation in small oak barrels amplifies its complexity, yet for all of its drama and theatrics, it finishes with tension and poise.

The Champagne Guide

BOLLINGER LA GRANDE ANNÉE ROSÉ 2007 $$$$$

97 points • TASTED IN AUSTRALIA

72% pinot, mainly from Aÿ and Verzenay; 28% chardonnay, mainly from Avize, Cramant and Oger; a blend of 14 crus, 92% grand cru and 8% premier cru; entirely fermented and matured in oak barrels; aged under natural cork 8 years on lees; 5% still red wine from La Côte aux Enfants; 7g/L dosage

LGA Rosé is LGA with a tiny inclusion of red wine from the same vintage. The effect is profound, beckoning from its radiant, full salmon-copper gown with exuberant, flamboyant and extroverted appeal. Its purity of red cherry fruits and violet fragrance are heightened even by its tiny dose of red wine, furnishing cherry kernel and anise nuances. Understated nuances of secondary complexity in golden fruit cake, roast almonds and fruit mince spice will heighten with age. Fine tannin grip and chalk minerality lace seamlessly on a very long and refined finish that lingers very long with red cherry purity.

BOLLINGER LA GRANDE ANNÉE ROSÉ 2005 $$$$$

96 points • TASTED IN CHAMPAGNE

72% pinot noir, 28% chardonnay; a blend of 13 crus, mainly Aÿ and Verzenay for pinot noir, and Avize, Chouilly and Le Mesnil-sur-Oger for chardonnay; 95% grand crus and 5% premier cru; 5% still red wine from La Côte Aux Enfants; entirely fermented and matured in oak barrels; aged under natural cork 8.5 years on lees; 7g/L dosage

Even a tiny dose of just 5% red wine heightens the purity and depth of La Grande Année to gorgeous black cherry fruits, succulent strawberries, cherry kernel and anise, hovering above a grand expanse of golden fruit cake, anise, vanilla, even Turkish delight. It intricately laces beautifully fine tannin structure with the grip and depth of the warm 2005 season, lingering very long and accurate with red cherry purity. Two years after release, it's built just the right amount of flesh to contrast the dry extract of the season. It's attained its full magnificence already, a vintage to drink early.

BOLLINGER LA GRANDE ANNÉE 2005 $$$$

95 points • TASTED IN CHAMPAGNE AND AUSTRALIA

70% pinot, mainly from Aÿ and Verzenay; 30% chardonnay, mainly from Avize, Chouilly and Le Mesnil-sur-Oger; a blend of 13 crus, 95% grand cru and 5% premier cru; a higher proportion of pinot noir than usual because 2005 was believed to be a great season for pinot noir; entirely fermented and matured in oak barrels; aged under natural cork 8.5 years on lees; 6g/L dosage

This is a vintage that captures the full magnificence of Bollinger exuberance, with a fruit integrity rarely seen in 2005, blossoming to even greater voluptuous succulence two years on from release. It glows with mirabelle plums, figs and red apples, oozes with ripe peach and resonates with the depth of black cherries, before launching into a universe of Bollinger complexity in golden fruit cake, spice, pâtisserie and roast nuts. The depth and body of Bollinger confidently steps up to the firm structure, dry astringency and grapefruit-like grip of the season, built more on phenolic presence than acid line, yet with the flesh, drive and persistence to carry it, and at this age more silkiness than ever, culminating in a crescendo of seamless persistence. An earlier-drinking Bollinger and a great take on 2005. One bottle was oxidised.

BOLLINGER R.D. EXTRA BRUT 2002 $$$$$

97 points • DISGORGED NOVEMBER 2015 • TASTED IN AUSTRALIA
98 points • TASTED IN CHAMPAGNE

R.D. is Bollinger's 'Récemment Dégorgé', which confusingly is not necessarily 'recently disgorged', but a vintage of La Grande Année that has aged longer on its lees. The blend has more chardonnay than usual, 60% pinot noir and 40% chardonnay from 16 grand crus and seven premier crus, with less dosage than the LGA rendition: just 3–4g/L. The 2002 was an exhilarating LGA of driving energy and a razor edge of structure that barely evolved across the years of its release cycle. It naturally makes for a brilliant and enduring R.D. – though double the price is a lot to pay. It's now had five more years on lees (13 all up) and will effortlessly take another decade in its stride. It still holds youthful dynamism and focus, projecting all the exuberance of pinot noir's red cherry and plum fruits, striking a wonderful interplay with the mixed spice of barrel fermentation and the integration of 15 years of age, creating creamy depth amidst tightly honed focus. It's charged with all the gingernut biscuits, Christmas pudding, nougat, brioche, dried pear and honey that we love from Bollinger, concluding in epic line and length. I love R.D. 2002 and have opened more than a dozen bottles to showcase at masterclasses and dinners around the country. Sadly its age under cork makes every bottle different and some display some oxidation. The freshest and most magnificent I've seen it is at the house itself.

BOLLINGER VIEILLES VIGNES FRANÇAISES 2006 $$$$$

98 points • DISGORGED JULY 2016 • TASTED IN CHAMPAGNE

100% Aÿ pinot noir; no chaptalisation; entirely fermented and matured in small oak barrels; aged under natural cork 9 years on lees; the maturity and body of 2006 warranted a very low dosage of 4g/L; 3300 bottles

Vieilles Vignes Française is one of Champagne's rarest, most legendary and most distinctive cuvées. It is the product of two tiny plots adjacent to the house within Aÿ, maintained in memory of the way champagne was grown pre-phylloxera: non-grafted and non-trellised, in the traditional 'en foule' (without order) layering system and worked entirely by hand and sometimes by horse. Dense planting and severe pruning reduces yields by as much as one-third, producing particularly ripe and concentrated juice. It's always the first vineyard that Bollinger harvests, and usually a special dispensation must be requested to harvest before picking is officially open. The aim is to harvest at 11 or 11.5 degrees potential, not over 12 or 13, to create a cuvée of power with personality and yet balance, freshness and approachable drinkability.

I was privileged to the very first tasting of VVF 2006 outside Bollinger's winemaking team, to the infinite delight and stunned surprise of the small group I was hosting in Champagne that week. Having just walked the vines themselves, we were enraptured by the sheer confidence of this cuvée, abounding with the inimitable presence of its unique site and unusual method. Projecting a full straw hue, this is a wine of profound depth and presence, with red Burgundy-like expansiveness and a peacock's-tail flourish of theatrical proportions. In volume and sheer persistence it takes champagne to an altogether higher plateau, layered with succulent mirabelle plums and figs, framed in epic spice, apple cake, gingernut biscuit and baked plum. Such dimensions in the warm 2006 season lend a sensation of ripe-fruit phenolic grip, which has been expertly controlled, melding seamlessly with fine mineral texture. A revelation of line and length, enduring into tomorrow, VVF 2006 is profound and strong, yet ever so fit.

The Champagne Guide

BRUNO PAILLARD

(Broo-no Peye-yard)

7/10

AVENUE DE CHAMPAGNE 51100 REIMS

www.champagnebrunopaillard.com

Champagne

BRUNO PAILLARD

Reims - France

*W*hen former Lanson-BCC director and CIVC communications director Bruno Paillard set out to establish his own champagne brand in 1981, he sold his Jaguar to finance the operation. 'It takes three generations to create a house,' he says. 'But there are some advantages starting three centuries after everyone else!' Three and a half decades on, his finely crafted cuvées are evidence of what can be achieved with sufficient connections and determination.

It's no simple thing to establish a champagne house, and when Paillard set out he had no land, no stock, no vineyards and no right to even purchase fruit. What he did have was a great network and considerable knowledge. Back then, a regulation banned any upstart from purchasing fruit, so, instead, he sourced wines from earlier vintages to establish his brand and gain purchasing rights.

A generation later, Paillard crafts 400,000–500,000 bottles annually – 'small enough to hand-craft, but large enough to make the hard decisions and to be selective!' he says. The freedom to be selective is fundamental for Paillard, and he sets the rare precedent of selling half the fruit he presses, all of his second pressings, and anything else that doesn't meet the standard for his blends.

Sourcing spans 35 villages, with 32 hectares of estate vines supplying an impressive 65% of requirements. Chardonnay is sourced exclusively from the Côte des Blancs, pinot from the Montagne de Reims and Les Riceys in the Aube, and meunier from the Montagne de Reims and the south-facing slopes of the eastern reaches of the Vallée de la Marne. Vineyards are ploughed to encourage deep roots and worked with no herbicides, calling for a vineyard worker for every two hectares, rather than the average three hectares. Paillard says it takes 5–8 years to get the results he wants. 'A lot of people thought we were crazy to work this way!' he admits.

Paillard has been progressive from the outset, leading the way in using a gyropalette in Champagne, and was the first in the region to publish the disgorgement date on every bottle – more than controversial when he set out in 1983. Today, his website is super informative.

He built his winemaking facility next door to Piper-Heidsieck in Bezannes on the outskirts of Reims in 1990, and expanded its capacity in 2000. Every parcel is vinified separately in 100 tanks and 400 old oak barrels purchased after three vintages, and kept for eight or nine. A further 100 barrels hold reserve wines. One-fifth of all base wines are fermented and matured in barrels, so as not to dominate the blends, with the exception of his Nec Plus Ultra cuvée, which is entirely barrel fermented. All cuvées are aged long, with

Brut NV and Rosé enjoying three years on lees, Blanc de Blancs four, Vintage eight and Nec Plus Ultra 11–12.

In 1985, Paillard established a reserve solera which today comprises between 25% and 51% of each of his multi-vintage cuvées (as he prefers to call them). All cuvées are extra brut, with low dosages of between 3g/L and 6g/L.

Paillard devotes 10–20% of his time to responsibilities to support the region, and is currently chair of the Appellation Committee of the CIVC, overseeing the monumental task of updating the region's boundaries. He is ably assisted by his daughter, Alice, who takes responsibility for sales and marketing of the house.

BRUNO PAILLARD PREMIÈRE CUVÉE BRUT NV $$

93 points • DISGORGED APRIL 2016 • TASTED IN AUSTRALIA
94 points • DISGORGED APRIL 2013 • TASTED IN AUSTRALIA

45% pinot noir from the Montagne de Reims and Les Riceys, 33% chardonnay from the northern Côte des Blancs, 22% meunier from the Vallée de la Marne; majority from 89 estate parcels; 40% reserve solera of 25 vintages back to 1985; 20% fermented in old barrels; sourced from 35 villages; 3 years on lees; less than 6g/L dosage; 60% of the production of the house

Complexity meets character in a style led by pinot noir in primary red cherry and wild strawberry fruit, backed by the lemon zest of chardonnay and the subtle brioche and roast almond notes of at least four years of lees age. Lingering acidity draws out a long finish, with subtle dry earthiness in the April 2016 disgorgement rescued by bright acid line.

BRUNO PAILLARD BLANC DE BLANCS GRAND CRU NV $$$

92 points • DISGORGED SEPTEMBER 2015 • TASTED IN AUSTRALIA

36 parcels in Oger and Le Mesnil-sur-Oger; reserve solera of 25 vintages back to 1985; at least 4 years on lees; 4.5 atmospheres of pressure; 5g/L dosage

Grapefruit, apple and pear fruit define a style of structure, concentration and drive, with at least four years of bottle age contributing notes of nutmeg. The depth of Oger lends notes of orange, yet it retains its lemon focus in a long finish of grainy chalk minerality. A blanc de blancs of body, depth and character.

BRUNO PAILLARD PREMIÈRE CUVÉE ROSÉ EXTRA BRUT NV $$$

94 points • DISGORGED MARCH 2016 • TASTED IN AUSTRALIA
96 points • DISGORGED SEPTEMBER 2014 • TASTED IN AUSTRALIA

Majority pinot noir with a little chardonnay and pinot noir red wine; majority sourced from 89 estate parcels in 12 crus; reserve solera of 25 vintages back to 1985; 3 years on lees; less than 6g/L dosage; 22-24% of the production of the house

A pretty and restrained rosé of ultra-pale salmon hue and elegant pomegranate, strawberry and watermelon flavours. In time, flickers of black cherries emerge. It's lighter on its feet and more subtle than previous blends, with a delicate and graceful air, driven by a structure of fine chalk minerality. The September 2014 disgorgement is a delightful union between elegant structure, expressive fruit presence and characterful intrigue.

Bruno Paillard Blanc de Blancs Brut 2004 $$$

95 points • Disgorged March 2012 • Tasted in Australia

100% Côte des Blancs with 40% Le Mesnil and 40% Oger; 4.5 atmospheres of pressure; 8 years on lees; 5g/L dosage

Testimony to the heights of Bruno Paillard's fruit sources, craftsmanship and long ageing, this is a blanc de blancs of allure, finesse, elegance and grand persistence that has evolved magnificently in the years since its release, even now from an earlier disgorgement than I tasted two years ago. It's grown into a beautifully textured and focused cuvée of white peach and lemon zest, brushed with subtle toasted brioche development, underlined by beautifully fine chalk mineral structure, and outstanding line and length.

Bruno Paillard Assemblage 2008 $$$

95 points • Disgorged June 2015 • Tasted in Australia

42% chardonnay, 42% pinot, 16% meunier; blend of 10 crus; 7 years on lees; disgorgement dates on back labels; 5g/L dosage; 23,000 bottles

The tense acidity of 2008 drives a taut structure that contrasts subtle biscuit and toasted brioche development of seven years on lees. Testimony to grand fruit sources, a core of strawberry and lemon fruit translates bright energy, enduring structure, and well articulating prominent, fine, salty chalk mineral mouthfeel. A cuvée that sings with the stamina of the season, propagating with sensational line and persistence. It needs at least another few years before approaching and will happily live for a decade and beyond.

Bruno Paillard N.P.U. Nec Plus Ultra 2003 $$$$$

91 points • Disgorged March 2015 • Tasted in Australia

50% pinot noir, 50% chardonnay from Oger, Chouilly, Verzenay and Mailly-Champagne; fermented and aged for 10 months in small oak barrels; at least 10 years on lees; 3g/L dosage; 4200 bottles

Perhaps the last, lingering release of the tiny, sweltering harvest of 2003, this cuvée of full straw-yellow hue shows grand concentration of pineapple and custard apple, framed in the toasty, coconut and even caramel notes of barrel fermentation. It looks a little oxidised, with burnt-orange flavours and the first suggestions of dry contraction to the finish. Nonetheless, it upholds good length and impressive integrity for the season.

Bruno Paillard N.P.U. Nec Plus Ultra 1999 $$$$

96 points • Disgorged January 2012 • Tasted in Australia

50% pinot noir from Verzenay, 50% chardonnay from Chouilly, Oger and Le Mesnil-sur-Oger; fermented and aged 9 months in small oak barrels; aged 12 years on lees; 4g/L dosage; 12,500 bottles

The ripe yellow fruit succulence of 1999 shines amidst the generosity of fig and the grip of lemon zest. At a grand 18 years of age, it has evolved toward calm layers of toast and butter, against a backdrop of charcuterie complexity from small-barrel fermentation. For all its multifaceted complexity, it possesses inherent control and focus, giving full limelight to yellow fruits and well-defined chalk mineral structure. A cuvée of great persistence and longevity.

CAMILLE SAVÈS

(Cah-mill Sah-ves)

7/10

4 RUE DE CONDÉ BP 22 51150 BOUZY
www.champagne-saves.com

Eugène Savès began estate-bottling champagne in Bouzy in 1910 and his 1880 press still stands proudly in front of the press house. Today, fourth-generation grower Hervé Savès riddles bottles for an hour every morning before carefully tending 10 hectares of family vineyards across 25 plots on the famed Montagne de Reims terroirs of Bouzy, Ambonnay, Tours-sur-Marne and Tauxières-Mutry.

When I visited Savès in 2014 I was impressed by the spotless order of his facilities, which are climate-controlled to 10–12°C. 'The precision of the vinification and cleanliness of the cellar are important for sustaining the minerality of our terroirs,' he explains. For the same reason, Savès has fully blocked malolactic fermentation in all of his cuvées since 1982. 'This respects the wine and you can feel the terroir and minerality.'

He points out that many other good growers in Bouzy are now also blocking malolactic, prompted by warmer vintages due to global warming. 'I would like to conserve the acidity and freshness,' he says.

Mature pinot noir (85%) and chardonnay (15%) vines are managed naturally with respect for the soil and crop-thinned to emphasise site character. Savès cultivates the soil and propagates grasses in the mid-rows. No insecticides or herbicides are used, but a synthetic fungicide prohibits a fully organic approach.

Wines are fermented and aged cool in climate-controlled small enamel-lined stainless steel tanks and oak barrels. In tasting reserves with Savès, I was impressed with the freshness, liveliness and fruit presence of his wines and at the very elegant influence even of new oak barrels. Savès is impressed with the effect of oak vinification and plans to buy more barrels and foudres. Wines spend at least four years on lees. An annual production of about 85,000 bottles includes a still pinot noir from old Bouzy vines. Red wine is a specialty for Savès and he makes the rouge for Alfred Gratien Cuvée Paradis.

Savès' attention to detail is exacting, right down to laser etching disgorgement dates on every bottle. His precise approach and mineral attentiveness is well matched with his bold terroirs, producing champagnes of confident, intense, pinot-led character, which are impeccably crafted, honed by malic acidity, and excellent value for money.

CAMILLE SAVÈS BRUT PREMIER CRU CARTE BLANCHE NV $

90 points • 2011 BASE VINTAGE • DISGORGED SEPTEMBER 2016 • TASTED IN AUSTRALIA

75% pinot noir and 25% chardonnay from Bouzy, Ambonnay, Tauxières-Mutry and Tours-sur-Marne; 10% oak fermented; aged 3 years on lees; 9g/L dosage

Hervé Savès calls Bouzy 'the Chambertin of Champagne', and to temper its strength and dominance he adds a touch of chardonnay to his entry blend. The result is a focused expression of some of Champagne's most powerful villages, alive with deep red cherry and strawberry fruits, freshened with pretty lemon notes and lively malic acid line, and deepened with the brioche and roast nuts of three years of lees age and a touch of oak fermentation. The 2011 vintage leaves its mark in dusty notes and firm structure on the finish, though this is less pronounced than most from this harrowing season.

CAMILLE SAVÈS BRUT GRAND CRU ROSÉ NV $$

88 points • 2011 BASE VINTAGE • DISGORGED FEBRUARY 2016 • TASTED IN AUSTRALIA

60% chardonnay, 40% pinot noir white and red wine from Bouzy; no oak; aged 3 years on lees; 9g/L dosage

The definition of malic acidity and Savès' restraint make Bouzy rosé a naturally elegant hit, surprisingly but intelligently led by chardonnay. Savès' deeply coloured red wine infuses a pretty, medium-salmon hue and notes of red apple and watermelon. This is a release marked by the challenges of its 2011 base vintage, a dusty style of coarse, firm structure. It nonetheless holds good persistence, vibrant acid line and well-integrated dosage.

CAMILLE SAVÈS BRUT GRAND CRU VINTAGE 2009 $$

94 points • DISGORGED APRIL 2015 • TASTED IN AUSTRALIA

80% pinot noir and 20% chardonnay from old vines in the middle of the slope at Bouzy; 100% oak fermented; aged 5 years on lees; 8g/L dosage

A full straw hue with a blush tint heralds a fully oak-fermented, pinot-led cuvée that rumbles with the voice of some of Champagne's most powerful villages in a rich and warm vintage. Red cherry, strawberry and red apple fruit are underlined by the biscuit and ginger notes of five years lees age. For all its succulent exuberance, it's toned exactingly by finely poised and vibrant malic acid line. Hervé Savès has been masterful in deploying full oak fermentation to build fine texture, mouthfeel and integration, without for a second interrupting fruit purity, delicacy or fine chalk mineral structure. The result is a benchmark cuvée for 2009.

CANARD-DUCHÊNE

(Cah-nah Dew-shen)

---

61 RUE DEMOND-CANARD 51500 LUDES

www.canard-duchene.fr

CHAMPAGNE

Canard-Duchêne

MAISON FONDÉE EN 1868

FRANCE

From its home in the village of Ludes on the northern slopes of the Montagne de Reims, Canard-Duchêne draws pinot noir and chardonnay from a significant spread of growers, spanning 60 communes in Ludes, the Marne Valley, Côte des Blancs, Sézanne, and a significant proportion from the Aube. Purchased in 2003 by entrepreneur Alain Thiénot (see page 333), the house upholds a sustainable focus, including a certified organic champagne. Canard-Duchêne has traditionally been an inexpensive champagne, and remains relatively affordable. These are largely simple, fruity champagnes.

CANARD-DUCHÊNE CUVÉE LÉONIE BRUT NV $

89 points • TASTED IN AUSTRALIA

Red apple and raspberry fruit declare the lead of pinot noir in this style of subtle bouquet and firm palate texture, finishing dry and astringent, lacking in fruit presence and persistence. Acidity is bright and dosage is well balanced.

CANARD-DUCHÊNE CUVÉE LÉONIE BRUT ROSÉ NV $

91 points • TASTED IN AUSTRALIA

DIAM closure

The body and medium-salmon hue of pinot noir create a complex rosé of subtle bouquet and nuances of red apple, red cherry and a hint of pipe smoke on the palate. Its fleshy pinot lead is compelling, and handles a touch of fine tannin texture, concluding with good acid balance and well-integrated dosage.

Canard-Duchêne Brut Millésime Authentic Vintage 2009 $$

85 points • Tasted in Australia

A yeasty style with distinctive and unexpected notes of hops; finishes with bitter grip and astringency. Awkward.

Canard-Duchêne Charles VII Blanc de Blancs Brut NV $$

91 points • Tasted in Australia
DIAM closure

With a bright, medium-straw hue, this is a cuvée of subtle bouquet and reserved apple and pear flavours, with some dry phenolic structural grip, yet upholding good acid definition and reasonable persistence on the finish.

Canard-Duchêne Charles VII Blanc de Noirs Brut NV $$

87 points • Tasted in Australia
DIAM closure

Pink pepper and red apple fruit make for a blanc de noirs of crunch and structure, though let down by a dry, dusty grip that diminishes fruit purity and makes for a grainy structure.

Canard-Duchêne Charles VII Smooth Rosé Sec NV $$

86 points • Tasted in Australia
DIAM closure

A bright salmon-pink rosé of primary strawberry and musk flavours and a sweet finish. It's clean, simple, primary, short, and sweeter than it ought to be.

CATTIER

(Ca-tiay)

6 RUE DOM PÉRIGNON 51500 CHIGNY-LES-ROSES

www.cattier.com

Every summer, roses burst into colour along the streets and premier cru vineyards of the romantic village of Chigny-les-Roses, on the northern slopes of the Montagne de Reims. The family-owned house of Cattier is the most famous in the village, a small négociant house with an annual production of 800,000 bottles and no fewer than 19 cuvées, which just might be the most extensive portfolio in all of Champagne.

The Cattier family has long had its roots in the vines, owning vineyards in Chigny-les-Roses since at least 1763, and probably earlier, and selling its own wines since 1918. It now tends 33 hectares of mainly premier cru vineyards, mostly in Chigny-les-Roses and nearby Ludes, Rilly-la-Montagne and Taissy, half planted to pinot noir, and the remainder equally to chardonnay and meunier. Vineyards are managed with an environmentally sustainable philosophy, supplying around one-third of the needs of the house, and supplemented with grapes from across Champagne, particularly from the Montagne and chardonnay from the Côte des Blancs.

Cattier's production reached a little over a million bottles prior to the economic crisis. The launch of Armand de Brignac (see page 46) in 2006 was timely, proving to be quite a boost to the company's profile.

Allocation of cuvées is made to each house prior to blending. 'The best for Armand de Brignac, of course,' highlights head of the house and winemaker, Jean-Jacques Cattier. He upholds that the growth of Armand de Brignac to a production of 100,000 bottles has not had a derogatory impact on the standard of Cattier, though my tastings over the past decade would suggest otherwise.

Jean-Jacques handed over responsibility to his son Alexandre in 2011, though still remains actively involved in the tastings, which he describes as the nicest part of the job. Alexandre takes responsibility for winemaking. A stock of 2.5 million bottles for both houses is matured in some of the region's deepest cellars in their 150-year-old facility in neighbouring Rilly-la-Montagne. Space is supplemented with a 3600m² warehouse in Reims.

Cattier's Blanc de Noirs is on form this year, and its Clos du Moulin cuvées exemplify the character and elegance of the northern Montagne.

Cattier Brut Icône NV $

91 points • 2013 base vintage • Disgorged February 2016 • Tasted in Australia
50% meunier, 30% pinot, 20% chardonnay; 9g/L dosage

This is not a Cattier cuvée I've tasted before, and its composition is very different to that of the Brut Premier Cru cuvée. It's a young and fresh style, declaring its pinot noir lead in a medium-straw hue and red cherry flavours, a cuvée of flesh, power and body, built around deep pinot noir red fruits and layered with fig, toast and spice. It concludes with good persistence and fine acid/dosage balance. A hint of mushroom on the finish detracts from an otherwise pure and balanced style.

Cattier Brut Antique Premier Cru NV $

88 points • Disgorged March 2016 • Tasted in Champagne and Australia
40% meunier, 35% pinot, 25% chardonnay from the villages of Ludes through Villers-Allerand; 3 years on lees; 9g/L dosage

Purposely a powerful and rounded style, this is a fleshy, buttery and creamy cuvée of toasty, biscuity complexity, concluding in a finish diminished by dry extract and dusty phenolic grip. The bottle tasted in Champagne showed apple, pear and grapefruit notes, with more lively fruit focus and tangy acidity. It needs its full dosage to counter its grip, and its sweetness sits comfortably enough, holding its persistence on the finish.

Cattier Blanc de Blancs Premier Cru Brut NV $$

87 points • 2012 base vintage • Disgorged January 2016 • Tasted in Champagne and Australia
Northern Montagne de Reims; the house would like to be known for its blanc de blancs, intentionally a different style to the Côte des Blancs; 3 years on lees; 9g/L dosage

Notes of star fruit and golden delicious apple add an exotic edge to a core of lemon, grapefruit and crunchy apple, let down by the tell-tale mushroom notes of imperfect fruit on the finish. Green capsium notes point to underripe fruit. Acid and dosage are well married and it finishes short and a little firm.

Cattier Blanc de Noirs Brut NV $$

93 points • 2012 base vintage • Disgorged January 2016 • Tasted in Australia
70% pinot, 30% meunier; 9g/L dosage

This is one of Cattier's cleaner and more precise cuvées this year, confidently articulating the primary voice of its black grapes in nuances of black cherry and plum. With a full-straw hue, it's a softly structured style that effortlessly marries fine northern Montagne de Reims acidity with well-gauged dosage, concluding even and persistent. A compelling blanc de noirs.

Cattier Brut Vinothèque 2007 $$

87 points • Tasted in Australia

One-third each of pinot noir, meunier and chardonnay; 80,000 bottles

A blend of two-thirds pinot noir and one-third chardonnay, this is a dark, complex and engaging style that unites the red berries of pinot, the citrus of chardonnay and the pronounced honey and ginger-biscuit complexity of lees age, culminating in a finish with a little more dosage sweetness than it really needs.

Cattier Rosé Premier Cru Brut NV $$

89 points • 2012 base vintage • Disgorged October 2015 • Tasted in Australia

50% pinot, 40% meunier, 10% chardonnay; 9g/L dosage

Now the second-largest selling cuvée in the extensive portfolio of the house, this is a rosé that achieves its aspiration of a light, refreshing style in a pretty medium-salmon hue, expressing the medium-bodied mood of northern Montagne de Reims pinot noir and meunier, though let down by tannin grip and bitter phenolics.

Cattier Clos du Moulin Brut Premier Cru NV $$$$

94 points • 2008 base vintage • Disgorged December 2015 • Tasted in Champagne and Australia

50% chardonnay, 50% pinot from a single 2.2 hectare site on a gentle, windy ridge at the bottom of the village of Ludes, owned by the house since 1951; always a blend of three vintages; 40% 2007 and 10% 2006 reserves; 6.5 years on lees; 6g/L dosage; 17,933 bottles

Clos du Moulin remains the most famous and most engaging cuvée of Cattier. Its medium-straw hue is the brightest and palest of the Cattier range this year. A wonderful assemblage of white citrus, wild strawberry and red cherry fruits and rose petal lift celebrates the understated presence of Ludes chardonnay and pinot noir, accented with hints of pink pepper, even a suggestion of guava. A fine struck-flint reductive edge coalesces with the toast and brioche of bottle age. The palate is refined and fine, an excellent expression of the understated restraint of the northern Montagne de Reims. The tension of the 2008 vintage cuts through the finish, honed and angular, with chalk minerality, soft phenolic grip and the dry crunch of reductive complexity uniting to compelling effect. It's elegantly fruit-focused and understated.

Cattier Clos du Moulin Rosé Brut NV $$$$

95 points • 2008 base vintage • Disgorged December 2015 • Tasted in Australia

60% pinot noir, 40% chardonnay; 2007 and 2006 reserves; 3185 bottles; 7g/L dosage

A new concept launched for Christmas 2013, this is a wonderfully compelling and characterful rosé of full, bright salmon hue, eloquently capturing the delicacy and finesse of the northern Montagne de Reims in bright red cherry, raspberry, pomegranate and wild strawberry character. The fine chalk minerality under this special site in Ludes unites evenly with fine tannin texture to form a full mouthfeel, which carries a long finish of well-poised 2008 acidity and evenly integrated dosage. Nuances of struck-flint reduction and the toasty complexity of bottle age hover elegantly beneath the fruit. An excellent Clos du Moulin.

The Champagne Guide

CHARLES HEIDSIECK

(Shahl E-dseek)

12 ALLÉE VIGNOBLE 51000 REIMS

www.charlesheidsieck.com

Among the greatest of all champagne houses there is no common recipe for success, and the rise and rise of Charles Heidsieck over the past decades, and in particular the last six years, has been defined by an especially unique and turbulent journey. There are three champagne houses named Heidsieck, all from families once related, and Charles is the smallest and the best of them. With an annual production of just half a million bottles, Charles Heidsieck is made alongside the larger Piper-Heidsieck, and it is this unique coexistence that has springboarded Charles to its current heights. But, more than this, the house has been privileged to a lineage of particularly dynamic and remarkably talented chef de caves since 1976, and a current director as charismatic and sharp as any in the region. The new Charles Heidsieck is built on deep, autumnal complexity, juxtaposed with vibrant energy and astonishing poise. Its cuvées have never looked finer.

Charles and Piper-Heidsieck admirably uphold distinctly unique styles, thanks to their insightful and talented chef de cave, Régis Camus, who has focused the vision of both houses for 24 years. 'We cannot make Charles without Piper,' he reveals. 'There is a brotherhood of the two. The magic is to arrange their coexistence.'

Camus distinguishes Charles by likening its mood to late summer and early autumn, describing its floral spectrum in tones of aromatic flowers, dried flowers and leaves. 'Charles is more about generosity and fleshy expression of late summer fruits, like biting into a peach and having the juice run down your face,' he says. 'It evokes dates, cream and a toasty register of warm brioche just out of the oven, or a crusty Parisian baguette.' This is a contemplative, mature, darker champagne style for cooler weather.

The late Daniel Thibault was the visionary mastermind behind Charles Heidsieck from 1976 until his untimely passing in 2002. In its heyday in 1985, the production of the house reached 4 million bottles, equal to that of Veuve Clicquot at the time.

The global financial crisis hit Piper and Charles Heidsieck hard, throwing the company into some €240 million of debt, and forcing it to lay off a quarter of its staff. Owner Rémy Cointreau sold the brand to French fashion-led luxury company Société Européenne de Participations Industrielles (EPI) in early 2011. President Christopher Descours named Régis Camus as one of the key reasons the company committed to the purchase.

The dynamic and sharp Stephen Leroux was brought on as director of Charles Heidsieck in early 2013. 'We are recuperating after many years in which Rémy Cointreau were not focusing at all on Charles Heidsieck, so we disappeared from many markets,' he admits.

With the relaunch of Charles Heidsieck in 2012, Thierry Roset was appointed chef de cave under Camus, after 25 years with the house. He had already refined the style by honing its sourcing from 120 villages to the 60 finest crus, with a particular focus on Ambonnay for pinot noir, Oger for chardonnay and Verneuil for meunier, three strong villages which Camus dubs 'the three pillars of Charles'. Roset simultaneously increased the average age of reserve wines for Brut Réserve NV from an already considerable eight years to an incredible 10 years – monumental figures for a blend comprising a high 40% of reserves.

Leroux describes the effect of Roset's vision. 'When I joined Charles, I expected this to produce an even more powerful cuvée,' he admits. 'But the longer ageing of reserves gives more complexity and more depth, and honing the selection of crus makes the wines cleaner, fresher and more precise. The intensity of the old Charles was enormous, but the wines could be a bit weighty. The new Charles is powerful but not heavy.'

Roset passed away tragically and suddenly at the end of harvest 2014, and the talented, insightful and articulate Cyril Brun was appointed as his successor. With 15 years overseeing wine development and communication at Veuve Clicquot, Brun is well qualified to define the next chapter of Heidsieck, and his appointment was something of a dream come true.

'When I first became a winemaker, I applied at my two favourite wineries, Veuve Clicquot and Charles Heidsieck,' he reflects. 'And Clicquot got in first!'

In 2015, his very first vintage at Charles, Brun surprised many by not making a vintage champagne from a season he himself described as 'very good' and Camus as 'a vintage more in the Charles style than the Piper style', instead electing to build the reserve stocks.

Brun has a long-term vision for the house. 'We are rebuilding to get Charles on track and we need excellent reserve wines for the future,' he explains. 'The reserves are the fundamentals of our non-vintage wines.' The generosity of the Charles style relies not only on extended lees age but on its deep reserve stocks, stored on fine lees in stainless steel tanks at 15–16°C to retain freshness.

A broad sweep of 10–11g/L dosage across the range may seem heavy-handed in these days of low dosage across champagne. While there has been a small decrease from 11 to 10g/L since 2005, lower dosage is not the aspiration.

'Many people have brainwashed consumers into thinking "the lower the dosage, the better the champagne", but this is not the case,' points out Brun. 'Sugar is not the enemy of champagne. When you have a style like Charles that lies long in the cellar, with deep, rich expression, sugar is on your side.'

Charles Heidsieck has a vision to grow its production slowly, bottling a little more than the half a million bottles it currently sells each year. Leroux's mantra is to rebuild its markets. 'If we do our job well, we might grow to 1.5 million bottles in 10 or 15 years time,' he suggests.

'Within the supply of the two houses, we have room to manoeuvre to achieve this growth in Charles,' Leroux explains. Just 5% of production is currently sourced from a total of 60 hectares across both houses, with the balance provided by some 400 growers. 'We are always looking for new vignerons, and our president, Christopher Descours, is looking to acquire some more land.' One or two hectares have been acquired each year since Descours purchased the company, and he has empowered his team to be active in acquiring more. 'He gave me his mobile number the week I started and said, "If you need a fast decision on purchasing vineyards or anything else, call me,"' Brun reveals.

For all its complexity and depth, the Charles Heidsieck style has always relied exclusively on stainless steel tanks for fermentation and ageing, though Brun is planning the introduction of oak for complexity in the coming years. For him, oak must be very well managed. 'The oak I like is the oak you cannot detect,' he explains. 'More to play with textures rather than flavours, through micro-oxygenation, with more impact on the palate than the nose – though most in Champagne are doing the opposite.'

Another of Brun's visions is to bring back Champagne Charlie, the famous flagship of the house, discontinued in 1985. 'When we have a great vintage in the future, I will put it aside as a Charlie,' he says. He plans to uphold the historical Charlie philosophy of no rules, sometimes pinot dominant and sometimes chardonnay. 'We will take our time and do it properly.'

In addition to sporting smart new front labels, Charles Heidsieck's back labels are now some of the most informative among champagne houses, detailing bottling and disgorgement years (with the quarter of the year in which it was disgorged recently added), proportion of reserve wines, and number of crus in the blend. The base vintage can be easily ascertained as the year before the bottling date.

With Brun's appointment completing a talented and dedicated team, I am quietly excited to see where Charles Heidsieck is headed. Two years go I announced its current cuvées as its finest yet. This year, these deeply contemplative yet thrillingly engaging cuvées have ascended yet another leap and now confidently rank among the finest in all of Champagne.

Charles Heidsieck Brut Réserve NV $$

96 points • 2008 base vintage • Disgorged variously 2014 & 2016 • Tasted in Champagne and Australia
95 points • 2007 base vintage • Tasted in Australia

Base wine one-third each of pinot noir, chardonnay and meunier from 60 villages; 10% estate vineyards; 40% reserve wines of 50% pinot noir and 50% chardonnay, aged an average of 10 years in tanks; full malolactic fermentation; aged 7 years on lees; 11g/L dosage

The delectable Charles Heidsieck mood is nothing short of winter-time generosity, full-straw hue, mellow autumn-leaf character, contemplative appeal, waxy, creamy, fleshy and brimming with juicy stone fruits, fig, pear and crunchy red apples, declaring a magnificent seven years on lees in grand maturity of dried peach, coffee, cocoa, nougat, even smoke and truffles. The current release is delightfully every bit of this and more, a jubilant accord between the reverberating complexity of old reserves and the radiant freshness of 2008. The thrilling energy of this splendid season charges it with a vibrancy and definition that places this blend on a plateau elevated high above even the lofty heights that this cuvée has attained under the new Charles Heidsieck. In searching for any other entry non-vintage cuvée to which to compare it, I can fathom none short of the mesospheric heights of Krug itself. In sheer age (current Krug Grande Cuvée is only one year older) and depth of reserves, this Charles Heidsieck splendidly upholds its elevated position among Champagne's richer NVs, yet does so in the 2008 season with a vivacity, a pronounced, fine chalk mineral mouthfeel, a seamless harmony and astonishing line and length like never before. In sheer, breathtaking calibre for the price, this is the greatest Charles Heidsieck Brut Réserve I can remember. It deserves to be the house champagne we all have chilled perpetually at the ready this year.

The 2007 base still holds its own in a rich and creamy mood, contrasting grilled pineapple with vibrant preserved lemons.

Charles Heidsieck Rosé Réserve NV $$$

96 points • Base vintage 2008 • Disgorged mid-2015 • Tasted in Champagne and Australia

Aiming for a fresher style; 80% 2008, one-third of each of the varieties; 20% reserves of 50% pinot noir and 50% chardonnay of up to 5-6 years of age; 5% red wine from Les Riceys from 2007 (mostly), 2006 and 2005; 11g/L dosage

For Cyril Brun, Les Riceys produces the ideal red wine for Charles Heidsieck Rosé, soft and fruity, never angular or aggressive, respectful of the base wines and deeper in colour than the red wines of the north of Champagne. The result is a medium-copper hue, though colour is not the focus for this style. The gloriously splendid complexity of long lees age and deep reserves infuses wonderful allure of roast chestnuts, baked apples, anise, pipe smoke and freshly baked pâtisserie, even suggestions of olives, tomatoes and crème caramel, yet presented with a dynamism and definition of newfound heights thanks to the dizzying stamina of the brilliant 2008 season. Radiant freshness of bright acid drive serves to heighten precise red cherry and tangy strawberry fruit and rose petal fragrance, as well as lifting its mouthfilling chalk mineral structure, intricately entwined with superfine, expertly handled tannin structure. The result exudes all the creamy, silky delight that we adore of Charles, with definition, freshness and astonishing persistence like never before.

CHARLES HEIDSIECK MILLÉSIME VINTAGE BRUT 2005 $$$

93 points • DISGORGED JUNE 2016 • TASTED IN AUSTRALIA
95 points • DISGORGED JUNE 2016 • TASTED IN CHAMPAGNE

First release since 2000, with 2001 and 2003 write-offs and the more elegant 2002 and 2004 reserved for Piper-Heidsieck; 60% pinot noir, 40% chardonnay from just 11 villages, with a strong base of Ambonnay, then Verzy, Verzenay, Bouzy, Avize, Oger, Cramant, Vertus, Mailly and Vindey; 10g/L dosage

My first tasting of this cuvée was its first showing following its release in late 2014. After a five-year hiatus, 2005 is a bold vintage to choose for this cuvée, and it's not shy on muscle, nor the wood spice notes, almond-skin grip, drying phenolic texture and firm, chewy structure that defines the season. As Brun explains, '2005 allowed us to capture lots of phenolics, and this is the signature of the season.' For many years, this wine was austere and unfriendly, and now it is starting to open up. Heidsieck has conjured a flattering take on this season, cunningly using creaminess, golden layers of ripe yellow summer fruits and honeyed dosage to counter its drying mouthfeel. The volume of the season and its pinot noir lead are well expressed in emerging notes of black cherry, notes of spice and hints of pepper, with a decade of maturity defining the aged complexity of coffee, roast chestnuts, mushrooms, wood smoke and the classic autumn-leaf character of the house. It's at once succulent, silky and exuberant and at the same time structured and dry, repeatedly showing stronger fruit integrity in Champagne than in Australia.

CHARLES HEIDSIECK MILLÉSIME ROSÉ 2006 $$$$

96 points • DISGORGED JUNE 2016 • TASTED IN CHAMPAGNE AND AUSTRALIA

63% pinot noir and 37% chardonnay, including 8% pinot noir red wine; a blend from 15 villages including Oger, Le Mesnil-sur-Oger, Cramant and Vertus for chardonnay; Avenay, Louvois, Tauxières, Ambonnay and Aÿ for pinot noir; and Bouzy, Ambonnay, Les Riceys, Verzenay and Hautvillers for pinot noir red wine

Released prior to the 2005 – which was deemed too tannic and opulent to be unleashed just yet – this is a rosé blended from red wine, half from the Côte des Bar (for smooth, fleshy fruitiness), and half from the Montagne de Reims (for minerality, smoky, spicy complexity and edgy, angular tannins).

The first surprise of this cuvée, on my first sneak preview prior to its release in early 2015, was its captivating delicacy for both the house and the vintage. The second surprise, following two more years on lees, is its freeze-frame evolution and elegant freshness. Its medium salmon copper–hue is undeviating, as are its refined rose petal fragrance and wild strawberry, cherry and pink grapefruit flavours, melting seamlessly into a vortex of brioche, pink pepper and ginger, effortlessly capturing a complex array of diverse rosé personalities with seamless finesse, at once vivacious, lively, contemplative and complex. Texture is marvellous, at once creamy and vibrant, all the while projecting pronounced yet seamless chalk minerality as the defining theme. A delightful champagne for long conversations on cool nights.

CHARLES HEIDSIECK BLANC DES MILLÉNAIRES 1995 $$$$$

98 points • DISGORGED VARIOUSLY IN 2014 AND 2015 • TASTED IN CHAMPAGNE AND AUSTRALIA

20% each of Cramant, Avize, Oger, Le Mesnil-sur-Oger and Vertus; stored in Charles Heidsieck's crayères at 11°C and disgorged successively for release; 10.5g/L dosage

The oldest currently available champagne in all three of the last editions of this guide is miraculously still on the shelves after nine years! With each passing year, it evolves and unravels to reveal a little more of its remarkable personality, and the house discloses a little more of its incredible story. 'I knew Daniel Thibault well,' reveals Cyril Brun. 'And when he made Blanc des Millénaires 1995 he could tell that the potential was enormous, and it would be at its best from 15 or 20 years. He was probably only asked to make what was needed for the market, but he would have thought, if that were the case, nobody would drink it in its prime. So he would have thought, "F#$%, I'll make more so that it will be at its best when it is finally enjoyed!"'

And so, 15 years after his passing, after a glorious 22 years of maturity, Thibault's gift lives on.

Before he himself passed away in 2014, Thierry Roset declared that he would probably never again be able to make another wine like this. Interestingly, he did make a small batch of 1996, but it did not meet expectation and was sold off to an airline some years ago.

The 1995 is an enigma, a grand testimony to the eternal Peter Pan endurance of the greatest crus of the Côte des Blancs, and it will live for decades yet. Its medium-straw hue is shot with a brightness that eludes its age, the freshest bottles upholding green tints, and there's still yellow fruit crunch and lemon zest freshness here, rumbling in tones of impeccable, soft chalk minerality, backed by succulent depth of grilled pineapple, white peach and butter. It's spicier and richer than ever, its voice having deepened as it's emerged from adolescence, taking on the understated, magical allure of grand maturity in bees wax, sweet pipe smoke, truffles, golden fruit cake, green olives and warm hearth. For all of its glorious maturity and silken magnificence, it has retained dizzying vivacity framed in epic salt minerality and vibrant acidity nothing short of mindblowing at 22 years of age. Who knows what might yet be in store in the decades to come? Sit back and enjoy the enthralling spectacle with the one you love, in the largest glasses you can procure.

CHARLES HEIDSIECK BLANC DES MILLÉNAIRES 1983

97 points • DISGORGED SEPTEMBER 1993 • TASTED IN CHAMPAGNE

This medium-gold cuvée is infused with a fantastic panoply of golden fruit integrity of grilled pineapple and glacé fig of enduring persistence, overlaid with all the smoky, tertiary fascination of more than 30 years in the bowels of the earth, in truffles, roast nuts and smouldering hearth. After 10 years on lees and more than 20 years on cork it retains the utmost integrity.

CHARLES HEIDSIECK CHAMPAGNE CHARLIE BRUT 1982

96 points • FROM THE END OF THE ORIGINAL DISGORGEMENT • TASTED IN CHAMPAGNE EN MAGNUM

One of the final vintages of the infamous Champagne Charlie is apparently beginning to decline in standard bottles, but upholding a remarkably bright and lively demeanour amidst depth and power in magnum. It has attained a full-yellow hue with a copper tint, layered with grand complexity of orange, apricot, marmalade and buttered toast. It concludes long and dry, yet retains great integrity and enticing fullness.

CHARTOGNE-TAILLET

(Shah-tone Tie-yair)

6/10

37–39 GRANDE RUE 51220 MERFY
www.chartogne-taillet.com

CHAMPAGNE

CHARTOGNE-TAILLET

Vigneron à *Merfy* depuis 1683

'*I didn't make this wine, the plants gave it to me,' the young Alexandre Chartogne proclaimed as he hand-disgorged a bottle of single-vineyard pinot meunier from 50-year-old vines. Fanatical about drawing every detail of expression from his family vines, he's conducted in-depth studies of root growth and microbiological life, experiments with planting at different densities, cultures yeasts from the vineyards, vinifies in anything that produces the best result (including concrete eggs and clay pots), and even pulled a vineyard out a few years ago because it didn't produce a wine of 'vibration' — his translation of 'terroir.' I like that.*

The Chartogne family has been growing wine on its 11-hectare domain spanning the villages of Merfy and Chenay, just to the north of Reims, since the 16th century. Today, young Alexandre Chartogne, with his parents Elisabeth and Philippe, are the only grower producers in their village.

Once a famed winegrowing district, this area was ravaged during both world wars and has never been replanted to its former glory. The bombings claimed all of the family's vines, their home, the cuverie behind, and all but a small section of the original cellar below.

Replanted and rebuilt, the estate's wines today showcase the area's style: less fruity, more rounded, more complex than the wines of the southern Montagne de Reims.

The chalk in Merfy lies a metre or more below the surface, much deeper than in, for instance, Cramant and Avize, where Alexandre has also worked vintages with fellow terroirist and mentor Anselme Selosse. The soil is far more variable here, too, with pockets of limestone, clay and sand, producing some parcels of inferior fruit, and others of grand cru heights. It takes experience, diligence and talent to draw distinguished wines from such terroirs. Chartogne-Taillet is blessed with all three.

'My most important goal is to present the village,' declares Alexandre, whose range includes five single-vineyard wines. In an era in which the holdings of many Champagne growers are sprawling into other villages, Chartogne-Taillet champions a more traditional philosophy, all the more noble in a village in which no other grower makes champagne. The fruit of two hectares of Chartogne-Taillet vineyards in the Vallée de la Marne is sold every year.

'How could I say that I produce good wine in the Marne Valley when I live in Merfy?' Alexandre

The Champagne Guide

questions. 'Making our own wine is not about making money,' he reveals.

Since he began working his family's estate in 2006, Alexandre has adopted a low-intervention, hands-on, organic approach to encourage soil health, ploughing soils by horse to reduce compaction. He has called on the assistance of famed Burgundian soil expert Claude Bourguignon, and their analyses have shown that when herbicides are not used and the soil is aerated and not compacted, micro-organisms are active at all levels, encouraging deep roots and expressive, terroir wines.

Alexandre pulls out vineyards with shallow roots and replants with ungrafted vines. Yields are kept in check by green harvesting (crop thinning) to maintain an average of just 60hL/hectare – two-thirds of the regional average – and as little as 20hL/hectare in his oldest vines. This produces 80,000–100,000 bottles annually, a conservative yield from 11 hectares.

When I visited in 2016, Alexandre was proud to show me the new cuverie he'd built. 'It's fundamental,' he reflected, 'but the most important work for the interpretation of the terroir is in the vines. It is the vineyards that explain the harmony of the wines,' he emphasises.

He sources wild yeast from each plot, which he upholds as crucial for maintaining the purity of his cuvées. So much so that when he was recently offered two hectares to rent in nearby St Thierry, he resolved to buy another cuverie on the other side of the road, just to keep the fruit separate and avoid cross-contamination of wild yeasts.

Since 2008, fermentation has taken place mostly in concrete eggs and old barrels (aged 4–9 years), and occasionally in stainless steel. He considers the reductive character of stainless steel and the woody notes of oak to be a distraction from terroir, favouring concrete eggs for wines requiring more air and lees

A 12th century church stands sentinel over a walled vineyard in Saint-Thierry, to the immediate north-west of Reims.

contact, without the influence of wood. Low sulphur and low dosage are used in every cuvée.

Alexandre's interactive website is one of the best in Champagne, detailing the philosophy and vinification of each cuvée, vineyard maps and soil strata. Back labels are also refreshingly informative, stating base vintage, blend, vinification and disgorgement date. A clean, sophisticated front label brings a Burgundian feel to the brand, in tune with its terroir focus.

These are champagnes of precision, harmony and grace that represent exceptional value for money. It's no surprise that the full production sells out every year.

CHARTOGNE-TAILLET SAINTE ANNE BRUT NV $

92 points • 60% 2013 BASE VINTAGE • DISGORGED FEBRUARY 2016 • TASTED IN CHAMPAGNE

65% pinot, 35% chardonnay; 40% 2012 reserves; tasted 1 month after disgorgement; 4g/L dosage

Chartogne-Taillet's entry wine is always good value, a blend from across estate Merfy vineyards. An ever-increaasing reliance on pinot noir is showcased in depth and presence of red cherry, strawberry and lemon fruit. It presents fine minerality supported by well-integrated acidity, finishing long and fine with nicely textured mouthfeel and a fine bead. Notes of charcuterie sit behind the fruit. An enticingly full, fleshy finish contrasts with its salt mineral texture and bright acidity. Definitive Merfy.

CHARTOGNE-TAILLET LE ROSÉ BRUT NV $$

93 points • 2012 BASE VINTAGE • DISGORGED FEBRUARY 2016 • TASTED IN CHAMPAGNE
60% chardonnay, 40% pinot; 55-year-old vines; 5.5g/L dosage

The understated definition of Merfy fruit is well suited to graceful rosé, and Le Rosé is consistently one of Champagne's finest at a very enticing price. It's a pretty thing of medium crimson-salmon hue and expressive red berry, red cherry and pomegranate fruit, with a savoury hint of tomato and pink pepper on the finish. Gentle, fine mineral structure and a fine bead define a long finish of well-integrated, subtle dosage and gentle, supportive acid line. It's light-footed, delicate, well composed and finely crafted.

CHARTOGNE-TAILLET BEAUX SENS EXTRA BRUT 2011 $$$

84 points • TASTED IN CHAMPAGNE
Ungrafted meunier planted between 1955 and 1957 on a flat site with chalk 1 metre below the surface; 5g/L dosage

Alexandre is frank in declaring 2011 the worst vintage ever. The result is a wine of dry and earthy character, with notes of wet wood and tilled earth, concluding coarse and short.

CHARTOGNE-TAILLET COUARRES CHÂTEAU EXTRA BRUT 2010 $$$

92 points • TASTED IN CHAMPAGNE
35-year-old pinot noir planted on organic sand over chalk; vinified in 1, 2 and 3-year-old oak barrels

A savoury and honeyed cuvée, layered with grilled pineapple and the nutty, roasted notes of oak barrels sitting neatly behind the fruit. A characterful and engaging wine of fine, gently salty minerality and lingering persistence.

CHARTOGNE-TAILLET LES COUARRES EXTRA BRUT 2010 $$$

90 points • TASTED IN CHAMPAGNE
Pinot noir planted on clay soil over chalk; identical vinification to Couarres Chateau

Les Couarres is the neighbouring lieu-dit to Les Couarres Chateau, and the two wines make for a fascinating comparison of the complex effects of Champagne's diverse geologies. Les Couarres presents rounded stone fruits and charcuterie with honeyed, toasty complexity and a soft, supple finish drawn out long by balanced acid drive.

The Champagne Guide

CLAUDE CAZALS

(Clawd Cah-zahl)

6/10

28 RUE DU GRAND MONT, 51190 LE MESNIL-SUR-OGER

www.champagne-cazals.fr

'I don't know if I am from Oger or from Le Mesnil-sur-Oger!' exclaims Delphine Cazals, who oversees nine hectares of prime chardonnay vineyards in both villages, Vertus and Villeneuve with her mother Michèle. Their family estate has been based in Le Mesnil for four generations since 1897, and in the 1950s her grandfather purchased from French President Léon Bourgeois the famous walled vineyard in the heart of Oger, which also encloses their family home, naming it Clos Cazals. A portfolio of masterfully composed blanc de blancs contrasts the broad-shouldered stature of Oger with the vertical tension of Le Mesnil.

Grape sourcing is exclusively from the family's estate vineyards, with the exception of Verzenay red wine for rosé, though Delphine muses that such is the warm generosity of Oger that she might one day secretly plant pinot noir here!

Her father, the late Claude Cazals, was controversial in arguing that Le Mensil and Oger are best when blended together, a style confidently maintained by the house for decades, and still to this day.

When Delphine joined the estate in 1995, she noted that the ripeness of their prized Clos Cazals was a full degree higher than other parcels, and hence proposed a special standalone bottling from this glorious 3.7 hectares of chardonnay enclosed by one kilometre of wall more than a century of age.

Three different parcels within the clos are allocated separately, one hectare planted by her grandfather in 1957 as 'Clos Cazals'; one small upper part of the clos with a small chapel, planted by Delphine and her father in 1981, as 'La Chapelle du Clos'; and the remainder blended with Le Mensil in her other cuvées.

Delphine releases Clos Cazals every vintage, in good seasons as many as 8500 bottles and in poor seasons as few as 2000. These old vines produce great concentration, but yield just half of the appellation average.

All cuvées are vinified in stainless steel, with the exception of four barrels. 'I don't like wood in chardonnay – I prefer the real chardonnay!' Delphine declares unashamedly.

Claude Cazals' other claim to fame was the co-invention of the gyropalette for riddling bottles in 1969.

Few houses produce standalone Oger cuvées and Cazals' rank among the most distinctive and well-balanced of all.

Claude Cazals Grand Cru Cuvée Vive Blanc de Blancs 2007 $

94 points • Tasted in Champagne

Le Mesnil-sur-Oger and Oger; 3g/L dosage; DIAM closure

All the flamboyance of Oger leaps forth in rich, concentrated, exotic orange flesh, contrasting magnificently with the lemon and apple tension and the inimitable fine chalk minerality of Le Mesnil. Long age completes this dramatic picture with brush strokes of anise and biscuit.

Claude Cazals Millésime Grand Cru Blanc de Blancs Brut 2008 $$

95 points • Tasted in Champagne

70% Le Mesnil-sur-Oger, 30% Oger; majority of old vines; 7g/L dosage; DIAM closure

The luminescent 2008 vintage presents a great case for Claude Cazals' conviction to blend Le Mesnil and Oger. The tension of the season is backed with impressive Oger fruit depth of apple, lemon and pear, and the toast, brioche and honey complexity of eight years of maturity. The chalk mineral structure of Le Mesnil sings on a long finish that froths with deeply penetrating minerality. It's magnificently poised, with a long future before it.

Clos Cazals Blanc de Blancs Extra Brut 2005 $$$$

93 points • Tasted in Champagne

3.7 hectare walled clos in the heart of Oger; from vines planted in 1957; 3g/L dosage; DIAM closure

A champagne of body and richness true to Oger and the old vines in this prized site, heightened by the rich 2005 vintage. Layers of fig, peach and pineapple linger long amidst mixed spice complexity. The dry extract of the season marks the finish, though the fine salty minerality of the village shines through admirably.

La Chapelle du Clos Delphine Cazals Blanc de Blancs Brut NV $$$$

95 points • Tasted in Champagne

1 hectare parcel planted in 1981 by Delphine and her father in the upper part of the walled clos in the heart of Oger; 100% 2007; 8g/L dosage; DIAM closure

The second release of Delphine's baby is, like the first, exclusively from a single season, though not labelled as a vintage wine (although it will be in the future). The characterful ripeness of Oger is on grand parade, amplified by the intensity of the site and its low-yielding vines, in exotic presence of orange, fig and spice. It is pulled effortlessly into line by soft salty chalk minerality, less pronounced in its mineral texture than Le Mesnil, but with a similarly salty mineral profile. In fruit richness and body it is magnificent and expansive, even suggesting notes of golden fruit cake, ginger and pineapple, yet toned and honed into wonderful precision thanks to its fine acidity and mineral definition.

COLLET

(Coh-lay)

14 BOULEVARD PASTEUR 51160 AŸ

www.champagne-collet.com

CHAMPAGNE

COLLET

AŸ - FRANCE

DEPUIS 1921

ollet sits alongside Jacquart and Montaudon as the brands of Champagne's longest-standing and third largest cooperative, Coopérative Générale des Vignerons. The group has enjoyed considerable development in recent years, with a new headquarters built in its home town of Aÿ, and a new production facility constructed in Oger in 2004 and significantly expanded in 2011, to a capacity of 27 million bottles. The cooperative sources from 162 villages, of which 100 are utilised in the Collet blends. A production of 500,000 bottles makes Collet less than one-fifth the size of Jacquart, and its distribution consequently focuses more toward restaurants than supermarkets. These are generally long-aged cuvées of fruit integrity, though at times lacking polish.

COLLET BRUT NV $$

89 points • 2012 BASE VINTAGE • DISGORGED AUGUST 2016 • TASTED IN AUSTRALIA

50% meunier, 30% chardonnay, 20% pinot; a blend of 100 crus, including meunier from Bonneil, Reuil, Festigny and Vallée de l'Ardre; chardonnay from Étoges, Epernay and Vitry-le-François; pinot mainly from Côte des Bars; 35% reserves; 10g/L dosage; DIAM closure

The red apple, peach and strawberry fruit of meunier is supported by subtle lees age character reminiscent of almond meal. It's clean and balanced, though simple and short, with a touch of phenolic texture on the finish.

COLLET EXTRA BRUT NV $$

88 points • 2009 BASE VINTAGE • DISGORGED SEPTEMBER 2016 • TASTED IN AUSTRALIA

40% chardonnay, 40% pinot, 20% meunier; a blend of 20 crus, including chardonnay from Côtes des Blancs and Villers-Marmery; pinot noir from Aÿ, Hautvillers, Rilly-la-Montagne; meunier from Ville-Dommange; 10% reserves; 3g/L dosage; DIAM closure

There's quite some maturity here, boasting more than six years on lees. Lower dosage brings out lemon accents but accentuates the phenolic grip of the finish, and a lack of fruit persistence makes for a firm and somewhat callow feel. It's nonetheless clean and focused.

COLLET BRUT ART DECO NV $$

90 points • 2009 BASE VINTAGE • DISGORGED MAY 2016 • TASTED IN AUSTRALIA

40% chardonnay, 40% pinot, 20% meunier; same base as Extra Brut but with higher dosage; 10% reserves; 9g/L dosage; DIAM closure

A little more dosage in Collet's Extra Brut heightens red apple, black cherry and peach fruit, bolstered by rich lees-derived complexity of honey, gingernut biscuits and mixed spice. Bottle age has built impressive persistence and mouth-filling texture, too, elevating this cuvée confidently ahead of Collet's entry NVs. It's ready to drink now.

COLLET ESPRIT COUTURE BRUT NV $$$$

90 points • 2007 BASE VINTAGE • DISGORGED MAY 2016 • TASTED IN AUSTRALIA

50% pinot, 40% chardonnay, 10% meunier; 4 crus of pinot noir (Mailly, Hautvillers, Louvois, Tauxières), 1 cru of chardonnay (Louvois) and 1 cru of meunier (Ville-Dommange); 7.5g/L dosage

Reductive struck flint and gun smoke notes ride over a core of lemon and grapefruit, in a dry and tense style bolstered by layers of roast almond and nougat complexity, thanks to eight years on lees. Phenolic grip makes for a grainy finish, though accurate acid line draws out persistence, and low dosage is well integrated.

COLLET MILLÉSIME BRUT 2006 $$$

92 points • DISGORGED APRIL 2016 • TASTED IN AUSTRALIA

54% chardonnay from Avize, Oger and Villers-Marmery; 46% pinot from Aÿ and Verzenay; 6g/L dosage

Pinot noir from Aÿ and Verzenay jumps out of the glass in its characterful cherry and strawberry manner, backed with the full ensemble of a decade of maturity in roast nuts and spice. It upholds its freshness and primary fruit purity admirably for this ripe and fast-maturing season, supported by nicely poised acidity and fine chalk minerality. A good result for the season, and, unlike some, it won't fall over tomorrow.

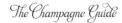

The Champagne Guide

De Saint Gall

(union champagne)

(Der Sahn Gahl)

7 Rue Pasteur 51190 Avize

www.union-champagne.fr

CHAMPAGNE
DE SAINT GALL

*D*e Saint Gall is the brand of the Union Champagne cooperative, an enormous conglomerate of 13 member cooperatives of 2150 member growers controlling more than 1260 hectares of champagne vineyards. Half of these are located in grand cru villages, encompassing half the surface of the Côte des Blancs and many of the great pinot villages of the southern Montagne de Reims, and 40% in premier crus. The cooperative operates from substantial, state-of-the-art facilities in Avize and Vertus and a (relatively) smaller site in Oger, where it produces the equivalent of 12 million bottles annually. The majority of production is sold to other houses, including highly sought after components of such cuvées as Taittinger Comtes de Champagne, Laurent-Perrier Grand Siècle and Dom Pérignon, and a sizeable number of bottles to member growers. Since 1984, the Union has marketed its own brand in De Saint Gall, steadily growing to a production of some 2.2 million bottles, which can represent good value in an at times reductive style.

De Saint Gall Extra Brut Blanc de Blancs Premier Cru NV $$

90 points • Tasted in Australia

100% Côte des Blancs; DIAM closure

The incisive cut of Côte des Blancs chardonnay charges a tense, crunchy lemon, grapefruit and apple fruit core, well softened by the toasty, biscuity, roast almond and brioche complexity of lees age and accented with smoky, struck-flint reductive character. It concludes with good length and well-balanced dosage, quite a contrast in personality to the Brut Blanc de Blancs, lacking just a little in polish on the finish, as phenolic grip lends a little firmness.

De Saint Gall Brut Millésime Premier Cru 2009 $$

90 points • Tasted in Australia

100% Côte des Blancs; DIAM closure

The voluptuous and fast-maturing nature of the hot, dry and ripe 2009 season is on full display in this cuvée, very much in the secondary phase of its life already, layered with toast, roast nuts, even golden fruit cake. It holds its balance on the end, with gentle support from acidity and chalk mineral texture, holding good persistence and plenty of character. Drink soon.

De Saint Gall So Dark Grand Cru 2008 $$

92 points • Tasted in Australia

75% pinot noir, 25% chardonnay; DIAM closure

Thanks to the tension of the 2008 season, this is a pale-straw cuvée that belies its three-quarters pinot noir predominance, leading out reductive with enticing struck flint and gun smoke notes, even a hint of tinned corn that quickly dissipates, more reminiscent of chardonnay. The palate is streamlined and honed, layered with smoked almond and subtle almond meal and toasty nuances of bottle age, with great potential for the future. It finishes long, with crunchy lemon and red apple fruit and the focus of 2008 acidity defining impressive line, underlined by fine chalk mineral texture, subtle, integrated dosage and a little dry phenolic grip.

De Saint Gall Orpale Grand Cru Blanc de Blancs Brut 2002 $$$$

90 points • Tasted in Australia
89 points • Tasted in Australia

One-third Avize and Cramant for lightness and finesse, two-thirds Oger and Le Mesnil-sur-Oger for expression and vitality; aged on lees 8-10 years; DIAM closure

An impressively bright medium-straw hue does little to betray 14 years of maturity. The bouquet and palate have more to reveal, edging into a tertiary charcuterie place, while upholding the tense lemon notes of youth and the lemon meringue and even vanilla and coconut of middle age. It struggles on the finish, with tart acidity standing at odds to its otherwise mature profile. One tasting showed more development in a tint of golden yellow colour and more mature marmalade complexity, leaving the finish a little dried out and bitter, though nonetheless retaining well-defined acidity and low, seamlessly integrated dosage.

De Saint Gall Brut Blanc de Blancs Premier Cru NV $$

89 points • Tasted in Australia

100% Côte des Blancs

De Saint Gall Brut Rosé NV $$

89 points • Tasted in Australia

DIAM closure

De Sousa

(De Soo-za)

12 Place Léon Bourgeois 51190 Avize

www.champagnedesousa.com

Un Champagne de Précision

If you could write the perfect recipe for the greatest champagnes it might read something like this: a tiny grower based in Avize in the exact centre of the grand crus of the Côte des Blancs, sourcing chardonnay from estate vineyards on the finest slopes of the grand crus of Avize, Oger, Cramant and Le Mesnil-sur-Oger, and pinot noir and meunier from the grand crus of Aÿ and Ambonnay. Vines would be very old and painstakingly tended biodynamically by an experienced artisan, fanatical about drawing every detail of character and minerality from every site. Crop levels and dosage would be low, oak would be used generously when the fruit called for it and sparingly when it did not, blending would be performed from a deep pool of reserve wines, cuvées would mature long on their lees in cold cellars, and bottling and disgorgement dates and dosages would be printed on every bottle. Welcome to the wonderful world of De Sousa.

On paper, this might be the finest recipe in all of Champagne. But do the wines live up to it?

I first met third-generation head of the house Erick de Sousa over the gigantic French oak table in his tasting room in the heart of Avize. 'My job is to maximise the minerality in the vines,' he commenced, and everything from this point served to demonstrate his vision – every cuvée opened, every vineyard technique expounded, every cellar procedure demonstrated.

Over 30 years, Erick has refined the best of traditional thinking and progressive methods to revitalise, transform and grow the estate to become one of the finest on the Côte des Blancs. Production has increased to 85,000 bottles annually and vineyard holdings have grown to 42 plots spanning 9.5 hectares, including 2.5 hectares of coveted old vines in Avize, Cramant and Oger. With the exception of his entry Brut Tradition, every vineyard source is grand cru, with 70% of vines over 40 years of age and a significant percentage 50–60 years old. Some planted by his grandfather are more than 80 years old. 'I must give my wine the minerality that can only come from old vines,' he emphasises.

The roots of these old vines plunge deep into the soil, even as far as 35–40 metres into the chalk, he suggests. Here they extract the salts and trace elements that are fundamental to the structure of these wines.

'Minerality comes from the chalk,' he says. And his wines sing with crystal clear mineral fidelity.

Old vines have a natural moderating effect on yields, which generally average just 60hL/hectare from 8000 vines, 25–30% less than the average of the appellation. Such yields provide greater concentration and permit him to harvest only when the grapes have attained full ripeness. 'I want to maintain the maturity in the sugar level at harvest, but not too high, so as to keep a balance of acidity and minerality,' he explains. 'High maturity at harvest provides opulence, while minerality maintains freshness.' When I visited towards the end of harvest 2014, I was impressed with the cleanliness and purity of the juices, displaying intensity of flavour and great acid balance.

In his own words, Erick de Sousa 'lives in the rhythm of the vines' and regards his work in the vineyards as the key to the quality of the grapes. Respect for the vine and the earth is paramount, and he spent a decade converting the domaine to biodynamic viticulture, with full certification granted in 2010. Biodynamics for him is about equipping his old vines to capture minerality, 'to encourage the vine to draw deeply the trace elements specific to each terroir and provide different characteristics to each cuvée'. The soil is ploughed for ventilation and to restore microbial life, with a horse in some vineyards.

To increase production, de Sousa purchased new cellars on the opposite side of the village square in 2004 for his négociant label, Zoémie de Sousa. With walls at least half a metre thick, the stable temperature is ideal for ageing wines. When he showed me through, I was surprised by the small scale of production. His enamelled tanks are tiny; he owns one foudre for ageing red wine, a small wooden vat for red wine fermentation, and little 225-litre barrels made from oak harvested in Avize and from a cooper friend in Burgundy.

Fruit from vines older than 50 years is fermented in small oak barrels, with regular bâtonnage to enhance depth and breadth. He has used about 15% new barrels for his top cuvées, and increased the proportion slightly in 2004. Such is his sensitive and masterful use of barrels that fruit flavours always take precedence over oak flavours, and texture is enhanced, amplifying minerality and definition. Chaptalisation is performed when necessary, the first fermentation is initiated with natural yeasts, and all wines pass through malolactic fermentation. Sulphur dioxide is used sparingly.

Narrow and atmospheric, the 200-year-old cellars under the house run 800 metres directly beneath the square in the middle of the village. A stable temperature of 10°C is ideal for long ageing. Here, the old method of poignettage is practised, in which autolytic flavours are enhanced by shaking the bottles by hand to stir up the lees. Bottles are also riddled by hand.

De Sousa's profound prestige Cuvée des Caudalies' claim to uniqueness is not so much that it is a prestige cuvée of non-vintage blend, but just how this blend is assembled. Sourced from chardonnay vines exceeding 50 years of age in Avize, Oger, Le Mesnil-sur-Oger and Cramant, and vinified in small barrels with no chaptalisation, it is blended as a solera of reserve wines that currently spans the 11 harvests from 1995 to 2005. Cuvée des Caudalies is also released as an ultra-complex vintage wine and a mesmerising rosé.

De Sousa's substantial and diverse portfolio is growing, with the introduction of tiny production cuvées like Umami and Mycorhize. This year has seen the unveiling of a Grand Cru Blanc de Noirs and Rosé de Saignée. If ever proof was needed of the masterful dexterity of this estate far beyond the realm of mineral-rich blanc de blancs, these two stunning first attempts are surely it.

In addition to disgorgement dates, back labels now disclose the bottling date, which is a useful insight as the base vintage of NV cuvées is always the year prior.

De Sousa has decided to phase out Zoémie de Sousa as it perceives that trading under two brands has confused the market. The status of De Sousa has changed to Négociant-Manipulant and purchased grapes are now included in some cuvées. There are some who would lay judgement for such a move. But, as always, the ultimate test lies in the bottle, and I am yet to detect any cause for alarm under De Sousa or Zoémie.

De Sousa has risen to a rightful place among Champagne's greatest producers under Erick's visionary guidance over the past quarter century, now ably assisted by his three children, Charlotte, Julie and Valentin, all of whom have completed degrees at the local wine school. Theirs are masterfully grown and crafted wines, every one of which is brilliantly mineral, profoundly exact and beautifully fresh. At the end of a long tasting and vigorous conversation over that massive oak table, I once told Erick as much.

'It's all about mature vines with roots that go deep into the soil,' he replies with unassuming humility.

And it must also have a little to do with what is indeed one of the finest recipes in Champagne.

Zoémie De Sousa Précieuse Grand Cru Brut NV $$

93 points • 2012 BASE VINTAGE • DISGORGED MARCH 2016 • TASTED IN AUSTRALIA
100% chardonnay from Avize, Oger and Cramant; aged 2.5 years on lees; 7g/L dosage

From the very first cuvée, De Sousa's grand terroirs in the great crus of the Côte des Blancs declare their fruit presence, harmony and mineral definition. The great 2012 base vintage lays out compelling lemon, pear and apple fruit, beautifully toned by two and a half years of lees age and its subtle almond meal and brioche influence. Oger and Cramant lend their stature in generous mid-palate presence. A soft and silky mouthfeel is impeccably underscored by fine, salty chalk minerality that sings of chardonnay, of Avize and of De Sousa.

De Sousa Tradition Brut NV $$

92 points • 2013 BASE VINTAGE • DISGORGED SEPTEMBER 2015 • TASTED IN
CHAMPAGNE
50% chardonnay, 40% pinot, 10% meunier; 15% reserves aged in barrel for 6 months; 7g/L dosage

A spicy style of red apple, cherry, cherry kernel and almonds, with good fruit integrity and freshness, uniting the red berries of pinot noir with the apple and citrus of chardonnay. It finishes long and fruity, with well-integrated dosage and expressive, fine chalk minerality. A young, fresh and fruity style made from good fruit sources.

De Sousa Grand Cru Réserve Blanc de Blancs Brut NV $$

90 points • 2011 BASE VINTAGE WITH 15–20% RESERVES • DISGORGED JUNE 2015
• TASTED IN CHAMPAGNE
96 points • 70% 2008 BASE VINTAGE, 30% 2007 RESERVES AGED IN BARRELS
• DISGORGED FEBRUARY 2016 • TASTED IN AUSTRALIA
35-45-year-old vines in Avize, Oger, Cramant and Le Mesnil-sur-Oger; 7g/L dosage

On its first release four years ago, I declared the 2008 base 'a breathtakingly refined De Sousa, the very definition of chardonnay from the heart of its finest terroirs'. Returning for a rousing encore, the captivatingly delicate yet energetically enduring 2008 base defines a spellbinding De Sousa. The dainty lemon blossom and anise of its youth remain, beginning to morph magnificently into nougat, almond and vanilla. A full seven years on lees has heightened its delightfully silky mouthfeel, without for a moment diminishing its mineral impact, a revelation of frothing, sea-surf chalk of impeccable definition. A blend of vines of 35–45 years of age is young by De Sousa standards, but an organic regime has encouraged deep root penetration and mineral pick-up. I predicted four years ago that it would age magnificently and, on current performance, there's no stopping it. The 2011 base is a stark contrast, a savoury and awkward style that reflects its challenging and cold year, with nuances of wood smoke and baked apple that juxtapose the tangy acidity and lemon notes of the season. It's clean and carries balance, with well-integrated, honeyed dosage, a good result for a difficult base year.

De Sousa Brut Rosé NV $$

93 points • 2013 BASE VINTAGE • DISGORGED SEPTEMBER AND OCTOBER 2015
• TASTED IN CHAMPAGNE AND AUSTRALIA

92% chardonnay from Avize, Grauves and Cuis; 8% pinot noir red wine from 2012 from estate vineyards in Aÿ and Ambonnay vinified in oak casks; aged 1.5 years on lees; 7g/L dosage

Freshness and fruitiness are the aspirations of this young blend, and it's quite thrilling to see just what an impact 8% pinot noir red wine can have in transforming chardonnay into a medium salmon-crimson tone, infusing seductive layers of rose petals, strawberries, pink pepper, even a suggestion of Campari. Barrel fermentation of the red wine adds a subtle, savoury, wood spice, herbal twist. In the midst of it all, the magnificent, salty chalk minerality of Avize makes a grand statement, uniting seamlessly with masterfully orchestrated, superfine tannins to create a delightful mouthfeel. A beguiling De Sousa Rosé of much more pronounced and characterful presence than the 2012 base, and none the less for it.

De Sousa Grand Cru Blanc de Noirs Brut NV $$

95 points • 2012 BASE VINTAGE • DISGORGED JANUARY 2016 • TASTED IN AUSTRALIA

Aged 2.5 years on lees; matured in small oak barrels; 7g/L dosage

For a house rooted deeply in the great chardonnay terroirs of the Côte des Blancs, De Sousa's command of grand cru pinot noir is handsome indeed, and this brand new cuvée, landing just in time for this edition, is perhaps the most resounding evidence of the dexterity of this incredible grower. There's no mistaking pinot noir, from its full-straw hue with a blush tint, to its gorgeous aromas and flavours of succulent black cherries, strawberries and violets. It's deep, fleshy and magnificent, yet at every moment fresh and dynamic, with a bright and lively line of ripe acidity and a prominent, omnipresent, thrillingly mouthfilling eruption of fine, salty chalk minerality. This cuvée singly eclipses a good many growers in the great pinot villages.

De Sousa Rosé de Saignée Grand Cru Brut NV $$

95 points • 2013 BASE VINTAGE • DISGORGED JANUARY 2016 • TASTED IN AUSTRALIA

100% pinot noir from Aÿ and Ambonnay; aged 2 years on lees; 7g/L dosage

De Sousa is forever innovating, and from its prized position in Avize, it might seem ludicrous to make a rosé de saignée from prime sites in Aÿ and Ambonnay. The colour ranks among the deepest in Champagne, a deep crimson, closer to Coteaux Champenois than rosé as we know it. Its aromas and flavours confidently meet the full expectation of its hue, deep in pink pepper, mulberry and raspberry fruit. For all of its depth, this cuvée is never for a moment broad, heavy or hard, exemplifying the masterful craftsmanship of De Sousa in capturing character and definition with precision. For its rich colour and red fruit presence, its tannins are astonishingly fine and intricately integrated, a fearsome accomplishment for a house that, to my knowledge, is completely inexperienced in the art of saignée. And, as always in the magnificent De Sousa way, it is the fine salt minerality of great terroirs that leads the structure and defines the finish, frothing, salty and precise. Is there nothing De Sousa cannot do?

The Champagne Guide

De Sousa Cuvée 3A Grand Cru Extra Brut NV $$

93 points • 2013 BASE VINTAGE • DISGORGED JANUARY 2016 • TASTED IN AUSTRALIA
94 points • 2012 BASE VINTAGE • DISGORGED JULY 2015 • TASTED IN CHAMPAGNE

A blend of the 3 'A' grand crus: 50% Avize chardonnay, 25% Aÿ pinot noir and 25% Ambonnay pinot noir, co-pressed and co-fermented to increase harmony; 50% vinified in old and new oak barrels

The trend in Champagne is towards keeping parcels separate to increase definition, but De Sousa has boldly co-fermented to created a profoundly seamless union of chardonnay and pinot noir from three of Champagne's most distinctive villages. The mood of 3A swings dramatically according to its base vintage, and the 2013 season presents quite a contrast to earlier blends. Ripe pinot noir leaps from the glass in pink musk stick, red cherry and candied strawberry exuberance, declaring a bold and fruity style. It pulls in line on the finish, thanks to well-defined acidity and a tremendous undercurrent of fine salt chalk minerality, the unifying highlight of De Sousa. The 2012 base, by comparison, is a rich style that declares the depth of Aÿ and Ambonnay pinot noir in plum and black cherry fruit, with the expansive mood of oak fermentation expressed in mixed spice, dark fruit cake and dark chocolate. The minerality of Avize triumphs, fine, tense and chalk-rich.

Zoémie De Sousa Précieuse Millésime Grand Cru Brut 2008 $$

96 points • DISGORGED MARCH 2014 • TASTED IN AUSTRALIA

A blend of Avize, Oger and Cramant; aged 7 years on lees; 5g/L dosage

A distinguished tribute to the precision and sheer beauty of the great crus of the Côte des Blancs in the brilliant 2008 season, given articulate voice by the mastery of De Sousa. Freshness of lemon, white peach, apple and pear mark out a breathtakingly primary bouquet, replicated in intricate detail on the palate, undeviating from delightful start to very long finish. The influence of seven years of lees age is understated, bringing textural seamlessness more than subtle almond meal and nougat complexity. Its minerality is an epiphany, frothing with sea surf, mouth-filling, deep-set and all-encompassing. As ever, the frothing, churning, salt-infused minerality of old vines rooted deeply into chalk is communicated in heightened stature by De Sousa's exacting regime in the vineyards and winery. It's irresistible now, but has the stamina to live for decades. Précieuse, indeed.

De Sousa Cuvée des Caudalies Millésime Grand Cru Extra Brut 2008 $$$$$

95 points • DISGORGED NOVEMBER 2014 • TASTED IN CHAMPAGNE AND AUSTRALIA

From vines more than 50 years of age in Avize and Oger; fully vinified and aged for 10 months in oak barrels; aged 5.5 years on lees; 5000 bottles

Erick De Sousa describes 2008 as a fantastic and perfect season, and bottled 5000 bottles of this cuvée rather than the usual 2000. This is a ripe and exuberant take on the year, a wine of grand stature and proportions, with layers of fruit presence of expressive ripe peach, apple, star fruit, grapefruit, even fig, framed in layers of barrel-fermented complexity of roast almonds, cherry kernel, dark fruit cake and dark chocolate. This is a blanc de blancs of tremendous dimension, juxtaposed consummately with the tension and focus of pure 2008 acidity, the high-tensile definition of Oger and, most especially, Avize, and an all-consuming shower of epic, cascading, salty chalk minerality as embracing as a dousing in an icy waterfall, dissolving fruit and oak perfectly in a finish of crystalline mineral definition.

Zoémie De Sousa Cuvée Umami Grand Cru Extra Brut Vintage 2009 $$$$$

95 points • Disgorged February 2015 • Tasted in Champagne and Australia

70% chardonnay from Avize, and a little from Oger and Le Mesnil-sur-Oger; 30% pinot noir from Aÿ and Ambonnay; vines more than 50 years of age; vinified in new and old barrels; 3g/L dosage; 7000 bottles and 1000 magnums to be released over 10 years, with only 500 bottles allocated each year

De Sousa associates the Japanese concept of 'umami' with the mouthfeel of salinity and sappiness derived from the chalk soils of the Côte des Blancs, drawn out by biodynamic viticulture. Coming from anyone else, I would dismiss such umami aspirations as a trite, contrived marketing line, but the texture and frothing sea salt minerality of this first release are an irrefutable testimony to the successful execution of an ambitious brief. Few estates in the world have the terroirs and the expertise to embody umami as emphatically as this. The 2009 was chosen for this first release for its strength, roundness and power, with a ripe fruit body of fleshy white peach, pear, apple, nuances of ginger and roast almond barrel toastiness, all encased in a brittle mineral shell. In the two years since its release it's grown in depth and stature, building in spicy, honeyed complexity, fleshy depth and creamy, silky appeal, though shedding nothing of its salty, iodine umami. A cuvée of breathtaking line and length, presenting a captivating alternative to the De Sousa style.

....

De Sousa Cuvée des Caudalies Blanc de Blancs Grand Cru Extra Brut NV $$$

95 points • 2010 base vintage • Avize • Aged 4 years on lees • Disgorged October 2015 • Tasted in Australia
94 points • 2009 base vintage • Avize and Oger • Aged 5 years on lees • Disgorged January 2015 • Tasted in Champagne

100% chardonnay from vines aged over 50 years; fermented entirely in small oak barrels, 15% new; 50% reserves from a solera of every vintage from 1995; matured 4 years on lees; 5g/L dosage

I tasted the Caudalies solera for the first time during the 2014 harvest and was stunned at its complexity. In the 2010 base – 50% reserves, a blend of 16 vintages, all oak fermented – it might appear that its recipe could play havoc with purity and focus. To the contrary, and to the credit of the genius of Erick de Sousa and the all-conquering presence of salt-infused Avize chalk minerality, this is a wine of remarkable purity. The pristine energy of Avize charges grapefruit and white fruits of all kinds, while a full 20 years of maturity brings a walk through an autumnal landscape in spicy complexity of red apple, golden leaves, fig, cherry kernel, dried pear and butter on toast. The 2010 base brings greater presence than the energetic 2008, yet in the midst of such complexity, it maintains utter control and poise through an undeviating finish of grand persistence and silky, caressing texture. The warmer and more generous 2009 vintage does not have the same stamina to energise the reverberating complexity of its deep solera, yet nonetheless upholds good freshness, vitality and chalk mineral definition. A prestige cuvée in every regard except price.

De Sousa Cuvée des Caudalies Brut Rosé NV $$$$

94 points • 2010 BASE VINTAGE • DISGORGED DECEMBER 2014 • TASTED IN CHAMPAGNE AND AUSTRALIA

90% Avize chardonnay from vines aged over 50 years; 10% Aÿ pinot noir vinified as red wine and matured in oak casks for 1 year; fermented entirely in small oak barrels; matured 3.5 years on lees; 50% reserves from a solera of every vintage since 1995; 2000 bottles

Such is the powerful colour, pure fruit and delicate structure of De Sousa's red wine that a 10% dose transforms a pristine blanc de blancs into a characterful and savoury rosé. Relentless beauty of haunting red cherry and wild strawberry fruits that hover in suspension long through the finish accented by fleeting glimpses of tomatoes. The 2010 base brings a mid-palate depth and presence of immediate appeal, without the energy or chalk mineral fanfare of 2008. A maelstrom of complexity of incense, cumquats, cherry kernel and ginger erupts in a riveting spectacle of understated presence framed in Avize tension and exacting mineral texture, impeccably laced with ultra-fine tannins. The layered spice and seamless texture of a deep solera and barrel work are intricately entwined and perfectly integrated. It concludes gracefully refined and eminently sophisticated, with pencil-lead definition.

De Sousa Mycorhize Grand Cru Extra Brut NV $$$

93 points • 2012 BASE VINTAGE • DISGORGED MARCH 2016 • TASTED IN AUSTRALIA
92 points • 100% 2010 VINTAGE • DISGORGED 2014 • TASTED IN CHAMPAGNE

Chardonnay vines of more than 50 years of age in Avize and Oger; wild fermented entirely in 225 barrels; 3g/L dosage; 2000 bottles (2010), 1212 bottles (2012)

Mycorhize is a fungus that metabolises the soil and helps plant roots to ingest minerality. By only ploughing these vineyards by horse, the theory is that soil compaction is reduced and hence the roots achieve greater penetration, while increased mycorhize enhances mineral character. The wine dramatically exemplifies the science as the mineral, saline, iodine definition of Avize is accentuated in De Sousa's exacting regime. So pronounced is its salty, oyster shell presence that it is impossible to miss, even on the bouquet. The palate heightens the theme, amidst the apple, grapefruit and lemon of chardonnay in the great 2012 season, massaged with the creamy texture and savoury allure of barrel fermentation. The result contrasts fleshy, ripe fruit with all the savoury complexity of salt minerality and barrel work, culminating in a finish of focused mineral definition. An intriguing and unique style that meets its brief and will captivate those fascinated by Champagne's extremes. The 2010 season has produced a toasty and spicy style of baked apple and dried fig character, while upholding citrus definition on a long, dry finish.

From enviably placed, meticulously tended biodynamic vineyards, De Sousa's fruit is afforded the utmost care, hand loaded into the press.

DELAMOTTE

(Deh-la-mot)

6/10

5–7 Rue de la Brèche d'Oger 51190 Le Mesnil-sur-Oger

www.salondelamotte.com

CHAMPAGNE
DELAMOTTE
Le Mesnil sur Oger depuis 1760

*D*elamotte is effectively the second label of Salon (page 321), though the house prefers to call them 'sister houses'. It has been Salon's neighbour for over a century, and celebrated its 250th birthday in 2010. The two joined forces in 1988, and the following year were bought by Laurent-Perrier, which handles the winemaking for both brands. 'Delamotte has long been in the shadow of Salon, but we are now very proud of Delamotte,' declares Salon Delamotte president Didier Depond. And so he should be, because the initiatives he's put in place have set this exciting house on the rise.

Delamotte produces 800,000 bottles annually from 35 hectares of its own vineyards, largely in Le Mesnil-sur-Oger, and a similar volume of purchased fruit. Chardonnay is sourced principally from the grand crus of Le Mesnil-sur-Oger, Oger, Avize and Cramant, and pinot noir for its Brut NV and Rosé primarily from Bouzy, Ambonnay and Tours-sur-Marne. While Delamotte has shared production with Laurent-Perrier under Michel Fauconnet for more than 30 years in the house's substantial facility in Tours-sur-Marne, the vineyard resources of the house are distinct.

Delamotte also receives all the leftovers from Salon, and in years when Salon doesn't declare (two in five, to date), the entire Salon harvest is dedicated to Delamotte Blanc de Blancs NV (not the vintage, so as to avoid the perception of a declassified Salon). All the fruit of the Jardin de Salon went to Delamotte until the 2012 vintage, as it was replanted in 2003 and the average age for Salon is 35–40 years. For other parcels, the ultimate destiny of each tank (there are no barrels

here) is quickly determined post-fermentation, since Delamotte undergoes malolactic fermentation while Salon does not.

Delamotte has been riding a steep growth curve for the past couple of decades, more than trebling its output from 250,000 bottles, spurred by strong demand across Asia. Depond discloses that he could increase production to 1 million bottles, but this is not his aspiration.

His vision, instead, is to make Delamotte the reference house for blanc de blancs. Since Salon is blanc de blancs, it's no surprise that Delamotte's blanc de blancs cuvées are its soaring highlights. 'My dream is to produce only blanc de blancs, but it is impossible!' Depond exclaims.

When he commenced with the house in 1997, he streamlined the portfolio from seven to four cuvées. 'It was a nonsense!' he exclaims. 'Everyone wants to create new cuvées in Champagne now, but I prefer to be focused on just four.

The Champagne Guide

Depond has no interest in following the Champagne trends to make zero dosage or oak-fermented cuvées. 'Zero dosage is like a recipe without salt,' he proclaims. 'And the taste of wood is nonsense in champagne. For me, champagne is about freshness and elegance.'

In tune with this vision, he has been proactive in changing the balance of production of Delamotte, astutely reducing the volume of Brut NV, which represented the majority of the output of the house in 1997. Today, Blanc de Blancs NV and Blanc de Blancs Vintage comprise an impressive 50% of production. He has also been successful in gradually shifting the blend of Brut NV over more than a decade, in tune with his philosophy, from equal thirds of pinot noir, chardonnay and meunier when he commenced with the house, to 55% grand cru chardonnay and pinot noir from Bouzy, Ambonnay and Tours-sur-Marne today.

Disgorgement dates can be decoded from cork codes. The letter is the trimester and the year is inverted, so A61 denotes the first trimester of 2016.

Delamotte Brut NV $$

85 points • Base vintage 2010 • Disgorged April 2015 • Tasted in Champagne

55% grand cru chardonnay from Le Mesnil-sur-Oger, Avize and Cramant; 35% grand cru pinot noir mostly from Tours-sur-Marne, Bouzy and Ambonnay; 10% meunier from Reuil and Fleury-la-Rivière; 15 villages in all, 90% grand cru; 20% reserve wine; aged 3 years on lees; 7g/L dosage

There is no denying the progress made in the rise of chardonnay in this blend over the past decade, not to mention its laudable vineyard sources, though the tricky 2010 season has regrettably foiled its aspirations. I have long been disturbed by the dusty, dry extract, tilled earth, firm phenolics and mushroom notes that render its finish austere, and another couple of years of age have not rescued it. It upholds memories of apple and citrus fruit, with rising biscuity complexity.

Delamotte Blanc de Blancs NV $$

94 points • 2008 base vintage • Tasted in Australia
94 points • 2009 base vintage • Disgorged July 2014 • Tasted in Champagne
90 points • 2010 base vintage • Disgorged 2015 • Tasted in Champagne
     En magnum

Roughly equal proportions of Le Mesnil-sur-Oger for focus and attention, Oger for body and flesh, Avize for aromaticity and Cramant for harmony; 40% estate vineyards; 20% reserve wines; aged at least 4 years on lees; 7g/L dosage

The sublime 2008 base vintage sings with energetic, pristine vibrancy and a pale hue that eludes its age. Focused and primary lemon, grapefruit and white peach propagate with driving persistence, underscored by prominent, fresh chalk mineral structure. Subtle struck-flint reduction is characteristic of the style, while age has built nougat and toasted marshmallow complexity, finishing with great persistence and well-integrated dosage. The warmer 2009 season exhibits the same bright, chalk mineral glory, touched with golden delicious apple exoticism, while the lesser 2010 base shows toasted corn reduction and upholds good acid tension through a finish slightly distorted by this imperfect season.

DELAMOTTE ROSÉ NV $$$

93 points • TASTED IN CHAMPAGNE

80% pinot noir from Bouzy, Ambonnay and Tours-sur-Marne, co-fermented with 20% chardonnay mainly from Le Mesnil-sur-Oger; similar saignée process as Laurent-Perrier; aged 3-4 years on lees; a small production of just 30,000 bottles, so as not to compete with Laurent-Perrier; 8g/L dosage

The personality of southern Montagne de Reims pinot noir and the dexterity of Michel Fauconnet with rosé are both on display here. There's a copper tint to its crimson hue, but there is no hint of fading on the bouquet or palate, which are very much alive with pretty, fruity character reminiscent of red cherries, strawberries, pink pepper and pomegranate. A tightly honed and mineral finish is accented with gentle yet well-managed tannin grip.

DELAMOTTE BLANC DE BLANCS 2007 $$$

95 points • JUNE 2014 DISGORGEMENT • TASTED IN CHAMPAGNE AND AUSTRALIA

45% Le Mesnil-sur-Oger, remainder Oger, Avize and Cramant; 30% estate vineyards; 7 years on lees; 7g/L dosage

To Didier Depond, 2007 is the perfect Champagne vintage for chardonnay, light, airy and fresh, with acidity and presence. This cuvée exemplifies his impressions to the letter, a graceful and understated Delamotte that sings with the pronounced chalk mineral core of Le Mesnil-sur-Oger. It's bright and airy with magnificent expression of white peach, lemon and apple, becoming brioche, nougat, marzipan and vanilla bean. True to this elegant and cool season, a long finish is propelled by energetic acidity and lingering minerality, promising great things in the cellar.

DELAMOTTE COLLECTION BRUT 1970

96 points • DISGORGED 2012 • TASTED IN CHAMPAGNE EN MAGNUM

A rare treat from the Delamotte cellar, this is a complex and exotic blend exuding marmalade, tarte tatin, honey, dried apricot, and hints of resin. At a magnificent 46 years of age, tertiary suggestions of pipe smoke and green olives are but subtle hints, with secondary characters very much taking the lead. A magnum in magnificent form, evolving ever so slowly, glorious now, and with years of potential in it yet.

DEUTZ

(Derts)

9/10

6 RUE JEANSON 51160 AŸ

www.champagne-deutz.com

FONDÉ EN 1838

Champagne

DEUTZ

AY- FRANCE

'*Fabrice, you are crazy!' came the response when Deutz president Fabrice Rosset joined the house in 1996 and set a mandate to grow sales from 576,000 bottles to 1.5 million in just six years. 'As long as I could find the grapes, I could do it,' he reflects. 'And not only did we do it, we exceeded it!' Deutz continued to grow like a mad thing, more than tripling production to more than 2 million bottles every year from 2004 to 2008, dipping only slightly in response to the global economy and reaching 2.2 million bottles today. For such a breathtaking pace of expansion, the standards it has maintained are not only admirable, they're downright remarkable. There isn't one wine out of place in this line of crisp, pure champagnes, impeccably crafted in a style of elegant finesse.*

Deutz is still setting a cracking pace. The main press house in Aÿ was razed in 2010 and two new layers of cellars dug underneath. An investment of some €20 million was made in the cuverie alone, with a completely new press house erected just in time for vintage 2011, with new four- and eight-tonne presses, a new bottling line and increased capacity for reserve wines. These extensions increased cellar capacity from 8 million to 11.5 million bottles, and Deutz is now bottling its annual production target of 2.5 million bottles, having secured the grape supply to sustain it.

Owned by Louis Roederer, the house lays claim to just 42 of the total 200 hectares from which it sources fruit, all in grand and premier cru villages in the Marne.

Chardonnay and pinot noir are the focus for Deutz, with meunier comprising just 5% of its fruit. 'We are looking for vineyards to buy, but the availability of good vineyards is not high,' reveals Rosset, still very much the dynamic powerhouse behind the house. Most of the supply increase in recent years has come from purchased fruit. 'There is as much rivalry and fighting upstream in searching for good grapes as there is downstream in our markets!' he discloses. To reward quality, growers are paid based not only on the standard of their terroir, but the quality of grapes delivered. Growers are hearing of Deutz's reputation and calling the company to offer their grapes. 'This is the highest compliment we could be paid!' exclaims Rosset.

Can the house continue to maintain quality while following such a steep trajectory of growth? 'It is crucial that we maintain the same quality of supplies,' chef de cave Michel Davesne emphasises. The intention is to uphold the same suppliers, continuing to source from within 35 kilometres of Aÿ and using only the first pressings. He is confident the investments in the new winery and cellars will only aid the pursuit of quality.

Assuming the house can maintain reliable supply channels, Deutz will be well equipped to uphold its production target. Recently modernised disgorgement and warehousing facilities are already in operation, and 10 million bottles wait in anticipation for between three and 12 or more years in three kilometres of cellars extending into the hill, up to 65 metres deep beneath the vineyard behind Aÿ.

With sustainable agriculture a priority, Deutz is trialling organics and even biodynamics in the plot immediately above the winery. Chemical pesticides have been abandoned, and grasses cultivated in the mid-rows of some plots to avoid the use of herbicides and reduce yields. Pruning techniques and green harvests have also been adopted to reduce yields to slightly below the average.

Even in its young vins clairs, the clean, crisp, fresh, pristine focus of the house is abundantly clear. Deutz preserves the purity of its fruit through fermentation plot by plot in 350 stainless steel tanks (no barrels, apart from five for *liqueur d'expédition*, introduced in the austere 2011 vintage), temperature controlled to 16–17°C. Malolactic fermentation is encouraged systematically. Non-vintage wines are aged for two and a half years on lees, and are rested in the cellar for a further six months post-disgorgement. Dosages of around 9g/L are well matched to the graceful style of the house.

In vintages not up to standard, the prestige cuvées of William Deutz and Amour de Deutz are sacrificed to provide fruit resources to maintain the calibre of the non-vintage cuvées of the house. 'No way are we going to make Brut Classic with the leftovers!' Rosset exclaims.

Rosset personally joins the winemaking team at every blending session throughout the year, tasting every vat. Most batches of tailles are discarded, but even these are tasted four times, to ascertain which to sell. 'We must uphold our integrity and standards by selling off any parcel not up to standard,' he emphasises. When I visited during blending tastings in February 2016, Rosset and his team had already identified 776hL to sell off (from a total production of 17,000hL). It is such exacting attention to detail that defines the purity and precision of the house.

'The key to Deutz is elegance,' expounds Rosset. 'The Deutz style is made on refinement and harmony – this is the quintessence of champagne.' Then he checks himself and grins warmly. 'I am exaggerating!'

But he's right. In its classic, eloquently labelled bottles, Deutz has upheld its air of consistently refreshing, pure lemon sunshine.

DEUTZ BRUT CLASSIC NV $$

93 points • 2012 BASE VINTAGE • DISGORGED JANUARY 2016 • TASTED IN CHAMPAGNE AND AUSTRALIA

One-third each of chardonnay, pinot noir and meunier; 35% reserves of 2-4 years of age; a blend from 20-30 villages across the Marne, with a focus on Aÿ and Mareuil-sur-Aÿ; aged 3 years in the cellar; 9.5g/L dosage; around 1.8 million bottles annually

Brut Classic is the barometer of Deutz, representing 80% of the volume of production, and the house gives it first priority. Even in the wake of steady growth, it remains as pure and true as ever. This is the quintessential, refreshing apéritif, presenting an engaging contrast between the presence and volume of red apple and strawberry fruits of pinot, the racy tension of lemon and grapefruit of chardonnay, and the complexity of bottle age in nuances of nougat, brioche and honey. It finishes fine and long, with well-integrated dosage and gentle chalk minerality. There is presence and flesh here, well presented in the vivacious and subtle style that defines the signature of Deutz.

The Champagne Guide

Deutz Brut Rosé NV $$

95 points • 2012 BASE VINTAGE • DISGORGED FEBRUARY 2016 • TASTED IN CHAMPAGNE AND AUSTRALIA

90% pinot noir, including 8% red wine from Aÿ; 10% chardonnay; 30% reserves from the previous two vintages; aged almost 3 years on lees; 9g/L dosage

The pure, fresh style of Deutz is perfectly suited to elegant and restrained rosé, and the house is unusual in producing the style at three different levels. Right from the start, the entry cuvée is a gorgeous, bright, pale salmon, with a delightful air of rose petals and a pristine palate of exact red cherry, raspberry and strawberry fruit. The 2012 base represents a particularly graceful blend, a dazzling showpiece of pinot noir in all its radiant glory, yet with a refreshing elegance instilled by profound chalk mineral texture. It's long, refined and exactingly pinpoint accurate, a profound demonstration of the accomplishment of Deutz in crafting pristine rosé.

Deutz Brut Millésime 2010 $$$

92 points • DISGORGED APRIL 2016 • TASTED IN AUSTRALIA

75% pinot from Aÿ, Bouzy and Verzenay, 20% chardonnay from Avize, 5% meunier mainly from Pierry; 8.5g/L dosage

There's an intensity and a generosity to this vintage for Deutz, reflective of a confident lead from pinot noir from grand terroirs, and the result is commendable for a tricky season. Layered with grapefruit, fennel and fleshy peach, it's backed by the rising baked bread complexity of lees age. The purity of red fruit expression and the finesse of chalk mineral mouthfeel are marked by the challenges of the vintage, though it nonetheless upholds integrity, poise and balance.

Deutz Brut Millésime 2009 $$$

94 points • DISGORGED OCTOBER 2015 • TASTED IN CHAMPAGNE AND AUSTRALIA

67% pinot from Aÿ, Bouzy, Verzenay and Ambonnay; 29% chardonnay from Avize, Chouilly and Villers-Marmery; 4% meunier mainly from Pierry; 9.5g/L dosage

For a two-thirds pinot noir lead in a warm vintage, an impressively pale-straw hue is testament to the precision of Deutz. The personality of pinot is gloriously displayed in deep and rich layers of black cherries, strawberries, mixed spice and anise. It upholds impeccable poise and purity in the midst of riveting fruit power, with the ever-present texture of fine chalk minerality energising a long and fragrant finish, well married with subtle phenolic structure true to the ripeness of the season. Lees maturity has built seamless integration of brioche, toast and honey.

Deutz Blanc de Blancs Brut 2010 $$$

94 points • DISGORGED FEBRUARY 2016 • TASTED IN AUSTRALIA

55% Avize, 40% Le Mesnil-sur-Oger and Oger, 5% Villers-Marmery; 9.5g/L dosage

A gorgeous hue of ultra-pale, bright straw heralds a refined Deutz that transcends a less than easy season. There is body and presence here, with ripe white peach, fig, even a subtle hint of tropical exoticism, yet framed elegantly in the veil of subtlety and precision that define Deutz. The finish is long and focused, riding on a fine and pronounced sea of chalk minerality, the inimitable signature of Avize and Le Mesnil-sur-Oger.

Deutz Blanc de Blancs Brut 2009 $$$

94 points • Disgorged December 2015 • Tasted in Champagne and Australia

51% Avize; 23% Bergères-lès-Vertus; 21% Le Mesnil-sur-Oger; 5% Villers-Marmery; 7% Cramant, Oger and Chouilly; 9g/L dosage

Fabrice Rosset is brutally frank in admitting that 2009 isn't his favourite season, preferring the precision of 2008 and even the balance of the 2009 Brut compared with the Blanc de Blancs. I agree on every point, but kudos to the restraint and subtlety of Deutz in standing even a warm and generous season like 2009 in confident stead. The exuberance of white peach, and even star fruit, grilled pineapple and fig, are toned with the focus of beach-fresh lemon and the crunch of granny smith apple. The flesh and body of the front palate is honed consummately on a finish defined by the chalk mineral structure and acid tension of Avize. Time has built complexity of mixed spice, brioche, gingernut biscuits and even golden fruit cake. A rich and ripe vintage that holds its balance and perspective, concluding long and enticing.

Deutz Brut Rosé Millésimé 2012 $$$

96 points • Disgorged May 2016 • Tasted in Australia

80% pinot from Aÿ, Mareuil-sur-Aÿ, Bouzy, Ambonnay, Ludes, Rilly-la-Montagne and Verzenay; 20% chardonnay from Vertus, Avize, Le Mesnil-sur-Oger and Villeneuve-Renneville

The parade of vintages of Deutz rosé is like a ravishing catwalk line-up of elegant splendour, and the latest outfit is as drop-dead gorgeous as ever. Dressed in an ultra-pale salmon silk ballgown, it's a rousing celebration of pinot noir in all its red cherry and strawberry succulence, yet transcended with a remarkable, long-legged gracefulness. It culminates in a long train of bright acidity and fine, pronounced chalk mineral lace. Transfixing, adorable and downright delicious.

Deutz Brut Rosé Millésimé 2010 $$$

92 points • Disgorged June 2015 • Tasted in Champagne and Australia

78% pinot, including 9% pinot noir red wine from Aÿ and Bouzy; 22% chardonnay; 9g/L dosage

There is a faint copper tint to the ultra-pale salmon hue of this vintage, and a secondary complexity that takes it to a place of more pronounced savoury development, without the fresh precision of other recent vintages. This tricky season brings a mood change for Deutz Rosé. Strawberry hull, red cherry and red apple fruit are underlined by toasty, honeyed, roast nut maturity, flowing evenly into a balanced finish of fine chalk minerality and subtle phenolic texture. The flesh of pinot noir provides compelling mouthfeel and harmony despite the challenges of the vintage.

Deutz Demi-Sec 2007 $$

92 points • Tasted in Champagne

65% pinot noir, 30% chardonnay, 5% meunier; the same base as Brut Vintage; 35g/L dosage; just 1000 bottles

A demi-sec vintage of a decade of age is a rare thing (Philipponnat is the only other one I know), and all the more unusual to find such clean purity, freshness and persistence. It's honeyed, candied and toasty, filled with stone fruits, citrus and plenty of sweetness. True to the exacting regime of Deutz, though the 2007 Brut shows much greater finesse and poise in its standard, low-dosage rendition.

Deutz Cuvée William Deutz Brut Millésimé 2008 $$$$

98 points • Disgorged March 2015 • Tasted in Champagne and Australia en demi-bouteille

65% pinot mostly from Aÿ, Bouzy, Ambonnay and Verzenay; 32% chardonnay mostly from Avize and Le Mesnil-sur-Oger; 3% meunier mostly from Pierry; 9.5g/L dosage; currently only in half bottles, with full bottles coming soon

The finest vintages of William Deutz display profound contrasts and contradictions, juxtaposing the exacting precision of the house with the intensity of pinot noir, and it is in the most energetic vintages that this accord finds its most alluring expression. No season exemplifies this more magnificently than 2008. It is built around depth and breadth, charged with an incredible display of the freshness of Deutz, and elevated and energised by ultra-fine, chalk-rich minerality that attains new heights of expression in this profound season. For all of its contrasts, it crucially maintains seamless persistence and breathtaking lightness. Youthful endurance is declared in vibrant lemon zest and young summer-fruit freshness, quietly touched with depth of brioche, ginger, vanilla nougat and toast. A prominent, mouth-enveloping, silky cloud of chalk dust is the grand highlight of a mesmerising finish, riding a laser-line of acidity of the utmost elegance. In a full bottle, it will live for decades, but in a half, it's irresistible right away. One of the greatest Deutz cuvées of the modern era.

Deutz Cuvée William Deutz Brut Millésimé 2006 $$$$

96 points • Disgorged April 2015 • Tasted in Champagne and Australia

66% pinot mostly from Aÿ, Bouzy, Ambonnay and Verzenay; 29% chardonnay from Avize, Vertus, Chouilly and Villers-Marmery; 5% meunier mostly from Venteuil; 9g/L dosage

In the exuberant 2006 season, the generous and fast-evolving mood of pinot noir from some of Champagne's finest crus sits eloquently in the refined style of Deutz to captivating and mesmerising effect. It's fast evolved to a comfortable place of secondary complexity of toast, vanilla custard, nougat, golden fruit cake and roast hazelnuts, while upholding the soft, supple mirabelle plum spice of the season, touched with subtle struck-flint reduction. Gentle phenolic presence on the finish is true to the warmth of the year, and melds comfortably with surprisingly pronounced fine chalk minerality for such a voluminous vintage. It's ready to drink now, a standout for the season. Kudos, Deutz.

Deutz Cuvée William Deutz Brut Millésimé 1988

96 points • Disgorged 2004 • Tasted in Champagne

The energetic and enduring 1988 season bears grand testimony to the stamina of Deutz, and this once austere cuvée has evolved to a wonderful place of savoury complexity reminiscent of no less than coffee bean, cocoa, green olive, preserved lemon and spice. Even after almost three decades, it projects remarkable lemon zest freshness with an incredible persistence, purity and elegant restraint that articulate the signature of the house.

Deutz Amour de Deutz Brut Millésimé 2008 $$$$

98 points • Disgorged January 2016 • Tasted in Champagne and Australia
en demi-bouteille

100% chardonnay; 57% Avize, 38% Le Mesnil-sur-Oger, 5% Villers-Marmery; 9.5g/L dosage;
currently only in half bottles, with full bottles coming soon

In the delicately masterful hands of Deutz, the zesty vibrancy, energetic freshness and effortless grace of two of the most profound chardonnay terroirs on earth rise to mesospheric heights in the scintillating 2008 harvest. Chalk mineral tension explodes like a stark white firework in the dark of night, illuminating ultra-fine definition and a pronounced, glittering shower of salty chalk texture. Apple, pear and lemon fruit glistens in the flickering glow, toned by the toasted brioche, ginger cake and nougat accents of bottle age, accentuated in a half bottle. A cuvée of profound definition and precision, yet possessing a substance and succulence that make it irresistible from the outset. I can't wait to taste it from a full bottle.

Deutz Amour de Deutz Brut Millésimé 2007 $$$$

97 points • Tasted in australia

100% chardonnay; 51% Avize, 44% Le Mesnil-sur-Oger, 5% Villers-Marmery

Magnificent chalk mineral definition declares the grand terroirs of Avize and Le Mesnil in profound, articulate detail. Stunning lemon, apple and pear fruit has evolved gracefully into toasted brioche, nougat and roasted almond complexity, accented by appealing struck-flint reduction, supported by well-integrated acid poise and balanced dosage. It's attained a compelling and enticing peak in its curve, where primary vivacity and secondary complexity propel each other forth, never competing, never dominating. It's ready to thrill right away and any time in the next two years.

Deutz Amour de Deutz Brut Millésimé 2006 $$$$

97 points • Disgorged variously in 2015 • Tasted in Champagne and Australia

100% chardonnay; 53% Le Mesnil-sur-Oger, 39% Avize, 8% Villers-Marmery; 9g/L dosage

There are no sparkling chardonnay terroirs more profound than Le Mesnil-sur-Oger and Avize, and the exacting and sensitive hands of Deutz unite the two to profound effect. Subtle struck-flint reduction flows into apple, pear, white nectarine and lemon fruit well evolved to the toasted brioche and roasted almond complexity of 11 years of maturity. Profound, salty, brilliant chalk mineral texture froths effortlessly amidst finely structured acidity and balanced dosage. It carries generosity and presence true to the warm 2006 season, though it transcends the vintage, never for a moment dropping its gaze from the effortless poise that sets Deutz apart. It's ready to enrapture right away, and will hold for a couple of years still.

Deutz Amour de Deutz Rosé Millésime Brut 2008 $$$$

99 points • Disgorged March 2015 • Tasted in Champagne and Australia en demi-bouteille

64% pinot from Aÿ, Verzenay, Ambonnay and Bouzy, including 9% red wine from Aÿ and Mareuil-sur-Aÿ; 36% chardonnay from Avize and Le Mesnil-sur-Oger; 9.5g/L dosage

Uniting the very greatest pinot terroirs with the pinnacle chardonnay crus in the greatest season in decades, with the exacting precision of Deutz and all of its wizardry with rosé, should produce a cuvée of dizzying heights, but there is no anticipating the sheer, graceful beauty that has been captured in this little bottle. A radiant, pale-salmon hue heralds the most delicate and expressive aromas of rose petals, freshly picked red cherries and cherry kernel, flowing into a palate of the most delightful strawberry and red cherry flavours. Understated elegance meets the brief for Amour de Deutz Rosé, and yet these profound pinot noir terroirs possess a deep, even powerful presence, a line and a breathtaking persistence beyond words. For all of its delight, it saves its most riveting declaration until the end: a chalk mineral structure that rises like a frothing wave on the finish, of such complete, mouth-filling presence and fine chalk mineral texture that it should overwhelm such delicate, elegant demeanour, yet it is effortlessly, profoundly and perfectly integrated. Even after nine years in a half bottle, it is still exactingly primary and fresh. Such is its beauty it brought me to tears. Could it possibly be any finer in a full bottle?

Deutz Amour de Deutz Rosé Millésime Brut 2007 $$$$

96 points • Disgorged November 2015 • Tasted in Australia

60% pinot mostly from Aÿ, Verzenay, Ambonnay and Bouzy; 40% chardonnay mostly from Avize and Villers-Marmery; 9g/L dosage

The refined grace of Deutz is exemplified nowhere more exactly than in Amour de Deutz Rosé, capturing an A-list of many of Champagne's finest terroirs with all the delicate grace that defines this great estate. Primary, understated red cherry fruit has begun to evolve into the toasty, honeyed spectrum of bottle age, as its pale-salmon hue has started to take on a subtle copper tint. It upholds effortless flow and spectacular persistence, ever supported by the omnipresent texture of finely structured grand cru chalk mineral mouthfeel.

Deutz Amour de Deutz Rosé Millésime Brut 2006 $$$$

97 points • Disgorged March 2015 • Tasted in Champagne and Australia

55% pinot mostly from Aÿ, Verzenay and Bouzy, including 8% red wine from Aÿ and Mareuil-sur-Aÿ; 45% chardonnay mostly from Avize, Chouilly and Villers-Marmery; 9g/L dosage

A new star has risen in the dazzling firmament of Deutz rosé, a brand new release, replacing William Deutz Rosé with an intentionally more elegant style and inadvertently offering a profound insight into the motivation of this house and its president, making the tough and costly decision never to release Amour de Deutz Rosé 2005.

It takes all the wizardry and resources of Deutz to create a new rosé of such thrilling, towering magnificence. It is at once ethereal in its elegance, precise in its definition and fairy-light on its feet, yet there is grand presence and depth of fruit power driving it long and full on the finish. Capturing such a definitive platform of chalk mineral texture within a style of breathtakingly graceful elegance elevates it to another spiritual plane. In the two years since its release it has shed its primary, lively red berry and cherry fruits and evolved to a more complex and secondary place of Burgundian-like complexity, with hints of truffles, forest floor, toasted brioche, honey, even an understated hint of fruit mince spice. It has lost nothing of its impeccably crafted shape of exuberant yet immaculate refinement, all-embracing, fine chalk minerality and mesmerising persistence. A triumph, and an instant addition to Champagne's top rosé tier — and who else can claim that with a new cuvée?

DEVAUX

(Deh-voh)

6/10

DOMAINE DE VILLENEUVE, 10110 BAR-SUR-SEINE

www.champagne-devaux.fr

1846

CHAMPAGNE
VEUVE A. DEVAUX

Champagne Devaux is the label of the large Union Auboise cooperative based in Bar-sur-Seine in the heart of the Champagne outpost of Côte des Bar. Owned by more than 800 growers, with some 1400 hectares under vine, the cooperative is the largest grower in the region and sells a substantial quantity of juice to other houses. Its headquarters are located in the country, on the banks of the Seine, where the soil is too moist for subterranean storage, so air-conditioned, industrial warehousing is employed. This hardly reads like an endorsement, but the cooperative is innovative and progressive, and its value-for-money champagnes are well made, living up to its aspiration of flagship Côte des Bar cuvées of long-aged pinot noir and chardonnay with no tailles, showcasing the fruit power and definition of the region.

The Union Auboise dedicates just 100 hectares to the production of Devaux, and even this is more than 1.5 times the requirement for producing 650,000 bottles each year. Twenty percent of volume is lost through avoidance of tailles in the blends. Chef de cave Michel Parisot visits every vineyard prior to harvest to decide which will be rejected.

Twenty-five years at Devaux have blessed Parisot with a keen insight into the diversity of terroirs across the many valleys of the large region of the Aube. He compares some with the soils of Chablis, and others with those of Burgundy – which comes as no surprise, with many of his vineyards closer to both than the Côte des Blancs.

'We are not about comparing the Côte des Bar with the Côte des Blancs,' he emphasises. 'We have vineyards in both, and we focus on the diversity of Champagne in its villages, landscapes and finished products.'

Pinot noir rules in the Côte des Bar, and leads most of Parisot's cuvées, but chardonnay is increasing in the region, showing particular promise in Urville, and finding representation in the wines accordingly. Since 1987, Devaux has turned its attention more resolutely towards the Aube, focusing on pinot noir and chardonnay, removing meunier from its cuvées.

Parisot works closely with his many growers, though a team of six full-time liaison officers is required to help them better manage their vineyards.

'We decided some years ago that we want to have a large representation of organic vines, and we tell our growers that this is how they should manage their vineyards,' Parisot reports. Devaux performs extensive

The Champagne Guide

experimental work, investigating different techniques in its vineyards.

Growers are paid a premium for fruit destined for the premium D de Devaux range, which currently represents 30% of the brand. There is an aspiration to increase this to 50%, and to slowly grow production by 5% every year, a conservative target given the vineyard resources at Devaux's disposal.

The house is equally progressive in vinification, creating a vast array of different parcels from every vintage. Parisot compares his philosophy to that of a perfumer, creating different flavours to assemble a blend of great complexity. 'The first work is in the vineyard; the second is to create many different possibilities for fermentation and vinification, so as to produce a large palette of flavours,' he says.

This defines an interesting and unusual house style that encompasses a bit of everything – tank ferment-ation, barrel fermentation, large barrels and small, bâtonnage, full malolactic, no malolactic, even reserve soleras back to 1995. With 500 tanks and barrels of all sizes at his disposal, the permutations for Parisot's experimentation are vast, and in the rare and privileged position of selling an enormous 95% of every harvest to other houses, he is afforded the luxury of keeping only those ferments that suit his blends.

Malolactic fermentation is completed for the Devaux range, and carried out or blocked for D de Devaux, according to the parcel and the year. Parisot likes the complexity of blending with the two so much that he will sometimes split parcels and allow part to go through malolactic fermentation.

The D de Devaux wines are fermented in oak barrels, and large stocks of reserve wines are kept in large oak tuns of 3000–7000-litre capacity for up to three years. This allows the opportunity for slow, natural oxidation. 'I don't like oxidative wines, I like well-developed wines,' Parisot emphasises. 'A good champagne should have just the beginning of oxidation flavours, but always maintain its freshness.' To further preserve freshness, malolactic fermentation is blocked on all oak-fermented parcels.

A small percentage of reserves are fermented in small barrels and matured on lees with weekly bâtonnage for four months. After extensive trials, Parisot was surprised to discover that 300-litre barrels produce finer and more elegant wines than 600-litre demi-muids.

Parisot's latest pursuit has been in pioneering the use of local oak from the Côte des Bar, motivated by an imperative to improve the company's carbon footprint. He is working with the University of France to compare oak from the Côte des Bar, Montagne de Reims and Argonne, but it's still early days and he admits he is yet to identify any differences in flavour. 'We would like to determine whether a certain forest suits a particular parcel of pinot noir or chardonnay, but it will take us many years, and maybe we will find that the place of origin doesn't matter!' he admits. His latest pursuit has been in trialling new Burgundian toasting techniques, favouring long toasting at low temperature to achieve an elegant result.

A focus on raising quality since 1987 has seen a trend towards increasing use of reserve wines, an impressive increase in bottle age of non-vintage cuvées from two years to between three and five, and a progressive decrease in dosage to under 10g/L. Each of three or four different disgorgements for each cuvée receives a different dosage, generally 7–9g/L.

An increased focus on the D de Devaux range has seen its production double since its release in 1999 to an impressive 40% of the brand. New and unique metal neck labels declare admirable durations of lees age.

A number of cuvées are sealed under DIAM closures and Parisot is delighted. 'We have only had two complaints in four years regarding the look of these closures,' he says. Unfortunately, the D de Devaux range is still consigned to natural cork, but Parisot believes he's close to convincing the company's president to move the entire range across to DIAM.

Since 2014, disgorgement dates have been laser etched into every bottle. The last digit of the bottling code is the base year, so, for instance, LYD6 is 2006 base.

Parisot's innovative and progressive spirit continues to drive advancement at Devaux. 'It is always possible to improve,' he maintains. 'We can't sit on our reputation. We must always look for ways to improve.'

Devaux: one of the Aube's most innovative, progressive producers.

Devaux Grande Réserve Brut NV $$

92 points • 2010 BASE VINTAGE • DISGORGED MARCH 2016 • TASTED IN AUSTRALIA

70% pinot, 30% chardonnay; 20% reserves partially aged in oak foudres; 100% malolactic fermentation; aged at least 3 years on lees; 9g/L dosage; DIAM closure; ~400,000 bottles

Another enticing rendition of this impeccably assembled blend, showcasing the inviting lusciousness and definition of the Côte des Bar at an affordable price. Pinot noir is the perpetual theme of this blend, declaring its rounded, primary generosity of succulent cherry, plum and peach fruit. It's backed with all the fanfare of long lees age in layers of mixed spice, toast, honey, even dark fruit cake depth, impeccably enlivened with a vibrant acid backbone and soft minerality, bringing poise and focus to the finish. It's well made and great value.

D de Devaux Cuvée D NV $$

94 points • 2008 BASE VINTAGE • DISGORGED MAY 2014 • 60% PINOT, 40% CHARDONNAY
   • 7G/L DOSAGE • TASTED IN AUSTRALIA
94 points • 2010 BASE VINTAGE • DISGORGED JANUARY 2016 • 55% PINOT, 45% CHARDONNAY
   • 8G/L DOSAGE • TASTED IN AUSTRALIA

Pinot from the Côte des Bar, chardonnay from the Côte des Blancs, a small component vinified in small oak barrels; 40% reserves aged in oak foudres; partial malolactic fermentation; 5 years on lees

A captivating celebration of the spicy, luscious generosity of Aube pinot, enlivened with Côte des Blancs chardonnay and polished with long bottle age while upholding vibrancy and the energetic tang of partial malolactic fermentation. Michel Parisot has maintained a reserve solera in large oak tuns since 2002, showcasing the complexity of maturity that can be built in a solera, while upholding wonderful purity, freshness and finesse. For its age and pinot noir lead, the 2010 base presents a bright pale-straw hue and pretty freshness of crunchy red apple, pure lemon juice and all the flavour of wild strawberries. Youthful fruit purity and vibrancy are charged with electric acidity, creating an energising effect that belies five years of age on lees. The finish proclaims its maturity not in flavour but in fine, mouth-filling, lees-derived texture and effortlessly harmonious persistence. The 2008 juxtaposes secondary and primary expression, rejoicing in the concentration of the Aube, perfectly honed with a touch of malic acidity. A showcase for the intelligent winemaking of this underrated outfit in top form.

Devaux Sténopé 2008 $$$$

95 points • TASTED IN AUSTRALIA

3400 bottles and 600 magnums

In 2007 Devaux teamed up with Rhône superstar Michel Chapoutier to purchase a vineyard in Les Riceys. In 2008 this site provided the core of a new prestige cuvée which the two houses designed together, to be created every vintage, 'even in bad years'. The precise details have not been disclosed. It is a blend of pinot noir and chardonnay of undisclosed proportions, predominantly barrel fermented ('a high proportion'), with no malolactic fermentation in these components.

The first iteration is a characterful and engaging wine of medium, bright straw hue that leads out with the savoury, charcuterie complexity of barrel ferment, supporting the depth of red fruit fleshiness of pinot noir, energised by the cut of chardonnay and the bolt of 2008 acidity. Chalk minerality meets chewy barrel ferment texture, producing an engaging mouthfeel that contrasts delicacy with mouth-filling presence. It finishes very long and accurate, promising a grand future.

The Champagne Guide

D de Devaux D Rosé Brut NV $$$

94 points • 2009 BASE VINTAGE • TASTED IN AUSTRALIA
94 points • 2010 BASE VINTAGE • DISGORGED JANUARY 2016 • TASTED IN AUSTRALIA
55% pinot, 45% chardonnay; aged at least 5 years on lees; 6g/L dosage

A purposely light and fresh apéritif style, so much so that it does not rely on any reserves, though it is still only labelled as a non-vintage cuvée in spite of five years of lees age. The 2010 vintage meets the brief, as a pretty pale salmon hue announces an elegantly characterful style that captures the musk, wild strawberry and raspberry personality of Côte des Bar pinot noir and frames it beautifully in fine chalk mineral texture. More than five years on lees has built wonderfully seamless integration and a fine and creamy bead, without diminishing primary focus or refined purity. The 2009 remains equally lively and bright, with more black cherry and anise personality, refined by lively acid line and gentle tannin grip. A fragrant and delightfully crafted Devaux Rosé.

D de Devaux Millésime 2008 $$$

95 points • DISGORGED JUNE 2015 • TASTED IN AUSTRALIA
52% chardonnay from the Côte des Blancs, 48% pinot from the Côte des Bar; fermented in stainless steel tanks; full malolactic fermentation; 6 years on lees; 8g/L dosage

The cuddly generosity of Côte des Bar pinot noir is the perfect foil for the tension of Côte des Blancs chardonnay in the magnificently high-strung 2008 season. The result is a fine-tuned accord between the juicy peach and red cherry fruit of pinot, the citrus attack of chardonnay and the toasty, spicy, brioche enticement of more than six years on lees. It finishes with fine, creamy texture, well-composed, subtle salt minerality and captivating immediacy and appeal.

D de Devaux Millésime 2006 $$$

92 points • TASTED IN AUSTRALIA
50% chardonnay from the Côte des Blancs, 50% pinot from the Côte des Bar; 7 years on lees; 6g/L dosage

This cuvée encapsulates the luscious generosity of the ripe 2006 vintage in succulent peach, black cherry and mirabelle plum fruit, layered in the spicy complexity of the Aube. A touch of phenolic texture on the finish reflects its warmer season, but it upholds acid balance, persistence and appeal.

D de Devaux Ultra Extra Brut NV $$

91 points • 2008 BASE VINTAGE • DISGORGED OCTOBER 2014 • TASTED IN AUSTRALIA
90 points • 2009 BASE VINTAGE • DISGORGED MARCH 2016 • TASTED IN AUSTRALIA
D de Devaux with just 2g/L dosage; 60% pinot, 40% chardonnay; 40% reserves from solera back to 1995, aged in large oak foudres; aged more than 5 years on lees

Devaux purposely avoids a zero-dosage cuvee, favouring a dosage of 2g/L to provide better balance and persistence. The result is a more taut, metallic and coiled expression of Cuvee D, accenting lemon zest and chalk mineral structure on a firmer, tenser finish in the 2009 base. The 2008 base preserves the prominent plum and black cherry of Aube pinot, though low dosage likewise makes for a more biscuity, coarse, firm and tense finish. A searing, ultra-dry champagne for the brave, and a case for the foils of a dry style from a base built for a higher dosage.

DOM PÉRIGNON

(Dom Pe-ri-ngon)

8/10

20 AVENUE DE CHAMPAGNE 51200 ÉPERNAY
www.domPérignon.com
www.creatingdomPérignon.com

Dom Pérignon is the prestige cuvée of Moët & Chandon, but so distinct are the production, style and sheer class of the wines that the two brands are best considered completely autonomous. The two are made in the same premises in Épernay, and some facilities are shared, but the winemaking teams are distinct. Of Moët's colossal resource of 1180 hectares of estate vineyards, some are designated as Moët, others Dom Pérignon, and the rest are vinified by Dom Pérignon and allocated at the time of blending. 'The Dom' is a wine of tension, power and long-ageing endurance, the king of the most readily available and perpetually discounted prestige cuvées.

Dom Pérignon is the vision of the talented and in-sightful Richard Geoffroy, dedicated to this cuvée since 1990, and who today also oversees the entire production of Moët & Chandon ('piloting the cruise liner!'). The man who deserves much of the credit for the rise of one of Champagne's most famous and celebrated brands of the modern age carries his responsibility with unassuming humility. When I congratulated him on his 25th year in early 2015, he praised the positive energy of his team and the extensive resources at his disposal. 'I must be the most privileged winemaker in the world!' he grinned.

Geoffroy works painstakingly to draw out the best wines he can in each season, while juggling the politics of big business and a frenetic travel schedule to intro-duce his wines to the world. While deeply embedded in the history and tradition of Champagne, he steers this sizeable house with a courageous sense of daring (more on this later), and there is no doubt he is one of the great minds of modern Champagne.

Alongside Louis Roederer Cristal, Dom Pérignon was the very first of champagne's prestige cuvées, introduced in the mid-1930s with the 1921 vintage. There are only two wines: a vintage and a vintage rosé, traditionally produced less than one year in two, released after a minimum of seven years' bottle ageing on lees, and again selectively in later life recently renamed, less than romantically, Dom Pérignon P2 and P3 (formerly 'Oenothèque'). There are no non-vintage wines. Every vintage is harvested and vinified, and the decision is made at the blending table as to whether the wine will be made and released, or the entire vintage sold off.

Dom Pérignon's production is a closely guarded secret and rumours abound in Champagne, with some putting annual sales at 3.5 million bottles, and others suggesting as many as 8 million each vintage. The company maintains it is very much less than this, divulging only that it's more than Krug's 600,000 bottles. There is a desire to increase production, but opportunities to increase estate holdings are extremely limited. 'I would love to have more grand cru vineyards!' Geoffroy exclaims. 'We're already making as much as we can.'

VAST VINEYARD RESOURCES

Dom Pérignon is based on a core of five grand cru villages of pinot noir: Aÿ, Ambonnay, Bouzy, Verzenay and Mailly-Champagne; and four of chardonnay: Le Mesnil-sur-Oger, Avize, Cramant and Chouilly, in which the company owns 'huge' resources. In all, there are about 20 villages in the blend, including the premier crus of Hautvillers and Vertus. Estate vineyards in 14 of Champagne's 17 grand crus are called upon, and fruit is sometimes purchased from two of the others, but over the past decade more than 98% has come from estate sources, including the oldest vines of the premier cru of Hautvillers, the historical and spiritual home of Dom Pérignon.

The key to Dom Pérignon's sourcing is the vast diversity of vineyards at its disposal. Historically, particular sites have been dedicated to each Moët Hennessy house, and Dom Pérignon has had first choice. 'There are core grand crus for Dom Pérignon and we have a privilege to access the fruit sources of the other houses as we desire,' Geoffroy divulges. He is afforded 'tremendous latitude' to change the plots and take the very best that a given year has to offer. Blending is fundamental to Dom Pérignon, and Geoffroy upholds that this is more important than ever in vintage champagne. 'If there is one house able to make vineyard-specific wine styles, surely it is Dom Pérignon – we own more vineyards than anyone else in every grand cru,' he points out. 'If anyone is capable of making Le Mesnil, it is Dom Pérignon! But I want to use Le Mesnil in the blend.'

The Dom Pérignon house style is about a tension between chardonnay and pinot noir, in a blend of roughly 50/50, though it can drift to 60/40 in either direction, according to the season. Chardonnay is the limiting ingredient in production, and in the current time of short supply, Geoffroy is pleased to have the security of a majority of estate vineyards and a single contract with a 'top cooperative'.

The precise moment of harvest is given the utmost attention, and the grapes are tasted twice every day. The window of picking is short – 'in 2008 it was vegetal on Monday and too ripe on Tuesday!' Geoffroy uses pH over acid, flavour and sugar as the most important indicator of properly ripe fruit. Waiting for sugar ripeness doesn't work in the wildly fluctuating vintages of current times. 'Ten degrees of sugar ripeness in 2003 was not like 10 degrees in 2004!' he points out.

Work is underway to redefine vineyard plots using observation tools such as aerial surveying, and to separately vinify each plot to further hone the detail of each parcel. Trials have also been conducted into an acceptable distance for fruit to be trucked between vineyard and press house, finding that a distance exceeding 15–20 kilometres can be problematic. Dom Pérignon is not afraid of some oxidation prior to fermentation in order to reduce phenolics in the juice, but this needs to be carefully controlled, according to the maturity of the grapes and their phenolic content.

REDUCTIVE WINEMAKING

'We are very dedicated to the fruit and the vineyards, but fermentation is just as important,' Geoffroy declares. Wines are fermented exclusively in stainless steel tanks, using a cultured house yeast strain, with sulphite added at the press to kill off indigenous wild yeasts. 'I love the idea of the yeast emptying into the wine to bring an added dimension; the organic meeting the mineral,' says Geoffroy. The wine is judiciously protected from oxidation post-fermentation. 'Our vision is to age our wine in a reductive way, as too much oxidation kills champagne's complexity, making it fat and heavy.'

Malolactic fermentation is run to completion using a culture co-inoculated with the primary fermentation, upheld as a key to achieving freshness as the wines build complexity and texture through long ageing. If vintages continue to warm, malolactic may be blocked in some parcels to maintain balance.

There is no rule for the dosage level in Dom Pérignon, which is determined through trials of different reserve wines and varying levels of sugar and sulphur dioxide six months prior to release. The dosage sweetness has diminished from 10g/L in 1996 to less than 7g/L today. 'Perhaps the maturity of the grapes is higher, or perhaps we're doing different things in the making?' postulates Geoffroy's offsider, Vincent Chaperon.

The decision to release a wine is made at the point of blending. 'Even in the lousiest years we go to the final blend with no preconceived ideas,' Geoffroy says. 'Since Dom Pérignon has been Dom Pérignon we have always harvested a vintage every year.'

First released in 1959, Dom Pérignon Rosé represents just a few per cent of the blanc volume, and typically sells for close to twice the price. Only made in seasons in which phenolics are in balance, there is an attempt to make rosé in every vintage, but it's typically released every second year. It displays a riper fruit profile than the blanc, since the pinot noir for the red wine for blending is picked riper, with more aromatics and more jammy character. 'The challenge is to balance this to maintain delicacy in the wine,' Chaperon explains. 'It's a highly bodied wine that needs to maintain an equilibrium between authority and seduction.' Since 2000, the mandate has been to make a more substantial rosé style. 'Burgundy is all the rage and the market is looking for a more substantial style,' Geoffroy explains.

The key to Dom Pérignon lies in blending to achieve 'a state of completeness', a perfect balance of white and black grapes. 'Harmony is so intense!' is Geoffroy's line. 'It's like playing tennis. If you're not experienced you try to make it up with power, but if you have the right swing, it's effortless. You can forget about power and deliver intensity. When you hit it right, you hear it because the sound of the ball is different. You hear the pop! That's my quest. Dom Pérignon is about the pop.'

THE NEW DOM PÉRIGNON

Prior to 1990, Dom Pérignon released 29 vintages in 70 years – one release every two and a half years. Since Geoffroy commenced in 1990, the frequency has almost doubled, to 13 vintages in 17 seasons. This has recently increased further still. Since 1997, so far only 2001 has not been released. This is the first time in its almost century-long history that Dom Pérignon has released eight out of nine vintages. 'My dream is to make Dom Pérignon every year,' Geoffroy reveals. 'I am a physician, my commitment is to bring vintages to life.'

Conspiracy theories abound, but he thanks an improvement in Champagne vintages for this trend. 'I have often been asked about global warming, and I am embarrassed to say that so far it has been for the better in Champagne!' he exclaims. 'Good crop sizes, more consistent yields, good consistency of quality, good levels of ripeness, lower acids and more rounded wines, which I'm very excited about.'

He admits he is not yet able to make Dom Pérignon every year. 'But if you cross global warming with smart viticulture and more precision in the winemaking, the only question is the volume of the blend.' In the difficult 2005 vintage, he released a smaller volume and suggested that in the most challenging years, a release

The celebrated sweeping slopes of Verzenay. The key to Dom Pérignon is its vast and unparalleled resource of grand cru vineyards.

The Champagne Guide

might represent one-quarter or even one-eighth of a large vintage such as 2004.

It is bewildering that Dom Pérignon released a full production volume of the controversial 2003 vintage, a difficult and atypical season, when the hottest summer to ever hit Champagne was recorded. Geoffroy admits that '2003 is high in phenolics, it's the key to the vintage'. The hard bitterness that this brings is my biggest concern with this vintage. He reveals it had the lowest acidity he's ever recorded, and then makes an unexpected announcement: 'I take it as it is. It's not about the style of Dom Pérignon, it's about the vintage. I am sick of the word "style". There is no style. Dom Pérignon is pushing the idea of vintage more than anything else.'

There's something noble and inherently authentic in this statement, something perhaps more Burgundian than it is Champenois: a wholesome celebration of the voice of the elements over the force of the hand of man. Yet in a climate as tumultuous and increasingly erratic as Champagne's, there is something deeply disturbing in this statement, too. It changes the game for Dom Pérignon.

The Dom Pérignon that we know and love has never been all about the vintage. Chaperon explained to me some years ago that 'Dom Pérignon is about creating a balance between the style of the vintage and the style of the house, and we are able to drive the vintage in the direction of our style by selecting the finest sites in each season. Whether we release a vintage is more a question of style than of quality.'

'Style' hasn't always been a dirty word for Dom Pérignon. Until recently, if the style of the vintage hadn't met the style of Dom Pérignon, it was never released. And there will always be Champagne vintages unworthy of standing alone. But it seems something changed in 2003. Geoffroy admits that '2003 is border territory for Champagne, as border as it can be. We took the risk, a technical risk. Frankly, we never lacked confidence, but we had to push harder.'

Is 2003 a one-off? Geoffroy alludes to a fundamental shift in the philosophy of the house. 'Some future vintages will be more than you might expect from Dom Pérignon,' he warns. 'In the past, Dom Pérignon has been very gentle and very accessible. But the decade of the 2000s is more about pushing the style. We are pushing the factor of vintage, covering a much broader span of scope than anything in the past, making wine in the character of the vintage by playing with the ripeness. We are not playing on the safe side as much as we used to, and as much as other champagne makers are, which implies that there is an element of risk. This is doing very good things for the brand, and I will keep taking the risks because it is the only way to keep the brand alive.'

Are we entering an era in which the consumer must exercise greater discretion in selecting vintages of Dom Pérignon? If 2003 suggested that we are, 2005 confirms it, and there are more vintages to come which are 'very much on the ripe side'.

THE PLENITUDES P1, P2 AND P3

Geoffroy speaks of three ages of peak maturity in Dom Pérignon's life, the first after 7–9 years (the standard release, formerly released at seven years of age and now nine or 10, the 'first plenitude,' dubbed P1), a second at 12–20 years (now P2, formerly 'Oenothèque') and a third at 35–40 years (P3, the 'plenitude of complexity').

Dom Pérignon makes these mature vintages available through an extremely limited library of releases, representing just 1–2% of only the most age-worthy vintages, and typically at double the price of the first release.

P1 and P2 are each disgorged as a single batch, and surprisingly not necessarily soon before release (1998 P2 was disgorged five years before release), but P3 tends to be disgorged progressively according to demand. P2 is released in vintage order and P3 in any order, as each vintage is ready. P2 and P3 are a testament to the remarkable battery pack of energy and vitality contained within the lees in a bottle of champagne, capable of sustaining a bottle for a lifetime. If a vintage is not deemed worthy of a P2 and P3 release, it is never released, even as P1. If it then didn't develop satisfactorily for P2 and P3, the theory is that they would not be re-released, though it hasn't happened yet.

P2 and P3 are based on the same wine as the standard release, sealed from the outset with a cork and cellared on lees for an extended time. Bottles are kept upside down so the lees settle inside the cork and impede oxygen ingress. Surprisingly, trials have found crown caps less reliable than corks beyond 10 years, perhaps due to phenolics and antioxidants leaching from the cork. 'After 10 years a cork is so superior to crown cap,' Geoffroy believes. 'There is a wonderful chemistry, which would be very difficult to reproduce with a different closure.'

The cork seal necessitates manual disgorgement of P1 and P2 releases, and each bottle is checked for cork taint as it is disgorged. 'On tirage you have an added effect from the first and second cork,' he explains. 'You may not detect any problem from the first cork, but after you insert the second cork it may become noticeable.' Further, as in any wine style, long-ageing under natural corks creates bottle variation, and no two P2 and P3s are alike, adding an element of risk to a significant outlay. The house reports more variation due to oxidation and reduction than to cork taint.

Dom Pérignon's best buy is always its standard blanc.

DOM PÉRIGNON VINTAGE 2006 $$$$

95 points • TASTED IN AUSTRALIA

55% pinot noir, 45% chardonnay; 6g/L dosage

Immediately and unmistakably Dom, 2006 is a vintage that juxtaposes the smoky, flinty, gunpowder and grilled toast reduction that defines Dom, with a charge of tense, strong acidity, presented with a magnitude and generosity bolstered by a warm, dry vintage of scorching July and summery September. In the aftermath of the season, a touch of phenolic bitterness leaves a little firmness on the finish. A medium-straw hue proclaims its vibrancy even after 10 years, and a flattering succulence calms and contrasts its drying grip. The rumbling exuberance of a decade in the deep has evolved spicy, primary lemon and apple fruit into molten wax, brioche, gingernut biscuits, even the beginnings of coffee and dark chocolate. There is an extroverted confidence to 2006 which charges Dom with a larger-than-life, room-filling personality, toned with just the right level of acidity to keep the finish admirably determined and well defined. This is a Dom that will stand out and turn heads, though not forever – a vintage at its finest in the short to medium term.

DOM PÉRIGNON ROSÉ VINTAGE 2004 $$$$$

94 points • TASTED IN AUSTRALIA

40% chardonnay; 30% pinot noir white wine and 30% pinot noir red wine, from Bouzy, Aÿ and Hautvillers

At 30%, this represents one of the highest doses of pinot noir red wine in a blended champagne rosé, up from 17–20% in the past, in line with Geoffroy's mandate to create a more substantial style. One year after release it upheld tamarillo, blood orange, rose hip, pomegranate and strawberry exuberance. But in more recent tastings, two years after release, its hue has deepened to a medium crimson copper and its primary fruits have evolved to a more secondary and savoury demeanour of toast, mixed spice, liquorice and pipe smoke. The reductive style of the house speaks in flinty complexity. As fruit fades, the textural grip and bitterness of phenolic structure and not insubstantial pinot noir tannins are now more prominent on the finish, declaring that it has now past its finest days. It nonetheless holds outstanding persistence and character.

DOM PÉRIGNON P2 1998 $$$$$

98 points • TASTED IN AUSTRALIA

First release 9g/L dosage, P2 6.5g/L

Two years on from its release, P2 1998 has not dipped its gaze one iota, upholding definition and determination while building transfixing layers of creamy complexity. Through a hue of bright, medium-straw, the youthful luminescence of lemon zest and white fruits hold their radiance, accented seamlessly with gunflint reduction and the billowing maturity of Parisienne baguette, toasted brioche, dried fig, nougat and roasted hazelnuts. Its creamy, silky, luscious mouthfeel and notes of vanilla and crème brûlée are gloriously heightened, culminating in a finish softly accented by tertiary, smoky, iodine nuances. Its tanginess integrates as its creaminess blossoms, yet it upholds just the right acid tension and softly textural grip on a finish of marvellous line and length. In sheer line and persistence, this is a Dom Pérignon of the highest order. Two years ago I announced that it had atttained an incredible plateau, with plenty of life to ascend higher still. My goodness, it has, and it's in no hurry to move on.

The Champagne Guide

DOSNON

(Do-noh)

4 BIS RUE DU BAS DE LINGEY 10340 AVIREY-LINGEY

www.champagne-dosnon.com

*T*he small cellar run by the young Davy Dosnon in his home town of Avirey-Lingey in the south-western reaches of the Côte des Bar is built on his principles of modernity and ecological sustainability. A small annual production of just 50,000 bottles reflects a comfortable disposition of integration of low dosage and old oak. There is refinement, skill and craftsmanship on display in every cuvée, though in recent tastings barrel fermentation characters have tended to dominate.

Less than 50 kilometres north-east of Chablis, a little over a half-hour drive, Avirey-Lingey perhaps has more in common with the northern end of Burgundy than it does with other parts of Champagne. The local clay-limestone soils make for particularly rich fruit, and pinot noir takes a confident lead, as it does across the region, though this estate also takes pride in showcasing the rising credentials of Côte des Bar chardonnay in flying solo.

Complexity and fullness are the goals here. Dosnon cultivates 2.15 hectares of 25-year-old estate pinot noir vines (and a little chardonnay) in the village and nearby Urville and Polisy, supplementing supply from 3 hectares of other growers.

Harmony is the buzz word for Dosnon and vines are essentially worked organically, while maintaining the flexibility to apply treatments in adverse seasons. Grasses are grown in the mid-rows, soils are tilled for

aeration, no chemical treatments are used, and yields are controlled.

Minimal intervention is the philosophy in the winery, too, and fermentation and ageing take place exclusively in 228-litre Burgundian barrels (minimum age five years).

Indigenous yeasts are increasingly employed for primary fermentation, to build character and complexity. An intuitive philosophy sees malolactic fermentation allowed or blocked and bâtonnage performed or not, according to the character of the wine. A high 40% of reserve wine is used, and bottle maturation is never less than two years.

These are cuvées to enjoy young and fresh, as bottle age tends to induce oxidation. Back labels declare disgorgement dates and dosages. Ultra-modern labels appropriately set off the progressive approach of this boutique négociant.

DOSNON RECOLTE NOIRE NV $$

87 points • DISGORGED JANUARY 2016 • TASTED IN AUSTRALIA

100% Côte des Bar pinot noir; vinified and aged in barrel; 5g/L dosage

The fleshy plum and cherry fruit of Aube pinot noir contrasts the savoury, charcuterie notes of barrel fermentation, culminating in a finish of fine, bitter grip that produces a firm astringency.

DOSNON RECOLTE ROSÉ NV $$

89 points • DISGORGED DECEMBER 2015 • TASTED IN AUSTRALIA

95% pinot, 5% meunier; 100% Côte des Bar; vinified and aged in barrel; 7g/L dosage

A pretty, pale salmon hue with an orange tint announces a savoury rosé of blood orange fruit overlaid with the nuttiness of barrel vinification. This lends some tannin grip to the finish, supported by soft acidity and well-integrated dosage.

Midsummer sunset over the village of Rizaucourt-Buchey in the Haute-Marne.

The Champagne Guide

DUMANGIN J. FILS

(Dew-mohn-zhan J. Feess)

6/10

3 RUE DE RILLY 51500 CHIGNY-LES-ROSES

www.champagne-dumangin.com

CHAMPAGNE
DUMANGIN
J. Fils

'The secret to making great wine is attention to the fine details at every stage' is the mantra of Gilles Dumangin. The fifth-generation chef de cave must be the hardest worker in Chigny-les-Roses. When I visited late one Sunday afternoon in July, he'd been at the bottling machine since 4am, as he had been every morning for the previous two weeks. The week before, his air-conditioner had died, then his brine chiller, then his labelling machine. He fixed all three himself. A self-confessed control freak, Gilles works 20–22 hours every day during harvest. And he loves it.

Such fanaticism defines every stage of production at Dumangin J. Fils. 'My wife spent one harvest with me and declared, "You are in love with your presses! You do not leave them for a moment!"' Gilles recounts. And he doesn't disagree. His old Coquards are 'the Rolls Royce' of champagne presses. 'The week and a half of harvest is a lovely time. I listen to my presses the whole time. I know them so well that if anything sounds different, I know something is wrong. If you can't press well, you can't make good champagne.'

I spent a day shadowing Gilles in the middle of harvest 2014 and I have not seen more focused attention to detail anywhere in Champagne. There was a subtle change in the sound of the press and he stopped mid-sentence and jumped to its attention.

These are handmade champagnes, and a production of just 150,000 bottles permits every step in the process to be performed manually by Gilles and his small team, including riddling (by transfer between pallets). Every parcel is kept separate, thanks to tiny tanks, some not much larger than a bar fridge. 'A house this size would normally have 20 tanks,' Gilles points out. 'I have 80.'

Based in the romantic little village of Chigny-les-Roses, on the northern slopes of the Montagne de Reims, in the old school building that Gilles's grandfather converted, the estate sources from 15 hectares in this and the surrounding villages. Gilles owns a little more than three hectares of his own vines; he purchases from his parents' two hectares of vineyards and a further nine hectares from growers with long-term contracts.

Irrespective of ownership, Gilles's principles for the management of the vines are consistent across all of his sources. 'I work mostly organically when I can, but I will save my harvest when I have to.' He interacts with each of the vineyards in the same way, monitoring the vines during the year, going into the rows to determine the optimal time for harvest, and supporting his own managers throughout the year in the same manner as he supports his growers. He is therefore technically a négociant-manipulant, but very much with the approach of a dedicated récoltant-manipulant. 'Would I produce better wines if I grew all the grapes myself?' he asks. 'No. I'd do everything the same way.'

This is pinot country, and both pinot and meunier feature heavily in the Dumangin style. Chardonnay finds its place, too, and the local quality is impressive, as his expressive single-vineyard, single-vintage blanc de blancs attests. Meunier is more important here than it is in most champagne houses. 'This is the grape that makes champagne what it is, providing its fruit and its easy-drinking style,' says Gilles, whose entry Grande Réserve NV contains an impressive 50% of the variety.

Gilles is obsessive about preserving fruit in optimal condition. In 2008 he terminated some contracts with growers of inferior vineyards, and signed up other vineyards to bring all of his sources to within seven kilometres of his beloved old Coquard presses. 'They're so gentle,' he says, 'that the pips stay on the skins and the seeds remain inside!' The second-press cut is used only in Brut 17 and Grande Réserve.

Gilles pioneered 18-kilogram picking crates rather than the usual 50-kilogram crates, so as not to crush the fruit at the bottom. When fruit arrives it never spends more than five minutes in the sun before he brings it into his air-conditioned press room. He personally presses every grape. 'I don't believe you can make very good wine if you don't press your own grapes,' he explains.

Non-vintage cuvées rely on deep stocks of reserve wines, with a full year's production volume in reserve, and the Grande Réserve and Extra Brut cuvées each boasting a whopping 60%. In every vintage 40% is kept in reserve. Rosé production is on the rise, now Dumangin's key cuvée, representing 50% of production. Since Rosé doesn't call for large reserves, an ever-increasing proportion of reserves are available for Brut 17, now 43%. All cuvées have traditionally undergone full malolactic fermentation, but such was the acid and sugar balance of his 2012 fruit that he blocked malolactic fermentation in some parcels for the first time, necessitating rigorous cleaning and sanitisation in the winery. He has continued to block malolactic since, and has been very pleased with the results. He also started trialling barrel fermentation in 2012.

For the past 15 years, Gilles has invested all his income back into his stocks, and now boasts an incredible six years' supply in storage.

To preserve the elegance of the terroirs of the northern Montagne, Gilles disgorges every shipment

Gilles Dumangin works tirelessly to capture the elegance of his pretty village of Chigny-les-Roses.

of non-vintage wine to order, and seals every bottle with a DIAM cork. 'In my trials, the wines keep fresher under DIAM.' The dosage of every shipment is tweaked from its usual 10g/L sugar to suit. As length of time on lees has increased, dosages have been progressively lowered across the range over recent years. 'From my tests, the wines stay fresher if they're disgorged just prior to shipment,' Gilles says. It's different for the vintage wines, which he finds hold their freshness best if disgorged 3–4 years after bottling.

For champagnes disgorged to order, back labels are impressively informative, disclosing disgorgement date, blend and dosage. Each disgorgement now receives a unique QR code to provide a great depth of information, including disgorgement date, blend, reserve wines, vineyards, food matches, reviews and importer's details.

Gilles's painstaking attention to detail shines in every bottle. I have been following his champagnes for more than a decade now, and they are cleaner, fresher, more precise and more focused than ever. As a result, they effortlessly handle lower dosage than before, and all but the Brut 17 and Rosé are Extra Brut. These rank high among the best-value small-producer champagnes.

The Champagne Guide

Dumangin J. Fils La Cuvée 17 Brut NV $

90 points • 2011 BASE VINTAGE • DISGORGED OCTOBER 2015 AND MAY 2016 • TASTED IN AUSTRALIA
One-third each of pinot noir, meunier and chardonnay; 43% reserves; 8.8g/L dosage

Brut 17 took a step up in refinement and purity with the 2009 base, after changing contracts to improve fruit sources, and 2010 followed impeccably, a beautifully refined apéritif style and a cracking entry champagne. Gilles discarded a lot of tailles in 2011 in an attempt to avoid the dusty notes of the vintage. It still shows the dusty and dry reflections of its harrowing season, but retains the crisp freshness of lemon juice purity characteristic of the northern Montagne, red apple crunch and strawberry freshness, good acid line, evenly integrated dosage and reasonable persistence.

Dumangin J. Fils L'Extra Brut Premier Cru NV $$

91 points • 2010 BASE VINTAGE • DISGORGED NOVEMBER 2016 • TASTED IN CHAMPAGNE AND AUSTRALIA
50% meunier, 25% chardonnay, 25% pinot noir; 2g/L dosage

Dumangin's Extra Brut is precise, clean and classy, with all the tension you'd expect from a dry take on northern Montagne finesse, yet sufficient red fruit generosity to hold its balance. It upholds the definition of crunchy lemon juice, lemon zest, pear and red apple fruit, accented with gentle layers of toasty, spicy, biscuity roast nut bottle development. Lingering, finely focused acid drive and fine mineral strucure keep the finish crisp and tense. Try it with oysters.

Dumangin J. Fils Le Rosé Brut NV $$

92 points • 2010 BASE VINTAGE • DISGORGED JULY 2016 • TASTED IN CHAMPAGNE AND AUSTRALIA
47% chardonnay, 37% pinot noir, 16% red wine from meunier; 4.4g/L dosage; 50% of production

Gilles's rosé is a reflection of his precision, one of Champagne's most finely crafted and elegant rosés at a refreshingly affordable price. Red wine from meunier is unusual in Champagne, yet his is well suited to his elegant rosé style, creating a pretty medium-salmon hue, neatly supported by the finesse of chardonnay and the fragrance of pinot noir. The result is a pretty and restrained style of subtle rose petal lift and gentle chalk mineral texture. It holds its integrity in pretty red cherry, red apple and cherry kernel character that lingers on a long, fresh, picture-perfect finish. In spite of the growing popularity of this cuvée, Gilles has resolved not to increase production, so as not to unbalance his other cuvées. There will be no 2011 base Le Rosé as he was dissatified with it and sold off the entire production. Kudos.

DUMANGIN J. FILS LE VINTAGE EXTRA BRUT PREMIER CRU 2004 $$

93 points • TASTED IN AUSTRALIA

54% chardonnay, 46% pinot noir; liqueur aged in oak barrels 1–2 years; 4.4g/L dosage; 15,000 bottles

Dumangin's vintage is blessed with 13 years of maturity, upholding primary integrity in the wake of rising complexity, testimony to Gilles's precision and the stamina of 2004. Such was the yield in this vintage that he produced three times the usual volume of this cuvée. Elegance, vivacity and tension heightened by low dosage are the themes here, alive with red apple and lemon fruit. Time has ushered in toasty, spicy allure, concluding long and focused, backed by great acid drive and soft chalk mineral presence.

DUMANGIN J. FILS PREMIUM SINGLE VINEYARD BLANC DE BLANCS DESSUS LE MONT EXTRA BRUT 2006 $$

92 points • TASTED IN AUSTRALIA

Harvested ripe and unchaptalised, so only made in years of sufficient ripeness; from a low vineyard on clay soils; 5g/L dosage

There's concentration here, and a medium- to full-straw hue, true to the ripeness of fruit targeted for this cuvée. It's morphed into a complex and exuberant style of golden delicious apples and even a hint of caramel, reflecting the generosity of the season and its clay soils. It concludes long, supple and smoothly textured.

DUMANGIN J. FILS CUVÉE FIRMIN BRUT NATURE 2000 $$$$

92 points • DISGORGED NOVEMBER 2016 • TASTED IN AUSTRALIA

100% chardonnay from Monthouzons vineyard in Taissy; wood aged 1 year; zero dosage; DIAM closure

Gilles's trio of single-vineyard, single-varietal, single-vintage champagnes make for a fascinating comparison. The charcuterie complexity and nutty, buttery wood characters of oak fermenation lead out here, making for a spicy, complex and savoury cuvée of creamy structure. The golden delicious apple and preserved lemon fruit of its youth has evolved into a lingering spectrum of secondary yellow summer fruits that define 2000. It maintains good acid line on a long and bright finish, quite refreshing for this rounded season.

DUMANGIN J. FILS CUVÉE HIPPOLYTE BRUT NATURE 2000 $$$$

93 points • DISGORGED NOVEMBER 2016 • TASTED IN AUSTRALIA

100% pinot noir from Cornes de Cerf vineyard in Rilly-la-Montagne; wood aged 1 year; zero dosage; DIAM closure

The fragant appeal of pinot noir projects from the glass even at 17 years of age, with violet aromas over a core of red and black cherry fruit. The oak flavours and aromas that dominated its earlier life have been subsumed, leaving the structural grip and firm, fine tannins of oak barrel fermentation on the finish, energised by lively acidity. It holds great persistence, layered with all the spicy, toasty, creamy, brioche complexity of bottle maturity.

The Champagne Guide

DUVAL-LEROY

(Dew-val-Lair-wah)

6/10

69 AVENUE DE BAMMENTAL 51130 VERTUS

www.duval-leroy.com

The scale of Duval-Leroy's modern winery is a physical statement of the rapid progress at this family-owned company. Recently celebrating its 150th birthday, it now ranks in the 15 largest champagne houses, thanks to its dynamic, visionary leader, Carol Duval-Leroy, who has grown the estate during the past two decades. Chardonnay takes the lead in these graceful and elegant wines, reflecting the bright fruit purity of the village of Vertus.

The imposing Duval-Leroy building looks more at home in Silicon Valley than a small village in Champagne. The entire façade is covered by 250 square metres of solar panels, sufficient for the electrical needs of the barrel room, tasting room and reception area. It makes a bold, immediate statement that Duval-Leroy has sunk a serious investment into its modernisation and growth. And that's just the beginning.

Step inside the largest facility in Vertus and you're greeted by lines of gleaming new tanks, all temperature controlled to between 16°C and 20°C to preserve delicacy during fermentation. Five gentle eight-tonne pneumatic presses are cleverly positioned above 30 settling tanks, delivering the must by gravity. Dug deep underground, this facility operates on multiple levels. Operations were modernised in 2009 when extensions were made to integrate the entire production under one roof to improve efficiency and quality. A new barrel room was also added for fermentation of grand cru parcels.

Estate holdings comprise 60% chardonnay. The house controls 200 hectares in the Côte des Blancs (including an impressive 150 hectares in Vertus, and holdings in every grand cru), Montagne de Reims and Côte de Sézanne, providing a generous one-third of all fruit required to produce 5–5.5 million bottles annually. It is serviced by five press centres, and 18 million bottles stored 30 kilometres away in Châlons-en-Champagne.

Duval-Leroy manages a sustainability regime that's more than just a solar panel façade. A 10-page document on its website details a diverse list of initiatives. Herbicide use has more than halved in the past decade, and all estate vineyards are cultivated organically or biodynamically – quite a feat for a house of this size. Fruit purchased from a number of organically certified growers finds its way into two organic champagnes.

It is apparently possible to ascertain the disgorgement date from the bottling code, but the house keeps this a closely guarded secret, for reasons I fail to understand.

Duval-Leroy achieves a lofty pinnacle in the towering magnificence of its prestige cuvée, Femme de Champagne. Its 1996 re-release is spellbinding.

DUVAL-LEROY CLOS DES BOUVERIES CHARDONNAY PREMIER CRU EXTRA BRUT 2006 $$$$

91 points • DISGORGED JUNE 2016 • TASTED IN AUSTRALIA

100% chardonnay from a single clos in the heart of Vertus, belonging to the company for more than a century; partially aged in oak barrels; 4g/L dosage; 15,888 bottles, less than half the production volume of 2005

The concept of releasing a single-variety, single-vineyard wine in every single vintage in a climate as fickle as that of Champagne is more than a little disconcerting. This is a Vertus of significant impact and proportions, colliding the rich, ripe power of 2006 with the full texture and flavour overlay of partial oak barrel ageing. It delivers white peach and succulent mirabelle plum fruit amidst quite some presence of toasty, nutty oak. It's released altogether too young for a wine with significant oak treatment, though the fruit presence of 2006 allows it to pull off this accord with much more confidence than the austere 2005 before it. Bright, well-defined acidity and prominent chalk minerality keep the finish fresh and lively, though the coarse grip of oak tannin threatens to foil its long-lingering flow.

DUVAL-LEROY CUMIÈRES PINOT NOIR PREMIER CRU BRUT 2005 $$$$

88 points • DISGORGED JANUARY 2016 • TASTED IN AUSTRALIA

Single vineyard; organic; vinified entirely in oak barrels; 5648 bottles

Joining Clos des Bouveries in Duval-Leroy's growing portfolio of single-clos releases, this is a powerful cuvée of full straw hue that encapsulates the impact of Cumières pinot noir in red apple and fig fruit. It is very much a child of its season, and the pronounced dusty, dry extract, dank peanut notes and coarse phenolic grip that define the vintage completely overwhelm the bouquet, palate and structure, heightened by full barrel fermentation. Nonetheless, it presents good persistence, well-defined acid line, integrated dosage and no lack of character.

DUVAL-LEROY BOUZY PINOT NOIR GRAND CRU BRUT NATURE 2005 $$$$

89 points • DISGORGED SEPTEMBER 2016 • TASTED IN AUSTRALIA

Single vineyard; vinified entirely in oak barrels; 3258 bottles

Duval-Leroy is joining the ranks of houses releasing more single-clos cuvées, inspired by the terroir focus initiated largely by the growers of Champagne. It's no easy task to achieve balance and appeal in single-vineyard champagne, particularly in vintages with their own inherent challenges. But the presence and generosity of the great pinot noir grand cru of Bouzy makes this a pretty solid attempt at this pursuit. All the generosity of the village, the variety, the vintage and full barrel fermentation are compacted into a full straw yellow thing layered with mixed spice, plum pudding, even malt and coffee. Oak presence adds a subtle, savoury, dank glimpse on the finish, but it upholds good acid drive and persistence. The phenolic grip of 2005 pokes through its generous fruit core in a little bitterness on the end.

The Champagne Guide

DUVAL-LEROY FEMME DE CHAMPAGNE BRUT GRAND CRU NV $$$$

96 points • DISGORGED JULY 2016 • TASTED IN AUSTRALIA

80% chardonnay from Avize, Chouilly and Le Mesnil-sur-Oger; 20% pinot noir from Ambonnay; aged at least 8 years on lees

The first I have seen Femme as a non-vintage release, this is a pale straw cuvée that juxtaposes wonderful fruit depth with mineral tension. Chardonnay takes the lead in grapefruit and white peaches, with subtle fig depth from pinot noir. Bottle age has built subtle brioche/nougat complexity, while upholding primary lemon juice purity. Mineral expression is profound, mouth-filling, deeply salty and chalk mineral, given full voice thanks to low dosage, articulating the full glory of the Côte des Blancs. A grand Femme that will be long lived.

DUVAL-LEROY FEMME DE CHAMPAGNE 1996 $$$$$

99 points • DISGORGED SEPTEMBER 2010 • TASTED IN AUSTRALIA

79% chardonnay, 21% pinot noir

The youthful endurance of grand cru Côte des Blancs chardonnay in this cuvée has long captivated me, but never has it reached the heights that it has attained in 1996, and with a larger dose than usual of grand cru pinot noir, too. Even on the occasion of its 21st birthday, and no less than seven years after disgorgement, it retains a bright glint to its full straw hue. The sheer, bombastic energy and towering concentration of 1996 are on grand display, yet with a harmony, focus, even an elegance and sheer allure so many failed to capture in this lauded yet controversial season. Primary apple, pear and lemon zest are still here, layered with the toast and nougat of middle age and hints of pipe smoke and green olives that declare its decades in the cellar. Tense acid line and fine chalk minerality unite on a finish of profound focus and endurance, holding every promise of yet another decade of life. I lined it up alongside more than 40 top prestige cuvées from all the famous houses and this wine singly topped the tasting. A triumph.

Le Mesnil-sur-Oger stands alongside Avize and Chouilly as the core of Femme de Champagne.

EGLY-OURIET

(Eglee-Ou-ree-yair)

10/10

15 Rue Trépail 51150 Ambonnay

CHAMPAGNE
Elaboré par SAS EGLY-OURIET à Ambonnay France

EGLY-OURIET
Propriétaire - Récoltant

BRUT TRADITION GRAND CRU

Issu des Grands Terroirs d'Ambonnay, Bouzy
et Verzenay Classés Grand Cru.

BRUT

ALC. 12.5% BY VOL.   750 ML

Egly-Ouriet enjoys a cult status shared by no other grower on the Montagne de Reims. This tiny, pristine operation in Ambonnay deserves its acclaim, capturing the profound complexity, intensity and grandeur of the Montagne's finest terroirs, without sacrificing the precision that underlies the most revered champagnes. These are ravishingly vinous sparkling wines, consistently among the most exactingly balanced of Champagne's power set, handcrafted by a creative, thoughtful artisan who painstakingly tends his vines naturally to low yields and full maturity. To uphold the calibre of his non-vintage cuvées even in the wake of the harrowing 2011 season calls for wizardry I have witnessed from no other grower or house. On this basis, Egly-Ouriet remains the finest grower in Champagne right now, and my only 10/10 grower.

Egly-Ouriet owns just under 12 hectares of grand cru vineyards planted to 70% pinot noir and 30% chardonnay, primarily in Ambonnay, 1.4 hectares in Verzenay, a few rows in Bouzy, and a two-hectare plot of very old meunier vines in Vrigny that produce a single-vineyard premier cru. Francis Egly, fourth-generation head of the estate, has bottled the entire harvest of 100,000 bottles since he took over in 1982. Previously, his father, Michel, bottled a small proportion since the 1970s, and his grandfather, Charles, bottled tiny quantities for family and friends since the 1950s.

'Champagne is like Burgundy,' Egly upholds. 'You go one kilometre and it is different. Ambonnay is completely different to Bouzy, where the soils are deeper. Ambonnay is a very "solaire" village, south-orientated, which is very important for maturity. The soil is very

poor, generally only 20 centimetres deep, so you can smell the minerality of the chalk.' Egly works intuitively to preserve the detail of his grapes and their terroirs.

His approach in the vineyards is as natural as possible, without aspiring to organic or biodynamic certification. 'It is too complicated to practise specific regimes,' he maintains. An eco-friendly approach has seen a radical reduction in the use of fertilisers and chemical pesticides. The soil is manured and ploughed for aeration, and green harvests reduce crop levels by up to 50% for red wine for rosé and Coteaux Champenois. Otherwise, his yields are at the full level of 10 tonnes per hectare.

From vines averaging more than 45 years of age, Egly harvests at full maturity, typically at 12 or 13 degrees of potential alcohol, extremely ripe for Champagne, and never chaptalises. His goal is to harvest grapes as ripe as possible, and he cites the best vintages as those of high maturity, naming under-maturity as Champagne's biggest problem. His aspiration is 'elegance and strength, but never heaviness'. He says champagne is like a bird; 'it has to stay aromatic and light'. Grapes are pressed slowly and fermented almost entirely in barriques, the balance in enamelled tanks (not stainless steel), using only natural yeasts. Egly maintains more than 200 barrels, in which his entire production is fermented (apart from 20% of Brut Tradition), not only for structure and longevity, but to facilitate vinification of different parcels separately to draw out more character of the terroir. Used barrels are purchased from his friend Dominique Laurent in Nuits-Saint-Georges.

Malolactic fermentation is allowed or barred depending on the vintage. Very low dosages are used – typically just 1–3g/L. 'I prefer to use a little sugar rather than following the fashion of no dosage,' he says. Long ageing on lees in barrel for 8–10 months and in bottle for at least 3–4 years furnishes considerable longevity.

A 2006 cellar expansion brought all winemaking operations together in the same building, with pressing, vinification and storage on successive levels, temperature controlled at every stage. In 2008, Egly acquired two new presses, which he says have improved quality.

The back labels are among Champagne's most informative, declaring disgorgement dates, terroirs and number of months on lees. Wines are bottled in July following harvest, so it's easy to determine the base vintage. Important details appear on every bottle, alongside the philosophy of the house: 'This champagne is the expression of a "family" style that comes first and foremost from perfectly tended vineyards. The quality of grapes, the precision of blending and long *élevage* in the cellar allows us to offer you non-filtered champagnes in the purest champagne style.' A breath of fresh air in a region saturated with marketing froth.

I first had the privilege of meeting Francis Egly in 2015, a man of generous warmth and careful precision, just like his champagnes.

Egly-Ouriet's inauspicious headquarters in Ambonnay.

EGLY-OURIET GRAND CRU BRUT TRADITION NV $$$

94 points • 2011 BASE VINTAGE • TASTED IN AUSTRALIA

70% pinot noir, 30% chardonnay; 50% 2011, 30% 2010 and 20% 2009; wild fermented; 50% vinified and aged in oak barrel; aged 48 months on lees; 3-4g/L dosage

From the very first cuvée, Egly-Ouriet is distinguished for its ability to preserve exacting precision and outstanding chalk mineral focus in the midst of magnificent generosity. This is a vinous wine of calm authority, carrying the full grandeur and complexity of carefully tended, old-vine pinot noir on some of Champagne's most revered grand crus. Even the rough 2011 vintage does little to thwart its distinguished poise. Depth and power of red cherry, plum and red apple fruit are supported eloquently by the toasty and spicy complexity of barrel fermentation. Its rippling intensity juxtaposes magnificently with marvellous acid line, underscored by prominent, fine chalk minerality, bringing wonderful focus and definition. A paradox of luxurious generosity and crystalline purity.

EGLY-OURIET GRAND CRU BRUT ROSÉ NV $$$$

96 points • 2011 BASE VINTAGE • DISGORGED JULY 2016 • TASTED IN AUSTRALIA

Similar composition to Brut Tradition, with 5% 2009 red wine from Ambonnay; 60% 2011, 20% 2010 and 20% 2009; aged 48 months on lees; 2g/L dosage

Rumbling power with delicate finesse, this is a rosé of medium-salmon hue, bursting with the exuberance and beguiling transparency of Ambonnay pinot noir. Sensational perfume of rose hip, red cherry and mixed spice heralds a rosé that sings with the magnificent red-fruits purity of the village, to a thundering undercurrent of grand complexity of dark fruit cake and spice. Yet at every instant it is light, refreshing and breathtakingly energetic. Francis Egly's genius is on grand display here in achieving acidity so lively and so focused and yet, at the same time, ripe, full and enticing. All the more profound in the traumatic 2011 season. Chalk minerality underscores every magnificent moment.

EGLY-OURIET GRAND CRU MILLÉSIME 2006 $$$$

97 points • DISGORGED MAY 2016 • TASTED IN AUSTRALIA

70% pinot noir, 30% chardonnay from 40-year-old vines in Ambonnay; aged completely in oak barrels; no malolactic fermentation; aged 106 months on lees

Some in Champagne can achieve grandeur of dizzying proportions, and the most talented can summons delicacy of light-footed grace, but no village marries the two as effortlessly as Ambonnay, and no practitioner as masterfully as Francis Egly. To achieve such a feat in the ripe and generous 2006 vintage is perhaps most remarkable of all. This is a cuvée that wells up with depth and power of the highest order. Full orchestral scoring of black cherries and plums reverberates with thundering complexity of dark fruit cake, cherry liqueur and dark chocolate. Its concentration embodies the full crescendo of pinot noir with epic line and length, underscored by all the spicy complexity of barrel fermentation. In the wake of such exuberance, to uphold pitch-perfect high notes of structural finesse is a breathtaking triumph. Intricately and exactingly structured with outstanding, bright malic acidity, it's awash with a cascade of mouth-filling chalk minerality that bears testimony to carefully tended old vines on shallow soils. Francis Egly starts picking when everyone else finishes, yet even in 2006, the definition of acidity and articulate expression of chalk minerality that he has upheld are nothing short of exhilaratingly thrilling.

From enviably positioned sites in Ambonnay, Francis Egly crafts the finest grower cuvées in Champagne today.

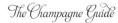

EGLY-OURIET GRAND CRU EXTRA BRUT VP VIEILLISSEMENT PROLONGÉ NV $$$$

98 points • 2008 BASE VINTAGE • DISGORGED MAY 2016 • TASTED IN AUSTRALIA

70% pinot noir and 30% chardonnay from Ambonnay, Bouzy and Verzenay; 60% 2008, 40% 2006; vinified and aged in oak casks; aged 82 months on lees; 3g/L dosage

In an age when single-vineyard, single-varietal, single-vintage champagnes are all the rage, it remains that blends triumph most often, even in an estate as tiny as Egly-Ouriet. Power meets effortless calm as Champagne's three finest pinot noir crus unite with breathtaking expression of lifted violet perfume and sensational purity of red cherry and strawberry fruit. Chardonnay injects energy and definition into a mouthfeel that bores to the core of grand cru chalk, intricately and seamlessly entwining a palate of glittering minerality of the finest texture. Magnificently defined acidity is at once bright, youthful and energetic, yet simultaneously ripe, full and integrated. The 2008 base propels with energy and purity, juxtaposing the grand depth and stature of 2006, yet never competing. Francis Egly has bottled the ultimate expression of the refinement and towering magnificence of Ambonnay, Bouzy and Verzenay.

EGLY-OURIET GRAND CRU BLANC DE NOIRS VIEILLE VIGNE NV $$$$$

98 points • 2009 BASE VINTAGE • DISGORGED MAY 2016 • TASTED IN AUSTRALIA

100% pinot noir; 50% 2009 and 50% 2008; fully vinified and aged in barriques; aged 70 months on lees

From a single lieu-dit, 'Les Crayères', planted in shallow soils in 1946, this warm amphitheatre high up the Ambonnay slope epitomises the golden sunlight, glowing warmth and magnificent mineral expression of Egly-Ouriet. Hedonistic aromas of black cherries, plum pie and violets erupt in grand cru red Burgundy proportions, backed with notes of dark chocolate and exotic spice. In sheer volume, depth and persistence, this cuvée pushes champagne into another world. Yet, crucially and mesmerisingly, it is never for a moment heavy or blowsy, pulled exactingly into tight line by gorgeous, bright yet perfectly ripe and generous acidity. With barely a foot of topsoil before the chalk, the mineral character of this hallowed site speaks articulately in softly salty tones that will stir the depths of your soul.

EGLY-OURIET GRAND CRU AMBONNAY ROUGE 2012 $$$$

96 points • TASTED IN AUSTRALIA

Single parcel of Ambonnay old vines; low yields of just 35hL/hectare; vinified and aged for 18-22 months entirely in oak barrels; minuscule production of 200 cases

Egly-Ouriet produces the finest Coteaux Champenois in all of Champagne, from a plot of very old pinot noir vines in a sun-catching amphitheatre on the mid-slope of Ambonnay. This is a red wine of integrity, character, immaculate line and sheer persistence that align it more closely with the greatest premier crus of Burgundy than anything in Champagne. It erupts in a glorious upwelling of pristine red cherry fruit of the utmost purity, accented with pink pepper and rose hip, laced together with fine chalk minerality and seductively silky tannins.

EMMANUEL BROCHET

(Eman-yoo-el Bro-sheh)

7/10

7 IMPASSE BROCHET 51500 VILLERS-AUX-NOEUDS

Champagne

EMMANUEL BROCHET

In the turning wheel of Champagne succession, it is virtually unheard of for a young grower-producer to be the first in his family to tend vines. All the more daring in the little-known premier cru village of Villers-aux-Noeuds, in which no one has made champagne for generations. Emmanuel Brochet defines a bold new frontier, bringing an old terroir to life with an intuition derived not from local knowledge, family history or personal experience, but from the sheer courage to respond to each plot, each season and each ferment individually. Most remarkable of all is the beautiful fruit character and pronounced terroir expression he has drawn from this place in a very short time. I know of no one in Champagne today who has achieved so much from so little so quickly as Emmanuel Brochet.

In the plains between the slopes of the Montagne de Reims and the sprawling southern suburbs of Reims, Villers-aux-Noeuds was once the proud custodian of 250 hectares of vines. The quaint little village is now home to just 27 hectares, planted on its best south-east slopes, spanning a wide diversity of soils, with chalk just 30 centimetres below the surface.

Emmanuel Brochet's family has owned vines here for generations, leasing them to others to tend until Emmanuel commenced in 1997. His mother's 2.5 hectare single vineyard 'Le Mont Benoit' is one of the better sites in the village, with a thin layer of 40 centimetres of topsoil directly over chalk, and just 25 centimetres at the top of the slope. The vineyard is visible from the motorway, under the power lines, adjacent to the toll station near Champfleury. Planted to 37% meunier, 30% chardonnay and 23% pinot noir dating from 1962, half the block was replanted in 1986 after devastating frosts.

Emmanuel manages the site for his mother, paying her a rent of 0.6 hectares of fruit, leaving 1.9 hectares for his modest production of 10,000 bottles.

Without the constraints of family and village history, Brochet is blessed with the freedom to forge a brave path with a spontaneity rarely possible in this staid region. 'As the first winemaker of the family, I am lucky I do not have my family telling me what to do!' he grins. 'I do things because I want to, not because I have to.' This affords full licence to pursue his elegantly simple philosophy: 'A wine is good because the grapes are good. If there is good balance in the soils and in the vine, there is good balance in the wine. Every year is different, and we work it according to the season, not because we did it that way last year,' he says, admitting he's never written down anything he's done each vintage. 'I practise biodynamics, but this is not the most important thing, no more important than the soil, the vines or my state of mind.'

To achieve a good balance of acidity and sugar, Brochet harvests his fruit ripe; many of his neighbours have finished picking before he even starts. In respect for the soil, he commenced biodynamic certification in 2008 and completely abandoned use of chemicals in 2009, though he has no intention of mentioning biodynamics on his labels once certification is granted. 'It is important that my wines have no residues of pesticides, but many other elements are equally important,' he explains. 'If I put biodynamic certification on my labels, then I should also include my press, the house, the grapes, the soil, the place and my state of mind!'

Brochet has found the period of transition to organic certification difficult, selling all his reserve wines prior to 2010 to a négociant, as they were not organic. An annual production of 10,000 bottles is little over half of what 1.9 hectares would normally produce in Champagne, even with some vins clairs sold to négocians for cash flow. Biodynamics has reduced Brochet's yields to a tiny 35hL/hectare. He does not perform a green harvest and upholds that balanced fruit relies upon yields that are neither too large nor too small. 'Perhaps it's not that we produce too little yield, but that conventional viticulture produces too much?' he pointedly suggests. The equilibrium he has achieved in his vines produces a balance of sugar and acidity sufficient that he has no need to chaptalise, unusual in Champagne, and virtually unheard of in a lesser premier cru village.

MINIMALIST WINEMAKING

With no winery to inherit, Brochet sold his grapes until 2002 to finance the purchase of his equipment. He found a traditional 1960s two-tonne Coquard press in 2006, half the size of a traditional champagne press, and restored it 'like an old car'. He admits he prefers driving a tractor to driving a horse. 'I am a boy and I love machines!' says this off-road rally driver. Grapes are pressed on the day they are harvested and settled overnight before fermentation with wild yeasts entirely in barrels, in which the wine remains for 11 months.

The soil and the vines are Brochet's first priority, and he says that with good fruit he has little to do in the winery. 'My winemaking is very simple: an oxidative vinification and ageing on lees, which consume the oxygen, creating a balance between oxidation and reduction.' Adamant champagne should not have a woody taste, he buys old barrels as well as new, and keeps wines in barrel on their lees for an extended period of 11 months to reduce pick-up of oak flavours. Brochet likens winemaking in barrels to biodynamics: 'It's easier than in tanks, and the wines are more natural.' There is no bâtonnage, no filtration and no cold stabilisation.

Brochet is continually experimenting and refining his style. 'I tried putting my reserve wines in barrel, but without lees they became tired and woody, so for the past three years I've kept reserve wines in tank.' Generally he blocks malolactic fermentation in his vintage wines, but in 2012 he allowed it to proceed. 'With our warming weather, some people are saying that we should stop malo so as to retain acidity, but if you don't have a lot of acidity it's very hard to stop malo,' he explains. 'I would have to use a lot of preservative, and I don't want to do that.'

Brochet uses very small levels of preservative, and an extra brut dosage of around 4g/L in his cuvées, and trialled a zero-dosage wine from the same blend as his Le Mont Benoit NV, but found the acidity too pronounced at low temperatures. 'Sugar is a mediator, and a little is a technical support if you drink champagne too cold!' he says. The blend of this cuvée changes each year. 'The *cépage* is not important,' he upholds, 'and we can achieve great consistency each year even with different proportions of each variety. The wines taste of the vineyard and the soil, and that's the important thing. The soil is more important than the varieties.'

He maintains the flexibility to release wines 'when they are good to drink, not because I need the money', a rare opportunity in any young business. His wines are aged long, NVs generally 2–3 years and vintages 5–8 years. He has also broken with Champagne

Emmanuel Brochet, the only grower-producer in the premier cru village of Villers-aux-Noeuds.

tradition in releasing vintage and even non-vintage blends non-sequentially, releasing 2009 before 2007 and 2008. He tastes vintages blind with his friends and releases those that are ready. Back labels are informative, specifying vintages, varieties and vinification details.

Brochet's wines showcase the unique mineral expression of his vineyard in a savoury chalk mouthfeel, a little coarser-grained in texture than that of the Côte des Blancs. I ask if this is unique to the village, or particular to the accessible chalk in his vineyard, and he says he has no idea. 'There is just one producer who makes wine in this village and it is me!' he exclaims. 'Everyone else sells their grapes to the cooperatives and négociants. Old winegrowers always said they could make very good wines in this village. Two generations ago they kept the grapes separate and made very good wines.'

To Brochet, state of mind is an important ingredient of terroir. 'There is no stress here during harvest,' he says, having employed his two best friends to assist. 'It's very important to enjoy your work and I like working in the vineyard on the tractor. When I was young I played with toys and now I like to have fun playing with bigger toys in the vineyard and the winery!' A refreshing mindset for one who has achieved so much so quickly.

EMMANUEL BROCHET LE MONT BENOIT EXTRA BRUT NV $$

93 points • 2013 AND 2012 VINTAGES • TASTED IN AUSTRALIA

39% pinot, 37% meunier, 24% chardonnay; 4g/L dosage; 9102 bottles

A focused and characterful expression of Brochet's finest site, expressing elegant pear and apple fruit and subtle grapefruit notes. Long barrel and bottle age have contributed less in complexing notes of charcuterie and spice, and more in a creamy, soft texture. The minerality of the accessible chalk of the village is prominent, soft, supple and deeply salty. A wine of well-defined acid line, impressive length and seamless coherence.

Champagne growers are increasingly sympathetic to the ecosystem of their vines, encouraging life by reducing herbicides and pesticides.

The Champagne Guide

ERIC RODEZ

(E-ri Roh-day)

7/10

RUE DE ISSE 51150 AMBONNAY

www.champagne-rodez.fr

ERIC RODEZ
CHAMPAGNE

*O*rganic viticulture has become something of a catch cry in the modern wine world, but never have I seen a more profound statement of its impact than in Eric Rodez's magnificently positioned vineyard of 6.5 hectares on the glorious mid-slopes of Ambonnay. Standing on the edge of his rows of vines, he showed me tiny, sparse bunches. In the very next row, not more than a metre away, his neighbour's vines were loaded with full-sized bunches. The fanatical approach of this eighth-generation winegrower permeates every detail of his work, which embraces vinification in barriques, light dosages and a colossal resource of reserve wines spanning 20 years. The aspiration is to let the salty minerality and generous expression of one of Champagne's greatest grand crus sing through every cuvée. And sing they do.

When I first met Eric Rodez, who moonlights as mayor of Ambonnay, he immediately admitted his English is very limited and, my French being far worse, he proposed, *Nous pourrons parler la langue des bulles! –* 'We can speak in the language of the bubbles!'

As I soon discovered, where his bubbles are concerned, a particularly fine language it is.

Rodez makes eight wines, which he thinks of as eight 'melodies'. He likens them to a concert, where every tune evokes a different emotion. 'There is not enough emotion in champagne today!' he exclaims. 'I will not be the Coca-Cola of champagne – I will make emotional wine!' He thinks of his 35 parcels as 35 notes of music, each expressing five emotions, in their grape variety, vintage, vineyard location, method of fermentation, and malolactic fermentation ('forte') or not ('allegro').

The Rodez family have grown grapes in Ambonnay since 1757, and have made their own champagnes since the time of Eric's grandparents, but things changed

when Eric began in 1984. 'That was not a good vintage,' he recalls, and it prompted him to do things differently in the vineyard, initiating a methodology that he prefers to call 'integrated' rather than 'ecological'.

He borrows practices of organics and biodynamics, without seeking certification under either. 'Every year it is a new logic,' he explains. 'I do not have only one vision or one consistent process. My philosophy is to be free. Real life is not about following a recipe.' Use of chemicals is limited, grasses are cultivated in the mid-rows and yields are restricted to a tiny 30–40% of the permitted levels. 'To achieve music in the wine you need music in the grapes to begin with, and to achieve this you cannot have too high a yield,' he maintains. He is working hard to reduce the use of copper sulphate as a fungicide, just six kilograms per hectare in 2014, and ultimately aiming for four kilograms per hectare.

'To my colleagues, I am a little crazy!' he exclaims. 'But I am very happy. When you want to see the soil in the glass, you need to get the vine roots to go into the chalk,' he says. In his vineyards, the chalk is just 40 centimetres below the surface, but this is still deeper than in many parts of the Côte des Blancs, and it took 10 years from when he commenced biodynamics in 1989 before the roots tapped deep into the minerality of the chalk.

His philosophy now translates accurately into his profoundly salty mineral champagnes. He showed me a stunning barrel sample of 2010 pinot noir that displayed none of the botrytis problems that dogged this wet vintage. 'Thanks to low vegetation in the canopy, we had good ventilation and no botrytis in the vineyard,' he explains.

Expression of terroir is everything to Rodez, and he cheerfully admits that he doesn't aspire to make consistent wine each year. 'Every year is different and I will adapt my processes in the vineyards and in the cellar to suit. It is very important to me to make a wine of terroir, where you can taste the emotion.'

Exclusively in the heart of Ambonnay's mid-slope, his vineyards are planted to 60% pinot noir and 40% chardonnay, with an average vine age exceeding 30 years. As we left his vineyard and passed Krug's Clos d'Ambonnay on the lower slopes, he commented, 'There is more complexity in the mid-slopes and more minerality lower on the slopes.' I asked which was better and he paused for a long time, smiled knowingly and responded, 'Both are very important for blending!'

There are few small growers who understand blending more intricately than Rodez. His annual production of 45,000 bottles comprises a very large range of 11 cuvées, including six non-vintage blends,

benefiting from a deep stock of reserve wines, currently extending as far back as 20 years. Disgorgement dates are clearly marked on every back label.

His 35 plots of two varieties are vinified separately to produce 60 different wines, 80% of which are fermented and matured in small Burgundian barrels, mostly aged between three and 20 years. Three vintages in Burgundy and one at Krug taught him how to use barrels 'for sensuality, not oak flavour'; Rodez maintains that new barrels are not good for the equilibrium and personality of champagne. He is currently increasing old barrel vinification, finding that it offers greater persistence and complexity.

His reserve stocks presently comprise barrels of every vintage since 2000 except the dreaded 2001 and 2003. He showed me a 2006 chardonnay with power and length resembling a great white Burgundy. 'It's too big for champagne,' he says, 'but five or seven per cent is very important for the blend.'

Rodez tactically utilises the generosity of Ambonnay and the complexity of barrel fermentation, then enlivens his cuvées with low dosage and selective use of malolactic fermentation, according to the parcel and the season. Grape juice rather than sugar is used to sweeten liqueurs, and all his wines currently contain no more than 5g/L dosage, allowing the character and minerality of these distinguished vineyards to sing with clarity and harmony.

I visited Rodez during and after the 2014 harvest, and the expression of salt minerality in his vins clairs was exceptional. For all they represent, the wines of Eric Rodez are largely undiscovered, and offer incredible value for money.

The mandate of Eric Rodez is to express the terroir of his enviably positioned vines on the mid-slopes of Ambonnay.

The Champagne Guide

ERIC RODEZ CUVÉE DES CRAYÈRES NV $$

92 points • 2011 BASE VINTAGE • TASTED IN AUSTRALIA

40% chardonnay, 60% pinot from Ambonnay; 35% 2011, 30% 2010, 15% 2009, 12% 2008, 8% 2007; close to 4 years on lees; 65% malolactic fermentation; 50-55% vinified in small oak barrels; 5g/L dosage

Eric Rodez captures the personality of Ambonnay from his very first cuvée, in depth, complexity and structure. Such is the weight of reserve wines (almost two-thirds here, a little more than usual, remarkable in an entry cuvée) that it has hardly been marked by its tricky 2011 base year, but captures the expression of fleshy white nectarine, red apple, pear and spice, and the structure of very fine, soft, bath-salts minerality. Its depth of reserves in concert with four years of lees age has built toasty, spicy complexity and fine integration. A touch of phenolic grip inherent to 2011 does not thwart its harmony or fine mineral texture.

ERIC RODEZ CUVÉE DOSAGE ZÉRO NV $$

92 points • 2009 BASE VINTAGE • DISGORGED FEBRUARY 2016 • TASTED IN AUSTRALIA
93 points • DISGORGED AUGUST 2015 • TASTED IN AMBONNAY

70% pinot, 30% chardonnay from Ambonnay; 2009 base has 46% 2009, 23% 2008, 22% 2006, 9% 2005; close to 6 years on lees; 25% malolactic fermentation; 95% barrel fermented; zero dosage

Rodez admits that it's very difficult to create a good equilibrium in zero-dosage champagne every year. Testimony to his intuitive flexibility, this riveting cuvée oscillates from pure blanc de blancs to now upholding its full magnificence with 70% pinot noir. What remains unchanged is that this is one of Champagne's richer zero-dosage offerings, and one of the most delicately balanced. While most create bone-dry champagne from taut, young fruit vinified in stainless steel and softened with malolactic, Rodez turns the entire concept on its head and ingeniously blends a tremendous depth of old wines vinified and aged in barrel from his wonderfully opulent Ambonnay fruit and kisses it with the lightest touch of malolactic. The ripe exuberance of the 2009 base makes for a more savoury and secondary style of rich, Ambonnay pinot noir mid-palate flesh. Already a magnificent nine years average age on release, the character he achieves is compelling, utilising the lively energy and vibrant lemon fruit of Ambonnay, tactically deploying the biscuity, toasty, ginger and charcuterie-accented complexity of barrel vinification and a deep stock of reserves to create internal harmony without the need for an iota of dosage. It finishes dry and structured, with beautiful flow, poise, profound persistence and the inimitable signature of Ambonnay salty minerality. The August 2015 disgorgement upholds primary red apple and fleshy fig fruit amidst pronounced secondary intrigue of roast nuts and buttered toast, concluding very long, dry and mineral-laden.

Eric Rodez Cuvée Blanc de Blancs NV $$

93 points • 2010 BASE VINTAGE • DISGORGED DECEMBER 2015 • TASTED IN AUSTRALIA

Ambonnay chardonnay; 29% 2010, 21% 2009, 22% 2008, 15% 2007, 7% 2006, 6% 2005; 4.5 years on lees; 20% malolactic fermentation; 83% barrel fermented; 4g/L dosage

Eric Rodez describes his blanc de blancs as more masculine and his blanc de noirs as more feminine. Strength here is derived from tremendous depth of reserves, bolstered eloquently this year by the vanillin and spice of oak. For such a recipe, it upholds a bright, medium-straw hue, energised by the acid line and permeating chalk mineral structure that defines Ambonnay. Layers of stone fruits, citrus and fig fill out a long and crafted palate of great integrity. Pinot noir may be the star of this village, but here is evidence that chardonnay can certainly perform here, upholding persistence and expression of salty mineral structure. A great release for Rodez.

Eric Rodez Cuvée Les Beurys Pinot Noir 2010 $$$$

92 points • TASTED IN AMBONNAY

100% pinot noir; single-plot Les Beurys; average vine age 35 years; vinified entirely in oak barrels; no malolactic fermentation; aged 4.5 years on lees; 3g/L dosage

I first tasted this single-vineyard, single-varietal cuvée as a very young release two years ago, when it screamed out for more time in bottle to mature and allow its prominent oak and malic acidity to soften and integrate. One more year on lees and one more on cork have aided it in this journey, its youthful plum liqueur, black cherry and ginger characters now fading, though its wood spice and firm tannin structure are still prominent. It upholds a fleshy palate of great persistence and will benefit from more time for its tannins to marry into the wine. It has the length and acid structure to go the distance. Patience.

Eric Rodez Cuvée des Grands Vintages Brut NV $$$

96 points • 2007 BASE VINTAGE • TASTED IN AUSTRALIA

30% chardonnay, 70% pinot from Ambonnay; 20% 2007, 30% 2006, 18% 2005, 12% 2004, 14% 2002, 6% 2000; close to 8 years on lees; no malolactic fermentation; 100% oak fermented; 3g/L dosage

An assemblage of the fruits of the first pressings of the best parcels across many years, this is a cuvée built on a mind-blowing roll-call of vintages, not only in that it averages 12 years of age on release, but that it plunders the greatest seasons of two decades, a line-up that must be unparalleled in Champagne, except perhaps in Krug itself, at three times the price. Its deep, layered complexity matches the recipe, countering the grand intensity of Ambonnay pinot noir with the finesse of chardonnay and the tension of malic acidity, upholding the churning salt minerality of the village on a long, dry finish. The 2007 base blend has attained a wonderful and enticing place of secondary complexity of fantastic, succulent depth, where the flesh of mirabelle plum and fig fruit is evolving to mocha, honey, golden fruit cake, butter and all manner of spices, sustained majestically by lively acidity and salty, chalk mineral freshness that proclaims grand terroirs tapped by great old vines. The harmony on show in this melody is a masterpiece of Rodez's talent as a composer.

The Champagne Guide

FRANCK BONVILLE

(Fronk Bon-vee)

9 RUE PASTEUR 51190 AVIZE

www.champagne-franck-bonville.com

Champagne
FRANCK BONVILLE
—GRAND CRU—

*A*s demand for the greatest Côtes des Blancs grand crus continues to spiral, the privilege of substantial, well-placed holdings cannot be overstated. Gilles and Ingrid Bonville and their son Olivier are in command of 20 hectares of prime grand cru turf, 15 in Avize, a little in Cramant, and old vines on the slope of Oger. The family have been growing grapes here for more than a century, and bottling their own champagnes since 1947. Olivier Bonville is the third generation of his family to make champagnes in Avize. Chardonnay is, of course, the theme of these tense, powerful champagnes, with red grapes for rosé sourced from the great estate of Paul Déthune in Ambonnay.

FRANCK BONVILLE BRUT BLANC DE BLANCS GRAND CRU NV $$

86 points • 2013 BASE VINTAGE • DISGORGED MAY 2016 • TASTED IN AUSTRALIA

Sourced from Avize and Oger; 2011 and 2009 reserves; 5.83g/L dosage

White peach and grapefruit of ripe, succulent depth is foiled by notes of stale peanut and dry extract, rendering the finish coarse and devoid of purity and harmony, with a confected sweetness more from ripe fruit than dosage.

FRANCK BONVILLE GRAND CRU AVIZE BRUT ROSÉ NV $$

90 points • 2012 BASE VINTAGE • DISGORGED MAY 2016 • TASTED IN AUSTRALIA

90% Avize chardonnay, 10% pinot noir red wine from Paul Déthune in Ambonnay, vinified in oak; 18% 2012, 67% 2011, 5% 2010; 6.67g/L dosage

A dry and savoury rosé of medium-straw hue, built primarily on the challenging 2011 harvest, and a pretty solid result considering. It's Avize blanc de blancs with 10% Ambonnay red wine, making for a style built more on the focus and fine, salty chalk mineral structure of chardonnay than on the aromatic roundness of pinot. True to the season, it lacks fragrance and life, yet upholds acid line, focus and balance.

FRANCK BONVILLE PRESTIGE GRAND CRU AVIZE BLANC DE BLANCS BRUT NV $$

88 points • 2011 BASE VINTAGE • DISGORGED APRIL 2016 • TASTED IN AUSTRALIA
Sourced from Avize; 2010 reserves; 5.83g/L dosage

The purity, vibrancy and sheer energy of Avize shines in lemon, grapefruit and apple, though the dry extract and stale imperfection of 2011 mark the finish and render it coarse and contracted.

FRANCK BONVILLE GRAND CRU AVIZE BLANC DE BLANCS BRUT MILLÉSIME 2010 $$

90 points • DISGORGED MAY 2015 • TASTED IN AUSTRALIA
Sourced from Avize; 5g/L dosage

Ripe notes of star fruit and white peach contrast tense notes of grapefruit and fennel. Bottle age has built fleeting suggestions of smoke and green olives unexpected at this young age. Acidity melds seamlessly with low dosage on a finish defined by the fine, salty chalk minerality of Avize. It lacks fruit line, reflecting its difficult season.

FRANCK BONVILLE GRAND CRU AVIZE BLANC DE BLANCS BRUT MILLÉSIME 2009 $$

92 points • DISGORGED JULY 2014 • TASTED IN AUSTRALIA
Sourced from Avize; 5.83g/L dosage

A beautiful juxtaposition of the tension of Avize and the generosity of the warm 2009 vintage makes for an enticing blanc de blancs of poise and purity. Accurate white peach, lemon and grapefruit shows backward freshness in magnum (94 points), supported by the fine, salty chalk mineral texture and focused acid line of Avize. The result is exactingly balanced and immediately appealing, without for an instant compromising tension or definition. A standard bottle displays more toasty development and notes of green olive, yet upholds fine, chalk mineral focus and excellent persistence.

FRANCK BONVILLE LES BELLES VOYES GRAND CRU BLANC DE BLANCS NV $$$

88 points • 2010 BASE VINTAGE • DISGORGED APRIL 2016 • TASTED IN AUSTRALIA
Sourced from Oger; aged 12 months in oak barriques; 2.5g/L dosage

This is a bold and bombastic blanc de blancs that parades the ripe mandarin and orange exuberance of Oger and bolsters it with a significant 12 months in oak barriques, throwing it into a spin of charcuterie, spice and gamey complexity. Salty minerality survives the ordeal, though it lacks grace and finesse.

The Champagne Guide

GATINOIS

(Ga-tin-wah)

8/10

7 RUE MARCEL MAILLY 51160 AŸ

www.champagne-gatinois.com

In the elegant reception room of Gatinois in the back streets of Aÿ, alongside a magnificent wine press still standing where it was constructed five generations ago, the Gatinois family tree is proudly displayed, tracing their history in the village back to 1696. Young Louis Cheval-Gatinois is the 12th successive generation to farm seven hectares of the family vineyards, enviably positioned on the majestic slopes of Aÿ. His family has made champagne here since probably the mid-1800s, which must place Gatinois among Champagne's oldest grower-producers. Gatinois's generously coloured champagnes are among the finest in this revered village, resonating with the history of the house and the thundering power of its grand cru slopes, at every moment retaining exceptional definition and freshness.

In the convoluted history of Champagne succession and inheritance, the vineyards of the ancient village of Aÿ have been divided into ever-smaller plots, creating what Louis Cheval-Gatinois describes as 'a mosaic on the hillside'.

Gatinois has been privileged to retain seven hectares that have scarcely changed since the inception of the house, divided into 27 parcels of exclusively south-facing vines. Old vines provide depth and structure, blended with young vines for freshness and vivacity. A wide spread of sites across the full breadth of the village creates complexity. 'Some respond better in particular seasons, so we can pick what we want in each vintage,' explains Cheval-Gatinois, who knows his vineyards so well that he can recognise each plot purely on the appearance of the grapes when they arrive at the press house.

Pinot noir comprises some 90% of plantings, with a little less than one hectare of chardonnay to add fresh-ness and endurance to pinot's fleshy structure and aromatic intensity. Fruit is green harvested if appropriate to give low harvests of 65hL/hectare, yielding an annual production of just 50,000 bottles. Less than 10% of the harvest is sold to a few houses, including Bollinger. Low yields enable Gatinois to pick at high maturity, bringing colour and intensity to its champagnes.

The house employs its own team of pickers, who are instructed to be very selective and, importantly, are paid by the hour and not by the kilogram. Every bad grape is sorted from each basket that is brought to the press.

'The quality of the grapes is the thing that makes our champagnes,' Cheval-Gatinois declares. 'The secret to the colour and style of our champagnes is what we put in our press. My father taught me to be proud of what is in the press before we close it, to be able to pick any grape and have the very best quality.'

Vinification is meticulously hands-on, shared between just three workers in the vineyards and cellars. The house still maintains its manual press. 'People are surprised to see me working with a traditional press, but this is important to ensure that we do not lose any quality,' he explains. 'We have a very humble vinification as we do not want to have too much impact on the taste.' Vinification takes place entirely in stainless steel tanks, to preserve purity of grape aromas. 'I produce wines more in an oxidative than a reductive style as I like generous champagnes, but with the freshness imparted by the acidity of Aÿ.' The only barrels in the house are for red wines, and these are very old, so as to produce gentle oxidation without imparting wood characters.

For Gatinois, debourbage (settling of juice prior to fermentation) is important for purity and elegance. All cuvées undergo full malolactic fermentation and receive low dosages of around 6g/L. Zero-dosage champagne is not the aim here, as 'dosage is important to produce smoothness and openness in the mouth without feeling the sweetness'. Blending is conducted slowly and carefully in May following the harvest, achieving very clear base wines by allowing plenty of time for natural settling prior to bottling. Bottles are matured in Gatinois's cellars under Aÿ, and all 50,000 are painstakingly hand disgorged on site every year. 'If it weren't for the history of the estate I wouldn't hand disgorge, but I watched my father and my grandfather do it, so I do the same!'

Since taking charge seven years ago, Louis has no desire to change the style. 'With such rich history behind me, I have a great opportunity to continue the philosophy of the house.' Skilfully capturing the exact character and great concentration of Aÿ, this tiny estate remains in capable hands. Eleven generations would be proud.

GATINOIS Aÿ GRAND CRU BRUT TRADITION NV $$

94 points • TASTED IN AUSTRALIA

80% pinot noir, 20% chardonnay; 30% reserves; part of the finished blend kept as reserve for the next year; 2 years on lees; 7g/L dosage

A full-straw hue with a slight blush tint declares the magnificent depth of character and concentration of Aÿ pinot noir. This is a cuvée of expansive, generous, primary depth of spicy red cherries, plums and figs, underscored by nuances of bottle maturity in spicy fruit cake. Yet for its considerable dimensions it is never heavy nor broad, toned by bright acidity and the signature fine, salty chalk mineral structure of Aÿ, drawing out a long and refined finish. Benchmark Gatinois and quintessential Aÿ.

GATINOIS Aÿ GRAND CRU BRUT RÉSERVE NV $$

95 points • TASTED IN AUSTRALIA

80% pinot, 20% chardonnay; aged 3 years on lees; 7g/L dosage

Made in the same manner and from similar parcels as Brut Tradition, and aged on lees for another year, this is purposely a more generous style that Cheval-Gatinois describes as more textural, more velvety and a more comfortable winter cuvée. A full-straw colour with a faint blush tint hints at its exuberance, trumpeting the magnificence of Aÿ in gloriously accurate red cherry and strawberry fruit which lingers with grand persistence and exacting line. Its fruit depth and definition are something to behold, charged with lively acidity and signature fine, salty chalk mineral texture. It epitomises the contrast between fruit depth and structural tension that only Aÿ can achieve. Brilliant and enthralling.

The Champagne Guide

Gatinois Aÿ Grand Cru Brut Rosé NV $$

95 points • Tasted in Australia

90% pinot, 10% chardonnay; aged 3 years on lees; 6g/L dosage

Rosé is Cheval-Gatinois's favourite cuvée and the tension between the elegant style of the house and the authority of Aÿ is captivating. With a full salmon crimson–hue, aromas and flavours of pretty red cherries, strawberries and raspberries leap from the glass. It's primary but not in any way simplistic, celebrating the structure and tension of Aÿ in bright acid line, fine and delicate tannin texture, and the rising, frothing salt mineral texture that can only be captured by great old vines on prime sites in Aÿ. In purity and persistence it is ravishingly magnificent.

Gatinois Aÿ Grand Cru Brut Millésimé 2009 $$

94 points • Tasted in Australia

90% pinot noir, 10% chardonnay; aged 6 years on lees; 7g/L dosage

Cheval-Gatinois's aspiration is to produce champagnes particular to Aÿ and to the season, blending parcels from the middle of the slope that best encapsulate this balance for the vintage. The generous 2009 season has produced a ripe, honeyed vintage wine with primary strawberry and red cherry fruit quickly evolving into secondary complexity of gingernut biscuits, mixed spice and brioche. The tension and definition of Aÿ is upheld confidently in a well-focused acid line and inimitable and pronounced salt chalk mineral texture. The result is definition and lively focus that transcends the dimensions of the season. Wow.

The majestic, sun-drenched, perfect south-facing slopes of Aÿ are the secret to Gatinois's thundering power and exceptional freshness.

GEOFFROY

(Zhof-wah)

6/10

4 RUE JEANSON 51160 AŸ
www.champagne-geoffroy.com

CHAMPAGNE
GEOFFROY

PROPRIÉTAIRE · RÉCOLTANT · ÉLABORATEUR

'*I am a winegrower,' says young, fifth-generation vigneron Jean-Baptiste Geoffroy. 'I need to be in the vineyard, this is my passion.' There is a well-considered sensibility about Geoffroy, and every detail of his work in the vineyard and winery follows a stringent regime, while maintaining practical common sense. With 11 glorious hectares in Cumières, and one in each of the nearby villages of Damery, Hautvillers and two in Fleury-la-Rivière, he is well placed to capture the fruit purity, poise and deep mineral fingerprint of some of the finer premier crus of the Vallée de la Marne. The sustaining presence of malic acidity makes his champagnes particularly long-lived.*

The finest grower in Cumières is no longer in Cumières. With winemaking facilities and cellars shared between his grandmother's house, his father's house and a neighbour, when the opportunity came to consolidate in 2008, Jean-Baptiste Geoffroy moved the whole operation 20 minutes (by tractor) down the road to a proud and spacious facility in Aÿ.

'Nothing has changed in the vineyards,' asserts Jean-Baptiste. 'I want to create a champagne of terroir, to achieve the best expression of the soil in the grapes.' To this end, his highest goal in the winery is to maintain freshness in every cuvée. This proved to be a challenge, working from three sites in Cumières, necessitating regular pumping and moving of bottles.

Now he can guarantee that his grapes are on the press less than an hour after they are harvested, in a facility ingeniously designed to do away with pumping altogether. Taking advantage of the hill behind, the harvest is delivered to the press on the third level of the building, and the juice flows by gravity to settling

tanks immediately below the press on the second level, then to fermentation on the first level, and finally to two levels of deep maturation cellars below. In 2012 he purchased a further 500 square metres of storage space in the village, not to increase production, but to relocate bottles to provide space to move his barrels deeper into the cellar, where the temperature is more stable.

Every step of production is geared towards maintaining freshness and vineyard character, which Geoffroy achieves with admirable consistency, even with low use of sulphur dioxide as a preservative. A traditional press is employed, which he admits is difficult to operate by hand, but worth every effort for quality. Each of 45 different parcels is pressed and vinified separately, and the tailles of each pressing separated and vinified independently.

Fermentation is conducted variously in the best vessels to facilitate controlled oxidation, generally small tanks for non-vintage wines, and small barrels and large foudres for vintage wines and the best pinot noir parcels, and Geoffroy has recently shown a preference for 350-litre barrels. Previously using only older barrels, he has recently introduced a turnover of younger barrels, purchased from Colin-Morey in Chassagne-Montrachet, though wild ferment and oak flavours and tannins can at times conflict with the elegance of his fruit.

Ferments rely on wild yeast, but are inoculated if they don't start naturally. To further preserve freshness, malolactic fermentation is avoided (but will occasionally start spontaneously). Only concentrated grape juice is used for dosage, because he says he couldn't find a good balance using sugar. 'This emphasises the taste of the grapes and the character of the soil,' he says.

Geoffroy generally uses extra brut dosages of less than 5g/L. As he puts it, 'A champagne must always be very fine, elegant and fresh. If you have good ripeness and good practice in the winery you don't need dosage.'

Ripeness is achieved through painstaking attention to every detail in the vineyard. Geoffroy's annual production of 130,000 bottles is sourced exclusively from his own vines, apart from 5% permitted under récoltant-manipulant registration. Pinot rules in this part of the world, and his holdings comprise 40% pinot noir, 40% meunier and 20% chardonnay.

EARTH-FRIENDLY APPROACH

His eco-friendly approach is close to organic, but falls purposely short of the constraints of certification. 'I like to say I am biological, without being biodynamic,' he says. To best express the soil in the grapes, vineyards are ploughed to discourage surface roots and drive the vines deeper into the subsoils. To the same end, several species of natural grasses are cultivated in the mid-rows to provide surface competition. He is currently introducing a horse to plough one vineyard in an attempt to reduce tractor compaction. Organic fertilisers encourage

Jean-Baptiste Geoffroy checks the fill on a barrel.

soil health, and herbicides are avoided. Sulphur and copper sulphate sprays are used where possible, but here he sometimes deviates from a strict organic regime, calling on other chemicals as required.

Geoffroy knows each of his 45 plots intimately, and treats each separately, regarding them variously as grand cru, premier cru or unclassified. The blanket classification of Cumières as premier cru makes no sense to him. 'On the poor soil and sand at the top of the hill near the forest, it is inferior to Damery, which is unclassified,' he clarifies. 'The early-ripening middle slope of the south-facing amphitheatre of Cumières north of the city is of grand cru quality, and to the west it is premier cru.' He points out each on a satellite photo, and his designations correspond precisely with green patches that betray the most vigorous vines. There is a natural regulation of vigour in Geoffroy's vines, with old vines and mid-row grasses limiting yields, ensuring earlier ripeness.

COTEAUX CHAMPENOIS RED WINES

This approach allows him to produce one of the most celebrated Coteaux Champenois still red wines, a passion he inherited from his father and grandfather. 'I make a red wine from the best grapes of my terroir, from the oldest vines and the lowest yields,' he says.

After experimenting extensively with red wine production in Beaujolais and Burgundy, Geoffroy produces red wine only in warmer vintages from Cumières pinot noir (meunier for the first time in 2008), releasing it as both a non-vintage and a vintage cuvée. The wines undergo malolactic fermentation and mature in 600-litre demi-muids for at least 12 months. These are long-ageing wines, with the potential to live for decades, and are only released when he deems them ready. Production is small and sporadic. 'It's good to make Coteaux Champenois when you don't need to!' he says. 'You can't make it to demand or in every vintage.'

In 2012, Geoffroy simplified the name of the estate from 'René Geoffroy' to 'Geoffroy' and introduced a new label, depicting the gate of the house in Aÿ to represent his new identity. 'It is not my philosophy to put my first name on the label, as I hope to one day pass the estate on to my children. There is no point changing the name with every generation,' he says.

Vintages, varieties, dosage and date of disgorgement are displayed on the back of every label, a laudable commitment for a small grower who disgorges every 2–3 months and tweaks the dosage for each disgorgement.

With undeviating attention to well-situated vineyards, an enviable production facility larger than his needs – and no intention to grow production – Cumières' finest grower is as fine as ever.

GEOFFROY EXPRESSION BRUT PREMIER CRU NV $$

92 points • 2011 BASE VINTAGE • DISGORGED DECEMBER 2015 • TASTED IN AUSTRALIA

50% meunier, 30% pinot noir, 10% chardonnay from Cumières and a little from Hautvillers; average vine age 20 years; tank fermented; 2010 reserves part aged in old casks; no malolactic fermentation; 8g/L dosage; 50% of production volume, ~65,000 bottles

Even in the difficult 2011 season, this cuvée rises to its brief of easy-drinking freshness. Meunier takes a confident lead in fragrant strawberry and red apple appeal, creating a compelling contrast with crisp malic acidity and tight grapefruit and lemon zest notes. It's fresher and more primary than ever, with more than three years on lees lending only subtle almond meal and spice notes. The dry grip of 2011 is refreshingly underplayed on a vibrant finish, thanks to the cut of malic acidity juxtaposed with well-rounded dosage.

GEOFFROY PURETÉ BRUT NATURE PREMIER CRU NV $$

92 points • 2010 BASE VINTAGE • DISGORGED MARCH 2016 • TASTED IN AUSTRALIA

50% meunier, 40% pinot noir, 10% chardonnay from Cumières, Damery and Fleury-la-Rivière; average vine age 25 years; 2009 reserves part aged in oak casks; no malolactic fermenation; no dosage

Pureté is Expression with another year on lees and no dosage. Full malic acidity and no added sugar makes for a tense and steely champagne with accentuated salt minerality. Yet the accord of 2010 and 2009 brings generosity of white peach and red apple to its crunchy lemon zest profile, bolstered by the biscuit and spice of five years lees age. It's clean, precise, taut and high-strung; an oyster-ready style driven by tense malic acidity. Perfect ripeness and great persistence make it alluringly enticing this year. Champagne die-hards, this one's for you.

GEOFFROY EMPREINTE BRUT PREMIER CRU 2009 $$

91 points • DISGORGED OCTOBER 2015 • TASTED IN AUSTRALIA

75% pinot noir, 20% chardonnay, 5% meunier from a selection of very early-ripening plots above Cumières on clay and chalk soils with fragments of flint; average vine age 30 years; 80% fermented in tuns, demi-muid casks and barrels; 6g/L dosage

Geoffroy is refining his style with each vintage, and upheld the lower dosage he introduced in the elegant 2008 season again in the richer 2009, though rose to the magnitude of this ripe vintage with a considerable 80% vinification in wood (it was just 24% in 2008). His aspiration is to portray the best expression of Cumières pinot noir, and in the bold 2009 season, these early-ripening plots above Cumières certainly deliver their distinctive personality. The result is as powerful as any Cumières I've tasted, a complex and secondary style brimming with baked apple, fig, even rockmelon, with barrel work contributing charcuterie and game (a little more funky than I'd like it to be) and bottle age layering butterscotch, gingernut biscuits and spice. The fine, salty minerality of Cumières defines a long finish, enlivened by a crunchy, focused drive that celebrates the vivacity and tension of malic acidity.

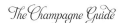

The Champagne Guide

GEOFFROY VOLUPTÉ BRUT PREMIER CRU 2007 $$$

93 points • DISGORGED DECEMBER 2015 • TASTED IN AUSTRALIA

58% chardonnay from Geoffroy's most beautiful Cumières plots of very chalky soil with shallow topsoil; 42% pinot noir; average vine age 35 years; 45% vinified in barrels and vats; no malolactic fermentation; 4g/L dosage

Two years ago I wrote that this beautifully focused style just needs time to soften and calm down. Another two years on lees has fulfilled its promise. Low dosage and a full serve of malic acidity in a chardonnay-focused style make for a tense and steely champagne of impressive stature. A high-strung lemon zest core is filled out with impressive complexity of fig, mixed spice and ginger cake, finishing long and dry, with firm minerality and prominent acidity. Time has made for a creamy mouthfeel and heighted vanilla nougat character, underlined with the fine chalk minerality of Cumières, drawing out a long and enticing finish. It's wonderful now and will only get better over the next decade.

GEOFFROY ROSÉ DE SAIGNÉE BRUT PREMIER CRU NV $$

94 points • 100% 2012 VINTAGE • DISGORGED OCTOBER 2015 • TASTED IN AUSTRALIA

Saignée of 100% skin-contact pinot noir, sourced from clay and silt soils with some marl; average vine age 25 years; no malolactic fermentation; 10g/L dosage

Renowned for his long-lived Cumières rouge Coteaux Champenois, it's no surprise that Geoffroy's Rosé de Saignée also improves with time. Now released with sufficient age for the vintage to be declared (on the back label) post-disgorgement, this is a style of medium, vibrant crimson salmon–hue and exuberant primary freshness of pink pepper, pomegranate, red cherry and tangy raspberry fruits. Beautifully ripe fruit expression is intricately supported and freshened by ripe, brightly poised malic acidity, fine, skilfully handled tannins, exactingly balanced dosage, and the salty chalk mineral expression of Cumières. The great 2012 season has given birth to one of Geoffroy's most enthralling Rosé de Saignées.

GEOFFROY ÉLIXIR DEMI-SEC NV $$

91 points • 2011 BASE VINTAGE • DISGORGED NOVEMBER 2014 • TASTED IN AUSTRALIA

2010 reserves; 35g/L dosage

Geoffroy's demi-sec is a refreshingly clean and well-balanced style, thanks to the energy and cut of malic acidity delivering balance rarely encountered with this level of dosage in Champagne. Baked apple and preserved lemon unite with the honey, gingernut biscuits and spice of three and a half years bottle age and more than two years cork age, drawing out a finish at once long, rich, sweet and lively. If you're chasing a sweeter style, this is a good bet.

GOSSET

(Goh-say)

7/10

3 RUE DE MALAKOFF 51200 ÉPERNAY
www.champagne-gosset.com

Established in 1584, centuries before the bubble was ever put into champagne, Gosset rightfully claims to be the oldest wine house in the region. Far from a staid, traditional establishment, Gosset is on the move, having relocated its production to the impressive Épernay cuverie and cellars of Château Malakoff, purchased from Laurent Perrier just in time for vintage 2009. In the midst of change, the house maintains an unwavering consistency, thanks largely to one man, the late Jean-Pierre Mareigner, its talented chef de cave of 33 years. Under his legacy, the house style of no malolactic fermentation, clean-cut structure and enduring longevity remains as fine as ever, with the exception of its Brut Excellence NV entry wine, which seems a strange misfit, in both philosophy and quality.

Previously operating from five different locations, Gosset is now basking in the opportunity to grow into the huge cuverie of Château Malakoff, with a capacity of 2.6 million litres, far exceeding the requirement for an annual production of 1.1 million bottles. There is a long-term hope to gradually increase to 1.2–1.4 million, but this will take a long time for a style as long-aged as Gosset.

The substantial premises, constructed in 1860 on two hectares of parkland next door to Pol Roger, came fully equipped with vinification facilities and disgorgement and labelling lines. Its 1.5 kilometres of deep cellars have a capacity for 2.5 million bottles, and house part of Gosset's stock of more than 4 million. The rest remain in Gosset's historic headquarters in Aÿ, where riddling and disgorgement are still conducted.

Gosset's roots in Mareigner's birth town of Aÿ remain strong in spite of the move and the company's tiny vineyard holdings. With just one hectare to its name, Gosset purchases 99% of its fruit from 200 growers in 60 different villages, exclusively premier and grand crus in the Marne department.

The consistency of supply is a credit to Mareigner's long-term relationships with growers, some of whom have supplied Gosset for three generations. He knew them all so well that when they phoned him they announced themselves by first name only. As evidence of its faith in these relationships, Gosset does not operate press houses in the villages, instead entrusting its growers to crush on its behalf.

Every village and grower is kept separate during vinification, which is performed in stainless steel tanks, the temperature regulated to maintain ferments below 18°C. 'Our goal is to keep what nature has given us,' explained Mareigner. 'No centrifuge, no filtering until immediately before bottling, and no malolactic fermentation.'

A little oxidation early in production builds resilience. No sulphur dioxide preservative is added at bottling, though a little remains in the wine from earlier in production. I have only ever encountered one oxidised Gosset – Celebris Extra Brut Vintage 2004 – in my tastings for this edition, and regrettably no back-up bottle was supplied.

The impressive freshness and remarkable ageing potential of malic acidity calls for long cellaring prior to release, and the great vintages of Gosset will live exceedingly long. The house has recently been tasting Jean-Pierre's very first blends of Grande Réserves from the 1980s, and reports that they are still magnificent.

Like Pol Roger next door, Gosset's deep cellars maintain a temperature below 11°C, drawing out the second ferment over six months to produce a very fine bead. A low dosage of 8g/L or less is used across the Grande range, and no more than 5g/L across the prestige Celebris trio, which accounts for a tiny 2% of the production of the house.

The beautifully poised Grande Réserve is on the rise, now representing more than 40% of production, pushing Brut Excellence down to just 40–45% (a tiny representation for an entry wine in the grand scale of champagne house production). The aim is to increase Grande Réserve and diminish Brut Excellence to just 20% in the next four to five years. This is just as well, because this cuvée is something of an ironic aberration in the excellence of the house, made using partial malolactic fermentation and a full dosage of 11g/L, and the house no longer shows me samples. There's quite a disparity between this bottle and the rest of the portfolio, which is referred to by the house as the 'antique' range. It is here that Mareigner's masterful skill was showcased, evidenced perhaps most demonstrably in his exceptional ability to achieve texture, finesse and harmony without malolactic fermentation.

Jean-Pierre Mareigner passed away in May 2016. The house remains in good hands, as Mareigner had been training a team around him for a decade, in anticipation of his intended retirement in January 2017. I will miss Jean-Pierre for his wit, his good humour, his cheeky grin, his generous kindness, and not least his masterful skill in crafting clean-cut and enduring cuvées. He will be fondly remembered and celebrated for decades to come through a deep and grand legacy which he has left in the cellars of Gosset – and one last surprise, in development for more than two decades. Join me in raising a glass to the life of a talented, humble soul who has made this distinguished old house what it is today.

GOSSET 15 ANS DE CAVE A MINIMA BRUT NV $$$$$

98 points • DISGORGED JUNE 2016 • TASTED IN AUSTRALIA

60% chardonnay from Le Mesnil-sur-Oger, Cramant and Villers-Marmery; 40% pinot from Ambonnay, Aÿ and Mareuil sur Aÿ; reserves from 1996 and 1995; aged 15 years on lees; 7g/L dosage; just 10,000 bottles produced, and only 5000 released so far

Mareigner has left a deep legacy in the cellars of Gosset, and one last surprise, a brand new cuvée in development for more than two decades, from experimental bottlings he developed as an extension to the Gosset style. He announced it to me at the end of what was to be my very last tasting with him. 'Grande Réserve is released at five years of age, but what if we were to make a wine with top sourcing, as a non-vintage blend of top vintages, built to age longer?' he asked. Of the late 1990s, the three greatest vintages are 1998, 1996 and 1995, and my only regret is that the seasons are not anywhere on the bottle, website or press releases. The charge of malic acidity jolts Gosset to a plane of incredible longevity, exemplified in this cuvée after almost 20 years of age, and counting. My first encounter with this remarkable innovation revealed a wine of beguiling allure, confidently poised in that special place midway between primary fruit definition, secondary complexity and the deep, reverberating presence of grand old age. In the context of the pale brilliance of Gosset, a medium straw yellow–hue declares its maturity, reinforced in notes of toast, butter, fruit mince spice, even subtle nuances of green olives, sweet leather and pipe smoke. In the midst of this maelstrom of character, ripe, primary citrus, white peach and apple fruit holds rock solid, carrying with sensational persistence. Malic acidity zaps everything into a state of frenzy with an ice shard of acidity that will sustain it for years yet. In sheer, undeviating persistence, exacting line and pure, unbridled joy, this is one of Mareigner's finest achievements. Vale Jean-Pierre.

GOSSET GRANDE RÉSERVE BRUT NV $$

94 points • 2011 BASE VINTAGE WITH 2010 AND 2009 RESERVES • TASTED IN
CHAMPAGNE
94 points • 2010 BASE VINTAGE WITH 2009 AND 2008 RESERVES • BOTTLED IN 2011
• DISGORGED 2014 AND 2015 • TASTED IN AUSTRALIA
91 points • 2010 BASE VINTAGE WITH 2009 AND 2008 RESERVES • BOTTLED IN 2012
• DISGORGED MARCH 2016 • TASTED IN AUSTRALIA

40% chardonnay, predominantly from Le Mesnil-sur-Oger, Villers-Marmery and Trépail; 40% pinot,
predominantly from Aÿ, Bouzy and Ambonnay; 20% meunier, predominantly from Cumières,
Damery and Tauxiéres; no malolactic fermentation; 8g/L dosage; more than 40% of production

Grande Réserve is the key focus of Gosset, progressively growing in volume to overtake Brut
Excellence, and the first priority for fruit allocation before vintage cuvées. It represents a blend
of 50 villages, all vinified separately, with reserves built both from single years and from the full
blend of the previous year, in what Mareigner likened to 'a partial solera system'.

Grande Réserve is perpetually among the most reliable NVs on the shelves, and retains
its full majesty even in the 2011 vintage. Mareigner cleverly bolstered reserves to a remarkable
two-thirds of the blend, including close to 40% of 2010, the balance from 2009. The result is a
more secondary take on the Grande Réserve style, filled with spice, toast and honey. The classic
malic acid drive of the house defines an impressive finish of enduring focus.

Mareigner admired the elegance and structure of the 2010 season and captured both
accurately. The tension and energy of Grande Réserve are on full display in this base vintage
in crunchy red apple and lemon fruit, illuminated by bright malic acidity and Gosset's signature
of prominent, gently rolling, fine chalk mineral finesse. I have bought and marvelled at many
bottles of 2010 base Grande Réserve over the past two years, and for reasons that elude me,
2011 bottled stock disgorged in 2014 and 2015 is consistently far superior to 2012 bottled stock
disgorged in 2016 (though the bottle regrettably offers no clue as to which is which). The latter
consistently displays subtle dry-extract dustiness that diminishes the finish, dipping from the
full majesty of earlier-bottled stock, though nonetheless admirably upholding the pale hue and
tightly coiled guise that defines the house. The 2012 base is coming soon. Bring it on!

GOSSET GRAND ROSÉ BRUT NV $$$

93 points • 2011 BASE VINTAGE WITH 2010 RESERVES • TASTED IN CHAMPAGNE
91 points • 2010 BASE • DISGORGED MAY 2016 • TASTED IN AUSTRALIA

50% chardonnay, predominantly from Avize, Chouilly, Villers-Marmery and Trépail; 50% pinot,
predominantly from Cumières, Bouzy, Ambonnay and Verzenay; 8% pinot noir red wine from
Ambonnay and Bouzy; 9g/L dosage; 130,000 bottles

The aspiration of Gosset Rosé is freshness, delicacy and elegance without too much structure.
A confident chardonnay lead, low proportion of red wine and signature cut of malic acidity fulfil
the brief for this delicate and graceful style. The 2011 base presents a medium-salmon hue and
accurate red fruits and spice, though the bottle the house showed me had been open for some
time and hence lacked a little in freshness. The 2010 base presents airy rose petal, red cherries
and pink grapefruit, though sadly foiled on the finish by dry-extract dustiness, a little more
prominent here than on the other NVs, very much paling from its grand elegance and exacting
freshness of its release two years ago. It nonetheless holds its integrity in even integration of
malic acidity and dosage, carrying long on the finish.

The Champagne Guide

Gosset Grand Millésime Brut 2006 $$$

94 points • Disgorged February 2016 • Tasted in Champagne and Australia

55% chardonnay, predominantly from Avize, Cramant, Le Mesnil-sur-Oger and Vertus; 45% pinot noir, predominantly from Avenay, Aÿ and Chigny-les-Roses; no malolactic fermentation; 6g/L dosage

Gosset's splendid mandate of beautifully ripe fruit in tension with the electric zap of malic acidity sets the rich and rounded 2006 season up for a powerfully characterful release, a Gosset of full straw with a gold tint, brimming with toffee, golden fruit cake, glacé peach, fig, ginger and nutmeg, characters not unfamiliar in vintage Gosset, yet here heightened by the amplitude of the season. For all of its exotic complexity and cuddly roundedness, it upholds poise and finesse, thanks to a long, drawn-out finish of well-composed malic acidity and the ever-present, ultra-fine texture of chalk minerality.

Gosset Celebris Rosé Extra Brut 2007 $$$$

96 points • Disgorged February 2016 • Tasted in Champagne and Australia

59% chardonnay from Avize, Chouill and Cramant; 33.5% pinot noir from Aÿ, Bouzy and Ambonnay; 7.5% pinot noir red wine from Ambonnay and Bouzy; no malolactic fermentation; 3g/L dosage

The most subtle rosés are the most enchanting, and Mareigner has conjured the epitome of elegance by seeking a small selection of what he called the most 'shy' villages in the very fresh vintage of 2007. Even four years post-release, this is an introverted wine, more about structure, mouthfeel and restrained lightness than it is about depth of fruit. Primary cherry and red berry fruits remain in Champagne, though in Australia have evolved to blood orange, mixed spice, toast, honey, almonds and brioche. Long lees age has brought a creaminess to its framework of chewy structure and tannin presence so fine it's impossible to tell where tannins finish and pronounced grand cru salt minerality begins. Now that its fruit has begun to subside, malic acidity lends some firmness to a tight finish, accentuated by lower dosage than its first release. It possesses ample energy to blossom for years yet. Don't drink it now, but if you must, give it plenty of time to wake up in the largest Burgundy glasses you can conjure.

Gosset Grand Blanc de Blancs Brut NV $$$

93 points • 2011 base vintage • Disgorged March 2016 • Tasted in Champagne and Australia

Two-thirds Côte des Blancs (predominantly Avize, Chouilly and Cramant) for freshness and finesse, one-third Montagne de Reims (predominantly Villers-Marmery, Trépail and Ambonnay) for body and structure; 10% 2010 reserves; no malolactic fermentation; 7g/L dosage

The Gosset house style of refined minerality and thrilling malic acidity shine in its blanc de blancs. Youthful purity and focus of lemon and beurre bosc pear highlight a primary style, with lees age tactically deployed to create creamy texture without malolactic fermentation. The tension of driving malic acidity and fine chalk minerality creates a seamless finish with the potential to hold its freshness for many years yet. A subtle dry-extract dustiness on the finish is but a faint hint of the challenging 2011 season, an impressive result, though Mareigner pointed out that the vintage was stronger for chardonnay than black grapes. It holds excellent harmony and poise on the finish, with fruit, minerality, dosage and malic acidity intricately entwined.

GUY CHARLEMAGNE

(Ghee Shar-le-mahn)

(6/10)

4 RUE DE LA BRÈCHE D'OGER 51190 LE MESNIL-SUR-OGER
www.champagne-guy-charlemagne.com

The Charlemagne family has made and sold its own champagnes since 1892, predating the house of Salon directly across the road in Le Mesnil-sur-Oger. The family is privileged to six glorious hectares of vines of average age 42 years in the village, one in neighbouring Oger and a little in Mancy and Cuis, yielding beautifully mineral chardonnay. This is a grower of two faces, with half its production of 130,000 bottles drawn from six hectares in the Sézanne and one in Glannes, producing more rustic blends of chardonnay and pinot noir. The purity of its terroirs is preserved through vinification in stainless steel tanks with full malolactic fermentation, with the exception of the cleverly named flagship of the house, Mesnillésime, of which 30% is vinified in 225-litre oak barrels without malolactic fermentation. Guy Charlemagne is astute in reserving Le Mesnil and Oger fruit for its refined and age-worthy blanc de blancs cuvées, and it is on these wines that this skilful and affordably priced grower rests its reputation.

GUY CHARLEMAGNE LE MESNIL-SUR-OGER GRAND CRU BLANC DE BLANCS BRUT RÉSERVE NV $$

92 points • 60% 2012 BASE VINTAGE • DISGORGED APRIL 2016 • TASTED IN AUSTRALIA

100% chardonnay from Les Mesnil-sur-Oger and Oger; 20% 2011 and 20% 2010 reserves; aged 3 years on lees; 8g/L dosage; DIAM closure

This is where the real business of Guy Charlemagne kicks off, an impressively mineral-driven wine, quite a contrast to the Sézanne cuvées of the house. The tension of Le Mesnil is bolstered by the power and depth of Oger, contrasting lemon and apple fruit with the ripe exoticism of oranges and mandarins. Honed acid cut and impressive chalk mineral mouthfeel keep the finish fresh and lively, with just a touch more dosage than the fruit ripeness of this season calls for. Subtle notes of brioche provide dimension.

GUY CHARLEMAGNE CUVÉE CHARLEMAGNE GRAND CRU BLANC DE BLANCS BRUT 2010 $$

91 points • DISGORGED MAY 2016 • TASTED IN AUSTRALIA

Sourced from Le Mesnil-sur-Oger; aged 5 years on lees; 6g/L dosage; DIAM closure

A full-straw hue heralds a rich, ripe and complex cuvée already declaring depth of secondary character. Ripe Le Mesnil chardonnay of lemon, white peach, mandarin and golden delicious apple fullness is layered with the toast, almond meal and brioche of bottle age. Le Mesnil acidity and soft chalk minerality meld seamlessly with low dosage and well-handled phenolics on the finish. A more than respectable result for a tricky season.

GUY CHARLEMAGNE MESNILLÉSIME LE MESNIL-SUR-OGER GRAND CRU BRUT 2005 $$$

90 points • DISGORGED APRIL 2016 • TASTED IN AUSTRALIA

100% Le Mesnil-sur-Oger chardonnay from old vines of average age 65 years; 70% vinified in stainless steel with malolactic fermentation, 30% in 225-litre oak barrels without malolactic; aged 10 years on lees; 3g/L dosage

It takes some tenacity to bottle Le Mesnil-sur-Oger with a dose of malic acidity, and even more to do so with some small oak fermentation. Guy Charlemagne has pulled off the challenge in the generous and powerful 2005 season, creating a wine of volume, impact and creamy succulence. It's rounded, rich and full, with impressive persistence and – crucially – upholding the salty chalk minerality of the village. Ripe orange and golden delicious apple fruit contrasts great complexity of custard, golden fruit cake, ginger and mixed spice. It's just beginning to tire and dry out on the finish.

The enduring grand cru of Le Mesnil-sur-Oger infuses Guy Charlemagne's finest cuvées with great stamina and poise.

Hatt et Söner

(At e Soh-neh)

10 Avenue des Comtes de Champagne 51130 Bergères-lès-Vertus
www.hatt-soner.com

CHAMPAGNE
HATT *et* SÖNER

When the Ruscon family established their small négociant business in the village of Bergères-lès-Vertus at the southern end of the Côte des Blancs in 2011, they were to become the first Swedish family to own a champagne house. Their recipe is daring to say the least. Sourcing from 40 parcels entirely in the premier and grand crus of the Côte des Blancs is certainly admirable, but to vinify these exclusively as vintage cuvées with low dosage and without malolactic fermentation makes for challenging wines in the lesser seasons.

HATT ET SÖNER LE GRAND-PÈRE OMNES OI 2012 $$$

91 points • Disgorged April 2016 • Tasted in Australia

100% chardonnay from Bergères-lès-Vertus single parcel 'Les Falloises' of 65-year-old vines; no malolactic fermentation; 50% vinified in third-use barrels; 3g/L dosage; 1000 bottles; DIAM closure

At this young age, the spicy exuberance of 50% oak vinification speaks louder than the gentle voice of the underrated premier cru of Bergéres-lés-Vertus. The fruit rises with time in glass, and it achieves the accord with seamless poise, presenting grapefruit and pear amidst barrel-induced notes of bacon fat and charcuterie. It finishes with well-focused malic acidity and finely structured phenolic grip accentuated by low dosage. Give it time in the cellar to expand and harmonise.

HATT ET SÖNER LE GRAND-PÈRE BRUT PRESTIGE 2006 $$$

90 points • Disgorged June 2014 • Tasted in Australia

100% chardonnay; 80% Oger, 20% Bergères-lès-Vertus; no malolactic fermentation; 6g/L dosage; 3500 bottles; DIAM closure

Packaged immaculately in a gorgeous proprietary bottle with evocative metal label plates, this tiny-production cuvée proclaims the fast-developing maturity of Oger in the warm 2006 season. Secondary complexity is the theme here, rejoicing in layers of buttered toast, quince, fig jam, even a hint of marmalade. It finishes dry, grainy and just a touch tired, though the ever-sustaining energy of malic acidity keeps it well focused.

HENRI ABELÉ

(On-ree Ab-leh)

50 RUE DE SILLERY 51100 REIMS

www.henriabele.com

Henri Abelé

· MAISON FONDÉE EN 1757 ·
A REIMS · FRANCE

CHAMPAGNE

Founded in 1757, Henri Abelé is the fifth oldest house in Champagne, and played a famous role in the history of riddling and disgorgement. In 1834, the house was joined by Antoine Müller, former chef de cave at Veuve Clicquot, where he developed the process of remuage with the Widow. When Henri Abelé himself took over in 1903, he fine-tuned the riddling rack and was the first to freeze the bottle neck in disgorgement. The house was bought by the Spanish giant Freixenet Group in 1985, though it has admirably shunned the trend to grow, capping production at a modest 500,000 bottles. With limited vineyard resources under its ownership, sourcing is primarily from growers spanning the Marne, Sézanne, Vitry and Aube. To celebrate its 250th anniversary in 2007, a new cuverie and vat room were constructed and a large supply of small vinification vats procured by new chef de cave Franck Nicaise. His aim then and now is for a fresher style, and to this end he has increased the presence of chardonnay as the leading varietal in all cuvées except his flagship blanc de noirs, Le Sourire de Reims Rosé.

HENRI ABELÉ BRUT NV $$

88 points • 2012 BASE VINTAGE • DISGORGED JULY 2016 • TASTED IN AUSTRALIA

40% chardonnay, 35% pinot, 25% meunier; Grande Montagne de Reims, Côte des Blancs, Massif de Saint-Thierry and Sézannais; 30% reserves from 2011, 2009, 2008 and 2007; 9g/L dosage; DIAM closure

Tangy grapefruit and lemon, crunchy red apple and strawberry fruit meet the biscuity complexity of bottle age, culminating in a firm finish of raw acidity and phenolic bitterness.

Henri Abelé Brut Rosé NV $$

90 points • 2012 BASE VINTAGE • DISGORGED JULY 2016 • TASTED IN AUSTRALIA

40% chardonnay, 40% pinot, 20% meunier; Grande Montagne de Reims, Côte des Blancs, Massif de Saint-Thierry and Sézannais; 30% reserves from 2011, 2009, 2008 and 2007; 9g/L dosage; DIAM closure

A medium salmon copper–hue accentuates a tangy rosé that contrasts red berry fruits with lively pink grapefruit acidity and the subtle biscuity complexity and soft texture of lees age. It concludes with well-integrated dosage and fine chalk mineral texture.

Henri Abelé Brut Millésimé 2007 $$$

89 points • DISGORGED MAY 2015 • TASTED IN AUSTRALIA

60% chardonnay, 40% pinot; Grande Montagne de Reims, Côte des Blancs; a tribute cuvée to celebrate the 250th anniversary of the house, the arrival of cellar master Franck Nicaise and the investment in a new winery; 8g/L dosage; DIAM closure

A rich, complex and ripe champagne of full straw yellow–hue, basking in the radiance of pineapple and juicy white peach fruit, meeting layers of brioche and candied almond complexity. For all of its exuberant ripeness, its acidity still carries a little firmness on the finish, contrasting candied dosage.

The village of Sacy overlooks Reims from its perch on the Petite Montagne de Reims.

The Champagne Guide

HENRI ABELÉ BRUT MILLÉSIMÉ 2006 $$$

92 points • DISGORGED JANUARY 2016 • TASTED IN AUSTRALIA

70% chardonnay, 30% pinot; Grande Montagne de Reims, Côte des Blancs; 8g/L dosage; DIAM closure

The magnificent, succulent richness of 2006 unites with all the creamy allure of more than a decade of age to produce a generous, chardonnay-led blend of caressing appeal. The ripeness of the season drips with succulent white peach and wild strawberry fruit, bolstered by generous lashings of honey, burnt toffee, roast almonds, dried apricots and fruit mince spice. It's just edging past the peak of its trajectory, so tuck in quick smart.

HENRI ABELÉ LE SOURIRE DE REIMS BRUT 2008 $$$$

94 points • DISGORGED JANUARY 2016 • TASTED IN AUSTRALIA

60% chardonnay, 40% pinot; Grande Montagne de Reims, Côte des Blancs; 7g/L dosage

The energy and dynamism of 2008 furnish a youthful and vivacious style alive with the primary definition of apple, pear and a suggestion of strawberry fruit. Reductive complextiy lends notes of flint and white pepper, quickly dissipating to make way for the toasty complexity of bottle maturity. It's structurally delightful – a jovial celebration of frothing chalk minerality, simultaneously heightened by the tension of 2008 acidity and softened by the creamy texture of lees age, culminating in a long and fine finish.

HENRI ABELÉ LE SOURIRE DE REIMS BRUT 2007 $$$$

91 points • DISGORGED FEBRUARY 2015 • TASTED IN AUSTRALIA

60% chardonnay, 40% pinot; Grande Montagne de Reims, Côte des Blancs; 7g/L dosage

Layers of toasty, bready, brioche and ginger celebrate a decade of maturity, while the primary grapefruit, pink lady apple and strawberry fruit of chardonnay and pinot noir define a long finish. Bright acidity and subtle dosage are well integrated, and it holds with good persistence, though phenolic grip lends a little firmness to the finish.

HENRI ABELÉ LE SOURIRE DE REIMS ROSÉ 2006 $$$$

94 points • DISGORGED JANUARY 2016 • TASTED IN AUSTRALIA

Maceration rosé entirely of 100% Les Riceys pinot noir; first launched from the 2003 vintage to commemorate the 800th anniversary of the Reims Cathedral in 2011; 7g/L dosage

Les Riceys is Champagne's largest cru and the most famous in the Aube, sought after by virtually every house with a keen interest in rosé. This saignée of 100% pinot noir pronounces a powerful and characterful expression of this village. With a medium to full crimson copper–hue, it leaps from the glass in exuberant characters of pomegranate, guava, wild strawberries, musk — even savoury, stalk-derived nuances of tamarillo, Campari and pipe smoke. Skin tannins lend bitter grip to the finish, not inappropriate or dominating in the presence of such juicy and extroverted fruit. It propagates with persistence and primary freshness impressive for this ripe season.

HENRI GIRAUD

(On-ree Zhi-row)

71 BOULEVARD CHARLES DE GAULLE 51160 AŸ

www.champagne-giraud.com

CHAMPAGNE
HENRI GIRAUD

The Giraud-Hémart family has diligently tended vines on the south-facing slopes of Aÿ since 1625, making this the oldest champagne house still owned by its founding family. It was not until the current head of house, 12th generation Claude Giraud, that champagnes were made under the family name. An annual production of about 250,000 bottles is sourced from the family's 10 hectares, spread across 35 small plots, supplemented with fruit purchased largely from family and friends, all of which is pressed by Giraud. Planted to 70% pinot noir and 30% chardonnay, the magnificence of Aÿ is captured, thanks to vines of a minimum 30 years of age, planted on thin topsoils and deep chalk, tended according to organic principles and harvested at full ripeness. Musts are cold settled at 10°C prior to fermentation, to enhance clarity and aroma, and all cuvées go through full malolactic fermentation. Stainless steel tanks have recently been completely rejected and all cuvées are now vinified in terracotta or 228-litre barrels from the Argonne forest south-east of Aÿ, an oak industry which Claude has been instrumental in reviving since 1989. He says his generous and silky Fût de Chêne and Code Noir cuvées are fresher and more lively as a result, though oak presence can compete with fruit purity.

HENRI GIRAUD ESPRIT DE GIRAUD BRUT NV $$

92 points • DISGORGED APRIL 2016 • TASTED IN AUSTRALIA

80% pinot, 20% chardonnay; 50% reserves matured in small Argonne oak casks and ovoid vats; aged 6 months in Argonne oak and concrete, plus 18 months on lees in bottle; 7.5g/L dosage

Previously named Esprit Nature, Giraud's line-up kicks off with a characterful cuvée that contrasts an invitingly rich, fruitful expression of Aÿ pinot noir with the depth and complexity of 50% reserves matured in small oak barrels. It's swimming with juicy strawberries and raspberries, accented with notes of sage and salt bush, underscored by salty chalk minerality and softly integrated acidity.

Henri Giraud Blanc de Craie Grand Vin de Champagne NV $$$

94 points • Disgorged June 2016 • Tasted in Australia

Montagne de Reims chardonnay, including 55% Aÿ and 30% Louvois; fermented and aged 12 months in Argonne oak and stainless steel tanks, followed by 2 years on lees in bottle; 7.5g/L dosage

The slopes of the Montagne de Reims are home to chardonnay of affable character, and this blanc de blancs of intensity yet finesse offers an enticing counterpoint to the cut of the Côte des Blancs. A bright, full-straw hue declares dimension and tension of grapefruit, apple and pear fruit, while a touch of oak barrel fermentation lends the faintest suggestion of coffee. Confident acidity, fine chalk minerality, creamy texture and long-lingering fruit lay out a spectacular finish, simultaneously succulent and lively.

Henri Giraud Dame-Jane Grand Vin de Champagne Rosé NV $$$

94 points • Disgorged July 2016 • Tasted in Australia

70% pinot, 30% chardonnay; aged in oak for 12 months and in bottle on lees for 2 years; 6% red wine from 70-year-old bush vines in Aÿ, fermented in amphora; 7.5g/L dosage

A medium salmon copper–hue announces a delightful accord between the succulent fruit expression and tense focus of Aÿ pinot noir and the creamy texture and dark chocolate nuances of barrel fermentation. It's alive with strawberry and raspberry fruit of juicy, ripe presence, impeccably cut with bright acidity and the frothing salt minerality of Aÿ old vines. Everything carries seamlessly with enduring harmony, line and persistence.

Henri Giraud Code Noir Brut NV $$$$

91 points • Disgorged February 2016 • Tasted in Australia

100% Aÿ pinot noir vinified and aged in Argonne oak for 12 months; aged 4 years on lees in bottle; 7.5g/L dosage

In its sleek, torpedo bottle, this full yellow-tinted blanc de noirs is a celebration of the bountiful grandeur of Aÿ. Its grand dimensions embrace the far-flung realms of champagne, brimming with ripe, juicy white peach, grilled pineapple and golden delicous apple. Full oak vinification and maturation lends butter, dark chocolate and coffee nuances, though the toasty, woody influence threatens to interrupt the finish with dry phenolic grip and oak tannins that hamper fruit purity and line. It nonetheless concludes with succulent generosity and grand persistence.

Henri Giraud Fût de Chêne MV09 Brut NV $$$$$

93 points • Disgorged June 2016 • Tasted in Australia

70% pinot, 30% chardonnay from Aÿ; aged in Argonne oak for 12 months, and in bottle on lees for 6 years; 7.5g/L dosage

The voluptuous curves of pinot noir are amplified three-fold, in the stature of Aÿ, the luscious warmth of 2009 and the voluminous character of small-barrel fermentation, flinging Fût de Chêne to the deep end of champagne concentration. The bombastic power of juicy white peach and pineapple is bolstered by all the toasty, dark chocolate and coffee exuberance of barrel fermentation, backed with all manner of complexity of ginger and roast nuts, declared in a full straw yellow–hue and grand fruit persistence. The sweet, ripe fruit of the warm 2009 season tussles with oak tannin structure, balanced acidity and fine, salty minerality in a compelling accord that lingers long and seamless with silky, slippery generosity. In the midst of this maelstrom, its fruit presence and structure holds its ground and the result is characterful, succulent, enticing and ready for main-course fare of entire turkey proportions.

Henri Giraud Argonne 2004 $$$$$

92 points • Disgorged July 2016 • Tasted in Australia

75% pinot, 25% chardonnay from Aÿ; aged in Argonne oak for 12 months, and in bottle on lees for 10 years; 7.5g/L dosage

A full-copper hue betrays immense fruit ripeness, oak vinification and some oxidative development that conspires with oak tannins to render the finish a little dry and contracted. A second bottle opened was the same colour, but showed better fruit expression without oxidation. Voluptuous Aÿ pinot noir of red cherry, strawberry and pineapple ripeness is underscored with layers of toasty, biscuity, chocolatey allure that declare oak and age. It has the sweet fruit body and power to coast long, buttery and succulent. Another main course–ready cuvée from Giraud.

Rising winter sun over the powerful grand cru of Aÿ. In summer, these south-facing slopes will capture the full radiance of perpendicular light.

The Champagne Guide

HENRI GOUTORBE

(On-ree Goo-tawb)

5/10

9 BIS RUE JEANSON 51160 AŸ

www.champagne-henri-goutorbe.com

The Goutorbe family ran a viticultural nursery before becoming winegrowers in their home town of Aÿ. The label, established in the late 1940s, has grown to encompass an impressive 25 hectares, including six in Aÿ, and good sites in Mareuil-sur-Aÿ, Mutigny, Bisseuil, Avenay-Val-d'Or and Hautvillers, providing for 200,000 bottles annually. Pinot noir makes up more than two-thirds of plantings, with the remainder largely chardonnay. Every cuvée is sourced exclusively from the estate, is fermented in stainless steel tanks, undergoes full malolactic fermentation and is aged at least three years on lees in Goutorbe's deep, cold cellar. Dosages are based on concentrated wine must rather than sugar. The result is a style that captures the rich expression of these privileged terroirs, while maintaining impressive control.

HENRI GOUTORBE BRUT TRADITION NV $

94 points • 2012 BASE VINTAGE • DISGORGED MAY 2016 • TASTED IN AUSTRALIA

70% pinot noir, 25% chardonnay, 5% meunier; aged 3 years on lees; 10g/L dosage; DIAM closure

This is a refreshing take on Aÿ pinot noir, with a lively medium-straw hue and well-focused ripe lemon zest, red cherry, red apple and crunchy pear fruit of excellent line and length. It's underscored by soft chalk mineral texture and long, ripe, well-poised acid line. Three years lees age has brought supporting complexity of spicy, biscuity, honeyed, roast nut appeal. Dosage and acidity unite seamlessly in a long and bright finish that lingers with pretty red cherry fruit. An excellent Goutorbe and a rousing celebration of the great 2012 vintage.

HENRIOT

(On-ree-oh)

6/10

81 RUE COQUEBERT 51100 REIMS

www.champagne-henriot.com

CHAMPAGNE
HENRIOT

MAISON FONDÉE EN 1808

Behind the magnificent 'Les Aulnois' 18th century manor house, home of Thomas Henriot in Pierry on the outskirts of Épernay, lies an immaculately ordered and symmetrical French garden. It offers a window into the mind of the eighth-generation managing director of Henriot. 'This is exactly the image of what we want to do at Henriot,' he told me as he rearranged his croquet set into precise position. Balance, order and a classic approach are his philosophy for gardening, for life and for champagne. 'I do not like wines that go in strange directions. I like to know where we are and where we are going.' This mindset defines what he refers to as the 'DNA of the house': meticulously assembled and long-aged cuvées built on a core of Côte des Blancs chardonnay.

In 2008 Henriot celebrated its 200th year of independent family ownership, one of the last remaining houses to be run continuously by the founding family from the outset. That same year, Thomas Henriot received an unexpected call from his father Joseph to join the company. He was appointed managing director in January 2014.

Family ownership has afforded the privilege of building a long-ageing house style that might otherwise be infeasible for a house producing 1.3 million bottles annually. This is achieved through a strong reliance on chardonnay and virtually no meunier. Long ageing on lees is reflected in a whopping 5–6 years of stock held continuously in the company's extensive cellars under Reims, as well as reserve wines back to 1990.

Thirty-three hectares of estate vineyards are located mainly in the great Côtes des Blancs villages, with smaller holdings in Avenay-Val-d'Or, Verzy and Verzenay. Vines averaging an impressive 25–30 years of age are tended respectfully, with grasses cultivated in mid-rows, and herbicides and fertilisers avoided. The family sources from a further 100 hectares of vineyards under long-term contracts. Every parcel is kept separate and fermented in small stainless steel vats, which can lead some cuvées to tend towards a reductive savouriness, not unusual for chardonnay-led blends. Full malolactic fermentation provides soft structures, with dosages between 8 and 11g/L.

Henriot's long-aged Cuvée des Enchanteleurs is a powerfully characterful flagship, recently accompanied by a new cuvée in secret production for 25 years.

The Champagne Guide

Henriot Brut Souverain NV $$

91 points • 2011 BASE VINTAGE • DISGORGED MARCH 2016 • TASTED IN AUSTRALIA

50% chardonnay, largely from the Côte des Blancs, particularly Le Mesnil-sur-Oger, Oger, Avize, Cramant and Chouilly; 50% pinot, mostly from the Montagne de Reims, particularly Aÿ, Verzy, Verzenay, Beaumont, Sillery and Mailly-Champagne; 20% reserves; aged 3 years on lees

Henriot's entry cuvée lands pre-charged with impressive, toasty bottle age, yet holding admirable vibrancy and energy thanks to its strong Côte des Blancs chardonnay lead. Lemon, red apple and white peach fruit are well progressed into the spectrum of toasty, nutty maturity, culminating in a lively finish of well-defined acid and integrated dosage. A faint hint of dry dustiness interrupts otherwise seamless flow.

Henriot Blanc de Blancs Brut NV $$$

93 points • 2012 BASE VINTAGE • DISGORGED OCTOBER 2015 • TASTED IN AUSTRALIA

Mainly from the Côte des Blancs, in particular Le Mesnil-sur-Oger, Avize, Chouilly, Vertus and also from Montgueux, Trépail, Épernay and Vitry; 30% reserves; aged 3-5 years on lees; 8g/L dosage; DIAM closure

A bright, medium-straw hue heralds a cuvée that strikes a compelling accord between the radiant lemon and white peach definition of the Côte des Blancs and the honeyed, nougat and biscuity appeal of long lees maturity and a touch of compelling struck-flint reductive complexity. Age builds a wonderfully creamy mouthfeel, while emphasising the fine chalk mineral texture of great terroirs. It's infused with more presence and character than this cuvée has delivered in the past.

Henriot Rosé Brut NV $$$

92 points • 2011 BASE • DISGORGED FEBRUARY 2016 • TASTED IN AUSTRALIA

60% pinot, mostly from the Montagne de Reims, particularly Mareuil-sur-Aÿ, Verzy, Verzenay, Avenay and Trépail; 40% chardonnay, from the Côte des Blancs, particularly Avize, Chouilly, Vertus and Épernay; 25% reserve wines; aged 2-3 years on lees; 8g/L dosage

Henriot Rosé occupies a place midway between the extremes of elegance and depth on the grand rosé spectrum, with a pretty medium-salmon hue, alive with rose hip and red cherry poise, yet celebrating the succulent fruit presence of pinot noir and the fine-grained structure of well-gauged tannin presence. Fine chalk mineral texture and bright acidity define a long finish of well-integrated dosage.

HENRIOT ROSÉ MILLÉSIME 2008 $$$

95 points • TASTED IN AUSTRALIA

55% pinot, majority from the Montagne de Reims, particularly Mareuil-sur-Aÿ, Verzy, Verzenay, Avenay and Trépail, 45% chardonnay, from the Côte des Blancs, particularly Avize and Vertus; aged 6 years on lees; 7g/L dosage

Two years ago I announced this as a rare 2008 to drink now, and it was certainly drinking beautifully on release, but such is the sheer stamina of the sensational 2008 season that it is still singing with full voice and has paled only the slightest fraction. Glorious restraint emanates in a pretty, glowing, pale-salmon hue, an almost invisible bouquet, and a palate exalting now more than ever in the wonderful texture of long lees age. Delicate red cherry and wild strawberry fruit have evolved from youthful verve, now relaxing into toasty, roast almond, creamy maturity, amid nuances of vanilla. Silky texture harmonises the magical touch of bottle age with soft chalk-infused minerality, and beautifully poised tannin support, drawn out by the fine acid line of the inimitable 2008 vintage.

HENRIOT BRUT MILLÉSIME 2006 $$$

92 points • TASTED IN AUSTRALIA

50% chardonnay, 50% pinot; from 15 crus including Mailly-Champagne, Verzy, Verzenay, Le Mesnil-sur-Oger, Avize, Chouilly, Mareuil-sur-Aÿ and Avenay; 6g/L dosage

On release two years ago, this exuberant and full-flavoured vintage was bang-on for drinking right away. Its intense yellow citrus and stone fruits have since evolved further still into a place of medium-straw hue and maturity of toast, spice, ginger, bread and a hint of marmalade. To its credit, it holds its head high, finishing fresh and well-defined, fully integrated, textural, rounded and succulent, yet holding its acid line and persistence.

A glorious midsummer afternoon in the premier cru of Trépail, whose east-facing slopes are planted to more than 90% chardonnay.

The Champagne Guide

HUGUES GODMÉ

(Oog Gurd-may)

6/10

10 RUE DE VERZY 51360 VERZENAY

www.champagne-godme.fr

CHAMPAGNE
HUGUES GODMÉ

Pinot noir rules the northern slopes of the Montagne de Reims, and it's unusual for chardonnay to account for half a grower's plantings. The Godmé family has tended its vines in the majestic grand cru of Verzenay on the northern slopes of the Montagne de Reims for five generations, bottling estate champagnes since as early as 1930. Today, 100,000 bottles are produced each year from 12 hectares, widely spread across 84 parcels spanning five villages.

Viticulture is the firm focus for Hugues Godmé, the fifth generation to tend his family's vines in Verzenay. When I visited, he was in the vineyards, where he spends much of his time.

'Organics takes time!' he grins, having maintained an organic approach since 2005, with full certification granted in 2013. His aspiration is to use organics to encourage deep roots that draw minerality and salinity from the soil. Insecticides and herbicides are avoided, organic treatments and composted manure are embraced, and mid-rows are ploughed and planted to cover crops, encouraging deeper roots. The result has been later ripening, producing wines that retain greater acidity at the same level of ripeness.

Parcels are kept separate and fermented by wild yeast largely in enamelled steel tanks, with an increasing proportion in oak barrels. Single-vineyard cuvées are fermented and aged for one year in barrels.

As the climate continues to warm in Champagne, malolactic fermentation is blocked in an increasing number of parcels, including all reserve wines. Godmé's blends finish between zero and 60% malolactic fermentation, maintaining freshness and focus.

Godmé maintains 400,000 bottles in its cellar, an impressive four times its annual production, reflective of long lees ageing for all of its cuvées. Non-vintage blends also receive generous proportions of reserve wines of between 40% and 70%.

Disgorgement dates are stamped clearly on back labels and in some cuvées also on corks. Concentrated grape must is used for dosage, retaining purity and clarity, the finishing touch to carefully balance cuvées that sensitively reflect the fine salt mineral texture of Verzenay, the greatest of all the terroirs of the northern Montagne de Reims.

Brut Vintage 2008 is the highlight this year.

HUGUES GODMÉ PREMIER CRU BRUT RÉSERVE NV $

92 points • 2010 BASE VINTAGE • DISGORGED JULY 2016 • TASTED IN AUSTRALIA

60% chardonnay, 30% meunier, 10% pinot noir from Ville-Dommange and Verzy; 60% reserves, half from 2009, the remainder 2008 and 2007; 20% fermented in barrels; 55% malolactic fermentation; aged 5 years on lees; 7g/L dosage

This cuvée has upheld impressive integrity with a further two years on lees since its first release. Characterful and well crafted, it finds a harmonious balance between the tension of chardonnay with malic acidity and the richness of deep and generous reserves. All the fanfare of figs, mixed spice, Christmas cake and citrus rind pull into a finish of well-focused acidity and fine-tuned salt minerality.

HUGUES GODMÉ PREMIER CRU EXTRA BRUT NV $

91 points • 2010 BASE VINTAGE • DISGORGED JANUARY 2016 • TASTED IN AUSTRALIA

60% chardonnay, 30% meunier, 10% pinot from Ville-Dommange and Verzy; 20% barrel fermented; partial malolactic fermentation; aged 5 years on lees; 3.5g/L dosage

The focused restraint of chardonnay and malic acidity are heightened by the absence of dosage, no trivial recipe in Champagne, yet Godmé pulls it off with balance and generosity. Red apple and fig fruit lingers amidst toasty, roast hazelnut complexity, concluding with good acid line and dry, phenolic grip.

HUGUES GODMÉ GRAND CRU BRUT ROSÉ NV $$

86 points • 2010 BASE VINTAGE • DISGORGED MAY 2016 • TASTED IN AUSTRALIA

65% pinot, 35% chardonnay from Verzy and Verzenay; 40% barrel fermented; partial malolactic fermentation; aged 5 years on lees; 4g/L dosage

This is a savoury rosé that pales in the wake of the difficult 2010 season, which renders the finish dusty, drying, phenolic and astringent, lacking in perfume and fruit definition.

HUGUES GODMÉ PREMIER CRU BRUT BLANC DE BLANCS NV $$

90 points • 2010 BASE VINTAGE • DISGORGED JANUARY 2016 • TASTED IN AUSTRALIA

100% chardonnay from Verzy and Verzenay; 65% reserves of 25% 2008, and 40% 2007 and 2006; 60% barrel fermented; 60% malolactic fermentation; aged 4 years on lees; 4g/L dosage

Since its release two years ago, the ripe yellow summer fruit and fig generosity of this blend have toned to a more contemplative mood of almond meal and nutmeg. Fading fruit has emphasised fine phenolic grip and a touch of dusty dryness on the finish. Nonetheless, it does carry a good acid line of bright yet well-balanced malic acidity and pretty good line and length. The 2010 base has never carried quite the crystalline grace of earlier blends, and this disgorgement has now passed its finest moment.

Hugues Godmé Blanc de Noirs Grand Cru Brut NV $$

91 points • 2010 BASE VINTAGE • DISGORGED JANUARY 2016 • TASTED IN AUSTRALIA

100% pinot from Verzy and Verzenay; 70% barrel fermented; partial malolactic fermentation; aged 6 years on lees; 4g/L dosage

Verzenay is the home of refined, structured pinot noir of definition and drive. Godmé has created a spicy, savoury and firm style of understated red cherry and strawberry fruits underscored by the toasty, biscuity complexity of barrel fermentation and bottle age. Its 2010 base has underplayed fruit presence and exaggerated dry, fine-grained phenolic grip, lacking the flamboyance of great seasons, though upholding persistence, balance and salty minerality on a long finish.

Hugues Godmé Grand Cru Brut Vintage 2008 $$

94 points • DISGORGED MAY 2016 • TASTED IN AUSTRALIA

60% chardonnay, 40% pinot from Verzy and Verzenay; 40% barrel fermented; partial malolactic fermentation; aged 6 years on lees; 2g/L dosage

The refined morello cherry and strawberry hull characters of Verzenay meet understated brioche, nougat and spice notes of a decade of lees age and the subtle toastiness and fig complexity of barrel fermentation. The tension of 2008 acidity in this chardonnay-focused style is heightened by both low dosage and partial retention of malic acidity, making for a taut finish, yet upholding enticing appeal and consummate balance. Wait at least another five years, and it will happily live longer still.

The north-east facing slopes of Verzenay are home to some of Champagne's most elegant yet characterful and enduring pinot noir.

HURÉ FRÈRES

(Oo-ray Frair)

2 IMPASSE CARNOT 51500 LUDES
www.champagne-hure-freres.com

CHAMPAGNE
HURÉ FRÈRES

Brothers Pierre and François Huré are third-generation viticulturist and winemaker, respectively, for their small family house in Ludes. A 10-hectare estate is located largely in their home town, in Ville-Dommange near Reims, and as far-flung as Serzy-et-Prin and Brouillet in the Vallée de l'Ardre and Vavray-le-Grand in the Vitry. Vines are managed sustainably, minimising herbicides and using organic composts and natural ground cover. Reserves are stored in oak vats and tanks, complementing the fruity appeal of meunier-led cuvées, which this year lack a little in polish.

HURÉ FRÈRES INVITATION BRUT NV $$

85 points • 2012 BASE VINTAGE • DISGORGED JUNE 2016 • TASTED IN AUSTRALIA

40% pinot, 40% meunier, 20% chardonnay; from Ludes, Ville-Dommange and Vavray-le-Grand; 40% reserves; partial malolactic fermentation; 6g/L dosage

A subtle bouquet of red apple fruit heralds a cuvée marked by hard phenolics and imperfect fruit, making for a dusty and dry finish that lacks fruit precision, unusual for the 2012 base vintage. Drink up.

HURÉ FRÈRES INSOUCIANCE ROSÉ BRUT NV $$

89 points • 2013 BASE VINTAGE • DISGORGED JUNE 2016 • TASTED IN AUSTRALIA

45% pinot, 30% meunier, 25% chardonnay; from Ludes, Ville-Dommange and Vavray-le-Grand; 30% reserves; partial malolactic fermentation; 10% fermented in old oak; 6g/L dosage

With a pale-salmon hue and subtle bouquet, this is an elegant rosé expressive of the northern slopes of the Montagne de Reims. Subtle red apple and strawberry fruit lacks in intensity, and hence a little overwhelmed on the finish by fine phenolic grip. Good acid line and well-integrated dosage keep things under control, allowing tangy pink grapefruit to linger on the finish.

The Champagne Guide

HURÈ FRÈRES INSTANTANÉE EXTRA BRUT 2008 $$

90 points • DISGORGED APRIL 2016 • TASTED IN AUSTRALIA

35% chardonnay, 35% pinot, 30% meunier; from Ludes and Rilly-la-Montagne; no malolactic fermentation; 3g/L dosage

The signature energy and cut of 2008 are well supported by layers of brioche, nougat and meringue, defining a faster-maturing expression of this great season, surprising for a style of full malic acidity, a cuvée ripe to drink right away. Chalk minerality and grainy phenolic grip meld on a finish of fine acid line and well-gauged dosage.

HURÉ FRÈRES MÉMOIRE EXTRA BRUT NV $$$

87 points • 2013 BASE VINTAGE • DISGORGED MARCH 2016 • TASTED IN AUSTRALIA

50% pinot, 50% meunier; from Ludes, Ville-Dommange and Vavray-le-Grand; reserve solera dating from 1982 until 2012; bottled in 2014; partial malolactic fermentation; 100% fermented in oak barrels; 2g/L dosage

A firm and structured cuvée of apple fruit and pear skin texture, with phenolic bitterness accented by the savoury grip of oak age and extra brut dosage, making for a firm and astringent finish. Lemon-like acidity lingers long.

The cool north-facing slopes of the Montagne de Reims define the elegant mood of the premier cru village of Ludes.

J. LASSALLE

(J. Lah-sahl)

7/10

21 RUE CHÂTAIGNIER 51500 CHIGNY-LES-ROSES

www.champagne-jlassalle.com

CHAMPAGNE
J. LASSALLE
— PROPRIÉTAIRE DE VIGNOBLES —

It takes great sensitivity to create wines that communicate the subtleties not only of the place that has given them birth, but also the very personalities of those who have brought them to life. When I first tasted the enchanting champagnes of J. Lassalle, I knew nothing of the estate or the family behind them and was immediately captivated by their dainty restraint and feminine beauty, arousing my curiosity to discover how such delicate sophistication could be achieved. It all made sense when I met the three generations of delightful women who, for more than 30 years, have nurtured this immaculate estate in the charming village of Chigny-les-Roses.

Ever since Jules Lassalle passed away in 1982, his wife, Olga, daughter Chantal and granddaughter Angéline Templier have worked closely together to treble the size of their family estate to 16 hectares and an annual production of 120,000 bottles. Angéline Templier oversees winemaking, ably assisted by her mother. Olga, now 96, still helps with management and administration. 'We don't need any men to help!' she grins.

The meticulous attention to detail of these women shines in every stage of production. The winery at their home in the village is pristine, bathed in white light, one of the cleanest little facilities I've visited anywhere. 'We do everything as my grandfather did, but because we are girls we have a feminine touch, and you can feel it in the wines,' says Angéline.

The Lassalles have been making champagnes exclusively from their premier cru vineyards since 1942. Their aspiration is to express the clay soil terroir of the northern slopes of the Montagne de Reims, so all vineyards are tightly located within 10 kilometres of the house. Meunier is king here, comprising 50% of plantings. Chardonnay (25%) takes a confident, if surprising, lead in Lassalle's most sublime cuvée, and pinot noir makes up the remaining 25% of the estate. The family is privileged to own a significant proportion of old parcels, upholding an average vine age of 40 years, none less than 30, and some up to 50. 'They make great wines, so we don't replant them!' Angéline exclaims. Any fruit of insufficient quality is sold to large houses.

Blends comprise all three champagne varieties in proportions varied according to the season, bolstered by a generous stock of five years of reserve wines. Preserving freshness at every stage is a high priority. Grapes are pressed on the first floor and the juice is piped directly to settling tanks below to avoid oxidation. Every cuvée undergoes full malolactic fermentation. The philosophy in the winery is to maintain the tradition of Angéline's grandfather, while growing progressively. 'I don't want to follow trends, I just want to be respectful of the traditional style of

The Champagne Guide

the product we make,' she says. 'The wine we make today is a tribute to my grandfather, and our work in the vineyards looks like the work he did 30 years ago.' Much of the historical equipment of the estate is still in use, including enamelled tanks, and all cuvées are still riddled by hand. New technology, including a modern press, was installed, 'to be more precise'.

Long ageing is inherent to the house style, and when rosé demand outstripped supply, the cuvée was put on allocation rather than releasing it earlier. 'The only thing we have to sell the house is our quality, and it is very important for us to respect this, so we told our clients to wait,' Templier explains.

Non-vintage cuvées are aged at least four years, and vintage cuvées 6–10 years, necessitating a large cellar stock of 400,000–450,000 bottles. The estate also holds back unusually large reserves, and currently holds as much reserve as new wine in storage. 'We're always full and running out of room!' says Templier.

To facilitate growth, the building next door was bought in 2007 and the winery expanded to a capacity of almost 100,000 litres. A new press was purchased, new cellars dug under the building, and temperature-controlled stainless steel tanks installed to allow separate vinification of the estate's many small parcels.

In late 2013, the Lassalles were presented with their biggest growth opportunity yet: an invitation to buy the neighbouring estate of a cousin in the village, providing much-needed production and cellar space and, most of all, 4.5 glorious hectares of vineyards in Chigny-les-Roses, Ludes and Rilly-la-Montagne, all conveniently neighbouring existing Lassalle plots.

When I visited during vintage 2014, the first of the new fruit was arriving and I was privileged to the first tour of the new premises. The Lassalles are excited about the opportunity to expand production from 100,000 to 150,000 bottles, but are cautious about maintaining quality, so are slowly evolving production progressively over four years.

Refined new labels were introduced in 2015, with elegant white space reflecting the graceful appeal of the house and courtyard. The bottling code laser-etched on every cuvée is the disgorgement date.

Don't miss these impeccably crafted cuvées of generous fruit presence, purity, and the most intricately judged balance.

J. LASSALLE CUVÉE PREFERENCE PREMIER CRU BRUT NV $$

93 points • 45% 2012 AND 55% 2011 • DISGORGED NOVEMBER 2016 • TASTED IN AUSTRALIA
60% meunier, 20% pinot noir, 20% chardonnay; aged 3.5 years on lees; 9g/L dosage; 60,000–70,000 bottles

Angéline Templier likes emphasising the aromas of meunier, structured with chardonnay and pinot noir. There is a delicacy, purity and more energy than ever to this lively, clean, fruit-focused style of pale-straw hue, with crisp lemon, apple and pear framed neatly in a fine, creamy bead, vibrant, bright acid line and soft, subtle mineral structure true to the premier cru villages of the northern Montagne. The great 2012 season is deployed in large proportion to bring finesse to 2011. A refined and fruit-focused finish lingers long and bright, a wonderful conclusion to an intricately crafted and graceful style.

J. LASSALLE PREMIER CRU BRUT ROSÉ NV $$

94 points • 45% 2012 AND 55% 2011 • DISGORGED OCTOBER 2016 • TASTED IN AUSTRALIA
70% pinot noir, 15% meunier, 15% chardonnay; 7% red wine from a parcel of 50-year-old vines in Chigny; 9g/L dosage

A tiny addition of red wine creates a gorgeous, delicate salmon colour. 'We want something light and delicate; maybe this is our feminine side!' says Templier. Based on the great 2012 season (completely trumping a slight majority of 2011 reserves), the current disgorgement is back to the dainty refinement and clean precision I love of this cuvée, with a fairy touch of rose petal perfume and pretty and subtle notes of red cherries and strawberries, invigorated by bright acidity and fine, soft chalk minerality that bears the stamp of the north-facing slopes of the northern Montagne. For all of its refinement, pinot noir shapes a wonderful mid-palate presence and intricate, effortless harmony. A breathtakingly subtle and primary apéritif, to showcase with as little culinary distraction as possible.

J. Lassalle Blanc de Blancs Millésime Premier Cru Brut 2007 $$$

95 points • Disgorged October 2016 • Tasted in Champagne and Australia

From a single parcel of 30–35-year-old vines in Villers-Allerand; aged 8 years on lees; 8g/L dosage; always less than 10,000 bottles

The mandate of this cuvée is to express the rounded, soft character of the clay soils of Villers-Allerand chardonnay that Templier describes as 'body built', very different in style to the Côte des Blancs. The 2007 transcends the village, the season and every vintage I've tasted to date, a compelling take on its brief, presenting a seamless accord between the tension of the lemon, grapefruit, crunchy pear and apple purity of the house, the fleshy generosity of white nectarine, the toasty, spicy, biscuity, honeyed, nougat allure and creamy texture of a decade on lees, and a fine salt minerality surprisingly pronounced for Villers-Allerand. It holds every detail in fine balance of impressive line through a long finish.

J. Lassalle Cuvée Angéline Millésime Premier Cru Brut 2009 $$$$

92 points • Disgorged October 21016 • Tasted in Australia

60% pinot noir, 40% chardonnay from old parcels in Chigny-les-Roses and Rilly-la-Montagne selected by Angéline's grandfather for this cuvée since 1973; 7g/L dosage; never more than 6000 bottles

The flagship of the house, created from the same parcels since 1973, epitomising the elegance of northern Montagne pinot noir and the exacting precision of Lassalle. True to the season, the generous 2009 plays out an altogether different mood to the tense 2008 before it. Raspberry, red apple and mirabelle plum fruit of fleshy, ripe presence has been blessed by a decade of maturity, building toasty, biscuity, honeyed complexity. The fine acidity and gentle chalk minerality of the northern Montagne premier crus provides life and definition to the finish, with a subtle hint of the phenolic grip of a warm vintage. An impressive result for the season.

J. Lassalle Special Club Premier Cru Brut 2007 $$$$

94 points • Disgorged October 2016 • Tasted in Champagne and Australia

60% chardonnay, 40% pinot noir, mainly from Chigny-les-Roses; a selection in the winery of the very best parcels of elegance, finesse and balance; aged 8.5 years on lees; 8g/L dosage

The philosophy here is of greater freshness and delicacy, hence a stronger representation of chardonnay, building a backward and refined core of grapefruit, lemon, crunchy red apple and pear. Pinot noir brings its presence to the finish in red cherry and strawberry fruits, well-measured body and lingering persistence. More than eight years on lees has built layers of roasted almond, honey and brioche character, energised by well-defined acidity, fine chalk mineral texture and a glimpse of phenolic grip comfortably subsumed into its folds. It's seamless, effortless and immediately engaging.

J.L. VERGNON

(J.L. Vair-ngoh)

(7/10)

1 Grande Rue 51190 Le Mesnil-sur-Oger

www.champagne-jl-vergnon.com

'Daring' is the only word to describe Christophe Constant, the talented chef de cave of this little estate in Le Mesnil-sur-Oger. In a village renowned for chardonnay of greater longevity than any other in Champagne, no other grower-producer dares avoid malolactic fermentation. And he goes further. Dosages are very low, never more than 7g/L, and often just 3g/L. His top cuvée, appropriately named 'Confidence', is vinified entirely in oak, a whopping 50% of which is brand new. With such an ambitious recipe, the proof of his skill is a well-crafted range of long-lived blanc de blancs that capture the vibrant, clean expression of the finest grand crus of the Côte des Blancs.

And herein lies the secret of J.L. Vergnon. With nothing but estate chardonnay harvested ripe from just five hectares of vines averaging more than 30 years of age, enviably situated in Le Mesnil-sur-Oger, Oger and Avize, he has no need of malolactic fermentation, chaptalisation, dosage, or any other trick to soften or mask such riveting fruit.

The aim at harvest is to achieve maximum maturity so as to produce balanced wines of vinosity and finesse. To this end, cover crops are used to naturally regulate yields, and there is a focus on sustainable viticulture, avoiding pesticides where possible.

With supply limiting current production to 50,000 bottles, J.L. Vergnon surrendered its grower-producer status in late 2012 to function as a négociant and purchase fruit from the 2013 harvest, with the plan to increase the volume of its Conversation cuvée.

'I buy grapes in the vineyard, like they do in Burgundy, though this is not done much in Champagne,' Constant explains. 'I don't want to buy must, only grapes, so we can press everything ourselves, with one exception. We have found an old vineyard in Le Mesnil managed by someone who works like me and makes wine without malolactic fermentation, and we would like to one day buy vins clairs from him.'

Constant vinifies in stainless steel tanks or oak, according to the cuvée, with all reserve wines fermented in oak since 2010. Disgorgement is by hand and disgorgement dates are printed on every back label and every cork. The first two digits are the month and the second two are the year.

These are engaging wines of characterful endurance and riveting structure that are not to be judged hurriedly. It takes some time to get to know these cuvées, and the longer I sip and swirl, the more I admire their harmony.

Blending of different plots creates distinct personalities in five cuvées, whose evocative names neatly sum up the character of the house in both French and English: 'Conversation', 'Éloquence', 'Résonance', 'Rosémotion' and, most of all, 'Confidence'.

J.L. Vergnon Conversation Grand Cru Blanc de Blancs Brut NV $

93 points • 2012 base vintage • Disgorged September 2015 • Tasted in Australia

Le Mesnil-sur-Oger, Oger and Avize; aged 3 years on lees; 20% reserve wines vinified in barrels; 5g/L dosage

This is an engaging Conversation, leading out with articulate apple and pear fruit of wonderful depth and expansive mouthfeel, nuanced with the complexity of toast and almond. Consummate ripeness takes the edge off malic acidity, producing harmony and integration in the wonderful 2012 vintage, even with very low dosage. Grapefruit character brings vibrancy to a finish of fine, salty minerality and lingering persistence.

J.L. Vergnon Éloquence Grand Cru Blanc de Blancs Extra Brut NV $$

93 points • 2012 base vintage • Disgorged October 2015 • Tasted in Australia

Le Mesnil-sur-Oger, Oger, Avize; aged 3 years on lees; 20% reserve wines vinified in barrels; the same wine as Conversation, with a lower dosage of 3g/L

Back in the days when Conversation held 7g/L dosage, there was a subtle distinction in the 3g/L dosage of Éloquence. Conversation has since progressively dropped to 5g/L, narrowing the gap. I love them both, Conversation built on the grand 2012 season, with a whisker more generosity, and Éloquence from the same base for its dazzling display of fine chalk minerality. Such subtle difference is testimony to the attention to detail of Christophe Constant and the articulate expression of the finest nuances in his cuvées.

J.L. Vergnon Rosémotion Grand Cru Extra Brut NV $$

94 points • 2012 base vintage • Disgorged December 2015 • Tasted in Australia

Chardonnay from Avize, touched with red wine from Mailly-Champagne; aged at least 2 years on lees; 20% reserve wines vinified in barrels; 3g/L dosage

Mailly-Champagne red wine blesses Avize chardonnay with a pale salmon-copper hue and nuances of red apple, raspberry, guava, tamarillo and a touch of pepper. Texture and structure are the game here, and the inimitable, fine, salty chalk mineral presence of Avize is all-encompassing, heightened by finely integrated malic acidity and invisibly low dosage. It carries with great persistence and savoury refinement. Masterfully crafted and consummately engaging.

The Champagne Guide

J.L. Vergnon Résonance Millésime Grand Cru Blanc de Blancs Extra Brut 2008 $$$

97 points • Disgorged February 2016 • Tasted in Australia

100% Le Mesnil-sur-Oger; aged at least 7 years on lees; vinified in stainless steel tanks; 3g/L dosage

One might be forgiven for feeling daunted by the sheer recipe of malic acidity and low dosage, without the calming influence of barrel vinification, in the electric 2008 season in one of Champagne's most enduring chardonnay grand crus of all. Yet it is grand testimony to the masterful art and skill of Christophe Constant that in the midst of a lightning bolt of tense definition and enduring longevity, this cuvée confidently delivers the ripe fruit presence and lees-aged texture that infuse harmony and balance. Crunchy apple, lemon and grapefruit sing with the high soprano notes of 2008, backed with the rumbling depth of toast, spice, vanilla bean and honey. Such depth and breadth attained amidst sheer tension can be achieved nowhere outside of Le Mesnil-sur-Oger. This cuvée demands at least 20 years before even contemplating an approach, and will easily outlive us all. It culminates in a crescendo that resonates profoundly with swirling, frothing salt minerality, embracing every corner of the mouth and the soul.

J.L. Vergnon O.G Millésime Grand Cru Blanc de Blancs Brut Nature 2010 $

93 points • Disgorged December 2015 • Tasted in Australia

100% Oger; aged 5 years on lees; zero dosage

The unique generosity and grainy structure of Oger are well toned by the malic acid tension and masterful touch of the Vergnon style, rendering this cuvée in no need of dosage, even in the less than ideal 2010 season. Orange, pear and apple fruit speak of the exuberance of the village, yet are impressively toned by lemon and grapefruit definition and taut yet consummately ripe malic acidity. It finishes long, spicy, full and tense.

J.L. Vergnon Confidence Millésime Grand Cru Blanc de Blancs Brut Nature 2009 $$$

94 points • Disgorged July 2015 • Tasted in Australia

100% Le Mesnil-sur-Oger; aged 5 years on lees; fully vinified in oak, 50% new; zero dosage

It takes confidence indeed to half vinify in a forest of new oak, and this tense and structured fruit of Le Mesnil is infused with no shortage of vanillin oak flavour and tannin. Zero dosage and malic acid heighten the tension of grapefruit and lemon fruit, pulled in firmly on a finish accented with wood spice. Yet for all of its stark, contrasting tension, this is a cuvée that immaculately and astonishingly finds a harmony and balance with ripe white peach and apple confidence, propagating long and true amidst the frothing salt chalk minerality that defines Le Mesnil. The result stands in stark contrast to the voluptuous and immediate 2009 vintage, and this is set to become one of the most enduring cuvées of the season. Hold off until at least 2025, and preferably longer.

JACQUART

(Zhah-khah)

5/10

34 BOULEVARD LUNDY 51100 REIMS

www.champagne-jacquart.com

CHAMPAGNE
JACQUART

*J*acquart is the brand of the Alliance Champagne Group, a cooperative representing one of Champagne's largest sources of grapes. The group is owned by 1800 growers, holding over 2200 hectares (and counting), vinifying 900 separate parcels spanning more than 150 crus across the Côte des Blancs, Vallée de la Marne, Montagne de Reims and Côte des Bar. Jacquart has grown dramatically since it was founded just over 50 years ago, selecting 300 parcels from 300 hectares of its vineyard pool to create 2.6 million bottles of pleasant chardonnay-led blends. Freshness, purity and elegance are the mandates of the house, upheld by 36-year-old chef de cave Florian Eznack, who left Veuve Clicquot to join the house in 2011. Its chardonnay-focused style calls for long ageing, and non-vintage cuvées are matured a minimum of four years, blanc de blancs at least six years and Cuvée Alpha seven or more.

In 2010, Jacquart ranked as the fifth largest house in Champagne, boasting a production of 5.8 million bottles. 'But Jacquart got lost in promotions and supermarket listings and so lost its image,' Eznack admits. With 18 different cuvées in the portfolio, the house was ready for a refocus. 'With 2200 hectares you could do anything you want to please the market, but we don't want to do this,' she says.

When Eznack came on board, production was slashed by more than half, aspiring 'to be recognised as a premium brand, though not a luxury brand – we are not trying to compete with LVMH or Pernod Ricard.' She is comfortable with the current production level to maintain consistency in Brut Mosaïque and to introduce the prestige Alpha cuvées. 'I could produce a little more volume if I wanted to, but to do much more would compromise quality,' she explains.

The complexity of this scenario is compounded because Eznack finds herself in a unique position in Champagne overseeing three winemakers, each responsible for their own distinct brand and their own production facility. The group makes Devaux in Bar-sur-Seine, Collet in Oger and Pannier in Château-Thierry. Each produces just 400–500,000 bottles, making the much larger volume of Jacquart the prime priority of the group.

Eznack's exclusive priority rests on Jacquart, and she says she gets to choose all the parcels she wants. She's the youngest in the team, yet enjoys strong relationships with each of her winemakers. 'Having three wineries is a weakness and the logistics can be hard to manage,' she reveals. 'But it is rare in Champagne to have the opportunity to create a brand together in addition to each of their own brands.'

Vinification of the cuvée (no tailles is used) for each of the group's 900 separate parcels takes place in small vats, no larger than 400 hectolitres. Of these, just 300 are preselected for blending for Jacquart and the remainder are sold to other houses.

The freshness, straightforward appeal and power of chardonnay are the aspirations, sourced predominantly from the Côte des Blancs (particularly Vertus) and the Montagne de Reims, fleshed out with the fruitiness of meunier from the very far west of the Vallée de la Marne and the premier crus around Épernay, and the finesse of pinot noir, half from the northern slopes of the Montagne de Reims and half from the eastern parts of the Aube.

This mandate of freshness and appeal does not call for a heavy reliance on reserve wines, which are used selectively to fill out the flesh of the blends for consistency and longevity. 'We are looking for refined texture, elegant bead and graceful and immediately accessible wines, with sufficient richness to enjoy,' Eznack sums up. Her current cuvées meet the brief with pleasant appeal.

JACQUART BRUT MOSAÏQUE NV $$

91 points • 2012 BASE VINTAGE • DISGORGED JUNE 2016 • TASTED IN AUSTRALIA

40% chardonnay, 33% pinot noir, 27% meunier; focus of selection on the grand crus of the Côte des Blancs and Montagne de Reims; 35% reserve wines an average of 2 years old; a blend of 60 villages; aged 3 years on lees; 9g/L dosage to give 9.5g/L total sugar; 1.1-1.2 million bottles

'The essence of Jacquart is to be a mosaic,' says Florian Eznack. A fresh and refreshing style, with a medium-straw hue, is true to her aspiration, accurately reflecting more elegant pinot and meunier parcels to highlight the structure and elegance of chardonnay in refined apple and lemon fruits. It concludes with accurate acid line and dosage that shows just a little, well gauged to counter a touch of phenolic grip. A fresh and lively apéritif style.

JACQUART BRUT MOSAIC SIGNATURE AGED 5 YEARS NV $$

93 points • 2010 BASE VINTAGE • DISGORGED APRIL 2016 • TASTED IN AUSTRALIA

38% chardonnay, 32% pinot, 30% meunier; 28% reserve wines; a blend of 60 crus; aged 5 years on lees; 7g/L dosage

The first release of Brut Mosaic after five years on lees is testimony to the endurance of these chardonnay-led blends. With a medium straw yellow–hue, it has upheld enticing freshness, an engaging accord between the crunchy apple and lemon of vivacious fruit and the subtle almond and toast of lees age. It carries well-defined acidity, fine chalk texture and nicely integrated dosage. An impressive result for the 2010 base, a wine of line, length, integrity and surprising liveliness for its age.

JACQUART MOSAÏQUE ROSÉ NV $$

88 points • 2012 BASE VINTAGE • DISGORGED APRIL 2016 • TASTED IN AUSTRALIA

45% pinot, 34% chardonnay, 21% meunier; 28% reserve wines; 18% pinot noir red wine selected from Neuville, Les Riceys, Vertus, Cumières and Aÿ; a blend of 63 crus; aged 3 years on lees; 9g/L dosage; more than 300,000 bottles

Jacquart builds its rosé on the same base as its white Mosaïque, with a mandate of impact and attack, achieved with a solid dose of pinot noir red wine, contributing a medium salmon colour, body and grip. This release is a savoury style and a little gamey, with a charcuterie suggestion, notes of roast almonds and toast, finishing short.

JACQUART BLANC DE BLANCS 2009 $$$

93 points • Disgorged June 2016 • Tasted in Australia
One-third each of Cramant, Le Mesnil-sur-Oger and Oger; aged 6 years on lees; 6g/L dosage

'Freshness, minerality, chalk, creaminess, ampleness and richness' are the diverse aspirations for Jacquart's Blanc de Blancs, tactically employing long lees age to tone low-dosage grand cru chardonnay. Sourcing is adjusted according to the season, always from the Montagne de Reims or the Côte des Blancs; in 2006 a premier cru blend and in 2009 grand cru. Eznack describes 2009 as a very solar' year, creamy, lacy and ripe, with perfect balance between fruit, minerality, freshness and acidity. The result is a wonderful celebration of the tension and expression of these three thundering grand crus, uniting a creamy silkiness with a cut of fresh, lively, vibrant, primary citrus zest and ripe apple. It upholds a medium-straw hue and carries an even finish of excellent fine chalk minerality.

JACQUART CUVÉE ALPHA BRUT VINTAGE 2010 $$$$

92 points • Disgorged March 2016 • Tasted in Australia
60% chardonnay from Avize and Vertus, 40% pinot from Chigny-les-Roses, Mailly-Champagne, Verzenay, Verzy and a little from Aÿ; aged 5 years on lees; 5g/L dosage

The Alpha aspiration is for 'perfect harmony, depth and finesse' without constraints to a specific blend. Each vintage is thus built around different cépages, crus and ageing. The 2010 rendition tones powerful fruit presence of star fruit, pineapple and golden delicious apple with the crunch and grip of grapefruit. Notes of marzipan have gathered over five years of lees age. It propagates with good line and length, contrasting fruit concentration with well-defined acid line and a touch of phenolic grip.

JACQUART CUVÉE ALPHA ROSÉ VINTAGE 2010 $$$$

93 points • Disgorged March 2016 • Tasted in Australia
51% chardonnay, 49% pinot; Chigny-les-Roses, Mailly-Champagne, Verzenay, Verzy, Avize and Vertus; 16% pinot noir red wine from Vertus; aged 5 years on lees; 5g/L dosage

The inaugural Alpha Rosé is built on the same base as the white Alpha, with a respectable dose of pinot noir red wine, intended to produce a pale hue, but here a medium salmon-copper tint. A touch of savoury reductive character quickly dissipates to reveal complex and deep notes of cassis, anise, wood spice and plum liqueur. This is an upfront style of front-palate volume and mid-palate presence, though its honed and elegant finish doesn't translate the same depth at first. With time in the glass, it builds to appealing black cherry persistence. Fruit volume is toned by the sea salt and iodine structure of Avize chalk.

JACQUES PICARD
(Zhak Pee-khah)

5/10

12 RUE DU LUXEMBOURG 51420 BERRU
www.champagnepicard.com

CHAMPAGNE
JACQUES PICARD

PROPRIÉTAIRE-RÉCOLTANT

From their home on the slopes of Mont Berru, seven kilometres north-east of Reims, the Picard family crafts champagnes with an insightful touch. Well-considered, strategic use of generous proportions of chardonnay, abundant reserve wines and selective employment of oak fermentation and maturation conspire to build fleshy, layered complexity, sensitively tweaked with low dosage and selective blocking of malolactic fermentation to preserve vivacity. With no other estate bottling champagnes in Berru, it is difficult to distinguish the skill of the maker from the potential of the place. Wherever the credit is directed, there is no denying that this beautifully complete set of champagnes transcends its terroirs.

The history of viticulture in Berru dates from at least the 12th century. On a gentle slope of easterly exposition 4 kilometres from Verzy and Verzenay, the geology is not dissimilar, with thin brown topsoil over deep chalk, producing chardonnay of body and roundness. On the strategic battlefront of World War I, the vineyards of the village were almost completely destroyed, to be replanted by Roger Picard, then mayor of the village, after World War II.

The estate has been run by the same family for three generations. Jacques Picard made his first sparkling wines in the early 1960s, and his daughters Sylvie and Corinne and their husbands took over in the 1990s. Corinne's husband, José Lieven, oversees the vineyards and winemaking.

The estate is privileged to own 17 hectares in Berru, meunier in Montbré and a small parcel of pinot noir in Avenay-Val-d'Or. Berru chardonnay is the focus, comprising 70% of holdings, supported by 20% meunier and 10% pinot noir.

The Picards believe in *lutte naturelle* (natural control) and practise *culture raisonnée* (reasoned culture), some time ago convincing the entire community of the village to use sexual confusion through the use of hormones for insect control, to reduce use of pesticides. Sustainable viticulture is the focus, and grasses have been planted in mid-rows to control erosion.

'We refuse to be strictly organic, not organic, or bio-dynamic, as one system is not an integrated approach,' says Lieven. 'There are good ideas within all three and I like to pick and choose.' He runs one vineyard organically so as to observe the impact on the wine over many years.

A sparkling-clean, gravity-fed winery has been strategically engineered to minimise their carbon foot-print. No air conditioning is installed, as air is able to pass by convection through a 150-metre underground pipe to cool. Lieven is more focused on the vineyards than on vinification. 'We aim to keep things clean and do as little as possible,' he says. Picard's wines are aged at least three years in cellars dug into chalk under the house.

Vinification is matched to the mood of the year, with selective use of barrel vinification, malolactic fermentation blocked or encouraged according to the parcel, and dosage tweaked to suit the disgorgement. Lieven visits Louis Latour in Burgundy every June, tastes from different barrels, cleverly marks those he likes, then returns in September to buy them. Impressive attention to detail.

The gentle eastern exposition of Berru retains freshness in chardonnay, making reserve wines important for balance; hence almost a full year of production is held in reserve. Freshness is further retained by holding a solera of reserves of Berru chardonnay below 16°C. Commenced in 1998, this solera is impressively characterful, tangy and taut, with a tight acid line. Such was its success that Lieven commenced a solera of Montbré meunier in 2008, which retains admirable fragrance and lively definition.

JACQUES PICARD BRUT NV $$

92 points • 2013 BASE VINTAGE • DISGORGED APRIL 2016 • TASTED IN AUSTRALIA

60% chardonnay, 35% pinot, 5% meunier from Berru and Montbré; 5 years on lees; 8g/L dosage

Picard successfully tones the fleshiness of Berru chardonnay with malic acidity and low dosage, building complexity with large proportions of reserve wines and long ageing on lees. A strong chardonnay lead retains the precision and focus of lemon zest, grapefruit and beurre bosc pear amidst the rounded generosity of red apples. A taut line of malic acidity and softly gentle, salty and slightly grainy chalk mineral texture provides impressive energy and definition to this lively style. Age has built subtle praline and almond complexity. It holds with good length and drive.

JACQUES PICARD ART DE VIGNE BRUT MILLÉSIME 2005 $$$

86 points • DISGORGED MARCH 2016 • TASTED IN AUSTRALIA

60% single-vineyard Berru chardonnay from 30-year-old vines; 20% single-vineyard Montbré meunier from 22-year-old vines; 20% single-vineyard Avenay-Val-d'Or pinot noir from 50-year-old vines; fully fermented and matured in old barrels with bâtonnage for 6 months; no malolactic fermentation; 4g/L dosage

Since its release two years ago, the bitter, dusty, dry-extract grip that characterises the 2005 season has only accentuated. True to a lesser season, this is a wine of firm, drying tension and taut acid structure accentuated by barrel work and malic acidity. It's dusty and dry, with star anise and wood spice notes.

JACQUES SELOSSE

(Zhak Sur-loss)

6/10

59 RUE DE CRAMANT 51190 AVIZE

www.selosse-lesavises.com

JACQUES SELOSSE

VINS DE CHAMPAGNE AVIZE

The expression of terroir has been one of the great advances of Champagne in the past three decades, and no grower has been more influential in its progress than Anselme Selosse. 'We should take what nature has given us and not interfere' is a philosophy he pursues more obsessively than any other, making him a visionary mentor who has inspired a generation of growers in Champagne. Since taking over from his father in 1980, his example has been a revolution in the region, radically pioneering lower yields farmed according to biodynamic principles and a handmade, Burgundian approach quite unlike any other in Champagne. His wines are as strong as the convictions behind them, and rank among the ripest and most expressive in all of Champagne. Regrettably, his approach too often pushes his wines beyond the realms of sound champagne and into the outer limits of oxidation. Yet the wines of Selosse rank high among the most prized sparkling wines of all, and each year his entire production of 57,000 bottles quickly vanishes into the cellars of collectors across the globe. These are rare champagnes, and priced accordingly.

There is no name in Champagne more talked about right now than Anselme Selosse, and no grower more controversial. He is one of the most profound thinkers in the modern wine world on the role of the soil as the interface between the terroir and the vine. 'The terroir expresses itself in the minerality, the flavour and the intensity of the wine,' he explains.

'The bedrock on which we plant our vines is rarely directly soluble, and it is only by the action of micro-organisms that it is able to be transformed to be absorbed by the roots and impart its mineral signature. The population of micro-organisms is specific to its location, and a short distance away, when the population changes, the terroir changes.'

For Selosse, terroir encompasses the entire eco-system, and anything that might disrupt the intricate balance of biodiversity is to be vigorously avoided. This is intuitive winegrowing of the highest order, a rigorous biodynamic regime, yet vigorously non-prescriptive, encouraging balance through such techniques as soil respiration by planting grasses in the mid-rows, abandoning pesticides, and hard pruning to limit yields.

The result is fruit of full ripeness, capturing the detail and character of spectacular estate holdings spanning 47 parcels across 7.5 hectares, located primarily in the grand crus of the Côte des Blancs, including four hectares of chardonnay in Selosse's home village of Avize, one hectare in each of Oger and Cramant and smaller plots in Le Mesnil-sur-Oger, and pinot noir in Aÿ, Ambonnay and Mareuil-sur-Aÿ. Selosse produces fewer than 60,000 bottles each year.

Selosse's Burgundian approach is particularly conspicuous in the winery. 'A lot of people consider vintage to be finished when the grapes are picked, but for me it continues through the vinification and all the way to bottling'.

In 2008 he purchased an old Avize château with 200-year-old cellars built on four levels. Each of 47 different plots is pressed separately in his press house at the level of the vines above the village, flowing by gravity into settling tanks below, then down to barrels on a third level. Every parcel is fermented using wild yeast in puncheons, foudres and Burgundy barrels of all sizes, purchased from some of Burgundy's finest estates.

Maintaining solids in the fermentation juices is an important element of the Selosse style. 'Solids in the juice provide nutrients and antioxidant protection for the wine,' he explains, 'adding texture, nutty flavours and deep colour.' These characters build as the wines are held in barrel over one year, enhanced with weekly bâtonnage (lees stirring).

Malolactic fermentation is free to occur (or not) as each parcel evolves. Minimal sulphur dioxide is used, and only ever prior to fermentation. This is fraught with danger in an oxidative, barrel-matured wine style, and every 2014 and 2013 barrel sample that I tasted was oxidised. Selosse has been at the forefront of low dosage in Champagne, using less than 7g/L, and usually less than 3g/L. Each cuvée is aged long on lees prior to release – up to eight years in the case of 'Substance', made using a true solera going back to 1986.

These radical methods make the wines of Selosse unique in flavour and stature in all of Champagne. These are inherently textural, vinous wines that have as much in common with white Burgundy as they do with champagne. Not to be hurried, they benefit tremendously from a decant and plenty of time to open up in a large glass to allow volatility to blow off.

They evolve dramatically and polarise even the most seasoned champagne drinkers.

Such big, oxidative, unashamedly broad styles with all too often vinegar or fino sherry-like development are more than confronting, yet there are bottles of some cuvées out there that are not oxidised, and these can be mesmerising. The trouble is, that's a very expensive chance to take. If you do choose to take the plunge, your best chances are with very large glasses and plenty of time to breathe.

Selosse's latest creations are four single-vineyard, single-varietal champagnes from Le Mesnil-sur-Oger, Aÿ, Ambonnay and Mareuil-sur-Aÿ. Produced in tiny volumes, they will fascinate those who enjoy his oak-driven, oxidative style.

Selosse's champagnes are as distinctive and original as the man who masterminded them. Anselme regularly travels to Spain, where he focuses on sherry production, 'because he is a bit obsessed with oxidation!' as one of his close grower friends put it.

His cuvées are powerfully ripe, deeply mineral, eminently characterful, and worthy of admiration on each count. When oxidation and oak are kept at bay, they have the potential to be profound.

Anselme's young son Guillaume returned to the estate in June 2012 and is assuming increasing responsibility.

Labels are impressively informative, detailing disgorgement dates, dosage and blends.

Selosse's luxury hotel, Les Avisés, goes from strength to strength, and his brilliant chef Stéphane Rossillon continues to serve up one of the most memorable and hospitable dining experiences in all of Champagne.

The Selosse revolution continues.

JACQUES SELOSSE INITIAL BLANC DE BLANCS BRUT NV $$$$

91 points • DISGORGED FEBRUARY 2016 • TASTED IN AUSTRALIA
95 points • DISGORGED OCTOBER 2015 • TASTED IN CHAMPAGNE

Chardonnay from three successive vintages from Avize, Cramant and Oger; 33,000 bottles each year

'Initial' accounts for more than 50% of Selosse's production, yet such is its variability that I find my impressions varying widely according to the level of oxidative degradation in each bottle. The mineral tension of Avize, Cramant and Oger meet the full fanfare of barrel fermentation. This is a powerful cuvée of full-yellow hue and characters of bruised apple, dried peach and grapefruit, layered with marmalade, toast, fruit mince spice and fruit cake. It upholds the persistence and acid definition of grand cru chardonnay commensurate with its proportions, though oxidation brought dry contraction to the finish in one bottle I tasted.

JACQUES SELOSSE V. O. VERSION ORIGINALE GRAND CRU BLANC DE BLANCS EXTRA BRUT NV $$$$$

93 points • DISGORGED JANUARY 2016 • TASTED IN AUSTRALIA

Avize, Cramant and Oger; three successive vintages from Avize, Cramant and Oger; vinified in oak barrels; aged 3.5-4 years on lees; zero dosage; 3600 bottles

Signature Selosse, such is the bombastic complexity and volume of V. O. that it resembles mature white burgundy as much as it does champagne. A full yellow copper–hue announces both ripeness and oxidation, with remarkable ripe-fruit intensity transcending Côte des Blancs chardonnay in its panoply of flavours of ripe mirabelle plum, pineapple and pear. Layers of toast and mixed spice proclaim its development, culminating in a finish that celebrates grand cru acidity and deep, characterful chalk minerality, propagating with grand persistence, though faltering just ever so slightly in dry oxidation on the close.

JACQUES SELOSSE ROSÉ BRUT NV $$$$$

92 points • DISGORGED MAY 2016 • TASTED IN AUSTRALIA

Chardonnay from Avize and pinot noir from Ambonnay; two successive vintages; 6000 bottles each year

This is a cuvée that fuses the signature mineral structure of Selosse's Avize chardonnay with the bold dimension of Ambonnay pinot noir and the oxidative development of barrel maturity. The medium copper–tinted result carries grand complexity of red cherry and strawberry fruits over a core of bruised apple and pear, layered with mixed spice and toast that linger with outstanding persistence. Fine salt chalk minerality builds impressive texture, though the dry, vinegary influence of burnt-orange oxidation leaves a touch of astringency on the end.

JACQUES SELOSSE MILLÉSIME GRAND CRU EXTRA-BRUT 2005 $$$$$

88 points • DISGORGED NOVEMBER 2015 • TASTED IN AUSTRALIA

Avize chardonnay; always the same two parcels since 1975; 4800 bottles

The power of the 2005 season collides with the ripe intensity of Selosse in a full yellow copper–hue. With aromas and flavours of fino sherry and a dry, contracted, vinegary finish, this is a cuvée that has tragically collapsed in the hands of oxidation. For what it's worth, it upholds fleshy mid-palate body, fair persistence and chalk mineral structure. A high price to pay.

Jacques Selosse Lieux-Dits Le Mesnil-sur-Oger Les Carelles Grand Cru Extra-Brut NV $$$$$

90 points • Disgorged February 2016 • Tasted in Australia

Single-vineyard Le Mesnil-sur-Oger; solera blend; aged 5-6 years on lees; less than 4g/L dosage

For its complexity, impact and full yellow copper–hue, this is a cuvée of subtle bouquet. The palate celebrates the fleshy presence of ripe chardonnay in flavours of fig, bruised apple, beurre bosc pear, peach and a hint of grapefruit tang, evolving into marmalade and mixed spice, collapsing into a dry, oxidative finish. The salt mineral mouthfeel of Le Mesnil holds out.

Jacques Selosse Lieux-Dits Mareuil-sur-Aÿ Sous le Mont Premier Cru Extra-Brut NV $$$$$

92 points • Disgorged February 2016 • Tasted in Australia

100% pinot noir; single-vineyard Mareuil-sur-Aÿ

A full copper salmon–hue and enticing aromas of red cherries, strawberries and cherry kernel declare pinot noir of presence and character. The toasty development of oxidative barrel maturity defines a dry palate of tamarillo flavours and subtle smoky complexity. It concludes firm and astringent, with the fine salt minerality of Mareuil poking through burnt-orange oxidation. It nonetheless upholds good persistence, line and character.

Jacques Selosse Lieux-Dits Aÿ La Côte Faron Grand Cru Extra-Brut NV $$$$$

87 points • Disgorged February 2016 • Tasted in Australia

100% pinot noir; single-vineyard Aÿ

A full yellow copper–hue declares an intense and powerful Aÿ pinot that has tragically collapsed into dry, astringent, vinegary oxidation that strips it of freshness, definition and character.

Jacques Selosse Lieux-Dits Ambonnay Le Bout du Clos Grand Cru Extra-Brut NV $$$$$

88 points • Disgorged February 2016 • Tasted in Australia

Single-vineyard Ambonnay

A dry and firm style of full orange copper–hue and prominent toasty, nutty flavours of oak, accented with notes of Old Spice. Oak and oxidation conspire in an astringent finish, though it does hold with persistence.

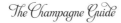

The Champagne Guide

Jacques Selosse Substance Grand Cru Blanc de Blancs Brut NV $$$$$

89 points • Disgorged December 2015 • Tasted in Australia

Chardonnay from Avize; solera of every vintage since 1986

This is a fully developed cuvée of fino sherry character and full yellow copper–hue. The fine salt mineral mouthfeel of Avize is prominent amidst the fleshy body of ripe chardonnay fruit. Nuances of pineapple and peach make fleeting appearances, though sadly diminished by overwhelming oxidation. Nonetheless, it carries ripe fruit body, mixed spice complexity and reasonable persistence.

Jacques Selosse Exquise Sec NV $$$$$

90 points • Disgorged February 2016 • Tasted in Australia

Chardonnay; 1000 bottles

In the presence of the ripe Selosse style, sweetness brings with it exotic overtones of lychee, locut and frangipane, even a suggestion of gooseberries, over the spicy complexity of barrel fermentation. Fine chalk mineral stucture brings definition to a long and sweet finish. A characterful sec.

Every parcel at Selosse is wild fermented and aged in barrels for one year with minimal sulphur dioxide and none after fermentation.

JACQUESSON

(Zhak-soh)

9/10

68 RUE DU COLONEL FABIEN 51530 DIZY
www.champagnejacquesson.com

CHAMPAGNE
JACQUESSON
— FAMILLE CHIQUET —

No champagne house today is on a trajectory of ascent as steep as Jacquesson. While many houses are on the prowl for more fruit to increase production, Jacquesson has drastically slashed its yields and its contracts to radically improve quality in spite of lowering quantity. When others set out to make a consistent blend every year, Jacquesson throws uniformity to the wind to draw the best blend out of every vintage. Each time I look, this little house in the village of Dizy appears more like a fanatical grower-producer. Purely on the refinement of its current cuvées, Jacquesson has leapt from ranking among Champagne's top 20 houses to a lofty position among its top 10.

The concept of non-vintage champagne has never sat quite right with me. Blending multiple vintages to deal with the ups and downs of the seasons makes sense. But creating a consistent style that tastes the same every year seems unambitious or at best an elusive ideal.

When a particularly blessed season arrives, why must it always be dumbed down for the sake of uniformity? Or must it?

'We were making a regular non-vintage at Jacquesson until we became progressively frustrated with it,' Jean-Hervé Chiquet told me when we first tasted his oddly named Cuvée No 734 in the tasting room of the family estate in Dizy.

'We face such vintage variation at this extreme, with fantastic vintages followed by disasters, that our ancestors found that the only way to handle the seasons was to blend vintages to produce consistent wine. This is why 90% of Champagne's production does not carry a vintage. In spring 1998 we were working on our non-vintage from 1997 base and we found a blend that was

very nice, but not the same as the previous non-vintage and not able to be reproduced. At the time, we made an inferior wine to match the consistency of the house. We decided then that there should be a better rule. We thought, what happens if we don't try to imitate what we did last year, but start from a blank sheet of paper and make the best wine that we can every year?'

And so Cuvée 728 was born from 2000 vintage base. 'A vintage with reserve wine,' as Jean-Hervé calls it. A different blend every year is reflected by a consecutively rolling number (1272 less than the vintage year) – a 'stupid number', according to Jean-Hervé. 'But two things don't change: the fruit sources and the taste of the two guys who do the blend!'

RADICAL CHANGE

Those two guys are brothers Jean-Hervé and Laurent Chiquet, whose family purchased the company in 1978 and transferred its headquarters to their own family's historic estate. 'I spent 10 years campaigning to my

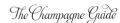
The Champagne Guide

father that we could do something differently,' Jean-Hervé says.

'Then in 1988 he allowed me and my brother to take over and we spent 12 years changing everything about the structures of the company and the vineyards. But in 2000 we realised that the changes were not reflected in the wines, so it was then that we changed the entire range. We took big risks in changing the style to introduce the 700 series. A risk of losing most of our customers and a risk of big investment with no return for some years. We had to be good friends with our bank manager!'

While 2002 marked the turning point of what Jean-Hervé describes as 'deconstructing Jacquesson', a champagne house is like an ocean liner and it takes a generation to turn around. 'Our last Late Disgorged 2002 will be sold between 2019 and 2021, from a regime we started talking about in 1978, so it takes 43 years for the change to fully take effect.' And the Jacquesson revolution is far from over yet.

The house has introduced a series of drastic changes to raise quality in recent vintages. At a time when many houses are seeking to extend their fruit sources, Jacquesson has radically initiated just the opposite. Yields were lowered in 2008 at the same time as fruit purchases were strategically slashed from 40 hectares to just eight, lowering annual production from 350,000 bottles to 250,000–260,000 today, with estate vines now supplying almost 80% of needs. 'The quality of what we grow means we are less satisfied with the fruit we buy, so we dropped those vineyards that were not up to the standard of our rising expectations,' Jean-Hervé declares. Any parcels vinified that don't meet their standards are sold.

Further, the age of release of the 700 series has been progressively stepped up, from three years on lees for Cuvée 733 (2005 base) to four years for Cuvée 736 (2008), though back to 3.5 years for Cuvée 740 (2012). Meanwhile, allocations have been further lowered by holding back an average of 15,000 bottles from each release since Cuvée 733, to release as a Late Disgorged 700 series, with an additional 4–5 years of bottle age.

'We may be the only champagne producer to take the risk of releasing their entry wine at nine years of age!' Jean-Hervé suggests. These are radical measures for any wine region, unheard of for a champagne house, and reflect resoundingly in the calibre of the 700 series today.

FANATICAL GROWER

Jacquesson's cuvées are complex blends that age impressively and reflect the intricate attention to detail applied at every step of their creation. This begins in the vineyards. According to Jean-Hervé, there are five factors in wine: 'Terroir, viticulture, viticulture, viticulture and winemaking!' He describes Jacquesson as a grower more than a champagne house, and himself and his brother as 'frustrated growers'. It is this philosophy that underpins the recent transformation of the house. I visited Jacquesson's vineyards towards the end of harvest 2014 and was stunned at how immaculately they are kept.

Their goal in the vineyards is to grow less fruit, slightly riper, to draw out the mineral character of the terroir. 'The detail of our terroirs in Champagne is every bit as sharp as that of Burgundy,' Jean-Hervé points out. Jacquesson directly controls 28 hectares of enviably located premier and grand cru vineyards, 17 in Dizy, Aÿ and Hautvillers, and 11 in Avize, with an additional eight hectares sourced from contract growers in the same villages, who Jean-Hervé describes as 'neighbours and friends'. Jacquesson harvests half the fruit it purchases, and now only buys from its neighbours, 'because we want to see every single berry with our own eyes'. The house today is 40% smaller than it was 25 years ago, now producing just 280,000 bottles. 'Of course, we aim to increase the price.' We may see a price rise when Cuvée 740 lands.

The estate has experimented with organics, with 10 hectares now fully organic, and the remainder run under a minimal-sulphur regime. When I questioned why full organic certification was not the agenda, Jean-Hervé's sensible response was, 'We are here to make good wine as our primary priority.' And 2012 was a strong case in point, with his organic fruit lost to mildew. 'I have always been convinced that a 100% organic system is not reasonable in Champagne's climate,' he explains.

Traditional methods are used throughout: little or no soil improvers, no herbicides or pesticides, minimal spray regimes, use of ploughing, cover crops between rows, and pruning to control vigour, increase ripeness, and limit yields to an average of around 60hL/hectare – just two-thirds of Champagne's average. 'The problem with Champagne is that every grower considers the maximum yield permitted by the appellation to be an economic minimum,' he admits. He describes cover cropping as particularly effective in controlling yields, but acknowledges that until recent environmental priorities became prominent, this was practised by significantly fewer than 1% of Champagne growers. Selection is very important to Jacquesson, and all tailles is sold, as well as any declassified parcels.

Jacquesson's attention in the vineyard allows its cuvées to capture the expression of the soil, exemplified in its trilogy of single-vineyard, single-varietal, single-vintage wines produced in minuscule volumes (never more than 10% of production in total), from three special little plots in Aÿ, Dizy and Avize. 'Terroir is the most unfair part of the wine business – you either have the right place or you don't!' Jean-Hervé says. 'It is very important to talk about terroir in champagne.' And talk terroir these cuvées do, articulating chalk mineral textures of disarming clarity. Jacquesson's single-vineyards and late-disgorged 700 series cuvées are tiraged under cork.

HANDS-OFF WINEMAKING

Jacquesson's scrupulous practices in the vineyard are mirrored in its hands-off approach in the winery. All fruit is pressed in its own press houses. 'Pressing is very important in champagne because we have this stupid idea of making white wine from red grapes!' he exclaims. 'We must hand pick and press close to the vineyard or we'll end up with jam.'

Gentle vertical presses are used, and the very first juice is removed 'because it has washed the outside of the grapes'. No chaptalisation has been performed since 2007. 'You only need to chaptalise when there is a problem,' Jean-Hervé points out.

Each parcel is vinified separately in large 45hL oak foudres to allow the wine to breathe, after which it is left on lees and stirred until a relatively late bottling in June or July. Lees stirring produces creaminess and body, and has an antioxidant effect, and so no sulphur dioxide is added between pressing and disgorgement.

'Malolactic fermentation is the eternal debate in Champagne,' Jean-Hervé suggests. 'We favour malolactic fermentation as we don't want to use heavy sulphur dioxide additions or filtration.' Traditionally, Jacquesson has run malolactic fermentation to completion, but more recently has blocked it in less than 20% of ferments by using cooling. There is also no fining, 'to maintain the aromatic potential of the fruit'.

To build complexity, reserves for the 700 series wines are the previous blends, kept separate in foudres, demi-muids and enamelled tanks, with reserves back to Cuvée 735 (2007 base) currently in stock. No single parcels are kept as reserves, which makes allocation of parcels a simple choice between the 700 series, the three single vineyards or discarding them to sell. 'Our blending is very easy because we sort of blend everything except the single vineyards,' Jean-Hervé explains. A trial blend is created using the single vineyards, and if the blend needs them, no single vineyard cuvées are made.

All Jacquesson cuvées have been extra brut (less than 6g/L dosage) since 2000, although only recently declared on labels. 'We never intended to make extra brut, but we just don't think our wines need more dosage,' says Jean-Hervé.

Dosages have become progressively lower, but this trend has never been a conscious decision. 'Some of our wines have no dosage, not because we wanted to make zero-dosage wine, but because they were better wines this way,' he says.

Back labels are among the most informative of any champagne house, shamelessly declaring disgorgement date, dosage, base vintage, blend and even precise production quantities.

There are no secrets here, just great champagnes, and better than ever. As Jean-Hervé puts it, 'At Jacquesson, we just want to grow great fruit and make great wines.'

JACQUESSON CUVÉE NO 740 EXTRA-BRUT NV $$

94 points • 2012 BASE VINTAGE • DISGORGED JULY 2016 • TASTED IN AUSTRALIA

43% chardonnay, 30% meunier and 27% pinot noir from Aÿ, Dizy, Hautvillers, Avize and Oiry; 20% reserves (usually more than 30%); majority of reserves from older 700 series blends for the first time; 1.5g/L dosage; 211,978 bottles

To properly respect the 700 series, treat it like a vintage wine, and don't be alarmed when it's introverted and tightly restrained on release. It will open beautifully a year later, and truly blossom five or 10 years on. The 740 is built around a core of grapefruit, nashi pear and almost ripe fig, with a dry focus that accentuates wonderfully present, salty oyster-shell chalk minerality. Large barrel fermentation brings impressive coherence, creamy seamlessness, fine-tuned texture and the slightest charcuterie nuances. It lingers with great line, persistence and integrity. A very classy 700 series.

The Champagne Guide

Jacquesson Cuvée No 738 Extra-Brut NV $$

94 points • 2010 base vintage • Disgorged November 2014 • Tasted in Champagne

61% chardonnay, 21% meunier, 18% pinot noir; 33% reserves; 2.5g/L dosage; 275,936 bottles

Jean-Hervé Chiquet is the first to admit that Cuvées 738 and 739 proved to be a challenge, based on the difficult vintages of 2010 and 2011. He pulled out every stop for 738 in this challengingly warm and wet season, producing no single-vineyard wines and using a very high proportion of chardonnay to build finesse and elegance. 'The idea of this cuvée is to give the identity of the base vintage, but we had to put a lot of things in here to make it work!' exclaims Jean-Hervé. And work it does, an impressive result for the season, albeit, inevitably, a lesser example of 700 series. I suggested on its release two years ago that it would benefit from a few more years to develop, and that it has. Chardonnay takes its lead with impressive citrus freshness, fleshed out by the stone fruit succulence of meunier and pinot noir. Skilfully managed barrel work spins beautifully woven texture without oxidation or oak character, building a fine, creamy mouthfeel that amplifies salty minerality. A well-crafted and characterful wine of driving structure, charged with excellent acid line, finishing even, dry and long.

Jacquesson Cuvée No 735 Dégorgement Tardif Extra-Brut NV $$$$

91 points • 2007 base vintage • Disgorged November 2015 • Tasted in Australia

47% chardonnay, 33% pinot, 20% meunier from grand and premier crus in the Grande Vallée de la Marne and Côte des Blancs; 28% reserves; more than 7 years on lees; 3.5g/L dosage; 16,220 bottles

735 has returned for an encore, transforming into a complex style in which secondary development is the theme in toast and roast brazil nut characters, touched with tertiary notes of sweet pipe smoke and black olives. Long lees age has brought wonderfully creamy seamlessness, supporting prominent, fine, frothing, salty chalk minerality. The finish is beginning to show some dryness and a little contraction, signalling the close of life for this bottle.

Jacquesson Dizy Terres Rouges 2012 $$$$

98 points • Disgorged March 2016 • Tasted in Champagne

52% chardonnay, 24% meunier, 24% pinot noir; 22% reserves; 2.5g/L dosage; 16,000 bottles

In a sneak preview of the first release of Dizy Terres Rouges as a white champagne, Jean-Hervé Chiquet disgorged this bottle on the day of my visit in 2016 and wowed me with a remarkable cuvée that transcends the terroir of Dizy. In its youthful guise it led out with layers of wood spice, pineapple core, grapefruit and white nectarine, opening into a breathtaking red cherry purity of exceptional line and length. Profound chalk minerality permeated the palate with remarkable distinction. I have long admired Terres Rouges as a powerfully distinctive rosé, and had always wondered at Jean-Hervé Chiquet's suggestion that this terroir would sit better as a white. Now, finally and emphatically, I understand.

JACQUESSON DIZY TERRES ROUGES ROSÉ EXTRA-BRUT 2009 $$$$

96 points • DISGORGED JANUARY 2016 • TASTED IN CHAMPAGNE AND AUSTRALIA

Skin-contact rosé of pinot noir; 1.35-hectare single vineyard on the boundary of Dizy and Hautvillers, planted 1993; vinified in oak foudres; aged 5.5 years on lees; zero dosage; 9496 bottles

The aspiration of Terres Rouges is a pronounced expression of pinot noir, yet with finesse. For Jean-Hervé, the 2009 transcends even the great 2008, with greater balance and more volume, while retaining brightness. He's right. It's a uniquely full-bodied and tightly stuctured rosé of deep-crimson hue — think halfway between champagne rosé and full-blown red Burgundy. It has the struture to match, with a firm, fine tannin backbone, grippy and chewy, yet harmonious and confident, ready for protein-rich pink meats. For all of its structure, it projects a gorgeous complexity of rose petal and musk aromas over a palate of deep and pronounced fresh red cherry, strawberry and raspberry fruit, and even a hint of tomato bush. A contrast between the focused tension of bright acid line and the structural grip of tannins and wonderful chalk minerality is no easy juxtaposition to juggle, yet Jacquesson has pulled it off with exacting precision. It's powerfully seductive and characterful. And it will age long, too.

JACQUESSON DIZY CORNE BAUTRAY EXTRA-BRUT 2007 $$$$$

96 points • DISGORGED JANUARY 2016 • TASTED IN CHAMPAGNE & AUSTRALIA

South-west facing single-vineyard Dizy on the boundary with Aÿ, planted in 1960 on millstone-grit gravel over clayey marl and Campanian chalk; 100% chardonnay; vinified and aged in oak casks on lees; unfiltered; aged 7.5 years in bottle; zero dosage; 5760 bottles

Jean-Hervé has no idea why his father planted chardonnay in Dizy, but a half-century later these old vines have tapped so deep into the terroir that the voice of the soil speaks above the tones of the fruit and the expression of the barrels. The 2007 proves that the inexplicable chalk mineral impression of the preceding vintages was no fluke, speaking in profound, deep and irrefutable notes of salty chalk texture and flavour, from a site with chalk no less than 2.5 metres under the surface, in a village unrecognised for chardonnay of structure. Crunchy apple, nashi pear, bright lemon and grapefruit are backed with the subtle almond meal, brioche, anise, lemon meringue and even coffee nuances of long lees age, finishing structured and scaffolded by salty chalk minerality and acid tension, unified by the calming influence of barrel fermentation. In length, energetic drive, poise and sheer character of personality, this is one of the greats. As ever, all it calls for is time, and it promises to blossom in a decade.

JACQUESSON DÉGORGEMENT TARDIF EXTRA-BRUT MILLÉSIME 2000 $$$$$

94 points • DISGORGED JANUARY 2016 • TASTED IN AUSTRALIA

50% chardonnay, 50% pinot from the Grande Vallée de la Marne, Côte des Blancs and Montagne de Reims; 1.5g/L dosage; 1688 bottles

A glowing, full straw yellow–hue proclaims the radiant, sun-drenched 2000 season. The generosity of the year prevails, now well developed into the buttered toast, roast almonds and spice of maturity, with some of the smoky, olive-like notes of grand old age beginning to materialise. The fleshy mood of the season contrasts a dry, savoury and structured finish that proclaims the prominent salt minerality that Jacquesson so accurately preserves. Though now toward the end of its life, it grasps its integrity and hovers with great length and alluring character.

The Champagne Guide

JÉRÔME PRÉVOST

(Zheh-rowm Preh-voh)

7/10

2 RUE DE LA PETITE MONTAGNE 51390 GUEUX

CHAMPAGNE
La Closerie

Across every style and region of the wine world, the very greatest makers share an intuitive approach that transcends any prescriptive grapegrowing or winemaking regime. Besides Anselme Selosse (of Jacques Selosse) himself, no one in Champagne personifies this more dramatically than Jérôme Prévost. When others follow regimes of traditional viticulture, organics or biodynamics, Prévost adopts a natural approach, keeping his senses attuned to the vines and responding gently. In a region that strives to mould every vintage into a house style, Prévost makes only a vintage wine and sees it as his role to support the vines to maximise the expression of the season, though sadly releases it too early to label it as a vintage. He harvests not on sugar or acidity, but on the sensation of the skins of the grapes in his mouth. He can't tell you if his wines go through malolactic fermentation ('I don't do analysis – the wines do what they want'). And he doesn't add dosage, not because this is his philosophy, but because the wine doesn't need it. 'Wine is not about philosophy,' he declares. This is winemaking by emotion, a world away from the formal, clinical approach of Champagne. With a big smile and a genuine, warm and unflustered approach, Prévost makes wines much like himself. Fleshy, vinous and brimming with exotic spice, these are some of the finest expressions of pure, single-vineyard, single-vintage meunier in all of Champagne.

In 1987, at the age of 21, Prévost inherited the 2.2 hectare vineyard planted in the 1960s by his grandmother in Gueux on the Petite Montagne. There is only one vineyard and one variety and, until a recent foray into rosé, there was only one wine, too.

Prévost made his first wine in 1998, with the help of his friend, Anselme Selosse. It was a sign of the regard in which Anselme held the young Jérôme that he lent him space in his winery in Avize to make his first four vintages. There is a clear synergy of philosophy between the two.

Prévost treasures the 55-million-year-old soils of his village in Champagne's youngest geological area, and proudly showed me a sample, teeming with fossils of ancient sea life like some geology museum artefact – the secret, he says, to the minerality of his wine. Here, the chalk is deep, starting 80 centimetres below the surface, and he has spent 12 years working the soil to encourage deeper roots to build minerality in his wines. This is very much a lesser terroir of Champagne. 'I cannot understand how Jérôme Prévost can make wines as good as he does where he is,' Jacquesson's Jean-Hervé Chiquet told me recently. 'He is very talented.'

And he pays close attention to his vineyard. 'The soil used to be very hard, but now it is very easy to work.

I plough the mid-rows and avoid herbicides. It's all about building up the micro-organism population in the soil, and that takes time,' Prévost says.

He is emphatic that this is not biodynamics. 'Biodynamics is like a religion and I don't agree with that,' he explains. 'It's too much like a recipe, but every plot of land is different. You have to work with emotion and sensation and learn from nature, not from a book. You have to go out in the vines and feel the sun and the wind, with all of your senses attuned, to taste with your eyes and your ears.'

Grapes are harvested at a high level of maturity, achieved with tiny yields of 45hL/hectare, less than half Champagne's average. His role is to support his vines to draw out the expression of the year. 'I do not know which years are good years because for me every year is different,' he says. 'I have two girls, educated in the same way, but each is different and I love them both with the same love. My wines are the same. In the vineyard, every year is very different and this is what I enjoy about it.

'I do not understand the philosophy of making champagne taste the same every year. It is not my role to determine the style of the wine. The wine is the wine and it has its own way. In the winery, I do not want my stamp to show. I have to work very softly. To make a white wine I do nothing in the cellar – I work hard in the vineyard, press and put it in barrels,' he says.

Fermentation relies exclusively on natural yeasts from the vines. 'Different yeasts give different aromas, so you have to use natural yeast to make complex wines,' he explains. Since different yeasts have different tolerances to sulphur, he uses only very low levels of sulphur, so as not to inhibit weaker strains. Fermentation takes place entirely in barrels, three-quarters in Burgundy barrels, the remainder in larger barrels of up to 600 litre capacity, including a few acacia barriques for the first time in 2012, and wines remain in barrel for 10 months, so as to breathe and not develop reductive characters. There is only one wine (the rosé is made from the same base as the white and named 'Fac-simile', because 'in Latin it means to do the same thing – and for me it is all about the vineyard, not the cellar'), so the blend is made up of every barrel. Prévost prizes the complexity achieved by blending many small ferments of parcels from one vineyard. Every wine receives the same dosage of a minute 2.5g/L. 'I don't think about that, they all get the same!' he says.

It's a shame Prévost's wines are released so young, as it takes years for them to blossom. My scores are uniformly higher years later than they are on release. Bottles are not vintage dated, but the year of harvest is coded in the fine print of the front label, beginning 'LC'.

Prévost was excited to make red wine for rosé from meunier for the first time in 2007. A tiny volume of a single barrel is worked by hand, even using a bucket to 'pump' over twice a day. 'It's a marvellous thing!' he exclaims. 'Working directly with the grapes to make red wine is like a gift for me. In Champagne traditionally we never put the skin in the wine, but I don't understand this because all the good things about the grape are just under the skin!' Harvesting at full ripeness is the key, because maturity of the skin is more important to him than sugar and acid levels. This is achieved by sourcing red wine from an old part of the vineyard affected by a virus which produces very small and very few berries, reducing yields and intensifying the fruit. He always adds 10% to the white of the vintage to produce a rosé of slightly different colour each year.

Prévost makes just 13,000 bottles every year in the outhouses of his charming 1924 cottage in Gueux and a little cellar on his street. It's a small space, containing his barrels, one small blending tank, one forklift and a cellar in an old World War I armaments store. He riddles by hand twice daily in the same little space. 'It is very small, but enough for my two hands,' he says. Such is his tiny scale that he refers to his friend Pierre Larmandier's small estate of Larmandier-Bernier as 'a factory'.

The scarcity of Prévost's wines makes them hard to find, but the hunt is richly rewarded. Don't look for a bottle with his name on it. The name of the vineyard is prominent and his name is lost in the fine print.

This is just as he would have it.

Jérôme Prévost's intuitive approach elevates a lesser terroir.

The Champagne Guide

Jérôme Prévost La Closerie les Béguines LC13 NV $$$

89 points • Tasted in Champagne

2013 base vintage; 100% meunier; 2.5g/L dosage

2013 was the first year in which Jérôme commenced harvest in October. Regrettably, the bottle he showed displayed some oxidised green olive characters. It's difficult to ascertain whether this was representative, or simply because this bottle had been open for five days, though he said it tasted normal to him. It upheld spicy red berry fruits of good persistence, supported by softly salty minerality and hints of coffee from barrel fermentation.

Jérôme Prévost La Closerie les Béguines LC08 NV $$$

93 points • Tasted in Champagne

2008 vintage; 100% meunier; 2.5g/L dosage

This bottle had been open for a full two weeks before Jérôme poured it for me, and while I have no doubt my notes and score would look very different from a fresh bottle, this showed good bead and no sign of oxidation. It was a full straw yellow–hue, with a creamy, toasty and biscuity palate, finishing dry, with character, complexity and persistence.

Jérôme Prévost La Closerie les Béguines LC07 NV $$$

93 points • Disgorged late 2009 • Tasted in Champagne

2007 vintage; 100% meunier; 2.5g/L dosage

Testimony to the stamina of Prévost's cuvées, this original disgorgement bottle was in good condition, even after having been open for five days before he showed me. It was toasty and rich, with layers of stone fruits, spice, toffee and preserved lemon, finishing long, characterful, dry and creamy, with a soft bead and finely textured mouthfeel.

Jérôme Prévost La Closerie Fac-simile LC13 NV $$$

92 points • Tasted in Champagne

2013 vintage; 100% meunier; 10% still red wine; 2.5g/L dosage

This cuvée has held confidently since my first preview long before its release, having now evolved to a medium crimson salmon–hue. It's upheld tomato, strawberry and pink pepper character on a long palate of charcuterie barrel-ferment complexity, bright acid line and finely textured structure. It's long, dry and characterful. Alexandre Chartogne kindly opened a fresh bottle to share with me after a tasting of his own Chartogne-Taillet cuvées. It looked identical to a bottle Jérôme showed me, which he'd opened five days prior — a sure sign it has the endurance to age.

JOSEPH LORIOT-PAGEL

(Zhoh-sef Loh-ree-oh-Pah-zhel)

(5/10)

33–40 RUE DE LA RÉPUBLIQUE 51700 FESTIGNY
www.champagne-loriot-pagel.fr

CHAMPAGNE

Joseph Loriot-Pagel

The Loriot family has tended vines for more than a century and made its own wines for 80 years from Festigny in the Marne Valley. Almost nine hectares of estate vines span the surrounding villages and the Côte des Blancs grand crus of Cramant, Avize and Oger. Meunier comprises more than two-thirds of the estate, the balance made up by chardonnay and pinot noir from vines averaging 28 years of age, farmed using integrated techniques that care for the soil and its people. Fermentation takes place in small stainless steel tanks, with reserve wines matured in wooden barrels.

JOSEPH LORIOT-PAGEL BLANC DE BLANCS GRAND CRU BRUT 2008 $$

93 points • DISGORGED MARCH 2016 • TASTED IN AUSTRALIA

Oger, Cramant, Avize; aged at least 7 years on lees; 9g/L dosage; DIAM closure

This is a blanc de blancs that contrasts the body, depth and complexity of ripe fruit and lees age with the tension and definition of bright 2008 acidity and grand cru chalk minerality. Rich flavours of fig, baked apple and even blood orange are underscored by layers of mixed spice, fruit mince spice and gingernut biscuits. It's full, fleshy and ready, with just the right level of ripe acidity and gently integrated chalk minerality to uphold focus on the finish.

....

JOSEPH LORIOT-PAGEL CUVÉE DE RÉSERVE BRUT 2008 $$

93 points • DISGORGED NOVEMBER 2015 • TASTED IN AUSTRALIA

40% chardonnay, 30% pinot, 30% meunier; aged at least 6 years on lees; 9g/L dosage; DIAM closure

Pinot noir and meunier command a strong lead here, abounding with beautifully primary strawberry and red cherry fruit that coasts through a supple and attractive palate. A fine, creamy texture and hints of savoury, biscuity complexity are derived from lees age. The focus and energy of 2008 mark out a long and vibrant finish of well-integrated acidity and soft, gentle, salty chalk mineral structure. A beautifully approachable 2008 that will impress the masses and connoisseurs alike.

KRUG

(Khroo-k)

10/10

5 RUE COQUEBERT 51100 REIMS

www.krug.com

CHAMPAGNE

To those of us gazing in from the outside in wide-eyed wonder, Krug is to Champagne as Domaine de la Romanée-Conti is to Burgundy and Pétrus is to Bordeaux. It possesses a grandeur, an other-worldliness, an amplitude that is as lofty as its mesospheric price. Krug's grand hierarchy of prestige begins at a higher price than any other in Champagne, and its single-vineyard wines rank among the most expensive in the world. Krug is the king of champagnes. And it has something mystical, too.

I've always wondered if the magic of Krug is real. If one worked here for long enough, would the sparkle evaporate, the cellar turn into just a dank, dark hole, the barrels become just dirty old kegs, the cracks in the walls reveal these old buildings for what they are, and the day-to-day reality expose the hyperbole of one of the most clever of all French marketing spiels?

I'm not the only one who has wondered. Julie Cavil, one of four in a talented young winemaking team headed by Eric Lebel, made a flippant passing comment when I first met her in 2010.

'When I joined here, I went behind the scenes because I suspected that not everything was done as it is said to be. But I found that it is,' she said. The sparkle in her eye and that glimmer of don't-pinch-me-in-case-I-wake-up wonder told me this was no marketing line. The magic, it seems, is real.

And it has to be, hasn't it? Some can fake wines of mediocre standards – but no one, anywhere, ever, can fake wines at this level. The wines of Krug are among the most revered in the world.

'I've been talking about Krug for over 20 years, but in 2011, I really discovered what it is about!' exclaims sixth-generation director, Olivier Krug. The revelation was the discovery of a book buried in the company archives for more than 160 years. The personal note-book of Olivier's great-great-great-grandfather was written to document the philosophy of Krug just five years after he founded the house in 1843. In it he expounded the principles of creating a champagne of great richness and yet great elegance, of selecting only the finest elements from the greatest terroirs, rejecting mediocre fruit and, revolutionary at the time, making both a non-vintage and a vintage cuvée. To this day, a resolute commitment to these very ideals has secured Krug's position as the most luxurious, most exclusive and most decadent of all champagnes. And, most extra-ordinary of all, its champagnes are only getting better.

PERFECTIONISM BEFORE TRADITION

From the outset, Krug has courageously pursued perfectionism ahead of traditionalism.

'Joseph was not a non-conformist, he was a very serious German guy, but he was ready to go beyond the rules to create something different,' Olivier reflects. 'He left the stability of the largest house in Champagne in 1842, with a vision to create a champagne that didn't exist.'

That same daring spirit flows in Olivier's blood, relentlessly pursuing the very finest grapes, regardless of variety, vineyard classification or village reputation, and fanatical vinification, regardless of cost.

Meunier is prized, even in these wines of untiring longevity. Classification tastings are conducted blind, with no regard for a vineyard's cru. Krug purposely does not constrain itself to grand cru, nor even to premier cru, and its reach has extended as far even as the village of Les Riceys at the most southerly extreme of the Côte des Bar, on the border of Burgundy.

In a region not traditionally associated with longevity, its winegrowers were amazed when Krug invited them to taste their reserve wines at two, three, five and even 15 years of age. 'They were astounded that their wines could be kept all that time, and were extremely moved and very emotional,' Julie recalls.

Krug owns just 21 hectares, less than 35% of the vineyards required to meet an annual production of an undisclosed figure somewhere in the vicinity of 650,000 bottles. Olivier says that Krug is not selling any more bottles today than it was 15 years ago, though production has increased by an undisclosed amount to facilitate a slow future growth in sales.

Estate vineyards are supplemented with fruit from some 70–100 loyal growers, some of whom have supplied the house since its foundation. Olivier explains that they have recently formalised contracts based on individual plots, but with the flexibility to maintain quality in difficult vintages.

'One grower called us in 2010 and said, "I have a different plot for you because yours was done by rot",' he says. Few champagne houses can claim such loyalty. Olivier personally visits the vineyards every day during harvest.

I was privileged to tag along for a day during vintage 2014 and witness the calibre of their plots and pristine condition of their fruit. Olivier is warm and friendly with his growers and workers in the press houses, showing them photos on his phone when he visits.

Krug pays a premium for higher quality grapes, and pays its picking teams mostly by the hour rather than the usual rate by the kilogram, an important distinction in ensuring stringent selection in the vineyards. Pickers are instructed to drop anything with rot and burnt or weak berries. I was surprised by just how much fruit was dropped in the mid-rows of Clos d'Ambonnay.

OBSESSED WITH DETAIL

Krug's long-ageing style begins with fruit harvested with more acidity and less sugar, so pHs are usually lower than the rest of the region.

'In 2010 we started in Clos du Mesnil two days before the official regulated start of harvest,' Olivier explains. 'Everyone in the village said we were mad, but they were all watching for when we started because they know we are obsessed with detail!'

The secret at Krug lies in the detail. 'Joseph set some rules for absolute detail for everything,' Olivier says. 'And we focus even more intently on the details today.' Grapes are selected plot by plot and pressed individually by their growers. 'Even if a grower chooses grapes from the same part of the village, we ask him to press as many parcels as he can.'

Olivier's late father, Henri Krug, told him, 'If you have a chance to vinify a wine on its own, you will express more of its personality. The more individuality you get, the more precise you can be with your selection.'

'It is as if I have a friend who paints the most beautiful panorama covering a wall, so lifelike and so detailed that it is as if the wall is not there,' says Olivier. 'And he paints the sky using 200 different shades of blue. Pale for the horizon, grey-blue for the east and deep blue for the west. But if he mixed all 200 shades of blue together and used the same proportions to paint the sky, it would have nothing of the same detail. So it is with blending champagne. We make 240 separate vinifications of parcels that could all be blended into just three vats.'

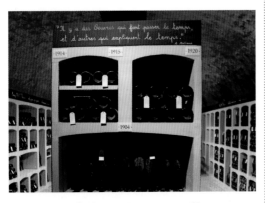

Krug's museum cellar bears testimony to its grand longevity, nurturing vintages back to 1880.

To facilitate this, 36 stainless steel double vats of small capacity were installed in 2007, increasing the small-batch storage capacity of the winery. In keeping each plot separate, reserve wines can be kept fresher. 'Some plots have more potential to age than others, and if they were all vinified together, the blend would lose the freshness of the freshest parcels,' he explains.

Last year one of Krug's largest growers in Avize came to taste his six reserve wines back to 1998. 'He knows which plots are in each sample and we don't,' Oliver recounts. 'He went white when he tasted them. Out of 20 plots that he has supplied us over 13 years – more than 250 wines in all – five of those six reserves were from the same plot. None of us had any idea, because what we do is by taste, not by recipe. Such is our attention to detail in the tasting room.'

Krug's winemaking team admits to an obsession with numbers. Krug works with 200–250 very small parcels of fruit every vintage, all of which are tasted after vintage and again the following year. Any not up to Krug's exacting standards go somewhere else in the Louis Vuitton–Moët Hennessy (LVMH) group. Since 1990, Krug has more than doubled its reserves, without increasing production. In the past 15 years, it has grown reserves from 60 to 150 different wines, dubbed 'treasures' by Olivier.

At any time, all of these are under consideration for Grande Cuvée, and all are tasted annually. Olivier and his uncle Rémi join the winemaking team for the tastings. The final blend comprises more than 100 parcels, spanning eight to 10 vintages, reflecting a different recipe every year. 'Our job every year is to recreate the most generous character of champagne,' says Olivier. A particular 1995 reserve wine from Bouzy has been tasted every year for 16 years and is yet to be allocated to the blend. There are still two 2001 reserve wines in Krug's cellar. As always, taste before reputation. 'Even in a crap vintage there are still great wines,' grins Olivier. Reserves are kept fresh in 150 small tanks, deep in the cellar at a stable 11–13°C. At any given time there are 5 million bottles in the cellar, 10 times the annual production, a massive ratio that reflects this long-ageing style.

MAGNIFICENT LONGEVITY

Krug attributes its longevity to the primary fermentation of all its wines in more than 4000 small, 205-litre oak barrels. When I arrived in September 2015, I was confronted by a sea of barrels in preparation for vintage packed tightly into Krug's large courtyard. And Krug has more barrels on site at its Clos du Mesnil and Clos d'Ambonnay vineyards. It uses these not for oak flavour

or aroma, but to build richness, complexity, balance and a 'high fidelity' not possible in stainless steel.

This is achieved by using only old casks, of average age 20 years, currently dating back to 1964. They are decommissioned after about 50 years, when they become too difficult to repair. Seguin Moreau barrels were used exclusively in the past, but Taransaud have been introduced recently. 'It took six years of tasting trials to establish the best coopers for Krug,' Julie tells me. Such is the attention to detail here. All barrels are purchased new and are seasoned for a few years by fermenting the second and third press before it is sold for distillation. A waste of a new barrel, but that's Krug!

Olivier is adamant that Krug is not special just because it is fermented in oak. 'When we started, every champagne was fermented in oak, and it still was 50 years ago!' he points out. When I asked to take his photo in front of the barrels, he politely proposed a different backdrop, eager to downplay the focus on oak.

To uphold freshness, Krug's wines spend just a few weeks in cask and are transferred to tanks following fermentation. Contact with oxygen during fermentation furnishes Krug with a resilience when it contacts oxygen as it ages, infusing its wines with rock-solid consistency. I have not seen the degradation of freshness in Krug bottles that plagues many other champagnes as they travel around the world. These are wines capable of ageing magnificently for decades.

When a bottle in Krug's museum cellar popped as its cage was replaced a few years ago, the board and winemakers were immediately assembled to taste the wine blind. Vigorous debate ensued as to whether it was from the 1950s or the 1960s, but it was decided it was too fresh for the 1960s. It turned out to be 1915 – all the more remarkable because the Côte des Blancs was under occupation during World War I and the wine was made exclusively from pinot noir, without the structural longevity of chardonnay.

Olivier doesn't like talking about malolactic fermentation, but lab analysis reveals the presence of malic acid as a key agent in Krug's longevity. 'Eric Lebel says he doesn't care about malolactic, but of course he cares,' reveals Olivier. 'Nothing is done to start it and nothing is done to stop it.' In 2013, just two or three of Krug's 240 fermentations went through malolactic fermentation. Even some parcels of the searingly high-acid 1996 vintage retained full malic acidity.

Although Grande Cuvée is released when it is ready to drink, after a long ageing process, Olivier has been intrigued by the number of collectors who age it further. 'Visitors now talk about Grand Cuvées from the '40s, '50s, '60s and '70s,' he reports. 'Many of our customers now put it down for five years or more.' He enjoys hosting dinners around the world for Krug lovers to bring their oldest Grand Cuvée.

It is now finally possible to ascertain the age of Krug's cuvées, firstly thanks to an ingenious ID code printed above the barcode of every bottle, the first three digits of which indicate the trimester (first digit) and year (second and third digits) in which it was disgorged. Using this code, Krug.com and the new Krug app will reveal the season and year in which the bottle was shipped, the number of years over which it has aged, the blend and the vintage story for vintage wines. For non-vintage blends, it will reveal the number of wines and each of the vintages. There is even a Twitter robot that will reply with the details when you tweet #KrugID with the code.

Secondly, in 2016 Krug began printing the edition number on the front label of every Grande Cuvée. Edition 163 is based on the 2007 harvest, the 163rd release in its history. This editon number comes with another exciting promise from Krug, the release of older editions of Grande Cuvée in the future.

Such disclosure ushers in a brand new era for Krug. 'I was resisting the concept of disclosing the disgorgement date,' admits Olivier. 'But the world has changed. People want to know. I have changed. And we are keen to be more transparent now.' Bravo.

RELENTLESS PURSUIT OF QUALITY

Krug's quest for quality in spite of the cost knows no limits. Krug Clos du Mesnil 1999 was to be released in 2010, but the final tasting pre-labelling was a disappointment. 'It did not have extravagant purity, it was shy and boring, you don't want to sit next to this wine!' Olivier explains.

So the decision was made to cancel its release, in spite of an offer from China to purchase the entire production of more than 10,000 bottles at full price. Olivier opened a bottle for me, 'to show that there is no compromise at Krug'. It was tense, introverted, deeply mineral and magnificent, though not as coherent as the 1998 or 2000. A secure 96 points. 'We will destroy the bottles and blend it away,' he declared.

'The first thing you learn here is patience,' admits Julie. 'There is a different time here. The clock in the courtyard is a symbol of the house. Time is very important in this place.'

Long ageing prior to release makes it impossible for Krug to follow trends, even if it wanted to. It takes 20 years to make a bottle of Grand Cuvée, since reserve wines are built up over 10 years, and seven or eight years of stock is perpetually ageing on lees.

Ownership of Krug rests with LVMH, which has remained sufficiently detached to leave most of the decisions in the hands of the family. Since he joined the company in 1989, Olivier has built the Japanese market into the most important for Krug. 'Everyone in Champagne was laughing when we went to Japan,' he said. 'And that's the reason they are still not there today!'

Krug's respect for a timeless tradition of rigorous selection, genius winemaking and masterful blending secures its inimitable position at the pinnacle of sparkling wine in the world today.

The clock in the courtyard of Krug's historic premises in Reims is a symbol of the house and the grand longevity of its cuvées.

The Champagne Guide

Krug Rosé Brut NV $$$$$

98 points • 2007 BASE VINTAGE WITH RESERVES BACK TO 2000 • DISGORGED AUTUMN 2014 • TASTED IN AUSTRALIA

47% pinot noir, 37% chardonnay, 16% meunier; ID 414068; about two-thirds malolactic fermentation; 7g/L dosage

98 points • 2006 BASE VINTAGE WITH RESERVES BACK TO 2000 • DISGORGED WINTER 2013/2014 • TASTED IN CHAMPAGNE

59% pinot noir, 33% chardonnay, 8% meunier; ID 114016

Like Grande Cuvée, Krug Rosé is a multi-vintage blend, but the association strictly ends here. This is a much smaller volume, representing less than 10% of the production of the house, assembled from the ground up. Pinot noir is treated to a short fermentation on skins and then blended with pinot noir, meunier and chardonnay fermented in small oak casks as white wine, before ageing for a minimum of now six years in bottle. Rosé is a relative newcomer at Krug, first released in the 1980s. Such was the visionary daring of Olivier's late father Henri Krug, and his brother Rémi, that when their father opposed the creation of a pink wine, they secretly produced a trial rosé. On pouring it blind for their father in 1976, he exclaimed, 'It is finished for us because someone in Champagne has copied Krug!'

Its ethereal restraint and delicate air seem a paradox in the grand decadence of Krug, but such is the detailed intricacy of this medium salmon tinted–cuvée that it dances with light-footed grace on a stage of epic complexity. It basks in the opportunity to warm up in large glasses to reveal pretty red cherry and strawberry fruit and rose petal fragrance, unravelling to a world of spicy complexity of truffles, sweet pipe smoke and game. An impeccable, energetic malic acid profile and pinpoint bead define a remarkable finish of mind-blowing seamlessness, impeccable line, reverberating depth and unrelenting persistence. Tannins are super fine and intimately meshed with thrilling minerality of all-encompassing presence, mouth-embracing fullness and emphatic, chalk-infused definition.

Krug Vintage 2003 $$$$$

96 points • DISGORGED AUTUMN 2014 AND WINTER 2014/2015 • TASTED IN CHAMPAGNE AND AUSTRALIA

46% pinot noir, 29% chardonnay, 25% meunier; ID 115023 and 414070

No one expected Krug to release a vintage from this record hot, tiny-yielding season, and certainly not with an unusually high proportion of meunier. Eric Lebel described 2003 as the most difficult vintage to blend, the most difficult intellectual challenge of his career, because they had everything in nature against them. The result is as astonishing on paper as it is in the glass. 'If you look at this blend on paper, it looks like the opposite of what you'd expect in a prestige cuvée!' Olivier admits. 'Our impressions of the wines were the opposite of what we were hearing from others in Champagne. And the more we tasted the wines, the more we fell in love with some, though not all. So we decided to express the character of the year and make one of the smallest vintages at Krug in 60 years. The trick with 2003 is that we chose parcels on the aromatics of the grapes, not on the acidity, and we found some truly great wines with surprising balance, freshness, aromatic expression and vivacious fruit.' With Avize and Le Mesnil-sur-Oger largely wiped out by spring frost, the blend is built on chardonnay from Villers-Marmery and Trépail, the elegance of pinot noir from the northern Montagne de Reims and the depth of Clos d'Ambonnay (with no Clos d'Ambonnay released this vintage), and the vivacity and expression of meunier from Sainte-Gemme, Villevenard and Courmas. In memory of its intense sun, Krug dubbed the vintage 'vivacious radiance'.

In a vintage when most houses didn't release a prestige cuvée, or shouldn't have, I was apprehensive when Olivier first introduced this cuvée. At this age, the wines of 2003 are characterised by dry extract and firm phenolic structure, but Krug takes this mood and presents it gracefully rather than aggressively. I have retasted it many times over the two years since its release and have been amazed every time at the integrity it has upheld. Its lemon zest and grapefruit purity and a wonderfully tense, energetic vitality remain, completely transcending a season that has generally not held its freshness. It delivers signature Krug impact with clarity seen nowhere else in 2003, layered with fig, dried peach and apple. Over time, its personality is progressively unfolding into bees wax, butterscotch, biscuits, dark chocolate, nougat, roast hazelnuts, vanilla, anise, wood smoke and incense. It holds impossible balance for the season, at once golden and ripe, generous, powerful and magnificent, yet really comes into its own on the finish, projecting integrity, precise line, profound persistence and exact, salty, super-fine chalk mineral definition like no other. How has Krug pulled off such a feat? Stringent selection and tiny production enlivened by malic acidity. The toughest seasons define the greatest estates. This was my top wine of the vintage. And then along came Clos du Mesnil (page 212).

KRUG VINTAGE 2002 $$$$$

99 points • DISGORGED AUTUMN 2014, WINTER 2015 AND SUMMER 2015 • TASTED IN CHAMPAGNE AND AUSTRALIA

40% pinot noir from Ambonnay, Bouzy, Aÿ and Mareuil-sur-Aÿ; 39% chardonnay from Le Mesnil-sur-Oger, Oger, Avize, Trépail and Villers-Marmery; 21% meunier from Saint-Gemme, Villevenard and Coulommes; aged more than 12 years on lees and 1 year on cork; ID 115012, 314064 and 315043

Krug's vintage comprises just 4–5% of production, making a statement to reflect the story of the year, rather than a creative expression. It comes as a surprise that the house dropped more fruit during green harvest than usual in the magnificent and bountiful season of 2002. 'We don't green harvest every year, but when we do so, we do it to reduce the yield and avoid wastage, rather than to concentrate the fruit,' Olivier explains. Eric Lebel describes the vintage as extremely serene and generous, consistently warm and relatively dry. To Olivier, every still wine was great, with both structure and richness. 'The trick for Eric,' he says, 'was to avoid falling into the trap of using everything; it was more about fine-tuning. 2002 is very much a vintage in which nature is talking, so we call it the "Ode to Nature".'

Krug 2002 is one of the most anticipated releases of the year, and it surpasses even its lofty expectations. This is a vintage that unites remarkable definition with grand generosity, and Krug encapsulates this dramatic contrast with thrilling flair. Even at 14 years of age it finds a new lease on life in Krug's capable hands, singing with brilliant focus, remarkable vitality and breathtaking freshness of lemon, locut, fig and glacé peach. A taut yet silky line of malic acidity charges it with phenomenal energy and endurance, yet at every moment stunningly integrated and enticingly captivating. It resonates with all the signature layers of Krug in rumbling depth of molten bees wax, incense, truffle, nougat, white Christmas cake and fruit mince spice. Yet for all of its exuberance and sheer, expansive proportions, it pulls gracefully into a tightly honed finish of deep-set mineral presence that rises, churns and froths for minutes upon minutes. This is a Krug of magical poise, in which profound concentration meets impossible tension. I bought every bottle Krug would allow me, poured them at every tasting I could, and only wish I could hold every one of them for another decade yet. That is when the true magic will begin.

The Champagne Guide

Krug Grande Cuvée NV $$$$

97 points • 163ème Édition • 2007 base vintage with 183 wines from 12 vintages back to 1990 • Disgorged Summer 2014 and Spring 2015 • Tasted in Champagne and Australia

37% pinot, 32% chardonnay, 31% meunier; ID 215031 and 314057

96 points • 159ème Édition • 2003 base vintage with 120 wines from 10 vintages back to 1988, in particular 1996 • Disgorged spring 2015 • Tasted in Champagne

51% pinot noir, 30% chardonnay, 19% meunier; a blend of 120 wines; ID 215040

98 points • 158ème Édition • 2002 base vintage with 76 wines from 10 vintages back to 1988 • Disgorged Spring 2008 • Tasted in Champagne and Australia

44% pinot noir, 36% chardonnay, 20% meunier; ID 108001

Krug leads off where most other champagne houses end, and this is every bit a prestige cuvée. Krug is adamant that it has no hierarchy in its cuvées, but price and style dictate that Grande Cuvée is always the starting point. Interestingly, the house pours in reverse order, tasting Grande Cuvée last. 'My father said, "Red carpet for every Krug!"' explains Olivier. 'There is no special treatment here, and every grape at Krug is given the same respect.'

Krug's winemaking team describes Grande Cuvée as its most exciting and most challenging wine to produce each year. It is a blend of the three champagne varieties, but there is no formula or recipe except to maintain not so much the consistency of the style (as the house has claimed in the past), but the best that can be produced each year, a philosophy reinforced first by the ID code on the back label and now by the edition number on the front. Krug Grande Cuvée and Rosé are built on a high proportion (30–50%) and wide spectrum (6–12 vintages) of reserve wines. Reserves are kept in tank for five, 10 and even 20 years. After blending, Grande Cuvée spends at least a further six years on lees in bottle to build its characteristic golden amplitude. An additional year of ageing was added thanks to slow sales during the financial crisis of 2008 and 2009 (formerly five years). It is aged a further year after disgorgement (formerly six months). Grande Cuvée now accounts for 90% of the production of the house.

Grande Cuvée is a paradox of tense freshness, profound maturity and inimitable complexity. In its current 163ème Édition it sings with marvellous layers of lemon and lemon zest, strawberries, figs and tangelos. It opens with a fanfare into a maelstrom of molten wax, wisps of smouldering truffle, incense, freshly tanned leather, Christmas spice and kirsch. Decadently rich, extravagantly complex and thunderingly expansive, Grande Cuvée is a vinous champagne of multifaceted personality, yet ever-heightened tension, breathtaking persistence and unerring focus, tapping into deep wells of scintillating, swirling minerality and, no question, no small retention of malic acidity. Every bit as enchanting as its legendary reputation promises, this is a champagne to drink slowly from large glasses, to witness an entire universe of captivating theatrics unfold as it warms.

Older disgorgements served at the house and around the world demonstrate the enduring consistency of this cuvée and its profound propensity to retain its vitality. The house has re-released the 2003 base (159ème Édition) for special tastings to coincide with the launch of its vintage wine from the same season, making the resounding point that this controversial season has the capacity to age marvellously. An even more dramatic statement was made when the house repeated this tactic with the astonishing 2002 base (158ème Édition), upholding astounding freshness and poise amidst the marvellous allure of truffle and smouldering hearth. The precision of recent releases is unprecedented, and just how many decades they might hold in the cellar is anyone's guess. One bottle in nine opened for a large tasting was corked.

KRUG CLOS DU MESNIL BLANC DE BLANCS BRUT 2003 $$$$$

96 points • DISGORGED AUTUMN 2014 • TASTED IN AUSTRALIA

8671 bottles and 679 magnums, less than the usual 11,000-12,000 bottles; ID 214027

Clos du Mesnil is the most famous vineyard in all of Champagne, and one of the world's finest chardonnay sites outside the grand crus of Burgundy. An inscription in the vineyard states that vines were planted and the wall built in 1698. Olivier discovered recently that Krug has bought grapes from Clos du Mesnil since 1864. The 1.85 hectare clos is divided into five or six plots and 19 separate vinifications. On pure chalk in the heart of the finest and most age-worthy of Champagne's chardonnay villages, this east-facing slope achieves less ripeness than some of Le Mesnil-sur-Oger's due south-facing slopes, all the more suited to Krug's long-ageing style.

'My father purchased the plot in 1971 to secure a supply of chardonnay,' Olivier explains. 'They didn't expect this plot to produce amazing wines, but when they tasted all the still wines that year, they realised this little clos behind the big rusty gate in the middle of the village did not taste the same as the other wines from Le Mesnil. It was used in the blend at the time, but the same story repeated until the outstanding 1979 harvest, when my father suggested they should make a single wine. My grandfather said, "Never! You will ruin the philosophy of Krug! This is only one grape and one year and one little garden!" But my father made a test and they fell in love with it.'

There's something remarkable about Clos du Mesnil that is infused in its fruits from the outset. The powerful, intoxicating aroma of the cask hall at the vineyard mid-vintage is enthralling. A taste of the 2014 vintage from barrel mid-ferment, just eight days old, revealed the most concentrated and structured champagne of the season.

If Krug Vintage 2003 was unexpected, Clos du Mesnil 2003 was downright preposterous, if not for the record heat of the season, then for the devastating spring frosts that wiped out 90% of the village, though the clos itself fared better. There is no fingerprint of place more pronounced than the mineral voice of the soil that resonates in the most distinctive champagnes. Even this bad-tempered season could not dampen the earth-shaking minerality of Clos du Mesnil. It rumbles to the very core of the earth deep below this mesmerising site, then rises on the finish, like a shard of pure chalk erupting from the surface of the clos itself. It utterly trumps the phenolic grip of the season, which fades into complete oblivion. It is instead seamlessly composed, even silky, and two years on from its release it has toned from its white citrus brilliance into voluptuous expression of pure pear, dried fruits and mixed spice of all kinds, unravelling into a universe of complexity of bees wax, almond, nougat, toast, fennel and hints of smoke and truffles. This is not just the wine of the vintage, it is an entrancing champagne by any standards, vintage aside. The throne remains secure for the queen of blanc de blancs.

KRUG CLOS DU MESNIL BLANC DE BLANCS BRUT 2002 $$$$$

100 points • TASTED IN AUSTRALIA

As above; 14,000 bottles

There are some who would proclaim that anointing any creation with a perfect score is but the stuff of foolish dreamers. But if there is one champagne this year that singly and emphatically trounces any sceptical pontifications around subjective perfection, that champagne is Krug Clos du Mesnil 2002. I remember my first encounter with Etienne Sauzet Le Montrachet 2006 from barrel in the little domaine in Puligny-Montrachet a decade ago. Such was its sheer force of haunting persistence, building and spiralling with no end, that it was only after I had farewelled its maker Gérard Boudot and was well down the road that its true greatness revealed itself and I increased my score to 100 perfect points. My first encounter with Krug Clos du Mesnil 2002 was nothing like that. From the first molecule of hedonistic aroma and time-arresting sip, this cuvée instantly and unequivocally

The Champagne Guide

projected itself so far beyond anything else I have tasted this year that awarding it 100 points was no wishful triumph, but simply a necessary formality. And yet Clos du Mesnil was everything like Etienne Sauzet, instantly transporting me back to Le Montrachet, for no other vineyard infuses chardonnay with such explosive concentration and force with a shining white sabre of razor precision. Its youthfulness at 15 years of age is disarming, a blinding flash of white sunshine, of lemon freshness and white pepper, layered with molten wax, even glimpses of green olives. Grand malic acidity of dizzyingly heightened proportions is swept up in an immense, all-consuming tidal wave of frothing, sea salt minerality, crashing with such structure that any mortal wine would collapse breathless in its wake. Yet herein lies the triumph of 2002, the vintage more than any other that reverberates with looming structure, yet meets it commandingly with awe-inspiring fruit presence. This sets it with a life expectancy of a century, no less. For all this, the one irrefutable trait that sets Krug Clos du Mesnil 2002 apart as one of the most profound wines of our era is a line and length so undeviating and enduring that it hovers, unwavering, for minutes, teasing and beckoning, as if taunting any who might have missed the point in that first spellbinding moment. None will miss it now. Here's to the ones who dream, foolish as they may seem.

KRUG CLOS D'AMBONNAY 2000 $$$$$

97 points • DISGORGED AUTUMN 2013 • TASTED IN AUSTRALIA

54% pinot noir, 30% chardonnay, 16% meunier; original disgorgement

When Olivier joined Krug in 1989, his father suggested that perhaps the challenge of his generation would be to find another clos with terroir worthy of another Krug single vineyard. Just two years later, a clos surrounded by a protective wall since 1766 was found in Ambonnay, Krug's favourite village and largest source of pinot noir. The tiny site of only 0.68 hectares, just one-third the size of Clos du Mesnil, was purchased in 1994, and the first vintage was made in 1995. 'We called it ABC as a codename to keep it an absolute secret until it was released in 2007,' Olivier reveals. 'We even kept it a secret from Moët for some years!' The result is the most expensive current-release champagne, with a four-digit price tag in any currency.

Clos d'Ambonnay is one of Champagne's most opulently voluminous creations, a sky with no ceilings in the radiant warmth of 2000. It's a powerfully complex and exotic cuvée of glorious, bright straw-yellow hue, brimming with exact truffle fragrance, vegetal notes, dried fruits, red cherries and all manner of spice. It concludes very long, deep and expansive, layered with the biscuits and brioche of 17 years of age, yet toned with focused lemon freshness and outstanding malic acid poise. Texture is creamy and ripe, evocative of the golden sunshine of 2000, freshened with impeccable, fine chalk mineral structure. This bottle showed hints of burnt-orange development on the nose, yet held its poise and integrity long on the finish.

Clos du Mesnil, built in 1698, and sourced by Krug since 1864, is the birthplace of the finest current-release champagne this year.

L. BÉNARD-PITOIS

(L. Bear-nah-Pee-twah)

(6/10)

23 RUE DUVAL 51160 MAREUIL-SUR-AŸ

www.champagne-benard-pitois.com

CHAMPAGNE

L. Bénard - Pitois

PROPRIÉTAIRE-RÉCOLTANT

Vignobles Premier Cru et Grand Cru

'*In Champagne's finest villages, the carving knife of succession is prone to shrinking the estate of each generation, but the Bénard-Pitois family has been blessed with something of the opposite. Laurent Bénard's paternal grandfather was privileged to holdings in Le Mesnil-sur-Oger and Oger, his mother in Avenay-val-d'Or and neighbouring Mutigny since 1850, and his wife in Bergères-lès-Vertus. The estate now draws from all five villages from its home in Mareuil-sur-Aÿ, one of the Vallée de la Marne's finest premier crus, and source of half its fruit. These are refreshingly affordable, terroir-driven wines, built around majestic pinot noir (two-thirds of the estate), from vines of average age exceeding 25 years.*

Bénard's grandfather made his own champagne in Mareuil-sur-Aÿ in small quantities from 1950. His father increased annual production to 20,000 bottles, and since 1991, Bénard has grown it to 70,000.

This is a conservative production for a 12-hectare estate. Meunier has very little place in these cuvées 'because I don't like it', Bénard admits candidly. Most is sold to Duval-Leroy, who reportedly love it.

Bénard-Pitois upholds a natural approach in its vines, cultivating grasses in the mid-rows of every vineyard. Two hectares have been tended organically and ploughed with a horse since 2009, with certification approved in 2012. Organic fruit has already shown greater floral aromatics and complexity, as well as a lowering of yields by 20–30%, to less than 60hL/hectare – under two-thirds of Champagne's average.

Yields in 2012 were even lower, after outbreaks of mildew and oïdium. There is a hope to convert all estate vineyards to organics, though Bénard acknowledges that this will be quite a challenge across 40 far-flung plots. He will release his first organic champagne from Mareuil-sur-Aÿ in 2014 under the label 'Laurent Bénard'. As a grower, he is not permitted to market certified organic wines under the same brand as his traditional wines.

This organic philosophy carries over into vinification, with minimal use of sulphur as a preservative, and an attempt to make sulphur-free wine for the past two years.

'We prefer to use just enough sulphur at the beginning of vinification and a tiny addition at disgorgement,' Bénard explains. All cuvées go through full

The Champagne Guide

malolactic fermentation, as it's very difficult to block with a low-sulphur regime.

This creates something of a dilemma for Bénard, concerned by declining acidity in the wake of global warming. Warm summers are building good sugar concentrations and he has very little need to chaptalise, if at all. Reconstituted grape must rather than sugar is used for dosage. To balance lowering acid levels, Bénard has lowered dosage from 15g/L to 9g/L over two decades.

Each parcel is vinified separately in small enamelled tanks, or oak barrels for chardonnay and reserve wines. To minimise oak influence, barrels are purchased after two or three vintages in Burgundy. Growth of production over the past two decades has put pressure on space, and bottles are now aged in a rented cellar.

Disgorgement dates aren't printed on labels, but the date is on the cork. If you have a good eye, the bottling code on the glass is also the disgorgement date.

L. Bénard-Pitois Brut Carte Blanche Premier Cru NV $$

92 points • 2012 base vintage • Disgorged October 2016 • Tasted in Australia

20% chardonnay, 75% pinot, 5% meunier; pinot noir from Mareuil-sur-Aÿ, Mutigny and Avenay-Val-d'Or; chardonnay from Bergères-lès-Vertus; meunier from Mareuil-sur-Aÿ; 2011 reserves; 8.45g/L dosage

Making up half the production of the estate, Bénard-Pitois' entry wine is a rousing celebration of the pinot noir of Mareuil and its surrounding villages, an enticingly fruit-focused blend of young, fresh red apple, strawberry hull and nashi pear. Bergères-lès-Vertus chardonnay contributes seamlessly integrated definition. Revelling in the great 2012 base vintage, this is a cuvée of restraint and definition, a clean, refreshing and well-made apéritif that balances fresh acidity with the soft definition of premier cru pinot noir and the gentle chalk minerality of Mareuil.

L. Bénard-Pitois Brut Réserve Premier Cru NV $$

94 points • 2011 base vintage • Disgorged November 2016 • Tasted in Australia

40% chardonnay, 60% pinot; pinot noir from Mareuil-sur-Aÿ and Mutigny; chardonnay from Le Mesnil-sur-Oger and Bergères-lès-Vertus; 2010 reserves; 8.45g/L dosage

Few champagne producers offer the chance to trade up from the entry NV for such a tiny outlay. With a larger representation of chardonnay and an extra year in the cellar, this is a cuvée that captures the red cherry and strawberry character of Mareuil pinot noir and melds it seamlessly with the definition of Le Mesnil and Bergères chardonnay, culminating in a finish of great persistence and accurate line. Age has brought subtle almond meal and nougat complexity, which linger on a finish defined by fine chalk minerality and beautifully poised acid line. The result transcends its 2011 base vintage and epitomises the friendly, fruit-focused bargain that this label has come to represent.

L. BÉNARD-PITOIS BRUT NATURE PREMIER CRU NV $$

90 points • 2010 BASE VINTAGE • DISGORGED JULY 2016 • TASTED IN AUSTRALIA

40% chardonnay, 60% pinot; pinot noir from Mareuil-sur-Aÿ and Mutigny; chardonnay from Le Mesnil-sur-Oger, Oger and Bergères-lès-Vertus; 2009 reserves; 0g/L dosage

Brut Nature exemplifies the ability of Bénard-Pitois Brut Réserve to both age confidently and stand up without added dosage. It upholds its red apple and red cherry fruit, with biscuity complexity from bottle age, though in the tricky 2010 base vintage it quickly switches mood to a dry and contracted finish, with a hint of dustiness.

L. BÉNARD-PITOIS BRUT ROSÉ PREMIER CRU NV $$

94 points • 2012 BASE VINTAGE • DISGORGED SEPTEMBER 2016 • TASTED IN AUSTRALIA

35% chardonnay, 65% pinot; pinot noir from Mareuil-sur-Aÿ and Mutigny; chardonnay from Le Mesnil-sur-Oger and Oger; 2011 reserves; 15% pinot noir red wine; 7.65g/L dosage

The pristine freshness, purity and chalk mineral expression of Brut Réserve is the perfect base for a beautifully elegant rosé in the great 2012 base vintage. A generous 15% red wine transforms it into a generously medium salmon crimson-tinted thing with a pretty air of strawberry and red cherry fruit. More exuberant than past incarnations, and none the less for it, Mareuil pinot noir takes a confident lead here, well-defined in its red cherry depth, fleshy mid palate and full, long-lingering finish. It's toned impeccably with prominent chalk minerality and consummately integrated acidity and dosage. Fine pinot noir tannins are delicately interwoven with its mineral texture on an enticing finish.

L. BÉNARD-PITOIS BRUT ROSÉ LB PREMIER CRU NV $$

93 points • 2011 BASE VINTAGE • DISGORGED SEPTEMBER 2016 • TASTED IN AUSTRALIA

85% chardonnay, 15% pinot; pinot noir from Mareuil-sur-Aÿ; chardonnay from Le Mesnil-sur-Oger, Mareuil-sur-Aÿ and Bergères-lès-Vertus; 2010 reserves; 15% pinot noir red wine; vinified partly in old oak barrels; 7.45g/L dosage

It takes keen eyes to spot the difference between Bénard-Pitois's two non-vintage rosés, but look for the little 'LB' in the border of the front label. There is no mistaking the distinction in the glass. The goal here is to contrast the vibrancy and mineral texture of chardonnay (an unusual 85% of the blend) with the red berry fruits of pinot noir red wine (15%) and the spicy complexity of barrel ageing. It meets the brief with flamboyance and confidence, contrasting the pronounced chalk mineral cut and acid tension of Le Mesnil-sur-Oger with the depth of pinot noir red wine and patently apparent savoury charcuterie complexity of barrel fermentation. With such grand fruit sources on display, its barrel work need not be quite so prominent, but there is no questioning the expert craftsmanship in assembling this beautifully medium salmon-tinted cuvée, even from the tricky 2011 base vintage, and it ultimately concludes beautifully balanced and harmonious.

The Champagne Guide

L. Bénard-Pitois Brut Millésime Premier Cru 2009 $$

89 points • Disgorged October 2016 • Tasted in Australia

20% chardonnay, 80% pinot; pinot noir from Mareuil-sur-Aÿ, Mutigny and Avenay-Val-d'Or; chardonnay from Le Mesnil-sur-Oger, Mareuil-sur-Aÿ and Bergères-lès-Vertus; vinified partly in old oak barrels; 4.55g/L dosage

A full-straw hue with a salmon tint heralds a confidently pinot noir–led cuvée that exemplifies a rich and powerful season. It leaps from the glass with ripe stone fruits prominently contrasting fast-rising baked cake, mixed spice and biscuit complexity. It's fleshy and honeyed on the front palate, pulling into a dry and slightly grainy finish that lacks freshness, verve and acid cut.

L. Bénard-Pitois Brut Blanc de Blancs Millésime Premier Cru 2006 $$

92 points • Disgorged March 2016 • Tasted in Australia

100% chardonnay; from Le Mesnil-sur-Oger, Oger and Mareuil-sur-Aÿ; vinified partly in old oak barrels; 6g/L dosage

At a decade of age, a bright medium-straw hue declares a cuvée of confidence and definition. Layers of complexity of honey, gingernut biscuits, roast almonds, vanilla and brioche declare both maturity and partial barrel vinification, while ripe white peach, pear and star fruit heralds the ripe 2006 season. It concludes with generous persistence and softly integrated acidity, with warm-season fine phenolic grip offering a little bite to its texture. Ready to drink now.

Laurent Bénard Vibrato LB Extra Brut 2011 $$

85 points • Disgorged 2016 • Tasted in Australia

Mareuil-sur-Aÿ vineyards in conversion to organics; vinified in barrels without sulphur

Organic certification was approved in 2012 for Bénard-Pitois's two hectares of organically tended and horse-ploughed (since 2009) vines in Mareuil. Oak asserts itself boldly in this woody, toasty, vanillin-accented cuvée of firm tannin structure. Regrettably, its elegantly defined and finely structured fruit is swamped with oak. Full oak vinification is too much.

Laurent Bénard Vendange LB Extra Brut 2010 $$$

91 points • Disgorged 2016 • Tasted in Australia

Mareuil-sur-Aÿ vineyards in conversion to organics; vinified in barrels and tanks

With a full straw yellow–hue, this is a generous and characterful cuvée of exuberant ripe fruits of succulent pear, orange and white peach, well cut with the tension of vibrant acidity. Partial vinification in oak barrels has contributed supportive savoury, biscuity complexity and fine tannin structure, well-integrated with the fine chalk minerality of Mareuil. It finishes a little dried out, though long and full.

Laherte Frères

(La-airt Frair)

5/10

3 Rue des Jardins 51530 Chavot-Courcourt
www.champagne-laherte.com
champagne-laherte.blogspot.com

CHAMPAGNE

DEPUIS 1889

The young Aurélien Laherte describes himself as a farmer, not a winemaker. 'More than anything, my father and I are trying to respect the soil, expressing the style of the clay and limestone,' he says. This is the soil of the historic little village of Chavot-Courcourt, on the border of the Côte des Blancs and the Vallée de la Marne. 'The clay gives us chardonnay that is fruitier than the Côte des Blancs, and the limestone meunier that is finer than the Vallée de la Marne,' he explains. For a production of less than 120,000 bottles, Laherte Frères boasts a very large portfolio of 12 cuvées that preserve the detail of its terroirs in wines of taut, linear persistence, and at times assertive structure.

With a history of grape-growing in the village spanning seven generations, the extended Laherte family accounts for almost one-third of Chavot's population of 350. The 10 hectares from which the estate sources across 75 parcels in 10 nearby villages have been passed down through the generations, and all are still owned and tended by members of the immediate family. French law dictates registration of the domaine as a négociant-manipulant, but for all practical purposes it should be considered a grower-producer, with the exception of its entry Brut Ultradition NV, for which supply is supplemented with two hectares of purchased fruit.

A complex array of vineyard parcels span the Coteaux Sud d'Épernay (Chavot, Moussy, Épernay, Vaudancourt and Mancy, with chardonnay, pinot noir and meunier), Côte des Blancs (Vertus and Voipreux, with chardonnay) and Vallée de la Marne (Le Breuil and Boursault, with meunier). In 2014, four hectares of Montagne de Reims vineyards were added to the sourcing pool.

'We would like our wines to express that they are not from the Côte des Blancs or the Montagne de Reims, but to be expressive of our village,' Aurélien says. In tasting young vins clairs, the distinctive saltiness of the chalk minerality and the north-facing freshness of Chavot are unique compared with his parcels from other villages. The oldest vines have been cultivated here by different generations of the family for more than 68 years.

An ecological approach is taken, with half the vineyard holdings managed biodynamically, and the rest essentially organically, 'to facilitate the natural expression of the vine and increase its aromatic potential,' Aurélien explains. He reports seeing increased mineral character in biodynamic plots as vines push deeper into the chalk, encouraged by ploughing by horse in spring and autumn to break up the surface. Natural pesticides and herbicides are used, and yields are limited.

'When we started with biodynamics in 2005, we found the fruit was cleaner and more consistent during vinification,' he says. 'The wines were fruity, held good acidities, and the bottles maintained their freshness for longer after they were opened.'

A vintage wine is made every year, even in the challenging 2010 season. 'If you work diligently, you don't need to be afraid of the quality of the vintage,' he suggests. 'In Champagne, many people just add more sugar or leave a wine on lees for longer if it's not right, but for us we simply make the wine.'

Villages, crus and varieties are separated, and matched to the age and style of one of 280 barrels as the musts leave one of two traditional presses. 'We have lots of complexity in the vineyard, so we try to obtain the same complexity in the winery using different fermentation vessels,' explains Aurélien. He considers the matching of parcels to the right vessels to be his most important task in the winery. 'The work we are doing in the vineyards has increased the potential of our fruit, so we have increased the quantity of oak in the last five years.' More than 80% of parcels are now fermented and aged in oak, as has been the tradition here for more than 25 years. Barrels vary from four to 40 years of age, and include several large 100-year-old foudres from Alsace for reserve wines. Five small barrels are purchased each year from Domaine de la Romanée-Conti, where they have aged Le Montrachet, no less. Since 2011, pinot noir and meunier have been selectively vinified in barrels used for red Burgundy in the hope of increasing red fruit character and tannins. Two new foudres were acquired in 2014.

In 2012, a cellar with capacity for 600,000 bottles was built, and Aurélien challenged his father that it was too big. 'A cellar is never too big!' came the response. A current stock of 250,000 bottles facilitates an average age of three years. 'It is the work of my generation to increase the ageing of our cuvées, and if I could extend it to four years by the end of my life, that would be an important step,' declares Aurélien, who aspires to add a month or two of age every year. An increase in production of 10,000 bottles in 2014 equated to an increase of four months of ageing in the cellar.

Some lees stirring is performed to build richness. Malolactic fermentation is blocked in most cuvées, but may proceed spontaneously or by design for particular years and varieties. In Laherte's structured and savoury terroirs, malic acidity makes for a tricky balance in young cuvées with increasing use of small-format oak, all too often resulting in assertive and drying structures. Laherte has trialled some barrels without sulphur, but is not yet convinced. 'Good acidity and low pH mean we don't need to use much sulphur, but without any we lose something of the soil and the precision of the fruit,' he says.

A unique 'Le Clos' vineyard of just 0.3 hectares in Chavot has been planted to seven varieties to preserve the heritage of the estate. 'We found the lost varieties of our ancestors in our old plots, and we have embarked on a project to recreate champagne with the same taste as 250 years ago,' Aurélien explained as he showed me through the prized site at the top of the village. Chardonnay, meunier, pinot noir, fromenteau, petit meslier, pinot blanc and arbane are harvested and pressed together, wild yeast fermented in barrel without malolactic fermentation, and blended with a reserve solera of every vintage since 2005 and bottled as 'Les 7'.

Attention to every detail is the key at Laherte, right down to the cork. Every wine has been sealed with DIAM for more than six years. 'I don't want to lose all our work to the cork!' Aurélien exclaims. 'Our goal is to preserve freshness, fruit and minerality in our wines, and our tests indicate that DIAM is most effective, providing protection against changes in temperature and humidity as our wines travel around the world.'

Aurélien has worked hard to slowly evolve the estate since he began working alongside his father, uncle and grandparents in 2005, and his spirit of experimentation and evolution continues. They now produce 12 cuvées each year, all but two of which are made in tiny volumes of just a few thousand bottles. Each boasts a refreshingly informative back label, detailing villages, assemblage, vinification, dosage and disgorgement date.

LAHERTE FRÈRES EXTRA BRUT ULTRADITION NV $

91 points • 2013 BASE VINTAGE • DISGORGED APRIL 2015 • TASTED IN AUSTRALIA

60% meunier, 30% chardonnay, 10% pinot noir from 10 villages in the Coteaux Sud d'Épernay and Vallée de la Marne; 40% reserves from 2012; fermented in barrels (80%), tanks and foudres; around 50% malolactic fermentation; 4.5g/L dosage

Cleverly named Ultradition, Aurélien explains, 'because our work in the vines and the winery now is not traditional. We are trying to do something different.' It is in this cuvée that he feels they have made their greatest progress in the vines and the barrels and foudres over the past decade, and still have the most potential to improve. 'People ask which is my favourite wine, and this is it because there is so much that we can do with the blend!' he discloses. This is certainly a complex expression of an entry cuvée, a characterful and representative take on the Coteaux Sud d'Épernay, with plenty of complexity of red apple and grapefruit. It captures the glassy, chalk mineral texture of the village, with some grip to the structure. Tense malic acidity marks out a long and fresh finish.

LAHERTE FRÈRES BLANC DE BLANCS BRUT NATURE NV $$

89 points • 2013 BASE VINTAGE • DISGORGED JULY 2014 • TASTED IN AUSTRALIA

Reserves from 2012; a blend of four villages, particularly Chavot and Épernay; vinified in foudres and 228-litre barrels; zero dosage; 30,000 bottles

The aspiration here is to draw out the salinity of young chardonnay through vinification in barrels and lees contact. Aurélien concedes that it's very young and hopes to work towards releasing it later. Vibrant malic acidity and salty chalk minerality define a tightly coiled, young, mineral-accented style, contrasting ripe fruit reminiscent of golden delicious apple and grapefruit. Barrel maturation lends some notes of charcuterie complexity. Fine, glassy, mineral texture and a fresh and focused acid line make for a tense, dry finish. It will benefit from a few years for its acidity to soften.

LAHERTE FRÈRES ROSÉ ULTRADITION BRUT NV $

88 points • 2012 BASE VINTAGE • DISGORGED SEPTEMBER 2014 • TASTED IN AUSTRALIA

50% meunier, 30% pinot noir, 20% chardonnay; 10% red wine from old-vine meunier; 40% reserves from 2011; partial malolactic fermentation; 7g/L dosage

Aurélien finds his blended rosé his most challenging wine to make, with the tannins of red wine clashing with the citrus of chardonnay, hence the blend is predominantly black grapes, including some from his wife's family in Bouzy. In future it will include a portion macerated on skins. For now, it's evolved to a medium-crimson hue and has taken on spicy, pepper complexity, while upholding its youthfully tense freshness and fine, glassy, quartz-like mineral texture. The earthy, dusty nuances of 2011 are reflected on the finish.

The Champagne Guide

LAHERTE FRÈRES ROSÉ DE MEUNIER EXTRA BRUT NV $$

93 points • 2014 BASE VINTAGE • DISGORGED MAY 2016 • TASTED IN AUSTRALIA

Vines of average age 25 years, and 40 years for the red wine; 30% saignée macerated fruit, 60% white, 10% red wine; of the white, 40% is 2013 reserves aged in barrels; fermented and aged for 6 months in vats, foudres and old demi-muid barrels

Uniting the best of all rosé methods, this is both a saignée and a blended style. Meunier speaks with bright expression of cherry, strawberry and red apple fruit, supported by fine, glassy minerality and bright acid line – a pleasant surprise for meunier. It's youthful and vibrant, with clean focus and lively, primary expression.

LAHERTE FRÈRES LES 7 EXTRA-BRUT 05-11 $$$

92 points • 2011 BASE VINTAGE • DISGORGED AUGUST 2014 • TASTED IN AUSTRALIA

Single-vineyard Chavot; previously labelled Les Clos; 18% chardonnay, 18% meunier, 17% pinot blanc, 15% petit meslier, 14% pinot noir, 10% fromenteau, 8% arbane; planted 2003; 60% 2011; blended at the press; 40% perpetual reserve blend of 2005 through 2010; co-fermented with wild yeast in Burgundy barrels of at least 10 years of age; matured in barrel for 6 months with regular lees stirring; no malolactic fermentation; 4g/L dosage

An opulent and multidimensional fruit salad anticipated by its recipe, spanning the contrasting expressions of intense fruit presence in citrus and stone fruits of all kinds, star fruit and unripe honeydew. It's exotic and complex, with a tight grapefruit-like malic acid that pokes out a little on the finish. It's shed the slight awkwardness of its youth and displays confident, idiosyncratic character and great length. It's evolving cheerfully and will only get better with more time to mellow. Great to see an NV cuvée sensibly named with a declaration of its vintages.

Aurélien Laherte maintains individual ferments in each of 280 different barrels to build complexity in his cuvées.

LALLIER

(Lah-liay)

6/10

4 PLACE DE LA LIBÉRATION 51160 AŸ

www.champagne-lallier.fr

DEPUIS 1906

CHAMPAGNE
LALLIER
À AŸ-FRANCE

The young house of Lallier was established in 1996, though the family's history in Aÿ spans five generations, having overseen Deutz from 1906 until Louis Roederer took ownership in 1996. Chef de cave since 2000, Francis Tribaut purchased Lallier when James Lallier retired in 2004. At the time, production totalled only 50,000 bottles; in just one decade, it mushroomed to a cool 400,000 bottles, where it remains today.

Such rapid growth necessitates space, and in 2011 production was moved from Aÿ to a new facility in Oger with a capacity for 1 million bottles. The heart of the company, its 18th-century vaulted cellars and the core of its sourcing, remain in Aÿ, whose pinot noir is the core of every cuvée. The estate is privileged to eight hectares in the village and four in Cramant, Chouilly and Vertus, providing for one-quarter of its production, the remainder sourced from across the Montagne de Reims and Côtes des Blancs. No meunier is used.

Fermentation takes place in stainless steel tanks using only natural yeasts, and partial malolactic fermentation maintains freshness in all cuvées. The entry NV blend has been cleverly re-engineered to reflect the character of its base vintage, with the year proudly displayed in the name of the cuvée. For the first time, back labels now disclose disgorgement dates, blends and crus.

Increasing quality in the midst of a rapid growth curve is a monumental calling in any house, but there is a dramatic leap in precision and finesse in every cuvée emerging from the Oger facility. Lallier is to be lauded for its clean, well-balanced and fruit-focused champagnes that have stepped up in this year's release, thanks to a refresh both inside and outside the bottles.

Winter draws to a close on the hillsides of Aÿ.

The Champagne Guide

LALLIER R.013 BRUT NV $$

92 points • 2013 BASE VINTAGE • DISGORGED AUGUST 2016 • TASTED IN AUSTRALIA

63% pinot from Aÿ, Verzenay, Bouzy and Ambonnay; 37% chardonnay from Avize, Cramant and Oger; 17% reserve wines; 7g/L dosage

The back label announces Lallier's new and noble philosophy: 'The "Série R" is the result of a deep reflection upon one year's harvest. A large majority of the cuvée R.013 comes from the vintage 2013.' The result is as magnificent as the mandate, a beautiful and enticing cuvée that seamlessly contrasts the depth and strength of pinot noir with the zest of chardonnay. It leads out strongly with baked apple and peach fruit and backs it with lemon and grapefruit. Lees age has contributed an enticing backdrop of brioche and nougat, culminating with succulent fruit generosity, balanced and well-integrated acidity and subtle dosage.

LALLIER R.012 BRUT NV $$

92 points • 2012 BASE VINTAGE • DISGORGED JANUARY AND FEBRUARY 2016 • TASTED IN AUSTRALIA

62% pinot mainly from Aÿ, Verzenay, Bouzy and Ambonnay; 38% chardonnay largely from Avize, Cramant and Oger; 19% reserves from 2008, 2005 and 2002; 8g/L dosage

A showcase for the rich, fleshy, red-fruited, spicy personality of grand cru pinot noir, this is a cuvée of stature and strength, from its medium-straw hue to its full-bodied palate of grapefruit, red apple and pear, and long, driving finish. Gentle, dry phenolic grip is subtle and does not interfere with fruit poise or persistence. Old reserves and bottle age bring a bready, biscuity backdrop of toasty, honeyed complexity. A great concept and a characterful expression.

LALLIER BLANC DE BLANCS GRAND CRU BRUT NV $$

94 points • 2012 BASE VINTAGE • DISGORGED FEBRUARY 2016 • TASTED IN AUSTRALIA

60% Aÿ; 40% Avize, Cramant and Oger; 36-48 months on lees; 9g/L dosage

Always a highlight of Lallier's portfolio, this is a cuvée that balances the expressive depth and intensity of Aÿ with the freshness of Côte des Blancs, and never has it looked more exact than it does from Lallier's new facility, basking in the glory of the great 2012 harvest. Aÿ brings a succulent white peach generosity to the citrus cut of the Côte des Blancs, beautifully overlaid with the lemon meringue and marzipan complexity of lees age, at every moment underlined by the pronounced chalk minerality of these profound grand crus. Dosage is well integrated on a finish of exacting line and seamless persistence.

LALLIER GRAND ROSÉ GRAND CRU BRUT NV $$

93 points • 2012 BASE VINTAGE • DISGORGED JANUARY AND FEBRUARY 2016
• TASTED IN AUSTRALIA

80% pinot noir from Aÿ and Bouzy; 20% chardonnay from Avize; 24-36 months on lees; a saignée of partial maceration of pinot noir and chardonnay and also a blend of red wine; 9g/L dosage

Pinot noir takes a commanding lead in this rosé of medium salmon copper tint, basking in the flesh and body of Aÿ and Bouzy pinot noir. Red apple, strawberry, raspberry and pink pepper fruit carry long, fragrant and full amidst a complexity reminiscent of strawberry flan and even a savoury hint of tamarillo. Maceration in union with assemblage of red wine provides fine tannin structure, which offers gentle support to a long finish. Chalk minerality and acidity rise to the occasion, toning the aftertaste with fine-grained structure and elegant drive.

LALLIER GRAND CRU BRUT MILLÉSIME 2008 $$$

92 points • DISGORGED JANUARY 2016 • TASTED IN AUSTRALIA

55% pinot from Aÿ; 45% chardonnay from Avize, Cramant and Oger; at least 5 years on lees; 7g/L dosage

A rich and voluptuous cuvée of medium-straw-yellow hue and fleshy stone fruits, fig, spice, even notes of golden fruit cake. There is a generously full richness here that verges on exotic fruits and fig, held confidently in place thanks to finely structured grip and well-integrated acidity. A 2008 ready to drink now, culminating in layers of gingernut and roast almonds. An attractive cuvée, albeit without the finesse or precision of the new regime of Lallier. One bottle tasted showed subtle burnt-orange oxidation character.

LALLIER OUVRAGE GRAND CRU NV $$$$

91 points • 2010 BASE VINTAGE • DISGORGED FEBRUARY 2015 • TASTED IN AUSTRALIA

70% pinot from Aÿ; 30% chardonnay from Avize and Cramant; partial malolactic fermentation; 5 years on lees under cork; 3g/L dosage

The house describes Ouvrage as Francis Tribaut's 'baby', the flagship of the house, built on a deep selection of the best crus. It's a complex and characterful style, with toasty, woody notes declaring the character of Aÿ pinot noir. This is a savoury cuvée of layered spice, grapefruit pith, bitter almond, even a hint of beetroot, amplified by the toasty complexity of bottle age under cork. It finishes with firm tension as much from dry extract as acidity, framed in low dosage.

LANSON

(Lohn-soh)

6/10

66 RUE DE COURLANCY 51100 REIMS

www.lanson.com

DEPUIS 1760

CHAMPAGNE *Lanson*

à REIMS FRANCE

*T*here is something about Lanson that has always struck me as quite extraordinary. For the ninth-largest Champagne house, with a 4 million bottle annual production (the majority of which is Black Label Brut NV, frequently discounted to one of the lowest prices of any champagne on the shelves), this is a house that has maintained remarkable consistency. All the more astonishing considering that it was purchased by Moët in 1991 and cunningly on-sold less than six months later, retaining just two of its 208 hectares of magnificent vineyards. It should take 15 years for a house of this magnitude to recover from such a blow, but I have enjoyed Black Label as my house champagne many times over the past decade, and in recent tastings of vintage wines spanning 30 years, that ominous dip that everyone anticipated simply never came. How is this possible?

One man. Jean-Paul Gandon commenced here in 1972, making his tenure of more than 40 years extraordinary, even in a region as historic as Champagne. More than this, he spent his first 15 years overseeing the sourcing of the grapes and must in the vineyards, a role which he retained when he was promoted to chef de cave in 1986.

His new owners astutely left him free rein to source, make and blend the wines as he saw best. He was a talented winemaker, certainly, but more than this, he was connected, and his relationships with the growers spanning 500 hectares of Lanson sourcing across Champagne have infused this house with a startling resilience in the midst of its tumultuous corporate ride of recent decades.

In 2013, Hervé Dantan joined Lanson as assistant chef de cave in anticipation of Jean-Paul Gandon's pending retirement.

Dantan came with an impressive track record of 22 years of innovation, transforming Mailly Grand Cru into one of Champagne's top cooperatives. And he has immediately ushered in an exciting new era at Lanson. Dantan's first priorities have been to facilitate small-parcel vinification and to increase texture in the wines. To this end, 55 new small tanks of 50–100hL capacity, a new reserve wine cellar and 23 new foudres were installed just in time for the 2014 vintage.

'Without malolactic fermentation, we need to add creamy texture, and we hope that the use of oak and micro-oxygenation can help with this,' he says.

'We want to keep the style fresh and crisp, while adding creamy complexity.' His foudres are thus for complexity and not for wood character, through ageing (not fermenting) chardonnay and pinot noir. 'I don't envisage making a special oak-matured cuvée, but expect that a very small contribution of just 5–6% will add complexity and depth to our blends.'

Following primary fermentation, the wine is cooled to 8°C and sulphur dioxide preservative is added to block malolactic fermentation. This creates a distinctive house style of excitingly high-strung, age-worthy champagne, true to Gandon's aspiration of 'maintaining freshness, power and fruit character'. In 2015, Dantan put 10% of Black Label components through malolactic, which he considers important, not to change the style, but for maintaining consistency in Black Label and Rose Label in certain vintages.

A considerable stock of 20 million bottles rests in 7 kilometres of galleries at a stable 10°C. The non-vintage receives complexity from a minimum of three years ageing on lees and a generous 20–30% reserves, power and structure from a 50% dose of pinot noir from the Montagne de Reims and Côte des Bar, minerality from chardonnay on the southern slopes of the Montagne de Reims, and a balancing touch of just 15% Vallée de la Marne meunier. Lanson uses meunier only in its entry non-vintage cuvées.

Thanks to Gandon, Lanson has been able to maintain grand cru fruit sources for all of its vintage wines, which are generally a 50/50 blend of pinot noir and chardonnay, aged a minimum of five years on lees prior to release, and usually considerably longer – remarkable for one of the lowest-priced vintage wines on the shelves.

Such maturation calls for a total cellar stock of 20 million bottles in Lanson's six kilometres of drives under Reims.

These are wines that age effortlessly, building slowly and purposefully in bottle, and I have recently been stunned by the stamina of late-disgorged 1979, 1983, 1988, 1990 and regular-disgorged 1996 and 1998.

Lanson is impressive in printing disgorgement dates on the back of every cuvée and its new website is refreshingly informative, with technical sheets detailing blends and villages for every cuvée.

To commemorate its 250th anniversary in 2010, Lanson launched a series of 'Extra Age' cuvées. The concept was unusual but inspired, a trilogy of three non-vintage cuvées, each from three mature vintages chosen to complement each other. These were not simply late-disgorged versions of its non-vintage cuvées, but purpose-assembled to age gracefully.

CLOS LANSON

In 2016, Lanson launched Clos Lanson from its unique single hectare alongside the winery in Reims. When Philippe Baijot purchased Lanson in 2006, he began conversion of the site to organic viticulture and resolved to create the first vintage from the only remaining vineyard in the city of Reims. 'It was here in the 18th century, and was on the edge of town at the beginning of the 19th,' reveals Dantan. Surrounded by development today, the environment of the city influences its microclimate, pushing temperatures 2–2.5°C warmer than the Montagne. The Clos is subsequently harvested as early as Avize and Oger.

It was planted to 100% chardonnay in 1962 and 1986 in 15 metres of topsoil above pure, white, friable, well-draining chalk. According to Dantan, it's the warmth and the chalk that make it possible for this site to produce a vintage every year.

The vineyard is divided into two plots, which ripen between three and seven days apart, and are hence harvested separately. The entire harvest of 8000

Clos Lanson, released as a dedicated cuvée for the first time this year.

The Champagne Guide

bottles (and as few as 5000) is fermented and matured in oak barrels of three to four vintages of age. True to Lanson, malolactic is fully blocked.

Clos Lanson is a generously expressive cuvée that captures the elegance of the Lanson style with ripe intensity. Its chalk salinity is the signature of its unique site.

It's a tricky calling to create a single-varietal, single-vintage wine from a single plot in every year, yet a vertical tasting of every vintage from 2006 to 2015 revealed a surprising consistency and impressive integrity. Oak impact is astonishingly subtle and colours are surprisingly pale, with fruit and oak presence diminished thanks to the absence of malolactic fermentation.

Lanson is the primary brand of the Lanson-BCC group, champagne's second-largest after LVMH.

Lanson Black Label Brut NV $

91 points • 2011 BASE VINTAGE • DISGORGED SEPTEMBER 2015 • TASTED IN CHAMPAGNE AND AUSTRALIA

50% pinot noir from the Montagne de Reims and Côte des Bar; 35% chardonnay from the Côte des Blancs, Montagne de Reims and a little from Sézanne and Vitry; 15% meunier from the Vallée de la Marne; a blend of around 100 villages; 25% reserve wines from 10 vintages from 2010 back to 2000, including part of the previous blend; no malolactic fermentation; aged 3 years on lees; 8g/L dosage; more than 3 million bottles

Lanson tactically doubled the dose of reserve wines to boost the tricky 2011 vintage. This cuvée accurately contrasts a profound statement of fresh apple, pear and lemon zest with the toastiness and brioche notes of bottle age, well-gauged honeyed dosage and the classic, tense, malic acid signature of the house. The dry extract grip of 2011 lends some firmness and savouriness, making for a lesser Black Label. The balance is nonetheless refined and the line and length are accurate, making Black Label one of the best of the readily available bargain champagnes. One bottle had lost most of its bead, but still maintained freshness.

Lanson Rose Label Brut Rosé NV $

90 points • DISGORGED JULY 2015 • TASTED IN CHAMPAGNE

53% pinot noir, 32% chardonnay, 15% meunier; a blend of 50-60 villages; 7% red wine reserves equally from Les Riceys, Bouzy and Cumières; 30% reserve of last year's blend; no malolactic fermentation; aged 3 years on lees; 8g/L dosage

Lanson first produced rosé in the 1950s and the style is increasingly important for the house, now representing an impressive 18% of its production, close to double the region's average. It's intentionally a fruity style, blended with red wine. The base wine is not the same as Black Label, but not far from it, with more grand and premier cru sourcing in the Rose Label, and more reserves.

There is a pretty elegance and an understated delicacy to this gorgeous rosé that its blatant strawberry mousse-coloured livery belies. Don't be put off by this or its teeny price, because this is a finely crafted rosé of purity and subtlety, one of the real bargains of rosé champagne. Pinot noir and chardonnay are blended from the most elegant premier and grand crus with a judicious dose of red wine of pretty aromatics and soft tannins to create a medium salmon copper–hue and a delicate freshness of strawberry and raspberry aromas. The palate has crunchy red apple and tangy morello cherry fruits of pretty and refined persistence. A little dry extract on the palate sits more comfortably than it does in the Black Label, finishing long, tangy and elegant.

LANSON WHITE LABEL DRY SEC NV $

87 points • 2011 BASE VINTAGE • TASTED IN CHAMPAGNE

38% chardonnay, 37% pinot noir, 25% meunier; Black Label with 25g/L dosage

With 25g/L of dosage, White Label is purposely not as sweet as demi-sec (35–50g/L). Since its release four years ago, the house has found it to be a popular style in a trendy category. To me, it stands as a case in point that champagne of different dosage should be built from the ground up rather than tampered with at disgorgement. Candied sweetness creates an awkward tension with the dry, extractive structure of 2011 and the malic acid tension of the house, making for a sweet and sour effect. It lacks the balance and poise of Black Label, though to its credit it's clean and not overtly sweet.

LANSON GOLD LABEL VINTAGE BRUT 2008 $$

96 points • DISGORGED JULY 2015 • TASTED IN CHAMPAGNE

53% pinot noir for body and vinosity, 47% chardonnay; sourced from premier and grand crus; no malolactic fermentation

If you're hankering to load up the cellar with a guaranteed long-term performer that won't break the bank, here is your answer. Lanson Gold Label is only made in the golden years, and with no 2006 or 2007, Hervé Dantan was nervous about releasing the 2008 last year. I can understand why. True to the season and its no-malolactic and low-dosage mandate, this is a tightly coiled cuvée of elegant refinement and astounding energy. I love the endurance of malic acidity in charging Lanson Vintage with tremendous potential in the cellar, and I cannot recall when this was more pronounced than in 2008, with the stamina to age confidently for three or four decades. Fine chalk minerality of pronounced presence supports pure, beach-fresh lemon fruit as radiant as high-noon sunlight. Grand persistence defines one of the most sublime Gold Labels of the modern era. I dare you to wait until at least 2030. Seriously.

LANSON EXTRA AGE BRUT NV $$$

95 points • DISGORGED JULY 2015 • TASTED IN CHAMPAGNE AND AUSTRALIA

A blend of 2002, 2004 and 2005; 60% pinot noir from Verzenay and Bouzy; 40% chardonnay from Avize, Chouilly, Cramant and Le Mesnil-sur-Oger; no malolactic fermentation; aged at least 8 years on lees; 8g/L dosage

The leader of Lanson's senior citizens owes its superiority to a predominance of the majestic 2002 vintage, boring deep into the chalk bedrock of six of Champagne's most profound grand crus to draw out intricate definition of mineral texture. It's a wonderfully enticing confluence of the flesh of white peach and white nectarine, the tang of lemon and the wonderful, rippling layers of texture and flavour that pronounce long lees age – brioche, meringue, nougat, honey and even a hint of vanilla. The whip-crack of malic acidity and the ravishing texture of scintillating chalk minerality keep everything energetic, refreshing and enduring. It exemplifies the calm sense of completeness that defines this label in its seamless harmony, layered with captivating multidimensional complexity, blessed with the fine-grained, silky, creamy texture of long lees age.

Lanson Noble Cuvée Blanc de Blancs Brut Millésimé 2000 $$$$

93 points • Tasted in Champagne

The sun-drenched 2000 season has been sustained wonderfully by malic acidity, clutching its succulent mirabelle and pear fruits and laden with brioche, mixed spice and even a hint of grilled pineapple. This cuvée is quite reductive at the moment, with notes of gunpowder and a hint of green olive. It has wonderfully fine, salty chalk minerality and great line and length.

Lanson Vintage Collection 1990 $$$$

89 points • Disgorged December 2015 • Tasted in Champagne en magnum
3g/L dosage

More developed than one would expect for 1990 *en magnum*, this is a cuvée of medium yellow-gold hue and aromas and flavours of green olive and burnt orange. Malic acidity is sadly the only element that has remained fresh.

Clos Lanson 2006 $$$$$

95 points • Disgorged December 2014 • Tasted in Champagne
100% chardonnay; one-hectare single vineyard in Reims; warm site on friable chalk; fermented and aged in oak barrels of 3-4 vintages of age; no malolactic fermentation; 3g/L dosage; ~8000 bottles; inaugural release

Medium-straw hue. There is a wonderfully seamless contrast here, between the understated generosity of this warm site, the ripe intensity of 2006, the enduring precision of the Lanson house style of blocking malolactic fermentation, the freshness of lemon and apple fruit, the toasty, spicy anise and praline nuances of almost a decade of age, and the salty and elegantly chalky texture that defines this unique Clos. It culminates in a mineral and dry finish, accented with very subtle smoky notes of barrel fermentation. A wine of great persistence and characterful singularity.

LARMANDIER-BERNIER

(Lah-mohn-diay-Bear-niay)

8/10

19 Avenue du Général de Gaulle 51130 Vertus

www.larmandier.fr

CHAMPAGNE
LARMANDIER-BERNIER

'*To create a wine that deeply expresses its terroir*' is Pierre Larmandier's aim, stated on the back of every one of the 140,000–150,000 bottles that leave his little cellar in Vertus each year. But to this fastidious grower, terroir in itself is not enough. 'Terroir is to wine what the score is to music,' he suggests. 'What's the point if the grape variety, the vine plant (the instrument) and the winegrower (the performer) are not up to standard?' Some growers are known for their focus on the vines, others for their attention in the winery, but few find a balance in every detail like Pierre Larmandier.

Since he came back to the family estate in 1988, Larmandier has grown holdings from 10 hectares to just over 16 hectares, blessed with impressive terroirs in the Côte des Blancs, spread across a total of 60 plots in the premier cru village of Vertus – including substantial holdings on the mid-slopes close to Le Mesnil-sur-Oger, supplemented with an impressive 2.5 hectares in the grand cru of Cramant, nearly 1 hectare in each of Avize and Chouilly, 0.2 in Oger, and 0.5 in the little villages of Bergères-lès-Vertus, Voipreux and Villeneuve-Renneville-Chevigny surrounding Vertus. Chardonnay is king here, and Larmandier tends just two hectares of pinot noir in Vertus for rosé and red wine.

'Chardonnay is very adaptable, and if you cultivate it carefully it will take its expression from the soil,' he explains, likening the diversity of his various plots to that of Puligny-Montrachet and Chablis.

'It would be a shame if we didn't bring our vineyards to your glass!' Larmandier says. And bring them he has, through one of the most sensible and diligent regimes anywhere in Champagne.

ORGANO-REALIST

Biodynamically certified since 2004, Larmandier describes himself as an 'organo-realist'. Every time I visit, he whisks me off in his four-wheel drive to one of his key plots in Vertus. One year, he'd heard rumours of an oïdium breakout around the village and wanted to get onto it right away. As we approached one of his plots, we passed other growers out treating for oïdium. 'That man', he said, pointing out one, 'is the worst in the village for always treating.' We found a little oïdium in Larmandier's plot, 'but it is not so bad so we will not treat yet. We're not too concerned about a little disease in the vineyards. Some people say grass is a disease, too!'

Larmandier cultivates grasses in the mid-rows during winter and ploughs until close to harvest. He considers an absence of herbicides to be the key in the vineyard. 'Organic or not is less important than abandoning herbicides,' he suggests. 'Everyone says they control weeds by ploughing, but I see them spraying with herbicide!' With neighbouring vines in such close proximity, it's impossible to conduct a biodynamic regime without some influence from those who do not farm naturally. Larmandier is matter-of-fact: 'We try to do the best we can, but it is not ideal. We still manage to be different to the others, even though we are among them.' Biodynamics is difficult to manage across so many plots, particularly the smaller ones, some just 200 square metres, spanning 15 kilometres north to south. 'We spend more time on the road than in the field with the tractor!' he says. And he calls his cousins in each village to check how much it has rained. 'We need to time our copper applications very carefully to combat disease.'

Since beginning conversion to biodynamic viticulture in 2000, Larmandier has noted a drop in yields, regulated by grasses in the mid-rows. He currently produces just 60–70hL/hectare. 'In the village, you are considered a bad grower if you do not produce 100hL/hectare,' he says. 'People produce too much in the Côte des Blancs, and the big houses just buy everything. They say I'm crazy to produce less than 100hL.'

He says 2012 was one of the toughest seasons he can recall in 25 years of managing his vines, yielding just two-thirds of his usual small harvest. Incessant rain made it difficult for him to get into the vineyards to cultivate the soil. 'We do our best with biodynamics, but when it's crazy, it's crazy!' he exclaims.

Larmandier likes old vines and tries to keep them as long as he can; some are as old as 80 years. 'My ideal is to never replace them, which is all very well, but then you don't have any grapes!' he says. In order to create more competition and push the roots deeper, he is slowly replanting at 10,000 vines per hectare, more than the regional average of 7500. 'This is contrary to the way of thinking in Champagne, but if I want to improve concentration without increasing my harvest, I think this is the way,' he explains.

'You can only extract so much minerality per square foot before it is diluted, but with more vines you can extract more.' While others focus on grapes per square metre of leaves to produce more aromatic wines, for Larmandier the key is the more Burgundian focus on grapes per square metre of soil.

'The soil is the most important thing,' he emphasises. 'With deep roots in good soils, 80% of the work is done.'

Pierre Larmandier and his meticulously tended vines in Vertus.

Here, on the lower slopes below the village of Vertus, the chalk lies 80 centimetres below the surface. He considers his average vine age of 35 years to be very important. 'The roots have a better depth and are better able to extract the minerality from the chalk. We are very lucky to have the place we do, and we work very hard in the vineyard to make the most of it,' he says.

Along with an expression of minerality, his priorities are roundness and linearity achieved by harvesting grapes at optimal ripeness of around eleven degrees of potential, compared with most in Champagne who aim for around nine. 'It is important for us to work the soil to achieve a lower pH in the wine, allowing us to wait longer to harvest, to achieve ripeness without lacking freshness.'

Even in the record heatwave of 2003 he was able to achieve freshness. 'Attention to the soil is increasingly important in these warmer vintages, so as to achieve phenolic maturity and not just sugar ripeness.' Larmandier harvests on taste rather than sugar levels.

NON-INTERVENTIONIST WINEMAKING

His sensitive and non-interventionist approach informs all he does. 'My philosophy used to be that terroir was everything and the hand of man was nothing, that our work in the vineyard was all that mattered,' Larmandier clarifies. 'But now we understand that the work we do and the choices we make in the winery are important, too.' Larmandier did not study oenology and says it's impossible to simplify winemaking to a recipe. 'If you work in the vineyards, your mind is not only on acid and alcohol numbers but on expression,' he says. 'Every year I have an oenology student come to work with me and they want to measure everything but I say, "First, you must taste!"'

To draw out the character of each site, wild yeast is used for primary and malolactic fermentations, with every ferment relying exclusively on its own natural yeasts. There is no filtration, 'because every time you filter or fine you lose a part of what you have worked hard to achieve in the vineyard'. Very low levels of preservative (sulphur dioxide), and ever lower dosages of around 4g/L are used. 'After all the care lavished on our wines, we are not going to add anything which might go against them!' Larmandier exclaims. Low sulphurs dictate that every wine is free to proceed through malolactic fermentation, and reserve wines are kept in tank under temperature control to maintain freshness.

Larmandier doesn't like the 'austerity' of stainless steel fermentation, and has increased the proportion of oak vinification from 40% to 70%, for controlled oxidation and complexity. He is very careful with barrel hygiene, having had 10% of his wines turn volatile when he first started with barrels, and now cleans them carefully and sulphurs them three times in the lead-up to harvest. He appreciates the expression achieved in oak, and has experimented with egg fermenters for rosé for some years (though finds the result too rounded and intense, so balances this with an equal proportion fermented in tank); recently, a new amphora arrived for rosé. 'Perhaps it can give us a little bit more complexity for the blend?' he suggests. He confesses he likes to follow fashions 'a little bit', but won't go too far as he doesn't like oxidation.

'In Champagne we are blenders, and different fermentation vessels give us more components for the blends. With more concentration in our fruit, stainless steel is too closed and there's more risk of reduction,' he explains. He maintains a delicate balance to keep his wines fresh, admitting that he's afraid of oxidation.

When I first visited in 2011, he was putting the finishing touches on a new building to provide space to work with more barrels. He still uses the first barrels he purchased in 1988, and has bought new barrels every year since 1999, 'because a used barrel has a personality of the wine, but we only want to express the personality of our vineyards'.

He doesn't want new oak characters to interfere, so new barrels comprise just 3% of his larger non-vintage blends for their first two years. Even tastings of his young vins clairs from second-use barrels display very subtle oak influence. He has purchased large foudres of the more subtle Austrian oak since 2001, and three more arrived in 2013.

Extra space also provides an opportunity to hold stock in bottle for longer, and his cellar now houses 500,000 bottles, sufficient for an average of 3.5 years on lees across his cuvées, with the aim of increasing his non-vintages from two years to three.

Larmandier's non-vintage philosophy is to let every vintage express its character. 'We are not blessed with making our non-vintage wines taste the same every year,' he says. Bottling codes are easy to decode, with the last four digits denoting the month and year of disgorgement. The other digits in the code are the base year.

Larmandier-Bernier exemplifies the levels of purity and mineral focus that can be drawn out of primarily premier cru terroirs with sufficient care and attention. These exceedingly fine wines rightfully rank high among the finest of Champagne's grower-producers.

LARMANDIER-BERNIER LATITUDE BLANC DE BLANCS À VERTUS EXTRA-BRUT NV $$

93 points • 2013 BASE VINTAGE • DISGORGED MAY 2016 • TASTED IN AUSTRALIA

35% reserves; vinified and aged in casks, wooden vats and stainless steel tanks on lees for almost 1 year with bâtonnage; unfined and unfiltered; aged in bottle at least 2 years; 3-4g/L dosage

Sourced exclusively from the same 'Latitude' of the generous terroir of southern Vertus, this is intentionally a less mineral, easy to drink blanc de blancs. The mandarin and orange exoticism of Vertus leaps from the glass, providing appeal and immediacy, magnificently pulled into line by well-focused acidity and outstanding salty chalk minerality. With enduring persistence and effortless line, this is a wonderful example of a fine-tuned, articulate expression of southern Vertus.

LARMANDIER-BERNIER LONGITUDE BLANC DE BLANCS PREMIER CRU EXTRA-BRUT NV $$

93 points • 2012 BASE VINTAGE • DISGORGED MAY 2016 • TASTED IN AUSTRALIA

40% reserves; two-thirds Vertus, one-third Avize, Cramant and a little Oger; vinified and aged in casks, wooden vats and stainless steel tanks on lees for almost 1 year with bâtonnage; unfined and unfiltered; aged in bottle at least 2 years; 4g/L dosage

A captivating wine, blended from four of chardonnay's most beguiling villages, sharing roughly the same 'longitude'. As always, the tremendous chalk minerality of these terroirs is most engaging. Apple and grapefruit with all the spicy complexity of barrel fermentation, lingering with excellent persistence and pronounced, frothing, salty chalk minerality. Barrel work contributes creamy harmony, while upholding the bright tension of chardonnay in this great season. Impressive.

LARMANDIER-BERNIER ROSÉ DE SAIGNÉE PREMIER CRU EXTRA-BRUT NV $$$

95 points • 100% 2013 • TASTED IN CHAMPAGNE AND AUSTRALIA

Vertus single-vineyard pinot noir; too young to be labelled as a vintage; old vines harvested ripe at very low yields; cold macerated 2-3 days for colour without tannin; fermented and aged 1 year in enamel-lined steel vat; aged 2 years in bottle; full malolactic fermentation; 3g/L dosage

This wine is a paradox of the highest order, a salute to the genius of its maker and the depth of its old-vine sources. How a 100% Côte des Blancs rosé from an elegant east-facing Vertus site can land midway between a graceful champagne rosé and an expressive red cherry pinot noir is truly astounding. Pierre Larmandier set out to make 'a rosé, not a white champagne with colour', marrying the power of pinot noir with the elegance of the village and, goodness, has he done it! It's magnificently youthful, alive with jubilant rose petal, pink pepper, strawberries, raspberries and greengage plums, vibrant, primary and characterfully expressive, layered with mixed spice and white pepper. It's framed in refreshingly elegant yet perfectly ripe acidity and wonderful chalk minerality of deeply penetrating structure that integrates seamlessly with super-fine tannins. Delightful harmony and persistence top off a brilliant rosé.

LARMANDIER-BERNIER TERRE DE VERTUS PREMIER CRU BLANC DE BLANCS BRUT NATURE 2009 $$$

94 points • TASTED IN CHAMPAGNE

Several parcels on similar terroirs spanning 2.5 hectares of Vertus mid-slopes; vinified and aged in casks, wooden vats and stainless steel tanks on lees for almost 1 year with bâtonnage; unfined and unfiltered; aged in bottle for at least 4 years; zero dosage

The intense mineral texture and layers of mouth-filling chalk of the northern slopes of Vertus learn much from the neighbouring grand cru of Le Mesnil-sur-Oger, and Larmandier is astute in separating these from the more rounded character of southern Vertus. Terre de Vertus is all about preserving this salt mineral fingerprint, which it does with laudable prowess, even in the ripe, 'solar' 2009 vintage. The precision of salty Vertus chalk provides definition to the flamboyant ripeness of Vertus, now evolved to a complex, toasty, spicy spectrum, accented with hints of liquorice. A wine of poise and balance, finishing very long and more creamy than ever. Signature Vertus.

LARMANDIER-BERNIER LES CHEMINS D'AVIZE GRAND CRU BLANC DE BLANCS EXTRA-BRUT 2010 $$$$

94 points • TASTED IN CHAMPAGNE

Single-vineyard Avize; vinified in casks and wooden vats and aged on lees with bâtonnage for almost 1 year; unfined and unfiltered; 2g/L dosage

'2010 was not supposed to be so good!' Larmandier exclaims, recalling grapes dripping with rain water as they were picking them, and losing 10–20% of volume to botrytis-infected grapes squashed in the picking bins. The result he's achieved is not only impressive for the harvest, it's a decent expression of the great terroir of Avize, infused with classic tension of salt minerality and surprisingly well-defined acid line for the season. It holds the freshness in apple and lemon fruit of extended persistence, backed with all the bottle-infused complexity of spice, honey, toast and anise. I predicted on first tasting in its desperate youth two years ago that it would benefit from short-term ageing to build complexity. That it has.

LARMANDIER-BERNIER LES CHEMINS D'AVIZE GRAND CRU BLANC DE BLANCS EXTRA-BRUT 2009 $$$$

95 points • TASTED IN AUSTRALIA

The evolution of champagne in bottle can represent a dramatic and at times unexpected transformation, and the reappearance of this vintage in my guide for the third edition running represents a stark contrast to its earlier showings. This small blend necessitated use of small barrels, and Larmandier thought the oak was a bit strong on release four years ago, but it found its happy place two years later in subtle almond complexity. It's since taken a turn, heightening the theatrics of oak-barrel fermentation in prominent toasty, caramel oak flavours and a touch of oak tannin structure. Elegant fruit from the flat of Avize in the intense 2009 season has built quite some stature in bottle, now powerful and generous with stone fruit, fig and baked apple fruit holding out amidst the oak onslaught on a long, full and generous finish, underscored by the refined, soft salt mineral texture of Avize chalk.

LARMANDIER-BERNIER VIEILLE VIGNE DE CRAMANT GRAND CRU EXTRA-BRUT 2007 $$$$

87 points • DISGORGED JANUARY 2014 • TASTED IN AUSTRALIA

Two nearby vineyards in the heart of Cramant; vines aged between 50 and 77 years; vinified and aged on lees in casks and wooden vats with bâtonnage for almost 1 year; unfined and unfiltered; aged in bottle at least 5 years; 2g/L dosage

To Larmandier, Cramant is a different world that deserves to be showcased solo. Like the Terre de Vertus, he prints the vintage only on the back label, 'because the place is more important than the vintage'. He says that in this special part of Cramant, his carefully cultivated old vines are less sensitive to seasonal fluctuations, and he could make a vintage every year. There's inherent power here, indicative of the intensity of one of the Côte des Blancs' strongest villages, tamed with the classic finesse of Larmandier's sensitive touch. It's showing significant development now, particularly from this older disgorgement, with honeycomb notes and orange rind, finishing with some vinegary notes. It has faded from its vibrant high point of two years ago.

LAURENT-PERRIER

(Lohr-rohn-Peh-riay)

6/10

51150 TOURS-SUR-MARNE

www.laurent-perrier.com

CHAMPAGNE

Laurent-Perrier

MAISON FONDÉE
1812

*L*aurent-Perrier is on a steep growth curve. Substantial expansion in recent years has seen the house climb to number five in Champagne by volume. A new cuverie, constructed in time for the 2009 harvest, added capacity for another 150 vins clairs and now handles production for the group, including de Castellane, Delamotte and Salon. With an annual production of 7 million bottles (almost two-thirds of which are L-P Brut), Laurent-Perrier is unusual in having found a reasonably comfortable equilibrium in that precarious balance between volume and finely tuned quality. These are champagnes with a flattering demeanour of precision, delicacy, elegance and tension, though some inconsistency has recently begun to creep into some cuvées.

Laurent-Perrier's success is less by virtue of its domain vineyard holdings, which supply just 11% of its total needs of 150 hectares, than of the skill and vision of its people. The talented Alain Terrier was its longstanding chef de cave from 1975 to 2005, and was succeeded by Michel Fauconnet, his offsider for more than 20 years. I have requested an audience with Michel countless times when visiting Champagne, and I very much look forward to meeting him. Hopefully next time.

The secret to Laurent-Perrier's wines today is buried deep within the history of a house that recently celebrated its 200th birthday. The late Bernard de Nonancourt, founding president of the Laurent-Perrier Group, was a visionary who spent half of the last century transforming and expanding the company. His innovations changed the face of modern champagne. Under his leadership, the house boldly launched its

non-vintage prestige cuvée, Grand Siècle, in 1957, a rosé well ahead of its time in 1968 (then considered a joke by the Champenois, now the best-selling champagne rosé in the world). Perhaps most influential of all, inspired by brewers of beer, Laurent-Perrier was the first house in Champagne to use stainless steel tanks in the 1960s.

De Nonancourt's vision was one of freshness, finesse and elegance based on chardonnay, which to this day maintains the majority stake in every cuvée (representing double Champagne's average) except rosé. No meunier is used, apart from a 15–20% touch in L-P Brut. This creates a house style of precision and tension, unusual among houses of this scale.

To celebrate its bicentenary in 2012, the house commissioned a major addition and renovation to its cuverie. In the same location as Champagne's first stainless steel tanks, the Grand Siècle winery is an atmospheric display of stainless steel reserve tanks custom-built with graceful curves, no seams, and narrow spouts to reduce oxidation.

Laurent-Perrier has a very real commitment to sustainability: former vineyard manager Christelle Rinville refused to fly in aeroplanes, encouraging workers to use bicycles, plant grasses in the mid-rows and use only non-invasive chemicals in all estate vineyards. The winery is almost self-sufficient in its use of water.

The tight, chardonnay-driven house style is softened through malolactic fermentation in all cuvées, and long lees ageing of at least four years at 11°C in 10 kilometres of cellars under the house in Tours-sur-Marne.

Regrettably, consumers remain oblivious to Laurent-Perrier's long ageing. The house fails to disclose disgorgement dates and base vintages on labels, and also refuses to provide this information when requested, for reasons I fail to understand. I was declined this information yet again this year, though I did discover how to decode the cork codes. The two digits represent the year (inverted) and the first letter (A–D) is the quarter – so, for instance, A31HO was disgorged in the first quarter of 2013.

These are long-ageing wines of a clean sophistication that transcend the scale of this operation.

LAURENT-PERRIER LA CUVÉE BRUT NV $$

90 points • DISGORGED APRIL–JUNE 2016 • TASTED IN AUSTRALIA
91 points • DISGORGED JANUARY–MARCH 2013 • TASTED IN AUSTRALIA

50-55% chardonnay, 30-35% pinot, 15-20% meunier; 20-30% reserves; aged 4 years on lees; 10g/L dosage

At 62% of Laurent-Perrier's production, this cuvée alone accounts for around 5 million bottles annually, which makes its high proportion of chardonnay and long ageing all the more impressive. A new name and evolution in the cépage and reserves were top secret when this bottle reached me, but its contents remain true to the original L-P Brut style. This is a happy party quaffer in a fresh and fruity style, with primary lemon zest, red apple, white peach and strawberry fruit of fragrant appeal. Tangy acidity is comfortably balanced by well-integrated dosage, finishing with a touch of phenolic bitterness in a 2016 disgorgement, but clean and fresh in 2013.

LAURENT-PERRIER ULTRA BRUT NATURE NV $$$

91 points • DISGORGED OCTOBER–DECEMBER 2016 • TASTED IN AUSTRALIA
93 points • DISGORGED APRIL–JUNE 2014 • TASTED IN AUSTRALIA

55% chardonnay, 45% pinot noir; bunch selection of grapes with high sugar and low acidity from 15 villages in ripe vintages; aged 6 years on lees; zero dosage

Laurent-Perrier has a very long history with zero dosage, having first launched its 'Grand Vins Sans Sucre' in the 1800s, relaunched by Bernard de Nonancourt in 1981. Today, this cuvée is champagne's best-selling brut nature, in a well-balanced and highly strung apéritif style. Clean nashi pear, lemon and grapefruit are accented, with subtle flinty reductive notes and almond meal complexity beginning to build in older disgorgements. It's razor tight in its lemon-juice acid line, finishing bracingly dry, yet upholding freshness and purity. Zero dosage gives full voice to pronounced salt mineral definition. This is a well-assembled zero dosage for champagne die-hards to drink with oysters.

The Champagne Guide

GRAND SIÈCLE BY LAURENT-PERRIER NV $$$$$

95 points • DISGORGED APRIL–JUNE 2016 • TASTED IN AUSTRALIA
97 points • TASTED IN AUSTRALIA

55% chardonnay from Avize, Cramant and Le Mesnil-sur-Oger; 45% pinot from Ambonnay, Bouzy and Mailly-Champagne; aged 7-8 years on lees

De Nonancourt's vision was to produce a multi-vintage prestige cuvée able to maintain consistent quality. This is achieved by blending only grand cru fruit from the best crus in the finest years declared by Laurent-Perrier. The blend places it among the oldest champagnes on the shelves. Sadly, the consumer is oblivious to all this, as the bottle gives no clue to either its disgorgement date or its splendid maturity. Despite a huge internal debate, the house refuses to budge on this, and declines to disclose base vintages even on my request. This makes managing collections a challenge, which is a shame, as Grand Siècle ages magnificently, long beyond its release.

Even in its grand maturity, this wine displays great poise and definition. Crunchy grapefruit and nashi pear are accented with an enticing reductive note of gunflint. It simultaneously celebrates long lees age in layers of buttered toast, vanilla nougat and a creamy, silky texture amidst mineral-driven structure. It closes with excellent persistence, marked by subtle phenolic bitterness. One bottle was fine, focused, coiled, reticent and enduring, while another at a different time and place lacked something of the vibrancy it has displayed in the past. With no hint as to the vintage composition of either, it's difficult to ascertain why.

LAURENT-PERRIER MILLÉSIMÉ BRUT 2007 $$$

92 points • DISGORGED JULY–SEPTEMBER 2016 • TASTED IN AUSTRALIA

50% chardonnay from Chouilly, Cramant, Oger and Le Mesnil-sur-Oger; 50% pinot from Verzy, Verzenay, Mailly, Louvois and Bouzy

This is an approachable vintage for Laurent-Perrier, having already attained a wonderful apogée in its development curve at nine years of age. It upholds a bright medium-straw hue and primary lemon zest, nashi pear, fennel, even white pepper nuances, opening into black cherry notes, prominently supported by the creamy, cuddly complexity of lees age in roast nuts, vanilla and nougat. It holds good persistence on the finish, marked by a subtle phenolic bitterness.

LAURENT-PERRIER MILLÉSIMÉ BRUT 2006 $$$

92 points • TASTED IN AUSTRALIA

The warm and immediate 2006 vintage makes for a soft and creamy Laurent-Perrier, with notes of white peach, grapefruit, pear, even mint. Its structure relies equally on acid drive as subtle phenolic grip and finely structured, chalk-infused minerality, having built softly textural, creamy, nutty character and a hint of nutmeg during time on lees. It shows relaxed balance and appeal, without persistence or endurance for further ageing.

LAURENT-PERRIER CUVÉE ROSÉ BRUT NV $$$

93 points • DISGORGED APRIL–JUNE 2016 • TASTED IN AUSTRALIA
91 points • DISGORGED JULY–SEPTEMBER 2014 • TASTED IN AUSTRALIA

100% pinot noir from 10 different crus, predominantly in the Montagne de Reims, including Ambonnay, Bouzy, Louvois and Tours-sur-Marne; hand sorted; aged 4 years on lees

Laurent-Perrier macerates its rosé for 48–72 hours, depending on fruit ripeness, until the colour is fixed and the aroma resembles freshly picked raspberries. So crucial is timing, legend has it that the first chef de cave, Edouard Leclerc, slept by the tank to stop it just in time! This wine has achieved that elusive ideal of volume and finesse; the world's best-selling rosé champagne epitomises the ultra-restraint of rosé's finest expressions. All the more remarkable for the challenging saignée method. Its latest incarnation carries a little more colour, character and structure, a medium- to full-salmon hue and layers of wild strawberries, raspberries, red cherries and pink pepper. There's more tannin structure here than this cuvée has presented before, with finely structured grip that melds seamlessly with gentle chalk mineral structure. Such prominent mouthfeel confidently steps this cuvée up to protein-rich fare. Earlier disgorgements show some dry dustiness yet uphold mineral mouthfeel and good persistence.

LAURENT-PERRIER ALEXANDRA GRANDE CUVÉE ROSÉ 2004 $$$$$

95 points • TASTED IN AUSTRALIA

80% grand cru pinot noir from Ambonnay, Bouzy and Verzenay; 20% grand cru chardonnay from Avize, Cramant and Le Mesnil-sur-Oger; macerated together; aged 10 years on lees; 7–8g/L dosage

Now in its fourth year in the market, this cuvée is in an enticing place in a fresh new disgorgement. From its disposition of calm maturity on release, I'm again surprised and impressed with how evenly it has evolved, upholding its medium-salmon hue and copper tints and its elegant and balanced complexity. Red cherry, raspberry and red liquorice fruits are evolving evenly as secondary, savoury complexity of anise and roast tomato rises, and enticing, smoky, tertiary complexity begins. A long finish is carried by a textural mouthfeel, mineral texture and soft tannin structure, with dry extract lending subtle firmness. This cuvée continues to blossom with time, and I have never seen it more complex, balanced and irresistible.

Laurent-Perrier's grand new reserve tanks celebrate the first house in Champagne to use stainless steel tanks in the 1960s.

The Champagne Guide

Le Brun-Servenay

(Ler Bru-Sair-veh-nay)

14 Place Léon Bourgeois 51190 Avize

www.champagnelebrun.com

*W*hen Patrick Le Brun's parents were married in 1955, they brought together the house of Le Brun in Avize and the estate of Servenay in Mancy in the Coteaux Sud d'Épernay. His estate remains a seamless, if somewhat unusual, union of the two families, maintaining the Le Brun cellars directly next door to Erick de Sousa in Avize, and the Servenay press house and cuverie, six kilometres over the hill in Mancy, rebuilt in 2013. Le Brun's almost six hectares of enviably positioned chardonnay in Cramant, Oger and (especially) Avize provide 80% of the estate's needs, supplemented by about 1.5 hectares of pinot noir and meunier from Mancy and its surrounding villages. These are distinctive champagnes in their remarkable freshness, pristine purity and staggering longevity, particularly expressive of the salty chalk mineral signature of Avize, heightened through the blocking of malolactic fermentation across all cuvées.

It wasn't many generations ago that malolactic fermentation became commonplace in Champagne, before which every wine of the region was blessed with the sustaining endurance, if at times disarming austerity, of malic acidity.

Those houses and growers who have conscientiously retained malic acidity while upholding carefully balanced ripeness are due high admiration.

Patrick Le Brun struggled to convince his father to block malolactic fermentation, maintaining that malic acidity is crucial for preserving the freshness and smoothness in his grapes' aromas. It also charges his cuvées with tremendous sustaining power. I have tasted Patrick's cuvées back to the 1970s on more than one occasion with him, and it is breathtakingly apparent

that these champagnes mature at but half the pace that one might expect. Even pre-1982 cuvées with full malolactic fermentation still look backward in their evolution.

Built on majestic grand cru chardonnay and finished with low dosages of typically 5–7g/L, with most cuvées also available as extra brut of typically 3.5g/L dosage, these could be challenging champagnes were it not for Le Brun's meticulous attention to picking at perfect ripeness, his exacting precision in vinification, and his patience in long ageing in the cellar. Freshness is preserved through vinification in tank, with just a small amount of red wine in barrel for rosé.

'Our purpose is to translate in the glass the elegance and minerality of the terroir of our vineyards,' declares

Le Brun, the fifth generation of the Servenay family, and the fourth on the Le Brun side to tend grapes in these sites. His vines are old by Champagne standards, some older than 80 years, with roots that plunge 10–12 metres into the chalk. 'We plough and plant grass in the mid-rows to encourage competition and force the roots deeper,' he explains. Yields of 60–80hL/hectare (60–80% of Champagne's average) are important for achieving full ripeness.

The champagnes of Le Brun-Servenay live up to their brief with exacting clarity, and represent outstanding value for money.

Le Brun-Servenay Brut Sélection Blanc de Blancs Grand Cru NV $$

94 points • 35% 2015 base vintage • Tasted in Australia

25% 2012, 20% 2011 and 20% 2010 reserves; 90% Avize and Cramant, 10% Oger; vines of average age 25 years; no malolactic fermentation; aged at least 3 years on lees; 7g/L dosage; DIAM closure

The pristine delights of Le Brun-Servenay are proclaimed for all to relish even in its refreshing, entry apéritif. It's a beautifully pale, fresh and pure expression of perfectly ripe chardonnay, alive with pristine lemon and granny smith apple and the subtle complexity of almond nougat. Impressively concentrated fruit presence is supported by a creamy bead and subtle dosage, striking an exacting balance for a style of tension and definition. The salty chalk minerality of (mostly) Avize and Cramant define a beautifully structured palate, charged with the coiled potential of electric malic acidity, making for an exceptionally affordable and accurate expression of the Côte des Blancs.

Le Brun-Servenay Cuvée Chardonnay Vieilles Vignes Extra-Brut 2006 $$

95 points • Tasted in Australia

Blanc de blancs from Avize for elegance, Oger for minerality and Cramant for body and freshness; 80–100-year-old vines; no malolactic fermentation; aged 9 years on lees; 4.5g/L dosage; DIAM closure

Le Brun-Servenay's malic freshness and exceptionally mineral grand crus unite to energise even the otherwise rounded and early-drinking 2006 season with a definition and stamina that lifts it above most from this vintage. It will confidently outlive most, too. The talent of old vines to tap into the deep, salty chalk mineral structure of Avize, Oger and Cramant is proclaimed resoundingly in a magnificently structured palate of bright malic acidity and enduring chalk minerality. Struck-flint reduction meets notes of white pepper and the toasty development of a generous vintage at more than a decade of age to create an enticingly complex and seamless accord. Lemon and apple fruit coast long and effortlessly through a finish that froths and foams with pristine bubbles of chalk minerality.

Le Brun-Servenay Cuvée Exhilarante Vieilles Vignes Millésime 2008 $$$

95 points • Tasted in Australia

80% chardonnay from Avize, Cramant and Oger; 10% pinot noir for structure; 10% meunier for fruitiness; Le Brun's oldest vines 60–80 years old on soil 15cm above chalk; no malolactic fermentation; aged 8 years on lees; 4g/L dosage; DIAM closure

The recipe of full malic acidity in chardonnay from the austere village of Avize in the electric 2008 season, with extra-brut dosage, should be enough to instil terror even in the most fanatical champagne die-hard. And yet, testimony first to the fruit depth and ripeness of Le Brun's old vines, second to strategically placed tweaks of pinot noir and meunier, and third but not least to Le Brun's mastery in both the vines and the cellars, this is a cuvée infused with a presence and generosity that define seamless balance. Lemon and grapefruit are tickled with the red apple and strawberry fruit of pinot noir and meunier, blessed with all the brioche, honey and nougat character of eight years of lees age. Bright, focused malic acid churns magnificently amidst the signature salt chalk minerality of Avize through a very long and full finish. It would be worthy of an even higher rating if it carried a touch more freshness on the finish.

Le Brun-Servenay Blanc de Blancs X.B. Extra Brut 2.5 NV $$$

94 points • Tasted in Australia

Chardonnay from Avize, Cramant and Oger; no malolactic fermentation; aged at least 3 years on lees; 2.5g/L dosage; DIAM closure

Patrick Le Brun teamed up with Les Crayères sommelier Philippe Jamesse to create his X.B. (Extra Brut) cuvées. In the hands of mere mortals, the chalk mineral texture of the great Côte des Blancs grand crus in concert with the vivacity of chardonnay's malic acidity would scream out for the calming presence of dosage. But this talented duo has infused this dashing cuvée with a core of fruit presence and depth, an outstanding acid line and precise chalk mineral spine, with just an invisible dash of sweetness, without any hint of hardness or austerity. Enticing, exact lemon and granny smith apple fruit is evolving steadily into layers of spice, gingernut biscuits, even hints of dried nectarine. It all rolls and propels with determination and energy on a long finish.

The long, sweeping, east-facing slope of Avize defines some of Champagne's finest and most age-worthy terroir for chardonnay.

LOUIS ROEDERER

(Loo-ii Roh-dehr-air)

8/10

21 BOULEVARD LUNDY 51053 REIMS

www.champagne-roederer.com

MAISON FONDÉE EN 1776

LOUIS ROEDERER

CHAMPAGNE

Louis Roederer is unlike any other champagne house of its magnitude. The largest independent, family-owned and managed champagne maker of all is privileged to 240 hectares of superbly located vineyards, supplying a grand 70% of its needs for an annual production of 3 million bottles. With 410 blocks and 450 tanks and casks at his disposal, chef de cave Jean-Baptiste Lécaillon describes his role as 'à la carte winemaking'. He hates the word 'blend'. 'We don't blend, we combine,' he says. 'I love art, and like a great painter we add colour rather than blending.' There are few in Champagne today with an intellect as sharp, an attention to detail as acute and a nerve as strong as Lécaillon. For 17 years, he has championed extraordinary initiatives in Roederer's vineyards unparalleled in the region, and a regime in the winery to match. Never have his wines looked more characterful, or more precise.

There was once a time when Louis Roederer was purely a négociant house, but over the years it has strategically acquired vineyards to amass one of the largest proportions of estate vines among the big champagne houses. These are well situated across some 16 villages, spanning the Montagne de Reims, Vallée de la Marne and Côte des Blancs. More than two-thirds are grand cru level.

All of Louis Roederer's vintage wines are assembled exclusively from estate properties, and even its entry Brut Premier NV now boasts 55% estate fruit, and rising.

'I do not say that Roederer is a champagne house for the vintage wines,' says Lécaillon. 'We are three growers, one in Montagne de Reims, one in Vallée de la Marne and one in Côte des Blancs.'

Roederer is continuing to expand its estate and has averaged an additional two hectares every year for the past decade, all on chalk soils. 'Chalk is the style of

Roederer,' Lécaillon declares. 'It produces more focused wines, while clay produces more round and soft styles.'

The vast majority of estate vines are on chalk, with a particular focus on the chalk-rich Côte des Blancs, home to 80 hectares of Roederer vines. The company owns no vineyards beyond Cumières in the Vallée de la Marne because of the higher clay content here. Some 45 parcels spanning 50 hectares are devoted to Cristal, all on chalk.

'We have wonderful terroirs and our goal is to express each of them,' Lécaillon says. 'We have a new era in Champagne today, coming back to the terroir; forgetting about all the know-how in the cellar, forgetting about the salt and the pepper, but getting back to the raw ingredients.' For an operation of this scale, the attention to detail in the vineyards is unprecedented. Old vines are used to limit yields

The Champagne Guide

(Cristal vineyards average a huge 42 years of age and some date from 1930), as is green harvesting, in what Lécaillon dubs 'haute couture viticulture'. Over the past 15 years, he has customised the pruning, budding, trellising, ploughing and harvesting of each vineyard to suit the cuvée to which it is destined.

A team of 800 pickers sorts fruit in the vineyard, and it is sorted again before it is pressed. 'The only way I can get quality is by paying pickers by the hour, not by the kilogram,' he emphasises. This is rare in Champagne.

BIODYNAMICS ON A GRAND SCALE

Most remarkably, Roederer now tends 87 hectares of vineyards biodynamically (though only 10 hectares are certified biodynamic), including more than half of those that contribute to Cristal, with a goal of reaching 100% by 2020. An incredible 25 hectares are ploughed by horse. Biodynamics on such a scale is unheard of in Champagne, and Roederer's operation is the biggest in the region by an order of magnitude, and one of the biggest in France.

'I am not a biodynamicist,' Lécaillon reveals. 'But I think biodynamics is the best school. Organics simply says "No to chemicals", but biodynamics says "Yes to life"! I am not a believer in biodynamics as such, but I believe what I see. I have been doing trials of biodynamic and organic wines for 16 years and there is always more texture in the biodynamic wines.' In tasting his 2015 vins clairs, I was amazed just how much more seamless integration and chalk minerality was expressed in biodynamic plots compared with traditional viticulture in the same vineyard.

In the village of Cumières, where Roederer has a strong presence, the tiny, fanatical biodynamic grower Vincent Laval recently mentioned that he prefers Roederer's attention to viticulture to that of small growers using industrial methods. High endorsement.

Lécaillon has set aside plots for experimentation in each of the three regions of Champagne, and fruit from biodynamic vines is compared with traditional viticulture from the same village. I was surprised at just how much more salty minerality and texture was evident in 2012 vins clairs from biodynamic sources.

'When the soil looks better, the vines look better, the fruit looks better, and we get more ripeness, more acidity and more iodine salinity to the minerality,' explains Lécaillon, for whom ripeness is 'the game'. His aim is to pick ripe and 'make wine first, champagne second'. He believes that 'dry extract, ripeness and fruitiness are the key, and a great champagne needs phenolics from oak or from fruit', and goes so far as to suggest that ripe skin phenolics are more important than acidity for ageing potential, though he does qualify this by emphasising that acidity and phenolics must be in balance.

He attributes greater precision in biodynamic fruit to decreased vigour in the vines, and greater mineral expression to deeper roots. 'We cannot explain this with measurements, but this is the way with biodynamics – we can only see it by tasting.'

Roederer began experimenting with biodynamics in 2003, after a false start in 2000. Seventeen years on, Lécaillon says it will take 40 years to draw any solid conclusions. But he has discovered that a different approach is necessary in each region, easier on well-draining chalk in the Côte des Blancs and Montagne de Reims, and harder on clay in the Vallée de la Marne.

'There are some years in which biodynamics is much better and some years in which it is not so effective,' Lécaillon explains. 'It performs well in vintages in which the vines struggle under particularly wet or dry conditions.' In the wet 2011 and 2014 seasons, he harvested his best fruit in biodynamic vineyards. He suspects this may be a result of thicker skins providing greater resilience in biodynamic fruit.

While he is convinced of the philosophy of biodynamics, certification is not the goal. 'We see it as just one means of achieving terroir expression,' he says. 'We are constantly learning.'

This learning curve was particularly steep in 2012, and Roederer reported losses of 30–50% in some plots, and greater under biodynamics. 'It involves so much risk,' Lécaillon explains. 'Biodynamics removes all the safety of chemicals, and if it's not done properly you can really get caught quickly.' He accepts the loss of 2012 and suggests that the experience was helpful for his team to really get on top of biodynamics.

At the end of vintage 2014, I shadowed Lécaillon for a day in his vineyards and was stunned by a stark difference between healthy biodynamic vines and struggling organic plots on neighbouring sites. I took 7500 words of notes and learnt more about viticulture in Champagne that day than ever before. 'In order to survive we must decrease the chemicals that we use,' he told me. 'By removing the comfort of chemicals, my team has to work like vignerons, to really understand the terroir, not like robots. It really is a culture of coming back to the terroir.'

À LA CARTE WINEMAKING

Lécaillon's aim is to emphasise terroir and downplay house style and varietal character, which he achieves by pushing for ripeness, encouraging a little oxidation at harvest, and blocking malolactic fermentation.

'My work in the vineyards is more important than my job in the cellar,' he emphasises.

Roederer's focus on its vineyards opens up opportunities for greater refinement in the winery. Regulated yields allow harvesting at full ripeness, rendering chaptalisation unnecessary, unless the season is very difficult – an impressive mandate, and I believe unprecedented at this scale in Champagne. In recent years, wild yeast ferments have been introduced. Biodynamic plots are harvested early, fermented wild, and used to seed other ferments.

Malolactic fermentation is generally avoided, except in some higher-acid parcels destined for the non-vintage Brut Premier, generally just 20–25% of the blend. 'The only way to avoid malo is to produce fruit in the vineyard that doesn't require it – ripe fruit with soft malic acid,' notes Lécaillon, who prefers to obtain the right acid balance in the vineyard than the winery.

'Malolactic fermentation was first conducted in Champagne in 1965,' he points out. 'It can be useful in a difficult year, but it must be a safety tool, not a systematic procedure, and this is especially true with global warming.' The house completely blocked malolactic fermentation on all estate and contract fruit in 2016, 2015, 2012, 2009, 2006, 2003, 2002 and 1999.

'Malolactic and oak are not the house style,' he reveals. 'Terroir is the house style, and malolactic and oak are just there according to what the grapes need.'

Basket presses run 24/7 throughout vintage, as it takes three hours to press the first cuvée. Unusually, the solids are retained, producing a cloudy juice. 'We feel this expresses terroir better and gives greater protection against oxidation,' Lécaillon explains.

A new cuverie was built in 2007 to enable every block to be vinified separately in a custom-made tank or large oak vat, according to the power of the fruit tasted in the vineyard. 'Each tank and vat is a vineyard with a roof!' Lécaillon suggests. 'My workers must think of each parcel in the winery as a site, not as a lot.' Oak fermentation was reintroduced in 1999, and today about 20% of the vintage is fermented in oak, and aged on lees with bâtonnage for texture, phenolics and roundness.

Lécaillon does not consider phenolics to be a dirty word in Champagne. 'Oak phenolics and the right fruit phenolics draw out salinity on the sides of the tongue and bring out another dimension to the flavour. We hate oxidation – it is a betrayal of terroir,' adds Lécaillon. 'Lees contact and bâtonnage protect from oxidation.'

This creates a reductive style, which has at times produced savoury overtones that distract from fruit purity in Roederer's vintage wines, though this has been

There are few in Champagne with an intellect as sharp, an attention to detail as acute and a nerve as strong as Jean-Baptiste Lécaillon.

better controlled in recent years. 'I make wines reductively because I want them to age.' Vins clairs fermented in oak show richer texture, without taking on oak flavour. Reserve wines are aged in 150 large old oak foudres (15–50 years of age), and *liqueur d'expédition* is kept in casks for as long as a decade. Four vintages of *liqueur d'expédition* are kept in vat at all times to allow the dosage for each blend to be tweaked. Dosages of typically 8–11g/L sometimes appear a little high for the natural ripeness of Roederer's fruit.

Non-vintage wines are aged on lees in bottle for three years, vintage wines for four years, and Cristal for six or seven (with the enduring 2008 Cristal due to land in 2017, after the 2009, the first ever non-sequential release). This requires a large stock of 18 million bottles squirrelled away in Roederer's cellars, with 3 million leaving every year.

Roederer's attention to detail in its vineyards and winery shine even in its non-vintage Brut Premier. In 2007, Lécaillon constructed a gleaming, state-of-the-art, all-new facility devoted exclusively to this cuvée (and a dedicated rosé facility in the same year). This facilitated its own dedicated team, earlier classification of fruit, fewer bottlings (just five each year of an identical blend) and less pumping, all of which he credits for the rise in Brut Premier. Representing 80% of the production of the house, this is a masterfully assembled cuvée.

Lécaillon describes champagne as a 'permanent innovation'. Such is his attention to tuning the finest details that he sells 5–10% of his crop that is not up to standard every year. He also tweaks the pressure to suit each cuvée, bottling riper vintages at five atmospheres, sometimes as low as four, and more classic, lean seasons at six.

The Champagne Guide

He emphasises that age in bottle on cork is crucial for his cuvées, and after three years he prefers the effect of natural cork to DIAM. His batch testing of corks is the most rigorous I have seen anywhere. Of every batch of 100,000 corks, 460 are agitated in water for 45 minutes and the water then tasted. This is repeated for 200 batches every year, and sometimes a batch is tested twice, and if a single tainted cork is found, the entire batch is rejected. His team rejects one batch in three. No doubt this is why, in all my years of tasting, I've only ever found one cork-tainted bottle of Roederer. If only every house were so stringent in its cork testing.

In a fantastic development in disclosure, Louis Roederer has followed Krug's lead, and its website and app now reveal the base vintage, year of bottling and year of disgorgement from the bottling code or QR code of any cuvée. May more houses do likewise!

Louis Roederer Brut Premier NV $$

93 points • 2012 BASE VINTAGE • DISGORGED MARCH 2016 • 40% CHARDONNAY, 40% PINOT, 20% MEUNIER • A BLEND OF 40 PLOTS FROM 6 VINTAGES • TASTED IN CHAMPAGNE AND AUSTRALIA
93 points • 2011 BASE VINTAGE • 46–47% PINOT, 37% CHARDONNAY, 16–17% MEUNIER • 30% RESERVES FROM 2010, 2009, 2008, 2007, 2006, 2005 AND 2002 • TASTED IN AUSTRALIA

5% of base wines from estate vines fermented and matured in oak casks with weekly bâtonnage; reserves fermented in tanks and matured in large oak casks for up to 8 years; 30% malolactic fermentation; 5-5.5 atmospheres of pressure; aged 3 years on lees; 9.5g/L dosage; 2.4 million bottles

I've long adored Brut Premier, a masterful presentation of impeccably ripe fruit of intricate balance and abundant appeal: a dependable bargain in the non-vintage champagne stakes. Until the 2009 base, Brut Premier reserves came from a solera, in Lécaillon's view, lacking focus and 'showing too much character of having been made in the cellar'. The solera is no more, bringing greater focus, more precise mineral articulation and greater emphasis on ripe fruit. Dosage was sensibly dropped from 10–11g/L to 9.5g/L. The 2012 base represents a Brut Premier that upholds the signature accord of this blend, uniting pretty lemon blossom, apple and pear fruit, the spicy, toasty, nutmeg allure of barrel fermentation and bottle age, the racy freshness of malic acidity and a fine cage of chalk mineral structure. There's a subtle note of dusty dryness that I've not seen in Brut Premier before, slightly marking purity of fruit expression and lending a hint of phenolic dryness to its texture on the finish. The 2011 base is a triumph for its difficult season, an excellent Brut Premier that captures the depth of Roederer in red fruits, proclaiming a little more pinot noir than usual, with all the biscuity, brioche and ginger complexity of deep reserves in barrels. The vintage lends its characteristic touch of dry grip to the finish, yet less pronounced than in most from this season. A cuvée of excellent acid drive and well-integrated dosage. Bravo.

Louis Roederer Brut Vintage 2009 $$$

94 points • TASTED IN AUSTRALIA

70% pinot noir, 30% chardonnay; 18% vinified in oak casks; no malolactic fermentation; aged 4 years on lees; 9g/L dosage; 5% of Roederer's estate fruit is devoted to this cuvée

The glowing aura of the hot and ripe 2009 season has given birth to a Roederer vintage of generous proportions of fig, peach, red apple, grapefruit and even pineapple, singing with all the depth of pinot noir, bolstered by rich layers of ginger, freshly baked butter cake and spice. It's succulent and enticing, and for all of its confident generosity, it's well tempered by masterfully integrated malic acidity, prominent, salty chalk minerality and impeccably gauged phenolic grip. The accord is compelling, finishing very long and linear, making for an accurate, captivating and eminently drinkable take on the season.

LOUIS ROEDERER BLANC DE BLANCS 2010 $$$

93 points • TASTED IN AUSTRALIA

20% vinified in oak casks; 9g/L dosage; 5% of Roederer's estate fruit is devoted to this cuvée

Enticing reductive nuances of struck flint and gunsmoke provide an alluring complexity to a wonderful contrast between the succulent white peach generosity of ripe fruit, the crunch of grapefruit and the tension of malic acidity. Partial oak fermentation and five years on lees have built impressive depth of roast nut and mixed-spice complexity, with a subtle nuance of smoked ham. Fine, pronounced chalk minerality proclaims the chalk of great grand cru sites. A generous and rounded vintage to drink right away.

LOUIS ROEDERER BLANC DE BLANCS 2009 $$$

94 points • TASTED IN AUSTRALIA

Avize, Le Mesnil-sur-Oger and Cramant; plots chosen because they are the ripest in their villages, to give the full expression of chardonnay; 10% matured in oak tuns with weekly bâtonnage; no malolactic fermentation; aged 5 years on lees; a low 4.5 atmospheres of pressure to heighten creaminess in the mousse; 9g/L dosage

Beautifully complex, contrasting the immense chalk minerality of Avize with the energy of full malic acidity and the subtle spice of large barrel fermentation. The tension and mineral expression in this wine are magnificent, balancing gentle phenolic texture and drawing the finish out very long and linear. Low pressure brings a creaminess to this textured and focused style. As always, it will benefit from years to build complexity and integration.

LOUIS ROEDERER VINTAGE ROSÉ 2011 $$$

89 points • DISGORGED JANUARY 2014 • TASTED IN AUSTRALIA

63% pinot, 37% chardonnay; 22% vinified in oak casks; saignée method, blended after cold maceration according to colour; aged 4 years on lees; 9g/L dosage; about 10% of Roederer's estate fruit is devoted to this cuvée

The elegance and multidimensional complexity inherent to the Roederer style is well articulated in this pale rosé of subtle strawberry hull and watermelon character. Regrettably, this release is inevitably marked with the challenges of the 2011 season, with the dusty, stale peanut aromas and flavours and the coarse texture of imperfect fruit making for an astringent and challenging style.

LOUIS ROEDERER VINTAGE ROSÉ 2010 $$$

95 points • TASTED IN CHAMPAGNE
93 points • TASTED IN AUSTRALIA

62% pinot noir from the south-facing slopes of Cumières, 38% chardonnay from the north-facing slopes of Chouilly; cold macerated for 5-8 days; 15% vinified in oak tuns without malolactic fermentation; age 4 years on lees; 9g/L dosage

Lécaillon says north-facing Chouilly chardonnay is the New World equivalent of adding acid and life. The result unites the body and flesh of Cumières pinot noir with the tension of Chouilly chardonnay in this pretty pale salmon-tinted rosé. My first encounter in Champagne revealed a gorgeously fresh style of vibrant acid tension and excellent red cherry and strawberry fruit definition, at every moment elegant and refined. Fine salty chalk mineral texture defined beautiful structure, which lingered long and graceful, promising a long life. A triumph for a difficult season. A year later in Australia, it had grown into a more creamy and generous style, its colour taking on a faint copper tint, its structure showing more pronounced texture and its flavours revealing touches of savoury complexity.

LOUIS ROEDERER ET PHILIPPE STARCK BRUT NATURE MILLESIMÉ 2009 $$$

94 points • TASTED IN AUSTRALIA

66% Cumières pinot noir, 34% Cumières chardonnay; picked and pressed together; half fermented in tanks and half in oak barrels; aged on lees prior to bottling for 8-9 months; no malolactic fermentation; low pressure of 4.5 atmospheres to heighten creaminess; zero dosage; about 5% of Roederer's estate fruit is devoted to this cuvée

Roederer's first new cuvée since 1974 was conceived in the estate's remarkable 10-hectare biodynamic vineyard in Cumières. 'The terroir had to be the key,' Lécaillon told me as we stood in the heart of the vineyard. 'This was the secret to making this wine. I didn't set out to make a zero-dosage wine, I just found that the terroir didn't need it. The paradox of this cuvée is that the marketing is about Philippe Starck, but the cuvée is all about the terroir.' After the inaugural 2006 release heralded a remarkably well balanced wine thanks to its warm and ripe season, Lécaillon has tactically waited until the sunny 2009 vintage to repeat the same act.

There is generosity here of yellow summer fruits, pear and apple, pulling into a tensely honed tail that highlights brilliant, glistening minerality even from Cumiérés' dark clay soils, impeccably framed by tight yet delightfully ripe and pure malic acidity. Here is evidence that the masterful harmony achieved with malic acidity without dosage in the first release was no fluke, and kudos to Lécaillon for pulling off the same tactical act again. Lingering complexity of brioche and roast almonds coast through a long and honed finish that flitters with spice. A unique and crafted cuvée that will benefit from at least five years to fully come together. It's again definitively Roederer and characteristically Cumières. I don't mind the uncharacteristic informality of its love-or-hate label, but I wish it declared its Cumières origins and the remarkable story of the most incredible biodynamic vineyard in all of Champagne. That's what this cuvée is really all about.

LOUIS ROEDERER CRISTAL BRUT 2009 $$$$$

95 points • DISGORGED OCTOBER 2014 • TASTED IN CHAMPAGNE AND AUSTRALIA

60% pinot noir, 40% chardonnay; a pool of 50 hectares of vines averaging 42 years of age on the most chalky mid-slopes, yielding 50% less than the appellation; 60% biodynamic vineyards, with a goal of 100% by 2020; 16% fermented in 60-hL casks with bâtonnage for power, vinosity and a touch of spice and vanilla complexity; no malolactic fermentation; 8.5g/L dosage; typically 150,000-300,000 bottles

The secret of Cristal is that it's built to age, and its reductive style screams out for some years of post-disgorgement to truly blossom. For its price and reputation, Cristal is a relatively early release in the world of prestige cuvées, though Lécaillon points out that 30 years ago it enjoyed only three years on lees, when he joined the company 20 years ago it only had four, and now it has six or seven. Notwithstanding, Cristal is the first 2009 prestige cuvée to hit the streets.

Lécaillon describes 2009 as a 'tutti-fruity year', yet holding its freshness, luminous and bright. He has given it the lowest dosage of any Cristal ever. It's a generous and creamy cuvée, true to its dry, hot, sunny and ripe vintage. It leads out succulent and complex, with juicy peach and apple fruit, even hints of pineapple, and the complexity of age in fresh, spicy ginger, honey biscuits and nougat. Subtle gunflint reduction brings complexity, while respecting the purity of its fruit. It changes up a gear on the finish, gaining velocity and energy from the tension of malic acidity and the pronounced texture of grapefruit pith that embodies a seamless accord between fine, salt chalk minerality, the mouthfeel of lees age and subtle phenolic bitterness. These elements all settle comfortably into place in balance and harmony, albeit disparate at this youthful age. As ever with Cristal, all it asks for is time.

LOUIS ROEDERER CRISTAL BRUT 2007 $$$$$

96 points • TASTED IN CHAMPAGNE AND AUSTRALIA

As for the 2009, except 58% pinot noir, 42% chardonnay; 15% matured in oak barrels with weekly bâtonnage; no malolactic fermentation; aged 5 years on lees; 9.5g/L dosage

2007 is an enticing season for Cristal, contrasting a secondary bouquet that rejoices in the brioche, ginger, cake warm-out-of-the-oven, nougat and mixed-spice complexity of lees age with the palate vibrancy of lemon and crunchy red apple, and the generous depth of fig. Vibrant malic acidity pulls the whole fanfare into a toned and athletic finish of bright acid drive and fine chalk mineral texture, basking in the radiance of 2007 acidity and the pronounced minerality of chalk vineyards. It's a Cristal charged to age for the medium term.

LOUIS ROEDERER CRISTAL BRUT 1995

97 points • TASTED IN CHAMPAGNE

15-20% malolactic fermentation; 7-8g/L dosage

Just a few hundred bottles of the stunning 1995 vintage were held back for Roederer's first ever re-release of Cristal. This late-disgorged, lower-dosage rendition is testimony to the magical transformation of Cristal with bottle age. Few will have the chance to partake, but we can all be inspired to have the stamina to leave the great vintages of Cristal in our cellars for 20 years, the age at which Lécaillon finds an ideal balance of youth and evolution, after 10 years on lees and 10 years on cork. After more than two decades, this classic and benchmark season has attained a magical place of ravishingly silky refinement, perfectly seamless, yet with all the clarity and focus of citrus and preserved lemon. Since its release, tertiary hints of green olive and smoke have begun to gently rise to meet refined notes of grilled-toast reduction. Stunning poise and harmony define a finish of outstanding persistence, with an undercurrent of fine salty chalk acidity that ripples with grand complexity and drive.

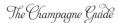
The Champagne Guide

LOUIS ROEDERER CRISTAL BRUT 1979

98 points • TASTED IN CHAMPAGNE

Original disgorgement; 12g/L dosage

Lécaillon regards 1979 to be Champagne's greatest vintage between 1969 and 1988, and aspires to make Cristal of this calibre today. It's a season that has now attained that magic moment where primary, secondary and tertiary complexity coexist in all the detail of cinematic 3D. A core of yellow mirabelle plums, pineapple and fig of astonishing definition at this age is overlaid by epic oyster shell complexity that bores to the core of the chalk mandate of Cristal. Time has coaxed out nuances of spice and polished every surface to silky seamlessness, culminating in a grand finale of breathtaking persistence.

LOUIS ROEDERER CRISTAL ROSÉ 2009 $$$$$

98 points • TASTED IN AUSTRALIA

55% pinot noir, 45% chardonnay; colour achieved by both saignée and blending; 12% vinified in oak casks; no malolactic fermentation; aged 6 years on lees; 8g/L dosage

Cristal Rosé is a towering monument to the grand juxtaposition between breathtaking finesse and surging concentration, rumbling with the power of grand cru pinot noir and mouth-storming chalk minerality. It propagates with consummate definition, exacting poise and undeterred persistence, reinforced by the tension of grand cru chardonnay. Its pretty, pale-salmon hue does nothing to anticipate such depth of glorious red cherry and wild strawberry character, with stunning complexity of pinot noir spice and the age-derived complexity of brioche and nougat. A captivating expression of this warm season, and ready to drink now.

LOUIS ROEDERER CRISTAL ROSÉ 2007 $$$$$

98 points • TASTED IN CHAMPAGNE

56% pinot noir, 44% chardonnay; a blend of just 4 parcels; saignée cold maceration for 5-8 days; 15% vinified in oak tuns with weekly bâtonnage; no malolactic fermentation; aged 6 years on lees; 9.5g/L dosage

At a decade of age, Cristal Rosé displays a delightful medium-salmon hue. Every frame is seamlessly connected, like a masterpiece of cinematography. A spectacular panorama of chalk minerality is coloured with elegant red berry fruits, which transition in time to pure red cherries. The effect is a wonderful juxtaposition between refined elegance and understated presence and intensity, culminating in grand persistence. The fine chalk mineral aspiration of Cristal is articulated with profound depth on a finish of tension and thrilling endurance.

MAILLY GRAND CRU

(My-ii Groh Khrew)

5/10

28 RUE DE LA LIBÉRATION 51500 MAILLY-CHAMPAGNE

www.champagne-mailly.com

Of Champagne's 137 cooperatives, only Le Mesnil rivals Mailly Grand Cru as the fairest of them all. Mailly's 75 owners supply fruit for 500,000 bottles each year, from some 730 parcels on 73 hectares, exclusively in one village, representing one-third of the glorious Mailly-Champagne grand cru on the northern slopes of the Montagne de Reims. Mailly is unusual in dedicating 90% of its fruit to its own label, selling just 10% to négociants and none back to its own growers. Mailly's non-vintage cuvées showcase the deep colour and up-front fruit character of this celebrated cru, while its finest prestige cuvées capture the elegant mineral precision of the northern Montagne.

In the erratic climate of Champagne, the inability to blend with other villages makes a single-cru estate particularly challenging.

Wine critic Michel Bettane upholds Mailly-Champagne and Aÿ as the two villages in Champagne with sufficiently varying exposition and soils to confidently produce a monocru. Half of Mailly's slopes are north-facing, and the remainder have easterly and even southerly aspects, since the hill slopes gently back up below the village. Soils likewise vary dramatically from the top of the village to the bottom, in some places with chalk very close to the surface, and in other areas two metres below.

Mailly has taken strategic advantage of this diversity and Hervé Dantan, its talented and longstanding chef de cave from 1991 to 2013, set up the cooperative with some 150 tanks, an incredible number for its size, to facilitate individual vinification of small parcels. In 2012, a new area of the winery was dug to provide space for more small tanks, providing for a blending palette of

more than 60 wines, including reserves back to 2002, stored in small stainless steel and enamelled tanks and oak foudres. A solera system for reserves has been in operation for 20 years. The house sources two-year-old barrels from Bordeaux and Burgundy.

The cooperative describes its approach as 'Burgundian', with so many plots in the same village, all within two kilometres and all pressed at the cooperative. Its vineyards are managed by 25 families, with whom it works closely. It has divided the village into 30 areas and has established a test plot in each, which it has analysed since 1998. The results have enabled it to better support its growers, setting the start of harvest for each part of the village, and decreasing use of chemicals in the vineyards by 75% over 15 years.

Mailly's north-facing slopes on chalk subsoils draw out the mineral freshness of pinot noir, which comprises 75% of plantings, with chardonnay making up the remainder. The cooperative is proud to uphold an average vine age of 25 years, though has been asking

its growers to plant more chardonnay. The old growers in the village say that their pinot noir has the elegance and minerality of chardonnay, and their chardonnay has the weight of pinot noir.

The cooperative's glass building stands proudly in the village, above seven levels of cellars and a kilometre of chalk crayères, dug by hand 20 metres below the surface by the founders of the cooperative every winter from 1929 to 1965. This is now the home of two million bottles, representing an impressive four years of stock.

Hervé Dantan accepted a position at Lanson in February 2013. He was replaced at Mailly by Sébastien Moncuit, from a family of growers in the Côte des Blancs, with a decade of experience at Château Malakoff and three years consulting for growers, including Pascal Agrapart, Francis Egly and Anselme Selosse.

MAILLY GRAND CRU BRUT RÉSERVE NV $$

92 points • 2013 BASE VINTAGE • DISGORGED JUNE 2016 • TASTED IN AUSTRALIA

75% pinot noir, 25% chardonnay; 35% reserves from 10 vintages; a tiny proportion of barrel fermentation; aged 2.5 years on lees; 9g/L dosage

Mailly's entry blend is on wonderful form in the 2013 base, an exacting juxtaposition of the tension and presence of Mailly pinot noir. Succulent wild strawberry and red cherry fruit lingers long on a palate subtly accented by the biscuity complexity of lees age and underlined by fine chalk minerality and bright, focused acid line.

MAILLY GRAND CRU EXTRA BRUT NV $$

88 points • 2011 BASE VINTAGE • DISGORGED MARCH 2016 • TASTED IN AUSTRALIA

75% pinot noir, 25% chardonnay; vinified in tanks; aged 4 years on lees; zero dosage; 30,000 bottles

Far ahead of the trend, Mailly has been making Extra Brut since 1955 and it now accounts for 6–7% of production. The philosophy is a blend of plots of high maturity, reflected in a full-straw hue with a copper tint. The dominance of pinot noir, the richness of the village and the ripeness of the fruit ordinarily make the zero-dosage style sit comfortably, though even the best intentions are thwarted by the coarse, dry grip and dusty character of imperfect fruit in the tough 2011 season. Nonetheless, it holds good acid balance and reasonable persistence.

MAILLY GRAND CRU BLANC DE NOIRS NV $$$

92 points • 2010 BASE VINTAGE • TASTED IN MAILLY-CHAMPAGNE

100% pinot noir, selected from plots known for their finesse; full malolactic fermentation; some oak fermentation; 15% reserves; 8g/L dosage

A classic expression of northern Montagne pinot noir, at once rich, fleshy, voluminous, powerful and full-bodied in its full yellow-gold hue and its mirabelle plum and red cherry fruit, and mixed spice and honey flavours, underlined by the roast almond and gingernut biscuit complexity of age. Soft acid line and gentle chalk mineral texture provide life to a succulent and rounded finish. For its depth of colour and flavour, it retains balance, impressive seamlessness and good persistence. Ready to drink now.

Mailly Grand Cru L'Intemporelle Millésimé Brut 2010 $$$$

95 points • Disgorged June 2016 • Tasted in Australia

60% pinot noir, 40% chardonnay; a blend of just four or five plots; vinified in tanks; 8g/L dosage; 20,242 bottles

Crafted as an apéritif style of freshness, finesse and elegance, the 2010 vintage is rather a showpiece for the exuberant expression of this generous village. A full straw yellow—hue, true to the deep tone of the house, it mounts waves of mirabelle plums, white peach and grapefruit, accented with hints of white pepper. Amidst the nougat and brioche allure of bottle age, it upholds its poise in the magnificent acid cut of the village, energised by the fine chalk minerality. In line and persistence, this distinguished expression of grand terroirs transcends its season.

Mailly Grand Cru L'Intemporelle Rosé Brut 2009 $$$$

94 points • Disgorged January 2016 • Tasted in Australia

60% pinot noir, 40% chardonnay; the base of L'Intemporelle with a minuscule 2.5-3% red wine of Coteaux Champenois rouge; a little barrel fermentation; 8g/L dosage; 10,337 bottles

It is a profound lesson in the intricacies of champagne blending to see the tremendous impact that less than 3% of red wine can make in transforming a cuvée. The colour has shifted to a pale-copper hue, and aromas and flavours have adopted nuances of subtle strawberries, red cherries and fruit mince spice. Age has infused layers of freshly baked biscuits, ginger and mixed spice. The warm 2009 season is devoid of the acid line that invigorated the 2008, though fine chalk mineral texture happily sustains a harmonious finish. Ready to drink now.

Mailly Grand Cru Les Échansons Millésimé Brut 2007 $$$$

95 points • Disgorged June 2016 • Tasted in Australia

75% pinot noir, 25% chardonnay, mostly from 80-year-old vines; vinified in tanks; 6g/L dosage; 11,655 bottles

Les Échansons is intentionally a contrast to the elegance of L'Intemporelle — and a powerful village, large majority of pinot noir, old-vine concentration and a decade of bottle age make for a compelling foursome, conspiring in a full straw yellow—hue and grand intensity of grilled pineapple, butter, grapefruit, fig, apple and mixed spice. The chalk minerality of the village and the acid cut of 2007 come to the rescue, providing delightful definition and focus to a long and full finish of chewy texture and harmonious integration. A jubilant and ravishing cuvée of main-course proportions, yet at every moment poised and dignified.

Mailly Grand Cru Exception Blanche Blanc de Blancs 2004 $$$$$

96 points • disgorged June 2016 • Tasted in Australia

100% chardonnay from Mailly-Champagne and Avize; vinified in tanks; 6g/L dosage; 11,607 bottles

Mailly's 'Exception' to its rigorous monocru status is the injection of Avize into its Mailly chardonnay. The result is one of the greatest cuvées to emerge from this laudable estate in the modern era, a tribute to grand terroirs, fastidious blending and magnificent bottle age. The exuberance of the house is encapsulated in grilled pineapple, juicy white peach, fig and grapefruit, delightfully pampered with glorious layers of brioche, vanilla and marzipan. The elegant focus of 2004 defines an acid line that eloquently tones its proportions, charged with the prominent yet intimately integrated chalk mineral definition of both villages. It concludes refined, creamy and ever so long.

Marc Hébrart

(Mark E-brah)

6/10

18 Rue du Pont 51160 Mareuil-sur-Aÿ

Champagne
MARC HEBRART
PROPRIÉTAIRE-RÉCOLTANT

Marc Hébrart has been making his own champagnes in Mareuil-sur-Aÿ since 1964, and his son Jean-Paul from the age of nineteen in 1983, taking over in 1997. The estate is privileged to 15 hectares of vines of average age 28 years, spread across 65 plots of 75% pinot noir in Mareuil-sur-Aÿ, Avenay, Bisseuil, Mutigny and Aÿ, cunningly married with 25% chardonnay from Chouilly and Oiry. No meunier is used. Sustainable viticulture is the mandate, and synthetic treatments are avoided. All parcels are vinified separately, mostly in stainless steel, with some small barrel fermentation since 2004. Jean-Paul Hébrart is married to Isabelle Diebolt of Diebolt-Vallois, though the businesses function autonomously. His annual production of around 70,000 bottles contrasts elegant fruit expression with the mineral signature of great terroirs.

MARC HÉBRART SÉLECTION BRUT PREMIER CRU NV $$

92 points • 55% 2011 BASE VINTAGE • DISGORGED MAY 2016 • TASTED IN AUSTRALIA

70% pinot noir from Mareuil-sur-Aÿ vieilles vignes; 30% chardonnay from Oiry and Chouilly; vines 45–50 years of age; 24% 2010 and 21% 2009 reserves; aged 54 months on lees; 7g/L dosage

For its age, pinot noir predominance and depth of reserves, the hue is an impressive pale straw. The body, depth and poise of Mareuil shine in a style of red apple and strawberry fruit, supported by the fine texture and subtle almond-meal notes of long lees age. Fine acid line and soft minerality define a long finish of well-integrated dosage. A triumph for 2011 and great value.

Marc Hébrart Blanc de Blancs Premier Cru NV $$

89 points • 72% 2012 base vintage • Disgorged May 2016 • Tasted in Australia

85% Mareuil-sur-Aÿ; 15% Oiry and Chouilly; 11% 2011 and 17% 2010 reserves; aged 38 months on lees; 7.5g/L dosage

There is a ripe, spicy exoticism resembling star fruit and kiwi fruit, expressing the exuberance and body of Mareuil-sur-Aÿ in this fleshy and flamboyant blanc de blancs. Ripe fruit sweetness is the theme here, and acidity, dosage, minerality and structure dissolve in its wake on a long, fruity finish.

Marc Hébrart Brut Rosé Premier Cru NV $$

94 points • 2013 base vintage • Disgorged April 2016 • Tasted in Australia

50% 2013 chardonnay and 50% 2012 and 2011 pinot noir from Mareuil-sur-Aÿ; 6.5% 2012 Mareuil-sur-Aÿ rouge vinified in oak barrels; aged 2 years on lees; 7g/L dosage

A small dose of Mareuil-sur-Aÿ rouge vinified in oak lends a delicate and pale salmon pink–hue to this pretty and finely poised rosé. Mareuil is an elegant base for rosé, with chardonnay and pinot noir uniting seamlessly in a primary style of strawberry and red cherry fruit, underlined by chalk minerality and fine tannin texture. The result is refined and enticing.

Marc Hébrart Noces de Craie Aÿ Blanc de Noirs 2012 $$$

94 points • Disgorged March 2016 • Tasted in Australia

100% pinot noir from 45+ year-old vines spanning five parcels in Aÿ; aged 4 years on lees; 5g/L dosage; 4000 bottles

Aÿ pinot noir is on full parade in a style that encapsulates presence and definition, with red cherry, mirabelle plum, red apple and fig fruit underlined by the biscuity, nougat development and creamy texture of bottle age. There is exuberance to its expansive palate, well controlled by the fine salt mineral texture of the village, bright acid line and well-toned dosage on a long finish. An accurate and compelling representation of one of Champagne's most celebrated grand crus.

Marc Hébrart Rive Gauche Rive Droit Extra Brut 2010 $$$

93 points • Disgorged 2016 • Tasted in Australia

50% Aÿ pinot noir and 50% Oiry, Chouilly and Avize chardonnay; fully fermented and matured in old 205-litre oak barrels; aged 4 years on lees; 5g/L dosage

This is a spicy and characterful cuvée of pale-straw hue that accurately accomplishes its aspiration of expressing the two sides of the river, by confidently uniting the depth of Aÿ pinot noir, the definition of ripe northern Côte des Blancs chardonnay, and the spicy, toasty, coffee bean complexity of well-handled old barrel fermentation. Oak is sensitively handled, making more of a contribution in creamy, seamless texture than in flavour or colour. The result has body, power and flesh, tempered by fine phenolic grip, well-integrated acidity and invisible dosage on a long finish.

The Champagne Guide

MOËT & CHANDON

(Mo-wet e Shon-don)

20 AVENUE DE CHAMPAGNE 51200 ÉPERNAY

www.moet.com

I thought I had Moët & Chandon figured out. We all know the wines, we've witnessed the PR machine in full grind, and I've visited command central in Épernay countless times over 16 years. But when chef de cave Benoît Gouez granted my request to shadow him for a day at the height of harvest 2014, I witnessed sparkling wine production like I had never conceived. The sheer magnitude of this operation is mind-boggling, but we all knew that. What astounded me most was the groundbreaking technology in play and an attention to detail no one thought possible on this scale. This is one of the most exciting wine outfits on earth. And it's downright terrifying.

THE GIANT OF CHAMPAGNE IS ON THE MOVE

In just 12 days, 15,000 pickers harvest an incredible 5000 hectares of vines spanning 230 villages for Moët & Chandon, Dom Pérignon and Mercier. Of these, 1180 hectares are estate vineyards, half of which are grand crus and one-quarter premier crus, making Moët not only the largest vineyard holder, but privileged to more of the best sites than any other.

No human hand touches the picking crates after they leave the vineyards, arriving at Moët's headquarters in Épernay or its grand new and ever mushrooming Mont Aigu winery in Oiry, to be unloaded by robotic arms and carried up to the presses on an airport luggage system. A computerised sorting system to classify each picking box on visual quality is currently being trialled. When I visited Mont Aigu, an ocean of 6000 picking crates was queued ready to be pressed.

Meanwhile, a fleet of 80 tankers delivers juice from press houses in the villages, each equipped with nitrogen to inhibit oxidation. When they back up at Mont Aigu, a computer automatically directs juice to one of 250 shining new fermentation tanks, without a human hand touching a hose or a tap. In a world first, every ferment is computer monitored every five seconds, allowing Gouez's team to manage each ferment precisely, anticipating when they will peak, and speeding up or slowing down their pace to avoid reductive or oxidative characters. On the day I visited, 80,000 litres of juice arrived at this facility. Such is its efficiency that the place felt quiet and calm.

On grand display to the stream of traffic on the main road from Épernay to the Côte des Blancs, behind floor-to-ceiling glass on every side, Moët's Mont Aigu winery must be the most sophisticated, sparkling facility in the world, boasting Death Star–like automation on every front, dedicated exclusively to Moët Brut Impérial NV. To extend the capacity of Moët's 28 kilometres of historic cellars under Épernay, its new 50 million bottle cellar at Mont Aigu is also the world's first in which bottles are transported to disgorgement by unmanned laser-guided vehicles.

After recent expansions, the total storage capacity of this facility reached 14.5 million litres in time for vintage 2014, bringing the total capacity across the two sites to a whopping 60 million litres, the equivalent of 80 million bottles of Moët, Dom Pérignon and Mercier. The house added a further 22 million litres (30 million bottles) of tank capacity in time for the 2017 harvest. 'It is crazy!' exclaims Gouez.

Precisely how many bottles the house sells today is a closely guarded secret, but my estimate is at least 38 million across the three brands annually, with production somewhere in the order of 50 million. To put this in perspective, the other 5000 houses, cooperatives and growers in Champagne between them produce about 250 million bottles. All the brands of Moët's owner, luxury giant Louis Vuitton–Moët Hennessy (or LVMH, including Veuve Clicquot, Ruinart and Krug) between them account for a whopping 61 million bottles, 20% of all champagne sales. Rumours in the region are consistent with recent expansion in production facilities, pointing to a target of 100 million bottles within a decade, in strategic anticipation of rising global demand for champagne. The group is already so far ahead in both value and volume that it more than exceeds its two nearest rivals, Lanson-BCC and Vranken-Pommery, put together.

UNPRECEDENTED ANTICS
Mont Aigu is a striking monument to Moët's growth and ambition, and the company is working overtime to secure supply to fill it, even door-knocking growers with enticing incentive offers. In June 2012, LVMH made a tactical and unprecedented play. An advertisement placed in local newspapers announced that it would pay 4% more for its grapes in the 2012 vintage.

An aggressive buyer in the champagne market for some years, this was the first public announcement of its intentions. There are loud grumblings in Champagne about this brazen wielding of power. As the largest purchaser in the region, when Moët sets a price, everyone follows.

Some perceive the move as a strategic attempt to put pressure on grape supply and push smaller players out of the market. It's not as simple as this. Champagne has long paid its growers like no other appellation in France, and higher grape prices are ultimately to their benefit, shoring up the foundation of the region. Moët's commitment to purchasing fruit rather than vins clairs made by other producers can only be a good thing, both for the growers and for quality. And the rise of Moët to date has been for the greater good of Champagne in another way, too.

In conversations across the region, from the largest houses and cooperatives to the smallest growers, I am continually impressed by the high regard in which Moët & Chandon is held. 'I cannot think of another producer in the world who has produced wine as well as Moët on such a scale,' Jacquesson's Jean-Hervé Chiquet remarked.

The Champenois salute Moët as an ambassador for their region, for its groundbreaking and ongoing work in breaking into emerging markets such as China and India. There is genuine gratitude that this trail-blazing paves the way for other champagne brands to follow.

And growing markets demand growing supplies. This is nothing new for Moët. Founded in 1743, the company claims to be the first house of champagne. It came into international prominence under Jean-Remy Moët, who inherited the house from its founder, his grandfather, Claude Moët, in 1789. It is said Jean-Remy was already dreaming about Asian markets before the end of that century.

Since this time, Moët has mushroomed like no other champagne house, and the real danger today is that its explosive growth may topple the balance in Champagne. The biggest question of all is how Moët can sustain quality in the wake of such unprecedented growth.

PERPETUAL EVOLUTION
'For me it is not a matter of size, but a matter of paying attention to the details,' Gouez says. 'To be able to adapt and to fight every year, to get the best out of what nature gives you.'

The precision of the technology at his disposal to analyse this detail is groundbreaking in sparkling wine production. He now has hand-held analysers to instantly measure the sugar, acid and pH of a bunch of grapes without picking a single berry, tools to measure the pressure in a bottle without opening it, even a centrifuge that has replaced the press for rosé. Vineyards are analysed by satellite to pinpoint areas to fertilise. With 12 full-time staff, his Épernay R&D lab was the only one of its kind in Champagne, until he replicated it at Mont Aigu. 'Some people will see all this and think it's all very industrial, but it's all for the sake of maintaining the character of the grapes,' Gouez explains.

Technology and resources aside, by far the most important initiative that he has introduced since he commenced at Moët in 1998 has been in tasting and testing every press sample that arrives during vintage. This may seem trivial, but such is the scale of this operation that no one believed he could pull it off. I witnessed the long lines of samples assembled in the vintage lab and could hardly believe it myself. Gouez works 14-hour days during harvest (16 hours or more on bad days) and during that time he and his team of four taste and test every one of up to 800 press samples that arrive. He personally tastes half of them.

'This is so important,' he tells me. 'It's impossible to assess the quality of a parcel by simply looking at the analysis.' Across vintage, his team tastes and allocates some 7500 batches to 800 tanks, filling every tank within 24 hours, and adapting their classification according to the vintage. On this scale, it's not possible to vinify village by village as it would take too long to fill each tank. Notes on each batch are beamed to the iPads of workers in the winery.

'I believe bigger is better,' Gouez says. 'I don't consider quality and quantity to be mutually exclusive in Champagne. A small grower in one village has nothing to compensate for difficult weather. Grower wines are very good, and I have friends among many of them, but by nature the quality of champagne is uneven. The more grapes you can access, the more you can be consistent.'

It's a principle that appears to have worked for Moët in recent years. At more than 20 million bottles every year, its Brut Impérial is the biggest blend in Champagne, and currently as fresh as I've seen it. 'This is a wine that is always evolving, because the climate, the technology, the market, the consumers and the world have changed,' Gouez explains.

Of course, quality does not automatically come with quantity, and his team has embraced innovation and worked hard to refine the style.

'We have worked on the preparation of our ferments to provide the right level of oxygenation so they don't get too stressed,' Gouez says. 'This reduces the reductive flavours, allowing room for the expression of the precision and cleanliness of the fruit.' Lower dosage has also been a refreshing trend in recent years, and more refined than ever in his current cuvées. 'In the past, we were known for higher dosage, but today Brut Impérial is 9g/L, one of the lowest among the grande marques,' he points out. This comes in response to both riper fruit and a changing consumer palate, seeking elegance and purity. 'We will continue to evolve,' he says. 'It's perpetual, and we need to continually revisit our style and our values.'

The Moët ambition is a fruit-driven style of freshness, brightness and purity. He prizes the ripeness and phenolic maturity of warmer vintages over acid definition, not a philosophy I subscribe to, but nonetheless a valid house style. 'Eighteen years ago, when I started here, phenolic bitterness was "no way!",

Benoît Gouez and his team of four taste and test every one of up to 800 press samples every day at the height of harvest.

but now I think that this is the next thing for us,' he reveals. He considers it something of a quest to build structure with bitterness and not just acidity. 'Since we are looking for fruitiness and roundness, we tend to harvest our grapes at a higher level of ripeness, so sometimes the acidity might be lower. We are looking for structure through phenolic bitterness rather than acidity.'

'We want our champagnes to taste of the grapes they're made of,' he says, pointing out that 90% of winemaking is simply getting the grapes and the pressing right. He tries not to do too much in the winery. To this end, the winemaking is purposely reductive, vigorously minimising oxidation and religiously avoiding oak. 'The size and diversity of our vineyard sources is the key to consistency,' he says.

Richard Geoffroy, who oversees Moët's production, names tightening up consistency and improving viticulture as the two key focus areas for the future of the house. Complexity is built through fermentation using yeasts produced in its own lab. All Moët & Chandon cuvées are blends of the three champagne varieties, and all undergo malolactic fermentation.

Moët has introduced DIAM closures and two other brands of micro-agglomerate corks, first with its vintage wines, so as to send the message that this is a quality initiative. All corks are batch tested 200 at a time, and rejected if more than 2.5% defects or 1% critical defects are detected. Gouez maintains that it's impossible to ask for zero defects for fear of rejecting everything (though Louis Roederer successfully maintains zero tolerance).

These are rounded, commercial champagnes, but recent efforts have certainly refined the style in spite of the monumental scale of production. The phenolic maturity of the Moët house style is not my favourite in Champagne, but the more I get to know Gouez and Geoffroy and their philosophies, and the more I see behind the curtain of this incredible operation, the more profound respect I have for their attention to detail while producing tens of millions of bottles. The philosophy, the technology and the execution are, quite simply, unprecedented on this scale anywhere on earth.

'Whatever we do at Moët, we like to do it big and bold, to share Moët with the world!' Gouez rejoices. That they do.

MOËT & CHANDON IMPÉRIAL BRUT NV $$

88 points • 2013 BASE VINTAGE • DISGORGED APRIL 2016 • TASTED IN AUSTRALIA

30-40% pinot, 30-40% meunier, 20-30% chardonnay; first blend of the year 35-50% reserves, second 30%, third 20-25%, mostly from the previous year; a blend of more than 100 different wines; aged 24 months on lees; 9g/L dosage

At well over 20 million bottles, and rising steeply, this one wine accounts for more than 7% of Champagne's production. To put this in perspective, the vines that supply this label alone would cover an area close to 4000 rugby fields! This is a blend of everything from everywhere, on an oceanic scale that makes a single blend impossible, dictating three quite different blends every year. Gouez and his team blend from December until June. The aim is to use young and fruity reserves of two vintages to build consistency by contributing any elements missing from the latest harvest. On average, the proportion of reserve wines in this blend is much higher than in the past (another reason for Moët's recent huge investment in storage capacity), particularly in the challenging vintages of recent years, as much as 50% in the first blend of the year, though fruitiness remains the goal, not maturity. There is thus no recipe, with a different dosage and different liqueur for every batch. 'I call this tailor-made winemaking,' says Gouez. 'We have to adapt and be flexible. How can a house of this size be flexible? For me, craftsmanship is not about being small, but about having an ambition to focus on every detail.'

The mind-boggling scale of Brut Impérial makes its improvement in recent years all the more impressive, and it's as lively and fresh as ever. Grapefruit zest, lemon pulp and red apple unite in a style underlined by the toasty, nutty influence of bottle age. Acid line more than dosage defines the finish, with some dry grip to the structure.

MOËT & CHANDON ROSÉ IMPÉRIAL BRUT NV $$$

88 points • 2012 BASE VINTAGE • DISGORGED SEPTEMBER 2015 • TASTED IN AUSTRALIA

40-50% pinot noir, 30-40% meunier, 10-20% chardonnay; 10% pinot red wine and 10% meunier red wine; 20-30% reserve wines; 9g/L dosage; DIAM closure

Moët has a very long history with champagne rosé, evidenced by a letter of order from Napoléon Bonaparte dated 1801. Today, rosé represents a phenomenal 20% of total sales, which Gouez has grown from just 3% when he commenced in 1998, prompting the recent opening of a new facility to double red wine production capacity. It's intentionally in the same style as Brut Impérial, though crafted from a unique blend. To create intensity of colour and lightness on the palate, Moët is unique in Champagne in employing a Beaujolais technique of heating and macerating meunier at 70°C for a couple of hours to extract colour and flavour without tannins. In a ground-breaking initiative, the press has now been replaced with a horizontal centrifuge to produce a more rounded style of intense colour and aroma without phenolic grip. Short macerations produce red wines of lighter colour, which explains a large dose of 20–25% red wine.

A full salmon crimson–hue heralds a rosé of generous and well-defined red apple, red cherry and strawberry fruit, and a suggestion of tomato. Pinot noir declares its lead in mid-palate fruit presence, upholding an impressive brightness. Soft, drying tannin texure and a note of phenolic grip and firmness are neatly offset with well-tuned dosage on the finish. This is the finest I have seen this cuvée.

MOËT & CHANDON NECTAR IMPÉRIAL NV $$

85 points • 2014 BASE VINTAGE • DISGORGED APRIL 2016 • TASTED IN AUSTRALIA
DIAM closure

A cuvée of honeyed, candied sweetness that jostles with phenolic grip and reductive earthiness on a palate of apple, pear and stone fruit character. It concudes short, firm and oh so sweet.

MOËT & CHANDON ICE IMPÉRIAL NV $$

85 points • TASTED IN AUSTRALIA

True to its name and arctic-white livery, this is a cuvée engineered to be served on ice in large glasses. At this temperature, its medium level of sweetness will sit better with its soft acidity, but there's no escaping its grubby imprecision, let down by earthy/mushroomy notes and phenolic grip that detract from what little fruit definition it presents.

MOËT & CHANDON GRAND VINTAGE 2008 $$$

90 points • Disgorged November 2015 • Tasted in Champagne and Australia
40% chardonnay, 37% pinot, 23% meunier; aged 7 years on lees; 5g/L dosage; DIAM closure

Vintage production is just 1% of the house, making this cuvée significantly less than 300,000 bottles. Gouez has replaced 'Moët & Chandon Vintage' with 'Vintage by Moët & Chandon', with labels of bold vintage declaration, to focus more on the style of the season than the house. He is looking for four things in a vintage: sufficient maturity of at least 9.5 degrees potential, no rot, ageing potential from either acidity or phenolic structure, and finally character – something special, not simply the stamp of the season. 'The idea is not to follow a recipe, but to listen to the wines and create a vintage with uniqueness and charisma,' he says. The blend and the selection of parcels change to reflect the character of the season, looking for those that are most interesting and original. 'We start from scratch. I choose the grapes from anywhere I want, and I don't care if it's meunier or if it isn't grand cru.' The maturation has also evolved, with Grand Vintage previously released after five years on lees and now after seven, allowing the dosage to be lowered to just 5g/L. Disgorgement date, dosage and blend are clearly displayed on the back label – impressive detail for a house of this magnitude.

The vivacious 2008 season leads out with fresh, dynamic lemon, apple and pear fruit, defining a style of well-focused acid line and tension. It's ageing slowly and incrementally, upholding a primary freshness and taut acid line that call for time to soften. The biscuity, spicy, honeyed, brioche complexity of almost a decade of age is yet subtle, supporting nuances of struck-flint reduction, finishing dry, with some bitter phenolic grip. Will live long.

MOËT & CHANDON GRAND VINTAGE COLLECTION 1998 $$$$

92 points • Disgorged April and June 2013 • Tasted in Champagne and Australia
40% chardonnay, 35% pinot, 25% meunier; 5–7g/L dosage; DIAM closure

A bright, medium straw yellow-hue heralds the freshness and poise of this great season, impeccably balanced at almost two decades of age, contrasting the struck flint and gunpowder reductive character of Moët, the almond meal, freshly churned butter, nougat, wild honey, toast and subtle truffle and smoke notes of maturity, and the grapefruit and nashi pear of primary fruit. Reductive maturity brings a suggestion of green olive. Low dosage emphasises a lively and bright acid line, though the finish is defined more dramatically by firm, bitter phenolic grip. Nonetheless, it upholds impressive acid line and persistence.

MOËT & CHANDON GRAND VINTAGE COLLECTION 1988 $$$$$

95 points • Disgorged October 2003 • Tasted in Champagne en magnum and Australia
50% pinot, 30% chardonnay, 20% meunier; 7.5g/L dosage

Testimony to the tension and grand endurance of the brilliant 1988 season, this is a vintage that has attained its glorious heyday. Almost three decades have created a bright, full-straw hue and tertiary complexity of green olives, while upholding the freshness of preserved lemons and layers of finely integrated, toasty complexity. Its bright acid line accounts for its youthful vibrancy that belies 15 years on lees and almost the same on cork, promising years of potential yet. Hints of iodine and oyster shell speak of the chalk terroir of Champagne, while a creamy texture bears witness to long lees and cork age. It concludes tight, refreshing and very long. One magnum was corked.

The Champagne Guide

Moët & Chandon Grand Vintage Collection 1978 $$$$$

93 points • Disgorged October 2004 • Tasted in Champagne en magnum

With a full-yellow hue and a gold tint, this is a beautifully nutty old Moët, with long lees age furnishing a creamy palate and a long and buttery finish. Nuances of smoke and toast declare magnificent maturity, yet it culminates in a finish of vitality, freshness, excellent acid line and wonderfully seamless persistence.

Moët & Chandon Grand Vintage Rosé 2008 $$$

89 points • Disgorged April 2015 • Tasted in Champagne and Australia

46% pinot noir, 32% chardonnay, 22% meunier; 20% pinot noir red wine; 5g/L dosage; DIAM closure

Moët harvests red wine for its vintage rosé from its best estate pinot noir plots of low-yielding old vines, green harvested to reduce yields when necessary. Twice the necessary vineyard area is prepared, to permit choice of the grapes with the best phenolic maturity to provide structure. Red wine is macerated for 5–7 days to draw out ripe, soft character, without hard tannins.

A full-crimson hue with a copper tint announces a tangy and savoury rosé that contrasts the acid drive and tension of the season with the savoury, reductive style of Moët. Red apple, tomato and tart morello cherry notes declare its pinot noir lead, accented with gentle spice, and reinforced by a dry finish of bitter, dry grip. Gentle phenolic bitterness and bright 2008 acidity conspire to create a firm ending that calls for further age to soften. A characterful and age-worthy release for Moët.

Moët & Chandon Rosé Grand Vintage Collection 1998 $$$$

92 points • Disgorged April 2013 • Tasted in Champagne

43% chardonnay, 35% pinot, 22% meunier

A savoury style of medium-copper hue and characters of tomato, green olive and roast nuts. Age has produced a creamy palate, concluding with reasonable length and gentle tannin grip.

Moët & Chandon Rosé Grand Vintage Collection 1988 $$$$$

94 points • Disgorged September 2004 • Tasted in Champagne en magnum

60% pinot, 25% chardonnay, 15% meunier; 7.5g/L dosage

A beautiful old rosé of iodine, smoke, toast, roast nuts and a hint of green olives. The finish is driven by the tense acid of this great season, with creamy texture built by 16 years on lees. It falls into that comfortable place where secondary and tertiary complexity marry evenly and linger with impressive persistence.

MOUZON-LEROUX

(Moo-zoh-Leh-roh)

6/10

16 RUE BASSE DES CARRIÈRES 51380 VERZY
www.champagne-mouzon-leroux.com

*B*iodynamic practices are labour intensive to uphold in the vagaries of Champagne's climate at the
best of times, all the more so spread across 50 separate plots spanning 7.5 hectares of vineyards. The
Mouzon family has been growing vines since 1776 and bottling its own champagnes since 1930, sourced mostly
from the revered grand cru of Verzy on the north-eastern edge of the Montagne de Reims. Vines have been farmed
organically since 1997 and biodynamically since 2008, with certification achieved in 2011. The youngest vines
are tended with a horse to minimise soil compaction, and plants and flowers are encouraged in the mid-rows.
Today, Pascale, Philippe and Sébastien Mouzon achieve the impressive feat of vinifying all 50 plots separately.
Their natural approach continues in the winery, where every cuvée is wild fermented before ageing in vats or
barrels. Back labels are particularly informative in declaring the villages, blend, base vintage, disgorgement date
and dosage. These are cuvées of low dosage that articulately proclaim the fine signature of Verzy.

MOUZON-LEROUX L'ATAVIQUE TRADITION GRAND CRU EXTRA BRUT NV $$

93 points • 60% 2012 BASE VINTAGE • DISGORGED JANUARY 2016 • TASTED IN AUSTRALIA

55% pinot , 45% chardonnay from Verzy; 35% reserves from 2011, 2010 and 2009; aged 30-40 months on lees;
wild fermented; 25% fermented in barrels and demi-muids; 3g/L dosage

The dynamism and depth of Verzy are communicated in a style replete with fruit presence and structural
definition. Red apple and morello cherry fruit are underlined by the subtle coffee and dark chocolate notes of
partial barrel fermentation. This is a cuvée that articulates its terroir accurately, spelling out the definition of the
north-easterly outlook of Verzy in a fine acid line and soft salt chalk mineral mouthfeel.

262   *The Champagne Guide*

MUMM

(Moom)

29 RUE DU CHAMPS DE MARS 51199 REIMS

www.mumm.com

An annual production of now 8.5 million bottles ranks Mumm number four by volume in Champagne after Moët, Clicquot and Feuillatte. Despite a turbulent history of acquisitions over the past century, Mumm has retained almost 218 hectares of vines, mostly planted to pinot noir, meeting 25% of its needs. The house has come a long way since my first visit during the snowfalls of Christmas 2001, recovering from its dark days of the 1980s and 1990s, due in part to the appointment of the 31-year-old Dominique Demarville as chef de cave in 1998 and his 35-year-old successor, Didier Mariotti, in 2006. Mumm now enjoys a higher percentage of chardonnay in its 'Cordon Rouge' house blend, as well as more reserve wine, longer maturation times and lower dosages. And there is more at hand.

In 1995, Mumm launched a 12-year plan to resurrect Cordon Rouge, encompassing harvesting, pressing and vinification, with a focus on building reserve wines since the late 1990s, but it was not until Pernod Ricard purchased the company in 2005 that sufficient funds were injected to fully realise this vision.

'The quality of Cordon Rouge was so bad 10–15 years ago, because of insufficient reserve wines, short ageing in the cellar and inconsistent blends for each vintage,' Mariotti admits.

A gleaming new winery was constructed in Reims in 2008 and extended in 2010 to house row after row of sparkling new stainless steel tanks, new disgorgement and bottling lines, and space for greater stocks of reserve wines. 'With a new winery and smaller vats we are able to home in on the terroir more accurately by producing smaller parcels for the blends,' Mariotti explains. New press centres were constructed in Mailly-

Champagne and Verzy in 2010 to address concerns with fruit waiting for up to 10 hours to be pressed. Grapes can now be moved just a few kilometres between press houses to avoid these delays.

Cordon Rouge is moving from 20% to an impressive 30–35% reserve wines, spanning six vintages, which Mariotti upholds as crucial for maintaining the consistency of the blend. It spends a minimum two and a half years on lees in the cellar, and Mariotti has worked to lower the dosage from 10g/L to 8g/L. 'I am very proud of this dosage, one of the lowest of any of the houses,' he claims. Every other Mumm cuvée is just 6g/L.

The magnitude of his new winery is sufficient that all 8 million bottles of Cordon Rouge are now the same blend each year, a remarkable feat of logistical engineering. An identical blend is made once a week for 15–20 weeks. An extra 30% is produced, and kept in tank as the reserve for the following year.

Enthusiastic about raising quality, Didier Mariotti brings acute attention to detail to every part of the process, from vineyard to market. He spends 70% of his time during harvest visiting growers, building relationships, seeing the quality of the fruit and gaining insight into the vintage. At the other end of the process, he tastes every wine from each warehouse in most export markets every six months, and checks the disgorgement date of cuvées in every restaurant he visits. He binned a couple of pallets of Rosé NV from the warehouse in Australia a few years ago and reserved some de Cramant 2006 for internal use only because they were too old.

'It is important to be sure that the quality is maintained at every step,' he emphasises. 'You can work hard on the blend, ageing and disgorgement, but if you don't focus on the supply chain you can destroy everything.' Mumm now prints bottling and disgorgement dates on the back labels of its de Cramant, Blanc de Blancs and Blanc de Noirs, as well as its Brut Selection for the French market, as Mariotti believes it is always best to disclose the disgorgement date.

In a region where change comes slowly, Mariotti is eager to embrace innovation, even appointing a new winemaker dedicated to this purpose last year, with a focus on testing stoppers, lightstruck damage, matching champagne glasses to particular cuvées, as well as driving all manner of experiments in the winery.

'If you are not trialling, you are not moving,' declares Mariotti. 'Global warming, the markets and other things are changing, so we need to be asking questions about winemaking all the time.' This philosophy has inspired small trials of bâtonnage, malolactic fermentation, barrel ageing of liqueurs, even barrels of different coopers and varying levels of toast. All Mumm cuvées currently undergo full malolactic fermentation, though parcels with no malolactic are trialled each vintage. 'We need to be prepared for global warming,' Mariotti reveals, 'but so far our only response has been to harvest earlier.'

Mariotti has a vision to bring more structure and complexity to non-vintage cuvées, by increasing ageing on lees, facilitated by maintaining 25 million bottles maturing at any time, and through greater proportions of reserve wines. 'With five years of wines in reserve I'm able to think about which reserves I use for each blend,' he explains. Barrel ageing with bâtonnage may in future be the third step, though Mariotti admits that 'in some of our experimentation with barrels, the results have been very, very bad! But it's good for the kids to play!'

Mumm has bottled half bottles of Cordon Rouge under DIAM closures for two years and is hoping to do the same for full bottles for export markets. Mariotti is convinced of DIAM's superiority. 'If we can guarantee no more cork problems, I don't know why we are waiting!' he exclaims. (This can't come too soon, as I've seen some cork effect in this cuvée.)

'It takes a long time to turn things around in Champagne!' he adds. This is especially true in a house the size of Mumm. Its non-vintage cuvées are on a slow ascent, with hope for further gains in years to come.

Mumm's evolution continues. In 2016, the house launched new bottles, classy new labels and a change of branding from G.H. Mumm to Maison Mumm.

MUMM CORDON ROUGE BRUT NV $$

89 points • 2012 BASE VINTAGE • TASTED IN AUSTRALIA
85 points • 2011 BASE VINTAGE • TASTED IN CHAMPAGNE

45% pinot noir, 30% chardonnay, 25% meunier from the Montagne de Reims, Grande Vallée de la Marne, Vallée de l'Ardre, Côte des Blancs, Sézannais and Côte des Bar; 30-35% reserves spanning 6 vintages; 15-20% of the final blend is kept as reserve; 8g/L dosage; 8 million bottles

Cordon Rouge is a massive blend of between 300 and 450 tanks from more than 100 villages, representing more than 85% of Mumm's production. After a couple of rough base vintages, Cordon Rouge is back on form in 2012, displaying the youthful, primary red apple, peach and lemon fruit character and the subtle biscuit, almond meal and vanilla complexity typical of this cuvée. There's a touch of earthy complexity along the way, and phenolics are very well handled. The finish sings with energy and vibrancy thanks to refreshing acid tension, well-integrated dosage and accurate focus, making this as fine as any Cordon Rouge I can remember. The challenging 2011 base pales in comparison, dry, short and simple, an unfortunate victim of a tough season.

The Champagne Guide

Mumm Le Rosé Brut NV $$

90 points • 2012 BASE VINTAGE • TASTED IN AUSTRALIA

60% pinot noir, 22% chardonnay, 18% meunier; 13-15% red wine from Bouzy, Verzenay and Les Riceys; 6g/L dosage; DIAM closure

Mumm Le Rosé is built on the Cordon Rouge blend. A bright, full-salmon hue heralds an expressive and fruit-focused style, back to the form of the 2010 base, a flamboyant celebration of crunchy red apples, tangy morello cherries, strawberries, grapefruit, tamarillo and pink pepper with a subtle, enticing edge of struck flint. It's primary, fresh, fruit-focused, clean and lively, with acid and dosage finding harmony on a short finish, with dimension furnished by an appropriate touch of tannin grip. As fresh, balanced and persistent as ever.

Mumm 6 Ans Édition Limitée NV $$

91 points • TASTED IN AUSTRALIA

73% pinot noir, 27% chardonnay; Grande Montagne de Reims and Côte des Blancs; 6 years on lees; 6g/L dosage

This is not late disgorged Cordon Rouge, but rather a cuvée stripped back to racing spec, sans lesser terroirs and meunier. Bright and fresh lemon aromas introduce a palate that revels in the complexity and texture of extended lees age, filled with layers of baked bread and brioche character and creamy mouthfeel, while upholding confident grapefruit freshness. Fine acidity and low dosage unite to create a fresh and long finish. Some phenolic grip threatens to hamper the harmony on the end, yet it upholds itself with energy and tension.

Mumm Le Millésimé 2009 $$

90 points • DISGORGED MARCH 2015 • TASTED IN AUSTRALIA

68% pinot noir, 32% chardonnay; majority of Aÿ pinot noir and Avize chardonnay; 6g/L dosage; DIAM closure

Since its release two years ago, the warm and dry 2009 season for Mumm has expanded into a secondary and savoury style of wild honey, gingernut biscuits, dried fruits, roast nuts and even tertiary notes of coffee, upholding the red apple, grapefruit, pear and lemon of its youth, though sadly still a textural and chewy thing, now showing a little more dry grip on the finish. Rich, rounded, voluptuous and ready, this is a vintage to drink up quick. Mariotti has intelligently released the fast-maturing 2009 vintage before the enduring 2008.

Mumm RSRV Cuvée Resérvée Blanc de Blancs Brut Grand Cru 2012 $$$

92 points • DISGORGED FEBRUARY 2016 • TASTED IN AUSTRALIA

100% Cramant; 6g/L dosage; DIAM closure

RSRV replaces de Cramant, the front label at last proclaiming both the vintage and '100% chardonnay du Village de Cramant'. This is a textural and grainy style of grapefruit pith bitterness and layers of apple and pear flavour, subtly accented with creamy lees texture more than secondary flavour. It's a very young vintage release for this long-ageing village, and is yet to reach a flattering point in its arc of development. It has the right ingredients to get there, with a finely focused acid line, good fruit persistence and purity of white-fruit definition. Give it at least a couple more years of bottle age before approaching.

Mumm RSRV Cuvée Réservée Blanc de Noirs Brut Grand Cru 2008 $$$$

86 points • Disgorged November 2015 • Tasted in Australia
100% Verzenay pinot noir; 6g/L dosage; DIAM closure

This is a dry and dusty cuvée that lacks the fruit brightness and definition that should denote Verzenay, the historic stronghold of the house, especially in the scintillating 2008 harvest. By contrast, both bottles I tasted were savoury and lifeless, grainy and grubby in both flavour profile and coarse phenolic grip. It's even less than the disappointing 2002 base NV from the same village that preceded it, such a shame for a cuvée that promises so much.

Mumm de Cramant Blanc de Blancs Brut $$$$

93 points • 2010 base vintage • Tasted in Champagne and Australia
100% Cramant chardonnay; DIAM closure; 6g/L dosage; 50,000-100,000 bottles

In philosophy and pedigree, de Cramant is an altogether different tier in the world of Mumm, and it's their only cuvée that I buy. A rather young release, it's bottled at 4.5 atmospheres of pressure rather than the usual 6, to soften the impression of acidity. It's always been one variety (chardonnay), one village (Cramant) and one vintage, though never labelled as a vintage as it's sometimes released too young. De Cramant has now been replaced by RSRV Cuvée Reservée Blanc de Blancs, which refreshingly declares both village and vintage on the front label. To maintain consistency, Mumm plays with selection of plots, fermentation temperature, addition of lees, blocking of malolactic fermentation and, unique in Champagne, even micro-oxygenation on some tanks. The 2010 is an excellent release for de Cramant, with a tight backbone of lemon citrus fruit, overlaid with the complexity of lees age in almond meal and brioche notes, even a touch of toasted coconut. It finishes long and tense with very fine dry extract providing structure and dimension, offering a compelling contrast to its acid structure. Its phenolic grip and earthy dryness reflect the season, yet it nonetheless upholds the lemon purity, persistence and acid line of Cramant. An energetic and age-worthy wine, and a good result for the 2010 season.

Mumm Cuvée R. Lalou Brut 2002 $$$$$

95 points • Tasted in Champagne and Australia
54% Ambonnay, Verzy and Verzenay pinot noir; 47% Avize and Cramant chardonnay; 6g/L dosage; DIAM closure

Lalou was the prestige wine of the house from 1969 to 1985, but the bottle mould and recipe were lost in the wild ride of ownership changes, and revived by Demarville in 1998. Only at the point of blending is the decision made of which 12 potential parcels of estate grand cru vineyards will win the golden ticket (as few as two, if the vintage is deemed worthy at all). The 2002 is a blend of eight parcels of vines more than 30 years of age in Mailly-Champagne, Bouzy, Verzenay, Verzy and Ambonnay for pinot noir, and Cramant and Avize for chardonnay. A liqueur of Cramant and Bouzy is aged in new and used barrels to build sufficiently to meet the power of the wine. Lalou is unashamedly built as a strong wine, and 2002 is a wonderfully complex rendition, seamlessly marrying the primary, secondary and tertiary phases of development. The richness of yellow mirabelle plum, quince, nectarine, fig, tart citrus, even plum liqueur, are evolving into dried peach, mixed spice, marzipan, toast, honey and brioche of silky, buttery smoothness. Fifteen years of maturity have built a full straw yellow–hue and creamy mouthfeel, while retaining brightness and integrity of acid line. This bottle shows less of the tertiary development it displayed two years ago, with just subtle nuances of coffee and pipe smoke. It's signature 2002, with generosity and presence held comfortably in place thanks to finely structured, well-integrated and brilliantly persistent acidity, upholding its integrity admirably in great acid line and well-defined structure and length. A Lalou of main-course stature that will live a few years yet.

Mumm Collection du Chef de Caves Cordon Rouge Brut 1996 $$$$$

96 points • Disgorged May 2014 • Tasted in Australia en magnum

63% pinot noir, 37% chardonnay; 4g/L dosage; DIAM; 150 magnums

A powerful and rich old champagne of toffee, dark chocolate, coffee, dried fig, grilled pineapple and even star anise. Luscious, buttery and rich, with a hint of fresh mushroom on the finish, the palate unites flamboyant, exotic power with the lively charge of 1996 acidity that Mariotti descibes as 'amazing and refreshing', carrying with outstanding persistence and poise. In time the black cherry fruits of pinot noir rise in commanding stature. All hail the great 1996 season, declaring its magnificent contrast between concentration and energetic structure. It will improve even further with time.

Mumm Collection du Chef de Caves Cordon Rouge Brut 1990 $$$$$

95 points • Disgorged May 2014 • Tasted in Australia en magnum

81% pinot noir, 19% chardonnay; 4g/L dosage; DIAM; 150 magnums

A wonderfully exotic and mature champagne of full yellow-gold hue and notes of wild honey, bees wax, dried candied fruits, anise, toffee, even suggestions of pipe smoke and musty sofa. It finishes with good length and the grand complexity of maturity, tempered by bitter grapefruit crunch.

Mumm Collection du Chef de Caves Cordon Rouge Brut 1985 $$$$$

94 points • Disgorged May 2014 • Tasted in Australia en magnum

75% pinot noir, 25% chardonnay; 4g/L dosage; DIAM; 150 magnums

A tertiary wine of full golden yellow hue and a panoply of complexity in aromas of sautéed mushrooms, hints of game, notes of bouquet garni and suggestions of tomato and coffee, even a hint of mint, becoming smoked ham in time. The palate is surprisingly fresh and unexpectedly energetic for such a tertiary nose, with secondary citrus fruits and focused, well-defined acidity. It boasts drive, texture and structure, and will hold for some years yet.

The iconic Moulin de Verzenay stands sentinel over the dormant vines of Mumm during winter 2013.

NAPOLÉON

(Nah-poh-lee-o)

---

30 RUE DU GÉNÉRAL LECLERC 51130 VERTUS
www.champagne-napoleon.fr

CHAMPAGNE

NAPOLÉON

Napoléon is a brand of the growers' cooperative of Vertus, producing 100,000 bottles annually from the fruit of 100 growers, with vineyards largely in Vertus and neighbouring Le Mesnil-sur-Oger and Bergères-lès-Vertus. Covering the second-largest area of any village in Champagne, and the largest in the Marne, Vertus offers great diversity of sites and micro-climates, and Napoléon vinifies its many parcels separately in small stainless steel tanks. The brand draws on equal proportions of pinot noir and chardonnay to produce long-ageing wines, with non-vintage cuvées typically matured for four years on lees, and vintage cuvées much longer, generally released around 13 years of age — extraordinarily old for a cooperative. Managing director and chef de cave Jean-Philippe Moulin brings significant experience from his former positions as chef de cave of Ruinart and inaugural head of the CIVC Research & Development unit. Napoléon produces soft, fruity and creamy champagnes, also sold as Prieur in some markets. Its long-aged vintage wines represent good value.

NAPOLÉON RÉSERVE BRUT NV $$

89 points • TASTED IN AUSTRALIA

DIAM closure

Layers of toasty, bready, roast nut complexity provide a strong dimension of secondary complexity to gentle lemon and peach fruit, concluding in a finish of well-matched dosage and acidity, with a touch of phenolic dryness.

....

NAPOLÉON BLANC DE BLANCS BRUT NV $$

90 points • TASTED IN AUSTRALIA

The vanilla and toast notes of bottle maturity have built dimension and texture to the citrus notes of chardonnay, with the inimitably exotic personality of Vertus expressed in notes of star fruit and pear. Chalk minerality melds with subtle phenolic texture on the finish.

NICOLAS FEUILLATTE

(Ni-khoh-lah Fer-yat)

CD 40A PLUMECOQ 51530 CHOUILLY
www.feuillatte.com

CHAMPAGNE

Nicolas Feuillatte

'*Centre Vinicole—Champagne Nicolas Feuillatte' is Champagne's oldest and largest cooperative, and Nicolas Feuillatte is its key brand. The gargantuan operation comprises a collective of 82 cooperatives, with some 4500 growers tending 2100 hectares of vines across more than 300 villages, covering 7% of Champagne's surface. Production facilities span a full 12 hectares of high-tech buildings, with a capacity of 30 million litres — so large that they act as a second production and storage site for Moët & Chandon. Extensions were added in 2007 and 2012 to facilitate growing production. Once focused on producing champagnes for its growers and other houses, today the key priority has shifted to 60—70% of production for Nicolas Feuillatte. In 2015 it produced 18—19 million bottles and sold 11 million, up from 9 million just a few years ago, making the brand Champagne's third largest and the best selling in France. At any time 65 million bottles of Nicolas Feuillatte are ageing here, with a capacity of 100 million. It's a primary, fruity style, with dosage now evenly balanced.*

Most cooperatives in Champagne were based in the Vallée de la Marne and the Aube when Nicolas Feuillatte was established in 1972, and to this day these areas remain the focus of the sourcing of the house. This explains its reliance on a high proportion of meunier (45%), and lesser amounts of pinot noir (35%) and chardonnay (25%). This is slowly changing (from 50% meunier a few years ago) as the region moves away from meunier towards chardonnay. In 2007 chardonnay overtook meunier as the most planted variety in the Marne.

Palmes d'Or is the prestige brand of the house.

NICOLAS FEUILLATTE BRUT RÉSERVE NV $$

88 points • 2012 BASE VINTAGE • TASTED IN CHAMPAGNE AND AUSTRALIA

40% pinot noir, 40% meunier, 20% chardonnay; a blend of 150 crus; aged 3 years on lees; 7.7g/L dosage

There's a more exotic and sweet-fruited mood to this release of Brut Réserve, with notes of musk and apricot underscored by a pear and lemon citrus core. Time has contributed biscuity, bready complexity, though its focus remains on youthful fruit and lemon-infused acidity. Complexity of vanilla and anise provide dimension. Dosage is lower than ever, though it still carries confectionery notes of boiled sweets and finishes simple and short.

NICOLAS FEUILLATTE BRUT ROSÉ NV $$

89 points • TASTED IN CHAMPAGNE AND AUSTRALIA

60% pinot noir, 30% meunier, 10% chardonnay; 9.8g/L dosage

For its full, vibrant crimson hue, this is a cuvée that has developed a grace and seamless appeal devoid from this label in the past. It meets its mandate of being as fruity as possible, in fresh raspberry, strawberry and red apple flavours of sweet fruit appeal, with a subtle tomato nuance contributing savoury complexity. Tannins and phenolics are better handled than ever, and while there is a little apple skin–like grip here, it makes tactical use of sweet dosage to keep things approachable. Well improved.

NICOLAS FEUILLATTE BRUT CHARDONNAY BLANC DE BLANCS MILLÉSIMÉ 2006 $$

88 points • TASTED IN CHAMPAGNE

A core of white peach, wild honey and lemon is overlaid with the brioche and vanilla of a decade of age. A confident, ripe-fruit core of succulent stone fruits culminates in a sweet finish of honeyed dosage that dominates more than it needs to in the rounded 2006 season, masking a coarse phenolic structure.

NICOLAS FEUILLATTE GRAND CRU BLANC DE BLANCS BRUT MILLÉSIMÉ 2006 $$

92 points • TASTED IN CHAMPAGNE

A blend of Chouilly, Cramant, Les Mesnil-sur-Oger and Oger; 7g/L dosage

A core of even and well-balanced yellow fruits of lemon and white peach is laced with nuances of vanilla and even a musk lift. It's centred on the chalk minerality of its four grand cru villages, providing a fine chalk mouthfeel that lingers long and strong. A cuvée of great persistence and poise, with the rounded generosity of 2006 contrasting the chalk mineral freshness of the great grand crus of the Côte des Blancs. 7g/L dosage is well integrated.

Château de Boursault, the iconic, fairytale centrepiece of the Vallée de la Marne, the region where Nicolas Feuillatte focuses its sourcing.

The Champagne Guide

NICOLAS FEUILLATTE GRAND CRU BLANC DE NOIRS PINOT NOIR BRUT MILLÉSIMÉ 2004 $$$

92 points • TASTED IN CHAMPAGNE

A blend of Verzy, Verzenay, Aÿ, Ambonnay and Bouzy

A deep core of black cherry and plum liqueur fruit reflects ripe pinot noir of intensity and presence, with the biscuit, anise and ginger overtones of 12 years of bottle age. It is holding its balance well in spite of its maturity, and has attained its prime. It finishes with ripe sweetness contrasting fine chalk minerality and some fine phenolic structure, concluding with balance and persistence.

NICOLAS FEUILLATTE CUVÉE 225 BRUT MILLÉSIMÉ 2005 $$$$

86 points • TASTED IN CHAMPAGNE

50% chardonnay and 50% pinot noir, mostly from premier crus; fermented in tanks and aged for 10 months in oak barrels

A savoury style of charcuterie and boiled-sausage notes that speak more of the influence of oak maturation than they do of the expression of fruit or place.

NICOLAS FEUILLATTE CUVÉE 225 BRUT ROSÉ 2006 $$$$

87 points • TASTED IN CHAMPAGNE

100% pinot noir

Like the white, a savoury cuvée of smoky, charcuterie, woodsy notes that speak louder than its fruit. It's short and a little flat and dried out on the finish, with a hue of crimson with copper tints. This rounded vintage is not standing the test of a decade with confidence.

NICOLAS FEUILLATTE PALMES D'OR BRUT ROSÉ 2005 $$$$

93 points • TASTED IN CHAMPAGNE

Rosé de saignée of 100% pinot noir; 50% Bouzy and 50% Les Riceys; 7g/L dosage

Like the Palmes d'Or white, this cuvée tasted at the house upholds greater integrity than the same vintage displayed in Australia two years prior. The saignée process has produced a deeply coloured rosé of full-crimson hue. It's a rosé that captures powerfully fruity, expressive red cherries, cherry kernel and anise with exotic, smoky overtones. Having shed the musk stick associations of its youth, the palate delivers intense red cherry liqueur, cherry kernel, even marzipan, with body and exuberance met by firm, fine tannin presence and well-balanced, bitter structure. This is a full-bodied rosé for main-course fare, ready for pink meats.

NICOLAS FEUILLATTE PALMES D'OR VINTAGE BRUT 2004 $$$$

95 points • TASTED IN CHAMPAGNE

60% chardonnay from Chouilly, Cramant, Oger, Le Mesnil-sur-Oger, Avize and Montgueux near Troyes; 40% pinot noir from Bouzy, Verzy, Verzenay, Aÿ and Ambonnay; aged 9 years on lees; 7.5g/L dosage

I wrote two years ago, after multiple tastings of Palmes d'Or 2004 in Australia, that it had already attained the height of its maturity. Two years on, samples at the house have retained an impressive pale-straw hue for 12 years of age. This is an elegant and focused Palmes d'Or, capturing the depth of grand crus and the subtle exotic influence of Montgueux. There is beautifully even expression of lemon, white peach and red cherry fruit, the culmination of chardonnay and pint noir in equal voice, underlined by the fine chalk presence of prominent chalk minerality and well-focused acidity that articulates the integrity of 2004. The secondary complexity that it showed in Australia in the past was not present in this bottle. A touch of dosage shows on the finish, but it has the minerality and acidity to hold it. A great Palmes d'Or.

NICOLAS FEUILLATTE PALMES D'OR VINTAGE BRUT 2006 $$$$

92 points • TASTED IN AUSTRALIA

50% chardonnay from Chouilly, Cramant, Oger, Le Mesnil-sur-Oger, Avize and Montgueux near Troyes; 50% pinot noir from Bouzy, Verzy, Verzenay, Aÿ and Ambonnay

This vintage opens with a reductive complexity of struck flint and grilled bread unfamiliar in Palmes d'Or. Behind this, the fast-developing personality of the 2006 vintage is displayed in a toasty, secondary style of spice and roast nuts. It culminates in a finish of integrity, marked by just a touch of phenolic bitterness, yet allowing the vibrant acidity and fine chalk minerality of some of Champagne's most revered grand crus to define a long and well-focused close.

An idyllic September afternoon for harvest in Sézanne, south of the Côte des Blancs, where chardonnay rules.

The Champagne Guide

PALMER & CO

(Pal-mair e Co)

(5/10)

67 RUE JACQUART 51100 REIMS

www.champagne-palmer.fr

CHAMPAGNE

*P*almer is a Reims-based cooperative with 285 member growers spread across some 40 villages and 400 hectares of vineyards, almost half of which are classified as grand or premier crus. Chardonnay comprises a high 50% of sourcing, hailing from the Montagne de Reims premier crus of Trépail and Villers-Marmery, and it is the generous concentration and bright structure of these villages that define the house style (supplemented with a little chardonnay from Barbonne in the Sézanne), bolstered with 40% pinot noir and 10% meunier, sourced mostly from the villages of the northern Montagne de Reims (and a little from Les Riceys in the Aube). Liqueurs are made from reserve wines aged in oak barrels. About 70% of production is sold to négociant houses, leaving just 400,000 bottles for Palmer & Co, and the standard of the current releases suggests that the cooperative is diligent in reserving the finest for its own cuvées, the best of which represent great value for money.

PALMER & CO BRUT RÉSERVE NV $

92 points • 2010 BASE VINTAGE • DISGORGED MARCH 2016 • TASTED IN AUSTRALIA

50% chardonnay from Villers-Marmery, Trépail and Barbonne; 40% pinot noir from Verzenay, Mailly-Champagne, Rilly-la-Montagne, Ludes and Les Riceys; 10% meunier from Rilly-la-Montagne and Ludes; 30% reserves, including some from a 20-year-old solera; aged 4 years on lees; 8–9g/L dosage

Vibrancy and cut meet fruit presence in a distinctive style that well articulates the depth and brightness of the northern and eastern slopes of the Montagne de Reims. Chardonnay asserts its lead in a fresh, zesty fruit focus of lemon and pear, with pinot noir lending red fruits and mid-palate presence. Impressive lees age in the order of five years contributes toasted brioche and nougat notes to the back palate. A touch of phenolic grip is well tempered by lingering acid line and integrated dosage. Great value.

Palmer & Co Blanc de Blancs NV $$

90 points • 2011 base vintage • Disgorged June 2016 • Tasted in Australia

The northern slopes of the Montagne de Reims have defined a blanc de blancs of grapefruit and nashi pear, cut with elegant, zesty fruit focus and grainy minerality quite distinct to that of the Côte des Blancs. Regrettably, it's all interrupted by the dry, dusty impurity of 2011 that renders the finish astringent and firm.

Palmer & Co Blanc de Noirs NV $$

89 points • 2011 base vintage • Disgorged April 2016 • Tasted in Australia

The character of northern Montagne de Reims pinot noir carries understated strawberry, red apple and red cherry fruits with dynamic acid drive and restraint, foiled on the finish by the stale, earthy grip of imperfect 2011 fruit.

Palmer & Co Rosé Réserve NV $$

91 points • 2013 base vintage • Disgorged April 2016 • Tasted in Australia

A medium-salmon hue announces a rosé of pink grapefruit tang, strawberry and red apple fruit. Nuances of savoury tomato and a touch of game are derived from a portion of reserves from a 20-year-old solera. A little fine tannin provides grip to the finish, without disturbing its flowing acid line or well-integrated dosage.

Palmer & Co Vintage 2008 $$

94 points • Disgorged December 2015 • Tasted in Australia

85% Trépail and Villers-Marmery, 15% Barbonne; 8-9g/L dosage

The energy and endurance of 2008 are beautifully presented in a style evolving slowly and confidently since its release two years ago. The depth and body of northern Montagne chardonnay, with a touch of textural grip from Sézanne, looks flattering in the tense and brilliant 2008 season, upholding a bright, medium-straw hue and an intense, primary core of white peach and lemon zest. Almond meal complexity is rising, with nougat and brioche joining the parade, yet upholding its pure, primary verve, promising years of potential yet, thanks to a pronounced, well-focused, yet softly integrated acid line, gentle chalk mineral texture, creamy bead and excellent persistence.

Palmer & Co Amazone de Palmer NV $$$

92 points • Disgorged April 2015 • Tasted in Australia

A blend of reserve wines from 1995, 1996, 1997, 1998 and 1999; bottled in 2000

There is profound vintage depth to this non-vintage prestige cuvée, yet the bottle discloses no clue as to its grand maturity. Its contents reveal the full story, in a full-yellow hue and a universe of complexity of grilled pineapple, roast hazelnuts, glacé apricot, sweet pipe smoke and burnt butter. It has evolved gloriously into its tertiary spectrum, while upholding secondary fruit integrity and persistence. It's just starting to show some dry, grainy bitterness to the finish.

The Champagne Guide

PAUL DÉTHUNE

(Pawl Deh-tune)

7/10

2 RUE DU MOULIN 51150 AMBONNAY

www.champagne-dethune.com

The Déthune family has tended its vines on the privileged slopes of Ambonnay since 1610, and produced their own wines since 1890. Today, Pierre Déthune and wife Sophie sensitively manage seven hectares of 70% pinot noir and 30% chardonnay entirely within the village. Seven cuvées draw complexity and diversity from 34 different Ambonnay parcels vinified separately, some in large oak foudres and small oak 'pièces' from the forests of Champagne. 'We want to show that the same grapes from the same village can produce seven different styles by varying the blends, the ageing and the use of oak,' Sophie explains. Their 50,000 bottles confidently express the luscious power and characterful poise of Ambonnay and quickly sell out every year.

The Déthunes proudly uphold an average vine age of 34–36 years and effectively tend their vineyards organically, having employed organic composts and avoided insecticides and herbicides for 20 years, though they have purposely shunned organic certification over concerns surrounding copper sulphate fungicide.

'Pierre's grandfather was organic without knowing it, and 100 years later we still have copper in the vineyard from his treatments. This is not good for the vines,' Sophie explains. 'Champagne's difficult climate calls for liberal use of fungicides, particularly in wet vintages like 2012, but we do not want to use massive amounts of copper sulphate.'

Pierre is instead trialling essential oils in the vineyards. 'I need every grape I can harvest, so I cannot take risks that might jeopardise any of our crop.' The Déthunes harvest 11 tonnes per hectare, quite a contrast to the 28 tonnes of one of their neighbours. 'Other growers laugh at us for not having many grapes, but we laugh at them for not having deep colour in their skins!' Sophie reveals.

Pierre's father, Paul, introduced mechanisation in 1960. 'They had an easier job — and we are going backwards!' he exclaims, detailing the time and attention required to control grasses planted in the mid-rows since 2001. 'We intend to leave the vineyards for the next generation, so it is important for us to preserve the environment.'

Fifty-four square metres of solar panels on the roof of the 17th century buildings provide one-fifth of the winery's electricity, and rainwater services a similar proportion of water requirements.

The Déthunes are careful not to harvest too late, to hold freshness and check the exuberance of Ambonnay pinot noir. Sophie works with the picking teams to inspect the fruit and ensure a stringent selection.

They aim to complete harvest of all 34 parcels within eight days. All are vinified separately, those destined for Brut NV in stainless steel, and reserves and other cuvées in large 3200-litre vats and small 205-litre barrels of up to 20 years of age. Vats work harmoniously with the Déthunes' fruit, though small oak barrels have at times tended to assert themselves, but are finding a more harmonious balance recently. They buy a few new 205-litre champagne oak barrels each year. 'We have 50 in all, and that's all we have room for!' says Sophie.

Having invested significantly in vineyards (purchasing four hectares and taking 20 years to pay it off), the focus since 1990 has been on investment in the winery, particularly in the purchase of new barrels and five new temperature-controlled vats. Space constraints have necessitated storage of their longest-aged cuvées off-site. They recently purchased the house next door and dug an impressive new cellar, to double their storage capacity to 200,000 bottles (much more than current requirements of 50,000 bottles), increase reserve wine stocks, and introduce a few new foudres.

This will permit a small increase in production, enabling them to keep the 15% of their fruit that they currently sell to Veuve Clicquot for La Grande Dame.

Blends, bottling and disgorgement dates are printed on the back of every bottle. A dosage of 9g/L is used across all cuvées, suiting the strength and vitality of the house style.

PAUL DÉTHUNE BRUT NV $$

94 points • 2012 BASE VINTAGE • DISGORGED SEPTEMBER 2015 • TASTED IN CHAMPAGNE

70% pinot noir, 30% chardonnay; 50% reserves from oak barrels, including a solera of more than 40 different vintages; 9g/L dosage; 34,000 bottles

A full-straw hue, this is a wonderfully deep and complex celebration of Ambonnay pinot noir, in all of its alluring black cherry and black plum glory, even fragrant violet perfume. It rumbles with the depth of the village, then pulls gracefully into a refined finish of beautifully expressive chalk minerality that lingers and ripples long and true. A grand and alluring showpiece of one of Champagne's finest terroirs.

PAUL DÉTHUNE BRUT ROSÉ NV $$

93 points • 2010 BASE VINTAGE • DISGORGED AUGUST 2014 • TASTED IN CHAMPAGNE

80% pinot noir, 20% chardonnay; Brut NV with 10% pinot noir red wine; 9g/L dosage; 3000 bottles

Déthune blends rosé from its Brut NV rather than macerating pinot noir, to retain higher acidity and freshness in its rich Ambonnay fruit. The effect is a medium- to full-crimson hue and a spicy style that carries the full depth and expansive mood of Ambonnay in wonderful waves of deep red cherry, strawberry and red plum fruit and anise. It leads out expansive and contracts into a well-rounded tail, underlined by finely structured tannins that meld seamlessly with fine chalk minerality.

The Champagne Guide

PAUL DÉTHUNE BLANC DE NOIRS NV $$

91 points • 100% 2011 VINTAGE • DISGORGED APRIL 2015 • TASTED IN CHAMPAGNE

From the ancient Les Crayères part of Ambonnay towards Trépail, with excellent exposition and accessible chalk; vinified entirely in oak barrels; 9g/L dosage; 5000 bottles

The rounded generosity of this well-exposed site in Ambonnay fills a palate of succulent peach, even apple crumble, gaining charcuterie complexity from barrel fermentation. Maturity has united with oak to coax out toasty, spicy, honeyed complexity, culminating in a soft, creamy, custardy finish, with a little dry-extract grip difficult to dodge in the tricky 2011 season. Its fruit presence has the depth to handle it, carrying long and true with good fruit integrity.

PAUL DÉTHUNE CUVÉE PRESTIGE PRINCESSE DES THUNES BRUT NV $$$

96 points • 2007 BASE VINTAGE • DISGORGED JULY 2015 • TASTED IN CHAMPAGNE

70% 2007, 30% reserve from a perpetual solera of 40 vintages made and aged in oak vats; 50% pinot, 50% chardonnay from a mix of different vineyards of vines over 40 years of age; vinified entirely in 3200–3400L oak vats of at least 5 years of age; aged 7 years on lees; 9g/L dosage; 2500 bottles

More than 40 years ago, Pierre's father Paul commenced a solera to which every vintage since has contributed. The complexity that such depth of maturity contributes to a blend is mesmerising, evoking memories of crème brûlée and pâtisserie. One might expect a dissonance between such far-fetched exoticism and the primary fruit exuberance of Ambonnay's generous and supple black cherry, plum and red berry fruit, and the anise and spice of a decade of maturity. The true skill of this cuvée comes first in harmonising this maelstrom seamlessly, and second in bringing poise, silky, polished finesse and enchanting appeal unexpected in Ambonnay. For all its generosity it is carefully measured and magnificently expressive of the fine, mouth-filling chalk minerality that typifies Ambonnay.

PAUL DÉTHUNE CUVÉE A L'ANCIENNE BRUT 2008 $$$$

96 points • DISGORGED SEPTEMBER 2015 • TASTED IN CHAMPAGNE

50% chardonnay, 50% pinot noir from a single parcel of 40-year-old vines; vinified and aged in 205-litre oak barrels; aged under cork for 6 years; just 1000 bottles

There's more than a little tension in this complex and multi-layered champagne of inimitable character, colliding the depth and impact of Ambonnay with all the personality of small oak barrels. In power and sheer, joyful exuberance, it lands squarely at the extreme of champagne flamboyance and yet – crucially – the energy and focus of the stunning 2008 season brings consummate control to a strict finish of wonderfully present, all-conquering chalk minerality of the finest texture. A panoply of exoticism rolls in waves of French pâtisserie, grilled pineapple, butter, fig, even fruit-mince spice, glacé apricot and marmalade. Barrel fermentation in concert with cork age explodes in a crescendo of coffee, dark chocolate and toasty, spicy, nutty complexity. The finish carries remarkably long, riding on rails of 2008 acidity.

PAUL GOERG

(Pawl Gerg)

30 RUE DU GÉNÉRAL LECLERC 51130 VERTUS
www.champagne-goerg.com

*P*aul Goerg is the sister brand of Napoléon under the cooperative of Vertus. Together, the two labels comprise two-thirds of the production of the group, with the remainder sold. Vertus chardonnay is the theme of Paul Goerg, supplemented with a little fruit from neighbouring villages, particularly Le Mesnil-sur-Oger. While richer and more rounded parcels are destined for Napoléon, chef de cave Jean-Philippe Moulin sets aside those of pure, elegant delicacy for Paul Goerg, aspiring to a long-aged style of clean, mineral precision. Moulin has lowered dosage from 9g/L to 7g/L. These are simple, tightly structured cuvées that appreciate bottle age.

PAUL GOERG BLANC DE BLANCS BRUT NV $$$

92 points • 2011 BASE VINTAGE • TASTED IN AUSTRALIA
A blend of Vertus, Le Mesnil-sur-Oger, Verzenay and Avize; 9g/L dosage

An impressive Goerg Blanc de Blancs that transcends the 2011 base vintage, accurately articulating the fine salt chalk mineral texture of the Côte des Blancs, and presenting fresh lemon, apple and pear fruit, subtly supported by the almond and nougat notes of bottle maturity. The finish carries accurate line and gentle confidence. The best I've seen this cuvée and a triumph for 2011.

PAUL GOERG ROSÉ BRUT NV $$$

88 points • 2010 BASE VINTAGE • DISGORGED 2015 • TASTED IN AUSTRALIA
85% chardonnay and 15% pinot noir from Vertus, Le Mesnil-sur-Oger, Verzenay and Avize; 8g/L dosage

A pale-salmon hue heralds a savoury chardonnay-led rosé of spicy, brambly complexity and some coarse tannin grip, lacking in fruit lift and structural finesse, though finishing with compelling, refreshing acid/dosage balance.

PERRIER-JOUËT

(Per-riay Zhoo-ay)

5/10

28 AVENUE DE CHAMPAGNE 51201 ÉPERNAY

www.perrier-jouet.com

The past 20 years have been turbulent for Perrier-Jouët, changing hands three times before it was taken over by current owners, Pernod Ricard, in 2005. In the midst of this rollercoaster, the house has been fortunate to retain most of its vineyards, with 65 hectares now providing for one-quarter of its annual production of 3.5 million bottles, up from 2.5 million just a decade ago, now ranking as Champagne's 10th-largest house. From its founding just over 200 years ago, the vision of the house has focused on the floral elegance of chardonnay, and today more than half of the estate's holdings lie in the Côte des Blancs, particularly in the grand crus of Cramant (27 ha), Avize (9 ha) and, to a lesser extent, Chouilly. The jewel of the house is the glorious Cramant, where it is privileged to the very finest sites in the village. For chef de cave Hervé Deschamps, 'Perrier-Jouët is about the elegance, freshness, fruitiness and roundness of chardonnay, with power and biscuity complexity.' His is a house style of soft, rounded, creamy generosity.

For Deschamps, the origin of the fruit is of utmost importance, and he sources from no less than 70 villages across Champagne. 'It's all about which village and which location and which age of vines,' he says. 'The best chardonnay comes from the Côte des Blancs, Trépail, Villers-Marmery, the Sézanne and the Vitry, and for Perrier-Jouët, it's all about the Côte des Blancs,' he says, listing Cramant, then Avize, then Chouilly as the greatest villages, adding that Villers-Marmery is also an important source. He uses pinot noir for perfume rather than strength, favouring Mailly-Champagne (the most important source of pinot for the house, with nine hectares under its ownership), Verzy, Verzenay, Aÿ, Avenay-Val-d'Or and Les Riceys, and meunier from Dizy, Damery, Venteuil and Vincelles. Maintaining acidity and avoiding high ripeness is his priority in the vineyards, which he admits is a challenge in the wake of global warming.

A total of 300 tanks allows the flexibility to keep not only each village separate, but the early, middle and late picks also. 'For me, a blend is not about percentages of products, it is about a list of tanks. And to me, every tank has its own personality.' Everything is vinified in stainless steel, with full malolactic fermentation.

Since my very first meeting with Hervé I have been drawn to his warm smile, humility and candour. 'When I joined Perrier-Jouët 32 years ago, I knew about winegrowing, as my grandfather grew grapes, but I'd never blended a wine before!' he revealed. He learnt his art over a decade under his predecessor, André Bavaret.

Hervé's openness is rare and refreshing in the big-brand champagne world, and as he methodically presents each of the cuvées of the house, no topic is off limits, even production volumes of each cuvée.

Together with Mumm, its sister house within Pernod Ricard, Perrier-Jouët aspires to double volume in ten years. The biggest challenge lies in sourcing fruit, Hervé admits. Without space to extend its historic premises, the house has rented cellars off-site.

Symbolic of its focus on chardonnay's floral elegance, the Belle Epoque flagships are presented in a distinctive, enamelled bottle of Art Nouveau Japanese anemones. The luscious branding of the house is likewise a tribute to the Art Nouveau era.

Every bottle of Perrier-Jouët is now reliably sealed with DIAM, except those destined for the US.

PERRIER-JOUËT GRAND BRUT NV $$

90 points • 2012 BASE VINTAGE • TASTED IN CHAMPAGNE AND AUSTRALIA

40% pinot noir, 40% meunier, 20% chardonnay; 40-45 crus; almost 15% reserves; 9g/L dosage; DIAM closure; 2 million bottles

This is a fresh, vibrant release for Perrier-Jouët. The bouquet presents a compelling synergy between primary apple and white peach fruit, and the honeysuckle and nutmeg of age. The palate is toasty and biscuity, balancing lemon cut and acid drive with well-integrated dosage. A subtle touch of dusty dryness and gentle phenolic grip are apparent on the finish, though less pronounced and with greater freshness and integrity than in the past.

PERRIER-JOUËT BLASON ROSÉ NV $$

89 points • 2012 BASE VINTAGE • TASTED IN AUSTRALIA

50% pinot noir, 25% meunier, 25% chardonnay; Grand Brut base with 15% red wine from Vincelles and Les Riceys; 15% reserves up to 10 years of age; DIAM closure; 200,000 bottles

The aspiration for Blason Rosé is an elegant colour and fruity style, created with red wine of fruity aromas, strong colour and soft tannin. Perrier-Jouët has been making rosé since 1959 and is currently increasing its production, though only makes it in vintages in which the red wine is of sufficient quality. 2012 makes for a stronger base than the bad-tempered 2011 and 2010 seasons, a wine of medium-salmon hue and primary strawberry, raspberry and even persimmon fruit. Acidity and dosage are evenly married, though firm, grainy tannins lend grip, dusty dryness and texture to the finish.

PERRIER-JOUËT BELLE EPOQUE VINTAGE 2008 $$$$

95 points • TASTED IN AUSTRALIA

50% chardonnay from Cramant and Avize; 45% pinot noir from the Montagne de Reims; 5% meunier from estate vines in Dizy to bridge chardonnay and pinot noir; 9g/L dosage; DIAM closure; less than 1 million bottles

The generous, sunny, buttery mood of Perrier-Jouët is well countered by the tension and definition of the great 2008 season, creating a Belle Epoque of heightened lemon purity and elevating the chalk mineral emphasis of Cramant and Avize. True to the season, it's backward and primary, with only subtle Parisian pâtisserie complexity providing interest to its white-fruit purity. It upholds the silky succulence and creamy approachability of the house, yet does so with greater focus, line and energy than ever. The result is quite magnificent, the most compelling vintage under this label for as long as I can recall.

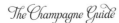

The Champagne Guide

PERRIER-JOUËT BELLE EPOQUE VINTAGE 2007 $$$$

93 points • TASTED IN CHAMPAGNE AND AUSTRALIA

50% chardonnay from Cramant, Avize, Le Mesnil-sur-Oger and Chouilly; 45% pinot noir from Mailly-Champagne and Verzy; 5% meunier from estate vines in Dizy to bridge chardonnay and pinot noir; 8g/L dosage; DIAM closure; almost 1 million bottles

Cramant and Mailly-Champagne are the pillars of Belle Epoque, and in the strong chardonnay year of 2007 they have yielded a powerful, rounded, sweet-fruited and succulent wine true to the Perrier-Jouët style. Chardonnay leads out with its cut of focused lemon and white peach fruit, layered with the depth of fig, ginger, vanilla, mixed spice, even English toffee. Its rounded fruit sweetness is contrasted with vibrant acidity, slightly grainy chalk mineral structure and gentle phenolic grip, culminating in a long finish of freshness, integrity and creamy fruit sweetness.

PERRIER-JOUËT BELLE EPOQUE ROSÉ 2006 $$$$$

93 points • TASTED IN CHAMPAGNE AND AUSTRALIA

50% Mailly-Champagne, Aÿ, Ambonnay, Mareuil-sur-Aÿ and Verzy pinot; 45% Cramant, Avize and Le Mesnil-sur-Oger chardonnay; 5% Dizy and Venteuil meunier; same base as Belle Epoque with 11% red wine, particularly from Vertus, Vincelles and Ambonnay; 8g/L dosage; DIAM closure

A floral style is the aspiration for Belle Epoque Rosé, but at more than a decade of age, the generous 2006 season delivers much more, now very much a complex style of secondary appeal. Medium salmon copper in hue, it upholds its primary strawberry and cherry liqueur characters, now evolving into a savoury realm of tomato and subtle vegetal reductive complexity. Maturity has brought allusions of toasted meringue, nougat and anise, and in more developed bottles, coffee bean, orange rind and dust. It's soft, gentle and creamy, having attained a comfortable balance of well-integrated acidity, even dosage, subtle mineral texture and firm, fine tannin grip.

PERRIER JOUËT BELLE EPOQUE BLANC DE BLANCS 2004 $$$$$

96 points • TASTED IN AUSTRALIA

Two legendary mid-slope lieux-dits in Cramant, Bouron Leroi and Bouron du Midi; 8g/L dosage; DIAM

It was celebrated grower Pierre Larmandier who once told me that Perrier-Jouët owns the finest terroir in Cramant. I suspect the two neighbouring plots of perfect south-easterly exposure in the glorious mid-slope of the village that contribute to this cuvée were part of what he was talking about. This is the second release of this label, and from the outset it steps up as the glittering triumph of the house. Cramant sings with full operatic gusto in grand power and complexity of yellow mirabelle plums, reverberating with magnificent depth and succulent breadth, enlivened with beautifully structured, impeccably fresh and definitively pronounced salt chalk minerality. With greater secondary complexity than the energetic, inaugural 2002, long bottle age piles on layers of ginger, honey, butter and brioche. It concludes with the same grand dimensions with which it led out, carrying a line of expansive volume from start to very long finish, yet at every moment tamed by impeccable salt minerality, the definitive Cramant. It's ready to drink right away. A classic. Alongside Perrier-Jouët's 2 million bottles of Grand Brut NV and 1 million of Belle Epoque, its 12,000 bottle production of this cuvée is minuscule.

PHILIPPE FOURRIER

(Fi-lip Faw-riay)

39 RUE DE BAR SUR AUBE 10200 BAROVILLE

www.champagne-fourrier.com

Maison fondée en 1847

CHAMPAGNE
PHILIPPE FOURRIER

CÔTE DES BAR BAROVILLE

The Fourriers have been growing grapes in the village of Baroville in the Côte des Bar for five generations since 1847, and were the first growers to produce their own champagne in the village by the early 1900s. Today, the family estate comprises 18 hectares in the village, planted predominantly to pinot noir (70%). Unusually for this part of Champagne, the balance is made up almost entirely of chardonnay (29%), with meunier comprising a tiny 1%. Sustainability is the mandate of not only the vineyards, where vines are ploughed manually and mulch is used to protect the soil, but also the winery, which is equipped with substantial rainwater recovery and solar systems. These are characterful wines, brimming with the personality of Côte des Bar pinot noir, at times lacking a little in polish, but with the propensity to shine in a great season like 2008.

PHILIPPE FOURRIER CARTE D'OR NV $$

90 points • DISGORGED APRIL 2016 • TASTED IN AUSTRALIA

100% Côte des Bar pinot noir; aged 3 years on lees; 11g/L dosage

This is Côte des Bar pinot noir in all of its glory, and one certainly feels closer to Burgundy than to the Marne in the presence of this cuvée. Blackberry and mulberry fruits of juicy freshness are supported by layers of spice, even a greengage plum tang. It's primary and lively, all about up-front fruit more than complexity or persistence.

The Champagne Guide

Philippe Fourrier Rosé NV $$

89 points • Disgorged April 2016 • Tasted in Australia

90% pinot noir, 10% chardonnay from Côte des Bar; aged 3 years on lees; 12g/L dosage

A dark-crimson hue heralds one of the deepest-coloured rosés of Champagne, fruity, exuberant and brimming with wild strawberries, freshly picked raspberries and pink pepper. Côte des Bar pinot noir sings with full voice here, supported by fine tannin structure. Tannin/sugar balance is always a precarious act in a deeply coloured rosé, and a full dosage is more than it calls for. The flamboyance of its fruit would stand better without it.

Philippe Fourrier Cuvée Prestige Brut NV $$

88 points • Disgorged May 2016 • Tasted in Australia

100% Côte des Bar chardonnay; aged 4 years on lees; 8g/L dosage

Grapefruit and strawberry-hull fruit character is evidence of chardonnay's ability to take on red fruit nuances in terroirs more commonly planted to pinot noir. It's underlined by the almond-meal notes of an additional year of bottle age, but what it gains in complexity and texture it unfortunately more than loses in fruit expression and character, finishing with dusty, dry phenolic grip.

Philippe Fourrier Cuvée Millésime Brut 2008 $$$

94 points • Disgorged May 2016 • Tasted in Australia

70% pinot noir, 30% chardonnay from Côte des Bar; aged at least 6 years on lees; 9g/L dosage

The confident presence and inimitable character of Côte des Bar pinot noir is well toned by the tension of the sensational 2008 season, culminating in a victory of harmony between primary red cherry, raspberry and strawberry fruit, layers of secondary complexity of mixed spice and dark fruit cake, finely textured structure and excellent, propagating acid line. Wonderful.

Philippe Fourrier Cuvée Millésime Brut 2007 $$$

91 points • Tasted in Australia

70% pinot noir, 30% chardonnay from Côte des Bar

Pinot noir speaks with full voice of black cherry and plum fruit, set against a backdrop of deep, rumbling, dark fruit cake and ginger and a swirling mass of spice. It's rich, rounded, succulent and ready, if a little lacking in freshness and tension.

PHILIPPONNAT

(Fi-li-poh-nah)

6/10

13 RUE DU PONT 51160 MAREUIL-SUR-AŸ

www.philipponnat.com

1522

PHILIPPONNAT

CHAMPAGNE

If the finest vineyard sites are the most important asset of any Champagne house, Philipponnat is particularly privileged. Its 17 hectares of mostly pinot noir span Mareuil-sur-Aÿ, and its neighbours Aÿ, Mutigny and Avenay-Val-d'Or, but its most prized is the splendid, sun-drenched Clos des Goisses, one of the most powerful and distinctive sites in all of Champagne. The walled vineyard of 5.5 hectares lies on the east of Mareuil-sur-Aÿ at the very heart of Champagne, the juncture at which the Côte des Blancs, the Vallée de la Marne and the Montagne de Reims meet. With perfect south-facing aspect, a dramatic slope of 30–45 degrees towards the Marne ('Gois' means 'very steep' in the local dialect), catching the sun in its full perpendicular strength, and shielded from the westerly winds, this is one of the warmest micro-climates in Champagne, boasting temperatures to equal those of Burgundy. The subsoil is pure chalk, following the gradient of the hill under a thin layer of poor topsoil, so roots quickly strike chalk, pervading the wines with minerality. Mareuil-sur-Aÿ is a mere premier cru, and Clos des Goisses is perhaps the most striking case of all for a much more detailed classification of Champagne vineyards.

Philipponnat's house style is particularly intense, relying primarily on the power of Montagne de Reims pinot noir from south-facing estate vineyards. Additional supplies are sourced from a further 60 hectares of vineyards, particularly from the Côte des Blancs and Vallée de la Marne, and excess is purchased each vintage to permit lesser parcels to be declassified.

Yields are restricted and optimal physiological maturity is sought through slightly delayed harvests. Clos des Goisses is 1–1.5°C warmer than other nearby vineyards, and is harvested at 13 degrees potential, the maximum permitted in the appellation.

The opulence of Philipponnat's ripeness can be disarming, and the phenolic coarseness that this creates can be disconcerting.

Fruit of high sugar ripeness calls for winemaking processes that preserve freshness in every detail. This begins with vinification close to the vineyards in Mareuil-sur-Aÿ. When Philipponnat owners Lanson-BCC invited Charles Philipponnat to return and manage the family business in 2000, his first initiative was to construct a new winery in Mareuil-sur-Aÿ and discontinue processing in Reims. He has since worked on improving viticulture through

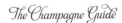

natural fertilisation and decreased use of chemicals, which have made for riper grapes, allowing for lower dosage, so every cuvée above the entry NVs are extra brut. Charles Philipponnat has also focused on longer oak ageing, cleaner blends, increasing pinot noir and decreasing meunier in the top cuvées, and finally, recently introducing new smart, minimalist, modern labels across the range. He remains personally actively involved in the tastings and blendings of the house.

Freshness is preserved through use of only the first pressings, cool fermentation in temperature-controlled stainless steel, blocking of malolactic fermentation in the most powerful parcels according to the vintage, use of a minimum of 30% chardonnay, and moderate dosage.

The strongest parcels of pinot noir and chardonnay (about 20% in all, representing 40–60% of vintage wines) are fermented in barrels, which vary between new and 5–6 years old, for complexity and oxidation. At least 50% of each cuvée is aged in barrels. Walking into the barrel hall, the aroma of oak is intoxicating, like nowhere else in Champagne. Such is the strength of Philipponnat's bold fruit that oak flavour does not tend to dominate, though its structure risks disrupting already heightened phenolics.

The barrel hall is climate controlled to block malolactic fermentation in every barrel. All reserve wines are matured for six months in small- and large-format oak. Reserve wines for Brut Royale are kept in a solera system of fractional blending in foudres for six months, then into small barrels, re-blended every year to incorporate mature wines without losing freshness. Non-vintage cuvées receive 20–30% reserve wines and are aged 3–4 years in bottle. The house doubles the minimum ageing times across its cuvées, necessitating a stock of 2.5 million bottles in its 1.5 kilometres of 17th-century cellars. It maintains some 250 barrels, purchased after two or three vintages in Burgundy, and upheld for about 10 seasons at Philipponnat.

Philipponnat sells 500,000 bottles annually, all of which boast some of the most informative back labels of any house, declaring the date of disgorgement (since 1997), the blend, barrel maturation and dosage. The house claims to be the first in Champagne to also indicate the base year of its blends. An excellent website adds more informative detail on every cuvée.

All 17 Clos de Goisses parcels are vinified separately, half in tank and half in barrel, as has been tradition since 1935. The vineyard comprises about two-thirds pinot noir and one-third chardonnay, from vines aged 8–45 years, with an average of 30.

While 5.5 hectares has the capacity to produce 55,000 bottles, on average just 17,000 bottles are made annually — sometimes as few as 5000 or as many as 20,000 — with the remainder declassified into other Philipponnat cuvées.

Clos des Goisses is produced every vintage, but not always released. The house believes that it represents the first single-vineyard bottling in Champagne, and it is testimony to the site that since 1936 all but seven vintages have been released.

Philipponnat Royale Réserve Non-Dosé NV $$

93 points • 2012 base vintage • Disgorged March 2016 • Tasted in Australia

Brut Royale without dosage; 65% pinot noir, 30% chardonnay, 5% meunier; mainly from grand and premier crus; 48% reserves; aged 3 years on lees; reserves aged in wooden-barrel solera system; partial malolactic; zero dosage

The 2012 season has produced a beautifully focused base wine whose purity shines in this no-added-sugar guise. That said, I eagerly await the 8g/L Brut version, as this comparison is always a strong case for the importance of dosage, and the inherent danger of making a zero-dosage champagne without designing it purposely from the ground up. If tense champagne is your vibe, this combination of crystal-clear lemon fruit, high-strung malic acidity and the subtle toastiness of a massive 48% of oak-aged reserves might be just your thing. It carries its purity and integrity long on the finish, and holds the stamina to age confidently for the medium term.

PHILIPPONNAT ROYALE RÉSERVE BRUT NV $

92 points • 2011 BASE VINTAGE • DISGORGED OCTOBER 2015 AND FEBRUARY 2016 • TASTED IN CHAMPAGNE AND AUSTRALIA

65% pinot noir, 30% chardonnay, 5% meunier; 30% reserves from a wooden barrel solera; a blend of 20 villages; partial malolactic fermentation; aged 3 years on lees; 8g/L dosage

Philipponnat has produced an admirable result for its entry cuvée in the tough 2011 season, and the savoury mushroom notes that were apparent pre-release two years ago have seemingly retracted into the wine, leaving a seamless, effortless and well-composed accord of primary lemon, ripe stone fruit and red apple, with intricately supporting and subtle roast nut and honey complexity. As predicted, it's fleshed out admirably, with malic acid lending tension and oak-aged reserves contributing depth and texture to the red fruit depth of Mareuil pinot.

PHILIPPONNAT ROYALE RÉSERVE ROSÉ BRUT NV $$

93 points • 2009 BASE VINTAGE • DISGORGED FEBRUARY 2016 • TASTED IN AUSTRALIA

75% pinot noir, 20% chardonnay, 5% meunier; 7-8% pinot noir red wine from Mareuil-sur-Aÿ and Les Riceys; 23% reserves from wooden-barrel solera; partial malolactic fermentation; aged 3 years on lees; 9g/L dosage

Philipponnat Rosé is on the rise, and this is a compelling and engaging follow-on to the wonderful 2008 base. A tiny dose of Mareuil-sur-Aÿ red wine produces a pretty pale-salmon hue, and heightens wonderful red cherry and wild strawberry accents of impressive depth and character, blessed by brioche complexity. Fleshy, creamy pinot noir takes a confident lead, well toned by the texture and fullness of a touch of barrel fermentation and more than five years of lees age.

PHILIPPONNAT BLANC DE NOIRS BRUT MILLÉSIMÉ 2009 $$

91 points • DISGORGED DECEMBER 2015 AND FEBRUARY 2016 • TASTED IN CHAMPAGNE AND AUSTRALIA

100% pinot noir from 5-6 Montagne de Reims premier and grand crus; 50% fermented in wooden barrels; partial malolactic fermentation; aged 5-7 years on lees; 4.25g/L dosage

A medium-straw hue declares the generosity of the house, confirmed by wonderful layers of black cherry and wild strawberry fruit, set against a backdrop of spice and toast and an undercurrent of fine chalk minerality. Rich and fleshy on the front, it contracts into a dry and firm finish in which phenolic grip, partial barrel fermentation, malic acidity and low dosage conspire to leave a firmness that screams out for protein-rich foods to soften.

PHILIPPONNAT GRAND BLANC BRUT 2007 $$

92 points • DISGORGED JANUARY 2015 AND SEPTEMBER 2015 • TASTED IN CHAMPAGNE AND AUSTRALIA

Côte des Blancs, Montagne de Reims and Clos des Goisses grand and premier crus; aged 5-7 years on lees; partial malolactic fermentation; 50% fermented in wooden barrels; 4.25g/L dosage

The 2007 returns a mood of focused composure after the generous 2006, though the style of Philipponnat is still very much upheld. The thundering depth of the all-conquering Clos de Goisses meets the dry grip of partial barrel fermentation, heightened by the tension of vibrant 2007 malic acidity, low dosage and the pronounced chalk minerality of Vertus, and especially Le Mesnil-sur-Oger and Chouilly. The result is a spicy, confident and well-bodied blanc de blancs, with a core of fresh lemon zest, and all the spectacle of vanilla, brioche, nougat, ginger cake, biscuits and even crème brûlée. It's enticing now and has a long and confident life before it.

PHILIPPONNAT SUBLIME RÉSERVE SEC 2005 $$

90 points • DISGORGED AUGUST 2014 • TASTED IN AUSTRALIA

Sourced mainly from grand and premier crus; partial malolactic fermentation; aged 8 years on lees; 30g/L dosage

A vintage champagne of such maturity is rare indeed in a sec style, so if sweet is your vibe, this is a good find. The effect of dosage in champagne is profound, and the candied lemon, peach and cane sugar notes contributed by four times Philipponnat's typical brut dosage make for a creamy and soft style, well masking the phenolic grip inherent to the 2005 season. It holds good persistence and all the toasty, roasty, nutty complexity of more than a decade of age.

PHILIPPONNAT LE LÉON AŸ GRAND CRU EXTRA BRUT 2006 $$$$

93 points • DISGORGED FEBRUARY 2015 • TASTED IN CHAMPAGNE

100% pinot noir; 45% aged in oak barrels without malolactic fermentation; 4.5g/L dosage; 2085 bottles

A cuvée that sings with the depth, width and red-fruited flamboyance of Aÿ pinot noir and sets it snugly in a backdrop of spicy, toasty, dark chocolate and coffee oak, culminating in a creamy and tangy finish. The result is a powerful cuvée that pulls obediently into line thanks to fine chalk minerality and refreshing malic acidity. It's well crafted and will age.

Philipponnat 1522 Grand Cru Brut 2007 $$$

91 points • Disgorged May 2016 • Tasted in Australia

65% pinot noir, 35% chardonnay from grand cru vineyards, majority from the Léon plot in Aÿ; partial barrel vinification; partial malolactic fermentation; aged 8 years on lees; extra-brut dosage of 4.5g/L, though labelled brut

The 1522 label commemorates the date of the first proof of the Philipponnats growing pinot noir in Aÿ. A full straw-gold hue declares a blend of grand proportions, the voluptuous curves of pinot noir amplified in the stature of Aÿ and the voluminous character of barrel fermentation. Fleshy and full, it's packed with golden fruit cake, grilled pineapple and white peach, colliding with the spicy, nutty, coffee bean presence of oak. Malic acidity pulls the finish into line, though also serves to heighten its dry phenolic grip.

Philipponnat 1522 Grand Cru Brut 2006 $$$

93 points • Disgorged November 2015 • Tasted in Champagne

65% pinot noir, 35% chardonnay from Aÿ, majority from the Léon plot; 50% barrel vinification; partial malolactic fermentation; aged 8 years on lees; extra-brut dosage of 4.5g/L, though labelled brut; 10,446 bottles

A toasty style that shows the coffee influence of oak barrel maturation, pulling into a finish at once creamy and tense with tangy malic acidity and simultaneously generous in the mood of the sun-drenched 2006 harvest. It's spicy, peppery and long.

Philipponnat 1522 Premier Cru Brut Rosé 2007 $$$

92 points • Disgorged June 2016 • Tasted in Australia

70% pinot noir, 30% chardonnay from Aÿ, majority from the Léon plot in Aÿ; 8.5% pinot noir red wine from Mareuil-sur-Aÿ; 50% vinified in barrels without malolactic fermentation; aged 8 years on lees; extra-brut dosage of 4.25g/L, though labelled brut

A full-salmon hue and an explosion of bright, characterful wild strawberry, red cherry and pink grapefruit declares all the theatrics of Mareuil and Aÿ pinot noir. The exuberance of the house is well tempered by the tension of malic acidity, while partial barrel fermentation heightens grip and tannin texture on the finish. The result is a complex and structured style that calls for protein-rich foods to temper its grip. Nonetheless, it carries long, with impressive line and coherence.

The Champagne Guide

PHILIPPONNAT CLOS DES GOISSES BRUT 2007 $$$$$

96 points • DISGORGED JUNE 2016 • TASTED IN AUSTRALIA

65% pinot noir, 35% chardonnay; 73% vinified in oak barrels; no malolactic fermentation; aged 8 years on lees; extra-brut dosage of 4.25g/L, though labelled brut

For its lofty credentials (and price to match), Clos des Goisses should consistently rank in the highest echelons of Champagne. If sheer, booming power were the only criterion, it would have no equal. The house describes it as a 'big, Burgundian style of champagne!' To me, its thumping ripeness can be alarming, creating disconcerting phenolic coarseness, though in some vintages it finds an alluring harmony, and 2007 is one of these.

   A full-straw hue with a yellow tint, this is a cuvée of voluminous power, rippling with the ripeness of juicy white peach, grilled pineapple and fig, layered with all the complexity of honey, gingernut biscuits and candied orange. Malic acidity upholds control and focus on the finish, projecting the full presence of fine, salty chalk minerality, and just the right touch of bitter lemon zest to control its dimensions. It concludes full and very long. This is inimitable Clos des Goisses, and a great vintage for this cuvée.

PHILIPPONNAT CLOS DES GOISSES BRUT 2006 $$$$$

95 points • DISGORGED MAY 2015 • TASTED IN CHAMPAGNE

65% pinot noir, 35% chardonnay; 40% vinified in oak barrels; no malolactic fermentation; aged 8 years on lees; extra-brut dosage of 4.5g/L, though labelled brut; 28,305 bottles

A wonderfully approachable, fruity and spicy Clos des Goisses of medium-straw hue, that marries the generous exuberance of this exceptional vineyard with the subtle chocolate, coffee and spice of oak-barrel fermentation. It finishes very long, creamy and well balanced, with full malic acidity sitting comfortably in the billowing generosity of the 2006 vintage. A great result for a warm season in a warm site.

PHILIPPONNAT CLOS DES GOISSES JUSTE ROSÉ BRUT 2005 $$$$$

95 points • DISGORGED NOVEMBER 2014 • TASTED IN AUSTRALIA

64% pinot noir, 36% chardonnay; 50% vinified in oak barrels; no malolactic fermentation; aged 8.5 years on lees; extra-brut dosage of 4.25g/L, though labelled brut

The thundering proportions of Clos des Goisses make a grand statement in this rosé of medium-salmon hue with a copper tint. It leads out with enticing, smoky complexity of 8.5 years of lees age, backed with beautifully poised strawberry hull and juicy yellow-peach fruit, intricately evolving into roast nut and brioche complexity. The salt chalk minerality of this lauded site speaks amidst the dry, grainy structure of 2005, but like the white Clos des Goisses 2005, the integrity and volume of its fruit counters this confidently, carrying through a long finish, well framed by impeccably ripe and evenly integrated malic acidity.

PIERRE GIMONNET & FILS

(Pee-yair Zhi-moh-neh e Feess)

8/10

1 RUE DE LA RÉPUBLIQUE 51530 CUIS

www.champagne-gimonnet.com

CHAMPAGNE
Pierre Gimonnet
& Fils

'*The difference between a good wine and an exceptional wine is only a question of very, very small details, but we must focus on every detail all of the time,' declares Didier Gimonnet, who oversees his family's glorious estate with his brother, Olivier. The champagnes of Pierre Gimonnet & Fils are intricately assembled by masterful hands exclusively from enviably positioned and painstakingly tended old vines. Every cuvée sings its aspiration of 'precision, purity and minerality', each speaking articulately of its place in the northern Côte des Blancs through expressive, chalky minerality, without one molecule of detail out of place. With high-strung tension, crystalline structure and rapier-sharp precision, these are blanc de blancs champagnes charged with an energy that will sustain them long indeed. They represent some of the best-value apéritif champagnes of all.*

'My father always told me the most important thing is to make wine, and after that to sell it at a reasonable price,' Didier explains. From one of Champagne's most intelligent growers, wines of such purity and fine-spun, mineral-laden precision should sell for much higher prices. Little wonder Gimonnet has experienced strong global demand in recent years, fully allocating its production of 260,000 bottles. There is not a champagne in this collection unworthy of your table this year.

GRAND VINEYARDS

'Our champagnes have a personality because of the vineyards they come from,' Didier says. 'In Champagne, as everywhere, the most important thing is the origin of the grapes.' The family owns a substantial estate of 28 hectares, most proudly located in the heart of each

of their village's terroirs, almost exclusively in the Côte des Blancs.

In a region afflicted with generally young vines, more than two-thirds of Gimonnet's are now more than 40 years old, close to half are more than 50, and one hectare more than a century – incredible numbers for a region that typically replants every 35 years. Every bottle of Gimonnet comes exclusively from these vineyards; not a single grape is purchased from growers.

'When you have great terroir, it is a child's game to create a great blend,' Didier says. Half of Gimonnet's vineyards are located in its premier cru home village of Cuis, which he is frank in admitting is the black sheep of the Côte des Blancs, not a great terroir. 'With less body and structure, Cuis does not have the character, body or structure of a grand cru, but it has higher acidity, giving

Its grand south- and east-facing amphitheatre makes Oger a distinctive style and tricky to blend for Didier Gimonnet.

us very fresh wines,' Didier explains. 'Without doubt, the best of our domains are in Cramant. I compare Cramant with lace – it is precise and delicate, with an interesting, chalky minerality, and it has a concentration but is not heavy.' He holds 5.5 glorious hectares in the village.

One hectare in the more stony soils of Oger contributes concentrated, spicy, smoky power and graphite minerality; two hectares in Vertus have less power, but more exotic tropical fruit character; while a substantial 5.5 hectares in Chouilly add a fruity elegance. A little pinot noir is derived from just half a hectare, shared between Aÿ and Mareuil-sur-Aÿ.

'Fruitiness, elegance, power and minerality can therefore be determined according to the villages that we use in each blend,' Didier clarifies. 'Our objective is to make wines of minerality, not of explosive fruit.'

UNCOMPROMISING MIXOLOGISTS

Of Gimonnet's considerable 12 hectares of grand cru holdings, three-quarters are located in the prized heart of the mid-slopes of their villages. Some in Champagne suggest Didier's blends do not do justice to the greatness of his terroirs. In the hands of others, these holdings could yield thundering single-cru old-vine cuvées from the grand crus of Cramant, Chouilly and Oger, but to do so would deprive Gimonnet of the powerful blending material that so eloquently lifts the mood of Cuis in all but the very first of his nine blends. He singles out the strength of Oger as an exception, making it tricky to blend without dominating.

'I created a single Oger cuvée last year, as I'm not clever enough to know how to blend all of it!' He defines the best terroirs as those that respect others in a blend. 'Champagne is a blend, and a grand terroir is one that can be blended without dominating,' says Didier, who has been dubbed a 'mixologist'. This blending is the key

to the philosophy of the house. 'I am against mono-terroir,' he says, 'but I am adept at very polished blends that combine the qualities of different terroirs to produce complexities. When I present the house I always say I'm not a winemaker, just an interpreter of terroir.'

Gimonnet owns 12 grand cru vineyards, but, apart from Oger, does not produce a single wine that can be labelled grand cru, 'because they're better balanced when blended with premier cru parcels to confer freshness of acidity and balance between concentration, finesse and elegance,' Didier explains. 'The blend is the highest ideal here, more than the sum of the parts.'

His mantra is to produce the most balanced wines, not those that can be labelled to command the highest prices. A noble pursuit, rare in Champagne, and it begins in the vineyards.

METICULOUS ATTENTION TO PURITY

When I visited at the height of harvest 2014 I found Olivier in the vineyards and Didier on the forklift unloading grapes in the winery. They are both very hands-on, and have the help of only two others in the winery. 'It is very important for the quality for me to be here,' Didier says.

'The date of harvest is very, very important,' he maintains. 'Just four days too early or too late and it will disrupt concentration, structure and elegance.'

He prizes minerality and freshness above concentration, so does not harvest at the maximum maturity, but at the optimum level of ripeness to give a good balance of alcohol potential and high acidity. To achieve this, yields are moderated to around 11–12 tonnes/hectare (equating to about 75hL/hectare), compared with a potential of 18–20 tonnes. Chaptalisation is performed only when necessary, and in the mature 2015 vintage, only in Cuis.

The goal of every stage of vinification is to preserve purity, freshness and minerality with the utmost precision. Gimonnet's winery is a pristine declaration of this mandate, a bathroom-fresh environment of floor-to-ceiling tiles and gleaming stainless steel. 'It is like cooking,' Didier suggests. 'To create purity you must have the freshest ingredients.' He upholds this mantra stringently, and most years sells or distils at least one tank that isn't up to standard. 'My father always explained to us that the most important rule of blending is to only use what you like,' he says.

Vinification is as simple as possible, 'so the expression is due only to the terroir and the maturity of the fruit'. With 90% of vineyards within four kilometres of the house, all grapes are pressed within six hours of harvest. Gimonnet presses more lightly than most, so of the little he harvests he extracts even less juice, but juice of finer quality. As at Billecart-Salmon and Pol Roger, the juice is clarified at 10°C for 24 hours prior to fermentation, a crucial procedure for the refined elegance of the style. Selected yeast is then added to achieve a rapid start to fermentation.

'My goal is to have the juice in fermentation less than two days after picking; this is very important for maintaining purity and freshness.' Fermentation and maturation take place only in temperature-controlled stainless steel tanks. 'Our grapes come from good terroirs, and we want no other taste than that of the fruit.' Every plot is vinified separately. There are 40 parcels in the estate, and hence 40 tanks. The tendency of Cuis chardonnay to oxidise quickly in tank dictates that reserve wines are instead kept on fine lees in magnums under crown seal, allowing them to mature and develop body, while retaining purity and freshness, without evolving too rapidly. An unusual and painstaking process, it takes six people to open 10,000 bottles a day.

Malolactic fermentation is employed in all wines to soften the high acidity of Cuis. A light dosage of 8g/L of sugar is used, as little as 5g/L in the vintage cuvées, and there is no impression of sweetness. 'Dosage is very important to avoid angular wines without introducing the taste of sugar,' Didier explains. He considers it crucial to oxidise the liquor before adding it to the bottle. 'It seems like nothing, but it makes a subtle difference to the taste.' He uses only a small amount of sulphur as a preservative, but sufficient to uphold freshness.

Timing of disgorgement is likewise given careful consideration, with every bottle freshly disgorged to order. Disgorgement dates are printed on bottles sent to countries that request them, including the US and Italy. 'The date of disgorgement is very important in champagne,' Didier points out. 'A cuvée is very different six months after disgorgement than it is two years after disgorgement.' More than half of Gimonnet's non-vintage cuvées are sealed with reliable Mytik DIAM closures, as his trials have found these to preserve freshness more reliably than natural cork.

Enviable vineyards and meticulous practices stir strong demand, and Gimonnet has been working to increase production to keep up, which is not as easy as it sounds. 'We don't want to be wine merchants by buying grapes to increase production,' he emphasises. 'We don't want to make volume, we want to make the quality that we like and then offer it on allocation. We therefore need to buy vineyards with the potential of our style. But there are not many vineyards on the market, and when they are they are too expensive.' Over the past decade, five hectares have been purchased in the Côte des Blancs to increase production by about 50,000 bottles.

Gimonnet's cuvées again represent some of the Côte des Blancs's best buys this year.

PIERRE GIMONNET & FILS CUIS 1ᴱᴿ CRU BRUT BLANC DE BLANCS NV $

93 points • 2013 BASE VINTAGE • DISGORGED MAY 2016 • TASTED IN AUSTRALIA

100% Cuis chardonnay; 70% 2013, 6% 2012, 9% 2011, 10% 2010, 5% 2009; reserve wines are the previous year's blend, stored in magnums; full malolactic fermentation; aged on lees 24-30 months; 6.5g/L dosage; 146,700 bottles; DIAM closure

Gimonnet's Cuis is the quintessential apéritif, and one of the most pristine champagnes for its price. Freshness and purity of lemon and crunchy nashi pear sing with primary vibrancy, pinpoint accuracy and Gimonnet precision. Bottle age has built seamless texture without yet contributing secondary complexity. The fine salt chalk minerality of the village is energised by crystalline acidity. It's signature Cuis, classic Gimonnet and fantastic-value champagne.

The Champagne Guide

Pierre Gimonnet & Fils Rosé de Blancs 1er Cru Brut NV $$

94 points • 2014 base vintage • Disgorged July 2016 • Tasted in Australia

92% chardonnay – 25.5% Chouilly for fruit and elegance, 16.5% Cramant for plumpness, 10% Oger for masculine structure and spicy minerality, 9% Vertus for exotic flavours, 32% Cuis for vivacity and freshness; 8% 2014 and 2013 pinot noir red wine from Bouzy; aged on lees 18–24 months; 6.5g/L dosage; 13,363 bottles; DIAM closure

Gimonnet's cracking and cleverly named rosé is just 8% red wine (not least because it costs him almost €15 a litre to buy) blended with his vintage Gastronome cuvée – his blanc de blancs with the most body. Charged with 50% grand cru chardonnay, the result upholds its mantra of sustaining the mouthfeel, persistence and surging bath-salts chalk minerality of the Côte des Blancs with great accomplishment, touched with the palest salmon pink hue and the lightest reflections of white cherries and strawberry hull. Delightfully restrained and refreshingly tense, it's more about crystalline precision than flavour. One of the most refreshing apéritif rosés this year, serve it like a delicate blanc de blancs, not like a rosé.

Pierre Gimonnet & Fils Cuvée Gastronome 1er Cru Blanc de Blancs Brut 2012 $$

94 points • Disgorged November 2016 • Tasted in Australia

50% Chouilly for fruit and elegance (mostly 1951 and 1960 plantings), 21.5% Cuis for vivacity and freshness, 15.5% Cramant for plumpness, 13% Oger for masculine structure and spicy minerality; aged on lees at least 36 months; 'petite mousse' of 4.5 atmospheres; 6g/L dosage; 15,406 bottles

The aspiration of Gastronome is to present the spirit, elegance and freshness of a non-vintage, with structure and body. The fruity depth and approachability of Chouilly Mont Aigu provides the core, balanced with the power of Cramant and Oger, the freshness of Cuis and a 'petite mousse' of 4.5 atmospheres for creaminess. 2012 is a wonderful personification of this aspiration, a vintage of purity, freshness and vivacity of lemon, grapefruit and crunchy granny smith apple and beurre bosc pear. Impressive grand cru concentration contrasts dynamic freshness. Even at five years of age, its youthful purity of fruit is everything, with no suggestion of secondary complexity beside the subtlest hint of almond meal and the gentle mouthfeel of lees texture. Its acid line is at once ripe and integrated, and simultaneously tense and enduring, heightening the presence of prominent, mouthfilling, glittering, salty minerality. One of the great vintages for Gimonnet, and certainly the finest Gastronome since 2008.

Pierre Gimonnet & Fils Cuvée Fleuron Brut 1er Cru Blanc de Blancs 2010 $$

93 points • Disgorged October 2016 • Tasted in Australia

40.5% Cramant, 27% Chouilly (mostly Mont Aigu), 6% Oger, 16% Cuis, 10.5% Vertus; aged on lees more than 4 years; 5.5 atmospheres of pressure; 4.5g/L dosage; 33,680 bottles

'Fleuron' means 'best of', created when there was only one non-vintage and one vintage wine in the house. Today it's Gimonnet's signature vintage cuvée, a blend of the best parcels from each village, boasting almost three-quarters grand cru Côte des Blancs, a preposterous proportion for a wine of this price. Gimonnet's goal here is to capture the taste of the domaine in a single blend, more about structure and focus than the immediacy of Gastronome. 2010 is a complex and immediate take on this mandate, a vintage fast developing into a medium-straw hue (bright by any standards, yet deep for Gimonnet) and grand complexity and presence of orange rind, mixed spice, toast, ginger and honey, while upholding a vivacious core of lemon and grapefruit. The impact of salty grand cru minerality defines a long finish of vibrant acid line, invisible dosage and subtle, well-handled phenolic grip.

PIERRE GIMONNET & FILS CUVÉE FLEURON BRUT 1ᴱᴿ CRU BLANC DE BLANCS 2009 $$

93 points • DISGORGED OCTOBER 2016 • TASTED IN AUSTRALIA

42.5% Cramant, 30% Chouilly, 18.5% Cuis, 9% Oger; aged on lees more than 4 years; 4.5g/L dosage; 28,800 bottles

2009 presents a very precise take on the Fleuron aspiration, launched before the 'more strict' 2008. Two years after release, it holds its head high, maintaining its primary, lingering apple and pear fruit, while a further two years on lees has built a creamy texture and layers of nougat, lemon butter and almond cream, retaining its fine chalk texture of mineral grip and character, providing structural precision.

PIERRE GIMONNET & FILS CUVÉE FLEURON BRUT 1ᴱᴿ CRU BLANC DE BLANCS 2008 $$

96 points • DISGORGED DECEMBER 2015 • TASTED IN AUSTRALIA

33.5% Cramant, 32.5% Chouilly, 22% Cuis, 10% Oger, 2% Vertus; aged on lees 6.5 years; 5g/L dosage; 53,300 bottles

The purity, precision and sheer energy of 2008 transposed upon an identical mandate of Gimonnet produces a result thrillingly electric, profoundly enduring and graced with sheer beauty. The full might of Gimonnet's enviably placed grand cru sites speaks in graceful voice of deep and full white fruits set amidst a pronounced sea of fine salt chalk minerality. More than six years on lees has built seamless texture, without yet any evolution into secondary complexity, a grand progression that will unfold for decades, to the delight of the patient. In length, line and sheer unbridled joy, this is a blanc de blancs of the highest order.

PIERRE GIMONNET & FILS EXTRA BRUT OENOPHILE 1ᴱᴿ CRU BLANC DE BLANCS NON DOSÉ 2008 $$

95 points • DISGORGED AUGUST 2016 • TASTED IN AUSTRALIA

Fleuron 2008 without dosage; 33.5% Cramant, 32.5% Chouilly, 22% Cuis, 10% Oger, 2% Vertus; aged 6 years on lees; 1.5g/L dosage; 5000-10,000 bottles of the 49,000 of Fleuron 2008

Didier Gimonnet's sincerity is refreshing. 'I am not a lover of champagne without dosage, as dosage is part of the tradition of our region, and even 4–5g/L rounds out the wine. Wine without dosage is interesting when it's recently disgorged, but when I pull them out of the cellar 18 months later I always prefer the same wine with a little dosage to add complexity and balance.' Still, sales of his zero-dosage Oenophile are on the rise. This is not a dedicated blend, but chosen from the cellar each year according to which cuvée has the natural balance to stand best without dosage. Olivier Gimonnet considers this cuvée too young for zero dosage. Two years after release, it's held its poise confidently, though without the harmony inherent even with just 5g/L dosage in the Fleuron. High-tensile definition contrasts depth of character in this exactingly crafted expression of an incredible vintage. Distinct oyster shell and sea breeze characters are present on the palate and – unusually for champagne – on the nose, its pronounced Côte des Blancs terroirs burst from the glass. There's all the unashamed grip and tension of grapefruit and lemon, defined by an incisive, steely acid line, contrasted cunningly with fine, creamy lees texture and a very fine bead. The result is a chiselled and highly sophisticated champagne, not for the uninitiated, but it will enthral oyster fanatics, and is certain to improve for many years to come.

Pierre Gimonnet & Fils Special Club Grands Terroirs de Chardonnay 2012 $$$

96 points • Disgorged November 2016 • Tasted in Australia

60% Cramant (mostly vines more than 50 years of age, with 15% planted 1911 and 1913) for structure and minerality, 30% Chouilly Mont Aigu (planted 1951) for elegance, 10% Cuis for freshness, the signature of Gimonnet; aged at least 4 years on lees; 5.5 atmospheres of pressure; 4.5g/L dosage; 21,516 bottles

Gimonnet's Special Club is a blend of the best of each vintage, with the aspiration of creating an elegant style that's greater than the sum of its parts. It's built on old vines of 40–100 years of age, relying on Cramant for structure, balanced with the silkiness of Chouilly Mont Aigu and the definition of Cuis. Didier Gimonnet considers 2012 greater even than 2008 and 2002, which is about as high as praise for any season could ever be. His Special Club presents a grand and captivating contradiction, on the one hand desperately subtle and delicately understated, with tightly clenched apple, grapefruit and lemon compressed into an infinitesimal singularity, yet simultaneously full of grand cru depth, enduring persistence and seamless, mouth-evading presence that marks out the most dramatic and unwavering line. The one detail that is not understated is the inimitable chalk mineral presence of enviable positions in the great crus of the Côte des Blancs, captured in full magnificence thanks to Gimonnet precision, frothing and churning with salty, chalky, mouth-filling texture from start to very long finish. Such is its infantile youthfulness that it is revealing little else right now, but do not be mistaken, for every detail is in precisely the right place to blossom into breathtaking greatness in many years to come.

Pierre Gimonnet & Fils Special Club Grands Terroirs de Chardonnay 2010 $$$

96 points • Disgorged July 2016 • Tasted in Australia

61% Cramant, 23.5% Chouilly, 14% Cuis, 1.5% Vertus; aged at least 5 years on lees; 4.5g/L dosage; 15,968 bottles

2010 meets the Gimonnet Special Club brief with all the commanding presence of old-vine grand cru concentration. Depth and power of white peach and ginger create a compelling interplay with the tension of grapefruit and lemon juice, defining a well-focused acid line that froths and churns with whitewater fury amidst pronounced salt chalk minerality. The toasty, praline and marzipan complexity of lees age is building slowly, lingering long and confident on a grand finish. A triumph for a tricky season.

Pierre Gimonnet & Fils Special Club Grands Terroirs de Chardonnay 2008 $$$

97 points • Tasted in Champagne

57% Cramant, 29% Chouilly, 14% Cuis and a little Vertus

There is an inherent subjectivity in the pricing of wine that rarely, oh so rarely, sees a prestige cuvée of the utmost finesse and the most enduring stamina hit the ground at a jaw-droppingly affordable price. The great vintages of Gimonnet Special Club represent some of the best value in Champagne today. If you're after one wine to discover the marvels of old champagne, buy a case now, promise you won't touch a bottle for 10 years, and keep one for at least 30. Two years on, it remains as absolutely beach-fresh as its release, upholding its stunning lemon freshness and raw, youthful, introverted and tightly coiled restraint. Beguiling transparency of pure, adroit acid propels an incredible finish that splashes long and strong with frothy, salty chalk minerality. Brilliant white cherries and citrus ring out in clear peals like church bells to an undercurrent of the most subtle nuances of almond and vanilla. A cuvée of effortless poise, unmitigated drive and breathtaking, scintillating, crystalline fidelity.

Pierre Gimonnet & Fils Special Club Oger Grand Cru Blanc de Blancs 2012 $$$

95 points • Disgorged August 2016 • Tasted in Champagne and Australia

Four plots spanning 1 hectare in Oger; aged on lees 3 years; no chaptalisation; 5.5 atmospheres of pressure; 4.5g/L dosage; 3027 bottles

Labelled 'Oger Grand Cru' in large letters, and 'Pierre Gimonnet & Fils Special Club' in fine print, because 'this is not the style of Gimonnet', Didier has found the southern Côte des Blancs character, smoky strength, graphite minerality and forward development of Oger difficult to reconcile with his northern blends. Hence a monocru cuvée by default. In the great 2012 season he elaborated three monocru Special Clubs, and while Oger is already ready to drink ('very mature for a three-year-old wine!'), Cramant and Chouilly are not yet ready for release. It's Gimonnet's finest Oger to date, toning the power of the village with the precision and definition of the house. The eloquence of the season is captured by pulling back the focus of Oger from its classical typicity of orange and spice, into a fresher and more refined spectrum of lemon, grapefruit, pear and apple, with subtle mature notes of spice, almond and nougat. The grainy, salty minerality of the village is all-conquering, more crystalline than ever, drawing long through a finish of exacting acid balance and brilliant line and length. One bottle was corked.

Pierre Gimonnet & Fils Millésime de Collection Vieilles Vignes de Chardonnay 2006 $$$

94 points • Disgorged October 2016 • Tasted in Australia en Magnum

Exclusively old vines of 40–90 years of age from the best sites of the domain; 65% Cramant (10% from vines more than 40 years old, and more than 30% from 1911 and 1913 plantings) for structure, minerality and laciness, 22.5% Chouilly (mostly Mont Aigu planted 1951) for elegance, 12.5% Cuis for freshness, the signature of Gimonnet; aged at least 8 years on lees; light chaptalisation; 5g/L dosage; 3713 magnums

In the fanatically precise style of Gimonnet, the acid line and all-encompassing chalk mineral structure of well-positioned sites throughout the Côte des Blancs spells out compelling longevity, even in a season as ripe and immediately approachable as 2006. At more than a decade of age it has evolved to a complex place of honey, toast, even notes of apricot, upholding a core of grapefruit, apple and pear. There is a rich approachability to this release that reflects the exuberance of the season, making it right for drinking right away, yet upholding the poised balance and mouth-filling, salty chalk minerality that define Gimonnet. A vintage to drink now.

Didier Gimonnet hard at work. A master blender of his suite of enviable terroirs, he has been dubbed a 'mixologist'.

PIERRE PÉTERS

(Pee-yair Peh-tair)

7/10

26 RUE DES LOMBARDS 51190 LE MESNIL-SUR-OGER
www.champagne-peters.com

PROPRIÉTAIRE-RÉCOLTANT

Very few champagnes more eloquently articulate their terroirs than those of Pierre Péters. Many encounters with the young Rodolphe Péters, exploring the fruits of three decades, have left me mesmerised by the remarkable capacity of the chardonnay vine to extract the salty minerality of the Côte des Blancs's finest grand crus and preserve it in its wines for time eternal. This little estate, more than any other, has given me the realisation of another dimension to champagne, one in which minerality assumes a personality all of its own. And I have discovered Les Chétillons, the Le Montrachet of Le Mesnil-sur-Oger.

The Péters family has tended its vines in Le Mesnil-sur-Oger for six generations, and made its own champagne since 1919. Today, the estate is the custodian of just over 19 hectares of well-placed vineyards spanning more than 60 plots in nothing but the finest grand crus of the Côte des Blancs: Oger, Cramant, Avize and, especially, Le Mesnil-sur-Oger.

ATTENTIVE VINEYARD CARE
Rodolphe Péters took control in 2008, but has been helping his father with the blending since 1994, and knows his vines as well as anyone in Champagne. I quickly discovered just how well when I first met him in late July 2011, four weeks before harvest, when he was about to depart for holidays.

'Everyone says I am a crazy man taking holidays until August 19, but I wrote in my book in May that we would begin harvest on August 23, 24 or 25 and I have not revised this since.' A remarkable insight in one of Champagne's most erratic years, in which others extended their projections by as much as four weeks. 'That's crazy,' he says, 'but I spend more time than any of them in my land.'

Péters' vines are lavished some of the most attentive care in all of Champagne. 'I am reluctant to walk in the vines for fear of crushing the chalk,' he says. I have never heard this from any other grower, but there are few other places that enjoy such ready access to chalk, just 10–30 centimetres below the surface in Le Mesnil-sur-Oger. For this reason, deep roots to access the minerality of the chalk are not the priority for Péters.

'Minerality deep in the chalk is not accessible to the plants, but the interface between the topsoil and the deep soil is where the roots are able to find it,' he explains. The role of micro-organisms and worms in mixing the deeper soils and making this minerality available to the roots is crucial, and he works hard to keep the soil alive with organic material. Grass is

Pierre Péters masterfully captures the endurance of Le Mesnil.

acidity.' He considers pH, rather than acidity, to be the best indicator of balance, always aiming for low pH as a sign that he has captured the minerality of the soil.

The racy acidity of Péters's cuvées has traditionally been softened by full malolactic fermentation, but since Rodolphe has been in command, he has selectively blocked malolactic in some tanks.

INNOVATIVE VINIFICATION

To preserve character and maintain freshness, Péters has recently commissioned a new cuverie, to allow him to focus more attention on the finer details of vinification. 'You cannot keep your two feet still on the ground!' he grins. New computer-controlled presses provide more precise control and allow him to keep smaller blocks separate. He personally tastes the juice as it comes off the press, and makes the press cuts by taste, not by the authorised volumes.

Péters stringently protects the juice from oxygen at all times, and ferments in small stainless steel tanks under temperature control. His recent passion has been experimentation with different vessels for storing reserves. A new room with natural temperature control is dedicated to concrete tanks, which he describes as the 'opposite concept to eggs', designed to decrease movement inside and produce fresher, earthier and less fruity wines. He has also introduced a large Croatian oak foudre, not for oak flavour, but for increasing the texture and creaminess of reserves. With two additional foudres commissioned in early 2015, he now maintains a balance of 50% reserves in stainless steel, 30% in concrete and 20% in foudres.

He considers structure and freshness to be derived from a combination of minerality, acidity and 'pleasant bitterness' from lees contact, and hence keeps wines on gross lees for long periods after alcoholic fermentation. The presence of gross lees keeps the wines fresh, permitting a low level of sulphur dioxide as a preservative.

FORGOTTEN RESERVE

Péters was concerned about the tendency of reserve wines to lose their freshness over time, necessitating use of the best wines as reserves, rather than in vintage and prestige cuvées. This led to a radical reinvention of the non-vintage blend in 1997. Every reserve wine, spanning 1988 to 1996, was blended into a modified solera which became the ongoing reserve, topped up every year except in 1999 and 2003; these were kept separate to preserve the purity of the reserve. Kept on fine lees in a stainless steel tank at 13–14°C, the reserve is kept lively through refreshing each year. I was amazed

planted in the mid-rows to provide competition for surface roots, forcing them down to the interface with the chalk.

He is adamant that he cannot keep his soils alive using certified organics. 'My philosophy is to follow the best procedures of the best of all philosophies,' he says, comparing the health of his vines with his own health, treating his allergies with a mixture of conventional medicine, vitamins and homeopathy. 'My first responsibility is to take care of my workers, the first people in contact with the chemicals I use – and by protecting them, I naturally take care of my customers, the vines and the environment.' His soil analyses have revealed high levels of copper sulphate from years of treatment by previous generations, detrimental to the soil, but permitted under biodynamics. He instead relies mainly on conventional treatments to protect his vineyards.

A natural balance is achieved in the vineyards, thanks to the regulating effect of old vines (averaging more than 30 years of age) and competition from grasses in the mid-rows. 'The fashion now is to say low yields and high maturity, but Champagne was not built on this – it was built on a comfortable balance of production to achieve the correct level of ripeness and that in 2011 (a sample up to and including the 2010 vintage), a wine of such complexity could still retain such purity of grapefruit and preserved lemon.

This reserve solera embodies Péters' philosophy of keeping the memory of the estate alive in his Cuvée de Réserve Blanc de Blancs Brut NV, which claims a generous 40% reserve wine. His aim is to showcase the terroir of grand cru blanc de blancs, achieved with 60% of the current vintage from 50 plots spanning all of his Côte des Blancs estate vineyards, including Les Chétillons.

'The reserve is the key to the quality, making it easy to maintain consistency,' he says. It's a genius concept, and such is the class of the reserve that he has released it as its own cuvée, aptly named La Réserve Oubliée – 'the forgotten reserve'.

Cuvée de Réserve and Péters's vintage blend L'Esprit draw estate chardonnay from across the Côte des Blancs's grand crus. 'I like to think of each of the villages as a season, according to how they make me feel when I taste the vins clairs,' Péters explains.

'Le Mesnil-sur-Oger is the grey of winter for its sharp, stony minerality – austere and cold in character, with a cold sea breeze that gives the feeling of being in Normandy in winter.

'Oger is spring, for its elegant white flowers and white fruits, the first white sunlight and the first blossoms of the fruit trees. Its amphitheatre concentrates the sunlight and provides warmth. It is very soft and feminine, giving you the feeling of spring after a long winter.

Twilight over a blanket of winter snow in Le Mesnil-sur-Oger, the enduring grand cru core of Pierre Péters.

'Avize is all about the character of summer, more orange than yellow in its full-bodied, showy and developed chardonnay of rich, ripe grapefruit, orange and mandarin. Its terroir is less chalky and more graphite in its structure.

'The south-east facing slope of Cramant is like the brown of fall, the perfect chardonnay, of similar profile to Le Mesnil, yet less cold. More lemony, with a creamy chalkiness and nuances reminiscent of vanilla, sweet spices, dried fruits and something dry, like dried flowers or cinnamon, that evokes autumn leaves falling before winter.

'I have parcels that really express each of these characters and I focus on these for my vintage blend. If a vintage expresses more summer and autumn, it is released as a vintage wine, but if it is more winter and spring I blend it as a non-vintage extra brut,' says Péters.

THE LE MONTRACHET OF LE MESNIL

Not far from the village itself, Les Chétillons is one of the finest sites for sparkling winegrowing in Le Mesnil-sur-Oger or, indeed, anywhere on earth. Here the chalk is never more than 10 centimetres from the surface, so the vines are effectively rooted in pure chalk. In slope and exposition, Péters describes it as perfect – not too much and not too little.

The family has nurtured three plots in these calcareous soils since 1930, with vines now an impressive 50 and 71 years old. Each has been vinified separately and blended to produce a single-vintage wine since 1971.

Péters speaks of the minerality of Les Chétillons as crushed oyster shells, sea salt, and flavours of the ocean that laid down the chalk millennia ago. 'If you taste a stone in the vineyard, it is salty,' he explains, and it is this that infuses the mineral texture in his wines.

The mesmerising minerality of this extraordinary site remains steadfast in every old vintage I have tasted, right back to 1985. Through changes of season and winemaker, flavours evolve, intensity builds and bubbles fade, but the minerality remains transfixed. 'It is a stake, it stays for a very long time,' he declares.

Such is the demand for Péters's wines that he is not able to offer every cuvée in every market. He is very concerned that his annual production of 160,000 bottles is no longer able to meet the demand of his loyal customers.

'I try my best to purchase more vineyards, but another two hectares is nothing in terms of increasing production. And it will cost €3 million.'

Since 2014, a QR code on every bottle reveals the disgorgement date, base vintage and dosage.

PIERRE PÉTERS CUVÉE DE RÉSERVE BLANC DE BLANCS BRUT NV $$

93 points • 2013 BASE VINTAGE • DISGORGED NOVEMBER 2015 • 6.7G/L DOSAGE
• TASTED IN CHAMPAGNE
91 points • 2012 BASE VINTAGE • DISGORGED AUGUST 2015 • 6G/L DOSAGE
• TASTED IN CHAMPAGNE

50% current vintage, 50% reserve solera dating from 1988; grand cru Côte des Blancs; DIAM closure

Rodolphe Péters loves the freshness and tension of 2013 even more than 2012, and likens it with 2008. It shines in this blend with clarity, precision and excellent lemon and pear freshness, flowing into generosity of crisp red apple fruit. All the theatrics of his masterful reserve solera build out a backdrop of deeply layered, biscuity complexity. It concludes with well-poised acid line, with the magnificent, frothing mineral structure of Le Mesnil singing loud and clear. The 2012 base is a tighter, drier and riper style of pear, apple and lemon, showing greater influence of the reserve in marzipan and biscuits, concluding with a touch more of the dry-extract effect of 2011 in the solera than it did on first release.

PIERRE PÉTERS RÉSERVE OUBLIÉE BLANC DE BLANCS BRUT NV $$

93 points • 2010 BASE VINTAGE • TASTED IN CHAMPAGNE

Perpetual reserve solera of 21 vintages spanning 1988 to 2010, missing only the inferior 1999 and 2003; stored in large oak casks, concrete and stainless steel tanks on lees before blending; 4g/L dosage from grape juice aged in a small barrel; DIAM closure

Few reserves can boast such ravishing integration, seamless internal harmony and sheer completeness, a credit to both the genius of this modified solera and the painstakingly tended vines that feed it. The 2010 base blend boasts bewildering complexity of stone fruits, baked apple and fruit mince spice, set against a deeply layered backdrop of toast and biscuits that proclaim its grand maturity. Its richness is profound, held in focus by the formidable presence of salt chalk mineral structure and a touch of fine tannin grip and grapefruit pith texture, serving to control its generosity rather than dominating.

PIERRE PÉTERS CUVÉE MILLÉSIME L'ESPRIT BLANC DE BLANCS 2012 $$$

95 points • DISGORGED FEBRUARY 2016 • TASTED IN CHAMPAGNE

A blend of four vineyards, one each in Le Mesnil-sur-Oger, Oger, Avize and Cramant; 3g/L dosage

A sneak preview 18 months prior to release heralds one of the great vintages in the lineage of L'Esprit. It's predictably tight and focused in its youthful guise, with pretty, focused notes of lemon blossom and lemon meringue. Lively acid line and prominent chalk minerality define great poise, endurance and persistence. Subtle nougat and gingernut complexity are beginning, and further time on lees will build these further. A great champagne in the making.

PIERRE PÉTERS EXTRA BRUT 2011 $$

88 points • DISGORGED DECEMBER 2015 • TASTED IN CHAMPAGNE

A blend of four vineyards, one each in Le Mesnil-sur-Oger, Oger, Avize and Cramant; 2g/L dosage

L'Esprit is rebadged as 'Extra Brut' in some vintages like 2011. Rodolphe accurately describes it as a 'herbal style' true to the vintage, which will evolve to coffee bean characters in time. It shows some exotic tropical fruits in its youth; a dry and tense style, built as much on the firm, fine tannin grip of the season as it is on mineral texture and lively acid line, exacerbated by low dosage. It will benefit from protein-rich fare to soften its tannins, but nonetheless represents a pretty good result for such a challenging season.

PIERRE PÉTERS CUVÉE MILLÉSIME L'ESPRIT BLANC DE BLANCS 2010 $$$

92 points • DISGORGED NOVEMBER 2015 • TASTED IN CHAMPAGNE

A blend of four vineyards, one each in Le Mesnil-sur-Oger, Oger, Avize and Cramant; 4.7g/L dosage

2010 has given birth to a dry and structured style, quite a contrast to the ripe and creamy 2009. It's built around an excellent core of apple and lemon fruit, even an exotic touch of orange. Lees age has furnished notes of nougat, honey and biscuit. Salty minerality and the firm, dry tannin texture of the 2010 harvest unite on a long finish.

PIERRE PÉTERS ROSÉ FOR ALBANE NV $$

95 points • 2012 BASE VINTAGE • DISGORGED DECEMBER 2015 • TASTED IN CHAMPAGNE
92 points • 2009 BASE VINTAGE • ORIGINAL DISGORGEMENT • TASTED IN CHAMPAGNE

Le Mesnil-sur-Oger chardonnay blended with a saignée of Damery and Cumières pinot meunier; DIAM closure; 7.3g/L dosage

Twelve years ago Péters discovered a rosé saignée of pinot meunier by a grower in Damery and Cumières, and was intrigued to find it tasted more like pink grapefruit than red berries — a style he felt would marry perfectly with the yellow citrus of a more fruity parcel of his Le Mesnil-sur-Oger chardonnay. This is the final release from this grower, who has since retired; the next will be with Jean-Baptiste Geoffroy, the master of Cumières pinot noir rosé saignée, who has enjoyed the challenge of making a meunier saignée for Péters. It's named in honour of Péters' daughter.

This is a fitting final release for this partnership, a pretty and elegant rosé of pretty medium salmon hue that marries the magnificent vibrancy and precise, fine chalk mineral texture of Le Mesnil-sur-Oger with the subtle red cherry and strawberry fruits of meunier maceration. Lees age has drawn out subtle nougat and brioche complexity, even a hint of marmalade, without for a moment disrupting freshness and finely poised balance. For interest, Péters also poured me a sample of the 2009 base from his personal oenothèque. It's evolved to a savoury place of tomato and pink pepper, but holds its poise of strawberry fruit with integrity and persistence.

PIERRE PÉTERS L'ÉTONNANT MONSIEUR VICTOR EDITION MK. 09 $$$$$

94 points • 2009 BASE VINTAGE • TASTED IN CHAMPAGNE

100% chardonnay; inaugural release, based on the Réserve Oubliée concept, blended from roughly 50% of the best large oak casks, stainless steel and concrete vats of each reserve since 1988, and 50% of the best vat from the latest harvest of Les Chétillons; aged 5 years on lees; 1110 bottles

Péters' new creation in honour of his son is a rousing celebration of the depth of his reserve solera and the inimitable chalk mineral character of Les Chétillons. It's an assemblage of all manner of stone fruits and citrus, married with the fleshy depth of the mature 2009 harvest and the grand complexity of deep reserves in honey, biscuits and roast nuts. A palate of enduring persistence and exacting line is carried by the ever-present, refreshingly fine chalk minerality of Les Chétillons, concluding dry and characterful.

PIERRE PÉTERS CUVÉE SPÉCIALE BLANC DE BLANCS LES CHÉTILLONS 2008 $$$$

99 points • DISGORGED NOVEMBER 2015 • TASTED IN CHAMPAGNE

4.7g/L dosage; 11,000 bottles

Les Chétillons articulates its mineral birthplace with greater precision than I have tasted anywhere in Champagne outside the thundering single vineyards of Krug itself, and no vintage expresses this more exhilaratingly than 2008. Released after 2009, it remains desperately youthful and stark, yet every element is perfectly integrated, like a choral effect in which individual voices are lost. Concentrate hard and you'll hear soprano top notes of pure lemon blossom and glorious white fruits over alto whispers of the most elegant almond nougat. The mineral signature of Les Chétillons is crystalline, like ground glass, yet impeccably creamy and enticing, permeating every corner of the palate with chalky sea salt and oyster-shell notes that heave and froth with the waves of the ocean that created this remarkable place 55 million years ago. Its length soars to new heights, navigating undeterred for minutes, propelled by an acid line that shimmers like jet exhaust. Patience is mandatory, and anyone with the discipline to hold out until it is at least 20 years old will be royally rewarded.

PIERRE PÉTERS CUVÉE SPÉCIALE BLANC DE BLANCS LES CHÉTILLONS 2007 $$$$

96 points • TASTED IN LE MESNIL-SUR-OGER

The 2007 was the first vintage in which Rodolphe was granted full control, and his first challenge came in holding back on harvesting after a cool summer. It proved to be the right decision, articulated most brilliantly in Les Chétillons. This is a wonderful result for a lesser season, a cuvée that sings with the introverted, focused restraint that endeared it on first release two years ago. It projects a precise aura of gleaming white peach, lemon and apple. Minerality rises above its fruit, with its cool season infusing a silky chalk presence that hovers like a still morning mist over deep-set salty texture. It's magnificently coiled, with an outstanding line, gripping persistence and a surprising approachability from the outset, yet holds a seemingly limitless reserve of energy to thrust it upward for some years yet.

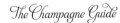

The Champagne Guide

PIPER-HEIDSIECK

(Pee-per E-dseek)

6/10

12 Allée du Vignoble 51000 Reims

www.piper-heidsieck.com

FONDÉ EN 1785 À REIMS, FRANCE

CHAMPAGNE

PIPER-HEIDSIECK

I first visited Piper-Heidsieck 15 years ago, and left more than a little bemused by its Disney-like automated tour. Thank goodness it is no more. Piper-Heidsieck has come a long way since then, transformed by champagne genius Daniel Thibault from an austere non-malolactic to a more appealing malolactic style, relying on meunier to bring roundness to the blend, and now ascending again in both quality and price under Thibault's friend and offsider, talented chef de cave Régis Camus.

Piper-Heidsieck is made alongside the smaller Charles Heidsieck (page 89) in an impressive cuverie at Bezannes on the southern outskirts of Reims, using the same production methods, from essentially the same pool of vineyards and reserve wines.

Camus's efforts begin in the vineyards, in liaising with vignerons, some of whom have been supplying Piper for five generations. It is a sign of his close relationships with some of his growers that he is godfather to their children and invited to their weddings.

Camus was nervous to fill Thibault's big shoes after his untimely death in 2002, but was determined to maintain his legacy in Charles Heidsieck and to take it further in revitalising Piper-Heidsieck. Since the mid-2000s, Charles and Piper have found their own separate lives in the selection of crus, styles and ages.

'It is all about the magic of the blend!' Camus explains. 'It is very important for me that the nuances of the wines speak so as to express the styles of the two different houses.' His goals for Piper are elegance and tenacity in a bright, fruity style, which he speaks of in terms of a floral register, a fruity register and a toasty register in each of the wines. 'I aim to evoke the first days of spring in Piper, with springtime flowers, sun, vegetal nuances, chlorophyll, fog and smoke.' The fruity register follows the floral register.

'Piper is all about apples, pears and citrus, like biting into a crunchy granny smith apple, with a nervousness, minerality and tension.' The vivacious, dynamic Piper style, with its lighter colour, is designed for warmer weather, to be poured at 6–8°C.

From an estate pool of some 60 hectares of vineyards, substantially supplemented by some 400 growers, Camus upholds some 15–20% of crus for Charles, about 30–40% as signature Piper and the remainder versatile according to the season. 'Many of the villages of the Côte des Bar, Les Riceys, Merville, and Sézanne for chardonnay are our classic Piper villages,' he points out.

'It could be perceived as a challenge to deal with both brands side by side, but we have transformed the challenge into an opportunity,' Camus explains. 'Allocating tanks is half the job of an architect and half the job of a banker!'

For him, the true measure of a house is the quality of its brut NV and he has worked hard to elevate Piper's Brut NV. In his frank and unpretentious manner he shares how much he had enjoyed Taittinger NV with friends.

'The NV wines are the real business for me,' he says. 'After that it's all about having fun! The vintage wines are the vacation photos of the season, signed by Piper or by Charles!'

Non-vintage wines are blends of all three champagne varieties. He uses pinot noir as the core of the blend, the 'vertebra' or 'DNA molecule'; chardonnay for its dynamic liveliness ('It's me on Saturday night!'); and meunier for its fruitiness and freshness, and because 'we particularly like its crunchiness'.

Reserve wines represent about half of the harvest, comprising a strong percentage of Charles, and Piper as little as 6% and as much as 18%. 'I want to see just how far certain wines will go,' Camus explains. Most of his reserves are chardonnay and pinot noir, but he is proud to show off a tank of 2004 meunier from Verneuil of stunning freshness and vivacity. 'This breaks the absurd impression that meunier can't age!' Reserve wines are stored in 300–500hL stainless steel tanks to guard their freshness, 'so we can use them whenever they're needed, frozen in time like an ice man!'

Fermentation and maturation are performed exclusively in stainless steel. 'The only wood here is the

The characterful premier cru of Cumières.

boardwalk above the tanks!' he quips. To balance their vivacity, all but one cuvée is finished with a broad sweep of full dosage of 10g/L, a touch less than it used to be, and better balanced than ever.

Sales of 4 million bottles make Piper Champagne's eighth-largest house, and third-largest exporter, though a mere shadow of its scale at its historic peak of 13 million bottles, prior to its dark days under Rémy Cointreau. President Christopher Descourts resolves to return the house to its former glory, and has sacrificed significant volume in this pursuit. This has been a long and at times uncomfortable journey for Piper-Heidsieck, but quality remains buoyant and value for money is as compelling as ever.

PIPER-HEIDSIECK BRUT NV $

91 points • 2011 BASE VINTAGE • DISGORGED JUNE 2016 • TASTED IN CHAMPAGNE
AND AUSTRALIA

**50-55% pinot noir, 20-25% meunier, 10-15% chardonnay; 18% reserves; a blend of more than
100 crus; aged 4 years on lees (previously 2-3 years); 10g/L dosage**

Fresh, lively, fruity and precise, Piper is a reliable champagne at a great price, and I recommend it all the time for weddings, parties, anything. The house has fulfilled its mandate to grow this cuvée into a more serious, textural and complex offering, thanks to longer lees age than ever, though balances this marvellously and unexpectedly with more bright fruit integrity and tension than before. Pinot noir takes the lead, laced with fresh, fruity red apple and strawberry hull, with the lemon zest of chardonnay contributing tension and a touch of struck flint adding complexity. Lees age brings plenty of toasty, roast nut, gingernut biscuits, spice and honey character. Refreshingly, bright acid tension is the theme of the finish rather than dosage. Bravo.

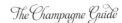

PIPER-HEIDSIECK ESSENTIEL CUVÉE BRUT ÉDITION NUMÉROTÉE S47263 NV $$

92 points • 2010 BASE VINTAGE • DISGORGED JUNE 2015 • TASTED IN CHAMPAGNE AND AUSTRALIA

Same as original Piper-Heidsieck Brut 2010 base; 50-55% pinot noir, 20-25% meunier, 10-15% chardonnay; 13% reserves; aged 4 years on lees; 6g/L dosage

Some years ago, while tasting different lots of the Brut NV blend, one lot stood out as particularly special. Based on the splendid 2008 vintage, it was left in the cellar for an additional year and bottled as a new, more serious extension of the label. The back label refreshingly features back vintage, reserves, dosage and bottling and disgorgement dates.

While the lesser 2010 base inevitably will never command the same respect, it does present a compelling accord of secondary toasty, spicy, nutty, honeyed complexity, even faintly smoky already, energised by a focused spine of fresh, bright, tangy, lemon-accented vitality. Additional time on lees has built a creaminess to its texture, though there is still some grip that harks back to a lesser base vintage. It's at once deeper yet fresher and more dynamic than the Brut.

PIPER-HEIDSIECK ROSÉ SAUVAGE BRUT NV $$

93 points • DISGORGED OCTOBER 2015 • TASTED IN CHAMPAGNE AND AUSTRALIA

Piper-Heidsieck Cuvée Brut with 20-25% pinot noir red wine; 50-55% pinot noir, 20-25% meunier, 10-15% chardonnay; 15-20% reserves; 10g/L dosage

The house goes a little far in describing this as 'the most extravagant and audacious rosé in the world', but when it was first released in the early 2000s, it may well have been. Camus resolved to create a distinctive rosé to contrast the Charles Heidsieck style, a wine of intense colour and dark fruit presence. That it is. In its full, unabashed crimson-red hue, it certainly floats far down the deep end of the champagne rosé pool. In colour, palate grip, concentration and food-matching versatility, it's best considered part-way between champagne rosé and red Burgundy, and should be served in big red wine glasses, as they do at the house. Distinctive, inimitable, potent and rustic, this is a champagne rosé with a personality all of its own. There's creaming soda here, sarsaparilla and liquorice, too, blood orange, strawberries, red cherris, tangelos and tamarillos, and this year an alluringly savoury twist of Campari, pink pepper and pipe smoke. True to its fluoro-pink label, it's ready for loud parties. For all its flamboyance, it's got length, tight acid line, the harmonious texture of lees age, well-integrated dosage and dry, finely textured tannin grip – just to prove it has a serious side, too.

PIPER-HEIDSIECK CUVÉE SUBLIME DEMI-SEC NV $$

91 points • DISGORGED DECEMBER 2015 • TASTED IN AUSTRALIA

50-55% pinot noir, 20-25% meunier, 10-15% chardonnay; 15-20% reserves; 40g/L dosage

This cuvée is clean and pristine, which may sound trite, but this in itself immediately places it among the best demi-secs in Champagne. More than that, it's charged with the bright acid structure to handle its sweetness. Succulent white stone fruits are slowly evolving into a place of butter and roast nut character, defined by boiled sweets in both sweetness and in flavour. A fine and elegant style with admirable fruit integrity makes this a top choice in the sweet stakes, and the finest I have ever seen this cuvée.

PIPER-HEIDSIECK VINTAGE BRUT 2008 $$

93 points • DISGORGED SEPTEMBER 2016 • TASTED IN AUSTRALIA

55% pinot noir, 45% chardonnay from 20 crus, including Verzy, Ludes, Aÿ, Avize and Vertus; aged 7.5 years on lees; 10g/L dosage

The backward, primary fruit focus, bright acid line and salty chalk mineral prominence of 2008 frame a delightful contrast to the toasty, spicy, honeyed bottle age of the Piper-Heidsieck style. The result is a 2008 poised to drink right away, at the perfect juncture between the vector of primary fruit and the arc of mature development, yet with the acid spine to hold its own for some years yet. Age has brought a creamy silkiness to its structure, while a little grainy phenolic texture does not hamper fine chalk mineral expression. It upholds integrity and poise.

PIPER-HEIDSIECK VINTAGE BRUT 2006 $$

92 points • TASTED IN CHAMPAGNE

51% chardonnay, 49% pinot noir from 17 premier and grand crus; aged more than 6 years on lees; 11g/L dosage

The hot summer of 2006 yielded muscular pinot noir ('too strong' for Camus) and fruity chardonnay, so he boosted chardonnay from 40% to a marginal 51% majority. It's a rich and fleshy expression of a ripe vintage, even showing apricot notes now, filled with aged complexity of toast, honey and brioche, just beginning to become tertiary for the first time, with nuances of wood smoke and a hint of green olive. I've tasted it more than a dozen times over the past six years, and while it peaked in early 2014, it has managed to uphold its integrity in a fleshy palate with citrus accents, balanced with a touch of fine phenolic grip. It's come to the end of the prime of its life now, just in time for the release of the 2008.

PIPER-HEIDSIECK RARE MILLESIME 2002 $$$$$

97 points • DISGORGED FEBRUARY 2015 • TASTED IN CHAMPAGNE AND AUSTRALIA

70% chardonnay from Avize, Vertus, Verzy and Villers-Marmery; 30% pinot noir from Aÿ; 11g/L dosage

This is indeed rare, the eighth vintage since 1976, and it keeps on coming, still current in the market six years after release. And, my goodness, it continues to radiate more than its quota of sheer joy! It still glows in elegantly medium-straw hues, impressively bright for 15 years of age. Its enticing gunflint reduction notes still lead out, carrying with them a wonderfully complex yet compact and elegant array of succulent yellow stone fruits, now beginning to show the complexity of glacé pear, with rising notes of wood smoke and buttered toast. Bottles opened in Champagne still uphold primary citrus vitality. Lees age has built seamless, creamy, silky integration, having finally attained its lofty pinnacle, which it will hold for some years yet. Its chalk minerality is fine, salty and pronounced, uniting the finesse of the Côte des Blancs with the firmer definition of the Montagne. It epitomises the gentle, textural minerality, the buttery allure of long age, and the harmonious personality and magnificent persistence of chardonnay in this epic vintage. The place of calm satisfaction to which it has evolved is all-encompassing. There is harmony here, and peace, like the gentle misty haze before dawn. A place that makes you slow down, and begs you to stay.

The Champagne Guide

POL ROGER

(Pol Roh-zheh)

9/10

1 RUE WINSTON CHURCHILL 51200 ÉPERNAY

www.polroger.com

CHAMPAGNE

POL ROGER

Stepping into Pol Roger's production facility in Épernay is like entering a different world. 'We call this the kitchen,' introduced managing director Laurent d'Harcourt. This was not like any kitchen I'd ever seen. Immaculately polished stainless steel tanks perfectly reflected shiny white tiles and snow-white surfaces. It was as if we were entering a brain surgery unit or a NASA assembly room, and I had an uneasy feeling that I might be asked to don a body suit, lest I contaminate this precision machine with a single molecule of foreign material. I have been buying Pol Roger for decades, but it was not until that moment that everything about this celestial estate suddenly snapped into perfect focus. The champagnes that emerge from this extraterrestrial building are as desperately precise, intricately delicate and flawlessly pristine as its polished interior, revealing the manifesto that defines all that lies within. And Pol Roger is on the rise.

It hasn't always been this way. The disorganised regime of the 1990s was 'a mess', according to d'Harcourt. The pace of transformation amazes me every time I visit Pol Roger. Since chef de cave Dominique Petit joined the company in 1999, after 24 years at Krug, more than €15 million has been invested in upgrading the winemaking facilities alone.

And it never seems to stop. The stainless steel fermentation space was updated in 2001, 2004, 2008, 2010 and 2011, and now provides full capacity to vinify every parcel separately. New cold-settling and fermentation halls were installed in 2011, alongside six new tiny 2200-litre tanks. The cellar was extended, and the cellar floors concreted to reduce vibrations from electric vehicles. More consistent and more precise disgorgement and dosage machines were also installed. In 2013, the old concrete tanks were refreshed, in 2014 a new cuverie for reserve wines was constructed, in 2015 a grand new reception room completed and in 2016 a state-of-the-art bottling line was commissioned. Even the address has changed, after the street was renamed. Pol Roger now proudly stands at 1 Rue Winston Churchill.

Pol Roger's investment is not to increase production, but to improve quality and consistency. Having already grown from 1.5 million to 1.8 million bottles annually, there is no immediate plan to increase further.

'Every year for the past 14 years we have seen results in the consistency of the wines from the work we are doing in the winery,' d'Harcourt explains. 'We have made a solid investment to ensure the family house remains secure in the family's hands into the 21st century.'

GRASS ROOTS RELATIONSHIPS

In 2014, I was privileged to an even deeper insight into the internal workings of this incredible company. Laurent d'Harcourt granted my request to shadow him for a full day mid-harvest, and I was surprised by what I discovered from the moment I sat down in his car as we set off in the morning. There on his passenger seat was the full harvest data of the company, which he was personally tracking and updating daily. 'I have more than 70 presses where our growers and our own vineyards press, and I spend all of harvest doing miles and miles visiting them,' he revealed. And these are not just flippant visits. 'Half of my visits are a breakfast, lunch or dinner. And sometimes two breakfasts a day!' Now *there's* a managing director who's engaged with the grass roots of his company. 'We have partnerships,' he explains, 'and we work with families for generation after generation.' It's dedication like this that sets Pol Roger apart.

Our first stop was Diebolt-Vallois, one of the finest growers in Cramant, where I witnessed some of the cleanest fruit I saw going into any press that vintage. Such is the demand for this famous grower that it sells its own wines on allocation, and yet it proudly supplies Pol Roger (as does Pierre Gimonnet in the next village, who is in the same situation). More than this, such is the pride of the Diebolt family in the partnership that its workers were proudly wearing Pol Roger t-shirts.

Pol Roger provides for an impressive 51% of its production from 90 hectares of estate vines. 'These holdings allow us to be more consistent over the long term,' clarifies d'Harcourt. The remainder is sourced exclusively from the Marne, and most importantly from Épernay and Chouilly, from long-term contracts under an arrangement that pays bonuses for quality. 'We are Pol Roger, we are not really growers,' d'Harcourt admits. 'Many of the growers from whom we source also care for vineyards that we own ourselves. They cultivate our vineyards, we press all the fruit and then give a portion back to them as payment.'

For some years, Pol Roger has been renewing its grower contracts to strengthen its sourcing in some grand crus, to enhance its capacity to make its Blanc de Blancs, Vintage and Sir Winston Churchill cuvées. The house already produces a higher proportion of vintage wines than virtually any other (in the order of 20%),

and this only bolsters its position. In 2015 it produced the largest volume of Sir Winston Churchill ever.

EXACTING PRECISION

The rise of Pol Roger is very much a credit to the exacting precision of Dominique Petit, who transformed a disorganised regime with an attention to detail learnt at Krug. The house preference for stainless steel over concrete and oak barrels rests on judicious temperature control of its musts during clarification and vinification. Musts undergo a double cold-settling process at just 5°C, producing the most pristine juice – a process that Petit's predecessor, James Coffinet, brought to Pol Roger from Billecart-Salmon. Held below 18°C, a cool primary fermentation is drawn out over 15 days, maintaining fruit freshness and aromatic definition.

Secondary fermentation is likewise cool, thanks to Pol Roger's 7.5 kilometres of cellars, which are among the coolest (9–11°C) and deepest (up to 33 metres) in Épernay. Most of the bottles rest in the deepest parts of the cellar. This slow fermentation produces wines of great finesse, fine effervescence and enduring longevity. 'Greater precision in the first and second fermentations have enabled a trend towards lower dosage,' explains d'Harcourt. The house tests dosages between 6g/L and 9g/L, and has currently settled around 8g/L.

Everything in the cellar is done by hand by a team of no more than 10. Pol Roger boasts four of the remaining 15 riddlers still working in Champagne. With each turning 50,000–60,000 bottles a day, it takes 4–5 weeks to riddle every bottle. Each is stacked in the cellar by hand, including every non-vintage wine – a painstaking process for a company with an incredible 9.5 million bottles in its care. 'Our neighbours think we are strange with such a huge inventory!' d'Harcourt exclaims.

With such a regime of excellence in the vineyard and winery, and having been under the ownership of the same family since the house was founded in 1849, Pol Roger's success is no surprise. 'We have been selling champagne in all of our markets under allocation in recent years,' d'Harcourt reveals. 'We could sell two or three times the volume in the UK, but we don't want to be too dependent on one market. We've been telling some markets to stop selling, particularly Blanc de Blancs and Sir Winston Churchill, because we don't have enough to send! We could increase our size, but we would lose our soul.'

That's a line you don't often hear from any medium-sized wine company in the current climate. And with ever-improving facilities every time I visit, this company is poised for even greater things to come.

It certainly is a different world at Pol Roger.

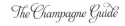

Pol Roger Brut Réserve NV $$

90 points • 2011 BASE VINTAGE • TASTED IN AUSTRALIA

A blend of the three champagne varieties in roughly equal proportions; 25% reserves from 2010, 2009 and 2008; 150 parcels from 30 crus; 42-54 months on lees in bottle (previously 36-48); 9g/L dosage; 1.3-1.4 million bottles; bottle code indicates packaging date, with the first digit denoting the year, and next three digits the day of that year

Pol Roger's infamous 'White Foil' is an attractive and refreshing apéritif, loaded with all the freshness of lemon and crunchy red apple fruit. Around four years on lees has built a creaminess to the mouthfeel. The imperfect fruit of the 2011 base vintage invariably leaves its mark in coarse, dusty phenolic grip that renders a hint of stale peanut to a firm finish. Nonetheless, it upholds some integrity in the vibrancy of lingering lemon fruit, bright acid line, finely honed chalk minerality and elegantly integrated dosage, the fingerprints that define Pol Roger.

Pol Roger Pure Extra Brut NV $$

91 points • 2012 BASE VINTAGE • TASTED IN AUSTRALIA

The 3 varieties in roughly equal balance; a different blend to Brut Réserve; more floral and less acidic; a blend of 30 crus; reserves from 2011, 2010 and 2009; zero dosage

This is a Pure of contrasts, juxtaposing the tension and structure of lemon zest and grapefruit with rich and full layers of toast, roast brazil nuts and anise. A shard of taut acidity meets expressive fine, salt-rich chalk minerality, and fine-ground phenolic presence, holding the finish in bone-dry tension, finding harmony thanks to the softening influence of lees age. It's a finely honed, oyster-ready apéritif.

Pol Roger Blanc de Blancs Brut Vintage 2009 $$$

95 points • DISGORGED JUNE 2016 • TASTED IN AUSTRALIA

100% Côte des Blancs grand crus: Chouilly, Oiry, Oger, Cramant and Avize; full malolactic fermentation; 7g/L dosage

For a house once led by pinot noir, Pol Roger is increasingly focusing on chardonnay in its vintage wines, and recent vintages of its Blanc de Blancs demonstrate why. The power and precision of the grand crus of the northern Côte des Blancs coalesce in the rich 2009 harvest to produce a beautifully refined blanc de blancs that captures the finesse and fragrant delicacy of Pol Roger. Dainty lemon and grapefruit lead out, backed by the understated succulence of white peach and the crunch of nashi pear in a long-lingering palate of bright acid line and frothing salt minerality. Almost a decade of lees age has begun to build a creamy texture and lingering, understated complexity of nutmeg, almond nougat and honey. It propagates with great persistence, sustained by the bright acidity of Pol Roger, even in such a warm vintage. A triumph of the season, and the vintage to drink over the next five years as we eagerly await the awakening of the sublime 2008.

POL ROGER BRUT VINTAGE 2008 $$$

96 points • Disgorged July 2016 • Tasted in Australia

60% pinot, 40% chardonnay; from 20 grand and premier crus in the Montagne de Reims and Côte des Blancs; full malolactic fermentation; 7g/L dosage

Pol Roger's vintage cuvées have long been highlights among the cuvées I most often recommend to friends, and I have many vintages from the past 25 years tucked into my cellar. I have long awaited the dawning of the release of the sensational 2008, a season I adore more than any other in recent history for its poise and energy. Pol Roger has done a fiendishly tactical thing, and while the recipe for this cuvée is always 60/40 pinot/chardonnay, it appears to have deployed pinot noir of particular presence and depth to rise to the tension of chardonnay in this electric season. The result is quite something to behold, with a profound core of the most sublime black cherries and black plums, intricately refined with exacting Pol Roger precision, energised by the lively acid line of 2008 and stirred vigorously by the brilliant chalk mineral structure of magnificently placed crus. In the slow-motion evolution of Pol Roger, age has brought just subtle nuances of biscuits and spice. It will age confidently, but it's irresistible from the outset. Do not miss this vintage. It's a revelation.

POL ROGER BRUT ROSÉ 2008 $$$$

95 points • Disgorged June 2016 • Tasted in Champagne and Australia

The same base as Brut Vintage, with around 15% Montagne de Reims pinot noir red wine, purchased by the company 'because we are not good at vinifying red wine ourselves'; 65% pinot noir, 35% chardonnay; from 20 grand cru and premier cru villages in the Montagne de Reims and Côte des Blancs; full malolactic fermentation; 8g/L dosage

A medium- to full-salmon hue heralds an expressive and characterful rosé of beautifully defined red and black cherries, blackberries, pink pepper, tamarillos and even a hint of pipe smoke. Pinot noir takes a confident lead, contributing elegant fragrance and succulent flesh and body within the strict and consummately controlled mood of Pol Roger. The fine chalk minerality of the great crus of the Côte des Blancs and Montagne de Reims draws out a long and refined finish, well supported by ultra-fine, impeccably handled tannins. A rosé of character and finesse, it looks smarter than ever in its new mushroom-purple livery.

POL ROGER CUVÉE SIR WINSTON CHURCHILL 2006 $$$$$

97 points • Disgorged September 2016 • Tasted in Épernay

Predominantly pinot noir, with some chardonnay, all from grand cru vineyards under vine at the time of Churchill; cold settled at 6°C; fermented below 18°C; full malolactic fermentation; secondary fermentation in the lowest part of the cellars (9°C); aged almost 10 years on lees

The blend of Sir Winston Churchill is a closely guarded secret. I ask d'Harcourt every time we taste a new vintage. 'I have not been drunk enough yet to tell you!' he replies. I'll keep working on it. Elusive details aside, Sir Winston steps up with a characterful presence in the powerful 2006 season, with pinot noir commanding a confident lead in spicy fig, mirabelle plum and red apple fruit, intricately toned by the bright lemon, grapefruit and crunchy pear of chardonnay. With time in the glass, a gorgeous presence of red cherry fruit rises and sweeps in a captivating display of youthful fruit integrity. Time moves slowly in Pol Roger's deep, cold cellars, and the tell-tale signs of maturity in nutmeg and almond are but fleeting glimpses, its age declared more dramatically in gorgeously seamless and silky texture. The signature, salty chalk minerality of the greatest crus of the Côte des Blancs and Montagne de Reims lays out a finish of outstanding line and enduring length, with a bright acid line that defines the finesse of the house and promises medium-term potential. A highlight of the season.

POMMERY

(Poh-mer-ee)

5 PLACE DU GÉNÉRAL GOURAUD 51053 REIMS

www.pommery.com

CHAMPAGNE
POMMERY
À REIMS-FRANCE

*C*hampagne's seventh largest house has had a rough ride, falling victim to buy-out after buy-out over recent decades, the most recent in 1996, when it was sold by Moët & Chandon to Belgian entrepreneur Jean-François Vranken, minus its exceptional vineyard holdings of 400 hectares, including more than 300 hectares of glorious grand crus. The inconsistency of its wines, particularly its non-vintage cuvées, is perhaps understandable in the context of this tumultuous history. To its credit, the house has now rebuilt its vineyard holdings to a respectable 255 hectares. 'Freshness, vivacity, fruit aromas and long length are the aspirations of Pommery, without being too strong,' explains chef de cave Thierry Gasco, who is this year celebrating his 25th anniversary with the house. Pommery claims to be the first house to make a brut champagne in 1874, when Madame Pommery made the gamble of producing a dry style to suit the British palate, and the aspiration has been low levels of dosage ever since, though 10g/L in Brut Royal and Brut Rosé are not particularly low by modern standards. Pommery sells close to 5 million bottles each year, and holds some 20 million at a stable, cold 10°C, 30 metres under its grand fairytale turrets in Reims in 120 glorious crayères, which Madame Pommery acquired between 1868 and 1878 and connected with 18 kilometres of tunnels. Pommery is the key house of the Vranken-Pommery group, Champagne's third largest after LVMH and Lanson-BCC.

POMMERY BRUT ROYAL NV $$

86 points • 2012 BASE VINTAGE • DISGORGED MARCH 2016 • TASTED IN AUSTRALIA
85 points • 2011 BASE VINTAGE • TASTED IN CHAMPAGNE

About one-third of each variety; a blend of about 40 crus; minimum 35% reserve wine, including reserves by cru and variety as well as 15% of the previous year's blend; 10g/L dosage

With a medium-straw hue and flavours of red apple, bruised pear and grapefruit, this is a cuvée of firm phenolic bite and redcurrant and lemon-accented acidity, with the toasty meringue notes of lees age contrasting the candied, honeyed effect of dosage. The result is short, simple, awkward and lacks finesse.

POMMERY BRUT ROSÉ ROYAL NV $$

89 points • 2012 BASE VINTAGE • DISGORGED MAY 2016 • TASTED IN AUSTRALIA
88 points • 2011 BASE VINTAGE • TASTED IN CHAMPAGNE

About one-third of each variety; Brut Royal with 7% Bouzy red wine; a blend of about 40 crus; minimum 35% reserve wine, including reserves by cru and variety as well as 15% of the previous year's blend; 10g/L dosage; 9% of production

'I don't want to have a very pink colour!' emphasises Thierry Gasco, whose aspiration for rosé is a very pale hue. 'When you see a pale colour, you anticipate an elegant wine,' he explains. A subtle 5% Bouzy rouge infuses a pale salmon hue, with a copper tint in the 2011 base, and gentle notes of red apple and pomegranate. Phenolic texture is coarse, making for a firm and astringent finish, though its small dose of red wine builds the palate nicely on the finish compared with the Brut Royal.

POMMERY GRAND CRU VINTAGE BRUT 2006 $$

88 points • DISGORGED DECEMBER 2015 • TASTED IN AUSTRALIA

50% chardonnay from Avize, Cramant, Oger and a little Verzenay and Sillery; 50% pinot from Aÿ, Verzenay, and a little Sillery and Bouzy; 8g/L dosage

The ripe 2006 vintage contributes a full straw hue and rich flavours of pineapple and stone fruits, balanced by an even acid/dosage accord. Reductive character lends savoury/vegetal notes. It carries with good persistence.

POMMERY GRAND CRU VINTAGE BRUT 2005 $$

84 points • 2012 BASE VINTAGE • TASTED IN CHAMPAGNE

50% chardonnay from Avize, Cramant, Oger and a little Verzenay and Sillery; 50% pinot from Aÿ, Verzenay, and a little Sillery and Bouzy; 8g/L dosage

Thierry Gasco describes the generosity, creaminess, body and softness of 2005 as a good balance for the style of Pommery. His vintage wine is a medium straw–coloured cuvée of firm phenolic grip, with notes of mushroom and a coarse structure, finishing dry, hard and short.

Pommery's fairytale castle sits atop 120 crayères nursing some 20 million bottles at a stable 10°C 30 metres underground.

The Champagne Guide

POMMERY CUVÉE LOUISE 2004 $$$$

95 points • DISGORGED NOVEMBER 2015 • TASTED IN CHAMPAGNE AND AUSTRALIA
65% chardonnay from Avize and Cramant; 35% pinot from Aÿ; a blend of 51 plots; 5g/L dosage

Louise is Pommery's blend of the finest plots of its best vintages. When Thierry Gasco commenced at Pommery in 1992, he made a selection of the best 85 plots on the mid-slopes of Avize, Cramant and Aÿ. Unusually, the selection for Louise is made a full three weeks before the harvest, and a second selection is made at the traditional point of blending post-fermentation. 'We are looking for the maturity of the grapes,' he explains. His pre-selection is necesary for a special pressing that he considers very important for the best extraction. Just 1800 litres of juice is pressed from each 4000 kg of marc, compared with the authorised 2550 litres.

A remarkably bright, pale-straw hue for 12 years of maturity heralds a cuvée of purity, focus and youthful spirit, singing with the white peach, grapefruit, lemon, beurre bosc pear and golden delicious apple definition of ripe Avize and Cramant chardonnay, backed sensitively with the depth of Aÿ pinot noir. Impressive concentration and definition of fruit are on grand display. A bright and energetic acid line accurately projects the character of the great 2004 season, charged with the fine, salty chalk minerality of Avize and Cramant. There is a touch of phenolic graininess in the texture, though it holds itself with evenness and confidence through a very long finish. Age has built subtle complexity of almond meal, toasted brioche, vanilla custard, wild honey and nougat. Impressive.

POMMERY CUVÉE LOUISE BRUT NATURE 2004 $$$$$

93 points • DISGORGED NOVEMBER 2015 • TASTED IN AUSTRALIA
Cuvée Louise with zero dosage

A lesson in the disproportionate influence of dosage, the absence of just 5g/L (the equivalent of less than one-third of a teaspoon of sugar in your cup of coffee) has a profound effect, diminishing the presence of the bouquet and tightening the finish to a dry and more grainy mouthfeel. This has the effect of accentuating its salt chalk minerality. It upholds its persistence and layers of brioche and almond-meal complexity. A cuvée of definition and structure for champagne purists.

POMMERY CUVÉE LOUISE 2002 $$$$

94 points • DISGORGED JANUARY 2015 • TASTED IN CHAMPAGNE
64% chardonnay from Avize and Cramant; 36% pinot from Aÿ; a blend of 50 plots; 5g/L dosage; less than 150,000 bottles

Encapsulating the personality of 2002, this is a compelling Louise that captures generous presence while upholding finesse and persistence. Apple and pear fruit meets the definition of lemon and grapefruit, with 14 years of age delivering a creamy and soft structure that contrasts the fine grip of gentle phenolic structure on the finish.

ROBERT MONCUIT

(Roh-beah Moh-kwee)

6/10

2 PLACE DE LA GARE 51190 LE MESNIL-SUR-OGER
www.champagnerobertmoncuit.com

ROBERT MONCUIT

'The Moncuit family has been growing chardonnay in the grand cru of Le Mesnil-sur-Oger since 1889, and making its own wines since the great vintage of 1928. Five generations later, Pierre Amillet, who has managed the estate since 2000, sustainably works the family's eight hectares of vineyards, located exclusively in the village. Insecticides are shunned, as are herbicides, in favour of ploughing for weed control. Grapes are harvested ripe to avoid chaptalisation, and every plot is pressed separately to maximise the palette of options for blending. Fermentation takes place in stainless steel tanks, with the exception of his vintage wine, Grande Cuvée, in barrels. The family's holdings are magnificent, none more so than a two-hectare parcel of the legendary Les Chétillons planted in 1956, and released as a single lieu-dit for the first time in the spectacular 2008 harvest. This family certainly has a knack of nailing the most sublime vintages for its new releases. These are wines of low dosage that capture the tension of Le Mesnil-sur-Oger. Disgorgement dates are printed on corks.

ROBERT MONCUIT GRAND CRU BRUT NV $

89 points • TASTED IN AUSTRALIA

A smartly packaged grand cru blend of layered complexity of golden delicious apple, quince, even tomato. Dusty notes and a slightly coarse texture make for a rustic style, but not bad for the price.

Robert Moncuit Grand Cru Blanc de Blancs Extra Brut NV $$

90 points • Tasted in Australia

Reserves are from a perpetual reserve from 2006 to 2012; 2–4g/L dosage

Freshness and definition are declared in a bright, pale-straw hue and crunchy apple, fennel and grapefruit, with an overlay of reductive complexity in struck flint and grilled toast. This is a dry and textural style that contrasts the salt minerality of Le Mesnil with gently grainy phenolic grip. It's unashamedly coiled and bony, yet gets away with it. A cuvée to match with fresh oysters.

Robert Moncuit Les Romarines Grand Cru Rosé Brut NV $$

96 points • 2013 base vintage • Tasted in Australia

Chardonnay from Le Mesnil-sur-Oger, pinot noir from Bouzy; 3–5g/L dosage

With a very pale salmon hue, this is a rosé that seamlessly synergises the tension and structure of Le Mesnil chardonnay with the enticing red fruits of Bouzy pinot. Bright and lively pink grapefruit, strawberry hull and delicate white cherries are underlined by a surge of frothing, salty chalk minerality that declares the unmistakable signature of Le Mesnil. To meld such light, airy delicacy with such chalk presence is a marvel indeed. The consummate apéritif rosé.

Robert Moncuit Grand Cru Grande Cuvée Le Mesnil-sur-Oger Blanc de Blancs 2006 $$

90 points • Tasted in Australia

The two oldest plots of the estate; vines of more than 50 years of age, low yields and maximum maturity; vinified in barrels; 6g/L dosage

Moncuit's aspiration to maximise maturity from these old, low-yielding vines produced especially luscious, ripe fruit in the sun-drenched 2006 season. The result is a toasty, honeyed, spicy, secondary style with candied notes and a short finish. An easy-drinking, crowd-pleasing style.

Robert Moncuit Les Chétillons Blanc de Blancs Grand Cru 2008 $$$$

97 points • Disgorged April 2015 • Tasted in Australia

Inaugural release; single 2-hectare plot planted 1956; 3g/L dosage

The remarkable Les Chétillons vineyard in Le Mesnil-sur-Oger attained legend status in 2008 in the hands of Rodolphe Péters (Pierre Péters). Robert Moncuit's take on the same site in this scintillating season upholds a bright medium-straw hue and magnificent definition of primary lemon, granny smith apple and fennel. Age has begun to bless it with brioche, roast almonds and honey, yet it upholds all the stamina of this enduring season in a high-tensile line of focused acidity and an epic snowfall of crystalline salt minerality, from pure white chalk just 20cm below the surface, boring to the essence of the very core of the Côte des Blancs. In exacting line, breathtaking length and sheer stamina, this is a thrilling cuvée with three decades of potential coiled into its core. A thrilling champagne by any standards, and a remarkable first release.

Ruinart

(Roo-ee-nar)

7/10

4 Rue des Crayères 51100 Reims

www.ruinart.com

Fréderic Panaïotis grew up between his grandparents' chardonnay vines in Champagne, and the variety remains close to his heart, making him very much at home as chef de cave at Ruinart since 2007. The longest-established champagne house of all has an affinity with chardonnay's freshness, finesse and elegance, and all of its finest cuvées lead with this variety, even its prestige rosé. Without the might of Moët & Chandon, the brand impact of Veuve Clicquot or the cachet of Krug, Ruinart lurks as the low-profile member of the Louis Vuitton–Moët Hennessy family. On Reims' famed Rue de Crayères, its premises hide behind the grand street presence of Pommery and Veuve Clicquot. This is just as Panaïotis would have it. 'In France we have a saying, if you live underground, you live happy!' he says. But on its performance, Ruinart has no need to lie low. Its cuvées are pure and pitch-perfect, singing with the crystalline precision of chardonnay.

Champagne is planted to just 28% chardonnay, making this the rarest of the region's three key varieties, and the hardest to source. Ruinart owns just 10% of its vineyards, including longstanding resources of 15 hectares of chardonnay in the grand crus of Sillery and Puisieulx on the eastern slopes of the Montagne de Reims, providing a richer and rounder style than the Côte des Blancs.

Long-term contracts with growers form the vast bulk of Ruinart's supplies, supplemented in recent times through vineyards acquired from Lanson and Joseph Perrier. This has enabled the house to increase its annual production from 1.4 million to 2.5–3 million bottles over the past two decades. 'Ruinart is in demand, so I'm getting all the chardonnay I can find!' Panaïotis exclaims. Annual growth today is under 5%.

To maintain the aromatic freshness and elegance of its fruit, the Ruinart house style is decisively reductive. 'We hate oxygen!' he declares, describing his approach as the antithesis of Bollinger and Krug. A pneumatic press is used instead of a traditional champagne press, to guard the juice against oxidation, and inert nitrogen gas protects the wine at every stage of production. Vinification takes place only in stainless steel. 'We have absolutely no need of oak in any of our wines,' Panaïotis states.

Ruinart's cuvées often carry flattering hints of struck flint or gunpowder, remnants of reductive winemaking. 'My goal is to take reduction even further!' proclaims Panaïotis. 'The stinky white Burgundy thing, I just love it! Like Domaine Roulot, but they use oak. The question is how to do it without oak!'

The Champagne Guide

To soften the austerity of young chardonnay, all cuvées undergo full malolactic fermentation, and non-vintage wines are balanced using respectable quantities of reserve wines. This makes for a style that permits refreshingly low dosages, declining admirably over recent years. The dosage is tweaked for successive disgorgements of Ruinart's prestige Dom Ruinart cuvée, typically lowering as the wine ages.

'For me, it's not a matter of numbers, but of balance,' Panaïotis explains.

Ruinart's distinctive rounded bottles make riddling challenging, and the house relies exclusively on gyropalettes, which Panaïotis claims give a far better result. The clear glass of these bottles renders the wine susceptible to lightstruck degradation, making it vital to store them in the dark.

Ruinart has occupied its premises in Reims since 1768, and was the first in Champagne to use the 3rd-century Roman crayères (chalk mines) under the city to age its champagnes.

Its location on top of the hill makes its eight kilometres of cellars some of the deepest and most spectacular in the region, plunging to depths of up to 38 metres. These are the only cellars in Champagne classified as a national monument – a distinguished home for such graceful champagnes.

R DE RUINART BRUT NV $$

88 points • 2011 BASE VINTAGE • DISGORGED 4TH QUARTER 2014 • TASTED IN AUSTRALIA

51% pinot noir, 40% chardonnay, 9% meunier; a blend of around 50 different crus across Champagne, though includes little Aube; reserves from 2010 and 2009; full malolactic fermentation; 9g/L dosage; 60% of the production of the house, hence more than 1.5 million bottles

After Panaïotis joined Ruinart, he recalls that 'it took a couple of years to figure out what was going on, and 2009 was the first year when I said, "Right, we can now start to do things! I don't think there's much I can do with the blanc de blancs or the rosé, but I can do things with R de Ruinart!"' This is a disappointingly old disgorgement of R de Ruinart, just a few months younger and derived from the same blend as the version I reviewed for the previous edition of this guide two years ago. It's shed its generous pinot noir accents of red apple and red cherry, with biscuity complexity rising. The dusty, astringent grip and bitter astringency of the wet and rot-plagued 2011 season is exacerbated now that fruit has faded on the finish.

RUINART BLANC DE BLANCS BRUT NV $$$

94 points • 2013 BASE VINTAGE • DISGORGED MID-2016 • TASTED IN AUSTRALIA

A blend of 20-25 crus, mostly premier crus from Côte des Blancs and Montagne de Reims, with Sézanne for maturity and the Massif de Saint-Thierry for freshness; 20-25% reserves from 2012 and 2011; full malolactic fermentation; aged 24-28 months on lees; 9/L dosage

Vivacity, elegance and enticing appeal unite in this fresh, young blend that exemplifies the exciting mood of Ruinart. The fine chalk mineral texture, pale colour and pure lemon and apple fruit of the Côte des Blancs define a honed and refreshing style, accented with subtle struck flint and grilled toast reduction that speaks Ruinart. Montagne de Reims chardonnay is strategically deployed to provide body and mid-palate fleshiness, without diminishing the line and mineral structure of the Côte des Blancs. Bottle age has built nougat and toast complexity, which mesh seamlessly with grand fruit persistence. An outstanding Ruinart Blanc de Blancs.

RUINART ROSÉ BRUT NV $$$

92 points • 2013 BASE VINTAGE • DISGORGED 3RD QUARTER 2016 • TASTED IN AUSTRALIA

55% pinot noir from the Montagne de Reims and Vallée de la Marne; 19% pinot noir red wine, with a short maceration of 5 days to extract colour but not tannin structure; 45% chardonnay from the Côte des Blancs and Montagne de Reims; 20-25% reserves from 2012 and 2011; 9g/L dosage

Ruinart's rosé is intentionally fresh, fruity, aromatic, approachable and full in colour. A light structure is the aspiration, but a strong inclusion of 18–19% red wine infuses a full-crimson hue, firm, fine tannin grip and a suggestion of bitterness to the finish. A large dose of chardonnay declares the house style of restraint and soft, chalk mineral mouthfeel, while pinot noir lends aromas and flavours of all shades of red: wild strawberries, raspberries, cherries and crab apples, with a rosehip lift.

DOM RUINART BLANC DE BLANCS BRUT 2004 $$$$$

96 points • DISGORGED JUNE 2013 • TASTED IN BRISBANE

100% grand cru chardonnay; 69% Côte des Blancs (predominantly Chouilly, Avize and Le Mesnil-sur-Oger), 31% Montagne de Reims (Sillery, Puisieulx, Mailly-Champagne and Verzenay); aged 8 years on lees; 5.5g/L dosage

Ruinart's flagship blanc de blancs plays the high strings of the Côte des Blancs to the thick orchestral scoring of Montagne de Reims, filling out chardonnay's pitch-perfect freshness with layers of creamy generosity. The 2004 has not moved since its release two years ago, delivering vitality and an edginess emphasised by prominent, diamond-cut acidity, underscored by the nostalgic timbre of inimitable Côte des Blancs chalk minerality. A distinctive and enticing air of reductive character blows through in gunpowder, white pepper and fennel notes, the signature of Ruinart and of chardonnay, while 12 years in Ruinart's ancient chalk mines has deepened its voice with rising tones of nougat, toasty complexity and a hint of smoked bacon. Its euphoric vigour and sheer stamina surpass even the masterpiece of 2002, promising two decades of potential in the cellar, though already drinking marvellously. Large glasses will be your best ally when it is finally time to awaken this sleeping beauty.

DOM RUINART ROSÉ BRUT 2002 $$$$$

95 points • TASTED IN AUSTRALIA

85% chardonnay from Avize, Le Mesnil-sur-Oger, Chouilly, Sillery and Puisieulx; 15% pinot noir red wine from Verzenay and Sillery; aged at least 10 years on lees

Panaïotis calls his Dom Ruinart Rosé 'blanc de blancs rosé', but the influence of 15% pinot noir red wine is profound, transforming its base Dom Ruinart 2002 almost beyond recognition. Its reductive complexity of struck flint and toast meets the secondary development of pinot noir and its notes of dried flowers, leather and truffles to produce a dry style of savoury allure. It's layered with toasty, bottle-derived complexity, though the grip of fine tannin structure on the finish calls for protein dishes.

SALMON

(Sahl-moh)

5/10

21–23 Rue du Capitaine Chesnais 51170 Chaumuzy

www.champagnesalmon.com

CHAMPAGNE
SALMON

*M*ichel Salmon produced his first champagne from his family's vineyards in 1958. Almost 60 years later, he remains in charge of the estate, ably assisted by his son Olivier and grandson Alexandre. The three tend 10 hectares sustainably on clay-limestone soils planted to 85% meunier in their village of Chaumuzy and the surrounding crus of the Vallée de l'Ardre in the west of the Montagne de Reims. Their cuvées well express the characterful exuberance of meunier. Full detail of cépage, disgorgement date and dosage are declared on back labels.

SALMON MONTGOLFIÈRE SÉLECTION BRUT NV $$

89 points • 2012 BASE VINTAGE • DISGORGED MAY 2016 • TASTED IN AUSTRALIA

50% meunier, 25% chardonnay, 25% pinot from Chaumuzy and the nearby villages of Chambrecy, Villes-en-Tardenois and Sacy; 50% reserves; 9g/L dosage

With a 50% meunier lead, this is a rich and mature NV that expresses the breadth of red berry and red apple fruit of the variety with heightened toasty, nutty complexity, culminating in a finish of soft acidity and some graininess in the structure. It concludes with good persistence and body.

Salmon 100% Meunier Brut NV $$

90 points • 2012 base vintage • Disgorged August 2016 • Tasted in Australia

100% Chaumuzy meunier; 35% reserves; 7g/L dosage

A statement of the fleshy exuberance of meunier, with juicy red cherry and succulent strawberry fruit evolving into the coffee bean and chocolate complexity of bottle age. Acidity is soft and dosage is well integrated, culminating in a finish of gently grainy phenolic grip, with plenty of flesh and body to hold its own.

Salmon 100% Meunier Brut Rosé NV $$

92 points • 2012 base vintage • Disgorged August 2016 • Tasted in Australia

100% Chaumuzy meunier; 50% reserves including 15% reserve red wine; 7g/L dosage

Meunier is on full parade in a cuvée of medium salmon copper hue and all the signature, spicy strawberry and raspberry fruits we love of this variety. It unites body and flesh with a well-composed structure comprised of both balanced, bright acidity and fine tannin grip, carrying an even and harmonious finish. In spite of higher reserves, it's even brighter and fresher than the 100% meunier blanc.

Salmon Rosé de Saignée Extra Brut 2012 $$$

93 points • Disgorged June 2016 • Tasted in Australia

100% meunier; single-plot Bouzin, the best of the estate in Chaumuzy; 18 hours skin contact; 3g/L dosage

Every one of 2152 bottles of this first-release cuvée has an individually handwritten front label. It's an enticing and characterful rosé de saignée of pretty medium salmon hue that epitomises meunier in its violet aromas and flavours of spicy wild strawberries, red cherries and even plum pudding. Red apple skin texture provides grip to the palate, sustained by good acid line and well-crafted tannin structure.

The Champagne Guide

SALON

(Sah-loh)

9/10

5–7 RUE DE LA BRÈCHE D'OGER 51190 LE MESNIL-SUR-OGER

www.salondelamotte.com

CHAMPAGNE

SALON

Le Mesnil

*T*here is only one Salon, and there has only ever been one. One wine of one variety from one vintage, sourced from one region (Côte de Blancs) and one village (Le Mesnil-sur-Oger). The romantic ideal ends abruptly here, however, because this is not a single-vineyard wine, nor even an estate wine. The fruit of the single-hectare estate vineyard of Jardin de Salon was declassified until 2012 to its lower-tier sister house, Delamotte, because the vines were replanted in 2003. Salon is sourced from 15 hectares of vines of average age 35–40 years, and some older than 90, owned by 19 longstanding growers, all of whom sell their fruit only to Salon. Winemaking is handled by the owner of both houses, Laurent-Perrier.

The minute scale of this operation sank in as I absorbed it from the homely tasting room in the house in Le Mesnil-sur-Oger. The windows framed the Jardin vineyard stretching up the gentle slope just outside. Directly below, a decade of future releases lay waiting in the small cellar, though most lie in warehouses off-site. There are only 10 employees: six in the cellar and four in the office. Production is typically about 50–60,000 bottles, and only in worthy vintages. There is no non-vintage wine, so production is limited to the finest years, of which the current release, 2004, is just the 39th since 1905.

It was in that year that Eugène-Aimé Salon created Champagne's first blanc de blancs, originally only for personal consumption. To this day it remains among the most celebrated and most expensive. Of the original vineyards from which Eugène-Aimé purchased, all but two are still part of Salon's sourcing. The philosophy from the start was to build a champagne that could age, with every element of its production honed towards this goal. The first pressing is used exclusively, fermented in stainless steel under temperature control. Its natural acidity is upheld by blocking malolactic fermentation, distinguishing it from Delamotte. Aged for an average of 10 years before release, the timing for each vintage is determined according to when it is ready. Riddling is performed by hand, and bottles are disgorged according to when they are released. This usually equates to four to six disgorgements across two years of release. Dosage is tweaked for each disgorgement, typically 5–6g/L.

Salon is usually among the last houses to release its vintage wine; even at this age, it is far from its peak. 'Whenever I produce a vintage I say, "This is not for me or for my children, but for my grandchildren",' declares Salon Delamotte president Didier Depond, who considers the perfect time to drink Salon to be after 20 years.

'It takes 20 years to truly define a great wine,' he suggests. 'We are always very surprised by the potential of Salons opened from the '70s, '60s and even '50s.'

Laurent-Perrier's vineyard manager, Christelle Rinville, follows each vineyard throughout the year, and monitors all cultures and treatments that are applied. Depond is afforded the freedom to manage the house independently, and feels no pressure to increase volumes, in spite of limited supply and high demand.

'It's difficult to increase the volume because the vineyards are limited,' he points out. 'And it would be a disaster to increase the number of vintages we release.' A noble stance at a time when some houses appear set on churning out flagship champagnes in lesser seasons.

Corks are coded with a letter to indicate the semester, and an inverted number for the year of disgorgement, so A61 is the first trimester of 2016.

There will be no 2000 Salon, after mid-August hail devastated the Le Mesnil harvest. The 2002

and 2004 will be followed by 2006, 2007, 2008 (10,000 magnums only) and 2012, bettering Salon's longstanding average of fewer than four vintages each decade. The 1996, 2002 and 2008 are upheld by the house to be the finest vintages for long ageing.

Salon ages a small amount of its production under the house in Le Mesnil.

SALON CUVÉE S BLANC DE BLANCS BRUT 2004 $$$$$

96 points • DISGORGED SEPTEMBER 2015 AND EARLY 2016 • TASTED IN CHAMPAGNE
19 parcels from Le Mesnil-sur-Oger; 5g/L dosage; 42,000 bottles

The talent of Salon to desperately cling to incisive youthfulness is electrifying, and 2004 has exploded into the world at 12 years of age with a flash of precision and tense, coiled lemon blossom and apple elegance. It is defined by a grand line of long, salty mineral texture that personifies Le Mesnil, accented with white pepper and a flourish of pear and apple, with just the subtlest glimmers of age in marzipan, almond meal, vanilla bean and pâtisserie, though the mood remains bright and primary. The record yields of 2004 alarmed many in Champagne, and Salon made the tough call of green harvesting not once but twice, slashing yields from the usual 60,000 to just 42,000 bottles. The ability of this season to shine and endure in spite of enormous yields has surprised us all, and I cannot help but wonder if Salon sacrificed something of the elegance of this release in this drastic decision, picking up a little firm, dry-extract structure that adds a touch of chewy, grapefruit pith-like grip to the finish.

SALON CUVÉE S BLANC DE BLANCS BRUT 1999 $$$$$

96 points • DISGORGED EARLY 2016 • TASTED IN CHAMPAGNE

Five years on from its release, the warm and sunny 1999 season has blossomed into the beautifully engaging prime of its life. The primary citrus and reduction of its early years have morphed gently into a wonderful complexity of mandarin, glacé fig, even a touch of musk, true to this generous season. It's full, rich, creamy and silky, supported by an ever-present undercurrent of fine Le Mesnil-sur-Oger chalk minerality. It will continue to bask in its glory days.

TAITTINGER

(Tet-ahn-zhay)

(8/10)

9 PLACE SAINT-NICAISE 51100 REIMS
www.taittinger.com

CHAMPAGNE
TAITTINGER
Reims

'My grandfather gave me a book when I was five years old,' Pierre-Emmanuel Taittinger recalls. 'In the dedication he wrote, "To my grandson, who will one day be an entrepreneur and be the guardian of the family tradition."' Little did he know how true his prophecy would prove to be, and just what it would take to achieve. In these days of corporate takeovers, it's a gutsy commitment to buy back the family business. When most of the heirs voted to cash in and Taittinger was sold in 2005, Pierre-Emmanuel launched a fierce, year-long buy-back for his branch of the family, to the tune of €550 million, with the help of family friends and French bank Crédit Agricole. The family has since built up its stake in the company to almost half, with the remainder mostly in the hands of its friends. Annual sales of 5.6 million bottles rank Taittinger as Champagne's sixth-largest house.

The fulfilment of his grandfather's prediction returned Taittinger to its place among the last big independent, family-owned houses that uphold the family name not only on the label, but in their management. Pierre-Emmanuel remains president of the company, his dynamic son, Clovis, is export director, and his delightful daughter, Vitalie, handles the company's artistic vision. The board and family are involved in each cuvée's tastings. 'My father leads the tasting, but it is a collective decision,' says Clovis.

It's a compelling story of fighting for the family business in the middle of one of the biggest corporate jungles anywhere in the wine world. It took Pierre-Emmanuel years to bring his buy-back to fruition,

and it was not until 2008 that it was complete. The vintage wines are only now beginning to emerge from the hallowed caverns of Taittinger, and they have never looked more refined.

NATURAL VITICULTURE

Taittinger's 288 hectares of vineyard holdings, predominantly in the Montagne de Reims and Côte des Blancs, provide for half of the company's annual production, with recent growth of around 7% each year. Half of its own vines are pinot noir, 35% are chardonnay and are 15% meunier. Chardonnay plays a significant role in the house style, sourced predominantly from the Côte des Blancs.

An increasingly eco-friendly approach is taken in the vines, with a reduction in the use of pesticides and elimination of herbicides. 'We are aiming to use half the usual dose of chemicals,' outlines Taittinger's young and talented Deputy General Manager, Damien Le Sueur, 'and in 2010 we used less than six treatments across all our vineyards.'

The house is not seeking organic certification, to retain the flexibility to use full doses when difficult seasons dictate. Nonetheless, natural treatments remain the preference, and attention has been given to trellising to provide ventilation to balanced canopies. Grasses are planted in the mid-rows of 80% of estate vineyards, believed to be an unprecedented proportion for an estate of this size, and ploughing is used for weed control, sometimes by horse. Green harvesting to limit yields is only used when necessary, such as in the high-yielding year of 2004, when as much as 40% of fruit was dropped in some vineyards.

Taittinger employs 700–800 pickers and is purposeful in paying them by their time, not by volume, which is rare in Champagne. 'It is more difficult to demand quality if we pay by volume, so we never do that,' explains Le Sueur. 'We explain to them what we want in terms of quality and tell them to be selective.'

Taittinger prizes its growers and takes an approach of building good relationships rather than supervising quality. 'To us, they are not just a number; a personal relationship is important,' says Le Sueur. 'It's about long-term relationships, of remaining loyal and maintaining confidence.' Pierre-Emmanuel Taittinger is actively involved during the harvests and visits all of Taittinger's press houses. 'They are proud to see him, as they appreciate the image of Taittinger and the family involvement.'

ATTENTIVE VINIFICATION

At the time of the family buy-back, the decision was made to work only with the finest juices, using around 10% of the tailles of chardonnay only in the Brut Réserve NV and Brut Prestige Rosé NV, and only the first pressing in the other cuvées. 'We only use the tailles from chardonnay, because the tailles of the black grapes are too heavy,' Le Sueur explains. 'Too much of the tailles in the blend makes them too strong and mature, but we want to produce very fine and accurate wines.' Excess tailles are exchanged for the cuvées of other houses.

In the winery, fermentation is conducted in tanks below 18°C to preserve freshness. Malolactic fermentation is allowed to complete on all cuvées, crucial for softening these chardonnay-led styles. 'I say we work with four varieties: chardonnay, pinot noir, meunier and

time!' says Le Sueur, emphasising the importance of maturity in allowing these nervy styles to develop. Non-vintage wines are aged on lees for at least three years, Prélude Grand Crus Brut NV for a minimum of five years, vintage wines for longer again, and the flagship Comtes de Champagne eight years or more (the current vintage is 2006).

Such long ageing necessitates large cellar stocks. Taittinger ages 3 million bottles of Comtes de Champagne at 9–10°C in its breathtaking four kilometres of galleries under its headquarters in Reims, including a section of 4th-century Roman crayères. Its remaining stores of some 23 million bottles are kept in a facility in town. This tremendous stock facilitates an average of more than 4.5 years on lees, a massive duration for any house.

Taittinger bottles under natural cork, since it hasn't found that its cuvées evolve in the same way under DIAM. Since mid-2014, all cuvées except Comtes de Champagne have boasted a QR code that reveals the bottling and disgorgement dates. I'm told there's also a way to locate this information on the website, but I couldn't find it.

COMTES DE CHAMPAGNE

Taittinger's flagship Comtes de Champagne holds an enviable position among the very finest blanc de blancs. It is sourced principally from Avize and Le Mesnil-sur-Oger, and to a lesser extent from Oger, Chouilly, Cramant, Vertus and Bergères-lès-Vertus.

'We are lucky to work with a huge quantity of wines from the Côte des Blancs, allowing us to choose the best samples for Comtes de Champagne each year,' explains cellar master Loïc Dupont. 'We look for the vats that represent the typicity of each cru, to build the expression of the vintage. Avize brings elegance, finesse and balance, Le Mesnil-sur-Oger contributes body and a subtle reduction akin to grilled bread, Chouilly delivers roundness, Cramant grilled almonds, and Oger elegant citrus.' Just 5% is aged for four months in oak barrels, one-third new, and the rest up to four years old – not for strength, but to bring subtle notes of toast and brioche to the delicacy of chardonnay.

Taittinger's depth of reach into the Côte des Blancs grand crus has made Comtes de Champagne one of Champagne's most consistent blanc de blancs, and every even-numbered vintage since 1996 has been nothing short of transcendental.

The Taittinger family tradition remains as alive and well as ever, Tattinger having just recorded five years of record sales in a row, thanks to the daring of Pierre-Emmanuel, his children, and their loyal, talented team.

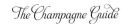

TAITTINGER CUVÉE BRUT RÉSERVE NV $$

93 points • 2013 BASE VINTAGE • DISGORGED AUGUST 2016 • TASTED IN AUSTRALIA
92 points • 70% 2012 BASE VINTAGE WITH 15% 2011 AND 15% 2010 • DISGORGED
LATE 2015 • TASTED IN CHAMPAGNE

40% chardonnay, 35% pinot noir, 25% meunier from more than 35 crus; aged at least 3 years on lees; 9g/L dosage

Taittinger always prepares its Brut Réserve blend first, and only if the vintage is deemed of sufficient quality are its other cuvées assembled. This philosophy, together with a generous inclusion of reserves, has produced another impressively poised rendition in 2013 that sings with the pretty white-peach fruit, apple and lemon zest vivacity of chardonnay, the delicate strawberry hull of pinot and the gentle almond and brioche notes of bottle age. This is a refreshing apéritif of persistence, poise, intricately integrated dosage and refreshing acid line, basking in the glory of more pronounced, fine chalk mineral structure than ever this year. 2012 represents a confident release, too, contrasting chardonnay's citrus freshness with the deep toastiness of long lees age.

TAITTINGER CUVÉE PRESTIGE BRUT NV $$

89 points • TASTED IN AUSTRALIA

A blend designed for on-premise venues; 40% chardonnay, 60% pinot and meunier; a blend of almost 50 components; aged 4.5 years on lees

This cuvée announces its extended maturity in a medium-straw hue and toasty, biscuity brioche complexity, which offers depth and texture to the focused apple and lemon of its chardonnay lead. It finishes with the dustiness and dry bitterness of fruit in less than perfect health, likely the victim of a tricky base vintage. Nonetheless, good acid line and well-integrated dosage linger on a long finish.

TAITTINGER FOLIES DE LA MARQUETTERIE NV $$

92 points • 2012 BASE VINTAGE • DISGORGED MAY 2016 • TASTED IN AUSTRALIA
93 points • 2009 BASE VINTAGE • TASTED IN CHAMPAGNE

55% pinot, 45% chardonnay; green harvested for optimum ripeness; 30% vinified in large oak foudres; aged 5 years on lees

Taittinger's first single-estate wine is blended from parcels surrounding its Château de la Marquetterie in Pierry, just south of Épernay. The typicity of the site is emphasised using viticulture to drop yields to around half of Champagne's average, through green harvest and elimination of soil supplements. The objective is to use no chaptalisation. Some parcels are vinified in large, 10-year-old, 4000-litre foudres to provide subtle oxygenation without oak character. No blend was produced between 2009 and 2012 as the house reflected on the philosophy of the style. From the release of the 2014 base it will be a 50/50 blend of Château de la Marquetterie and other vineyards.

  In 2012, this is a rounded, rich and generous cuvée, relying heavily on crop reduction to build depth and character of ripe peach fruit, and in this release reductive notes of white pepper, fennel and just a hint of brioche bottle development. It concludes with well-balanced acidity and good persistence. The 2009 harvest is more opulent than ever, brimming with apricots, dried peaches, honey and roast nuts, with a creamy and full palate balanced by gentle chalk minerality.

Taittinger Cuvée Brut Prestige Rosé NV $$$

94 points • 2012 base vintage • Disgorged July 2016 • Tasted in Australia

30% chardonnay, 70% pinot and meunier; 15% pinot noir red wine from Ambonnay, Bouzy and Les Riceys

With a pretty, medium-salmon hue, this is a rosé that contrasts a pitch-perfect, fragrant bouquet of rose petals, red cherries and elegant strawberries, with a palate built on a depth of roast nuts and toast complexity that belies just three years of bottle age. The result is a subtle and compelling change of mood for this cuvée, more secondary and more intriguing than ever, culminating in a finish that coasts in unison, evenly harmonising chalk mineral texture with fine tannin structure. Taittinger's aspiration with rosé is structure and a little touch of tannin, and this blend meets the brief with flair.

Taittinger Cuvée Nocturne NV $$

89 points • 2010 base vintage • Disgorged July 2016 • Tasted in Australia

Exactly the same blend as Brut Réserve, aged another year (4-4.5 years on lees), with 17.5g/L dosage

Nocturne has returned to more dignified livery after its swing as a pimped shiny iridescent purple disco ball (nothing wrong with that!). The recipe remains the same, a more mature and slightly sweeter version of Brut Réserve – not too cloying, and not a 'leftovers' cuvée of rotten fruit and too much tailles, as sweet champagnes all too often tend to be. By comparison, this is well made and fruity, with apricot, peach and pineapple fruit, boiled sweets and the honey and roast nuts of maturity. It's not too sweet, particularly when served well chilled. This base has now been in the market for a few years, and it's starting to lose freshness, with a touch of earthy complexity beginning to show on the finish, something I've not seen before. Turn down the lights, crank up the volume and give it a swing.

Taittinger Nocturne Rosé Sec NV $$$

93 points • 2011 base vintage • Tasted in Champagne

Exactly the same blend as Prestige Rosé, aged another year (3-3.5 years on lees), with 17.5g/L dosage; 34% pinot, 30% chardonnay, 20% meunier; 16% pinot noir red wine from the Montagne de Reims and Les Riceys

This is far more sophisticated than its shimmering night-club sleeve suggests: Taittinger has transcended the tribulations of 2011 to create one of the best sweeter champagnes I've tasted in years. As per the white Nocturne, the secret is firstly that it's a more mature version of the dry cuvée, and secondly that it's not too sweet. It's been in the market a couple of years now, and admirably upholds its pretty, clean, fresh and characterful style and medium-salmon hue. A confit of strawberry and cherry fruits and red apples is becoming toasty and nutty with the savoury notes of maturity. Creamy dosage contrasts well-structured acid line and fine chalk mineral texture. Give it a chill and it's ready to party.

The Champagne Guide

Taittinger Cuvée Prélude Grand Crus Brut NV $$$

89 points • 100% 2011 • Disgorged July 2016 • Tasted in Australia
94 points • 100% 2009 • Disgorged early 2015 • Tasted in Champagne

50% Côte des Blancs chardonnay, mainly from Avize and Le Mesnil-sur-Oger, with a little Chouilly; 50% northern Montagne de Reims pinot noir for freshness, mainly from Mailly-Champagne, then Ambonnay and Verzenay; grand cru parcels selected to show the characters of their crus, rather than the mood of the vintage; 9g/L dosage

Taittinger selects its grand cru parcels of elegance, finesse, delicacy and structure for its Prélude, reserving those with more power for the Comtes de Champagne Rosé. Prélude exudes a tightrope tension between power and precision; a particularly pale, bright straw hue and flavours of pear, grapefruit and fennel contrasting with the subtle bottle-developed complexity of almond meal and nougat. Alas, the challenging 2011 season marks this release with its dry-extract bitterness and pear skin–like phenolic grip, washing the wine out with the dustiness of imperfect fruit. Nonetheless, it upholds persistence and fine acid/sugar balance. Sadly, there is still no clue to the base vintage anywhere on the labelling, and the warm 2009 vintage makes for a striking contrast, a cuvée of body and volume, with toast and even toffee enveloping a generous core of succulent stone fruits, true to its rounded season and the exuberance of its grand cru villages. A vintage to drink now.

Taittinger Cuvée Brut Millésimé 2009 $$$

92 points • Disgorged May 2016 • Tasted in Australia

Equal parts of chardonnay from grand crus in the Côte des Blancs, and pinot noir from grand crus in the Montagne de Reims and the beginning of the Vallée de la Marne; parcels selected for their vintage typicity; 9g/L dosage

True to the dry and hot 2009 season, this is a powerfully rich rendition of vintage Taittinger, rejoicing in baked apple, black cherry and fig fruit, and even nuances of toffee. It pulls into a focused and poised finish of gentle acid structure and well-toned dosage, with phenolic bitterness admirably subtle and well handled. A vintage to drink right away.

Taittinger Comtes de Champagne Blanc de Blancs 2008 $$$$$

99 points • Disgorged October 2015 • Tasted in Champagne

50-60% Avize and Le Mesnil-sur-Oger, the pillars of Comtes, supported by Oger, Chouilly and Cramant; 5-6% (Chouilly component) aged in barrels for 4-5 months, to add body and subtle burnt vanilla and coconut character; 9g/L dosage

It is completely unfathomable to attempt to assess the most enduring Comtes since 1996 a full three years before its impending release in 2019 or 2020. And yet the inclusion of this desperately coiled and reticent thing here, even at this premature moment, is mandated, if not by the wonder of that first tasting with the team and the family in the reception room of Taittinger at Saint-Nicaise, permanently etched in my psyche, then for the imperative to inscribe its name at the top of your buying list when that magic moment finally comes when it is unleashed on the world. It evokes everything we adore of Comtes, bringing back all the innocence of a joyful childhood, of scaling lemon and apple trees to plunder their crunchy fruits, of a free-as-air dash through fields of lush grass in endless blue daylight, of a breathless plunge into an icy mountain rock pool. The subtle complexity of white pepper, almond and biscuit is but a fleeting glimpse, leaving the fanfare to a deep, frothing core of salty minerality which bores to the depths of Avize and Le Mesnil-sur-Oger, the most mineral of sparkling crus in the known universe. In breathtaking precison, zen-like focus and unmitigated drive, it is difficult to say just how many decades it may live and quite what dizzying heights it will attain. Be sure you're first in the queue to find out. I'll see you there.

Taittinger Comtes de Champagne Blanc de Blancs 2007 $$$$$

98 points • Disgorged October 2015 • Tasted in Champagne

After the might of 2005 and 2006, there is a pretty elegance to 2007 that I find thrillingly compelling, and it's captured in pinpoint detail in this enchanting Comtes. The theme here is fragrant finesse of youthful lemon blossom, touched with delightful notes of brioche, marzipan and almond. The chalk mineral signature of Comtes rumbles with the ancient geological history of the finest grand crus of the Côte des Blancs. Still pale in hue at a decade of age, this is my style of Comtes. Turn down the lights and the music and pour it for the one you love most.

Taittinger Comtes de Champagne Blanc de Blancs 2006 $$$$$

97 points • Disgorged January 2016 • Tasted in Champagne and Australia

In grand testament to Taittinger's profound reach into the Côte des Blancs' most enduring grand crus, the poise and stamina of Comtes even in the warm and ready 2006 season is nothing short of staggering. The lemon, lime, grapefruit, crunchy apple, pear and pineapple of its youth have softened as bottle complexity of nougat and almonds has begun to emerge. Nuances of grilled toast and brioche are considered by the house to be signatures of the season. The ripe, supple succulence of the vintage furnishes a fleshy mid-palate of immediate allure, making this a Comtes to enjoy while the 2002, 2004 and 2008 continue to evolve, though there is no immediate haste here. Its textural presence is mouth-embracing, permeating every crevice, masterfully uniting very fine phenolic grip with delightfully delicate, frothing salt minerality that bores to the very core of the finest chalkfields of the Côte des Blancs.

Taittinger Comtes de Champagne Rosé 2006 $$$$$

96 points • Disgorged March 2016 • Tasted in Australia

70% pinot noir from Ambonnay, Mailly-Champagne, Verzy and Verzenay, including 12% red wine from Bouzy; 30% chardonnay from Avize, Le Mesnil-sur-Oger, Oger and Chouilly; no oak; just 5–10% of the production of Comtes de Champagne

If the philosophy of Comtes de Champagne is that of restraint, the aim of its extroverted rosé sister is of aromatic explosiveness and energy. Previously released younger than the blanc, the house has discovered how magnificently the rosé ages, and now the releases coincide, with the aim of releasing the rosé even later in future. The finesse and grace of this release seem at odds with its brief and its full crimson copper–hue, particularly in the warmth of the 2006 vintage, which possesses a latent power only now unravelling two years after its release, making this a rare champagne rosé for the cellar. Primary red cherries, strawberries, guavas and pomegranates remain, while age ushers in a complexity akin to mature red Burgundy in notes of forest floor, truffles and subtle suggestions of smoked charcuterie. A rosé of excellent length, drive and presence, powered by considerable structure of firm, fine tannins, masterfully crafted to effortlessly support a long and harmonious finish of depth and breadth, underscored by beautifully defined bath-salts minerality.

Tarlant

(Tahr-lohn)

Rue de la Cooperative 51480 Oeuilly

www.tarlant.com

CHAMPAGNE
TARLANT
VIGNERONS DEPUIS 1687

'*Our goal is to express the personality of our unique place,' declares young Benoît Tarlant, and there are few in Champagne who have gone to greater lengths to do so. Within six years of taking the lead at his family estate in 1999, he had eliminated dosage in 80% of his annual production of 120,000–130,000 bottles, no mean feat in a house that preserves tension with malic acidity. 'I am not a cane sugar or beet sugar maker, I produce grapes!' he declares. His is an intuitive and sensitive approach that dares to ride the cutting edge of practice in the vineyard and the winery. 'There are no rules — it depends on the grapes!' he exclaims. A unique display of dried herbs in a corner of the winery celebrates a regime of cover crops and treatments that he dubs 'herbal therapy'. Fermentation is conducted mostly in barrels, some tanks and even small clay amphorae. 'The goal is not the method, the goal is to make great wine,' he sums up, exemplified in a large range of champagnes energised by malic acidity and characterised by the creamy generosity of ripe fruit, barrel fermentation, liberal use of reserve wines and long ageing. Tarlant's Zero is one of champagne's best brut natures.*

Benoît Tarlant's family has tended its vines in the Vallée de la Marne since 1687, made its own wine since the 1870s, and champagne since 1929. Today, the family is one of the most distinguished growers in its village of Oeuilly.

'Our priority is to take care of the vines and make our wines,' says Benoît, who has relished the opportunity to mark his own print on the estate while working alongside his grandfather Georges, his parents Jean-Mary and Micheline, and his sister Mélanie.

HERBAL THERAPY

Mostly on the southern side of the river, Tarlant's north-facing sites require meticulous attention, and even the use of a tractor winch to haul equipment up the rows of the steepest vineyards in the village. North- and east-facing slopes are prized for retention of acidity, particularly in meunier.

Benoît took me to the edge of the vines on the eastern side of the village. 'The Marne Valley is defined by the river, cutting like a knife and making many soil types,' he explained, pointing out six different soil varieties between us and the river, less than 800 metres away. 'Our job is to keep the character of each vineyard.' Tarlant's 14 hectares are spread across 57 plots, each of which are vinified separately. An extensive range of 2012 vins clairs exemplifies the distinctiveness of mineral expression and flavour profile of each plot.

Most of these vineyards were planted by his family and boast an average age of 34 years. The estate has had opportunity to increase slightly as the contracts on his grandfather's vineyards end, though only one hectare has been gained in this way in recent years. Benoît credits chalk in the soil for a diversity of grape selection.

'This area is best suited to black grapes, as chardonnay is quite rustic,' he points out, explaining his breakdown of 50% pinot noir, 30% chardonnay, 18% meunier and 2% petit meslier, arbanne and pinot blanc.

Benoît prizes the diversity of his plots, but admits it's a challenge to manage so many distinct sites using techniques sympathetic to organic practices. Three hectares are managed biodynamically, some organically, neither certified; the remainder rely on his ingenious regime of 'herbal therapy'. A wide range of herbs are planted in the vineyards, including oregano, which he harvests for pizzas and salads. Small concoctions are made from the plants and sprayed on the vines to protect against fungus attacks. He says 2012 was a good year to practise. 'We only lost 30% of fruit in our vineyards with herbal therapy, but 40% with organics and 50% with biodynamics.'

INTUITIVE WINEMAKING

The goal is to harvest ripe, tasty grapes with balanced acidity. To this end, malolactic fermentation is completely blocked. 'I think malolactic is an industry mistake from the 1960s and 1970s,' Benoît suggests. 'Traditionally, the majority of champagne was without malolactic fermentation. It makes sense to me to show the wine naturally, with its natural acidity.'

Intensity, precision and presence of texture are Benoît's priorities. Every transfer in the winery is performed by gravity. The traditional champagne pressing regime is taken one step further, by carefully splitting the juice from the first pressing into two separate components, and the tailles into two components. 'I hate pre-blending, so we vinify every parcel separately,' he explains. 'We should respect the origin of the place here in Champagne as much as they do in Burgundy.'

Two-thirds of the harvest is barrel fermented using wild yeast, without additions of enzymes or bentonite for clarification or stabilisation. The remainder is tank fermented in temperature-controlled stainless steel to preserve vitality. Inspired by friends in Italy, Benoît experimented with ageing in four 200-litre clay amphorae in 2012, for greater oxygen exchange than in barrels, though he's quick to point out he doesn't want to make orange wines.

Barrels are always purchased new and maintained until they are up to 30 years of age. 'I'm not a big fan of new barrels, but as a non-malolactic cellar, I don't want to bring the wolf into the sheep pen!' Benoît exclaims, in reference to the risk of introducing malolactic and other bugs from used barrels. Parcels fermented in new barrels are always blended. 'I prefer older barrels, but after long ageing of 7–10 years, the impact of a well-managed new barrel is not so scary!'

Bâtonnage is used to help finish fermentation and to build texture. 'I love working with barrels, so the wines can breathe and not look so monolithic,' he says. Reserve wines are aged in oak casks, and he incorporates at least three vintages in his Zero Brut, which he considers crucial for this style. Long bottle ageing is also critical in this process. Non-vintage wines are typically matured at least 3.5 years in bottle, and vintage wines around 10 years.

'When I was young, I wanted to hurry the disgorgement, but my grandfather taught me to wait six years by showing me the profound texture and character that developed as the wine breathed over time. I don't want to show a wine until it reveals its personality.'

ZERO DOSAGE

Benoît's ultimate goal is to make zero-dosage champagne. 'We don't need to add sugar to Chablis, so why do we need to do it with champagne?' He aims to pick grapes ripe when he can. 'We must always reach the prettiest maturity, not the highest maturity, so adding sugar should not be a question.' The point is not zero dosage, but to create wine of flavour and atmosphere. He chaptalises when he has to and uses low dosages of less than 6g/L in cuvées that require it, though he doesn't enjoy adding dosage.

Benoît's father has been making Zero Brut since the early 1980s, long before zero dosage was the rage in Champagne. 'Back then you could count on one hand all the people making this style in Champagne,' Benoît points out. 'I'm scared that it's becoming trendy now.'

It took him six years to build Tarlant Zero to the major cuvée of the estate, now representing around 100,000 bottles annually – a monumental feat for one of Champagne's better composed examples of this challenging style. He has also elevated Rosé Zero to the main rosé of the house.

'There are perhaps four or five zero-dosage rosés now, but when I began in 2000 it was a no-man's land,

and I had no one else's wines to look at,' he says. He made six trials of pinot noir and meunier, each with skin contact, blended from red and white wines and blended with chardonnay.

'The question with zero-dosage rosé was how to get acid and tannin to live together. I found the skin-contact wines too angular in their tannin expression, so I prefer to blend.'

Benoît chose chardonnay blended with pinot noir red wine, but the evolution continues. The current dilemma is an attempt to build greater persistence using white wine from black grapes – a challenge because even white pinot noir contributes tannins.

Benoît's single-vineyard wines are characterful expressions of his diverse terroirs. 'I'm not here to make single vineyards, but sometimes the taste of the samples makes it irresistible!' he exclaims. 'The first year I experienced real taste, explosiveness and length in single parcels was 2003.'

He recently added a new building to extend the winery, not to increase production but to provide space to work with his 57 plots and a portfolio now spanning 13 cuvées. All have boasted informative back labels since 2000, detailing terroirs, cépages, vintages, disgorgement and bottling dates and dosages.

His Millésime l'Aérienne 2004 is a highlight.

Tarlant Zero Brut Nature NV $

89 points • 2008 base vintage • Disgorged February 2016 • Tasted in Australia

One-third of each of the champagne varieties from the Vallée de la Marne; vines more than 25 years of age; fermented in stainless steel; no malolactic fermentation; aged almost 7 years on lees; zero dosage; ~100,000 bottles

Benoît Tarlant has sensitively honed every stage of viticulture and production to foster balance in his Zero Brut, aiming for an accuracy, purity and directness that he likens to playing darts. Flavour, not austerity, is a priority here, with ripe fruit, three reserve vintages and extremely long bottle ageing creating balance and presence. The magnificent and high-tensile 2008 season without malolactic fermentation or dosage is a harrowing recipe, making for a tense and electric style, toned with the depth of barrel-aged reserves. These add savoury, charcuterie complexity, which supports rather than disrupts fruit purity. It holds good persistence. A style for those sufficiently brave to face searing malic acidity.

Tarlant Zero Rosé Brut Nature NV $

93 points • 2009 base vintage • Disgorged April 2016 • Tasted in Australia

50% chardonnay, 44% pinot noir, 6% meunier from the Vallée de la Marne; 9% pinot noir red wine; fermented in stainless steel; 2008 reserve wines aged in oak barrels; no malolactic fermentation; aged more than 6 years on lees; zero dosage

Such is the intensity of Tarlant's red wine that even just 9% (it was 15% last year) infuses a full salmon crimson tone and full flavours of pink pepper, tamarillo and pink grapefruit. Finely textured yet prominent tannins meld seamlessly with gentle mineral structure and well-focused acid line, creating a compelling juxtaposition between tension, grip and characterful presence. The rounded ripeness of 2009 is perfectly suited to this zero dosage non-malolactic recipe. It lingers long with wonderful brightness and tangy morello cherry fruits. The result won't be for everybody, but it's a masterful take on a more than daring recipe.

Tarlant BAM! Blanc Arbanne Meslier NV $$$$

92 points • 2009 BASE VINTAGE • DISGORGED APRIL 2016 • TASTED IN AUSTRALIA

50% petit meslier, 27% pinot blanc, 23% arbanne; single-vineyard Oeuilly; 2008 and 2007 reserves; wild fermented and aged for 9 months in fourth-use oak barrels with regular lees stirring; no malolactic fermentation; aged 6 years on lees; zero dosage

Of all the Champagne varieties that fall outside the safe ground of the three usual suspects, this release of BAM! – in complete contrast to its name – is one of the most graceful and precise. This hasn't always been the case, and the progress of rapid evolution in this cuvée is a resounding credit to Benoît's dextrous flexibility to learn fast. Presenting a much more composed and settled demeanour than the searing 2008 base, this is a blend that captures the subtly exotic nuances and characterful, fleshy presence of its three varieties in glimmers of star fruit, honeydew and nashi pear, building notes of brioche and custard in the two years since its release, while admirably holding vibrant acid line. For young vines, its seamlessness, integration and lingering poise are more than impressive, thanks in no small part to clever use of barrel fermentation and lees stirring to create texture and harmony. Kudos, Benoît.

Tarlant Prestige Millésime l'Aérienne 2004 $$$$

94 points • DISGORGED JANUARY 2016 • TASTED IN AUSTRALIA

70% chardonnay, 30% pinot; wild fermented in oak barrels; no malolactic fermentation; aged 10.5 years on lees; 5g/L dosage

Delightfully fresh for its age, there's a surprising brightness to the medium salmon hue of this 13-year-old, oak-fermented cuvée. Chardonnay leads the charge in lemon rind and grapefruit character, energised by the grand tension of malic acidity. The savoury influence of wild barrel fermentation is subtle and well controlled, providing space for fruit to speak with articulate primary poise, gently supported by the almond meal and brioche nuances of maturity. Malic acidity holds a long and tense finish, underscored by gentle minerality and finely textured grip. Masterfully composed.

Tarlant Cuvée Louis Brut Nature NV $$

92 points • 2000 BASE VINTAGE • DISGORGED FEBRUARY 2016 • TASTED IN BRISBANE

50% chardonnay and 50% pinot noir from a single Oeuilly vineyard on the Marne river with vines of average age 65 years; reserves from 1999, 1998, 1997 and 1996; fermented and aged for 9 months in fourth-use oak barrels with regular lees stirring; no malolactic fermentation; zero dosage

Tarlant's original and chalkiest vineyard, 'Les Crayons', is closest to the cooling influence of the Marne, the quintessential expression of Oeuilly. The wine rises to its grand credentials, a radiant and monumental expression of the generosity of 2000 and the grand depth of decades of maturity. A glowing, medium golden-yellow hue declares its depth and age. The presence of fading pineapple and golden delicious apple is suspended in the gaping cavern between the dynamic cut of malic acidity and the deep, reverberating complexity of grand old age, pronounced in tones of sizzling tinder, green olives and exotic spice. It's attained the twilight of maturity, beginning to contract and dry out on the finish.

THIÉNOT

(Tea-e-noh)

4 RUE JOSEPH-CUGNOT 51500 TAISSY

www.thienot.com

CHAMPAGNE
THIÉNOT
REIMS.FRANCE

*S*ince establishing his eponymous house in Taissy in 1985, former broker Alain Thiénot has acquired a formidable empire encompassing champagne houses Canard-Duchêne, Joseph Perrier and Marie Stuart, and several Bordeaux châteaux. This small house of 350,000 bottles annually remains a family affair, and is the proud custodian of 27 hectares of estate vineyards in the Montagne de Reims, Côte des Blancs and Sézanne, supplying an impressive three-quarters of its needs. Use of oak has been abandoned to better express each cuvée's terroir.

THIÉNOT BRUT NV $

86 points • TASTED IN AUSTRALIA

45% chardonnay, 35% pinot, 20% meunier; 45% reserves

A firm champagne that contrasts simple lemon and stone fruit character with the biscuity complexity of age, culminating in a short finish marked by firm phenolics and candied dosage.

THIÉNOT BRUT ROSÉ NV $$

88 points • TASTED IN AUSTRALIA

45% pinot, 35% chardonnay, 20% meunier; 7% pinot noir red wine from old vines; 45% reserves

A medium salmon copper hue introduces a rosé lacking lift and energy. Strawberry and raspberry fruit is overlaid with the toasty complexity of bottle age, finishing soft, creamy and gently sweet.

Thiénot Vintage 2008 $

92 points • Tasted in Australia

50% chardonnay, 50% pinot noir

A full straw hue is a deep colour for the tense 2008 vintage, announcing a full and rich take on this season. Layered with succulent, ripe white peach and apple fruit, it's accented with the almond, nougat and honey of maturity. The acid drive of 2008 provides definition to a long finish, amidst subtle phenolic presence and well-rounded dosage. An unusually ready to drink 2008.

Thiénot Cuvée Alain Thiénot Millésimé Brut 2007 $$$

90 points • Tasted in Australia

With a full straw-yellow hue, this is a mature and rich blend of chardonnay and pinot noir, brimming with grilled pineapple, baked apple and ripe peach fruit. Secondary development is pronounced, markedly toasty and laced with roast almonds, finishing complex, full, a little sweet and just a touch dried out and tired, suggesting it has reached the end of its life.

Thiénot Cuvée Garance Blanc de Rouges Millésimé 2008 $$$

89 points • Tasted in Australia

The hue is brighter and paler than Thiénot's pinot chardonnay blends, hinting at the tension in this blanc de noirs style of 100% Montagne de Reims pinot noir. It's a savoury and biscuity style without the acid definition or brightness expected for 2008, instead reductive with grilled-bread notes that interrupt fruit purity. It concludes with creamy bead and some notes of phenolic grip.

Thiénot Cuvée Stanislas Blanc de Blancs 2006 $$$

89 points • Tasted in Australia

DIAM closure

At a decade of age, the silky smoothness of maturity is expressed in pronounced buttery notes and a creamy palate, accented with grapefruit and pear fruit that carries with good persistence. Phenolic grip on the finish interrupts an otherwise silky style.

Thiénot La Vigne aux Gamins Cuvée de 3614/1 Blanc de Blancs Brut 2005 $$$$

90 points • Tasted in Australia

Old-vine Avize chardonnay; 3614 bottles; DIAM closure

A powerful and full expression of old-vine Avize chardonnay that captures the full mood of 2005, for good and for bad, in ripe apple and grapefruit, toasty maturity and the firm, dusty, drying structure of the season. It pulls this off with depth, persistence and character.

The Champagne Guide

ULYSSE COLLIN

(Oo-lees Kohl-la)

7/10

21 RUE DES VIGNERONS 51270 CONGY

CHAMPAGNE
Ulysse Collin

Nestled into the gentle slopes between the Côte des Blancs and the Sézannais, west of Bergères-lès-Vertus, the district of the Val du Petit Morin is little known, yet holds important potential for the future of Champagne, according to young grower Olivier Collin. From his village of Congy in the heart of the region, his cuvées mount the most compelling evidence for the potential of the area. Unusually, Collin's cuvées are exclusively single varietal, single vineyard and non-vintage, each expressing the deeply characterful and distinctly mineral-driven personality of his unique terroirs.

It was after working with Anselme Selosse that Olivier Collin was inspired to reclaim a portion of his family's vines to produce his first vintage in 2004. He has since re-established the family winery and cellar and reclaimed 8.7 hectares in the village, neighbouring Vert-la-Gravelle and nearby Barbonne-Fayel, planted to chardonnay and pinot noir.

Midway between Épernay and Sézanne, the warm, south-facing slopes of Congy are among the first to begin harvest in Champagne. 'We are not part of the Sézannais or the Côte des Blancs here,' Collin points out. 'We have our own particularity that falls in between.'

The soils here vary from clay to limestone, with chalk as close as 1.5 metres below the surface. 'We have good chalk here, and it is the source of our most interesting wines,' Collin reveals. 'When we have 3–5 metre deep clay, we have less personality in the wines.'

He upholds the distinctive saltiness of his wines as the most particular character of the area, and is fascinated by deposits of flint in the chalk, though suggests it will take time to ascertain the impact these have on the wines.

Collin's aspiration is to capture the personality of his unique terroirs. 'I don't want to produce heavy wines,' he says. 'I want good maturity, but we are in Champagne, so I want to produce fresh wines. After ten years, they will become much more round, so they need to be fine but not sharp to begin.'

To this end, Collin aims to harvest at 10.5 degrees potential on average, sometimes as high as 11.2, but never higher, for fear of losing definition. His vines are privileged to be between 30 and 60 years of age, and are tended using a combination of organic and conventional practices, applying organic compost, ploughing and avoiding pesticides. 'We are 80% organic, but I don't like copper sulphate as a fungicide, so I don't use it,' he explains. In 2012, he attempted a 100% organic regime in his Les Enfers vineyard, but lost the entire crop.

Winemaking is likewise natural within sensible reason, relying on wild yeasts to complete very long fermentations exclusively in barrels and old casks, mostly around five years of age. Malolactic fermentation may proceed in part, though not by design. 'When the wine decides to go through malolactic, it goes through malolactic!'

he explains. Sulphur dioxide is used as a preservative to facilitate long ageing, and all cuvées are kept on gross lees for an unusually long period of 23 months. Reserves are stored in barrels five metres underground, and stainless steel tanks are used only for blending.

Collin's first two harvests of 2004 and 2005 were bottled as vintage cuvées ('because I had no choice') and since this time he has worked to increase reserves, which he upholds as very important for building complexity in his blends. Dosages are minuscule, between 1.7 and 2.4g/L. Back labels declare base vintages and disgorgement dates.

Smiling, laughing and extroverted, Olivier Collin is a master of characterful cuvées that have sparked great fascination in terroirs hitherto unknown to champagne lovers.

ULYSSE COLLIN LES PIERRIÈRES BLANC DE BLANCS EXTRA BRUT NV $$$

92 points • 2012 BASE VINTAGE • DISGORGED FEBRUARY 2016 • TASTED IN CHAMPAGNE AND AUSTRALIA

100% Les Pierrières lieu-dit in Toulon-La-Montagne; 100% fermented in barrels and casks; aged 3 years on lees; 1.7g/L dosage

A characterful and textural expression of the village of Toulon-la-Montagne, resonating deeply with fine, salty chalk minerality that Collin attributes to 90% of the roots delving into chalk. Crunchy nashi pear, fragrant lemon and fresh, tangy grapefruit are underscored by the subtle charcuterie and spice complexity of barrel fermentation, sitting neatly under the fruit. Tension and focus are upheld amidst a full straw hue and impeccable ripeness, with tense acid line accentuated by minuscule dosage. It concludes dry, salty and very long, with lingering lemon notes hovering just above the palate. A well-crafted cuvée, and the ultimate oyster match.

ULYSSE COLLIN LES MAILLONS ROSÉ DE SAIGNÉE EXTRA BRUT NV $$$$

95 points • 100% 2013 • DISGORGED FEBRUARY 2016 • TASTED IN CHAMPAGNE AND AUSTRALIA

100% pinot noir from 45-year-old vines in Les Maillons lieu-dit in Barbonne-Fayel; 100% fermented in barrels and casks; aged 3 years on lees; 2.4g/L dosage; 8000 bottles

Collin's aim is freshness in rosé and he finds rosé reserves too fragile and rapid in their evolution, hence his rosé is a single vintage, though labelled as non-vintage as it's sometimes released too early to be a vintage. He describes saignée rosé as the most difficult style of champagne to make, varying maceration from 1.5–3 days according to the harvest. 'If it's too quick or too long, we could lose a lot of character,' he explains. 'And when I drain the saignée, I have four hours before it finishes draining, so I need to anticipate it.' He nailed the colour in 2013, a full-throttle crimson hue heralding a pinot noir saignée loaded with presence and character. Outstanding character of pink pepper, raspberries, wild strawberries and musk lead out, drawn into the savoury complexity of barrel fermentation in nuances of roast tomato and sage. For all of its colour, tannins are masterfully handled, very fine and meld seamlessly with salty chalk minerality on a long and characterful finish, driven long and true by a bright and tightly focused yet well-integrated acid line. Masterfully crafted.

The Champagne Guide

ULYSSE COLLIN LES MAILLONS BLANC DE NOIRS EXTRA BRUT NV $$$$

94 points • 2012 BASE VINTAGE • DISGORGED FEBRUARY 2016 • TASTED IN CHAMPAGNE AND AUSTRALIA

100% pinot noir from 45-year-old vines in Les Maillons lieu-dit in Barbonne-Fayel; 100% fermented in barrels and casks; 20% 2011 reserves aged in 3-6-year-old barrels and foudres for 1 year; aged 3 years on lees; 2.4g/L dosage

2012 was a strong season for Collin, producing ripe fruit with darker, more mature skins. The result is ripe pinot noir in all of its red cherry, strawberry and pink grapefruit glory, taking on a full copper hue with a blush tint, underlined by a tense, fine line of acidity and a fine bed of accentuated chalky, glassy, salty mineral texture. Ripe fruit exuberance is juxtaposed with a high-tensile acid line energised by low dosage. Barrel fermentation lends subtle nuances of tamarillo, the slightest suggestion of charcuterie, nutmeg, anise, and even suggestions of coffee and dark chocolate. A serious, structured, characterful and complete pinot of graceful silkiness.

ULYSSE COLLIN LES ROISES BLANC DE BLANCS EXTRA BRUT NV $$$$

93 points • 2012 BASE VINTAGE • DISGORGED FEBRUARY 2016 • TASTED IN CHAMPAGNE AND AUSTRALIA

100% Les Roises lieu-dit in Congy, picked at 11.2 degrees potential and yielding just 45hL/ha, less than half the regional average; 100% fermented in barrels and casks; aged 3 years on lees; 1.7g/L dosage

One of the saltiest champagnes I've tasted, this is an intensely mineral blanc de blancs that contrasts the grainy chalk texture of Congy with the low-cropped exuberance of ripe chardonnay in pineapple, juicy white peach and locut. It's freshened with bright lemon and apple notes, and softened with the buttery, nutty, creamy influence of barrel fermentation and bottle age, uniting to create a full straw hue. It finishes very long, fine and focused, thanks to tense acidity heightened by low dosage. Wonderfully characterful and seamlessly composed, this is another consummate oyster match from Olivier Collin.

ULYSSE COLLIN LES ENFERS BLANC DE BLANCS EXTRA BRUT NV $$$$

89 points • 2010 BASE VINTAGE • DISGORGED FEBRUARY 2016 • TASTED IN AUSTRALIA

100% Les Enfers lieu-dit in Congy; 100% fermented in barrels and casks; aged 4 years on lees; 1.7g/L dosage

The tension of grapefruit juice and lemon zest contrast ripe tropical-fruit notes of pawpaw and golden kiwi fruit, finishing astringent and firm, with suggestions of burnt orange and vinegar-like development that truncate fruit flow. Nonetheless, it upholds good tension of acidity and structure, with toasty complexity infused from four years on lees. The child of a lesser base year, it appears to have passed its finest moment, and a second bottle was identical.

VAUVERSIN

(Vooh-veh-sah)

9 BIS RUE DE FLAVIGNY 51190 OGER

www.champagne-vauversin.fr

The Vauversin family has been growing chardonnay in the grand cru of Oger since 1640 and bottling its own champagnes since 1929. Fifteen generations later, Laurent Vauversin has worked alongside his father Bruno to tend their small estate of 3.15 hectares in the village organically since 2011, capturing the characterful and fast-maturing flamboyance of Oger. Disgorgement dates and dosages are printed on back labels.

VAUVERSIN ORPAIR GRAND CRU BLANC DE BLANCS EXTRA BRUT 2009 $$

91 points • DISGORGED OCTOBER 2016 • TASTED IN AUSTRALIA

Harvested at high ripeness from two plots in Oger; matured entirely in old oak barrels; aged at least 4 years on lees; 5g/L dosage

Aromas of vanilla, marshmallow and cream erupt from an expressive bouquet, announcing a palate unafraid of declaring its oak influence. The orange fruit and exotic flamboyance of ripe Oger chardonnay in a hot and dry season make for a rich and full style of ripe exuberance. The stony minerality of Oger melds seamlessly with the creamy texture of lees age on a long finish.

VAUVERSIN MILLÉSIMÉ GRAND CRU EXTRA BRUT 2010 $$

92 points • DISGORGED OCTOBER 2016 • TASTED IN AUSTRALIA

Vinified in tanks and barrels; aged 6 years on lees; 3g/L dosage

The personality of Oger stands in stark contrast to its nearby neighbours of Avize and Le Mesnil-sur-Oger, and this cuvée presents its mood as dramatically as any I have tasted. Orange fruit, ripe peach, star fruit and exotic spice meet vanilla, nougat and meringue. For all its flamboyance, it is well toned by bright acidity and fine, stony minerality on a finish well textured by the mouthfeel of lees age and subtle bitter grapefruit-pith texture. It's long and compelling.

The Champagne Guide

VAZART-COQUART & FILS

(Vah-zah Kho-khar e Feess)

6/10

6 RUE DES PARTELAINES 51530 CHOUILLY

www.champagnevazartcoquart.com

The Vazart family has sold champagne from its 11 hectares of estate vineyards exclusively in the Côte des Blancs grand cru of Chouilly for more than 60 years. Tall in stature and in warmth, Jean-Pierre Vazart is a gentleman with a broad smile and a very precise approach in the vineyards and the winery. Since he took charge of the estate more than 20 years ago, he has meticulously crafted a ripe fruit style in every cuvée that articulates the quintessential expression of Chouilly terroir. 'With soils like these, how could I do anything less?' he says graciously.

The story of Chouilly is all about the robust character and mineral expression of chardonnay, which makes up 95% of Vazart-Coquart's 30 plots of vines, averaging 30 years of age. 'My father has the récoltant-manipulant's mind, wanting to make everything himself, so after a few years of buying red wine, he hid some plantings of pinot noir in a lesser-known part of Chouilly,' reveals Jean-Pierre. Chouilly pinot noir was approved as grand cru in 2009. 'Next time I plant it, it will be on the road so everyone can see it!' he grins.

Perfectly ripe fruit is Jean-Pierre's goal, with a target of 10.5–11 degrees of potential, as he finds 11.5 too rich. 'I do all I can to avoid chaptalisation!' he declares. Fruit maturity is achieved through limiting yields by green harvesting and cultivating grasses between the rows. His 11 hectares yield more than he can make in his small winery and cellars, so he sells everything surplus to his 70,000-bottle requirements to Veuve Clicquot. 'Of course, the best parcels are for me, but they know what they buy!' he smiles. Veuve Clicquot chef de cave Dominique Demarville is a friend of Jean-Pierre's from school, and he enjoys a very flexible contract. 'If I have a small harvest, I can sell them less, and if I have a big harvest, they buy everything I don't need.' It doesn't get any better than that.

Jean-Pierre's aspiration in the winery is to preserve the character of his grapes, so he uses stainless steel vats 'for their neutrality' rather than oak barrels, and cultured yeasts rather than wild. Malolactic fermentation is carried to completion, and deep reserve stocks are employed to soften the robust character of Chouilly.

Reserve wines are stored as a perpetual blend in a 20,000-litre tank. Dating back to 1982, it's one of the oldest soleras in Champagne, held fresh at 12°C. Each year 50% is taken for Brut Réserve NV, Extra Brut NV, Rosé and for dosage liqueurs, and replenished with the current harvest. The solera is given priority over vintage cuvées and receives the estate's highest-potential fruit.

Jean-Pierre's production was spread across two premises in the village, which he integrated in 2016 into an impressive facility with a new press and tiny new tanks.

Jean-Pierre Vazart knows his craft intimately, and his sensible and sensitive approach makes him one of the most attentive growers in Chouilly. His terroir-driven cuvées are set off with stylish labels.

VAZART-COQUART & FILS BRUT RÉSERVE BLANC DE BLANCS GRAND CRU NV $$

93 points • 2013 BASE VINTAGE • DISGORGED JANUARY 2016 • TASTED IN AUSTRALIA
100% Chouilly chardonnay; 25% reserve solera dating back to 1982; aged 39 months on lees; 8.5g/L dosage; 40,000 bottles

Impeccably crafted and uncomplicated, this is a quintessential apéritif champagne that declares the signature of Chouilly and the precision of blanc de blancs. Pretty and refreshing lemon, crunchy red apple and beurre bosc pear flow into classic Chouilly richness of white peach and grapefruit, supported by subtle, well-integrated dosage and soft, characterful, salty chalk minerality. It's primary, uncomplicated and appealing.

VAZART-COQUART & FILS GRAND BOUQUET BLANC DE BLANCS BRUT 2009 $$

92 points • DISGORGED JANUARY 2016 • TASTED IN AUSTRALIA
100% Chouilly chardonnay; aged 75 months on lees; 8g/L dosage

In stark contrast to the tension of the 2008 before it, this is a cuvée of stature and rich body that encapsulates the ripe generosity of the 2009 harvest. Ripe yellow mirabelle plums, juicy white peaches and figs are well supported by layers of honey ginger cake and golden fruit cake. The salty chalk minerality of Chouilly keeps the finish in check, and it holds great persistence and a bright, pale hue, though this is not a vintage to keep. It's powerful, ripe and ready.

VAZART-COQUART & FILS GRAND CRU SPECIAL CLUB BRUT 2008 $$$

96 points • DISGORGED JUNE 2016 • TASTED IN AUSTRALIA
100% Chouilly chardonnay; aged 88 months on lees; 8g/L dosage

Grand Bouquet is tiraged on crown cap, and the same wine tiraged on cork is Special Club, because 'after ageing they are completely different, of course!' That they are. It takes Vazart half a day to disgorge 500 bottles (tasting every one for cork taint), the same time it takes to disgorge 3000 in crown cap. The vivacity, precision and fine chalk minerality of Chouilly chardonnay in concert with the high-tensile 2008 season infuses 20 years of potential into this cuvée. Fennel, lemon and white peach meet the glowing generosity of the village in notes of golden delicious apple. Cork age has built notes of vanilla custard and honey, creating a creamy succulence to the well-defined, frothing chalk minerality of the village. It holds grand persistence and exacting line.

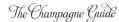

The Champagne Guide

VEUVE CLICQUOT

(Verv Khlee-kho)

7/10

1 PLACE DES DROITS DE L'HOMME 51100 REIMS

www.veuve-clicquot.com

Dramatic developments are underway in the bellows of Veuve Clicquot that are only just beginning to bubble to the surface. Its characterful, full-bodied, pinot-focused wines are more refined every time I look, an astounding feat for a house with a dizzying annual production of 18 million bottles, ranking a confident number two by volume behind Moët & Chandon in Louis Vuitton–Moët Hennessy's (LVMH's) champagne kingdom. Even Clicquot's conspicuous 'Yellow Label' non-vintage, in its inimitable, trademark, mango-orange livery, is looking trim and fit today, having lost its curvaceous sweetness – quite a workout for a cuvée that alone accounts for a whopping 15 million bottles every year. Its vintage wines are where Veuve Clicquot really steps up. For an operation of such a grand scale, the consistency of Veuve Clicquot is unrivalled in all of Champagne.

'Veuve Clicquot is a big house where we have a big responsibility to maintain the style, but every day we work to improve the quality,' chef de cave Dominique Demarville explains as he shows me through one of his two expansive wineries in Reims. With a glimmer in his eye he announces, 'The winery is like a kitchen where we can experiment!'

Then he thrusts open a gigantic door to reveal a grand spectacle of proportions I have never witnessed anywhere in Champagne. Oak barrels. Huge oak barrels. New foudres of 5000 litres and 7500 litres. Lots of them. I know of winemakers proud to show off just one of these beauties. And here, hidden in an enormous warehouse somewhere in the depths of Veuve Clicquot, are 30 of them, lined up in all of their towering magnificence of intricately crafted French oak, perfectly interconnected with arteries of polished stainless steel.

These 200,000 litres of oak-fermented wine – a tiny drop in the ocean of Clicquot – now comprise just 5–10% of its vintage wines, and 1–2% of non-vintage reserves. Leading me around the room to sample from his battalion of barrels, Demarville is as excited as a kid with a room full of new toys. 'Sometimes my team tells me I'm too involved in what I'm doing, but I work with my heart and not my head,' he confesses as he pours me an Oger chardonnay of which he's particularly proud. 'Barrel fermentation offers the chance to improve without changing the Clicquot style,' he explains. 'To add some spice!'

PROGRESSIVE TRANSFORMATION

It's a subtle twist, but it typifies the evolution that is slowly transforming one of Champagne's biggest players, leaving no stage of production untouched, revolutionising vineyards, vinification, and most notably its regimes of malolactic fermentation, reserves and dosage. 'The Veuve Clicquot style is about richness, but also about brightness: strong and full-bodied and at the same time fresh,' Demarville clarifies. It's in brightness and freshness that he has most demonstrably refined these wines since taking the helm in 2006, at just 39 years of age.

This has not been an easy time to drive such evolution. 'With climate change, we are seeing vintages which are more and more diverse,' he reveals. Since 2000, the house has declared just five vintages: 2002, 2004, 2006, 2008 and 2012 (and no Vintage Brut in 2006 or La Grande Dame in 2002). 'Managing reserves is the most important part of my job, and this is why I sometimes need to say I will not declare a vintage,' he reveals.

Demarville remains confident about the future. 'So many things have happened in Champagne over the past century, and we will adapt again. We will adjust our winegrowing and winemaking to ensure we can continue to make champagnes of elegance and minerality.'

PRIVILEGED VINEYARD RESOURCES

'Everything starts in the vineyard!' Demarville declares, and, for Clicquot, this represents a substantial and enviably positioned resource of 382 hectares of estate vines, including a wealth of grand crus, providing for just 20% of its needs, with a further 125 hectares supplied by LVMH vineyards, boosting the total to 30%. The remainder is sourced from 1200 growers with an average of less than one hectare each. Many have supplied fruit to no other company for some generations. Top price is paid when the quality warrants it.

One famous grower-producer in Ambonnay, who has trouble supplying demand for its own cuvées, and hence wants to keep as much of its fruit as it can, still sells to Veuve Clicquot because the company provides great support and expertise for managing their vineyards. 'Not every house is like this, but Clicquot is very good,' they revealed. Last year, the company created a new association to encourage its young growers.

Clicquot's own vineyards are planted to almost 50% chardonnay – a high proportion in Champagne, particularly for a house in which every cuvée is led by pinot noir. The Montagne de Reims has been the focus for Clicquot historically, and it is the proud custodian of some of the finest sites for pinot noir in Verzy, Verzenay and Bouzy. These form the core of La Grande Dame. 'Our goal is to showcase what we can do in the vineyards,' Demarville reveals. The 2008 La Grande Dame will be 95% pinot noir and 2012 will be 90%.

I was privileged to an inside perspective at Clicquot, shadowing Demarville on four separate occasions during harvest 2014, visiting growers and experiencing his press centre in Verzy and red winemaking facility in Bouzy. 'Most of my job during harvest is to go all over Champagne and taste and smell what is different in every terroir, because every village is different from one year to the next,' he explains. I was astounded by his dedication: over the three weeks of harvest, he visits every press centre and 15–20% of his vineyards to engage with his growers. 'Motivation, motivation, motivation!' He works long days from 6am each morning and spends 80% of his time in the vineyards, including in the Côte des Bar, where the house sources 15% of its needs. 'I have a dream,' Demarville announces. 'I hope that one day in Champagne we will pay for grapes according to quality, not according to volume and vineyard designation.'

Clicquot is working to enhance quality by reducing use of herbicides, and planting grasses in the mid-rows of its vineyards to encourage deeper roots. 'We are changing our view about grape-growing and what we're doing with the growers,' Demarville says. 'We are more aware of what happens in the soil, of how to follow the ripening of the grapes, and we are tasting the grapes more and more during the ripening season. This all helps to increase the quality of our wines.'

Outside of harvest, Demarville spends more than one-third of his year in the vineyards, the part of his job he loves the most. 'Champagne is a wine, and you can't make a good wine without understanding what happens in the vineyards. I believe that in the future, viticulture will make all the difference. Environmentally friendly sustainability will help us to achieve a higher expression of terroir.'

Demarville's goal is to encourage deeper roots to draw out better terroir expression by implementing an organic approach to the soils, herbicide-free and using only organic fertilisers in all estate and grower vineyards by 2020. 'Not to be organic for the sake of organics, but for the sake of the quality of the soil and the life in the soil, which is crucial in viticulture,' he emphasises. He admits that chemicals are sometimes necessary in protecting against disease and pests. 'I believe the ideal for us for the future is to use organic, chemical and biodynamic philosophies in perfect balance.'

EVOLUTIONARY WINEMAKING

'Our terroir is crucial in our approach, and this is why we vinify cru by cru and variety by variety, even though we blend at the end,' Demarville reveals.

Veuve Clicquot has trialled earlier harvesting and other means of retaining acidity. 'In the wake of climate change we must manage not only what happens in the vineyards, but also the winery,' Demarville clarifies. He has traditionally allowed every parcel to complete malolactic fermentation, but since 2007 has experimented with blocking malolactic in some parcels destined for its reserves and vintage cuvées. 'About 10–15% without malolactic fermentation will likely help our wines, without changing the style,' he suggests. This has created a dilemma in maintaining consistency, since malolactic fermentation also contributes texture.

The introduction of Demarville's prized foudres in 2007 may prove to be the answer, providing barrel fermentation texture without oak flavour to a house style that has traditionally relied on stainless steel tanks. He stepped up the regime in 2012 – a vintage of 'amazing acidity' – by blocking malolactic fermentation in half the foudres. These vins clairs looked incredible at just a few months of age, but the real proof came in the launch of the spellbinding 2008 vintage. He plans to introduce more foudres in the future.

The threat of more extreme vintages in the wake of climate change has also bolstered Demarville's resolve to increase his stocks of reserve wines. 'Look at four recent harvests – 2008 was exceptional, with high acidity and lots of structure; 2009 was ripe, with low acidity; 2010 was dilute, and 2011 was very inconsistent. If you don't have sufficient stocks of reserve wines, you can't make great non-vintage champagne,' he points out. On average, Yellow Label Brut Non-Vintage receives 35% reserve wines, increasing every year, and the 2012 base boasts a phenomenal 55% reserves.

'We have been increasing the level of reserve wines to increase both the consistency and the complexity in our blends,' he explains. 'Our style of lots of body, complexity and richness needs a lot of reserve wines.' Clicquot holds the biggest collection of reserve wines in Champagne besides Krug, currently comprised of 18 vintages. These are amazing wines, and at a full quarter-century of maturity, a 1988 Cramant was ravishingly concentrated and complex, with allusions of chocolate. Clicquot holds the equivalent of an entire year of production in more than 400 different reserve wines, each of which is tasted twice every year, and allocated before it begins to decline. All are held fresh on lees without filtration in tanks cooled to below 14°C.

Demarville points out that it's easier to control and refine wine in stainless steel tanks with temperature control, than under oak without temperature control. 'We are able to be more precise with our blending now, which has enabled us to reduce levels of dosage,' he says.

'We are not reducing dosage due to climate change, but because we have better control in the winery. Over the past 40 years we have been able to build greater purity and precision and so reduce dosage gradually.'

It's a flattering trend for Clicquot, embodied most emphatically in Yellow Label Brut Non-Vintage, which was candied and sweet with 12g/L dosage some years ago, now much more refreshing at 10g/L. Demarville has resisted the 'low-dosage lobby', as he calls it. 'We have a different vision in that the final sensation of sugar is affected not only by quantity, but by time in the cellar after dosage. Our vintage wine is released a year after disgorgement, so the impact of the sugar is diminished.'

Rosé is an increasingly important style for Clicquot, representing 5–6% of sales, with forecasts that this will double (and a strong precedent in Moët & Chandon, which grew rosé from 3% to 20% in less than 20 years). 'Our demand for rosé has been amazing!' he exclaims. 'It's growing as a category so much faster than white champagne, fuelled by incredible improvements in the style over the past five or six years.'

Ten hectares of estate pinot noir vines are allocated to red wine production for rosé in Bouzy alone, green harvested to reduce yields to 30–40% less than normal, and picked at high maturity. Clicquot also sources from 'top' growers in Bouzy and Ambonnay, and in 2012, for the first time, signed a contract with direct suppliers dedicated to red wines, to grow production. The house operates a state-of-the-art winery dedicated to red wine production in Bouzy, Demarville has created a new room for red wine storage in Reims, and a red wine facility was recently constructed in the Aube. When he showed me through his Bouzy facility I was stunned at its pristine cleanliness mid-vintage. Samples of red wine ferments displayed breathtaking violet and rose petal aromatics, culminating in the most profound Champagne red wine I've ever tasted. From the earth-shaking Clos Colin parcel on the mid-slope of Bouzy, there is complexity and depth that I have only ever seen in grand cru red Burgundy. It's fittingly reserved for La Grande Dame Rosé.

After much anticipation, I'm delighted Clicquot has introduced QR codes on its Cave Privées and La Grande Dame, hoping to one day roll these out across its full range, to reveal disgorgement dates, blends and dosages.

Veuve Clicquot has plans to grow slowly, expecting to outgrow its facilities on Rue des Crayères in Reims within the next few years and aspiring to ultimately increase capacity to 30 million bottles. To this end, a massive new €280 million facility commenced production in 2017 on a 44 hectare site on the road from Reims to Châlons, with the hope that it will be ready for vintage 2019. 'If the market is asking for more bottles, we will produce more,' Demarville reveals. 'And it is also a good opportunity for us to improve our logistics and efficiency. We are trialling many things in winemaking today, so we have the answers to design our new facility.'

The lack of pretence and big-company 'spin' of Dominique Demarville is refreshing in the world of corporate champagne. I ly respect what this man has achieved in his short time. There are few in Champagne who could seamlessly refine a house as enormous as this. The 2008 base Yellow Label was his first blend, and the finest I have seen.

'It is because 2008 is an amazing year!' Demarville responds with unassuming humility. 'And I am very fortunate to have a talented and passionate team.'

Veuve Clicquot Yellow Label Brut NV $$

91 points • 2012 BASE VINTAGE • DISGORGED JANUARY 2016 • TASTED IN AUSTRALIA
91 points • 2011 BASE VINTAGE • TASTED IN CHAMPAGNE

50-55% pinot noir, 28-33% chardonnay, 15-20% meunier; from 50-60 villages; 55% reserves in 2012 (with 36% of 2014 and 2013 and 19% older vintages), 42% in 2011; aged 2.5 years on lees; 10g/L dosage; 15 million bottles

It takes Demarville and his team four months of daily tastings to make Yellow Label, tasting 2000 different wines and selecting 400–500 to make up the final blend. Their expertise is reflected in a gentle trajectory of refinement over recent years, and the 2012 base represents a compelling Yellow Label. Since stronger vintages are demanded to resource Vintage and La Grande Dame production, levels of reserves are increased to sustain Yellow Label volumes, hence a record of a phenomenal 55% reserves in the great 2012 season. Pinot noir leads out confidently with a fleshy mid-palate and bright finish of red apple, strawberry and mixed spice, over a toasty and bready backdrop of bottle-derived complexity, finishing with touches of dry, dusty phenolic grip and good persistence. Lively acid line and well-integrated dosage make for a vibrant, well-assembled, accurate and appealing apéritif. Thanks to a strong representation of 42% reserves, the 2011 blend is a standout for its season, upholding balanced poise and a core of fresh fruit integrity.

Veuve Clicquot Rosé Brut NV $$

92 points • 2012 BASE VINTAGE • DISGORGED SEPTEMBER 2015 • TASTED IN AUSTRALIA

50-55% pinot noir, 28-33% chardonnay, 15-20% meunier; 55% reserve wines; Brut Yellow Label with 12% red wines from the villages that Demarville upholds as Champagne's best for red wine production: Bouzy, Ambonnay, Verzy, Verzenay, Dizy, Aÿ, Cumières and Les Riceys; 10g/L dosage; 1.4 million bottles annually

This is a lesson in what a difference 12% red wine can make in a blend, particularly in the hands of one of the finest red wine outfits in all of Champagne. In its medium salmon guise, this is an elegant, refined and pretty rosé, in an appealingly fruit-focused style of vibrant strawberries, red cherries and red apple. Pinot noir takes a confident lead in a fleshy and full mid-palate which coasts into a long finish of accurate line. The brioche, nougat and roast almond of lees maturity are more prominent in the 2012 base than usual, beautifully supporting its fruit presence. Tannins are impeccably handled, leaving lively acidity to define the structure, uninterrupted by well-integrated dosage. The 2012 base represents a particularly distinguished Clicquot Rosé. One bottle was corked.

Veuve Clicquot Vintage Brut 2008 $$$

94 points • Disgorged March 2015 • Tasted in Champagne and Australia

61% pinot noir, mostly from Ambonnay, Bouzy, Aÿ, Tauxières-Mutry, Avenay-Val-d'Or, Verzy, Verzenay and Ludes; 34% chardonnay from Le Mesnil-sur-Oger, Oger and Vertus; 5% meunier, mostly from Ludes and Dizy; 5% fermented and aged in large oak foudres for the first time; 8g/L dosage

Demarville lists 2008 in the top 10 vintages for Clicquot, ahead of 1996, a season of 'wonderful depth, minerality and a fine and delicate spirit'. The wine he has drawn from this is as great as any Clicquot vintage I have tasted. Its coiled tension and tightly clenched acidity have only just begun to unwind to reveal the expansive personality of pinot noir. Lemon top notes have subsided, making way for notes of blood orange rind, black cherries, plums and the beginnings of nougat and brioche. A glimpse of oak lends just a subtle, well-integrated toasty note, but the real highlight is its classic 2008 acid drive and beautifully fine, expansive, salty chalk mineral landscape. It concludes very long, spicy and magnificent. I wrote prior to its release two years ago that the secret to this vintage is to keep your hands off it for as many decades as you possibly can, as it possesses the euphoric freshness to outlive even the most disciplined willpower. Toward the end of its release cycle, this is more true than ever, having shed its beach-fresh, euphoric definition, without yet having built its secondary allure. Patience.

Veuve Clicquot Vintage Rosé 2008 $$$

94 points • Disgorged March 2015 • Tasted in Champagne and Australia

Veuve Clicquot Vintage Brut 2008, with 14% red wine from Bouzy; 8g/L dosage

It's in Clicquot's red wine facilities that I've encountered some of the most transcendental red wines in all of Champagne, but as they're reserved exclusively as rosé blending components, I've wished there were some way for the world to experience these enthralling wines. It took a vintage of the beguiling transparency of 2008 to provide the window. Two years after release, it has evolved to a subtly copper shade of salmon, its primary red cherry and red apple fruit and rose petals morphing into a spectrum of spice, tomato, sage and toasted brioche. Bright 2008 acidity and fine, salty chalk mineral structure hold strong amidst the body and presence of pinot noir from some of Champagne's finest crus. The true mastery of red winemaking in Champagne is tannin texture, and this wine is a case study in how it's done: so subtly that it does nothing to interrupt the profound chalk minerality of an elegant season, yet simultaneously furnishes the understated grip that promises enduring potential. Charged by a lightning bolt of brilliant acidity, the signature of this classic season, this is a vintage for the long haul.

Chardonnay and pinot noir arrive at Veuve Clicquot's press house in Verzenay, one of the most important villages for the house.

VEUVE CLICQUOT LA GRANDE DAME BRUT 2006 $$$$

95 points • DISGORGED JUNE 2014 • TASTED IN AUSTRALIA

53% pinot noir, largely from Verzy and Verzenay, with a touch of Bouzy, Ambonnay and Aÿ; 47% chardonnay, predominantly from Avize, Oger and Le Mesnil-sur-Oger; 8g/L dosage

In response to the generous, rounded, supple 2006 season, Demarville's predecessor, Jacques Péters, increased the share of chardonnay in his final La Grande Dame. Demarville confessed to some nervousness at launching the 2006 after the calibre of the linear and refined 2004. The two seasons certainly stand in contrast, and two years after release the 2006 has continued to power into its phase of secondary evolution. All of its generous, rich ginger, honey, toast, roast nuts and brioche remain, and notes of struck-flint reduction are now more prominent. A citrus zest liveliness to its acidity continues to uphold its focused, tangy finish, enlivened with fine chalk mineral structure. It propagates with admirable energy, endurance and persistence for this season, reinforced in a bright medium-straw radiance, though a hint of bitterness on the finish raises a question mark over its future. A vintage to drink while 2004 and 2008 rest in the cellar.

VEUVE CLICQUOT CAVE PRIVÉE BRUT 1989 $$$$$

94 points • DISGORGED MAY 2010 • TASTED IN AUSTRALIA

67% pinot noir, 33% chardonnay; a blend of 25 grand and premier crus; 6g/L dosage; 7000 bottles

Veuve Clicquot has the resourcefulness to set aside a respectable allocation of every vintage release for its late-disgorged Cave Privée, a remarkable collection of 700,000 bottles of a depth and magnitude that must be unmatched in all of Champagne. A bold venture, not least because vintages that don't age well will never surface. Demarville considers 1989 one of the best vintages of the last 30 years, with a ripe concentration that sustains it in spite of lower acidity. Two years ago I wrote that it had attained its peak. Today it upholds all the glorious complexity of secondary development, full of roast almonds, butter, brioche, ginger cake and honey, culminating in a flourish of pine sap, green olives and warm hearth. It's just beginning to show the signs of fading, starting to show dryness on the finish, which accentuates the chewy structure of a warm season, yet nonetheless upholding balance and persistence. One bottle was oxidised.

VEUVE CLICQUOT CAVE PRIVÉE ROSÉ BRUT 1979 $$$$$

93 points • DISGORGED MARCH 2011 • TASTED IN AUSTRALIA

61% pinot noir, 33% chardonnay, 6% meunier; a blend of 22 grand and premier crus; 19% red wine from Bouzy; 4g/L dosage; 1700 bottles

The 1979 has proven to be the most enduring vintage of the '70s, and happened to be privileged to the highest proportion of red wine of any Clicquot vintage (19%). This serves to draw out its Burgundian-like pinot noir personality, even at a dignified 38 years of age. Its primary fruit has now evolved to a spellbinding place of tertiary complexity, expressed in white truffles, balsamic vinegar, kirsch, even venison. Six years after disgorgement, it looks more tired than it did two years ago, though every bottle is different, and it upholds length and no lack of character.

The Champagne Guide

VEUVE FOURNY & FILS

(Verv Fawny e Feess)

6/10

5 RUE DU MESNIL 51130 VERTUS

www.champagne-veuve-fourny.com

CHAMPAGNE

V⁀ᵉ **FOURNY & FILS**

une Famille, un Clos, un Premier Cru

W hen a tiny plot on pure chalk in the coveted 'Le Mont Ferré' hillsides of the northern end of Vertus towards Le Mesnil-sur-Oger came up for sale in the summer of 2011, offers poured in from big houses, but the grower chose the brothers Emmanuel and Charles-Henry Fourny as its new custodians. The offer was indicative of the respect with which the young fifth-generation growers manage some of the finest terroirs in Vertus. Their location on Rue du Mesnil on the northern edge of Vertus is a clue to their success, with vineyards capturing the more mineral side of the premier cru village neighbouring the grand cru of Le Mesnil-sur-Oger itself.

When I first visited just four weeks before the scheduled start of vintage 2011, Rue du Mesnil was completely closed off. Veuve Fourny's winery was totally gutted and swarming with construction workers. Emmanuel Fourny emerged from an early-morning meeting with his builders.

'We are grateful for the cooler weather,' he said, 'because there's no chance our new winery would be ready for an early vintage!'

It was the beginning of a grand new era for a family who has tended vineyards at the southern end of the Côte des Blancs since 1856 and made its own champagne since 1931. Theirs is one of the most expressive champagnes of the character of their beloved village of Vertus.

VINEYARD FOCUS

Veuve Fourny's focus remains resolutely and exclusively on Vertus, apart from a small parcel in Cramant, contributing just 7% of production. 'I like to express the terroir of Vertus and show that you can have a lot of expression with just one village,' says Emmanuel, who has a self-confessed obsession with purity and precision.

The sunny, south-east-oriented slopes of Vertus are a great part of the Côte des Blancs for Emmanuel to bottle his vision. 'Vertus gives us better expression of fruit than the neighbouring grand crus of Le Mesnil-sur-Oger and Oger,' he explains. 'The chardonnay here has more of a pinot noir richness to it, which enables us to create blends exclusively from chardonnay that can be complete.'

The brothers are now harvesting riper than in the past, aiming for 10.4–10.5 degrees potential, diminishing the need for chaptalisation, but increasingly picking on flavour rather than sugar ripeness. In 2015 they started harvest five days after the rest of the village, achieving an average of 10.8 degrees potential. 'I am convinced that the riper you pick the grapes, the more pronounced the minerality,' says Emmanuel. This is evolving the house style towards the riper, more exotic fruit spectrum of Vertus, resembling notes of ripe oranges, while upholding freshness and mineral focus.

The east-facing slopes of the village nurture chardonnay of fresh definition, while its warmer south-facing aspects are among the only vineyards of the Côte des Blancs planted to pinot noir, leading the brothers to dub Vertus 'the paradox of the Côte des Blancs'. They own 8.7 hectares, predominantly on the mineral hillside of 'Le Mont Ferré' on the border of Le Mesnil-sur-Oger, where thin soils bless vines with easy access to chalk, and a south-east aspect imparts greater fruit expression than the more rounded style of south-facing slopes.

They manage a further 3.6 hectares of family vines now owned by their cousins, supplemented with almost eight hectares managed according to an organic philosophy, most of which were originally part of the family estate. The Fournys work closely with their growers, whom they describe as 'small, serious and interested in separation of plots for precision winemaking'. These are mostly young growers and friends, who are invited back to taste their plots after vinification. In all, the brothers manage the vineyards and harvests for a sizeable 60% of the grapes they purchase. A total of 20 hectares provides for an annual production of 200,000 bottles.

Estate vines now average a hefty 45 years of age. 'Vines over 30 years transform the minerality of the chalk into the salty minerality of the wine, which we feel is very important,' Emmanuel explains. Such old vines ensure that yields are very low for Champagne, averaging below 60hL/hectare, less than two-thirds of Champagne's average, 'to produce a balance in our wines'. Green harvests are conducted in high-yielding years like 2004, when 30% of the crop was dropped.

Veuve Fourny balances a resolute commitment to the environment with a realistic awareness of the limitations of viticulture in a climate as marginal as this. Vineyard practice is essentially organic, with the exception of sprays, which are used when necessary. Grasses are cultivated in the mid-rows of one-third of vineyards, another third is cultivated to bare soil, and herbicide has been reduced by 80%, with a goal to eliminate it altogether. Insect breeding is controlled using pheromones, canopy management is used instead of chemicals to control botrytis, and composting is used in place of fertiliser.

A normal spray regime is used to manage mildew, particularly in years like 2012, when it saved the crop. 'We like the organic philosophy, but we don't want to sacrifice our grapes to mildew,' Emmanuel says, referring to a trial the brothers conducted shortly after returning to the family estate in the mid-1990s. Synthetic chemicals were forsaken in two parcels, but the wild spread of mildew necessitated weekly sprayings with copper sulphate – permitted under biodynamics, despite its toxicity and detrimental effect on the soil and vine growth. Much of the crop was lost and they returned to non-toxic synthetic products.

On the same site as the house on Rue du Mesnil, Clos Faubourg Notre-Dame is a tiny plot of less than one-third of one hectare, purchased by the brothers' grandfather in 1920, but it was only in 1990 that Emmanuel and Charles-Henry proposed to their mother that the vineyard be bottled separately.

With just 40 centimetres of soil before the chalk, they consider it a good plot, 'not better, but different, holding its freshness as a long-ageing style'. Its micro-climate is protected by the enclosure. This plot is the source of their flagship cuvée. The brothers' grandmother built a house on part of the clos in 1965, which they removed in 2012 after she passed away. They have replanted this part of the vineyard to chardonnay, though won't use the fruit in this wine until the vines have reached 12 years of age.

MINIMAL-INTERVENTION WINEMAKING

The brothers are excited about the potential of their new winemaking facility to capture greater detail from every parcel. Previously, the press house was in a different location to the winery. Tanks and winemaking equipment that had gradually amassed over the years were not well suited to small-batch winemaking, so they boldly sold it all and created the new winery from scratch. A huge investment for a small company, and all the more impressive with no imperative to increase production.

Charles-Henry was initially sceptical about the outlay, preferring to see the investment poured into more vineyards, but he was impressed with the outcome, enabling them to separate every single parcel for the first time. 'The new winery is completely adaptive to the size of the plots, giving us greater precision in the details,' he said. 'It will help us make a more precise expression of each place, so you can expect our wines to be finer.'

The 60 plots from which the brothers source are quite distinct, and they showed me 2012 vins clairs that revealed that even parcels just 150 metres apart can show significant diversity. These can now be kept separate for the first time, thanks to a small press that runs 24 hours a day during vintage, and tanks to keep 20 blends, compared with just 12 previously.

Such is the diversity of their plots that Emmanuel quips, 'We need to add another 's' to Vertus!' The result is a total of nine cuvées, the largest portfolio in Vertus besides Duval-Leroy, though single-vineyard wines are not the aspiration.

Fourny's philosophy of respect and minimal intervention in the vineyards applies equally in the winery, an insulated building built from stone from northern Burgundy and wood from the nearby Vosges. Glass is utilised to capture natural light, all waste water is recycled on the gardens, and a natural cooling system pulls air in when it's cooler outside.

To preserve purity, only the first pressings are used, and the tailles are sold. Vintage wines are unfiltered, as are non-vintage wines since the 2012 base. They now use half the sulphur dioxide preservative of the past, but never so low that wines are at risk from oxidation, with wines held on lees for protection. To further

Chardonnay, the lifeblood of Veuve Fourny, ripe for harvest.

inhibit oxidation, barrels are topped weekly rather than monthly. Malolactic fermentation is used selectively, so as to maintain tension in each cuvée, with an average of about three-quarters of parcels completing malolactic, though in the warm 2015 season, this was decreased to around 60%. Wines are aged on lees with bâtonnage for 6–8 months after primary fermentation, and aged in bottle between 2.5 and 9 years. The purity of the house style permits refreshingly low dosages, never more than 6g/L, from grape liqueur rather than sugar.

Emmanuel learnt the craft of barrel fermentation with bâtonnage in Burgundy, and this has been a key element of the house style since he commenced in 1990. 'I don't like oxidative champagne, so I don't want to be extremist with wood,' he says. The goal is not to impart the taste of wood, but rather to create fresh, focused and textured wines. 'We do not want oak barrels to bring anything to the wine, but to enhance the characters and salty taste of the minerality. Micro-oxygenation in barrels vaccinates the wines against oxidation for the future, thus maintaining freshness and elegance for many years after disgorgement.'

Barrels are purchased from Marc Collin in Burgundy after 3–4 harvests and used for ageing a rich resource of some 200 reserve wines. A preference is given to small, 208-litre barrels to keep small plots separate and provide a balance of surface area and volume. Across the estate, 25% of parcels are fermented in old barrels of 5–15 years of age, and most cuvées are blended with more citrus-accented parcels from tanks.

Since 2014, a new 4000-litre foudre has been purchased each year for fermenting and storing reserve wines for Grande Reserve NV and Blanc de Blancs NV, with an aim to avoid oxidation and maintain freshness better than small barrels. Reserves are held on lees for complexity and texture.

This thoughtful approach produces wines that display sensitive oak influence, imparting great resilience and long-ageing potential.

Since 2006, all Veuve Fourny wines have been sealed with Mytik DIAM closures. A five-year trial of DIAM and natural cork revealed DIAM-sealed bottles to be consistent and fresh, with pure fruit, while those under natural cork were more evolved, and 'each bottle had its own personality'. The letter of reply when a corked bottle is returned has not been sent out once since the change was made. Emmanuel refers to natural cork as 'Russian roulette' and regards DIAM as a revolution, crucial for upholding the freshness and purity of the house.

Back labels have been updated to feature impressive detail, including disgorgement date, terroirs, cépage, vinification, assemblage, dosage and even the type of cork. 'More and more people consider champagne like they do table wine,' Charles-Henry explains. 'Our customers keep champagne in their cellars and need to keep track of it.'

Demand for Veuve Fourny has put supply on allocation in every market. The hope is to increase the bottle age of Grande Réserve and Blanc de Blancs from 2–2.5 years to 3 years, but this will take a decade to achieve, as these cuvées comprise 60% of production.

There is no goal to increase production, even with increased vineyard resources from the 2011 acquisition.

'Our goal is to grow the quality, not the volume, continuing to focus on the vineyards and the winery,' says Emmanuel. 'It depends on whether your goal in life is money or pleasure. My goal is to be able to host tastings and dinners in Japan and Australia and for people to say, "Your wines are wonderful!" That's the goal for me.'

It's a goal the brothers are capably translating into the bottle. The pristine champagnes of Veuve Fourny encapsulate their aspiration of purity, precision and freshness.

VEUVE FOURNY & FILS GRANDE RÉSERVE PREMIER CRU BRUT NV $$

92 points • 2012 BASE VINTAGE • DISGORGED MARCH 2016 • TASTED IN CHAMPAGNE AND AUSTRALIA

80% chardonnay, 20% pinot noir; 90% Vertus, 10% Cramant, Oger and Chouilly; average vine age more than 40 years; 40% reserves from 2011, 2010 and a little 2009, half aged in oak casks; 25–30% without malolactic fermentation; aged at least 2.5 years on lees; 6g/L dosage; DIAM closure

2012 returns to the glorious integrity of the Fourny entry cuvée. A pale straw hue does nothing to betray a glorious 40% of reserves, nor a little inclusion of pinot noir to bring flesh, body and strawberry accents to the finish. The focus here remains resolutely on Vertus chardonnay, in all of its crunchy apple and zesty lemon purity, with oak-aged reserves lending a subtle backdrop of spicy complexity and a creaminess to its textural mouthfeel. Fine, salty chalk minerality melds seamlessly with subtle phenolic texture on a long and endearing finish. A complete and engaging blend of immediate appeal.

VEUVE FOURNY & FILS BLANC DE BLANCS VERTUS PREMIER CRU BRUT NV $$

93 points • 2012 BASE VINTAGE • DISGORGED DECEMBER 2015 • TASTED IN CHAMPAGNE AND AUSTRALIA

Low-yielding vines of 50–56hL/hectare, about half of Champagne's average; predominantly from 1950s vines in Fourny's best terroir of Le Mont Ferré; harvested later and with higher concentration; 20% reserve wines from 2011 and 2010, aged in oak barrels on lees; 25% without malolactic fermentation; aged at least 2.5 years on lees; 6g/L dosage; DIAM closure

Fourny's mandate of purity and precision shimmers in delightful lemon blossom aromas and lemon juice flavours of soap-powder brightness and a pale straw hue. This is a cuvée that reaches deep into the mineral hillside of Le Mont Ferré. In the 2012 base year the privileged position of this plot on the border of Le Mesnil-sur-Oger is more pronounced than ever in its elegance and mouth-embracing chalk mineral completeness. There are nuances of fennel and star fruit along the way, true to the expressive, exotic personality of Vertus, lending body and depth, but, refreshingly, only faintly so, never compromising precision. A little oak vinification coaxes out nuances of spice, biscuit, nougat, even fig, coffee and chocolate, though never disturbing purity or drive.

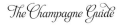
The Champagne Guide

VEUVE FOURNY & FILS BLANC DE BLANCS VERTUS PREMIER CRU BRUT NATURE NV $$

94 points • 2012 BASE VINTAGE • DISGORGED MARCH 2016 • TASTED IN CHAMPAGNE AND AUSTRALIA

Low-yielding Vertus vines of 50–56hL/hectare, about half of Champagne's average; predominantly from 1950s vines in Le Mont Ferré with a south orientation; harvested later and with higher concentration; 20% reserves from 2011, 2010 and a little 2009; 20% aged oak barrels on lees; zero dosage; DIAM closure

Under the command of old vines, the chalk soils of Le Mont Ferré hark more to the mineral structure of the thundering grand crus to their north than to the more fruity premier crus around them, and without the interruption of dosage, the strength of strong, salt-infused mineral texture is pronounced. This is more prominent than ever, thanks to the effortless precision of 2012, elevating this cuvée with an airy lightness of pinpoint lemon juice, lemon blossom, grapefruit, crunchy granny smith apple and pear, bolstered ever so delicately by the biscuity, spicy complexity of a touch of oak-barrel vinification. Its minerality is a revelation, defining a mouthfeel of pronounced and inimitable salt chalk texture. The result is one of the most complete and jubilant zero-dosage champagnes this year.

VEUVE FOURNY & FILS ROSÉ PREMIER CRU BRUT NV $$

92 points • 2012 BASE VINTAGE • TASTED IN CHAMPAGNE

A blend of roughly 50/50 chardonnay and pinot noir from different plots in Vertus; 12–15% red wine for fresh red fruits; less than 6g/L dosage; DIAM closure

Rosés are a new adventure for the Fourny brothers, and already their three new pink cuvées comprise a strong 12–13% of production. This is a light apéritif style of pretty medium salmon-pink hue, built on about 50% of chardonnay for freshness and elegance. It's restrained, tangy and fresh, with a strawberry hull core and notes of spice and pink pepper. There are notes of savoury appeal on a dry finish of gentle phenolic grip, while barrel-aged reserves lend a hint of coffee.

VEUVE FOURNY & FILS MONTS DE VERTUS BLANC DE BLANCS PREMIER CRU EXTRA-BRUT 2011 $$

89 points • DISGORGED APRIL 2016 • TASTED IN AUSTRALIA

Monts de Vertus lieu-dit, in the heart of Vertus near Le Mesnil-sur-Oger; vines more than 60 years of age; harvested late for ripeness; vinified in tanks; aged at least 5 years on lees; 3g/L dosage; DIAM closure

I don't expect there will be a lot of vintage cuvées unleashed from the harrowing 2011 harvest, marked as it is by the dry, dusty, coarse finish of imperfect fruit. Fourny's attention in the vines and the cuverie has produced a pretty good result under the circumstances, with the generosity of their later-harvest priority producing a fleshy mid-palate that goes some way toward alleviating the dry phenolic grip of the season. Five years age has built layers of toasty, biscuity, honeyed complexity that carry well on the finish.

VEUVE FOURNY & FILS MONTS DE VERTUS BLANC DE BLANCS PREMIER CRU EXTRA-BRUT 2009 $$

94 points • DISGORGED FEBRUARY AND MARCH 2015 • TASTED IN CHAMPAGNE AND AUSTRALIA

As per 2011, with full malolactic fermentation; aged 6 years on lees; just 1–2g/L dosage; DIAM closure

Since its release two years ago, this warm and exuberant vintage has held rock-solid, grounded by a remarkable terroir and the deft hands of the Fournys. The exoticism of Vertus is upheld in boiled orange, glacé fig, beurre bosc pear, mixed spice and grapefruit pith, yet not overtly so and, to its credit, precision of driving, lingering acidity, fresh lemon fruit and mineral structure remain its defining features. The soft, supple succulence of a ripe season is well offset by well-defined freshness and structural definition. Resonating with great soils tapped by the deep roots of grand old vines, salt minerality is gloriously pronounced.

VEUVE FOURNY & FILS ROSÉ VINOTHÈQUE PREMIER CRU EXTRA-BRUT 2011 $$

91 points • DISGORGED JUNE 2016 • TASTED IN CHAMPAGNE AND AUSTRALIA

Pinot noir and chardonnay from Vertus lieux-dits Les Barilliers and Les Gilottes, largely south facing; vines more than 50 years of age; pinot noir red wine; vinified in oak casks; 3–4g/L dosage; DIAM closure

A glorious full, bright salmon hue heralds a complex, spicy and savoury rosé that contrasts the flavour and bitter texture of crab apple with exuberant wild strawberry, tangy pink grapefruit, tomato and pink pepper exoticism. The result is quintessential northern Vertus, at once refreshing, exuberant and deeply chalk mineral, though it hasn't escaped the dry, dusty, bitter phenolic finish that marks the 2011 harvest. It's elegant and fine, with subtle tannin grip on the finish.

VEUVE FOURNY & FILS ROSÉ LES ROUGESMONTS EXTRA BRUT NV $$$

95 points • 100% 2012 VINTAGE • TASTED IN CHAMPAGNE

Single plot toward Bergères-lès-Vertus; east facing with a dramatic 47% slope; saignée of 20 hours on skins; DIAM closure

The aspiration here is ripeness with balance and without too much tannin. 'For me, tannin and bubbles is war – you cannot have this combination!' declares Emmanuel. The juice is taken off the skins the moment they feel the sensation of tannin in the mouth. It's released as non-vintage to permit the flexibility to release early if required. 'For us, rosé saignée is better at a young age to uphold its fruitiness.' The result fits the aspiration, a pretty and beautifully expressive rosé of medium salmon hue and strawberry hull and tangy morello cherry fruits. It's all laced together with refreshing acidity, bright and vibrant, underlined by fine chalk mineral texture that melds seamlessly and compellingly with the fine, supple tannins of pinot noir maceration. It's delightfully pure, refreshing and vibrant, with wonderfully expressive fruit character that holds long on a tangy, primary and vibrant finish.

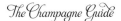

VEUVE FOURNY & FILS CUVÉE R DE VEUVE FOURNY PREMIER CRU EXTRA-BRUT NV $$

93 points • 50% 2012 AGED 1 YEAR IN OAK CASKS, 50% 2011 AGED 2 YEARS IN OAK CASKS • DISGORGED DECEMBER 2014 AND DECEMBER 2015 • 100% VERTUS CHARDONNAY • TASTED IN AUSTRALIA AND CHAMPAGNE

93 points • 50% 2011 AGED 1 YEAR IN OAK CASKS, 50% 2010 AGED 2 YEARS IN OAK CASKS • DISGORGED DECEMBER 2014 AND DECEMBER 2015 • 90% CHARDONNAY AND 10% PINOT FROM VERTUS • TASTED IN CHAMPAGNE

Predominantly from lieu-dit Les Barilliers; vines of more than 60 years of age; low-yielding vines of 50-56hL/ha; fully fermented and aged with bâtonnage in small oak barrels of 4-15 years of age; full malolactic fermentation; aged at least 4 years on lees; 3g/L dosage; DIAM closure

The honed restraint of Fourny's pristine fruit, meeting the ravishing complexity of old oak and swirling, tossing minerality, makes for quite a display. Fermentation in old oak barrels amplifies bath-salts minerality drawn from thin soils by grand old vines in the north of Vertus near Le Mesnil-sur-Oger. Carefully crafted old oak cranks things up a notch from Fourny's other non-vintage cuvées, with creamy texture and deep, ripe fruit presence of citrus, apple, pear and even dried peach complexity, richly overlaid with all the spicy, toasty, nutty, Parisian baguette and charcuterie personality of barrel work. For all its presence and flesh, it finishes dry and taut with grapefruit pith texture, and fruit sweetness perfectly married to finely honed acidity. An intricate and laudable accord between the great 2012 and the harrowing 2011 vintages. The 2011/2010 blend displays impressive definition for its lesser seasons, with notes of coffee flavour surrounding a core of stone fruits and citrus, finishing well defined and fresh, sustained by the chalk mineral mouthfeel of northern Vertus.

VEUVE FOURNY & FILS CUVÉE DU CLOS NOTRE DAME PREMIER CRU BLANC DE BLANCS EXTRA-BRUT 2006 $$$$

94 points • DISGORGED MARCH 2016 • TASTED IN CHAMPAGNE AND AUSTRALIA

Clos Faubourg Notre-Dame, monopole of the family; planted 1951; 0.29 hectares; 100% chardonnay; 100% vinified and aged for 9 months on lees in oak barrels of 5-6 years of age; full malolactic fermentation; aged 9 years on lees; 3g/L dosage; DIAM closure

The generous 2006 harvest has given birth to the most approachable Notre Dame yet, though this must be interpreted in the 'eternal' longevity in which the Fourny brothers define their flagship. The exoticism of Vertus shines in a full straw hue and glacé oranges, fig, succulent white peach and exotic spice, with a rumbling undercurrent of butterscotch reminiscent of 2005. The body and intensity of the Fourny Clos is pronounced in its fruits even as young vins clairs, and after full fermentation in barrels and a decade in bottle it grows into a wonderfully powerful and exuberant style of crème brûlée, vanilla, custard and almonds. For all of its flamboyance, its pure, prominent acid line draws out a finish of profound proportions, heightened at every moment by soft, creamy chalk minerality. This minerality defines its scaffolding more than its oak support, which furnishes a backdrop of roast hazelnuts, coffee and chocolate, and the welcome tension of faint phenolic bitterness. The result is a cuvée of effortless integrity that transcends this little plot in the village, and the best Clos Notre Dame since 2002.

VOLLEREAUX

(Voh-leh-roh)

5/10

48 Rue Léon Bourgeois 51530 Pierry

www.champagne-vollereaux.fr

CHAMPAGNE

Vollereaux

à Pierry près Épernay Marne (France)

The Vollereaux family has been based in Pierry just south of Épernay since 1805, and making their own champagne since 1923. Franck Vollereaux is the sixth generation to tend 40 hectares of family vineyards in the villages surrounding Pierry and the Sézanne. His cuvées undergo full malolactic fermentation and unite fruitiness and biscuity complexity in a style of immediate approachability. The 2008 Cuvée Marguerite exemplifies the potential of this small house.

VOLLEREAUX BRUT RÉSERVE NV $$

91 points • 2012 BASE VINTAGE • DISGORGED NOVEMBER 2015 • TASTED IN AUSTRALIA
One-third of each of the three varieties; reserves from 2011 and 2010; aged 3 years on lees; 9g/L dosage

A pleasant, even harmonious, blend that unites the cut of lemon with the depth of crunchy red apple and red cherry fruit and the roast nut, ginger and biscuit complexity of lees age. Tense acid envelops dosage on the finish. A nicely balanced style that's ready to drink now.

VOLLEREAUX BLANC DE BLANCS BRUT NV $$

91 points • 2013 BASE VINTAGE • DISGORGED JANUARY 2016 • TASTED IN AUSTRALIA
Reserves from 2012, 2011 and 2010; aged 3 years on lees; 9g/L dosage

A rich and concentrated blanc de blancs that delivers spicy white-peach intensity amidst well-developed complexity of roast nuts and biscuits. Bright acid keeps things toned on the finish, coasting with confidence and ready-to-drink appeal.

The Champagne Guide

VOLLEREAUX ROSÉ DE SAIGNÉE BRUT NV $$

88 points • 2012 BASE VINTAGE • DISGORGED JANUARY 2014 • TASTED IN AUSTRALIA
10g/L dosage

A rosé de saignée in all of its characterful distinctiveness, boldly medium crimson–copper in hue, and extroverted in its intense aromas and flavours of wood smoke, Campari, even ash, perhaps suggesting as much stalk impact as skin influence from the saignée. Acid and dosage are well matched to its red berry and cherry fruits, but that ashy smokiness dominates.

VOLLEREAUX CUVÉE MARGUERITE MILLÉSIME 2008 $$$

93 points • DISGORGED OCTOBER 2015 • TASTED IN AUSTRALIA
75% chardonnay, 25% pinot; aged 6 years on lees; 100% malolactic fermentation; 9g/L dosage; DIAM closure

There's compelling fruit body, succulence and ripeness on parade here, layered beautifully with mirabelle plum and strawberry fruit, impeccably contrasting the lemon citrus cut and finely composed acid drive that define this superlative season. Biscuity, vanillin, honeyed lees–age complexity announces a 2008 ready to drink now and over the next few years, with a creamy mouthfeel and long, long finish.

The outlook from the winding track from Aÿ to Mutigny is one of the most captivating spectacles in all of Champagne.

EPILOGUE
Authenticity

On a narrow vineyard track, brushing vines on both sides, winding up the steep hillside from Aÿ to the village of Mutigny, perched high atop the Montagne de Reims, is one of my favourite places in Champagne. I stop every time I visit and linger for hours, absorbing the breathtaking spectacle of the changing palette of the seasons in one of the most commanding panoramas anywhere in Champagne. Over the grand slopes of Aÿ, framed by the sprawling outskirts of Épernay on one side and the statue of the hill of Gruguet in Mareuil-sur-Aÿ on the other, the full spectacle of the Côte des Blancs disappears into the hazy horizon.

It is here, more than in a sterile tank or an ancient cellar, that the true romance of Champagne is born. To really understand Champagne, get under the surface, outface the elements and experience the tension of its climate, the diversity of its terroirs, the toil of its makers, the timeless patience of its cellars and the personalities of its characters.

It has been through these experiences that I have come to an incredible respect for this place and its people, a love that draws me back time after time, discovering a magic that leaves me in wide-eyed wonder again and again.

If I can bring a glimpse of this wonder to the champagne lovers of the world, I have achieved my aspiration. Only so much can be gleaned from words, so I am increasingly spending my time introducing Champagne's finest cuvées and telling their stories through dinners and tastings across the wine world.

And to ultimately experience this extraordinary place as I do, I have finally responded to requests from my readers in welcoming intimate groups to join me on my visits. It is my life ambition to share the remarkable experiences that I am privileged to enjoy in the world of wine. To bring people into the lives of the vines, the wines and the people and places that bring them to life.

In our modern world of virtual everything, we all yearn for real experiences. Not to buy them in shiny bottles from sterile supermarket aisles, but to shake the grubby hand that plucked them from the vine, to walk the ground in which they grew, to breathe the air of the cellar that brought them to life, to linger for hours on the twilight slopes of Mutigny as the pale northern sun is subsumed by the Côte des Blancs. To feel, to taste, to experience, to live.

'Today, luxury is all about authenticity,' Louis Roederer chef de cave Jean-Baptiste Lécaillon recently said to me.

His words have become my mantra. It intrigues and delights me that such a suggestion could come from one of the great houses of Champagne, the region that has long notoriously and unashamedly proclaimed its credentials in the romance of fabricated prestige and extravagant marketing.

Champagne, at last, is changing. Much has evolved since my first visit, in the snowfalls of the bitterly cold winter of Christmas 2001. Sixteen years on, the most over-hyped wine on earth is finally embracing an authenticity that celebrates its true, if unromantic, credentials for greatness.

The true magic of champagne is made from vines rooted into stark white chalk, grappling for survival in the most harrowing wine-growing climate on earth, transformed from an insipidly austere and unpalatably acidic juice into the most luxurious beverage of all.

It is my hope and wish that my words will guide you to a greater appreciation of the people, the places and the processes that make champagne sparkle like no other wine in the world.

This is the true story of luxury. This is the authentic champagne.

Drink it in, make the sojourn to experience it for real, and lose yourself high on the slopes of Mutigny.

Santé!

The Champagne Guide

INDEX
Rise to the Top

Duval-Leroy Femme de Champagne
Brut Grand Cru NV, $$$$, 137

Egly-Ouriet Grand Cru Ambonnay
Rouge 2012, $$$$, 141

Egly-Ouriet Grand Cru Brut Rosé
NV, $$$$, 140

Eric Rodez Cuvée des Grands
Vintages Brut NV, $$$, 148

Gosset Celebris Rosé Extra Brut
2007, $$$$, 161

Jacquesson Dizy Corne Bautray Extra
Brut 2007, $$$$$, 200

Jacquesson Dizy Terres Rouges Rosé
Extra Brut 2009, $$$$, 200

Krug Clos du Mesnil Blanc de Blancs
Brut 2003, $$$$$, 212

Krug Grande Cuvée 159ème Édition
NV, $$$$, 211

Krug Vintage 2003, $$$$$, 209–210

Lanson Gold Label Vintage Brut
2008, $$, 228

Louis Roederer Cristal Brut 2007,
$$$$$, 248

Mailly Grand Cru Exception Blanche
Blanc de Blancs 2004, $$$$$, 252

Mumm Collection du Chef de Caves
Cordon Rouge Brut 1996, $$$$$,
267

Paul Déthune Cuvée a l'Ancienne Brut
2008, $$$$, 277

Paul Déthune Cuvée Prestige
Princesse des Thunes Brut NV,
$$$, 277

Perrier-Jouët Belle Epoque Blanc de
Blancs 2004, $$$$$, 281

Philipponnat Clos des Goisses Brut
2007, $$$$$, 289

Pierre Gimonnet & Fils Cuvée Fleuron
1er Cru Blanc de Blancs 2008, $$,
294

Pierre Gimonnet & Fils Special Club
Grands Terroirs de Chardonnay
2012, $$$, 295

Pierre Gimonnet & Fils Special Club
Grands Terroirs de Chardonnay
2010, $$$, 295

Pierre Péters Cuvée Spéciale Blanc de
Blancs Les Chétillons 2007, $$$$,
302

Pierre Péters Cuvée Spéciale Blanc de
Blancs Les Chétillons 1996, $$$$

Pierre Péters Cuvée Spéciale Blanc de
Blancs Les Chétillons Oenothèque
2000, $$$$

Pol Roger Brut Vintage 2008, $$$, 310

Robert Moncuit Les Romarines Grand
Cru Rosé Brut NV, $$, 315

Ruinart Dom Ruinart Blanc de Blancs
Brut 2004, $$$$$, 318

Salon Cuvée S Blanc de Blancs Brut
2004, $$$$$, 322

Salon Cuvée S Blanc de Blancs Brut
1999, $$$$$, 322

Taittinger Comtes de Champagne
Rosé 2006, $$$$$, 328

Vazart-Coquart & Fils Grand Cru
Spécial Club Brut 2008, $$$, 340

95 POINTS

Alfred Gratien Brut Rosé NV, $$$, 37

AR Lenoble Grand Cru Blanc de
Blancs Chouilly Brut 2008, $$, 44

Ayala Blanc de Blancs Brut 2008,
$$$, 50

Bérêche & Fils Brut Réserve NV, $$,
54

Bérêche & Fils Raphaël & Vincent
Bérêche Cru Sélectionné Montagne
2004, $$$, 56

Bérêche & Fils Vallée de la Marne
Rive Gauche Meunier 2012, $$$, 55

Bernard Brémont Ambonnay Grand
Cru Brut Millésime 2008, $$$, 58

Billecart-Salmon Brut Rosé NV, $$$,
65

Billecart-Salmon Cuvée Sous Bois
Brut NV, $$$, 66

Billecart-Salmon Le Clos Saint-
Hilaire 1999, $$$$$, 69

Bollinger 007 Millésime 2009, $$$$,
76

Bollinger La Grande Année 2005,
$$$$, 77

Bollinger Special Cuvée Brut NV,
$$, 75

Bollinger Vintage 1830

Bruno Paillard Assemblage 2008,
$$$, 81

Bruno Paillard Blanc de Blancs Brut
2004, $$$, 81

Cattier Clos du Moulin Rosé
Brut NV, $$$$, 88

Claude Cazals La Chapelle du Clos
Delphine Cazals Blanc de Blancs
Brut NV, $$$$, 98

Claude Cazals Millésime Grand Cru
Blanc de Blancs Brut 2008, $$, 98

De Sousa Cuvée des Caudalies Blanc
de Blancs Grand Cru Extra Brut
NV, $$$, 108

De Sousa Cuvée des Caudalies
Millésime Grand Cru Extra Brut
2008, $$$$$, 107

De Sousa Grand Cru Blanc de Noirs
Brut NV, $$, 106

De Sousa Rosé de Saignée Grand Cru
Brut NV, $$, 106

De Sousa Zoémie De Sousa Cuvée
Umami Grand Cru Extra Brut
Vintage 2009, $$$$$, 108

Delamotte Blanc de Blancs 2007,
$$$, 112

Deutz Brut Rosé NV, $$, 115

Devaux D de Devaux Millésime 2008,
$$$, 123

Devaux Sténopé 2008, $$$$, 122

Dom Pérignon Vintage 2006, $$$$,
128

Gatinois Aÿ Grand Cru Brut Réserve
NV, $$, 152

Gatinois Aÿ Grand Cru Brut Rosé
NV, $$, 153

Henriot Rosé Millésime 2008, $$$,
174

J. Lassalle Blanc de Blancs Millésime
Premier Cru Brut 2007, $$$, 182

Lanson Clos Lanson 2006, $$$$$, 229

Lanson Extra Age Brut NV, $$$, 228

Larmandier-Bernier Les Chemins
d'Avize Grand Cru Blanc de Blancs
Extra Brut 2009, $$$$, 234

Larmandier-Bernier Rosé de Saignée
Premier Cru Extra-Brut NV, $$$,
233

Laurent-Perrier Alexandra Grande
Cuvée Rosé 2004, $$$$$, 238

Laurent-Perrier Grand Siècle by
Laurent-Perrier NV, $$$$$, 237

Le Brun-Servenay Cuvée Chardonnay
Vieilles Vignes Extra-Brut 2006,
$$, 240

Le Brun-Servenay Cuvée Exhilarante
Vieilles Vignes Millésime 2008,
$$$, 241

Louis Roederer Cristal Brut 2009,
$$$$$, 248

Louis Roederer Vintage Rosé 2010,
$$$, 247

Mailly Grand Cru L'Intemporelle
Millésimé Brut 2010, $$$$, 252

Mailly Grand Cru Les Échansons
Millésimé Brut 2007, $$$$, 252

Moët & Chandon Grand Vintage
Collection 1988, $$$$$, 260

Mumm Collection du Chef de Caves
Cordon Rouge Brut 1990, $$$$$,
267

Mumm Cuvée R. Lalou Brut 2002,
$$$$$, 266

Nicolas Feuillatte Palmes d'Or
Vintage Brut 2004, $$$$, 272

Perrier-Jouët Belle Epoque Vintage
2008, $$$$, 280

Philipponnat Clos des Goisses Brut
2006, $$$$$, 289

Philipponnat Clos des Goisses Juste
Rosé Brut 2005, $$$$$, 289

Pierre Gimonnet & Fils Extra Brut
Oenophile 1er Cru Blanc de Blancs
Non Dosé 2008, $$, 294

Pierre Gimonnet & Fils Special Club
Oger Grand Cru Blanc de Blancs
2012, $$$, 296

Pierre Péters Cuvée Millésime L'Esprit
Blanc de Blancs 2012, $$$, 300

Pierre Péters Rosé for Albane NV,
$$, 301

Pol Roger Blanc de Blancs Brut
Vintage 2009, $$$, 309

Laurent Bénard Vendange LB Extra Brut 2010, 217
Laurent-Perrier Ultra Brut Nature NV, $$$, 236
Laherte Frères Extra Brut Ultradition NV, $, 220
Lallier Ouvrage Grand Cru NV, $$$$, 224
Lanson Black Label Brut NV, $, 227
Mumm 6 Ans Édition Limitée NV, $$, 265
Nominé-Renard Brut Blanc de Blancs NV, $$
Palmer & Co Rosé Réserve NV, $$, 274
Paul Déthune Blanc de Noirs NV, $$, 277
Philippe Fourrier Cuvée Millésime Brut 2007, $$$, 283
Philipponnat 1522 Grand Cru Brut 2007, $$$, 288
Philipponnat Blanc de Noirs Brut Millésime 2009, $$, 286
Pierre Paillard Brut Rosé Grand Cru NV, $$
Pierre Paillard Millésime Brut 2004, $$
Piper-Heidsieck Brut NV, $, 304
Piper-Heidsieck Cuvée Sublime Demi-Sec NV, $$, 305
Pol Roger Pure Extra Brut NV, $$, 309
Vauversin Orpair Grand Cru Blanc de Blancs Extra Brut 2009, $$, 338
Veuve Clicquot Yellow Label Brut NV, $$, 344
Veuve Fourny & Fils Rosé Vinothèque Premier Cru Extra-Brut 2011, $$, 352
Vollereaux Blanc de Blancs Brut NV, $$, 354
Vollereaux Brut Réserve NV, $$, 354

90 POINTS
Augustin Cuvée CCCI NV
Ayala Brut Majeur NV, $$, 50
Barrat-Masson Grain d'Argile Extra Brut NV, $$, 51
Besserat de Bellefon Cuvée des Moines Brut NV, $$, 60
Camille Savès Brut Premier Cru Carte Blanche NV, $, 83
Chartogne-Taillet Les Couarres Extra Brut 2010, $$$, 96
Collet Brut Art Déco NV, $$, 100
Collet Esprit Couture Brut NV, $$$$, 100
De Saint Gall Blanc de Blancs NV, $$
De Saint Gall Brut Millésime Premier Cru 2009, $$, 102
De Saint Gall Extra Brut Blanc de Blancs Premier Cru NV, $$, 101

De Saint Gall Orpale Grand Cru Blanc de Blancs Brut 2002, $$$$, 102
De Sousa Grand Cru Réserve Blanc de Blancs Brut NV, $$, 105
Dumangin J. Fils La Cuvée 17 Brut NV, $, 133
Franck Bonville Grand Cru Avize Blanc de Blancs Brut Millésime 2010, $$, 150
Franck Bonville Grand Cru Avize Brut Rosé NV, $$, 149
Guy Charlemagne Mesnillésime Le Mesnil-sur-Oger Grand Cru Brut 2005, $$$, 163
Hatt et Söner Le Grand-Père Brut Prestige 2006, $$$, 164
Henri Abelé Brut Rosé NV, $$, 166
Hugues Godmé Premier Cru Brut Blanc de Blancs NV, $$, 176
Huré Frères Instantanée Extra Brut 2008, $$, 179
Jacques Selosse Exquise Sec NV, $$$$$, 195
Jacques Selosse Lieux-Dits Le Mesnil-sur-Oger Les Carelles Grand Cru Extra-Brut NV, $$$$$, 194
L. Bénard-Pitois Brut Nature Premier Cru NV, $$, 216
Lanson Rose Label Brut Rosé NV, $, 227
Laurent-Perrier La Cuvée Brut NV, $$, 236
Moët & Chandon Grand Vintage 2008, $$$, 260
Mumm Le Millésimé 2009, $$, 265
Mumm Le Rosé Brut NV, $$, 265
Napoléon Blanc de Blancs Brut NV, $$, 268
Nominé-Renard Blanc de Noirs NV, $$
Nominé-Renard Rosé NV, $
Palmer & Co Blanc de Blancs NV, $$, 274
Perrier-Jouët Grand Brut NV, $$, 280
Philippe Fourrier Carte d'Or NV, $$, 282
Philipponnat Sublime Réserve Sec 2005, $$, 287
Pol Roger Brut Réserve NV, $$, 309
Robert Moncuit Grand Cru Blanc de Blancs Extra Brut NV, $$, 315
Robert Moncuit Grand Cru Grande Cuvée Le Mesnil-sur-Oger Blanc de Blancs 2006, $$, 315
Salmon 100% Meunier Brut NV, $$, 320
Thiénot Cuvée Alain Thiénot Millésimé Brut 2007, $$$, 334
Thiénot La Vigne aux Gamins Cuvée de 3614/1 Blanc de Blancs Brut 2005, $$$$, 334
Vadin Plateau Blanc de Noirs NV, $

89 POINTS
Agrapart & Fils Terroirs Blanc de Blancs Grand Cru Extra Brut NV, $$$, 35
AR Lenoble Collection Rare Grand Cru Blanc de Blancs Millésime 1988, 45
Armand de Brignac Demi Sec NV, $$$$$, 48
Besserat de Bellefon Cuvée des Moines Extra Brut NV, $$, 60
Besserat de Bellefon Cuvée des Moines Grand Cru Blanc de Noirs Brut NV, $$, 60
Billecart-Salmon Demi-Sec NV, $$, 67
Canard-Duchêne Cuvée Léonie Brut NV, $, 84
Cattier Rosé Premier Cru Brut NV, $$, 88
Collet Brut NV, $$, 99
De Saint Gall Brut Blanc de Blancs Premier Cru NV, $$, 102
De Saint Gall Brut Rosé NV, $$, 102
Dosnon Recolte Rosé NV, $$, 130
Duval-Leroy Bouzy Pinot Noir Grand Cru Brut Nature 2005, $$$$, 136
Henri Abelé Brut Millésimé 2007, $$$, 166
Henri Goutorbe Cuvée Millésime Grand Cru Brut 2007, $$
Huré Frères Insouciance Rosé Brut NV, $$, 178
Jacques Selosse Substance Grand Cru Blanc de Blancs Brut NV, $$$$$, 195
Jérôme Prévost La Closerie les Béguines LC13 NV, $$$, 203
L. Bénard-Pitois Brut Millésime Premier Cru 2009, $$, 217
Laherte Frères Blanc de Blancs Brut Nature NV, $$, 220
Lanson Vintage Collection Magnum 1990, $$$$
Louis Roederer Vintage Rosé 2011, $$$, 246
Marc Hébrart Blanc de Blancs Premier Cru NV, $$, 254
Moët & Chandon Grand Vintage Rosé 2008, $$$, 261
Mumm Cordon Rouge Brut NV, $$, 264
Napoléon Réserve Brut NV, $$, 268
Nicolas Feuillatte Brut Rosé NV, $$, 270
Palmer & Co Blanc de Noirs NV, $$, 274
Perrier-Jouët Blason Rosé NV, $$, 280
Philippe Fourrier Rosé NV, $$, 283
Pierre Paillard Brut Grand Cru NV, $$
Pommery Brut Rosé Royal NV, $$, 312
Robert Moncuit Grand Cru Brut NV, $, 314

The Champagne Guide

GLOSSARY

ACIDITY A crucial element that gives champagne its tangy freshness, vitality and life, and a sharp, clean taste on the finish.

AGRAFE A large metal 'staple' to secure the cork during second fermentation and bottle ageing. Historically, used prior to the invention of capsules, and retained today by some houses and growers.

APÉRITIF A drink used to get the tastebuds humming before a meal (champagne, naturally!).

ASSEMBLAGE The process of blending a wine (see page 27).

AUTOLYSIS The breakdown of dead yeast cells during ageing on lees, improving mouthfeel and contributing biscuity, bready characters (see page 28).

BALTHAZAR 12-litre bottle (usually filled with champagne fermented in standard bottles or magnums). Be sure to have help on hand to pour it (and drink it!).

BARRIQUE Small oak barrel of 225-litre capacity.

BÂTONNAGE Stirring of the lees in barrel or tank.

BEAD Bubbles. The best champagne always has tiny bubbles, the product of the finest juice fermented in cold cellars.

BIODYNAMICS An intensive viticultural regime of extreme organics, eschewing chemical treatments and seeking a harmonious ecosystem.

BLANC DE BLANCS Literally translates as 'white from white'. White champagne made exclusively from white grapes, usually chardonnay, but may also include arbane, petit meslier, pinot blanc and/or pinot gris.

BLANC DE NOIRS Literally 'white from black'. White champagne made exclusively from the dark-skinned grapes pinot noir and/or meunier. This is achieved by gentle pressing to remove the juice from the skins before any colour leaches out.

BRETTANOMYCES 'Brett' is a barrel yeast infection, considered a spoilage character in champagne. It may develop further in bottle, manifesting itself as characters of boiled hot dog, antiseptic, horse stable, barnyard, animal or sweaty saddle, adding a metallic bite to the palate and contracting the finish.

BRUT Raw/dry, containing less than 12g/L sugar (formerly less than 15g/L sugar).

BRUT NATURE OR BRUT ZÉRO No added sugar (less than 3g/L sugar).

CAPSULE Crown cap.

CARBON DIOXIDE The gaseous by-product of fermentation that is responsible for the bubbles in sparkling wine.

CAVE Cellar.

CÉPAGE Grape variety or blend of varieties.

CHAMPAGNE Wine from the region of the same name in north-east France. Champagne with a capital 'C' refers to the region; with a lower-case 'c' to the wine. French law prohibits the name for sparkling wines grown elsewhere.

CHAPTALISATION The addition of sugar (yes, this is legal in France) or concentrated grape juice to increase the alcohol strength of the wine (see page 27).

CHEF DE CAVE The 'chief' or 'chef' in the cellar (champagne winemaker).

CIVC The 'Comité Interprofessionnel du Vin de Champagne', a semi-public agency of the French government to represent the growers and houses in overseeing the production, distribution, promotion and research of the wines of Champagne.

CLOS Historically a walled vineyard, though the walls may no longer exist.

COEUR DE LA CUVÉE 'Heart of the cuvée', the middle of the pressing, yielding the best juice.

COOPÉRATIVE DE MANIPULATION (CM) A co-op of growers who produce champagne under their own brand.

CORKED Cork taint is an all too common wine fault resulting from the presence of 2,4,6 trichloroanisole (TCA) in natural cork. It imparts an off-putting, mouldy, 'wet cardboard' or 'wet dog' character, suppressing fruit and shortening the length of finish (see page 19).

CORK TAINT See 'corked'.

COTEAUX CHAMPENOIS Champagne released as still wine, mostly red; typically made in tiny quantities, and mostly by smaller producers.

CRAYÈRES Roman chalk pits, now gloriously atmospheric cellars under Reims.

CRÉMANT Formerly used to describe slightly less fizzy champagnes (2–3 atmospheres of pressure), but no longer permitted on champagne, and instead often used for French sparkling wines

The Champagne Guide

produced outside of Champagne. Not to be confused with the village of Cramant in the Côte des Blancs. Mumm's de Cramant cuvée is both crémant (in the traditional sense) and exclusively sourced from Cramant.

CROWN CAP A metal seal like a beer cap, used to seal a champagne bottle during second fermentation and lees ageing.

CRU A commune, village, vineyard or officially classified 'growth'.

CUVÉE The first pressing of the grapes (2050 litres from 4000 kilograms of grapes), yielding the best juice. Also refers to an individual blend or style.

CUVERIE Tank room.

DÉBOURBAGE Settling of the solids from the must prior to fermentation (see page 27).

DÉBOURBAGE À FROID Cold settling to clarify the juice, as practised by Billecart-Salmon, Pol Roger and others.

DÉGORGEMENT Disgorgement.

DEGREES POTENTIAL The ripeness at which grapes are picked, which determines the alcohol content of the finished wine.

DEMI-MUID Large oak barrel of 500–600-litre capacity.

DEMI-SEC Half-dry or medium-dry (32–50g/L sugar).

DIAM Mytik DIAM is a brand of champagne closure made by Oeneo, moulded from fragments of cork which have been treated to extract cork taint. Its reliable performance has made it an increasingly popular choice for champagne in recent years (see page 19).

DISGORGEMENT Removal of a frozen plug of sediment from the neck of the bottle (see page 28).

DOSAGE The final addition to top up the bottle, usually a mixture of wine and sugar syrup called *liqueur d'expédition* or *liqueur de dosage*. A dosage of 8–10g/L of sugar is typical in champagne (see pages 19 and 28).

DOUX SWEET 50+ g/L sugar (Coca-Cola is 150g/L).

ÉCHELLE DES CRUS 'Ladder of growths', Champagne's crude classification of vineyards by village, expressed as a percentage.

ÉLEVAGE The process of 'bringing up' a wine, encompassing all cellar operations between fermentation and bottling.

EXTRA BRUT Extra raw/dry (less than 6g/L sugar).

EXTRA DRY OR EXTRA SEC Off dry (12–17g/L sugar).

FERMENTATION The conversion of sugar to alcohol by the action of yeasts. Carbonic gas is produced as a by-product.

FLUTE Narrow champagne glass.

FOUDRE Very large oak cask, typically with a capacity between 2000 litres and 12,000 litres.

GRAND CRU The highest vineyard classification. In Champagne, a classification is crudely applied to a village and all the vineyards within its bounds acquire the same classification. Seventeen villages are classified as grand cru.

GRANDES MARQUES An obsolete, self-imposed term for the big champagne brands. Still used informally.

GREY IMPORTS See 'Parallel imports'.

GROWER-PRODUCER A champagne producer who makes wines from fruit grown only on his or her own vineyards; 5% of fruit is permitted to be purchased. Olivier Krug defines a grower

champagne as one made from your garden.

GYROPALETTE A large mechanised crate to automatically riddle champagne bottles.

INOCULATE To seed a ferment with yeast.

JEROBOAM A 3-litre bottle, previously typically filled with champagne fermented in standard bottles or magnums. However, it is now a legal requirement that it must be made in its own bottle from first bottling.

LATE DISGORGEMENT A champagne that has been matured on its lees for an extended period.

LEES Sediment that settles in the bottom of a tank, barrel or bottle, primarily dead yeast cells.

LIEU-DIT Individually named plot or vineyard site.

LIGHTSTRUCK The degradation of wine exposed to ultraviolet light. Sparkling wines in clear bottles are most susceptible.

LIQUEUR D'EXPÉDITION The final addition to top up the bottle, usually a mixture of wine and sugar syrup.

LIQUEUR DE DOSAGE See 'Liqueur d'expédition'.

LIQUEUR DE TIRAGE A mixture of sugar and wine or concentrated grape juice added immediately prior to bottling, to produce the secondary fermentation in bottle (see page 28).

LUTTE RAISONNÉE Literally 'reasoned struggle', a middle ground between conventional viticulture and organic farming, reducing the use of herbicides and pesticides while retaining the right to employ them in times of need. Often a sensible approach in Champagne's erratic climate.

MACERATION Soaking of red grape skins in their juice in the production of red or rosé wine (see page 28).

MAGNUM A 1.5-litre bottle. According to the Champenois, the perfect size for two, when one is not drinking.

MAISON House.

MALIC ACID A naturally occurring acid in grapes and other fruits, particularly green apples. It is most pronounced in grapes in cold climates and is responsible for champagne's searing acidity, which is usually softened through malolactic fermentation.

MALOLACTIC FERMENTATION 'Malo' is the conversion of stronger malic (green apple) acid to softer lactic (dairy) acid (see page 27).

MARQUE D'ACHETEUR (MA) Buyer's own brand. An 'own label' owned by a supermarket or merchant.

MÉTHODE CHAMPENOISE An obsolete term for the traditional method of sparkling wine–making, now 'Méthode Traditionnelle' or 'Méthode Classique'.

MÉTHODE TRADITIONNELLE The official name for the traditional method of sparkling wine–making, in which the second fermentation occurs in the bottle in which the wine is sold.

METHUSELAH A 6-litre bottle, usually filled with champagne fermented in standard bottles or magnums.

MILLÉSIME Vintage.

MINERALITY The texture and mouthfeel of a wine derived from its soil.

MOUSSE See 'Bead'.

MUSELET Wire cage to hold a champagne cork in the bottle.

NEBUCHADNEZZAR A 15-litre bottle, usually filled with champagne fermented in standard bottles or magnums. Do not attempt while home alone!

NÉGOCIANT-MANIPULANT (NM) Champagne producer who purchases grapes and/or unfinished wines. A négociant may also include up to 95% estate grown fruit.

NON-VINTAGE (NV) A champagne containing wine from more than one vintage.

OENOTHÈQUE Literally a wine library or shop. Sometimes used to refer to bottles held back for extended ageing.

OÏDIUM Powdery mildew, a fungal disease that can have a devastating effect on grape crops.

ORGANICS A viticultural regime that avoids the use of any synthetic pesticides, herbicides, fungicides or other treatments. Copper is permitted, though criticised in some circles for a toxicity higher than that of some synthetic products.

OXIDISED A wine that has reacted with oxygen. At its most extreme, oxidation can produce browning in colour, loss of primary fruit, a general flattening of flavours, a shortening of the length of finish, or even a vinegar or bitter taste.

PARALLEL IMPORTS Champagne brought into a country by parties other than the usual agent, typically via a third-party country. Good for keeping pricing competitive, but can become problematic if transportation or storage are compromised.

pH The level of acid strength of a wine expressed as a number. Low pH equates to high acidity; 7 is neutral.

PHENOLICS A grape compound responsible for astringency and

My visiting group discovering riddling deep in the drives under Bollinger.

bitterness in the back palate. It is particularly rich in stems, seeds and skins, and especially prevalent in champagnes from warm vintages such as 2003 and 2005.

PIÈCE Small oak barrel of 205-litre capacity in Champagne (228 litres in Burgundy).

POIGNETTAGE The vigorous shaking of the bottle after corking to mix the wine and liqueur. It can also refer to the old practice of shaking the bottle by hand to stir up the lees and enhance autolytic flavours, rarely used today, though still upheld by De Sousa and Dumangin J. Fils.

PREMIER CRU The second highest vineyard classification, awarded to 41 villages. In Champagne, a classification is crudely applied to a village, and all the vineyards within its bounds acquire the same classification.

PRESTIGE CUVÉE The flagship champagne or champagnes of a brand, typically the most expensive. Olivier Krug says it should be defined as one that can age.

PRISE DE MOUSSE The second fermentation that creates the bubbles (see page 28).

PUPITRE Hand-riddling rack.

RÉCOLTANT-COOPÉRATEUR (RC) Champagne grower selling wine under his/her own brand, made by his/her cooperative.

RÉCOLTANT-MANIPULANT (RM) Champagne grower who makes wine from estate fruit; 5% of grapes may also be purchased to supplement production.

REDUCTIVE A wine made or aged with limited contact with oxygen may develop reductive characters, hydrogen sulphide notes akin to struck flint, burnt match and gunpowder. At their extreme, these can manifest

themselves as objectionable notes of rubber, rotten eggs, garlic, onion or cooked cabbage.

REHOBOAM A 4.5-litre bottle, usually filled with champagne fermented in standard bottles or magnums.

REMUAGE The riddling process (see page 28).

RESERVE WINES Wines held in the cellar for future blending in a non-vintage cuvée (see page 28). Usually aged in tanks, although sometimes kept in barrels or bottles.

RIDDLING The process of moving the lees sediment into the neck of the bottle prior to disgorgement, either by hand or by gyropalette (see page 28).

SABRAGE A technique for opening a champagne bottle with a sabre. Practice is recommended prior to attempting this in public. Not recommended for fear of wastage and glass shards in your flute.

SAIGNÉE A technique in which rosé is made by 'bleeding' off juice from just-crushed pinot noir or meunier grapes after a short maceration (soaking) on skins prior to fermentation (see page 28).

SALMANAZAR A 9-litre bottle, usually filled with champagne fermented in standard bottles or magnums.

SEC Dryish (17–32g/L sugar).

SOLERA A system of fractional blending using wines of different ages, with the bottled wine drawn from the last stage. Also used in Champagne to refer to a simplified system of perpetual blending, in which successive vintages are added to a single tank.

STALE Lacking in fruit freshness.

SUR LATTES See 'vins sur lattes'.

SUR POINTE The storing of bottles neck down, between riddling and disgorgement. Sometimes also used for long-term storage of undisgorged bottles. With the lees settled in the neck, it is believed the wine stays fresher for longer.

TAILLES Coarser, inferior juice that flows last from the press.

TCA See 'Corked'.

TERROIR A catch-all term for anything that defines the character of a vineyard – soil, micro-climate, altitude, aspect, exposure, slope, drainage, and even the hands that tend it.

TIRAGE Bottling of the blended wine with an addition of sugar and yeast, so as to provoke the second fermentation in bottle (see page 28).

TUN Large oak barrel, typically around 1000 litres in volume.

VENDANGE Vintage or harvest.

VIEILLES VIGNES Old vines.

VIGNERON Vine grower.

VIN CLAIR Still base wine that has undergone its primary fermentation and (potentially) malolactic fermentation, but not its secondary fermentation.

VINS SUR LATTES Champagne bottles laid on their side, having undergone second fermentation, but yet to be riddled. Also refers to the legal but shady practice by which champagne houses purchase finished but yet to be disgorged champagne made by another producer, to then market under their own label.

VINTAGE Wine from a single year.

ZERO DOSAGE No sweetness is added during the final addition to top up the bottle (see pages 19 and 28).

AUTHOR THANKS

I owe a great debt of gratitude to hundreds of champagne producers and their agents for their hospitality and generosity in inviting me into their homes, cellars, tasting rooms and vineyards, sending samples and offering the privilege of discovering their stories and their wines. A project of this magnitude is only possible with a cast of thousands. Here are just 200 of the many to whom I owe a special thanks.

Charlotte Agard, Pascal Agrapart, Daniel Arioldi, Sally Arnold, Eric Bailleux, Renaud Bancilhon, Laurent Bénard, Raphaël Bérêche, Katy Beurton, Philippe Bienvenu, Paul Boothby, Tim Boydell, Julien Breuzon, Emmanuel Brochet, Cyril Brun, Denis Bunner, Nat Burch, David Burkitt, Sabrina Cambray, Audrey Campos, Régis Camus, Elodie Caraskakis, Alexandre Cattier, Jean-Jacques Cattier, Xenia Charovatova, Alexandre Chartogne, Louis Cheval-Gatinois, Jean-Hervé Chiquet, Jean-François Clouet, Olivier Collin, Christophe Constant, Greg Corra, Sophie Couvreur, Paul Couvreur, Catherine Curie, Hervé Dantan, Mel De Barra, Antoine de Boysson, Nicoletta de Nicolo, Hervé Deschamps, Charlotte De Sousa, Erick De Sousa, Magda Debiec, Dominique Demarville, Eléonore Denieau, Didier Depond, Guy de Rivoire, Gilles Descôtes, Pierre Déthune, Sophie Déthune, Laurent d'Harcourt, Anne-Laure Domenichini, David Donald, Peter Dubourdieu, Nathalie Dufour, Gilles Dumangin, Olivier Dupré, Francis Egly, Tim Evans, Scott Evers, Florian Eznack, Emilie Ferguson, Charles-Henry Fourny, Emmanuel Fourny, Mathilde Fourrier, Inge Fransen, Emmanuel Gantet, Clément Gardillou, Thierry Gasco, Jean-Baptiste Geoffroy, Richard Geoffroy, Susanne Geppert, Didier Gimonnet, Jean-Noël Girard, Claude Giraud, Hughes Godmé, Diane Gonzalez, Benoît Gouez, Nicole Goutorbe, Jane Grant, Sandy Grant, Christelle Grivot, Tim Hampton, Tony Hancy, Charles Hargrave, Thomas Henriot, Caroline Henry, David Hervoil, Katri Hilden, Jessica Hill-Smith, Rachel Hofman, Linda Holmes, Christian Holthausen, Antoine Huray, François Huré, Melissa Irwin, Paul Jackson, Darren Jahn, James Johnston, Olivier Krug, Aurélien Laherte, Pierre Larmandier, Sophie Larmandier, Nicolas Laugerotte, Patrick Le Brun, Ian Leamon, Jean-Baptiste LeCaillon, Sylviane Lemaire, Stephen Leroux, Brigitte Lobet, Amy Looker, Antoine Malassagne, Anne Malassagne, Baptiste Marchal, Jean-Pierre Mareigner, Didier Mariotti, Joe Marsico, Craig McDonald, Loran McDougall, Sally McGill, Euan McKay, Julie-Amandine Michel, Xavier Millard, Stéphanie Mingam, Emma Morris, Jean-Philippe Moulin, Phoebe Murray, Bruce Nancarrow, Steven Naughton, Jo Newtown, Stephanie Noël, Jayden Ong, Alice Paillard, Bruno Paillard, Kaaren Palmer, Fréderic Panaïotis, Michel Parisot, Kristy Parker, Victor Pépin, Rodolphe Péters, Stéphanie Petizon, Jean-Jacques Peyre, Jérôme Philipon, Charles-Antoine Picart, Randall Pollard, Tom Portet, Mathieu Pouchan, Jérôme Prévost, Jody Rolfe, Matthew Quirk, Robert Remnant, Myriam Renard, Raymond Ringeval, Sandra Robbertse, Eric Rodez, Antoine Roland-Billecart, Jody Rolfe, Florent Roques-Boizel, Fabrice Rosset, Hervé Savès, Anselme Selosse, David Seymour, Chris Sheehy, Nesh Simic, Gary Steel, Melinda Steel, Huon Stelzer, Linden Stelzer, Rachael Stelzer, Vaughn Stelzer, Tim Stock, Pierre Stocks, Brooke Sullivan, Clovis Taittinger, Vitalie Taittinger, Benoit Tarlant, Angéline Templier, Marie-Agnès Thomas, Jean-Pierre Vazart, Maurizio Ugge, Gauthier Vecten, Chloé Verrat, Nicole Vezzola, Patrick Walsh, Rob Walters, Andy Warren, Steve Webber, Paige Wieselmann, Jane Willson, Scott Wilson, Danika Windrim, Matthew Withers, Jon Yarnall, Neville Yates

Research for this book is entirely self-funded, including all travel and accommodation in Champagne.

TYSON STELZER was named The International Wine & Spirit Competition Communicator of the Year 2015, The Wine Communicators of Australia Australian Wine Communicator of the Year 2015 and 2013, and The International Champagne Writer of the Year 2011 in The Louis Roederer International Wine Writers' Awards.

He is the author of 15 wine books and a regular contributor to 15 magazines including *Wine Spectator, Decanter, Australian Gourmet Traveller Wine Magazine* and *Wine Companion Magazine*. He contributes sparkling wine reviews to the *James Halliday Australian Wine Companion* and is a contributor to Jancis Robinson's *The Oxford Companion to Wine*, 3rd edition. He is the host of the television series *People of the Vines* and the founder of the Teen Rescue Foundation to address teen alcohol abuse.

As an international speaker, he has presented at wine conferences in the UK, Italy, Japan, Hong Kong, South Africa, New Zealand and Australia. Tyson is a regular judge and chairman at Australian wine shows.

Tyson personally hosts intimate champagne tours for an exclusive opportunity to explore, taste and dine at the finest houses and enjoy the best experiences that the region has to offer. See champagnetours.com.au.

Tyson is 41 years of age and lives in Brisbane with his wife Rachael and sons Linden, Huon and Vaughn.